Analysis and Design of Control Systems Using MATLAB

SECOND EDITION

RAO V DUKKIPATI
PhD, PE
Fellow of ASME and CSME
Former Professor and Chairman
Department of Mechanical Engineering
Ex-Director, Graduate Programme
Fairfield University
Fairfield, Connecticut
USA

NEW AGE
REFERENCE

An Imprint of

NEW AGE INTERNATIONAL (P) LIMITED, PUBLISHERS
LONDON • NEW DELHI • NAIROBI
Bangalore • Chennai • Cochin • Guwahati • Hyderabad • Kolkata • Lucknow • Mumbai
Visit us at **www.newagepublishers.com**

Published by New Age International (P) Ltd., Publishers
First Edition: 2006
Second Edition: 2010
Reprint: 2019

GLOBAL OFFICES

- **New Delhi** **NEW AGE INTERNATIONAL (P) LIMITED, PUBLISHERS**
7/30 A, Daryaganj, New Delhi-110002, (INDIA)
Tel.: (011) 23253771, 23253472, **Telefax:** 23267437, 43551305
E-mail: contactus@newagepublishers.com • Visit us at www.newagepublishers.com
- **London** **NEW AGE INTERNATIONAL (UK) LTD.**
27 Old Gloucester Street, London, WC1N 3AX, UK
E-mail: info@newacademicscience.co.uk • Visit us at www.newacademicscience.co.uk
- **Nairobi** **NEW AGE GOLDEN (EAST AFRICA) LTD.**
Ground Floor, Westlands Arcade, Chiromo Road (Next to Naivas Supermarket), Westlands, Nairobi, KENYA
Tel.: 00-254-713848772, 00-254-725700286
E-mail: kenya@newagepublishers.com

BRANCHES

- **Bangalore** 37/10, 8th Cross (Near Hanuman Temple), Azad Nagar, Chamarajpet, Bangalore- 560 018
Tel.: (080) 26756823, **Telefax:** 26756820, **E-mail: bangalore@newagepublishers.com**
- **Chennai** 26, Damodaran Street, T. Nagar, Chennai-600 017, **Tel.:** (044) 24353401, **Telefax:** 24351463
E-mail: chennai@newagepublishers.com
- **Cochin** CC-39/1016, Carrier Station Road, Ernakulam South, Cochin-682 016, **Tel.:** (0484) 2377303, **Telefax:** 4051304
E-mail: cochin@newagepublishers.com
- **Guwahati** Hemsen Complex, Mohd. Shah Road, Paltan Bazar, Near Starline Hotel, Guwahati-781 008,
Tel.: (0361) 2513881, **Telefax:** 2543669, **E-mail: guwahati@newagepublishers.com**
- **Hyderabad** 105, 1st Floor, Madhiray Kaveri Tower, 3-2-19, Azam Jahi Road, Near Kumar Theater, Nimboliadda Kachiguda, Hyderabad-500 027, **Tel.:** (040) 24652456, **Telefax:** 24652457
E-mail: hyderabad@newagepublishers.com
- **Kolkata** RDB Chambers (Formerly Lotus Cinema) 106A, 1st Floor, S N Banerjee Road, Kolkata-700 014
Tel.: (033) 22273773, **Telefax:** 22275247, **E-mail: kolkata@newagepublishers.com**
- **Lucknow** 16-A, Jopling Road, Lucknow-226 001, **Tel.:** (0522) 2209578, 4045297, **Telefax:** 2204098
E-mail: lucknow@newagepublishers.com
- **Mumbai** 142C, Victor House, Ground Floor, N.M. Joshi Marg, Lower Parel, Mumbai-400 013
Tel.: (022) 24927869, **Telefax:** 24915415, **E-mail: mumbai@newagepublishers.com**
- **New Delhi** 22, Golden House, Daryaganj, New Delhi-110 002, **Tel.:** (011) 23262368, 23262370, **Telefax:** 43551305
E-mail: sales@newagepublishers.com

ISBN: 978-81-224-2409-6
C-18-10-11633

Printed in India at Glorious Printers, Delhi.
Typeset at Akriti Graphics, Delhi.

NEW AGE INTERNATIONAL (P) LIMITED, PUBLISHERS
7/30 A, Daryaganj, New Delhi-110002
Visit us at **www.newagepublishers.com**
(CIN: U74899DL1966PTC004618)

Dedicated this book
to
'Lord Sri Venkateswara'

Preface to the Second Edition

It is a pleasure to bring out the second edition of the book. Efforts have been made to make this edition error free. Owing to the demand of valuable readers, solutions to problems in MATLAB Basics and also MATLAB Tutorials are given in Chapter 4 and 5. Bibliography has also been updated. With the additions, I hope the students will find it convenient to appreciate the topics of analysis and design of control systems and also test their calibre.

Thanks are to the management of New Age International (P) Ltd., Publishers to bring out this edition in a short span of time.

Rao V. Dukkipati

Preface to the First Edition

Control Systems Engineering is an exciting and challenging field and is a multidisciplinary subject. This book is designed and organized around the concepts of control systems engineering using MATLAB, as they have been developed in the frequency and time domain for an introductory undergraduate or graduate course in control systems for engineering students of all disciplines.

Chapter 1 presents a brief introduction to control systems. The fundamental strategy of controlling physical variables in systems is presented. Some of the terms commonly used to describe the operation, analysis, and design of control systems are described.

An introduction to MATLAB basics is presented in Chapter 2. Chapter 2 also presents MATLAB commands. MATLAB is considered as the software of choice. MATLAB can be used interactively and has an inventory of routines, called as functions, which minimize the task of programming even more. Further information on MATLAB can be obtained from: The MathWorks, Inc., 3 Apple Hill Drive, Natick, MA 01760. In the computational aspects, MATLAB has emerged as a very powerful tool for numerical computations involved in control systems engineering. The idea of computer-aided design and analysis using MATLAB with the Symbolic Math Tool box, and the Control System Tool box has been incorporated.

Chapter 3 consists of many solved problems that demonstrate the application of MATLAB to the analysis and design of control systems. Presentations are limited to linear, time-invariant continuous time systems.

Chapters 2 and 3 include a great number of worked examples and unsolved exercise problems to guide the students to understand the basic principles and concepts in control systems engineering.

I sincerely hope that the final outcome of this book helps the students in developing an appreciation for the topic of analysis and design of control systems.

An extensive bibliography to guide the student to further sources of information on control systems engineering is provided at the end of the book. All the end-of chapter problems are fully solved in the Solution Manual available only to Instructors.

Rao V. Dukkipati

Contents

CHAPTER 1

Introduction

1.1 INTRODUCTION

In this Chapter, we describe very briefly and introduce the topics on control systems, engineering mechanics, mechanical vibrations and electrical circuits.

1.2 CONTROL SYSTEMS

Control systems in an interdisciplinary field covering many areas of engineering and sciences. Control systems exist in many systems of engineering, sciences, and in human body. This chapter presents a brief introduction and overview of control systems. Some of the terms commonly used to describe the operation, analysis, and design of control systems are presented.

Control means to regulate, direct, command, or govern. A *system* is a collection, set, or arrangement of elements (subsystems). A *control system* is an interconnection of components forming a system configuration that will provide a desired system response. Hence, a control system is an arrangement of physical components connected or related in such a manner as to command, regulate, direct, or govern itself or another system.

In order to identify, delineate, or define a control system, we introduce two terms: *input* and *output* here. The *input* is the stimulus, excitation, or command applied to a control system, and the *output* is the actual response resulting from a control system. The *output* may or may not be equal to the specified response implied by the input. Inputs could be physical variables or abstract ones such as *reference*, *set point* or *desired* values for the output of the control system. Control systems can have more than one input or output. The input and the output represent the desired response and the actual response respectively. A control system provides an output or response for a given input or stimulus, as shown in Fig. 1.1.

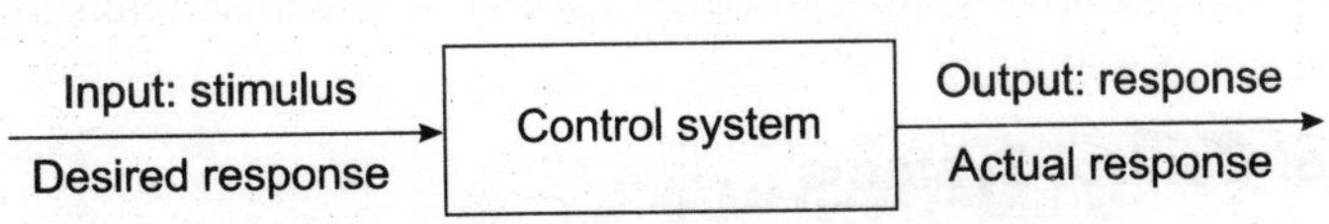

Fig. 1.1 Description of a control system

The output may not be equal to the specified response implied by the input. If the output and input are given, it is possible to identify or define the nature of the system's components. Broadly speaking, there are three basic types of control systems:

(*a*) Man-made control systems

(*b*) Natural, including biological-control systems

(*c*) Control systems whose components are both man-made and natural.

An electric switch is a man-made control system controlling the electricity-flow. The simple act of pointing at an object with a finger requires a biological control system consisting chiefly of eyes, the arm, hand and finger and the brain of a person, where the input is precise-direction of the object with respect to some reference and the output is the actual pointed direction with respect to the same reference. The control system consisting of a person driving an automobile has components, which are clearly both man-made and biological. The driver wants to keep the automobile in the appropriate lane of the roadway. The driver accomplishes this by constantly watching the direction of the automobile with respect to the direction of road. Fig.1.2 is an alternate way of showing the basic entities in a general control system.

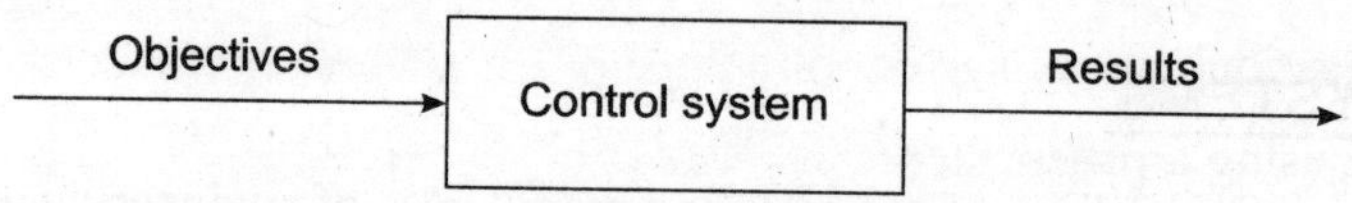

Fig. 1.2 Components of a control system

In the steering control of an automobile for example, the direction of two front wheels can be regarded as the result or controlled output variable and the direction of the steering wheel as the actuating signal or objective. The control-system in this case is composed of the steering mechanism and the dynamics of the entire automobile. As another example, consider the idle-speed control of an automobile engine, where it is necessary to maintain the engine idle speed at a relatively low-value (for fuel economy) regardless of the applied engine loads (like air-conditioning, power steering, etc.). Without the idle-speed control, any sudden engine-load application would cause a drop in engine speed that might cause the engine to stall. In this case, throttle angle and load-torque are the inputs (objectives) and the engine-speed is the output. The engine is the controlled process of the system. A few more applications of control-systems can be found in the print wheel control of an electronic typewriter, the thermostatically controlled heater or furnace which automatically regulates the temperature of a room or enclosure, and the sun tracking control of solar collector dish.

Control system applications are found in robotics, space-vehicle systems, aircraft autopilots and controls, ship and marine control systems, intercontinental missile guidance systems, automatic control systems for hydrofoils, surface-effect ships, and high-speed rail systems including the magnetic levitation systems.

1.2.1 Examples of Control Systems

Control systems find numerous and widespread applications from everyday to extraordinary in science, industry, and home. A few examples are given as follows:

(*a*) Home heating and air-conditioning systems controlled by a thermostat

(*b*) The cruise (speed) control of an automobile

(*c*) Manual control:

(*i*) Opening or closing of a window for regulating air temperature or air quality

(*ii*) Activation of a light switch to regulate the illumination in a room

(*iii*) Human controlling the speed of an automobile by regulating the gas supply to the engine

(*d*) Automatic traffic control (signal) system at roadway intersections

(*e*) Control system which automatically turns on a room lamp at dusk, and turns it off in daylight

(*f*) Automatic hot water heater

(*g*) Environmental test-chamber temperature control system

(*h*) An automatic positioning system for a missile launcher

(*i*) An automatic speed control for a field-controlled dc motor

(*j*) The attitude control system of a typical space vehicle

(*k*) Automatic position-control system of a high speed automated train system

(*l*) Human heart using a pacemaker

(*m*) An elevator-position control system used in high-rise multilevel buildings.

1.3 CONTROL SYSTEM CONFIGURATIONS

There are two control system configurations: open-loop control system and closed-loop control system.

(a) Block

A block is a set of elements that can be grouped together, with overall characteristics described by an input/output relationship as shown in Fig.1.3. A block diagram is a simplified pictorial representation of the cause-and-effect relationship between the input(s) and output(s) of a physical system.

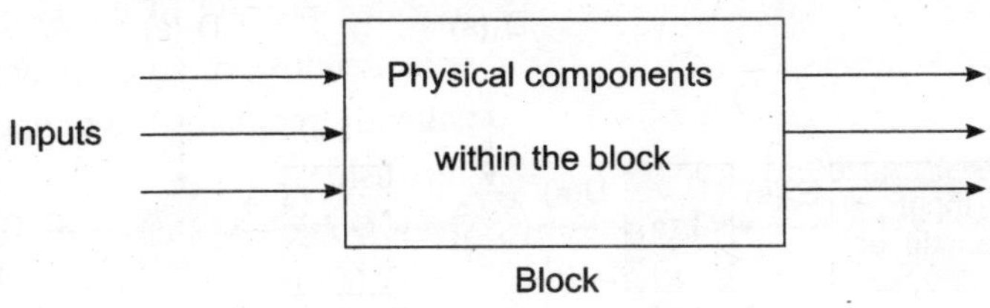

Fig. 1.3 Block diagram

The simplest form of the block diagram is the single block as shown in Fig.1.3. The input and output characteristics of entire groups of elements within the block can be described by an appropriate mathematical expressions as shown in Fig.1.4.

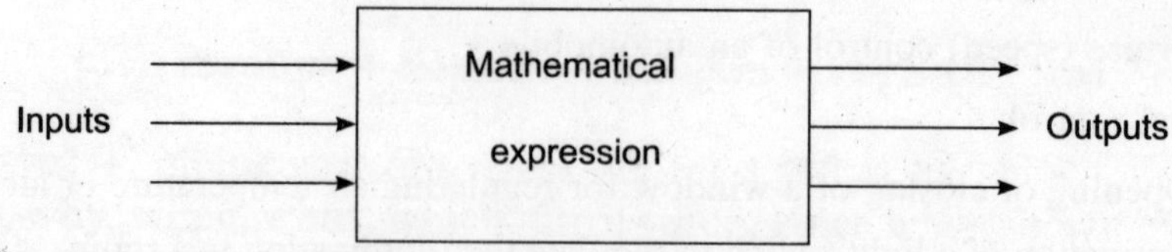

Fig. 1.4 Block representation

(b) Transfer function

The transfer function of a system (or a block) is defined as the ratio of output to input as shown in Fig.1.5.

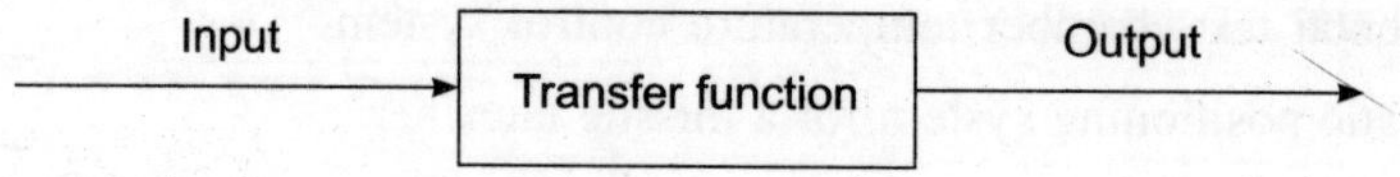

Fig. 1.5 Transfer function

$$\text{Transfer function} = \frac{\text{Output}}{\text{Input}}$$

Transfer functions are generally used to represent a mathematical model of each block in the block diagram representation. All the signals are transfer functions on the block diagrams. For instance, the time function reference input is r (t), and its transfer function is R(s) where t is time and s is the Laplace transform variable or complex frequency.

(c) Open-loop control system

A general block diagram of open-loop system is shown in Fig.1.6.

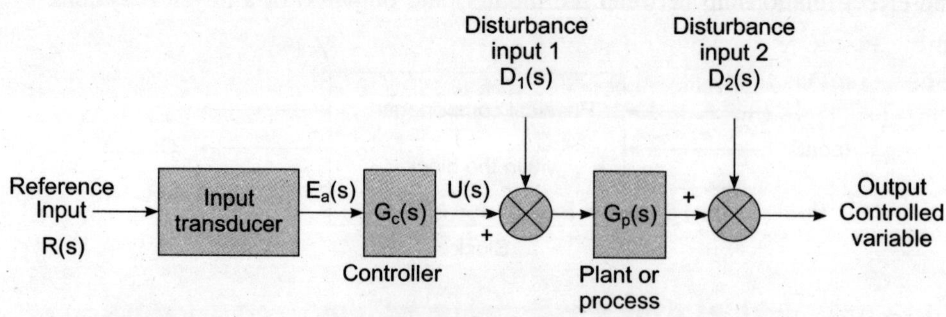

Fig. 1.6 General block diagram of open-loop control system

(d) Closed-loop (feedback control) system

The general architecture of a closed-loop control system is shown in Fig.1.7.

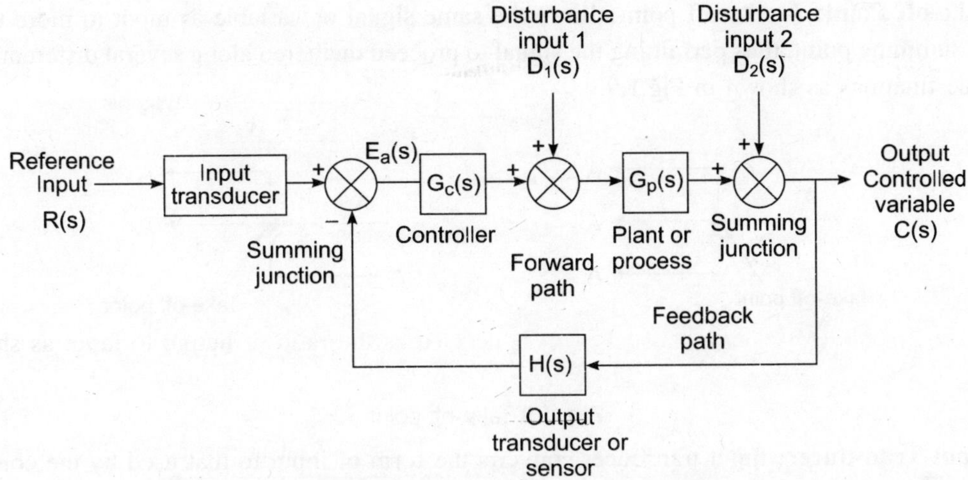

Fig. 1.7 General block diagram of closed-loop control system

1.4 CONTROL SYSTEM TERMINOLOGY

The variables in Figs.1.6 and 1.7 are defined as follows:

C(s) controlled output, transfer function of c (t)

D(s) disturbance input, transfer function of d (t)

$E_a(s)$ actuating error, transfer function of e_a (t)

$G_a(s)$ transfer function of the actuator

G_c (s) transfer function of the controller

$G_p(s)$ transfer function of the plant or process

H(s) transfer function of the sensor or output transducer = $G_s(s)$

R(s) reference input, transfer function of r (t).

Summing Point: As shown in Fig.1.8 the block is a small circle called a summing point with the appropriate plus or minus sign associated with the arrows entering the circle. The output is the algebraic sum of the inputs. There is no limit on the number of inputs entering a summing point.

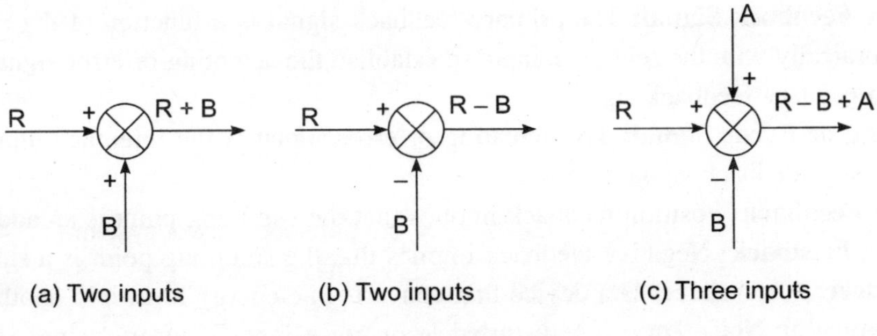

Fig. 1.8 Summing point

Take-off Point: A take-off point allows the same signal or variable as input to more than one block or summing point, thus permitting the signal to proceed unaltered along several different paths to several destinations as shown in Fig.1.9.

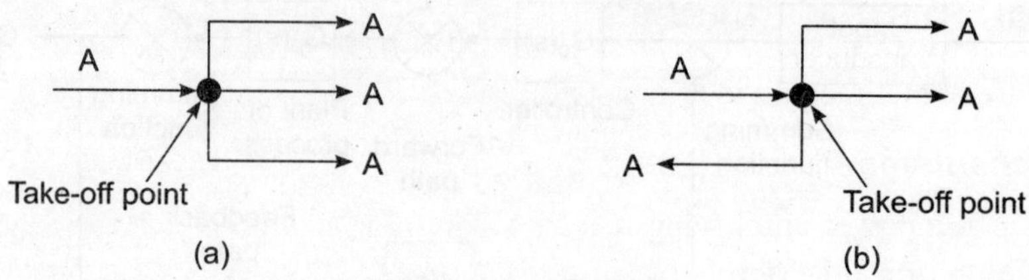

Fig. 1.9 Take-off point

Input Transducer: Input transducer converts the form of input to that used by the controller.

Controller: The controller drives a process or plant.

Plant, Process or Controlled System $G_p(s)$: The plant, process, or controlled system is the system, subsystem, process, or object controlled by the feedback control system. For example, the plant can be a furnace system where the output variable is temperature.

Controlled Output C(s): The controlled output C(s) is the output variable of the plant under the control of the control system.

Forward Path: The forward path is the transmission path from the summing point to the controlled output.

Feedback Path: The feedback path is the transmission path from the controlled output back to the summing point.

Feed Forward (Control) Elements: The feed forward (control) elements are the components of the forward path that generate the control signal applied to the plant or process. The feed forward (control) elements include controller(s), compensator(s), or equalization elements, and amplifiers.

Feedback Elements: The feedback elements establish the fundamental relationship between the controlled output C(s) and the primary feedback signal B(s). They include sensors of the controlled output, compensators, and controller elements.

Reference Input R(s): The reference input is an external signal applied to the control system generally at the first summing input, so as to command a specified action of the process or plant. It typically represents ideal or desired process or plant output response.

Primary Feedback Signal: The primary feedback signal is a function of the controlled output summed algebraically with the reference input to establish the actuating or error signal. An open-loop system has no primary feedback signal.

Actuating or Error Signal: The actuating or error signal is the reference input signal plus or minus the primary feedback signal.

Positive Feedback: Position feedback implies that the summing point is an adder.

Negative Feedback: Negative feedback implies that the summing point is a subtractor.

Transducer: A transducer is a device that converts one energy form into another.

Disturbance or Noise Input: A disturbance or noise input is an undesired stimulus or input signal affecting the value of the controlled output.

Time Response: The time response of a system, subsystem, or element is the output as a function of time, generally following the application of a prescribed input under specified operating conditions.

1.5 CONTROL SYSTEM CLASSES

Control systems are sometimes divided into two classes: (a) Servomechanisms and (b) Regulators.

(a) Servomechanisms

A servomechanism is a power-amplifying feedback control system in which the controlled variable is a mechanical position or a time derivative of position such as velocity or acceleration. An automatic aircraft landing system is an example of servomechanism. The aircraft follows a ramp to the desired touchdown point. Another example is the control system of an industrial robot in which the robot arm is forced to follow some desired path in space.

(b) Regulators

A regulator or regulating system is a feedback control system in which the reference input or command is constant for long periods of time, generally for the entire time interval during which the system is operational. Such an input is known as *set point*. An example of a regulator control system is the human biological system that maintains the body temperature at approximately 98.6°F in an environment that usually has a different temperature.

1.5.1 Supplementary Terminology

(a) Linear system

A linear system is a system where input/output relationships may be represented by a linear differential equation. The plant is linear if it can be accurately described using a set of linear differential equations. This attribute indicates that system parameters do not vary as a function of signal level.

Similarly, the plant is a lumped-parameter (rather than distributed parameter) system if it can be described using ordinary (rather than partial) differential equations. This condition is generally accomplished if the physical size of the system is very small in comparison to the wavelength of the highest frequency of interest.

(b) Time-variant system

A time-variant is a system if the parameters vary as a function of time. Thus, a time-variant system is a system described by a differential equation with variable coefficients. A linear time-variant system is described by linear differential equations with variable coefficients. A rocket-burning fuel system is an example of time-variant system since the rocket mass varies during the flight as the fuel is burned.

(c) Time-invariant system

A time-invariant system is a system described by a differential equation with constant coefficients. Thus, the plant is time invariant if the parameters do not change as a function of time. A linear time invariant system is described by linear differential equations with constant coefficients. A single degree of freedom spring mass viscous damper system is an example of a time-invariant system provided the characteristics of all the three components do not vary with time.

(d) Multivariable feedback system

The block diagram representing a multivariable feedback system where the interrelationships of many controlled variables are considered is shown in Fig.1.10.

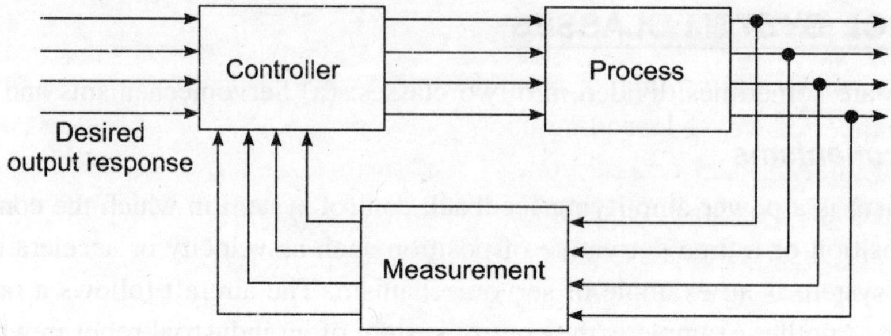

Fig. 1.10 Multivariable control system

1.6 FEEDBACK SYSTEMS

Feedback is the property of a closed-loop system, which allows the output to be compared with the input to the system such that the appropriate control action may be formed as some function of the input and output.

For more accurate and more adaptive control, a link or feedback must be provided from output to the input of an open-loop control system. So the controlled signal should be feedback and compared with the reference input, and an actuating signal proportional to the difference of input and output must be sent through the system to correct the error. In general, feedback is said to exist in a system when a closed sequence of cause-and-effect relations exists between system variables. A closed-loop idle-speed control system is shown in Fig.1.11. The reference input N_r sets the desired idle-speed. The engine idle speed N should agree with the reference value N_r and any difference such as the load-torque T is sensed by the speed-transducer and the error detector. The controller will operate on the difference and provide a signal to adjust the throttle angle to correct the error.

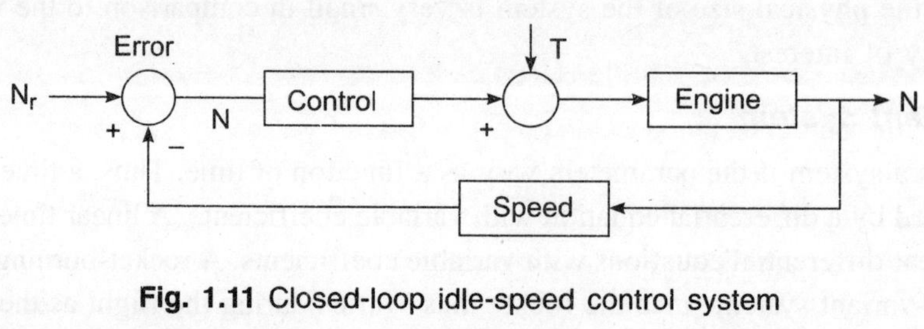

Fig. 1.11 Closed-loop idle-speed control system

1.7 ANALYSIS OF FEEDBACK

The most important features, the presence of feedback impacts to a system are the following:

(*a*) Increased accuracy: its ability to reproduce the input accurately

(*b*) Reduced sensitivity of the ratio of output to input for variations in system characteristics and other parameters (*c*) Reduced effects of nonlinearties and distortion

(*d*) Increased bandwidth (bandwidth of a system that ranges frequencies (input) over which the system will respond satisfactorily)

(*e*) Tendency towards oscillation or instability

(*f*) Reduced effects of external disturbances or noise.

A system is said to be *unstable*, if its output is out of control. Feedback control systems may be classified in a number of ways, depending upon the purpose of classification. For instance, according to the method of analysis and design, control-systems are classified as linear or non-linear, time-varying or time-variant systems. According to the types of signals used in the system, they may be: continuous data and discrete-data system or modulated and unmodulated systems.

Consider the simple feedback configuration shown in Fig.1.12, where R is the input signal, C is the output signal, E is error, and B is feedback signal.

The parameters G and H are constant-gains. By simple algebraic manipulations, it can be shown show that the input-output relation of the system is given by

$$M = \frac{C}{R} = \frac{G}{1+GH} \quad \text{...(1.1)}$$

The general effect of feedback is that it may increase or decrease the gain G. In practical control-systems, G and H are functions of frequency, so the magnitude of (1 + GH) is greater than 1 in one frequency range, but less than 1 in another. Thus feedback affects the gain G of a nonfeedback system by a factor (1 + GH).

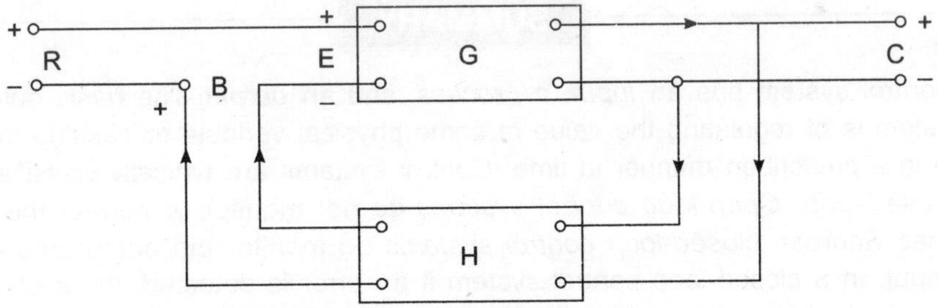

Fig. 1.12 Feedback system

If GH = –1, the output of the system is infinite for any finite input, such a state is called unstable system-state. Alternatively feedback stabilizes an unstable system and the sensitivity of a gain of the overall system M to the variation in G is defined as:

$$S_G^M = \frac{\partial M/M}{\partial G/G} = \frac{\text{Percentage change in M}}{\text{Percentage change in G}} \quad \text{...(1.2)}$$

where ∂M denotes incremental change in M due to incremental change in G (∂G). One can write sensitivity-function as:

$$S_G^M = \frac{\partial M/M}{\partial G/G} = \frac{1}{1+GH} \quad \text{...(1.3)}$$

By increasing GH, the magnitude of the sensitivity-function is made arbitrarily small.

1.8 CONTROL SYSTEM ANALYSIS AND DESIGN OBJECTIVES

Control systems engineering consists of *analysis* and *design* of control systems configurations. Control systems are *dynamic*, in that they respond to an input by first undergoing a transient response before attaining a steady-state response which corresponds to the input. There are three main objectives of control systems analysis and design. They are:

1. Producing the response to a transient disturbance which is acceptable
2. Minimizing the steady-state errors: Here, the concern is about the accuracy of the steady-state response
3. Achieving stability: Control systems must be designed to be stable. Their natural response should decay to a zero values as time approaches infinity, or oscillate.

Analysis is investigation of the properties and performance of an existing control system. Design is the selection and arrangement of the control system components to perform a prescribed task. The design of control systems is accomplished in two ways: *design by analysis* in which the characteristics of an existing or standard system configuration are modified, and *design by synthesis*, in which the form of the control system is obtained directly from its specifications.

SUMMARY

A basic control system has an *input*, *a process*, and an *output*. The basic objective of a control system is of regulating the value of some physical variable or causing that variable to change in a prescribed manner in time. Control systems are typically classified as *open loop* or *closed-loop*. *Open-loop control systems* do not monitor or correct the output for disturbances whereas *closed-loop control systems* do monitor the output and compare it with the input. In a closed-loop control system if an error is detected, the system corrects the output and thereby corrects the effects of disturbances. In closed-loop control systems, the system uses *feedback*, which is the process of measuring a control variable and returning the output to influence the value of the variable.

Block diagrams display the operational units of a control system. Each block in a *component block diagram* represent some major component of the control system, such as measurement, compensation, error detection, and the plant itself. It also depicts the major directions of information and energy flow from one component to another in a control system.

A block can represent the component or process to be controlled. Each block of a control system has a transfer function (represented by differential equations) and defines the block output as a function of the input.

Control system design and analysis objectives include: producing the response to a transient disturbance follow a specified pattern (over-damped or under damped), minimizing the steady-state errors, and achieving the stability.

GLOSSARY OF TECHNICAL TERMS

Terminology used frequently in the field of control systems is compiled here from various sources.

Action of the Controller: Another term used to describe the controller operations is the action of a controller.

Actuating or Error Signal: The actuating or error signal is the reference input signal plus or minus the primary feedback signal.

Actuator: The device that causes the process to provide the output. The device that provides the motive power to the process.

Angle of Departure: The angle at which a locus leaves a complex pole in the s-plane.

Asymptote: The path the root locus follows as the parameter becomes very large and approaches infinity. The number of asymptotes is equal to the number of poles minus the number of zeros.

Automatic Control System: A control system that is self-regulating, without any human intervention.

Automatic: Self-action without any human intervention.

Bandwidth: The frequency at which the frequency response has declined 3 dB from its low-frequency value.

Block Diagram: A block diagram is a simplified pictorial representation of the cause-and-effect relationship between the input(s) and output(s) of a physical system.

Block: A block is a set of elements that can be grouped together with overall characteristics described by an input/output relationship.

Block-Diagram Representation: In a block-diagram representation, each component (or subsystem) is represented as a rectangular block containing one input and one output in a block diagram.

Bode Diagram (Plot): A sinusoidal frequency response plot, where the magnitude response is plotted separately from the phase response. The magnitude plot is dB versus log w, and the phase plot is phase versus log ω. In control systems, the Bode plot is usually made for the open-loop transfer function. Bode plots can also be drawn as straight-line approximations.

Bode Plot: The logarithm of the magnitude of the transfer function is plotted versus the logarithm of ω, the frequency. The phase, ϕ, of the transfer function is separately plotted versus the logarithm of the frequency.

Branches: Individual loci are referred to as *branches* of the root locus. Also, lines that represent subsystems in a signal-flow graph.

Break Frequency: A frequency where the Bode magnitude plot changes slope.

Breakaway Point: A point on the real axis of the s-plane where the root locus leaves the real axis and enters the complex plane.

Break-in Point: A point on the real axis of the s-plane where the root locus enters the real axis from the complex plane.

Cascade Control: Two feedback controllers arranged in such a fashion that the output of one feedback controller becomes an input to the second controller.

Characteristic Equation: The resulting expression obtained when the denominator of the transfer function of the system is set equal to zero is known as the characteristic equation.

Closed-Loop Control System: A control system in which the control (regulating action) is influenced by the output.

Closed-Loop Feedback Control System: A system that uses a measurement of the output and compares it with the desired output.

Closed-Loop Frequency Response: The frequency response of the closed-loop transfer function T (jω).

Closed-Loop System: A system with a measurement of the output signal and a comparison with the desired output to generate an error signal that is applied to the actuator.

Closed-Loop Transfer Function: For a generic feedback system with G(s) in the forward path and H(s) in the feedback path, the closed-loop transfer function, T(s), is G(s)/[1 ± G(s)H(s)], where the + is for negative feedback, and the – is for positive feedback.

Compensation: The term compensation is usually used to indicate the process of increasing accuracy and speeding up the response.

Compensator: An additional component or circuit that is inserted into the system to compensate for a performance deficiency.

Configuration Space: Generally speaking, generalized coordinates, q_i (i = 1, 2, ..., n) define an n-dimensional Cartesian space that is referred to as the *configuration space*.

Constant M Circles: The locus of constant, closed-loop magnitude frequency response for unity feedback systems. It allows the closed-loop magnitude frequency response to be determined from the open-loop magnitude frequency response.

Constant N Circles: The locus of constant, closed-loop phase frequency response for unity feedback systems. It allows the closed-loop phase frequency response to be determined from the open-loop phase frequency response.

Continuous-Time Control Systems: *Continuous-time control systems* or *continuous-data control systems* or *analog control systems* contain or process only continuous-time (or analog) signals and components.

Contour Map: A contour or trajectory in one plane is mapped into another plane by a relation F(s).

Control System: A control system is an interconnection of components forming a system configuration that will provide a desired system response.

Control: Control means to regulate, direct, command, or govern.

Controllability: A property of a system by which an input can be found that takes every state variable from a desired initial state to a desired final state in finite time.

Controllable System: A system is controllable on the interval [t_0, t_f] if there exists a continuous input u(t) such that any initial state $x(t_0)$ can be driven to any arbitrary trial state $x(t_f)$ in a finite time interval $t_f - t_0 > 0$.

Controlled Output C(s): The controlled output C(s) is the output variable of the plant under the control of the system.

Controlled Variable: The output of a plant or process that the system is controlling for the purpose of desired transient response, stability and steady-state error characteristics.

Controller Action: The method by which the automatic controller produces the control signal is known as the control action.

Controller: The subsystem that generates the input to the plant or process.

Corner Frequency: See **break frequency**.

Critical Damping: The case where damping is on the boundary between underdamped and overdamped.

Critically Damped Response: The step response of a second-order system with a given natural frequency that is characterized by no overshoot and a rise time that is faster than any possible overdamped response with the same natural frequency.

Damped Frequency of Oscillation: The sinusoidal frequency of oscillation of an underdamped response.

Damped Natural Frequency: The frequency at which the system oscillates before settling down.

Damped Oscillation: An oscillation in which the amplitude decreases with time.

Damping Ratio: The ratio of the exponential decay frequency to the natural frequency.

dc Motor: An electric actuator that uses an input voltage as a control variable.

Decade: Frequencies that are separated by a factor of 10.

Decibel (dB): The decibel is defined as 10 log P_G, where P_G is the power gain of a signal. Equivalently, the decibel is also 20 log V_G, where V_G is the voltage gain of a signal.

Decoupled System: A state-space representation in which each state equation is a function of only one state variable. Hence, each differential equation can be solved independently of the other equations.

Delay Time: The delay time t_d is the time needed for the response to reach half the final value the very first time. The delay time is interpreted as a time domain specification, is often, defined as the time required for the response to a unit step input to reach 50% of its final value.

Delayed Step Function: A function of time (F(t – a)) that has a zero magnitude before t = a and a constant amplitude after that.

Design of a Control System: The arrangement or the plan of the system structure and the selection of suitable components and parameters.

Design Specifications: A set of prescribed performance criteria.

Design: The term design is used to encompass the entire process of basic system modification so as to meet the requirements of stability, accuracy, and transient response.

Digital Control System: A control system using digital signals and a digital computer to control a process.

Digital Signal: A signal which is defined at only discrete (distinct) instants of the independent variable t is called a *discrete-time* or a *discrete-data* or a *sampled-data* or a *digital signal.*

Digital-to-Analog Converter: A device that converts digital signals to analog signals.

Direct System: See **Open-loop system.**

Discrete-Time Approximation: An approximation used to obtain the time response of a system based on the division of the time into small increments, Δt.

Discrete-Time Control Systems: *Discrete-time control system*, or *discrete-data control system* or *sampled-data control system* has discrete-time signals or components at one or more points in the system.

Disturbance or Noise Input: A disturbance or noise input is an undesired stimulus or input signal affecting the value of the controlled output.

Disturbance Signal: An unwanted input signal that affects the system's output signal.

Disturbance: An unwanted signal that corrupts the input or output of a plant or process.

Dominant Poles: The poles that predominantly generate the transient response.

Dominant Roots: The roots of the characteristic equation that cause the dominant transient response of the system.

Eigenvalues: Any value, λ_i, that satisfies $\mathbf{Ax_i} = \lambda_i \mathbf{x_i}$ for $\mathbf{x_i} \neq 0$. Hence, any value, λ_i, that makes $\mathbf{x_i}$ an eigenvector under the transformation A.

Eigenvector: Any vector that is collinear with a new basis vector after a similarity transformation to a diagonal system.

Electric Circuit Analog: An electrical network whose variables and parameters are analogous to another physical system. The electric circuit analog can be used to solve for variables of the other physical system.

Electrical Impedance: The ratio of the Laplace transform of the voltage to the Laplace transform of the current.

Element (Component): Smallest part of a system that can be treated as a whole (entity).

Engineering Design: The process of designing a technical system.

Equilibrium: The steady-state solution characterized by a constant position or oscillation.

Error Signal: The difference between the desired output, R(s), and the actual output, Y(s). Therefore E(s) = R(s) – Y(s).

Error: The difference between the input and output of a system.

Feed Forward (Control) Element: The feed forward (control) elements are the components of the forward path that generate the control signal applied to the plant or process. The feed forward (control) elements include controller(s), compensator(s), or equalization elements, and amplifiers.

Feedback Compensator: A subsystem placed in a feedback path for the purpose of improving the performance of a closed-loop system.

Feedback Elements: The feedback elements establish the fundamental relationship between the controlled output C(s) and the primary feedback signal B(s). They include sensors of the controlled output, compensators, and controller elements.

Feedback Path: The feedback path is the transmission path from the controlled output back to the summing point.

Feedback Signal: A measure of the output of the system used for feedback to control the system.

Feedback: Feedback is the property of a closed-loop control system which allows the output to be compared with the input to the system such that the appropriate control action may be formed as some function of the input and output.

Flyball Governor: A mechanical device for controlling the speed of a steam engine.

Forced Response: For linear systems, that part of the total response function due to the input. It is typically of the same form as the input and its derivatives.

Forward Path: A *forward path* is a path that connects a source node to a sink node, in which no node is encountered more than once.

Forward-Path Gain: The product of gains found by traversing a path that follows the direction of signal flow from the input node to the output node of a signal-flow graph.

Fourier Transform: The transformation of a function of time, f(t), into the frequency domain.

Frequency Domain Techniques: A method of analyzing and designing linear control systems by using transfer functions and the Laplace transform as well as frequency response techniques.

Frequency Response Techniques: A method of analyzing and designing control systems by using the sinusoidal frequency response characteristics of a system.

Frequency Response: The steady-state response of a system to a sinusoidal input signal.

Gain Crossover Frequency: The frequency at which the open loop gain drops to 0 dB (gain of 1).

Gain Margin: The gain margin is the factor by which the gain factor K can be multiplied before the closed-loop system becomes unstable. It is defined as the magnitude of the reciprocal of the open-loop transfer function evaluated at the frequency w_2 at which the phase angle is –180º.

Gain: The gain of a branch is the transmission function of that branch when the transmission function is a multiplicative operator.

Heat Capacitance: The capacity of an object to store heat.

Ideal Derivative Compensator: See **proportional-plus-derivative controller.**

Ideal Integral Compensator: See **proportional-plus-integral controller**.

Input Transducer: Input transducer converts the form of input to that used by the controller.

Input: The input is the stimulus, excitation, or command applied to a control system, generally from an external source, so as to produce a specified response from the control system.

Instability: The characteristic of a system defined by a natural response that grows without bounds as time approaches infinity.

Integration Network: A network that acts, in part, like an integrator.

Kirchhoff's Law: The sum of voltages around a closed loop equals zero. Also, the sum of currents at a node equals zero.

Lag Compensator: A transfer function, characterized by a pole on the negative real axis close to the origin and a zero close and to the left of the pole, that is used for the purpose of improving the steady-state error of a closed-loop system.

Lag Network: See **Phase-lag network**.

Lag-Lead Compensator: A transfer function, characterized by a pole-zero configuration that is the combination of a lag and a lead compensator, that is used for the purpose of improving both the transient response and the steady-state error of a closed-loop system.

Laplace Transform: A transformation of a function f(t) from the time domain into the complex frequency domain yielding F(s).

Laplace Transformation: A transformation that transforms linear differential equations into algebraic expressions. The transformation is especially useful for modeling, analyzing, and designing control systems as well as solving linear differential equations.

Lead Compensator: A transfer function, characterized by a zero on the negative real axis and a pole to the left of the zero, that is used for the purpose of improving the transient response of a closed-loop system.

Lead Network: See **Phase-lead network**.

Lead-Lag Network: A network with the characteristics of both a lead network and a lag network.

Linear Approximation: An approximate model that results in a linear relationship between the output and the input of the device.

Linear System: A linear system is a system where input/output relationships may be represented by a linear differential equation.

Linearization: The process of approximating a nonlinear differential equation with a linear differential equation valid for small excursions about equilibrium.

Locus: Locus is defined as a set of all points satisfying a set of conditions.

Logarithmic Magnitude: The logarithmic of the magnitude of the transfer function, $20 \log_{10} |G|$.

Logarithmic Plot: See **Bode plot**.

Loop Gain: For a signal-flow graph, the product of branch gains found by traversing a path that starts at a node and ends at the same node without passing through any other node more than once, and following the direction of the signal flow.

Loop: A *loop* is a closed path (with all arrowheads in the same direction) in which no node is encountered more than once. Hence, a source node cannot be a part of a loop, since each node in the loop must have at least one branch into the node and at least one branch out.

Major-Loop Compensation: A method of feedback compensation that adds a compensating zero to the open-loop transfer function for the purpose of improving the transient response of the closed-loop system.

Manual Control System: A control system regulated through human intervention.

Marginal Stability: The characteristic of a system defined by a natural response that neither decays nor grows, but remains constant or oscillates as time approaches infinity as long as the input is not of the same form as the system's natural response.

Marginally Stable System: A closed-loop control system in which roots of the characteristic equation lie on the imaginary axis; for all practical purposes, an unstable system.

Mason's Loop Rule: A rule that enables the user to obtain a transfer function by tracing paths and loops within a system.

Mason's Gain Formula: Mason's gain formula is an alternative method of reducing complex block diagrams into a single block diagram with its associated transfer function for linear systems by inspection.

Mason's Rule: A formula from which the transfer function of a system consisting of the interconnection of multiple subsystems can be found.

Mathematical Model: An equation or set of equations that define the relationship between the input and output (variables).

Maximum Overshoot M_p: The maximum overshoot is the vertical distance between the maximum peak of the response curve and the horizontal line from unity (final value).

Maximum Value of the Frequency Response: A pair of complex poles will result in a maximum value for the frequency response occurring at the resonant frequency.

Minimum Phase: All the zeros of a transfer function lie in the left-hand side of the s-plane.

Minor-Loop Compensation: A method of feedback compensation that changes the poles of a forward-path transfer function for the purpose of improving the transient response of the closed-loop system.

Multiple-Input, Multiple-Output (MIMO) System: A multiple-input, multiple-output (MIMO) system is a system where several parameters may be entered as input and output is represented by multiple variables.

Multivariable Control System: A system with more than one input variable or more than one output variable.

Multivariable Feedback System: The multivariable feedback system where the interrelationships of many controlled variables are considered.

Natural Frequency: The frequency of oscillation of a system if all the damping is removed.

Natural Response: That part of the total response function due to the system and the way the system acquires or dissipates energy.

Negative Feedback: The case where a feedback signal is subtracted from a previous signal in the forward path.

Neutral Zone: The region of error over which the controller does not change its output; also known as dead band or error band.

Nichols Chart: Nichols chart is basically a transformation of the M- and N-circles on the polar plot into noncircular M and N contours on a db magnitude versus phase angle plot in rectangular coordinates.

Nodes: In a signal-flow graph, the internal signals in the diagram, such as the common input to several blocks or the output of summing junction, are called *nodes*.

Nonminimum Phase: Transfer functions with zeros in the right-hand s-plane.

Nonminimum Phase System: A system whose transfer function has zeros in the right half-plane. The step response is characterized by an initial reversal in direction.

Nontouching Loops: Loops that do not have any nodes in common.

Nontouching: Two loops are *nontouching* if these loops have no nodes in common. A loop and a path are nontouching if they have no nodes in common.

Nontouching-Loop Gain: The product of loop gains from nontouching loops taken two, three, and four, and so on at a time.

Number of Separate Loci: Equal to the number of poles of the transfer function, assuming that the number of poles is greater than or equal to the number of zeros of the transfer function.

Noise Input: A disturbance or noise input is an undesired stimulus or input signal affecting the value of the controlled output.

Nyquist Criterion: If a contour A, that encircles the entire right half-plane is mapped through G(s)H(s), then the number of closed-loop poles, Z, in the right half-plane equals the number of open-loop poles, P, that are in the right half-plane minus the number of counterclockwise revolutions, N, around –1, of the mapping; that is, Z = P – N. The mapping is called the *Nyquist diagram* of G(s)H(s).

Nyquist Diagram (Plot): A polar frequency response plot made for the open-loop transfer function.

Nyquist Path: The locus of the points in the s-plane mapped into G(s)-plane in Nyquist plots is called Nyquist path.

Nyquist Stability Criterion: The Nyquist stability criterion establishes the number of poles and zeros of 1 + GH(s) that lie in the right-half plane directly from the Nyquist stability plot of GH(s).

Observability: A property of a system by which an initial state vector, $x(t_0)$, can be found from u(f) and y(t) measured over a finite interval of time from t_0. Simply stated, observability is the property by which the state variables can be estimated from a knowledge of the input, u(i), and output, y(t).

Observable System: A system is observable on the interval $[t_0, t_f]$ if any initial state $x(t_0)$ is uniquely determined by observing the output y(t) on the interval $[t_0, t_f]$.

Observer: A system configuration from which inaccessible states can be estimated.

Octave: Frequencies that are separated by a factor of two.

Open-Loop Control System: A system that utilizes a device to control the process without using feedback. Thus the output has no effect upon the signal to the process.

Open-Loop System: A system without feedback that directly generates the output in response to an input signal.

Open-Loop Transfer Function: For a generic feedback system with G(s) in the forward path and H(s) in the feedback path, the open-loop transfer function is the product of the forward-path transfer function and the feedback transfer function, or, G(s)H(s).

Output Equation: For linear systems, the equation that expresses the output variables of a system as linear combinations of the state variables.

Output: The output is the actual response resulting from a control system.

Overdamped Response: A step response of a second-order system that is characterized by no overshoot.

Overshoot: The amount by which the system output response proceeds beyond the desired response.

Parameter Design: A method of selecting one or two parameters using the root locus method.

Partial-Fraction Expansion: A mathematical equation where a fraction with n factors in its denominator is represented as the sum of simpler fractions.

Path Gain: The *path gain* is the product of the transfer functions of all branches that form the path.

Path: A path is a sequence of connected blocks, the route passing from one variable to another in the direction of signal flow of the blocks without including any variable more than once.

Peak Time: The peak time t_p is the time required for the response to reach the first peak of the overshoot.

Peak Value: The maximum value of the output, reached after application of the unit step input after time t_p.

Per cent Overshoot, %OS: The amount that the underdamped step response overshoots the steady state, or final, value at the peak time, expressed as a percentage of the steady-state value.

Performance Index: A quantitative measure of the performance of a system.

Phase Crossover Frequency: The frequency at which the open loop phase angle drops to –180°.

Phase Margin: The amount of additional open-loop phase shift required at unity gain to make the closed-loop system unstable.

Phase Variables: State variables such that each subsequent state variable is the derivative of the previous state variable.

Phase-Lag Network: A network that provides a negative phase angle and a significant attenuation over the frequency range of interest.

Phase-Lead Network: A network that provides a positive phase angle over the frequency range of interest. Thus phase lead can be used to cause a system to have an adequate phase margin.

Phase-Margin Frequency: The frequency at which the magnitude frequency response plot equals zero dB. It is the frequency at which the phase margin is measured.

Phase-Margin: Phase margin of a stable system is the amount of additional phase log required to bring the system to point of instability.

PI Controller: Controller with a proportional term and an integral term (Proportional-Integral).

Pickoff Point: A block diagram symbol that shows the distribution of one signal to multiple subsystems.

PID Controller: A controller with three terms in which the output is the sum of a proportional term, an integrating term, and a differentiating term, with an adjustable gain for each term.

Plant, Process or Controlled System $G_p(s)$: The plant, process, or controlled system is the system, subsystem, process, or object controlled by the feedback control system. For example, the plant can be a furnace system where the output variable is temperature.

Plant: See **Process.**

Polar Plot: A plot of the real part of G(jω) versus the imaginary part of G(jω).

Pole of a Transfer Function: The root (solution) of the (characteristic) equation obtained by setting the denominator polynomial of the transfer function equal to zero; the value of s that makes (the value of) the transfer function approach infinity (hence the term *pole* (rising to infinity)); complex poles always appear as complex conjugate pairs.

Poles: (1) The values of the Laplace transform variable, s, that cause the transfer function to become infinite, and (2) any roots of factors of the characteristic equation in the denominator that are common to the numerator of the transfer function.

Pole-Zero Map: The s-plane including the locations of the finite poles and zeros of F(s) is called the pole-zero map of F(s).

Positive Feedback: Positive feedback implies that the summing point is an adder.

Primary Feedback Signal: The primary feedback signal is a function of the controlled output summed algebraically with the reference input to establish the actuating or error signal. An open-loop system has no primary feedback signal.

Process Controller: See **PID controller**.

Process: The device, plant, or system under control.

Productivity: The ratio of physical output to physical input of an industrial process.

Proportional Band: The maximum per cent error that will cause a change in controller output from minimum (0%) to maximum (100%).

Proportional-Plus-Derivative (PD) Controller: A controller that feeds forward to the plant a proportion of the actuating signal plus its derivative for the purpose of improving the transient response of a closed-loop system.

Proportional-Plus-Integral (PI) Controller: A controller that feeds forward to the plant a proportion of the actuating signal plus its integral for the purpose of improving the steady-state error of a closed-loop system.

Proportional-Plus-Integral-Plus-Derivative (PID) Controller: A controller that feeds forward to the plant a proportion of the actuating signal plus its integral plus its derivative for the purpose of improving the transient response and steady-state error of a closed-loop system.

Pulse Function: The difference between a step function and a delayed step function.

Ramp Function: A function whose amplitude increases linearly with time.

Reference Input R(s): The reference input is an external signal applied to the control system generally at the first summing point, so as to command a specific action of the processor plant. It typically represents ideal or desired process or plant output response.

Relative Stability: The property that is measured by the relative real part of each root or pair of roots of the characteristic equation.

Residue: The constants in the numerators of the terms in a partial-fraction expansion.

Resonant Frequency: The resonant frequency of a system is defined as the radian frequency at which the magnitude value of C(jω)/R(jω) occurs.

Rise Time: The rise time t_r is customarily defined as the time required for the response to a unit step input to rise from 10 to 90% of its final value. For underdamped second-order system, the 0% to 100% rise time is normally used. For overdamped systems, the 10% to 90% rise time is common.

Risk: Uncertainties embodied in the unintended consequences of a design.

Robot: Programmable computers integrated with a manipulator. A reprogrammable, multifunctional manipulator used for a variety of tasks.

Robust Control System: A system that exhibits the desired performance in the presence of significant plant uncertainty.

Root Locus Method: The method for determining the locus of roots of the characteristic equation $1 + KP(s) = 0$ as K varies from 0 to infinity.

Root Locus Segments on the Real Axis: The root locus lying in a section of the real axis to the left of an odd number of poles and zeros.

Root Sensitivity: The sensitivity of the roots as a parameter changes from its normal value. The root sensitivity is the incremental change in the root divided by the proportional change of the parameter.

Root: The term *root* refers to the roots of the characteristic equation which are the poles of the closed-loop transfer function.

Root-Locus Analysis: The root-locus method is an analytical method for displaying the location of the poles of the closed-loop transfer function $G/(1 + GH)$ as a function of the gain factor K of the open-loop transfer function GH. The method is called the root-locus analysis.

Root-Locus: Root-locus defines a graph of the poles of the closed-loop transfer function as the system parameter, such as the gain is varied.

Routh-Hurwitz Stability Criterion: The Routh-Hurwitz stability criterion states that the dynamic system is stable if both of the following conditions are satisfied: (1) all the coefficients of the characteristic equation are positive, and (2) all the elements of the first column of the Routh-Hurwitz table are positive.

Self-Loop: A self-loop is a feedback loop consisting of a single branch.

Sensitivity: The sensitivity of a system is defined as the ratio of the percentage change in the system-transfer function to the percentage- change of the process transfer function. In practice, the system sensitivity is expressed as the ratio of the percentage-variation in some specific quantity like gain to the percentage change in one of the system parameters.

Settling Time: The time required for the system output to settle within a certain percentage of the input amplitude.

Signal Flow Graph: A signal flow graph is a pictorial representation of the simultaneous equations describing a system. The signal flow graph displays the transmission of signals through the system just as in the block diagram.

Similarity Transformation: A transformation from one state-space representation to another state-space representation. Although the state variables are different, each representation is a valid description of the same system and the relationship between the input and output.

Single-Input, Single-Output (SISO) System: A single-input, single-output (SISO) system is a system where only one parameter enters as input and only one-parameter results as the output.

Sink Node: A *sink node* is a node for which signals flow *only toward* the node. Also known as *output node*.

Source Node: A *source node* is a node for which signals flow *only away* from the node. Hence, for the branches connected to a source node, the arrowheads are all directed away from the node. Also known as *input node*.

Specifications: Statements that explicitly state what the device or product is to be and to do. A set of prescribed performance criteria.

Stability: That characteristic of a system defined by a natural response that decays to zero as time approaches infinity.

Stabilization: The term stabilization is used to indicate the process of achieving the requirements of stability alone.

Stable Closed-Loop System: A system in which the open-loop gain is less than 0 db at a frequency at which the phase angle has reached -180°.

Stable System: A dynamic system with a bounded system response to a bounded input.

State Differential Equation: The differential equation for the state vector: $\dot{\mathbf{x}} = \mathbf{Ax} + \mathbf{Bu}$.

State Equations: A set of n simultaneous, first-order differential equations with n variables, where the n variables to be solved are the state variables.

State of a System: A set of numbers such that the knowledge of these numbers and the input function will, with the equations describing the dynamics, provide the future state of the system.

State Space: The n-dimensional space whose axes are the state variables.

State Variable Equations: When a system's equations of motion are rewritten as a system of first-order differential equations, each of these differential equations consists of the time derivative of the one of the state variables on the left-hand side and an algebraic function of the state variables as well as system outputs, on the right-hand side. These differential equations are referred to as state-variable equations.

State Variable Feedback: Occurs when the control signal, u, for the process is a direct function of all the state variables.

State Variables: State variables are the variables which define the smallest set of variables which determine the state of a system.

State Vector: State vector is a vector which completely describes a system's dynamics in terms of its n-state variables.

State: The property (condition) of a system.

State-Space Representation: A mathematical model for a system that consists of simultaneous, first-order differential equations and an output equation.

State-Transition Matrix: The matrix that performs a transformation on $\mathbf{x}(0)$, taking $\mathbf{x}$ from the initial state, $\mathbf{x}(0)$, to the state $\mathbf{x}(f)$ at any time, $\mathbf{t} \geq 0$.

Static Error Constants: The collection of position constant, velocity constant, and acceleration constant.

Steady-State Error: The difference between the input and output of a system after the natural response has decayed to zero.

Steady-State Response: The system response after the transients have died and output has settled (time response after transient response).

Step Function: A function of time, which has a zero value before t = 0 and has a constant value for all time $t \geq 0$.

Subsystem: A system that is a portion of a larger system.

Summing Junction: A block diagram symbol that shows the algebraic summation of two or more signals.

Summing Point: The summing point also known as a *summing joint* is the block used to represent the addition/subtraction of signals. It is represented as a small circle connected to arrows representing signal lines.

Synthesis: The process by which new physical configurations are created. The combining of separate elements or devices to form a coherent whole.

System Type: The number of pure integrations in the forward path of a unity feedback system.

System Variables: Any variable that responds to an input or initial conditions in a system.

System: A system is a collection, set, or arrangement of elements (subsystems).

Take-off Point: A takeoff point allows the same signal or variable as input to more than one block or summing point, thus permitting the signal to proceed unaltered along several different paths to several destinations. It is represented as a dot (solid circle) with arrows pointing away from it.

The Addition Rule: The value of the variable designated by a node is equal to the sum of all the signals entering the node.

The Design Specifications: The *design specifications* for control systems generally include several time-response indices for a specified input as well as a desired steady-state accuracy.

The Multiplication Rule: A single cascaded (series) connection of (n – 1) branches with transmission functions G_{21}, G_{32}, G_{43}, ..., $G_{n(n-1)}$ can be replaced by a single branch with a new transmission function equal to the product of the original ones.

The Steady-State Response: The steady-state response is that which exists a long time following any input signal initiation.

The Transient-Response: The *transient-response* is the response that disappears with time.

The Transmission Rule: The value of the variable designated by a node is transmitted on every branch leaving that node.

Time Delay: A pure time delay, T, so that events occurring at time t at one point in the system occur at another point in the system at a later time, t + T.

Time Domain: The mathematical domain that incorporates the time response and the description of a system in terms of time t.

Time Response: The time response of a system, subsystem, or element is the output as a function of time, generally, following application of a prescribed input under specified operating conditions.

Time-Domain Representation: See **State-space representation**.

Time-Invariant System: A system described by a differential equation with constant coefficients.

Time-Variant System: A system described by a differential equation with variable coefficients.

Time-Varying System: A system for which one or more parameters may vary with time.

Total Response: The response of a system from the time of application of an input to the point when time approaches infinity.

Trade-off: The result of making a judgment about how much compromise must be made between conflicting criteria.

Transducer: A device that converts a signal from one form to another, for example, from a mechanical displacement to an electrical voltage.

Transfer Function in the Frequency Domain: The ratio of the output to the input signal where the input is a sinusoid. It is expressed as G(jω).

Transfer Function: The transfer function of a system (or a block) is defined as the ratio of output to input.

Transient Response: That parts of the response curve due to the system and the way the system acquires or dissipates energy. In stable systems, it is the part of the response plot prior to the steady-state response.

Undamped Response: The step response of a second-order system that is characterized by a pure oscillation.

Underdamped Response: The step response of a second-order system that is characterized by overshoot.

Unit Step Function: A function of time that has zero magnitude before time t = 0 and unit magnitude after that.

Unstable System: A closed-loop control system in which one or more roots of the characteristic equation lie in the RHP (Right-Hand side of the s-Plane).

Zero of a Transfer Function: The root (solution) of the equation obtained by setting the numerator polynomial of the transfer function equal to 0; the value of s that makes (the value of) the transfer function equal to zero (hence the term *zero*).

Zeros: (1) Those values of the Laplace transform variable, s, that cause the transfer function to become zero, and (2) any roots of factors of the numerator that are common to the characteristic equation in the denominator of the transfer function.

Zero-State Response: That part of the response that depends only upon the input and not the initial state vector.

CHAPTER 2

MATLAB Basics

2.1 INTRODUCTION

This Chapter is a brief introduction to **MATLAB** (an abbreviation of **MAT**rix **LAB**oratory) basics, registered trademark of computer software, version 4.0 or later developed by the Math Works Inc. The software is widely used in many of science and engineering fields. MATLAB is an interactive program for numerical computation and data visualization. MATLAB is supported on Unix, Macintosh, and Windows environments. For more information on MATLAB, contact **The MathWorks.Com**. A Windows version of MATLAB is assumed here. The syntax is very similar for the DOS version.

MATLAB integrates mathematical computing, visualization, and a powerful language to provide a flexible environment for technical computing. The open architecture makes it easy to use MATLAB and its companion products to explore data, create algorithms, and create custom tools that provide early insights and competitive advantages.

Known for its highly optimized matrix and vector calculations, MATLAB offers an intuitive language for expressing problems and their solutions both mathematically and visually. Typical uses include:

- Numeric computation and algorithm development
- Symbolic computation (with the built-in Symbolic Math functions)
- Modeling, simulation, and prototyping
- Data analysis and signal processing
- Engineering graphics and scientific visualization

In this chapter, we will introduce the MATLAB environment. We will learn how to create, edit, save, run, and debug m-files (ASCII files with series of MATLAB statements). We will see how to create arrays (matrices and vectors), and explore the built-in MATLAB linear algebra functions for matrix and vector multiplication, dot and cross products, transpose, determinants, and inverses, and for the solution of linear equations. MATLAB is based on the language C, but is generally much easier to use. We will also see how to program logic constructs and loops in MATLAB, how to use subprograms and functions, how to use comments (%) for explaining the programs and tabs for easy readability, and how to print and plot graphics both two and three dimensional. MATLAB's functions for symbolic mathematics are presented. Use of these functions to perform symbolic operations, to develop closed form expressions for solutions to algebraic equations, ordinary differential equations, and system of equations was presented. Symbolic mathematics can also be used to determine analytical expressions for the derivative and integral of an expression.

2.1.1 Starting and Quitting MATLAB

To start MATLAB click on the MATLAB icon or type in MATLAB, followed by pressing the *enter* or *return* key at the system prompt. The screen will produce the MATLAB **prompt** >> (or EDU >>), which indicates that MATLAB is waiting for a command to be entered.

In order to quit MATLAB, type **quit** or **exit** after the prompt, followed by pressing the *enter* or *return* key.

2.1.2 Display Windows

MATLAB has three display windows. They are

1. A *Command Window* which is used to enter commands and data to display plots and graphs.
2. A *Graphics Window* which is used to display plots and graphs
3. *An Edit Window* which is used to create and modify M-files. M-files are files that contain a program or script of MATLAB commands.

2.1.3 Entering Commands

Every command has to be followed by a carriage return ⟨cr⟩ (enter key) in order that the command can be executed. MATLAB commands are case sensitive and *lower case* letters are used throughout.

To execute an *M-file* (such as Project_1.m), simply enter the name of the file without its extension (as in Project_1).

2.1.4 MATLAB Expo

In order to see some of the MATLAB capabilities, enter the *demo* command. This will initiate the *MATLAB EXPO*. *MATLAB* Expo is a graphical demonstration environment that shows some of the different types of operations which can be conducted with MATLAB.

2.1.5 Abort

In order to *abort* a command in MATLAB, hold down the control key and press C to generate a local abort with MATLAB.

2.1.6 The Semicolon (;)

If a semicolon (;) is typed at the end of a command the output of the command is not displayed.

2.1.7 Typing %

When per cent symbol (%) is typed in the beginning of a line, the line is designated as a comment. When the *enter* key is pressed the line is not executed.

2.1.8 The clc Command

Typing *clc* command and pressing *enter* cleans the command window. Once the *clc* command is executed a clear window is displayed.

2.1.9 Help

MATLAB has a host of built-in functions. For a complete list, refer to MATLAB user's guide or refer to the *on-line Help*. To obtain help on a particular topic in the list, e.g., inverse, type *help inv*.

2.1.10 Statements and Variables

Statements have the form

>> variable = expression

The equals ("=") sign implies the assignment of the expression to the variable. For instance, to enter a 2 × 2 matrix with a variable name A, we write

>> A == [1 2 ; 3 4] ⟨ret⟩

The statement is executed after the carriage return (or enter) key is pressed to display

```
A =
        1    2
        3    4
```

2.2 ARITHMETIC OPERATIONS

The symbols for arithmetic operations with scalars are summarized below in Table 2.1.

Table 2.1

Arithmetic operation	*Symbol*	*Example*
Addition	+	6 + 3 = 9
Subtraction	–	6 – 3 = 3
Multiplication	*	6 * 3 = 18
Right division	/	6/3 = 2
Left division	\	6\3 = 3/6 = 1/2
Exponentiation	^	6 ^ 3 (6^3 = 216)

2.3 DISPLAY FORMATS

MATLAB has several different screen output formats for displaying numbers. These formats can be found by typing the help command: help format in the Command Window. A few of these formats are shown in Table 2.2.

Table 2.2 Display formats

Command	*Description*	*Example*
format short	Fixed-point with 4 decimal digits	>> 351/7 ans = 50.1429
format long	Fixed-point with 14 decimal digits	>> 351/7 ans = 50.14285714285715
format short e	Scientific notation with 4 decimal digits	>> 351/7 ans = 5.0143e + 001
format long e	Scientific notation with 15 decimal digits	>> 351/7 ans = 5.014285714285715e001
format short g	Best of 5 digit fixed or floating point	>> 351/7 ans = 50.143
format long g	Best of 15 digit fixed or floating point	>> 351/7 ans = 50.1428571428571
format bank	Two decimal digits	>> 351/7 ans = 50.14
format compact	Eliminates empty lines to allow more lines with information displayed on the screen	
format loose	Adds empty lines (opposite of compact)	

2.4 ELEMENTARY MATH BUILT-IN FUNCTIONS

MATLAB contains a number of functions for performing computations which require the use of logarithms, elementary math functions, and trigonometric math functions. List of these commonly used elementary MATLAB mathematical built-in functions are given in Tables 2.3 to 2.8.

Table 2.3 Common math functions

Function	*Description*
abs(x)	Computes the absolute value of **x**.
sqrt(x)	Computes the square root of **x**.
round(x)	Rounds **x** to the nearest integer.
fix(x)	Rounds (or truncates) **x** to the nearest integer toward 0.
floor(x)	Rounds **x** to the nearest integer toward $-\infty$.
ceil(x)	Rounds **x** to the nearest integer toward ∞.
sign(x)	Returns a value of –1 if **x** is less than 0, a value of 0 if **x** equals 0, and a value of 1 otherwise.
rem(x, y)	Returns the remainder of x/y. for example, **rem(25, 4)** is 1, and **rem(100, 21)** is 16. This function is also called a **modulus** function.
exp(x)	Computes e^x, where *e* is the base for natural logarithms, or approximately 2.718282.
log(x)	Computes ln **x**, the natural logarithm of **x** to the base e.
log$_{10}$(x)	Computes $\log_{10}$ **x**, the common logarithm of **x** to the base 10.

Table 2.4 Exponential functions

Function	*Description*
exp.(x)	Exponential (e^x)
ln(x)	Natural logarithm
log$_{10}$(x)	Base 10 logarithm
sqrt(x)	Square root

Table 2.5 Trigonometric and hyperbolic functions

Function	*Description*
sin(x)	Computes the sine of **x**, where **x** is in radians.
cos(x)	Computes the cosine of **x**, where **x** is in radians.
tan(x)	Computes the tangent of **x**, where **x** is in radians.
asin(x)	Computes the arcsine or inverse sine of **x**, where **x** must be between –1 and 1. The function returns an angle in radians between $-\pi/2$ and $\pi/2$.
acos(x)	Computes the arccosine or inverse cosine of **x**, where **x** must be between –1 and 1. The function returns an angle in radians between 0 and π.
atan(x)	Computes the arctangent or inverse tangent of **x**. The function returns an angle in radians between $-\pi/2$ and $\pi/2$.
atan2(y, x)	Computes the arctangent or inverse tangent of the value *y/x*. The function returns an angle in radians that will be between $-\pi$ and π, depending on the signs of **x** and **y**.
sinh(x)	Computes the hyperbolic sine of **x**, which is equal to $\frac{e^x - e^{-x}}{2}$.
cosh(x)	Computes the hyperbolic cosine of **x**, which is equal to $\frac{e^x + e^{-x}}{2}$.
tanh(x)	Computes the hyperbolic tangent of **x**, which is equal to $\frac{\sinh x}{\cosh x}$.
asinh(x)	Computes the inverse hyperbolic sine of **x**, which is equal to $\ln\left(x+\sqrt{x^2+1}\right)$.
acosh(x)	Computes the inverse hyperbolic cosine of **x**, which is equal to $\ln\left(x+\sqrt{x^2-1}\right)$.
atanh(x)	Computes the inverse hyperbolic tangent of **x**, which is equal to $\ln\sqrt{\frac{1+x}{1-x}}$ for $\lvert\mathbf{x}\rvert \le 1$.

Table 2.6 Round-off functions

Function	*Description*	*Example*
round(x)	Round to the nearest integer	>> round(20/6) ans = 3
fix(x)	Round towards zero	>> fix(13/6) ans = 2
ceil(x)	Round towards infinity	>> ceil(13/5) ans = 3
floor(x)	Round towards minus infinity	>> floor(–10/4) ans = –3
rem(x, y)	Returns the remainder after **x** is divided by **y**	>> rem(14, 3) ans = 2
sign(x, y)	Signum function. Returns 1 if **x** > 0, –1 if **x** < 0, and 0 if **x** = 0.	>> sign(7) ans = 1

Table 2.7 Complex number functions

Function	*Description*
conj(x)	Computes the complex **conjugate** of the complex number **x**. Thus, if **x** is equal to a + ib, then **conj(x)** will be equal to a – ib.
real(x)	Computes the real portion of the complex number **x**.
imag(x)	Computes the imaginary portion of the complex number **x**.
abs(x)	Computes the absolute value of **magnitude** of the complex number **x**.
angle(x)	Computes the angle using the value of **atan2(imag(x), real(x);** thus, the angle value is between –π and π.

Table 2.8 Arithmetic operations with complex numbers

Operation	*Result*
$c_1 + c_2$	$(a_1 + a_2) + i(b_1 + b_2)$
$c_1 - c_2$	$(a_1 - a_2) + i(b_1 - b_2)$
$c_1 \bullet c_2$	$(a_1a_2 - b_1b_2) + i(a_1b_2 - a_2b_1)$
$\dfrac{c_1}{c_2}$	$\left(\dfrac{a_1a_2 + b_1b_2}{a_2^2 + b_2^2}\right) + i\left(\dfrac{a_2b_1 - b_2a_1}{a_2^2 + b_2^2}\right)$
$\lvert c_1 \rvert$	$\sqrt{a_1^2 + b_1^2}$ (magnitude or absolute value of c_1)
$c_1{}^*$	$a_1 - ib_1$ (conjugate of c_1)
(Assume that $c_1 = a_1 + ib_1$ and $c_2 = a_2 + ib_2$)	

2.5 VARIABLE NAMES

A variable is a name made of a letter or a combination of several letters and digits. Variable names can be up to 63 (in MATLAB 7) characters long (31 characters on MATLAB 6.0). MATLAB is case sensitive. For instance, XX, Xx, xX, and xx are the names of four different variables. It should be noted here that not to use the names of a built-in functions for a variable. For instance, avoid using: sin, cos, exp, sqrt, ..., etc. Once a function name is used to define a variable, the function cannot be used.

2.6 PREDEFINED VARIABLES

MATLAB includes a number of predefined variables. Some of the predefined variables that are available to use in MATLAB programs are summarized in Table 2.9.

Table 2.9 Predefined variables

Predefined variable in MATLAB	*Description*
ans	Represents a value computed by an expression but not stored in variable name.
pi	Represents the number π.
eps	Represents the floating-point precision for the computer being used. This is the smallest difference between two numbers.
inf	Represents infinity which for instance occurs as a result of a division by zero. A warning message will be displayed or the value will be printed as ∞.
i	Defined as $\sqrt{-1}$, which is: 0 + 1.0000i.
j	Same as i.
NaN	Stands for Not a Number. Typically occurs as a result of an expression being undefined, as in the case of division of zero by zero.
clock	Represents the current time in a six-element row vector containing year, month, day, hour, minute, and seconds.
date	Represents the current date in a character string format.

2.7 COMMANDS FOR MANAGING VARIABLES

Table 2.10 lists commands that can be used to eliminate variables or to obtain information about variables that have been created. The procedure is to enter the command in the Command Window and the *Enter* key is to be pressed.

Table 2.10 Commands for managing variables

Command	*Description*
clear	Removes all variables from the memory.
clear x, y, z	Clears/removes only variables **x, y,** and **z** from the memory.
who	Lists the variables currently in the workspace.
whos	Displays a list of the variables currently in the memory and their size together with information about their bytes and class.

2.8 GENERAL COMMANDS

In Tables 2.11 to 2.15 the useful general commands on on-line help, workspace information, directory information, and general information are given.

Table 2.11 On-line help

Function	*Description*
Help	Lists topics on which help is available.
Helpwin	Opens the interactive help window.
Helpdesk	Opens the web browser based help facility.
help *topic*	Provides help on *topic*.
lookfor *string*	Lists help topics containing *string*.
demo	Runs the demo program.

Table 2.12 Workspace information

Function	*Description*
who	Lists variables currently in the workspace.
whos	Lists variables currently in the workspace with their size.
what	Lists m-, mat-, and mex-files on the disk.
clear	Clears the workspace, all variables are removed.
clear x y z	Clears only variables x, y, and z.
clear all	Clears all variables and functions from workspace.
mlock *fun*	Locks function *fun* so that **clear** cannot remove it.
munlock *fun*	Unlocks function *fun* so that **clear** can remove it.
clc	Clears command window, command history is lost.
home	Same as **clc**.
clf	Clears figure window.

Table 2.13 Directory information

Function	*Description*
pwd	Shows the current working directory.
cd	Changes the current working directory.
dir	Lists contents of the current directory.
ls	Lists contents of the current directory, same as **dir**.
path	Gets or sets MATLAB search path.
editpath	Modifies MATLAB search path.
copyfile	Copies a file.
mkdir	Creates a directory.

Table 2.14 General information

Function	*Description*
Computer	Tells you the computer type your are using.
Clock	Gives you wall clock time and date as a vector.
Date	Tells you the date as a string.
More	Controls the paged output according to the screen size.
Ver	Gives the license and the version information about MATLAB installed on your computer.
Bench	Benchmarks your computer on running MATLAB compared to other computers.

Table 2.15 Termination

Function	*Description*
c (Control-c)	Local abort, kills the current command execution.
quit	Quits MATLAB.
exit	Same as **quit**.

2.9 ARRAYS

An array is a list of numbers arranged in rows and/or columns. A one-dimensional array is a row or a column of numbers and a two-dimensional array has a set of numbers arranged in rows and columns. An array operation is performed *element-by-element*.

2.9.1 Row Vector

A vector is a row or column of elements.
In a row vector the elements are entered with a space or a comma between the elements inside the square brackets. For example,

x = [7 –1 2 –5 8]

or x = [7, –1, 2, –5, 8]

2.9.2 Column Vector

In a column vector the elements are entered with a semicolon between the elements inside the square brackets. For example,

x = [7; –1; 2; –5; 8]

2.9.3 Matrix

A matrix is a two-dimensional array which has numbers in rows and columns. A matrix is entered row-wise with consecutive elements of a row separated by a space or a comma, and the rows separated by semicolons or carriage returns. The entire matrix is enclosed within square brackets. The elements of the matrix may be real numbers or complex numbers. For example to enter the matrix,

$$A = \begin{bmatrix} 1 & 3 & -4 \\ 0 & -2 & 8 \end{bmatrix}$$

The MATLAB input command is

A= [1 3 –4 ; 0 –2 8]

Similarly for complex number elements of a matrix B

$$B = \begin{bmatrix} -5x & \ln 2x + 7\sin 3y \\ 3i & 5-13i \end{bmatrix}$$

The MATLAB input command is

B = [–5*x log(2*x) + 7*sin(3*y); 3i 5 – 13i]

2.9.4 Addressing Arrays

A colon can be used in MATLAB to address a range of elements in a vector or a matrix.

1. Colon for a vector

Va(:) – refers to all the elements of the vector **Va** (either a row or a column vector).

Va(m:n) – refers to elements m through n of the vector **Va**.

For instance

```
>>    V = [2 5 –1 11 8 4 7 –3 11]
>>    u = V (2:8)
      u = 5 –1 11 8 4 7 –3 11
```

2. Colon for a matrix

Table 2.16 gives the use of a colon in addressing arrays in a matrix.

Table 2.16 Colon use for a matrix

Command	*Description*
A(:, n)	Refers to the elements in all the rows of a column n of the matrix A.
A(n, :)	Refers to the elements in all the columns of row n of the matrix A.
A(:, m:n)	Refers to the elements in all the rows between columns m and n of the matrix A.
A(m:n, :)	Refers to the elements in all the columns between rows m and n of the matrix A.
A(m:n, p:q)	Refers to the elements in rows m through n and columns p through q of the matrix A.

2.9.5 Adding Elements to a Vector or a Matrix

A variable that exists as a vector, or a matrix, can be changed by adding elements to it. Addition of elements is done by assigning values of the additional elements, or by appending existing variables. Rows and/or columns can be added to an existing matrix by assigning values to the new rows or columns.

2.9.6 Deleting Elements

An element, or a range of elements, of an existing variable can be deleted by reassigning blanks to these elements. This is done simply by the use of square brackets with nothing typed in between them.

2.9.7 Built-in Functions

Some of the built-in functions available in MATLAB for managing and handling arrays as listed in Table 2.17.

Table 2.17 Built-in functions for handling arrays

Function	*Description*	*Example*
length(A)	Returns the number of elements in the vector **A**.	>> A = [5 9 2 4]; >> length(A) ans = 4
size(A)	Returns a row vector [m, n], where m and n are the size m × n of the array **A**.	>> A = [2 3 0 8 11; 6 17 5 7 1] A = 2 3 0 8 11 6 17 5 7 1 >> size(A) ans = 2 5
reshape(A, m, n)	Rearrange a matrix A that has r rows and s columns to have m rows and n columns. r times s must be equal to m times n.	>> A = [3 1 4; 9 0 7] A = 3 1 4 9 0 7 >> B = reshape(A, 3, 2) B = 3 0 9 4 1 7
diag(v)	When v is a vector, creates a square matrix with the elements of v in the diagonal.	>> v = [3 2 1]; >> A = diag(v) A = 3 0 0 0 2 0 0 0 1
diag(A)	When A is a matrix, creates a vector from the diagonal elements of A.	>> A = [1 8 3; 4 2 6; 7 8 3] A = 1 8 3 4 2 6 7 8 3 >> vec = diag(A) vec = 1 2 3

2.10 OPERATIONS WITH ARRAYS

We consider here matrices that have more than one row and more than one column.

2.10.1 Addition and Subtraction of Matrices

The addition (the sum) or the subtraction (the difference) of the two arrays is obtained by adding or subtracting their corresponding elements. These operations are performed with arrays of identical size (same number of rows and columns).

For example if A and B are two arrays (2 × 3 matrices).

$$A = \begin{bmatrix} a_{11} & a_{12} & a_{13} \\ a_{21} & a_{22} & a_{23} \end{bmatrix} \text{ and } B = \begin{bmatrix} b_{11} & b_{12} & b_{13} \\ b_{21} & b_{22} & b_{23} \end{bmatrix}$$

Then, the matrix addition (A + B) is obtained by adding A and B is

$$\begin{bmatrix} a_{11}+b_{11} & a_{12}+b_{12} & a_{13}+b_{13} \\ a_{21}+b_{21} & a_{22}+b_{22} & a_{23}+b_{23} \end{bmatrix}$$

2.10.2 Dot Product

The dot product is a scalar computed from two vectors of the same size. The scalar is the sum of the products of the values in corresponding positions in the vectors.

For n elements in the vectors A and B:

$$\text{dot product} = A \bullet B = \sum_{i=1}^{n} a_i\, b_i$$

dot(A, B) Computes the dot product of A and B. If A and B are matrices, the dot product is a row vector containing the dot products for the corresponding columns of A and B.

2.10.3 Array Multiplication

The value in position $c_{i,j}$ of the product C of two matrices, A and B, is the dot product of row i of the first matrix and column of the second matrix:

$$c_{i,j} = \sum_{k=1}^{n} a_{i,k}\, b_{k,j}$$

2.10.4 Array Division

The division operation can be explained by means of the identity matrix and the inverse matrix operation.

2.10.5 Identity Matrix

An identity matrix is a square matrix in which all the diagonal elements are 1's, and the remaining elements are 0's. If a matrix A is square, then it can be multiplied by the identity matrix, I, from the left or from the right:

$$AI = IA = A$$

2.10.6 Inverse of a Matrix

The matrix B is the inverse of the matrix A if when the two matrices are multiplied the product is the identity matrix. Both matrices A and B must be square and the order of multiplication can be AB or BA.

$$AB = BA = I$$

2.10.7 Transpose

The transpose of a matrix is a new matrix in which the rows of the original matrix are the columns of the new matrix. The transpose of a given matrix A is denoted by A^T. In MATLAB, the transpose of the matrix A is denoted by A′.

2.10.8 Determinant

A determinant is a scalar computed from the entries in a square matrix. For a 2 × 2 matrix A, the determinant is

$$|A| = a_{11}\,a_{22} - a_{21}\,a_{12}$$

MATLAB will compute the determinant of a matrix using the **det** function:

det(A) computes the determinant of a square matrix A.

2.10.9 Array Division

MATLAB has two types of array division, which are the left division and the right division.

2.10.10 Left Division

The left division is used to solve the matrix equation Ax = B where x and B are column vectors. Multiplying both sides of this equation by the inverse of A, A^{-1}, we have

$$A^{-1}Ax = A^{-1}B$$

or

$$Ix = x = A^{-1}B$$

Hence

$$x = A^{-1}B$$

In MATLAB, the above equation is written by using the left division character:

x = A\B

2.10.11 Right Division

The right division is used to solve the matrix equation xA = B where x and B are row vectors. Multiplying both sides of this equation by the inverse of A, A^{-1}, we have

$$x \bullet AA^{-1} = B \bullet A^{-1}$$

or

$$x = B \bullet A^{-1}$$

In MATLAB, this equation is written by using the right division character:

x = B/A

2.10.12 Eigenvalues and Eigenvectors

Consider the following equation,

$$AX = \lambda X \tag{2.1}$$

where A is an n × n square matrix, X is a column vector with n rows and λ is a scalar.

The values of λ for which X are nonzero are called the *eigenvalues* of the matrix A, and the corresponding values of X are called the *eigenvectors* of the matrix A.

Eq. (2.1) can also be used to find the following equation:

$$(A - \lambda I)X = 0 \tag{2.2}$$

where I is an n × n identity matrix. Eq. (2.2) corresponding to a set of homogeneous equations and has nontrivial solutions only if the determinant is equal to zero, or

$$|A - \lambda I| = 0 \tag{2.3}$$

Eq. (2.3) is known as the *characteristic equation* of the matrix A. The solution to Eq. (2.3) gives the eigenvalues of the matrix A.

MATLAB determines both the eigenvalues and eigenvectors for a matrix A.

eig(A) Computes a column vector containing the eigenvalues of A.

[Q, d] = eig(A) Computes a square matrix Q containing the eigenvectors of A as columns and a square matrix d containing the eigenvalues (λ) of A on the diagonal. The values of Q and d are such that Q*Q is the identity matrix and A*X equals λ times X.

Triangular factorisation or lower-upper factorisation: Triangular or lower-upper factorisation expresses a square matrix as the product of two triangular matrices – a lower triangular matrix and an upper triangular matrix. The **lu** function in MATLAB computes the LU factorisation:

[L, U] = lu(A) Computes a permuted lower triangular factor in L and an upper triangular factor in U such that the product of L and U is equal to A.

***QR factorisation*:** The QR factorisation method factors a matrix A into the product of an orthonormal matrix and an upper-triangular matrix. The **qr** function is used to perform the QR factorisation in MATLAB:

[Q, R] = qr(A) Computes the values of Q and R such that A = QR.Q will be an orthonormal matrix, and R will be an upper triangular matrix.

For a matrix A of size m × n, the size of Q is m × m, and the size of R is m × n.

***Singular Value Decomposition (SVD)*:** Singular value decomposition decomposes a matrix A (size m × n) into a product of three matrix factors.

$$A = USV$$

where U and V are orthogonal matrices and *S* is a diagonal matrix. The size of U is m × m, the size of V is n × n, and the size of S is m × n. The values on the diagonal matrix S are called singular values. The number of nonzero singular values is equal to the rank of the matrix.

The SVD factorisation can be obtained using the **svd** function:

[U, S, V] = svd(A) Computes the factorisation of A into the product of three matrices, USV, where U and V are orthogonal matrices and S is a diagonal matrix.

svd(A) Returns the diagonal elements of S, which are the singular values of A.

2.11 ELEMENT-BY-ELEMENT OPERATIONS

Element-by-element operations can only be done with arrays of the same size. Element-by-element multiplication, division, and exponentiation of two vectors or matrices is entered in MATLAB by typing a period in front of the arithmetic operator. Table 2.18 lists these operations.

Table 2.18 Element-by-element operations

Arithmetic operators			
Matrix operators		*Array operators*	
+	Addition	+	Addition
–	Subtraction	–	Subtraction
*	Multiplication	•*	Array multiplication
^	Exponentiation	•^	Array exponentiation
/	Left division	•/	Array left division
\	Right division	•\	Array right division

2.11.1 Built-in Functions for Arrays

Table 2.19 lists some of the many built-in functions available in MATLAB for analyzing arrays.

Table 2.19 MATLAB built-in array functions

Function	*Description*	*Example*
mean(A)	If A is a vector, returns the mean value of the elements	>> A = [3 7 2 16]; >> mean(A) ans = 14
C = max(A)	If A is a vector, C is the largest element in A. If A is a matrix, C is a row vector containing the largest element of each column of A.	>> A = [3 7 2 16 9 5 18 13 0 4]; >> C = max(A) C = 18
[d, n] = max(A)	If A is a vector, d is the largest element in A, n is the position of the element (the first if several have the max value).	>> [d, n] = max(A) d = 18 n = 7

(Contd...)

Function	*Description*	*Example*
min(A	The same as **max(A)**, but for the smallest element.	>> A = [3 7 2 16]; >> min(A) ans = 2
[d, n] = min(A)	The same as **[d, n] = max(A)**, but for the smallest element.	
sum(A)	If A is a vector, returns the sum of the elements of the vector.	>> A = [3 7 2 16]; >> sum(A) ans = 28
sort(A)	If A is a vector, arranges the elements of the vector in ascending order.	>> A = [3 7 2 16]; >> sort(A) ans = 2 3 7 16
median(A)	If A is a vector, returns the median value of the elements of the vector.	>> A = [3 7 2 16]; >> median(A) ans = 5
std(A)	If A is a vector, returns the standard deviation of the elements of the vector.	>> A = [3 7 2 16]; >> std(A) ans = 6.3770
det(A)	Returns the determinant of a square matrix A.	>> A = [1 2; 3 4]; >> det(A) ans = –2
dot(a, b)	Calculates the scalar (dot) product of two vectors a and b. The vector can each be row or column vectors.	>> a = [5 6 7]; >> b = [4 3 2]; >> dot(a,b) ans = 52
cross(a, b)	Calculates the cross product of two vectors a and b, (a × b). The two vectors must have 3 elements	>> a = [5 6 7]; >> b = [4 3 2]; >> cross(a,b) ans = –9 18 –9
inv(A)	Returns the inverse of a square matrix A.	>> a = [1 2 3; 4 6 8; –1 2 3]; >> inv(A) ans = –0.5000 0.0000 –0.5000 –5.0000 1.5000 1.0000 3.5000 –1.0000 –0.5000

2.12 RANDOM NUMBERS GENERATION

There are many physical processes and engineering applications that require the use of *random numbers* in the development of a solution.

MATLAB has two commands *rand* and *rand* n that can be used to assign random numbers to variables.

The *rand* command: The *rand* command generates uniformly distributed over the interval [0, 1]. A *seed value* is used to initiate a random sequence of values. The seed value is initially set to zero. However, it can be changed with the *seed* function.

The command can be used to assign these numbers to a scalar, a vector, or a matrix, as shown in Table 2.20.

Table 2.20 The *rand* command

Command	*Description*	*Example*
rand	Generates a single random number between 0 and 1.	>> rand ans = 0.9501
rand(1, n)	Generates an n elements row vector of random numbers between 0 and 1.	>> a = rand(1, 3) a = 0.4565 0.0185 0.8214
rand(n)	Generates an n × n matrix with random numbers between 0 and 1.	>> b = rand(3) b = 0.7382 0.9355 0.8936 0.1763 0.9165 0.0579 0.4057 0.4103 0.3529
rand(m, n)	Generates an m × n matrix with random numbers between 0 and 1.	>> c = rand(2, 3) c = 0.2028 0.6038 0.1988 0.1987 0.2722 0.0153
randperm(n)	Generates a row vector with n elements that are random permutation of integers 1 through n.	>> randperm(7) ans = 5 2 4 7 1 6 3

2.12.1 The Random Command

MATLAB will generate Gaussian values with a mean of zero and a variance of 1.0 if a normal distribution is specified. The MATLAB functions for generating Gaussian values are as follows:

randn(n) Generates an n × n matrix containing Gaussian (or normal) random numbers with a mean of 0 and a variance of 1.

Randn(m, n) Generates an m × n matrix containing Gaussian (or normal) random numbers with a mean of 0 and a variance of 1.

2.13 POLYNOMIALS

A *polynomial* is a function of a single variable that can be expressed in the following form:

$$f(x) = a_0x^n + a_1x^{n-1} + a_2x^{n-2} + \ldots + a_{n-1}x^1 + a_n$$

where the variable is x and the coefficients of the polynomial are represented by the values a_0, a_1, ... and so on. The *degree* of a polynomial is equal to the largest value used as an exponent.

A vector represents a polynomial in MATLAB. When entering the data in MATLAB , simply enter each coefficient of the polynomial into the vector in descending order. For example, consider the polynomial

$$5s^5 + 7s^4 + 2s^2 - 6s + 10$$

To enter this into MATLAB, we enter this as a vector as

```
>>        x = [5  7  0  2  –6 10]
          x =  5  7  0  2  –6  10
```

It is necessary to enter the coefficients of all the terms.

MATLAB contains functions that perform polynomial multiplication and division, which are listed below:

conv(a, b) Computes a coefficient vector that contains the coefficients of the product of polynomials represented by the coefficients in **a** and **b**. The vectors **a** and **b** do not have to be the same size.

[q, r] = deconv(n, d) Returns two vectors. The first vector contains the coefficients of the quotient and the second vector contains the coefficients of the remainder polynomial.

The MATLAB function for determining the roots of a polynomial is the **roots** function:

root(a) Determines the roots of the polynomial represented by the coefficient vector **a**. The roots function returns a column vector containing the roots of the polynomial; the number of roots is equal to the degree of the polynomial. When the roots of a polynomial are known, the coefficients of the polynomial are determined when all the linear terms are multiplied, we can use the **poly** function:

poly(r) Determines the coefficients of the polynomial whose roots are contained in the vector **r**.

The output of the function is a row vector containing the polynomial coefficients.

The value of a polynomial can be computed using the *polyval* function, **polyval (a, x)**. It evaluates a polynomial with coefficients **a** for the values in **x**. The result is a matrix the same size ad **x**. For instance, to find the value of the above polynomial at s = 2,

```
>>        x = polyval([5  7 0  2  –6 10], 2)
          x =

          278
```

To find the roots of the above polynomial, we enter the command **roots (a)** which determines the roots of the polynomial represented by the coefficient vector **a**.

```
>>  roots([5 7 0 2 –6 10])
        ans =
              –1.8652
              –0.4641 + 1.0832i
              –0.4641 – 1.0832i
               0.6967 + 0.5355i
               0.6967 – 0.5355i
% or
>>          x = [5 7 0 2 –6 10]
            x =
               5   7   0   2   –6   10
>>          r = roots(x)
            r =
              –1.8652
              –0.4641 + 1.0832i
              –0.4641 – 1.0832i
               0.6967 + 0.5355i
               0.6967 – 0.5355i
```

To multiply two polynomials together, we enter the command *conv*.

The polynomials are: x = 2x + 5 and y = x^2 + 3x + 7

```
>>          x = [2 5];
>>          y = [1 3  7];
>>          z = conv(x, y)
            z =
           2 11 29 35
```

To divide two polynomials, we use the command *deconv*.

```
            z = [2 11 29 35]; x = [2 5]
>>       [g, t] = deconv (z, x)
            g = 1  3  7
            t = 0   0   0   0
```

2.14 SYSTEM OF LINEAR EQUATIONS

A system of equations is nonsingular if the matrix **A** containing the coefficients of the equations is nonsingular. A system of nonsingular simultaneous linear equations (**AX = B**) can be solved using two methods:

(*a*) Matrix Division Method.

(*b*) Matrix Inversion Method.

2.14.1 Matrix Division

The solution to the matrix equation **AX = B** is obtained using matrix division, or **X = A/B.** The vector **X** then contains the values of **x.**

2.14.2 Matrix Inverse

For the solution of the matrix equation **AX = B**, we premultiply both sides of the equation by $\mathbf{A^{-1}}$.

$$A^{-1}AX = A^{-1}B$$

or

$$IX = A^{-1}B$$

where **I** is the identity matrix.

Hence

$$\mathbf{X} = \mathbf{A^{-1}B}$$

In MATLAB, we use the command **x** = inv **(A)*B**. Similarly, for **XA = B**, we use the command **x = B***inv **(A).**

The basic computational unit in MATLAB is the matrix. A matrix expression is enclosed in square brackets, [ ]. Blanks or commas separate the column elements, and semicolons or carriage returns separate the rows.

```
>>      A = [1 2 3 4 ; 5  6 7 8 ; 9 10 11 12]
        A =
             1   2   3   4
             5   6   7   8
             9  10  11  12
```

The transpose of a simple matrix or a complex matrix is obtained by using the *apostrophe* key

```
>>      B = A'
        B =
             1    5    9
             2    6   10
             3    7   11
             4    8   12
```

Matrix multiplication is accomplished as follows:

```
>>      C = A * B
        C =
              30    70   110
              70   174   278
             110   278   446
```

```
>>      C = B * A
        C =

            107   122   137   152
            122   140   158   176
            137   158   179   200
            152   176   200   224
```

The inverse of a matrix D is obtained as:

```
>>      D = [1 2; 34]
        D =

            1   2
            3   4

>>      E = inv (D)
        E =

            -2.0000    1.0000
             1.5000   -0.5000
```

Similarly, its eigenvalue is

```
>>   eig (D)
     ans =

            -0.3723
             5.3723
```

Matrix operations require that the matrix dimensions be compatible. If A is an $n \times m$ and B is a $p \times r$ then $A \pm B$ is allowed only if $n = p$ and $m = r$. Similarly, matrix product A * B is allowed only if $m = p$.

EXAMPLES WITH SOLUTIONS

Example E2.1

Consider the two matrices;

$$A = \begin{bmatrix} 1 & 0 & 1 \\ 2 & 3 & 4 \\ -1 & 6 & 7 \end{bmatrix} \text{ and } B = \begin{bmatrix} 7 & 4 & 2 \\ 3 & 5 & 6 \\ -1 & 2 & 1 \end{bmatrix}$$

Using MATLAB, determine the following:

(*a*) **A + B**

(*b*) **AB**

(*c*) $\mathbf{A^2}$

(*d*) $\mathbf{A}^T$

(*e*) $\mathbf{B}^{-1}$

(*f*) $\mathbf{B}^T\mathbf{A}^T$

(*g*) $\mathbf{A}^2 + \mathbf{B}^2 - \mathbf{AB}$

(*h*) determinant of **A**, determinant of **B** and determinant of **AB**.

Solution

```
>>        A = [1 0 1; 2 3 4; -1 6 7]
          A =
                 1   0   1
                 2   3   4
                -1   6   7
>>        B = [7 4 2; 3 5 6; -1 2 1]
          B =
                 7   4   2
                 3   5   6
                -1   2   1
(a) >>    C = A+B
          C =
                 8   4   3
                 5   8  10
                -2   8   8
(b) >>    D = A*B
          D =
                 6   6   3
                19  31  26
                 4  40  41
(c) >>    E = A^2
          E =
                 0   6   8
                 4  33  42
                 4  60  72
(d)>> % Let F = transpose of A
>>        F =A'
```

```
F =

    1  2  -1
    0  3   6
    1  4   7
```

(*e*) >>
```
H = inv (B)
H =

    0.1111   0.0000  -0.2222
    0.1429  -0.1429   0.5714
   -0.1746   0.2857  -0.3651
```

(*f*) >>
```
J = B'*A'
J =

    6  19   4
    6  31  40
    3  26  41
```

(*g*) >>
```
K = A^2 + B^2 -A * B
K =

    53  52  45
    15  51  58
    -2  28  42
```

(*h*)
```
   det (A) = 12
   det (B) = -63
 det (A*B) = -756
```

Example E2.2

Determine the eigenvalues and eigenvectors of A and B using MATLAB

$$A = \begin{bmatrix} 4 & 2 & -3 \\ -1 & 1 & 3 \\ 2 & 5 & 7 \end{bmatrix} \quad B = \begin{bmatrix} 1 & 2 & 3 \\ 8 & 7 & 6 \\ 5 & 3 & 1 \end{bmatrix}$$

Solution

```
% Determine the eigenvalues and eigenvectors
   A = [4 2 -3; -1 1 3; 2 5 7]
```

```
A =

     4    2   -3
    -1    1    3
     2    5    7

eig(A)

ans =

    0.5949
    3.0000
    8.4051

lamda = eig(A)

lamda =

    0.5949
    3.0000
    8.4051

[V,D] = eig(A)

V =

   -0.6713    0.9163   -0.3905
    0.6713   -0.3984    0.3905
   -0.3144    0.0398    0.8337

D =

    0.5949         0         0
         0    3.0000         0
         0         0    8.4051
```

Example E2.3

Determine the values of x, y, and z for the following set of linear algebraic equations:

$$x_2 - 3x_3 = -5$$
$$2x_1 + 3x_2 - x_3 = 7$$
$$4x_1 + 5x_2 - 2x_3 = 10$$

Solution

Here

$$A = \begin{bmatrix} 0 & 1 & -3 \\ 2 & 3 & -1 \\ 4 & 5 & -2 \end{bmatrix} \quad B = \begin{bmatrix} 5 \\ 7 \\ 10 \end{bmatrix} \quad \text{and } X = \begin{bmatrix} x_1 \\ x_2 \\ x_3 \end{bmatrix}$$

$$AX = B$$
$$A^{-1}AX = A^{-1}B$$
$$IX = A^{-1}B$$
or
$$X = A^{-1}B$$

```
>>        A = [0 1 –3; 2 3 –1; 4 5 –2];
>>        B = [–5; 7; 10]
>>        x = inv (A) * B
          x =
              –1.0000
               4.0000
               3.0000
>>     check = A * x
       check =
                  –5
                   7
                  10
%   Alternative method
>>        x = A\B
          x =
                  –1
                   4
                   3
```

2.15 SCRIPT FILES

A *script* is a sequence of ordinary statements and functions used at the command prompt level. A script is invoked the command prompt level by typing the file-name or by using the pull down menu. Scripts can also invoke other scripts.

The commands in the Command Window cannot be saved and executed again. Also, the Command Window is not interactive. To overcome these difficulties, the procedure is first to create a file with a list of commands, save it, and then run the file. In this way the commands contained are executed in the order they are listed when the file is run. In addition, as the need arises, one can change or modify the commands in the file, the file can be saved and run again. The files that are used in this fashion are known as *script files*. Thus, a script file is a text file that contains a sequence of MATLAB commands. Script file can be edited (corrected and/or changed) and executed many times.

2.15.1 Creating and Saving a Script File

Any text editor can be used to create script files. In MATLAB script files are created and edited in the Editor/Debugger Window. This window can be opened from the Command Window. From the Command Window, select *File*, *New*, and then *M-file*. Once the window is open, the commands of the script file are typed line by line. The commands can also be typed in any text editor or word processor program and then copied and pasted in the Editor/Debugger Window. The second type of M-files is the *function file*. Function file enables the user to extend the basic library functions by adding ones own computational procedures. Function M-files are expected to return one or more results. Script files and function files may include reference to other MATLAB toolbox routines.

MATLAB function file begins with a header statement of the form:

function (name of result or results) = name (argument list)

Before a script file can be executed it must be saved. All script files must be saved with the extension ".m". MATLAB refers to them as m-files. When using MATLAB M-files editor, the files will automatically be saved with a ".m" extension. If any other text editor is used, the file must be saved with the ".m" extension, or MATLAB will not be able to find and run the script file. This is done by choosing *Save As*... from the *File* menu, selecting a location, and entering a name for the file. The names of user defined variables, predefined variables, MATLAB commands or functions should not be used to name script files.

2.15.2 Running a Script File

A script file can be executed either by typing its name in the Command Window and then pressing the *Enter* key, directly from the Editor Window by clicking on the *Run* icon. The file is assumed to be in the current directory, or in the search path.

2.15.3 Input to a Script File

There are three ways of assigning a value to a variable in a script file.

1. The variable is defined and assigned value in the script file.
2. The variable is defined and assigned value in the Command Window.
3. The variable is defined in the script file, but a specified value is entered in the Command Window when the script file is executed.

2.15.4 Output Commands

There are two commands that are commonly used to generate output. They are the *disp* and *fprintf* commands.

1. The disp *command*

The *disp* command displays the elements of a variable without displaying the name of the variable, and displays text.

disp(name of a variable) or disp('text as string')

```
>>      A = [1 2 3; 4 5 6];
>>      disp(A)

              1 2 3
              4 5 6
>>      disp('Solution to the problem.')
        Solution to the problem.
```

2. *The* fprintf *command*

The *fprintf* command displays output (text and data) on the screen or saves it to a file. The output can be formatted using this command.

Example E2.4

Write a function file Veccrossprod to compute the cross product of two vectors **a**, and **b**, where **a** = (a_1, a_2, a_3), b = (b_1, b_2, b_3), and a × b = ($a_2b_3 - a_3b_2$, $a_3b_1 - a_1b_3$, $a_1b_2 - a_2b_1$). Verify the function by taking the cross products of pairs of unit vectors: (i, j), (j, k), etc.

Solution

```
function      c = Veccrossprod(a, b);
% Veccrossprod : function to compute c = a x b where a and b are 3D vectors
% call syntax:
%             c = Veccrossprod(a, b);
c = [a(2) * b(3) – a(3) * b(2); a(3) * b(1) – a(1) * b(3); a(1) * b(2) – a(2) * b(1)];
```

2.16 PROGRAMMING IN MATLAB

One most significant feature of MATLAB is its extendibility through user-written programs such as the M-files. M-files are ordinary ASCII text files written in MATLAB language. A function file is a subprogram.

2.16.1 Relational and Logical Operators

A relational operator compares two numbers by finding whether a comparison statement is true or false. A logical operator examines true/false statements and produces a result which is true or false according to the specific operator. Relational and logical operators are used in mathematical expressions and also in combination with other commands, to make decision that control the flow a computer program.

MATLAB has six relational operators as shown in Table 2.21.

Table 2.21 Relational operators

Relational operator	*Interpretation*
<	Less than
<=	Less than or equal
>	Greater than
>=	Greater than or equal
= =	Equal
~ =	Not equal

The logical operators in MATLAB are shown in Table 2.22.

Table 2.22 Logical operators

Logical operator	*Name*	*Description*
& Example: A&B	AND	Operates on two operands (A and B). If both are true, the result is true (1), otherwise the result is false (0).
| Example: A|B	OR	Operates on two operands (A and B). If either one, or both are true, the result is true (1), otherwise (both are false) the result is false (0).
~ Example: ~A	NOT	Operates on one operand (A). Gives the opposite of the operand. True (1) if the operand is false, and false (0) if the operand is true.

2.16.2 Order of Precedence

The following Table 2.23 shows the order of precedence used by MATLAB.

Table 2.23

Precedence	*Operation*
1 (highest)	Parentheses (If nested parentheses exist, inner have precedence).
2	Exponentiation.
3	Logical NOT (~).
4	Multiplication, Division.
5	Addition, Subtraction.
6	Relational operators (>, <, >=, <=, = =, ~=).
7	Logical AND (&).
8 (lowest)	Logical OR (|).

2.16.3 Built-in Logical Functions

The MATLAB built-in functions which are equivalent to the logical operators are:

and(A, B) Equivalent to A & B
or(A, B) Equivalent to A | B
not(A) Equivalent to ~A

List the MATLAB logical built-in functions are described in Table 2.24.

Table 2.24 Additional logical built-in functions

Function	*Description*	*Example*
xor(a, b)	Exclusive or. Returns true (1) if one operand is true and the other is false	>>xor(8, –1) ans = 0 >>xor(8, 0) ans = 1
all(A)	Returns 1 (true) if all elements in a vector A are true (nonzero). Returns 0 (false) if one or more elements are false (zero). If A is a matrix, treats columns of A as vectors, returns a vector with 1's and 0's.	>>A = [5 3 11 7 8 15] >>all(A) ans = 1 >>B = [3 6 11 4 0 13] >>all(B) ans = 0
any(A)	Returns 1 (true) if any element in a vector A is true (nonzero). Returns 0 (false) if all elements are false (zero). If A is a matrix, treats columns of A as vectors, returns a vector with 1's and 0's.	>>A = [5 0 14 0 0 13] >>any(A) ans = 1 >>B = [0 0 0 0 0 0] >>any(B) ans = 0
find(A)	If A is a vector, returns the indices of the nonzero elements.	>>A = [0 7 4 2 8 0 0 3 9] >>find(A) ans = 2 3 4 5 8 9
find(A > d)	If A is a vector, returns the address of the elements that are larger than d (any relational operator can be used).	>>find(A > 4) ans = 4 5 6

The truth table for the operation of the four logical operators, and, or, X and not are summarized in Table 2.25.

Table 2.25 Truth table

Input		*Output*				
A	*B*	*AND A&B*	*OR A|B*	*XOR (A,B)*	*NOT ~A*	*NOT ~B*
false	false	false	false	false	ture	true
false	true	false	true	true	true	false
true	false	false	true	true	false	true
true	true	true	true	true	false	true

2.16.4 Conditional Statements

A conditional statement is a command that allows MATLAB to make a decision of whether to execute a group of commands that follow the conditional statement or to skip these commands.

if conditional expression consists of relational and/or logical operators

```
if      a < 30
            count = count + 1
            disp a
end
```

The general form of a simple **if** statement is as follows:

```
if   logical expression
        statements
end
```

If the logical expression is true, the statements between the **if** statement and the **end** statement are executed. If the logical expression is false, then it goes to the statements following the **end** statement.

2.16.5 Nested if Statements

Following is an example of *nested if* statements:

```
if        a < 30
             count = count + 1;
          disp(a);
                  if b > a
                     b = 0;
                  end
end
```

2.16.6 Else and Elseif Clauses

The else clause allows to execute one set of statements if a logical expression is true and a different set if the logical expression is false.

```
%         variable name inc
if        inc < 1
          x_inc = inc/10;
          else
          x_inc = 0.05;
 end
```

When several levels of **if-else** statements are nested, it may be difficult to find which logical expressions must be true (or false) to execute each set of statements. In such cases, the **elseif** clause is used to clarify the program logic.

2.16.7 MATLAB while Structures

There is a structure in MATLAB that combines the for loop with the features of the if block. This is called the *while loop* and has the form:

while *logical expression*

This set of statements is executed repeatedly as long as the logical expressions remain true (equals +1) or if the expression is a matrix rather than a simple scalar variable, as long as *all* the elements of the matrix remain nonzero.

end

In addition to the normal termination of a loop by means of the **end** statement, there are additional MATLAB commands available to interrupt the calculations. These commands are listed in Table 2.26 below:

Table 2.26

Command	*Description*
break	Terminates the execution of MATLAB for and **while** loops. In nested loops, **break** will terminate only the innermost loop in which it is placed.
return	Primarily used in MATLAB functions, **return** will cause a normal return from a function from the point at which the **return** statement is executed.
error (*'text'*)	Terminates execution and displays the message contained in **text** on the screen. Note, the text must be enclosed in single quotes.

The MATLAB functions used are summarized in Table 2.27 below:

Table 2.27

Function	*Description*
Relational operators	A MATLAB *logical relation* is a comparison between two variables **x** and **y** of the same size effected by one of the six operators, <, <=, >, >=, = =, ~=. The comparison involves corresponding elements of **x** and **y**, and yields a matrix or scalar of the same size with values of "true" or "false" for each of its elements. In MATLAB, the value of "false" is zero, and "true" has a value of one. Any nonzero quantity is interpreted as "true".
Combinatorial operators	The operators **&** (AND) and **|** (OR) may be used to combine two logical expressions.
all, any	If **x** is a vector, **all(x)** returns a value of one if *all* of the elements of **x** are nonzero, and a value of zero otherwise. When **X** is a matrix, all(**X**) returns a row vector of ones or zeros obtained by applying all to each of the columns of **X**. The function **any** operates similarly if *any* of the elements of **x** are nonzero.

(Contd...)

find	If **x** is a vector, **i** = **find(x)** returns the indices of those elements of **x** that are nonzero (i.e., true). Thus, replacing all the negative elements of **x** by zero could be accomplished by **i = find(x < 0);** **x(i) = zeros(size(i));** If **X** is a matrix, **[i, j]** = **find(X)** operates similarly and returns the row-column indices of nonzero elements.
if, else, elseif	The several forms of MATLAB **if** blocks are as follows: **if** *variable* block of statements executed if *variable* is "true", i.e., nonzero **end** block of statements *executed if variable* **end** block of statements **If** *variable* 1 block of statements executed if *variable* 1 is "true", i.e., nonzero **else** block of statements 1executed if *variable* 2 **else** executed if neither **If** variable 1 block of statements executed if *variable* 1 is "true", i.e., nonzero is **elseif** *variable* 2 is "false", i.e., zero is "true", **end** *variable* is "true"
break	Terminates the execution of a **for** or **while** loop. Only the innermost loop in which **break** is encountered will be terminated.
return	Causes the function to return at that point to the calling routine. MATLAB *M-file* functions will return normally without this statement.
error (*'text'*)	Within a loop or function, if the statement **error**(*'text'*) is encountered, the loop or function is terminated, and the *text* is displayed.
while	The form of the MATLAB **while** loop is **while** *variable* block of statements executed as long as the value of *variable* is "true"; i.e., nonzero **end** Useful when a function F itself calls a second "dummy" function "f ". For example, the function F might find the root of an arbitrary function identified as a generic f(x). Then, the name of the actual M-*file* function, say **fname**, is passed as a *character string* to the function F either through its argument list or as a global variable, and the function is evaluated within F by means of **feval.** The use of **feval(name, x1, x2, ..., xn)**, where **fname** is a variable containing the name of the function as a character string; i.e., enclosed in single quotes, and **x1, x2, ..., xn** are the variables needed in the argument list of function **fname.**

2.17 GRAPHICS

MATLAB has many commands that can be used to create basic 2-D plots, overlay plots, specialized 2-D plots, 3-D plots, mesh, and surface plots.

2.17.1 Basic 2-D Plots

The basic command for producing a simple 2-D plot is

plot(*x* values, *y* values, 'style option')

where

x values and *y* values are vectors containing the x- and y-coordinates of points on the graph.

style option is an optional argument that specifies the color, line-style, and the point-marker style.

The style option in the plot command is a character string that consists of 1, 2, or 3 characters that specify the color and/or the line style. The different color, line-style and marker-style options are summarised in Table 2.28.

Table 2.28 Color, line-style, and marker-style options

Color style-option		*Line style-option*		*Marker style-option*	
y	yellow	–	solid	+	plus sign
m	magenta	– –	dashed	o	circle
c	cyan	:	dotted	*	asterisk
r	red	–.	dash-dot	x	x-mark
g	green			.	point
b	blue			^	up triangle
w	white			s	square
k	black			d	diamond, etc.

2.17.2 Specialised 2-D Plots

There are several specialised graphics functions available in MATLAB for 2-D plots. The list of functions commonly used in MATLAB for plotting *x-y* data are given in Table 2.29.

Table 2.29 List of functions for plotting x-y data

Function	*Description*
area	Creates a filled area plot.
bar	Creates a bar graph.
barh	Creates a horizontal bar graph.
comet	Makes an animated 2-D plot.
compass	Creates arrow graph for complex numbers.
contour	Makes contour plots.
contourf	Makes filled contour plots.

(Contd...)

errorbar	Plots a graph and puts error bars.
feather	Makes a feather plot.
fill	Draws filled polygons of specified color.
fplot	Plots a function of a single variable.
hist	Makes histograms.
loglog	Creates plot with log scale on both *x* and *y* axes.
pareto	Makes pareto plots.
pcolor	Makes pseudo color plot of matrix.
pie	Creates a pie chart.
plotyy	Makes a double *y*-axis plot.
plotmatrix	Makes a scatter plot of a matrix.
polar	Plots curves in polar coordinates.
quiver	Plots vector fields.
rose	Makes angled histograms.
scatter	Creates a scatter plot.
semilogx	Makes semilog plot with log scale on the *x*-axis.
semilogy	Makes semilog plot with log scale on the *y*-axis.
stairs	Plots a stair graph.
stem	Plots a stem graph.

1. Overlay plots

There are three ways of generating overlay plots in MATLAB, they are:

(*a*) Plot command

(*b*) Hold command

(*c*) Line command

(*a*) *Plot command:* Example E2.7(a) shows the use of plot command used with matrix argument, each column of the second argument matrix plotted against the corresponding column of the first argument matrix.

(*b*) *Hold command:* Invoking hold on at any point during a session freezes the current plot in the graphics window. All the next plots generated by the plot command are added to the exiting plot. See Example E2.7(a).

(*c*) *Line command:* The line command takes a pair of vectors (or a triplet in 3-D) followed by a parameter name/parameter value pairs as argument. For instance, the command: *line* (*x data, y data, parameter name, parameter value*) adds lines to the existing axes. See Example E2.7(a).

2.17.3 3-D Plots

MATLAB provides various options for displaying three-dimensional data. They include line and wire, surface, mesh plots, among many others. More information can be found in the Help Window under Plotting and Data visualization. Table 2.30 lists commonly used functions.

Table 2.30 Functions used for 3-D graphics

Command	*Description*
plot3	Plots three-dimensional graph of the trajectory of a set of three parametric equations x(t), y(t), and z(t) can be obtained using **plot3(x, y, z).**
meshgrid	If **x** and **y** are two vectors containing a range of points for the evaluation of a function, **[X,Y] = meshgrid(x, y)** returns two rectangular matrices containing the x and y values at each point of a two-dimensional grid.
mesh(X, Y, z)	If **X** and **Y** are rectangular arrays containing the values of the x and y coordinates at each point of a rectangular grid , and if **z** is the value of a function evaluated at each of these points, **mesh(X, Y, z)** will produce a three-dimensional perspective graph of the points. The same results can be obtained with **mesh(x, y, z)** can also be used.
meshc, meshz	If the xy grid is rectangular, these two functions are merely variations of the basic plotting program **mesh**, and they operate in an identical fashion. **meshc** will produce a corresponding contour plot drawn on the xy plane below the three-dimensional figure, and **meshz** will add a vertical wall to the outside features of the figures drawn by **mesh**.
surf	Produces a three-dimensional perspective drawing. Its use is usually to draw surfaces, as opposed to plotting functions, although the actual tasks are quite similar. The output of **surf** will be a *shaded* figure. If row vectors of length n are defined by x = r cos θ and y = r sin θ, with $0 \le \theta \le 2\pi$, they correspond to a circle of radius r. If $\vec{r}$ is a *column* vector equal to **r = [0 1 2]'**; then **z = r*ones(size(x))** will be a rectangular, 3 × n, arrays of 0's and 2's, and **surf(x, y, z)** will produce a shaded surface bounded by three circles; i.e., a cone.
surfc	This function is related to **surf** in the same way that **meshc** is related to mesh.
colormap	Used to change the default coloring of a figure. See the MATLAB reference manual or the help file.
shading	Controls the type of color shading used in drawing figures. See the MATLAB reference manual or the help file.
view	**view(az,el)** controls the perspective view of a three-dimensional plot. The view of the figure is from angle "**el**" above the xy plane with the coordinate axes (and the figure) rotated by an angle "**az**" in a clockwise direction about the z axis. Both angles are in degrees. The default values are **az** = 37½° and **el** = 30°.

(*Contd...*)

axis	Determines or changes the scaling of a plot. If the coordinate axis limits of a two-dimensional or three-dimensional graph are contained in the row vector r = [x_{min}, x_{max}, y_{min}, y_{max}, z_{min}, z_{max}], **axis** will return the values in this vector, and **axis(r)** can be used to alter them. The coordinate axes can be turned *on* and *off* with **axis('on')** and **axis('off')**. A few other string constant inputs to **axis** and their effects are given below: **axis('equal')** x and y scaling are forced to be the same. **axis('square')** The box formed by the axes is square. **axis('auto')** Restores the scaling to default settings. **axis('normal')** Restoring the scaling to full size, removing any effects of *square* or *equal* settings. **axis('image')** Alters the aspect ratio and the scaling so the screen pixels are square shaped rather than rectangular.
contour	The use is **contour(x, y, z)**. A default value of N = 10 contour lines will be drawn. An optional fourth argument can be used to control the number of contour lines that are drawn. **contour(x, y, z, N)**, if **N** is a positive integer, will draw **N** contour lines, and **contour(x, y, z, V)**, if **V** is a vector containing values in the range of z values, will draw contour lines at each value of z = V.
plot3	Plots lines or curves in three dimensions. If **x**, **y**, and **z** are vectors of equal length, **plot3(x, y, z)** will draw, on a three-dimensional coordinate axis system, the lines connecting the points. A fourth argument, representing the color and symbols to be used at each point, can be added in exactly the same manner as with **plot**.
grid	**grid on** adds grid lines to a two-dimensional or three-dimensional graph; **grid off** removes them.
slice	Draws "slices" of a volume at a particular location within the volume.

Example E2.5

(*a*) Generate an overlay plot for plotting three lines

$$y_1 = \sin t$$

$$y_2 = t$$

$$y_3 = t - \frac{t^3}{3!} + \frac{t^5}{5!} + \frac{t^7}{3!}$$

$$0 \le t \le 2\pi$$

Use (*i*) the plot command

(*ii*) the hold command

(*iii*) the line command

(*b*) Use the functions for plotting x-y data for plotting the following functions.

(*i*) $f(t) = t \cos t \qquad 0 \le t \le 10\pi$

(*ii*) $x = e^t$

$y = 100 + e^{3t}$

$0 \le t \le 2\pi$

Solution

(*a*) Overlay plot

(*i*)
```
% using the plot command
t = linspace(0, 2*pi, 100);
y1 = sin(t); y2 = t;
y3 = t – (t.^3)/6 + (t.^5)/120 – (t.^7)/5040;
plot(t, y1, t, y2, '–', t, y3, 'o')
axis([0 5 –1 5])
xlabel('t')
ylabel('sin(t) approximation')
title('sin(t) function')
text(3.5,0, 'sin(t)')
gtext('Linear approximation')
gtext('4-term approximation')
```
Output is shown in Fig. E2.5(a)

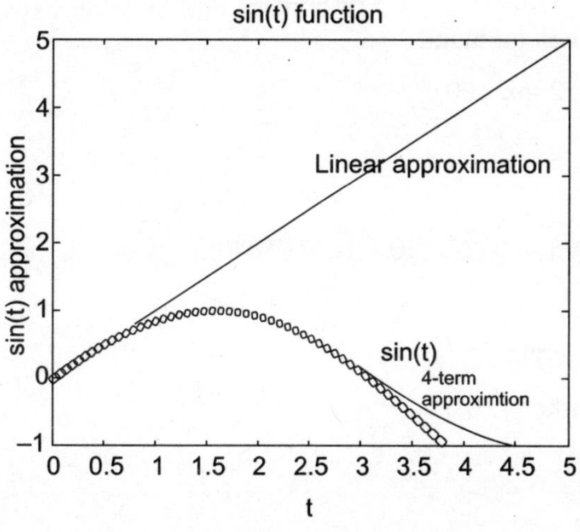

Fig. E2.5 (a)

(*ii*) % using the hold command

```
x = linspace(0, 2*pi, 100); y1 = sin(x);
plot(x, y1)
hold on
y2 = x; plot(x, y2, '–' )
y3 = x – (x.^3)/6 + (x.^5)/120 – (t.^7)/5040;
plot(x, y3, '0')
axis([0 5 –1 5])
hold off
```

Output is shown in Fig. E2.5(b).

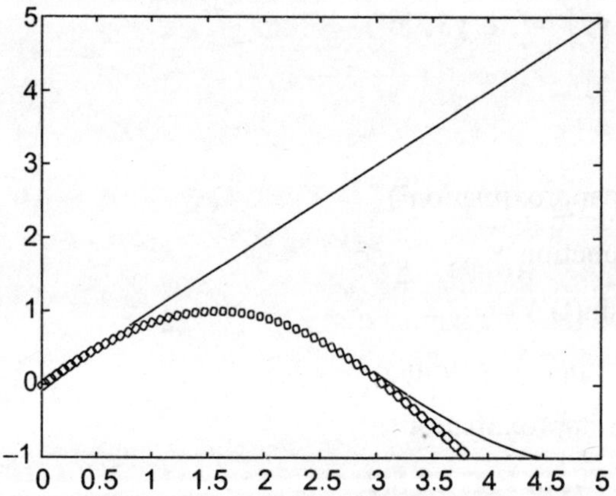

Fig. E2.5 (b)

(*iii*) % using the line command

```
t = linspace(0, 2*pi, 100);
y1 = sin(t);
y2 = t;
y3 = t – (t.^3)/6 + (t.^5)/120 – (t.^7)/5040;
plot(t, y1)
line(t, y2, 'linestyle', '–')
line(t, y3, 'marker', '0')
axis([0 5 –1 5])
xlabel('t')
ylabel('sin(t) approximation')
```

title('sin(t) function')

legend('sin(t)', 'linear approx', '7th order approx')

Output is shown in Fig. E2.5(c)

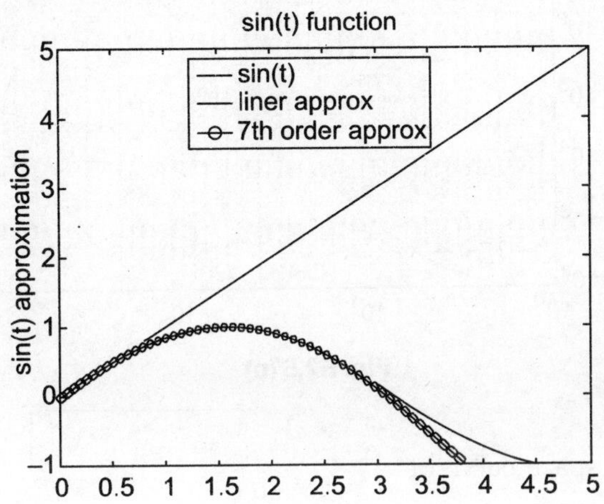

Fig. E2.5(c)

(*b*) Using Table 2.29 functions

(*i*) fplot('x.*cos(x)', [0 10*pi])

This will give the following figure (Fig. E2.5 (d))

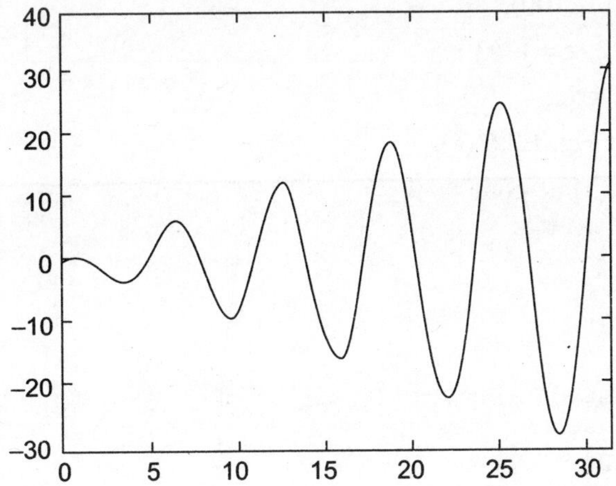

Fig. E2.5 (d)

(*ii*) t = linspace(0, 2*pi, 200);

x = exp(t);

y = 100 + exp(3*t);

loglog(x, y), grid

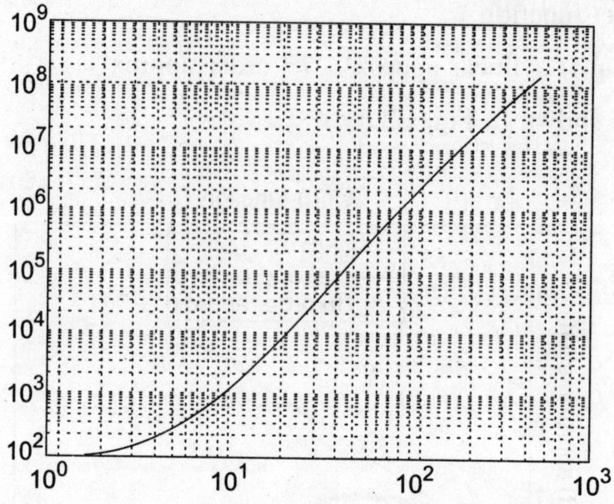

Fig. E2.5 (e)

Example E2.6

(*a*) Plot the parametric space curve of

$x(t) = t$

$y(t) = t^2$

$z(t) = t^3$ $\quad 0 \le t \le 2.0$

(*b*) $z = -7/(1+x^2+y^2)$ $\quad |x| \le 5,\ |y| \le 5$

Solution

(*a*)
```
>> t = linspace(0, 2,100);
>> x = t; y = t. ^2; z = t. ^3;
>> plot3(x, y, z), grid
```

The plot is shown in Fig. E2.6 (a).

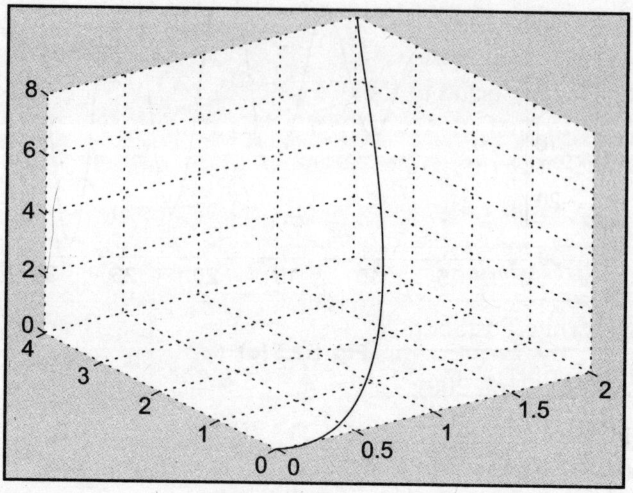

Figure E2.6 (a)

(*b*) >> t = linspace(0, 2,100);

```
>> x = t; y = t. ^2; z = t. ^3;
>> plot3(x, y, z), grid
>> t=linspace(–5,5,50);y = x;
>> z = –7./(1 + x.^2 + y.^2);
>> mesh(z)
```

The plot is shown in Fig. E2.6(b).

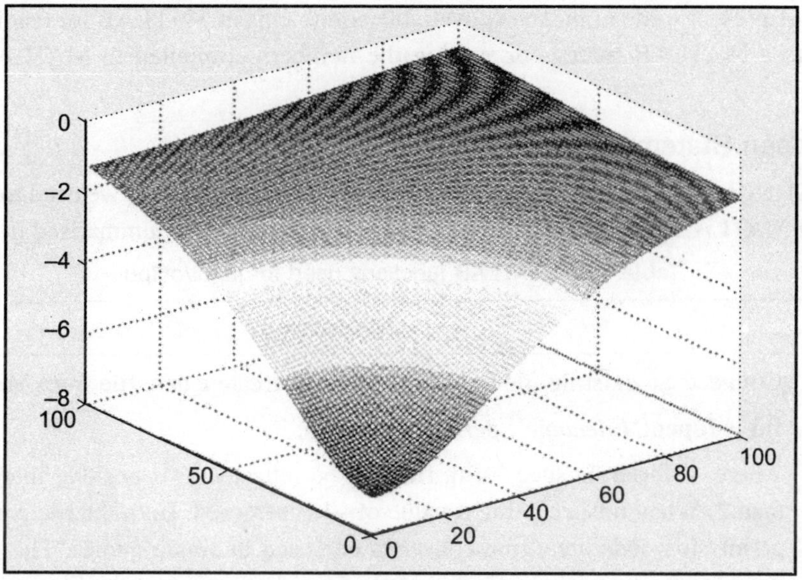

Fig. E2.6(b)

2.17.4 Saving and Printing Graphs

To obtain a hardcopy of a graph, type *print* in the Command Window after the graph appears in the Figure Window. The figure can also be saved into a specified file in the PostScripter or Encapsulated PostScript (EPS) format. The command to save graphics to a file is

print – d devicetype – options filename

where device type for PostScript printers are listed in the following Table 2.31.

Table 2.31 Devicetype for Postscript printers

Devicetype	*Description*	*Devicetype*	*Description*
ps	Black and white PostScript	**eps**	Black and white EPSF
psc	Color PostScript	**epsc**	Color EPSF
ps2	Level 2 BW PostScript	**eps2**	Level 2 black and white EPSF
psc2	Level 2 color PostScript	**epsc2**	Level 2 color EPSF

MATLAB can also generate a graphics file in the following popular formats among others.

–dill saves file in Adobe Illustrator format.

–djpeg saves file as a JPEG image.

–dtiff saves file as a compressed TIFF image.

–dmfile saves file as an M-file with graphics handles.

2.18 INPUT/OUTPUT IN MATLAB

In this section, we present some of the many available commands in MATLAB for reading data from an external file into a MATLAB matrix, or writing the numbers computed in MATLAB into such an external file.

2.18.1 The fopen Statement

To have the MATLAB read or write a separate data file of numerical values, we need to *connect* the file to the executing MATLAB program. The MATLAB functions used are summarised in Table 2.32.

Table 2.32 MATLAB functions used for input/output

Function	*Description*
fopen	Connects an existing file to MATLAB or to create a new file from MATLAB. **fid = fopen**('*Filename*', *permission code*); where, if **fopen** is successful, **fid** will be returned as a positive integer greater than 2. When unsuccessful, a value of –1 is returned. Both the file name and the permission code are string constants enclosed in single quotes. The permission code can be a variety of flags that specify whether or not the file can be written to, read from, appended to, or a combination of these. Some common codes are: **Code** — **Meaning** **'r'** — read only **'w'** — write only **'r+'** — read and write **'a+'** — read and append The **fopen** statement positions the file at the beginning.
fclose	Disconnects a file from the operating MATLAB program. The use is **fclose(fid)**, where **fid** is the *file identification number* of the file returned by **fopen.fclose('all')** will close all files.

(Contd...)

fscanf	Reads opened files. The use is **A = fscanf(fid,** *FORMAT, SIZE*) where *FORMAT* specifies the types of numbers (integers, reals with or without exponent, character strings) and their arrangement in the data file, and optional *SIZE* determines how many quantities are to be read and how they are to be arranged into the matrix **A**. If *SIZE* is omitted, the entire file is read. The *FORMAT* field is a string (enclosed in single quotes) specifying the form of the numbers in the file. The *type* of each number is characterized by a per cent sign (%), followed by a letter (**i** or **d** for integers, **e** or **f** for floating-point numbers with or without exponents). Between the per cent sign and the type code, one can insert an integer specifying the maximum width of the field.
fprintf	Writes files previously opened. **fprintf(fid,** *FORMAT*, **A)** where **fid** and *FORMAT* have the same meaning as for **fscanf**, with the exception that for output formats the string must end with **\n**, designating the end of a line of output.

2.19 SYMBOLIC MATHEMATICS

In Secs.2.1 to 2.18, the capability of MATLAB for numerical computations have been described. In this section some of MATLAB's capabilities for symbolic manipulations will be presented. Specifically, the symbolic expressions, symbolic algebra, simplification of mathematical expressions, operations on symbolic expressions, solution of a single equation or a set of linear algebraic equations, solutions to differential equations, differentiation and integration of functions using MATLAB are presented.

2.19.1 Symbolic Expressions

A symbolic expression is stored in MATLAB as a *character string*. A single quote marks are used to define the symbolic expression. For instance:

'sin(y/x)'; 'x^4 + 5*x^3 + 7*x^2 – 7'

The independent variable in many functions is specified as an additional function argument. If an independent variable is not specified, then MATLAB will pick one. When several variables exist, MATLAB will pick the one that is a single lower case letter (except i and j), which is closest to x alphabetically.

The independent variable is returned by the function *symvar*,

symvar(s) Returns the independent variable for the symbolic expression *s*.

For example:

Expression s	**symvar(s)**
'5 * c * d + 34'	d
'sin(y/x)'	x

In MATLAB, a number of functions are available to simplify mathematical expressions by expanding the terms, factoring expressions, collecting coefficients, or simplifying the expression. For instance:

expand(s) Performs an expansion of s.

A summary of these expressions is given in Table 2.33. A summary of basic operations is given in Table 2.34. The standard arithmetic operation (Table 2.35) is applied to symbolic expressions using symbolic functions. These symbolic expressions are summarized in Table 2.36.

Table 2.33 Simplification

collect	Collect common terms
expand	Expand polynomials and elementary functions
factor	Factorization
horner	Nested polynomial representation
numden	Numerator and denominator
simple	Search for shortest form
simplify	Simplification
subexpr	Rewrite in terms of subexpressions

Table 2.34 Basic Operations

ccode	C code representation of a symbolic expression
conj	Complex conjugate
findsym	Determine symbolic variables
fortran	Fortran representation of a symbolic expression
imag	Imaginary part of a complex number
latex	LaTeX representation of a symbolic expression
pretty	Pretty prints a symbolic expression
real	Real part of an imaginary number
sym	Create symbolic object
syms	Shortcut for creating multiple symbolic objects

Table 2.35 Arithmetic Operations

+	Addition
–	Subtraction
*	Multiplication
.*	Array multiplication
/	Right division
./	Array right division
\	Left division
.\	Array left division
^	Matrix or scalar raised to a power
.^	Array raised to a power
‘	Complex conjugate transpose
.‘	Real transpose

Table 2.36 Symbolic expressions

horner(S)	Transposes S into its Horner, or nested, representation.
numden(S)	Returns two symbolic expressions that represent, respectively, the numerator expression and the denominator expression for the rational representation of **S**
numeric(S)	Converts s to a numeric form (**S** must not contain any symbolic variables).
poly2sym(c)	Converts a polynomial coefficient vector **c** to a symbolic polynomial.
pretty(S)	Prints **S** in an output form that resembles typeset mathematics.
sym2poly(S)	Converts **S** to a polynomial coefficient vector. *
symadd(A, B)	Performs a symbolic addition, **A + B**.
symdiv(A, B)	Performs a symbolic division, **A/B.**
symmul(A, B)	Performs a symbolic multiplication, **A * B.**
sympow(S, p)	Performs a symbolic power, **S^p.**
symsub(A, B)	Performs a symbolic subtraction, **A – B.**

2.19.2 Solution to Differential Equations

Symbolic math functions can be used to solve a single equation, a system of equations, and differential equations. For example:

solve(f) Solves a symbolic equation **f** for its symbolic variable. If **f** is a symbolic expression, this function solves the equation **f** = 0 for its symbolic variable.

solve(f1, ... fn) Solves the system of equations represented by **f1, ..., fn.**

The symbolic function for solving ordinary differential equation is **dsolve** as shown below:

dsolve('equation', 'condition') Symbolically solves the ordinary differential equation specified by **'equation'**. The optional argument **'condition'** specifies a boundary or initial condition.

The symbolic equation uses the letter **D** to denote differentiation with respect to the independent variable. A **D** followed by a digit denotes repeated differentiation. Thus, **Dy** represents dy/dx, and **D2y** represents d^2y/dx^2. For example, given the ordinary second order differential equation;

$$\frac{d^2x}{dt^2} + 5\frac{dx}{dt} + 3x = 7$$

with the initial conditions $x(0) = 0$ and $\dot{x}(0) = 1$.

The MATLAB statement that determine the symbolic solution for the above differential equation is the following page:

```
x = dsolve('D2x = –5*Dx–3*x + 7', 'x(0) = 0', 'Dx(0) = 1')
```

The symbolic functions are summarized in Table 2.37.

Table 2.37 Solution of equations

compose	Functional composition
dsolve	Solution of differential equations
finverse	Functional inverse
solve	Solution of algebraic equations

2.19.3 Calculus

There are four forms by which the symbolic derivative of a symbolic expression is obtained in MATLAB. They are:

diff(f) Returns the derivative of the expression **f** with respect to the default independent variable.

diff(f, 't') Returns the derivative of the expression **f** with respect to the variable t.

diff(f, n) Returns the nth derivative of the expression **f** with respect to the default independent variable.

diff(f, 't', n) Returns the nth derivative of the expression **f** with respect to the variable t.

The various forms that are used in MATLAB to find the integral of a symbolic expression **f** are given below and summarized in Table 2.38.

int(f) Returns the integral of the expression **f** with respect to the default independent variable.

int(f, 't') Returns the integral of the expression **f** with respect to the variable t.

int(f, a, b) Returns the integral of the expression **f** with respect to the default independent variable evaluated over the interval **[a, b],** where **a** and **b** are numeric expressions.

int(f, 't', a, b) Returns the integral of the expression **f** with respect to the variable **t** evaluated over the interval **[a, b],** where **a** and **b** are numeric expressions.

int(f, 'm', 'n') Returns the integral of the expression **f** with respect to the default independent variable evaluated over the interval **[m, n],** where m and n are numeric expressions.

The other symbolic functions for pedagogical and graphical applications, conversions, integral transforms, and linear algebra are summarized in Tables 2.38 to 2.42.

Table 2.38 Calculus

diff	Differentiate
int	Integrate
jacobian	Jacobian matrix
limit	Limit of an expression
symsum	Summation of series
taylor	Taylor series expansion

Table 2.39 Pedagogical and Graphical applications

ezcontour	Contour plotter
ezcontourf	Filled contour plotter
ezmesh	Mesh plotter
ezmeshc	Combined mesh and contour plotter
ezplot	Function plotter
ezplot	Easy-to-use function plotter
ezplot3	Three-dimensional curve plotter
ezpolar	Polar coordinate plotter
ezsurf	Surface plotter
ezsurfc	Combined surface and contour plotter
funtool	Function calculator
rsums	Riemann sums
taylortool	Taylor series calculator

Table 2.40 Conversions

char	Convert sym object to string
double	Convert symbolic matrix to double
poly2sym	Function calculator
sym2poly	Symbolic polynomial to coefficient vector

Table 2.41 Integral transforms

fourier	Fourier transform
ifourier	Inverse Fourier transform
ilaplace	Inverse Laplace transform
iztrans	Inverse Z-transform
laplace	Laplace transform
ztrans	Z-transform

Table 2.42 Linear algebra

colspace	Basis for column space
det	Determinant
diag	Create or extract diagonals
eig	Eigenvalues and eigenvectors
expm	Matrix exponential
inv	Matrix inverse
jordan	Jordan canonical form
null	Basis for null space
poly	Characteristic polynomial
rank	Matrix rank
rref	Reduced row echelon form
svd	Singular value decomposition
tril	Lower triangle
triu	Upper triangle

2.20 CONTROL SYSTEMS

MATLAB has an extensive set of functions for the analysis and design of control systems. They involve matrix operations, root determination, model conversions, and plotting of complex functions. These functions are found in MATLAB's control systems toolbox. The analytical techniques used by MATLAB for the analysis and design of control systems assume the processes that are linear and time invariant. MATLAB uses models in the form of *transfer-functions* or *state-space equations.*

2.20.1 Transfer Functions

The transfer function of a linear time invariant system is expressed as a ratio of two polynomials. The transfer function for a single input and a single output (SISO) system is written as

$$H(s) = \frac{b_0 s^n + b_1 s^{n-1} + \ldots + b_{n-1} s + b_n}{a_0 s^m + a_1 s^{m-1} + \ldots + a_{m-1} s + a_m}$$

when the numerator and denominator of a transfer function are factored into the *zero-pole-gain form,* it is given by

$$H(s) = k\frac{(s - z_1)(s - z_2)\ldots(s - z_n)}{(s - p_1)(s - p_2)\ldots(s - p_m)}$$

The *state-space model* representation of a linear control system s is written as

$$\dot{x} = Ax + Bu$$
$$y = Cx + Du$$

2.20.2 Model Conversion

There are a number of functions in MATLAB that can be used to convert from one model to another. These conversion functions and their applications are summarized in Table 2.43.

Table 2.43 Model conversion functions

Function	*Purpose*
c2d	Continuous state-space to discrete state-space
residue	Partial-fraction expansion
ss3tf	State-space to transfer function
ss2zp	State-space to zero-pole-gain
tf2ss	Transfer function to state-space
tf2zp	Transfer function to zero-pole-gain
zp2ss	Zero-pole-gain to state-space
zp2tf	Zero-pole-gain to transfer function

Residue Function: The **residue** function converts the polynomial transfer function

$$H(s) = \frac{b_0 s^n + b_1 s^{n-1} + \ldots + b_{n-1} s + b_n}{a_0 s^m + a_1 s^{m-1} + \ldots + a_{m-1} s + a_m}$$

to the partial fraction transfer function

$$H(s) = \frac{r_1}{s - p_1} + \frac{r_2}{s - p_2} + \ldots + \frac{r_n}{s - p_n} + k(s)$$

[r, p, k] = residue(B, A): Determine the vectors **r, p,** and **k,** which contain the residue values, the poles, and the direct terms from the partial-fraction expansion. The inputs are the polynomial coefficients **B** and **A** from the numerator and denominator of the transfer function, respectively.

ss2tf Function: The **ss2tf** function converts the continuous-time, state-space equations

$$x' = Ax + Bu$$
$$y = Cx + Du$$

to the polynomial transfer function

$$H(s) = \frac{b_0 s^n + b_1 s^{n-1} + \ldots + b_{n-1} s + b_n}{a_0 s^m + a_1 s^{m-1} + \ldots + a_{m-1} s + a_m}$$

The function has two output matrices:

[num, den] = ss2tf(A, B, C, D, iu): Computes vectors **num** and **den** containing the coefficients, in descending powers of **s**, of the numerator and denominator of the polynomial transfer function for the **iu**th input. The input arguments **A, B, C** and **D** are the matrices of the state-space equations corresponding to the **iu**th input, where **iu** is the number of the input for a multi-input system. In the case of a single-input system, **iu** is 1.

ss2zp Function: The **ss2zp** function converts the continuous-time, state-space equations

$$x' = Ax + Bu$$

$$y = Cx + Du$$

to the zero-pole-gain transfer function

$$H(s) = k\frac{(s - z_1)(s - z_2)...(s - z_n)}{(s - p_1)(s - p_2)...(s - p_m)}$$

The function has three output matrices:

[z, p, k] = ss2zp(A, B, C, D, iu): Determines the zeros **(z)** and poles **(p)** of the zero-pole-gain transfer function for the **iu**th input, along with the associated gain **(k).** The input matrices **A, B, C,** and **D** of the state-space equations correspond to the **iu**th input, where **iu** is the number of the input for a multi-input system. In the case of a single-input system **iu** is 1.

tf2ss Function: The **ts2ss** function converts the polynomial transfer function

$$H(s) = \frac{b_0 s^n + b_1 s^{n-1} + ... + b_{n-1} s + b_n}{a_0 s^m + a_1 s^{m-1} + ... + a_{m-1} s + a_m}$$

to the controller-canonical form state-space equations

$$x' = Ax + Bu$$

$$y = Cx + Du$$

The function has four output matrices:

[A, B, C, D] = tf2ss(num, den): Determines the matrices **A, B, C,** and **D** of the controller-canonical form state-space equations. The input arguments num and den contain the coefficients, in descending powers of **s**, of the numerator and denominator polynomials of the transfer function that is to be converted.

tf2zp Function: The **tf2zp** function converts the polynomial transfer function

$$H(s) = \frac{b_0 s^n + b_1 s^{n-1} + ... + b_{n-1} s + b_n}{a_0 s^m + a_1 s^{m-1} + ... + a_{m-1} s + a_m}$$

to the zero-pole-gain transfer function

$$H(s) = k\frac{(s - z_1)(s - z_2)...(s - z_n)}{(s - p_1)(s - p_2)...(s - p_m)}$$

The function has three output matrices:

[z, p, k] = tf2zp(num, den): Determines the zeros **(z)**, poles **(p)** and associated gain **(k)** of the zero-pole-gain transfer function using the coefficients, in descending powers of **s**, of the numerator and denominator of the polynomial transfer function that is to be converted.

zp2tf Function: The **zp2tf** function converts the zero-pole-gain transfer function

$$H(s) = k\frac{(s-z_1)(s-z_2)...(s-z_n)}{(s-p_1)(s-p_2)...(s-p_m)}$$

to the polynomial transfer function

$$H(s) = \frac{b_0s^n + b_1s^{n-1} + ... + b_{n-1}s + b_n}{a_0s^m + a_1s^{m-1} + ... + a_{m-1}s + a_m}$$

The function has two output matrices:

[num, den] = zp2tf(z, p, k): Determines the vectors **num** and **den** containing the coefficients, in descending powers of **s**, of the numerator and denominator of the polynomial transfer function. **p** is a column vector of the pole locations of the zero-pole-gain transfer function, **z** is a matrix of the corresponding zero locations, having one column for each output of a multi-output system, **k** is the gain of the zero-pole-gain transfer function. In the case of a single-output system, **z** is a column vector of the zero locations corresponding to the pole locations of vector **p.**

zp2ss Function: The **zp2ss** function converts the zero-pole-gain transfer function

$$H(s) = k\frac{(s-z_1)(s-z_2)...(s-z_n)}{(s-p_1)(s-p_2)...(s-p_m)}$$

to the controller-canonical form state-space equations

$$x' = Ax + Bu$$

$$y = Cx + Du$$

The function has four output matrices.

[A, B, C, D] = zp2ss(z, p, k): Determines the matrices **A, B, C,** and **D** of the control-canonical form state-space equations. **p** is a column vector of the pole locations of the zero-pole-gain transfer function, **z** is a matrix of the corresponding zero locations, having one column for each output of a multi-output system, **k** is the gain of the zero-pole-gain transfer function. In the case of a single-output system, **z** is a column vector of the zero locations corresponding to the pole locations of vector **p.**

2.21 THE LAPLACE TRANSFORMS

The Laplace transformation method is an operational method that can be used to find the transforms of time functions, the inverse Laplace transformation using the partial-fraction expansion of B(s)/A(s), where A(s) and B(s) are polynomials in s. In this Chapter, we present the computational methods with MATLAB to obtain the partial-fraction expansion of B(s)/A(s) and the zeros and poles of B(s)/A(s).

MATLAB can be used to obtain the partial-fraction expansion of the ratio of two polynomials, B(s)/A(s) as follows:

$$\frac{B(s)}{A(s)} = \frac{num}{den} = \frac{b(1)s^n + b(2)s^{n-1} + \ldots + b(n)}{a(1)s^n + a(2)s^{n-1} + \ldots + a(n)}$$

where a(1) ≠ 0 and num and den are row vectors. The coefficients of the numerator and denominator of B(s)/A(s) are specified by the num and den vectors.

Hence

$$num = [b(1)\ b(2)\ldots b(n)]$$

$$den = [a(1)\ a(2)\ldots a(n)]$$

The MATLAB command

r, p, k = residue(num, den)

is used to determine the residues, poles, and direct terms of a partial-fraction expansion of the ratio of two polynomials B(s) and A(s) is then given by

$$\frac{B(s)}{A(s)} = k(s) + \frac{r(1)}{s-p(1)} + \frac{r(2)}{s-p(2)} + \ldots + \frac{r(n)}{s-p(n)}$$

The MATLAB command **[num, den] = residue(r, p, k)** where r, p, k are the output from MATLAB converts the partial fraction expansion back to the polynomial ratio B(s)/A(s).

The command **printsys (num, den, 's')** prints the num/den in terms of the ratio of polynomials in s.

The command **ilaplace** will find the inverse Laplace transform of a Laplace function.

2.21.1 Finding Zeros and Poles of B(s)/A(s)

The MATLAB command **[z, p, k] = tf2zp(num,den)** is used to find the zeros, poles, and gain K of B(s)/A(s).

If the zeros, poles, and gain K are given, the following MATLAB command can be used to find the original num/den:

[num, den] = zp2tf (z, p, k)

Example E2.7

Consider the function

$$H(s) = \frac{n(s)}{d(s)}$$

where

$$n(s) = s^4 + 6s^3 + 5s^2 + 4s + 3$$

$$d(s) = s^5 + 7s^4 + 6s^3 + 5s^2 + 4s + 7$$

(*a*) Find n(–10), n(–5), n(–3) and n(–1)

(*b*) Find d(–10), d(–5), d(–3) and d(–1)

(*c*) Find H(–10), H(–5), H(–3) and H(–1)

Solution

(*a*)
```
>> n = [1 6 5 4 3];     % n = s^4 + 6s^3 + 5s^2 + 4s + 3
>> d = [1 7 6 5 4 7];   % d = s^5 + 7s^4 + 6s^3 + 5s^2 + 4s + 7
>> n2 = polyval(n, [-10])
   n2 = 4463
>> nn10 = polyval(n, [-10])
   nn10 = 4463
>> nn5 = polyval(n, [-5])
   nn5 = -17
>> nn3 = polyval(n, [-3])
   nn3 = -45
>> nn1 = polyval(n, [-1])
   nn1 = -1
```

(*b*)
```
>> dn10 = polyval(d, [-10])
   dn10 = -35533
>> dn5 = polyval(d, [-5])
   dn5 = 612
>> dn3 = polyval(d, [-3])
   dn3 = 202
>> dn1 = polyval(d, [-1])
   dn1 =  8
```

(*c*)
```
>> Hn10 = nn10/dn10
   Hn10 = -0.1256
>> Hn5 = nn5/dn5
   Hn5 = -0.0278
>> Hn3 = nn3/dn3
   Hn3 = -0.2228
>> Hn1 = nn1/dn1
   Hn1 = -0.1250
```

Example E2.8

Generate a plot of

$$y(x) = e^{-0.7x} \sin \omega x$$

where $\omega = 15$ rad/s,

and $0 \leq x \leq 15$. Use the colon notation to generate the x vector in increments of 0.1.

Solution

```
>>          x = [0: 0.1: 15];
>>          ω = 15;
>>          y = exp (–0.7*x).*sin (ω*x);
>>  plot(x, y)
>>  title ('y(x) = e^-^0^. ^7^xsin\omegax')
>>  xlabel('x')
>>  ylabel('y')
```

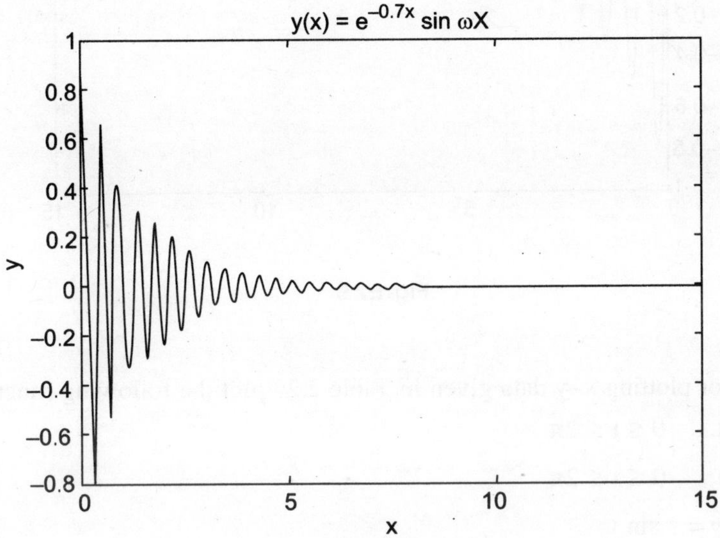

Fig. E2.8

Example E2.9

Generate a plot of

$$y(x) = e^{-0.6x} \cos \omega x$$

where $\omega = 10$ rad/s,

and $0 \le x \le 15$. Use the colon notation to generate the x vector in increments of 0.05.

Solution

```
>>          x = [0 : 0.1 : 15];
>>          w = 10;
>>          y = exp(–0.6*x).*cos(ω*x);
>>   plot(x, y)
>>   title ('y(x) = e^-^0^. ^6^xcos \omegax')
>>   xlabel('x')
>>   ylabel('y')
```

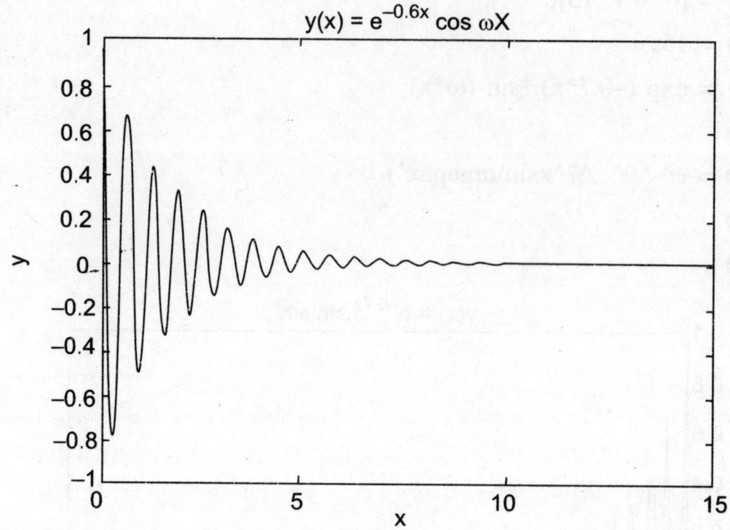

Fig. E2.9

Example E2.10

Using the functions for plotting x–y data given in Table 2.29 plot the following functions:

(*a*) $r^2 = 5 \cos 3t, \quad 0 \le t \le 2\pi$

(*b*) $r^2 = 5 \cos 3t, \quad 0 \le t \le 2\pi$

$x = r \cos t,\ y = r \sin t$

(*c*) $y_1 = e^{-2x} \cos x \quad 0 \le t \le 20$

$y_2 = e^{2x}$

(*d*) $y = \dfrac{\cos(x)}{x} \qquad -5 \le x \le 5\pi$

(*e*) $f = e^{-3t/5} \cos t \quad 0 \le t \le 2\pi$

(*f*) $z = -\dfrac{1}{3}x^2 + 2xy + y^2$

$|x| \le 7,\ |y| \le 7$

Solution

(*a*)
```
t = linspace(0, 2*pi, 200);
r = sqrt(abs(5*cos(3*t)));
polar(t, r)
```

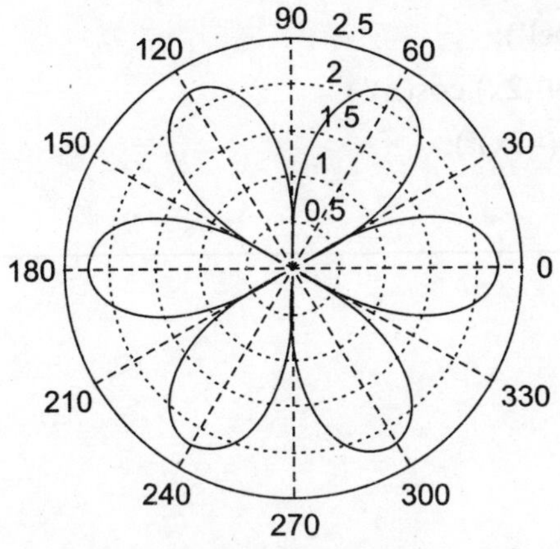

Fig. E2.10(a)

(*b*)
```
t = linspace (0, 2*pi, 200);
r = sqrt (abs (5*cos (3*t)));
x = r.*cos (t);
y = r.*sin (t);
fill(x, y, 'k'),
axis('square')
```

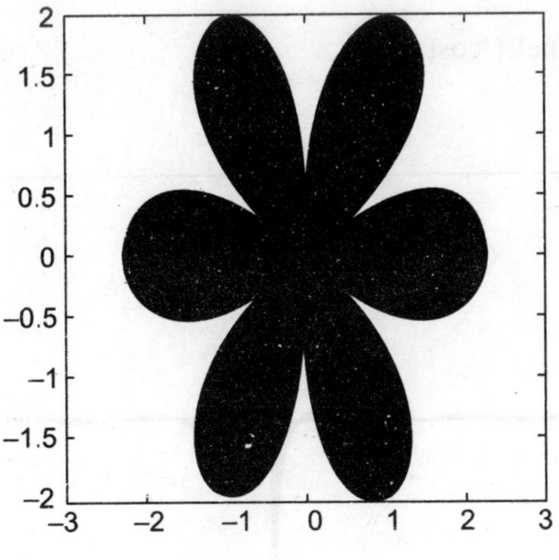

Fig. E2.10 (b)

(*c*)
```
x = 1:0.1:20;
y1 = exp (–2*x).*cos(x);
y2 = exp (2*x);
Ax = plotyy(x, y1, x, y2);
```

```
hy1 = get(Ax(1), 'ylabel');
hy2 = get(Ax(2), 'ylabel');
set(hy1, 'string', 'exp(-2x).cos(x)')
set(hy2, 'string', 'exp(-2x)');
```

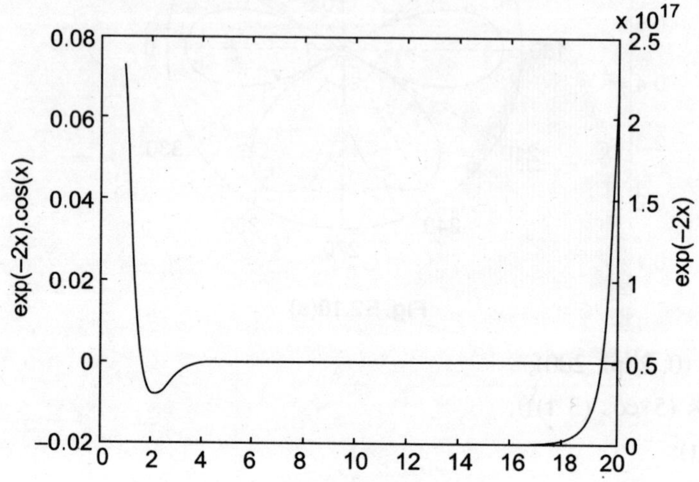

Fig. E2.10(c)

(*d*)
```
x = linspace (-5*pi, 5*pi, 100);
y = cos(x). /x;
area(x, y);
xlabel ('x (rad)'), ylabel ('cos(x)/x')
hold on
```

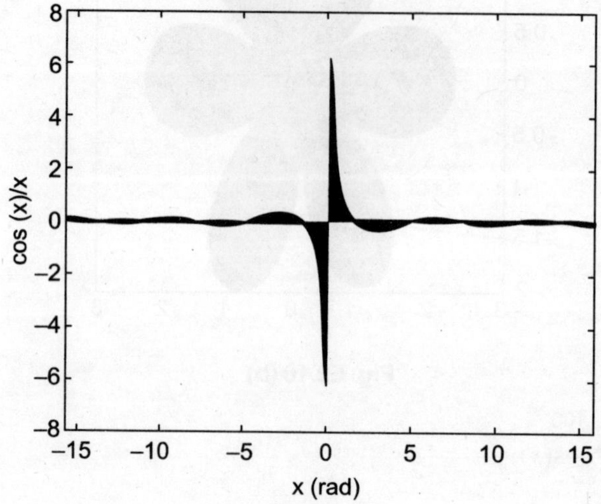

Fig. E2.10 (d)

(*e*)
```
t = linspace (0, 2*pi, 200);
f = exp(–0.6*t).*sin(t);
stem(t, f)
```

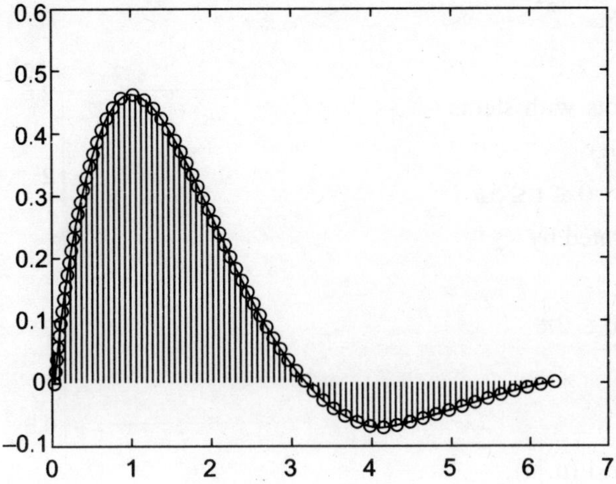

Fig. E2.10 (e)

(*f*)
```
r = –7:0.2:7;
[X, Y] = meshgrid(r, r);
Z = –0.333*X. ^2+2*X.*Y + Y. ^2;
cs = contour(X, Y, Z);
label(cs)
```

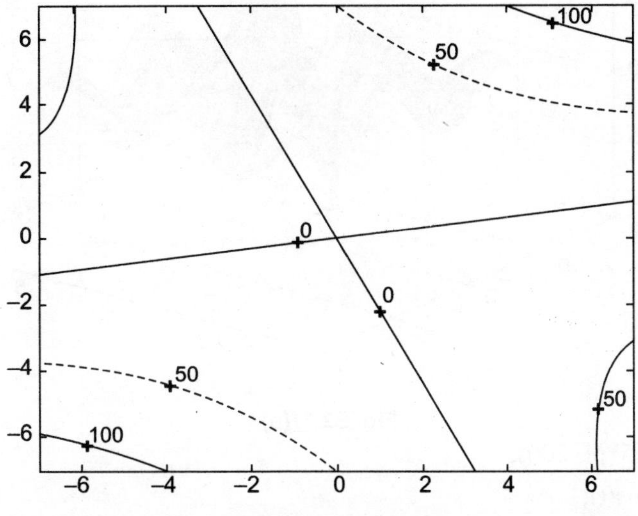

Fig. E2.10 (f)

Example E2.11

Use the functions listed in Table 2.30 for plotting 3-D data for the following.

(*a*) $z = \cos x \cos y\, e^{\frac{\sqrt{x^2+y^2}}{5}}$

$|x| \le = 7,\ |y| \le 7$

(*b*) Discrete data plots with stems

$x = t,\ y = t\cos(t)$

$z = e^{t/5} - 2 \qquad 0 \le t \le 5\pi$

(*c*) A cylinder generated by

$r = \sin(5\pi z) + 3$

$0 \le z \le 1 \quad 0 \le \theta \le 2\pi$

Solution

(*a*)
```
u = –7:0.2:7;
[X, Y] = meshgrid (u, u);
Z = cos(X).*cos (Y).*exp (–sqrt (X. ^2+Y. ^2)/5);
surf(X,Y,Z)
```

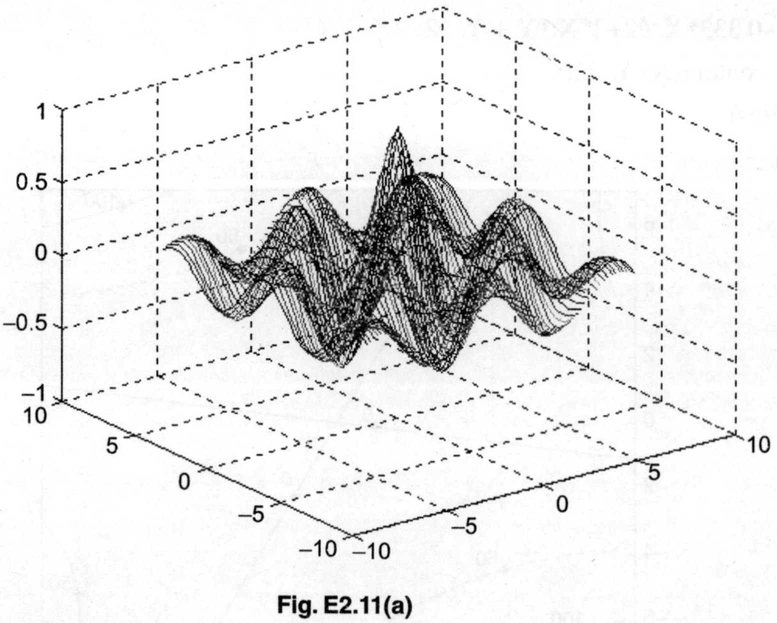

Fig. E2.11(a)

(*b*)
```
t = linspace(0, 5*pi, 200);
x = t; y = t.*cos(t);
z = exp(t/5)–2;
```

```
stem3(x, y, z, 'filled');
xlabel ('t'), ylabel ('t cos (t)'), zlabel ('e^t/5–1')
```

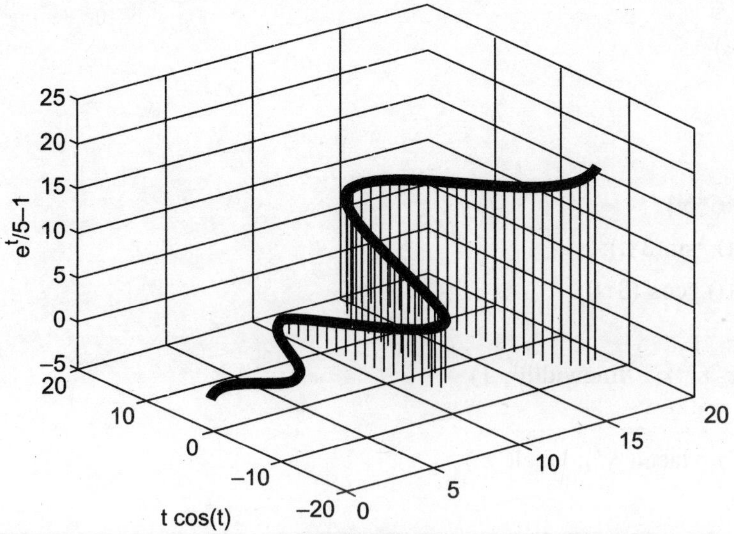

Fig. E2.11 (b)

(*c*) z = [0:0.2:1]';

```
r = sin (5*pi*z) + 3;
cylinder(r)
```

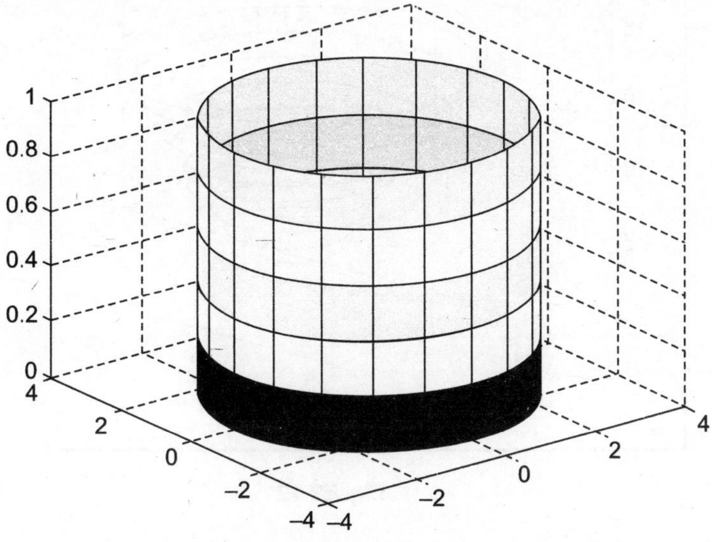

Fig. E2.11(c)

Example E2.12

Obtain the plot of the points for $0 \le t \le 6\pi$ when the coordinates x, y, z are given as a function of the parameter t as follows:

$$x = \sqrt{t}\sin(3t)$$

$$y = \sqrt{t}\cos(3t)$$

$$z = 0.8t$$

Solution

% Line plots

```
>> t = [0:0.1:6*pi];
>> x = sqrt(t).*sin(3*t);
>> y = sqrt (t).*cos (3*t);
>> z = 0.8*t;
>> plot3(x, y, z, 'k', 'linewidth', 1)
>> grid on
>> xlabel('x'); ylabel('y'); label('z')
```

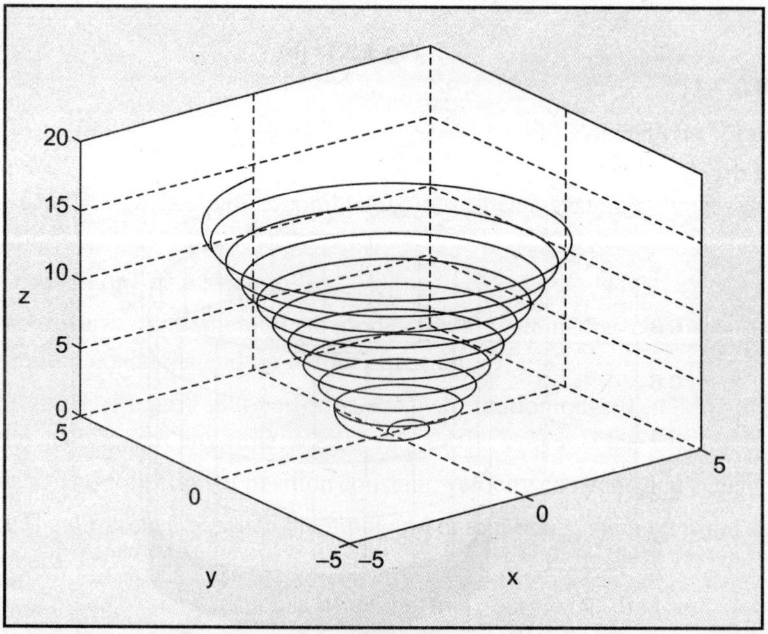

Fig. E2.12

Example E2.13

Obtain the mesh and surface plots for the function $z = \dfrac{2xy^2}{x^2 + y^2}$ over the domain $-2 \le x \le 6$ and $2 \le y \le 8$.

Solution

% Mesh and surface plots

```
   x = –2:0.1:6;
>> y = 2:0.1:8;
>> [x, y] = meshgrid (x, y);
>> z = 2*x.*y.^2./(x.^2 + y.^2);
>> mesh(x, y, z)
>> xlabel('x'); ylabel('y'); zlabel('z')
>> surf(x, y, z)
>> xlabel('x'); ylabel('y'); zlabel('z')
```

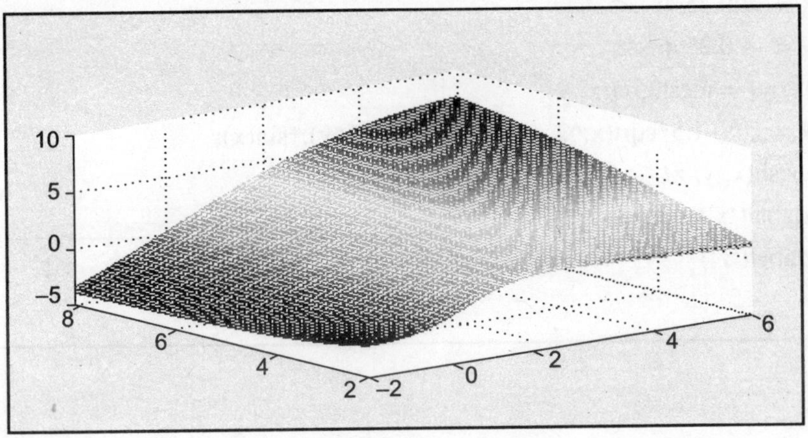

Fig. E2.13 (a)

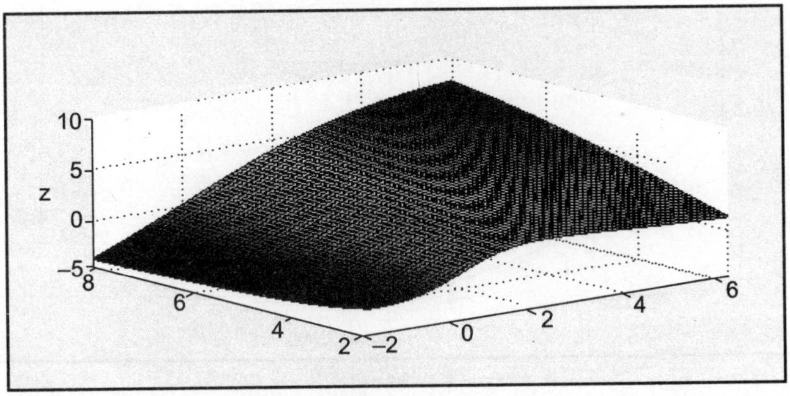

Fig. E2.13 (b)

Example E2.14

Plot the function $z = 2^{-1.5\sqrt{x^2+y^2}} \sin(x) \cos(0.5y)$ over the domain $-4 \le x \le 4$ and $-4 \le y \le 4$ using Table 2.30.

(*a*) Mesh plot
(*b*) Surface plot
(*c*) Mesh curtain plot
(*d*) Mesh and contour plot
(*e*) Surface and contour plot

Solution

(*a*) *% Mesh Plot*

```
>> x = –4:0.25:4;
>> y = –4:0.25:4;
>> [x, y] = meshgrid(x, y);
>> z = 2.^(–1.5*sqrt(x.^2 + y.^2)).*cos(0.5*y).*sin(x);
>> mesh(x, y, z)
>> xlabel('x'); ylabel('y')
>> zlabel('z')
```

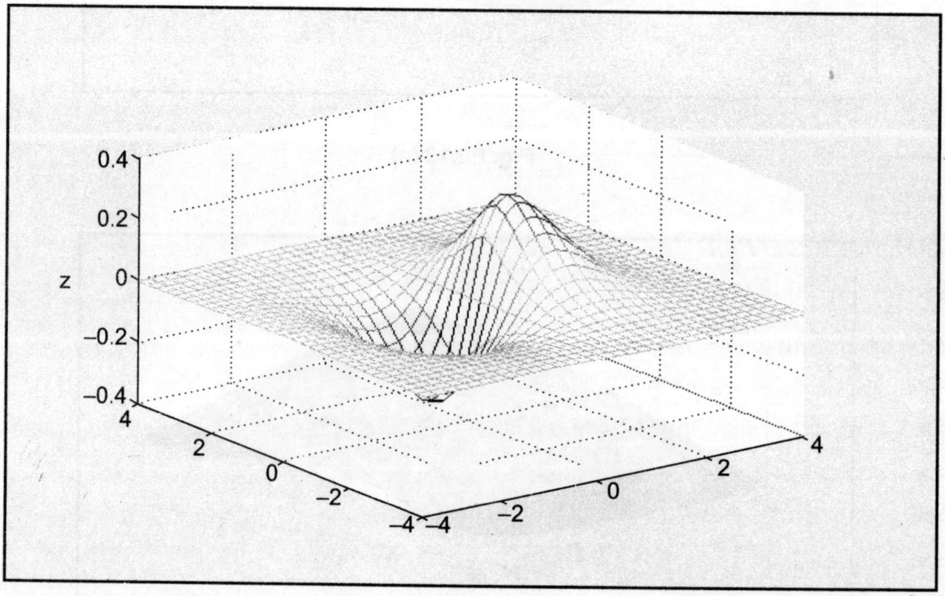

Fig. E2.14 (a)

(*b*) *% Surface Plot*

```
>> x = –4:0.25:4;
>> y = –4:0.25:4;
>> [x, y] = meshgrid(x, y);
>> z = 2.0.^(–1.5*sqrt(x.^2 + y.^2)).*cos(0.5*y).*sin(x);
>> surf(x, y, z)
>> xlabel('x'); ylabel('y')
>> zlabel('z')
```

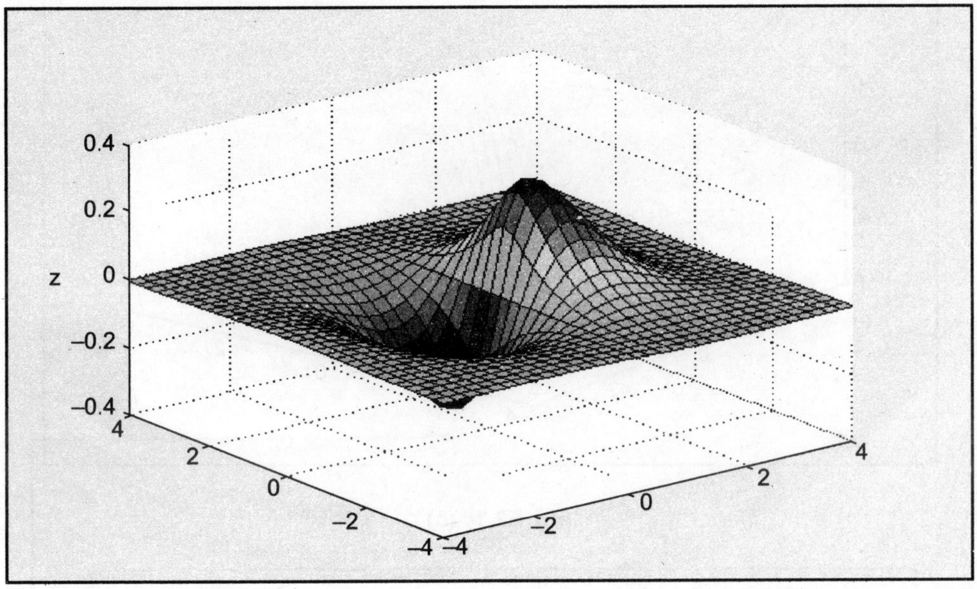

Fig. E2.14 (b)

(*c*) *% Mesh Curtain Plot*

```
>> x = –4.0:0.25:4;
>> y = –4.0:0.25:4;
>> [x, y] = meshgrid(x, y);
>> z = 2.0.^(–1.5*sqrt(x.^2 + y.^2)).*cos(0.5*y).*sin(x);
>> meshz(x, y, z)
>> xlabel('x'); ylabel('y')
>> zlabel('z')
```

(*d*) *% Mesh and Contour Plot*

```
>> x = –4.0:0.25:4;
>> y = –4.0:0.25:4;
>> [x, y] = meshgrid(x, y);
```

```
>>   z = 2.0.^(–1.5*sqrt(x.^2 + y.^2)).*cos(0.5*y).*sin(x);
>>   meshc(x, y, z)
>>   xlabel('x'); ylabel('y')
>>   zlabel('z')
```

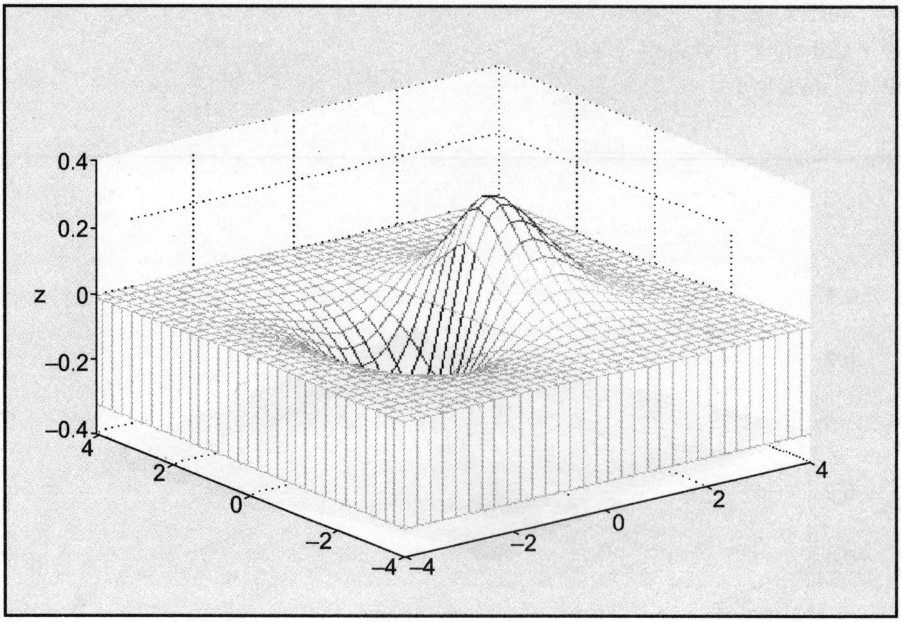

Fig. E2.14 (c)

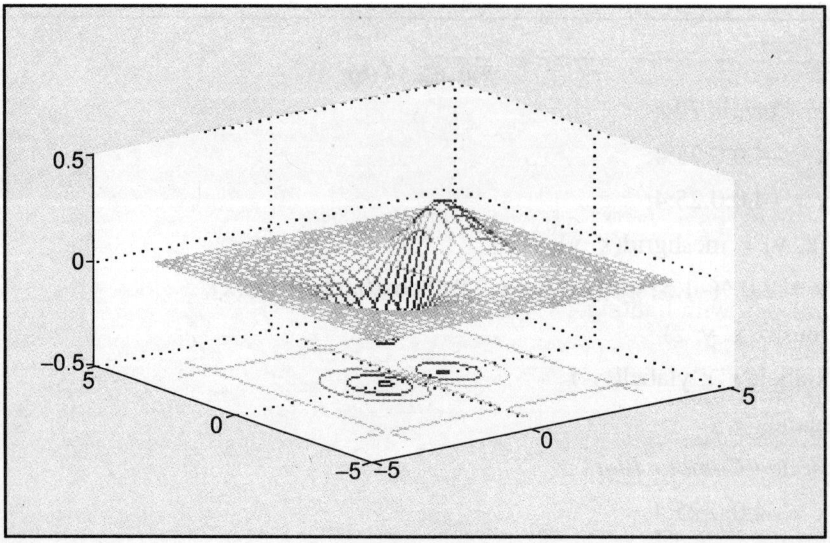

Fig. E2.14 (d)

(*e*) *% Surface and Contour Plot*

```
    >>   x = –4.0:0.25:4;
    >>   y = –4.0:0.25:4;
>>[x, y] = meshgrid(x, y);
>>z = 2.0. ^ (–1.5*sqrt (x. ^2 + y. ^2)).*cos (0.5*y).*sin(x);
>>surfc(x, y, z)
>>xlabel('x'); ylabel('y')
>>zlabel('z')
```

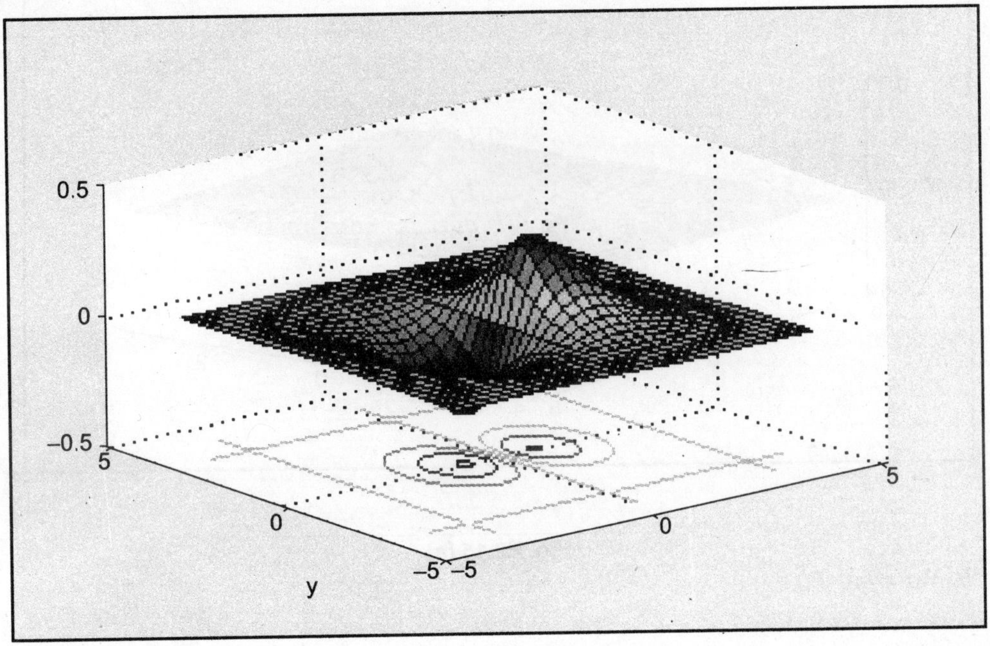

Fig. E2.14 (e)

Example E2.15

Plot the function $z = 2^{-1.5\sqrt{x^2+y^2}}\sin(x)\cos(0.5y)$ over the domain $-4 \le x \le 4$ and $-4 \le y \le 4$ using Table 2.30.

(*a*) Surface plot with lighting

(*b*) Waterfall plot

(*c*) 3-D contour plot

(*d*) 2-D contour plot

Solution

(*a*) *% Surface Plot with Lighting*

```
>> x = –4.0:0.25:4;
```

```
>> y = -4.0:0.25:4;
>> [x, y] = meshgrid(x, y);
>> z = 2.0.^(-1.5*sqrt(x.^2 + y.^2)).*cos(0.5*y).*sin(x);
>> surfl(x, y, z)
>> xlabel('x'); ylabel('y')
>> zlabel('z')
```

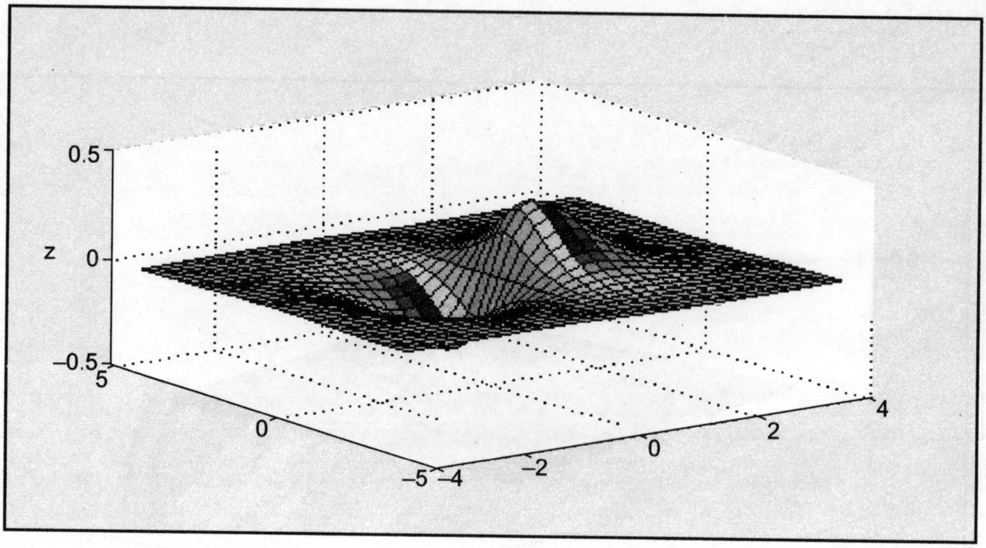

Fig. E2.15 (a)

(*b*) *% Waterfall Plot*

```
>>  x = -4.0:0.25:4;
>>  y = -4.0:0.25:4;
>>  [x, y] = meshgrid(x, y);
>>  z = 2.0.^(-1.5*sqrt(x.^2 + y.^2)).*cos(0.5*y).*sin(x);
>>  waterfall(x, y, z)
>>  xlabel('x'); ylabel('y')
>>  zlabel('z')
```

(*c*) *% 3-D Contour Plot*

```
>>  x = -4.0:0.25:4;
>>  y = -4.0:0.25:4;
>>  [x, y] = meshgrid(x, y);
>>  z = 2.0.^(-1.5*sqrt(x.^2 + y.^2)).*cos(0.5*y).*sin(x);
```

```
>>    contour3(x, y, z, 15)
>>    xlabel('x'); ylabel('y')
>>    zlabel('z')
```

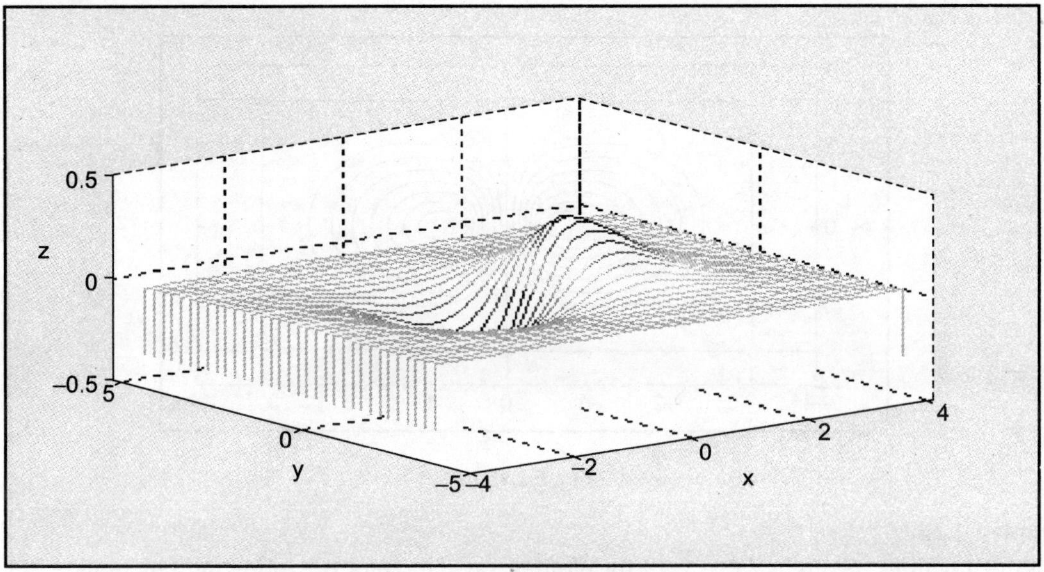

Fig. E2.15 (b)

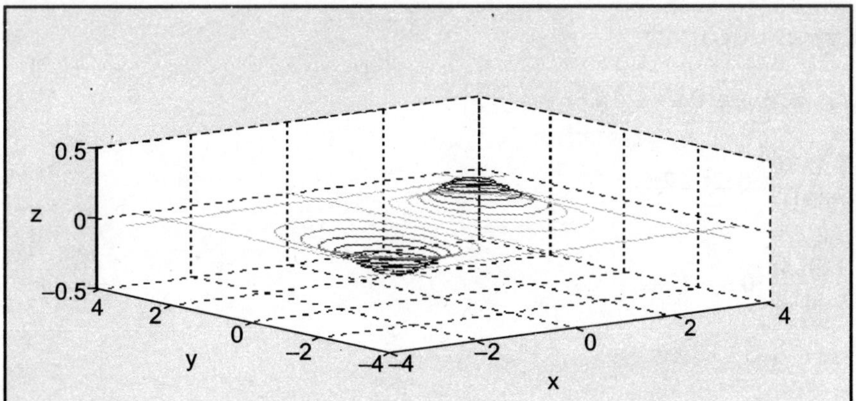

Fig. E2.15 (c)

(*d*) *% 2-D Contour Plot*

```
>>    x = –4.0:0.25:4;
>>    y = –4.0:0.25:4;
>>    [x, y] = meshgrid(x, y);
```

```
>>  z = 2.0.^(–1.5*sqrt(x.^2 + y.^2)).*cos(0.5*y).*sin(x);
>>  contour(x, y, z,15)
>>  xlabel('x'); ylabel('y')
>>  zlabel('z')
```

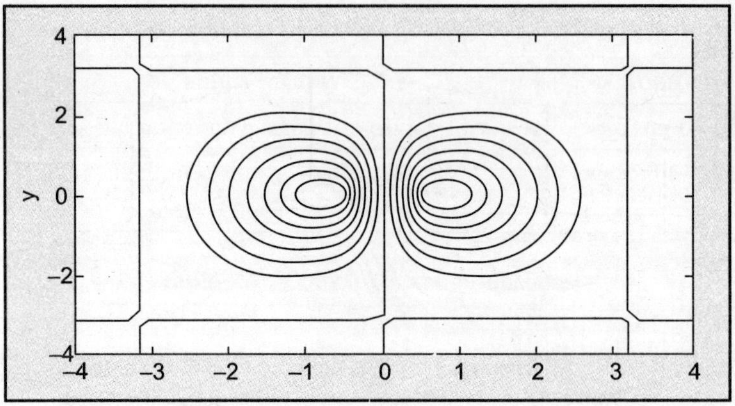

Fig. E2.15 (d)

Example E2.16

Using the functions given in Table 2.29 for plotting x-y data, plot the following functions:

(*a*) $f(t) = t \cos t \quad 0 \le t \le 10\pi$

(*b*) $x = e^{-2t},\ y = t \quad 0 \le t \le 2\pi$

(*c*) $x = t, y = e^{2t} \quad 0 \le t \le 2\pi$

(*d*) $x = e^{t}, y = 50 + e^{t} \quad 0 \le t \le 2\pi$

(*e*) $r^2 = 3 \sin 7t$, $y = r \sin t$ $\quad 0 \le t \le 2\pi$

(*f*) $r^2 = 3 \sin 4t$, $y = r \sin t$ $\quad 0 \le t \le 2\pi$

(*g*) $y = t \sin t \quad 0 \le t \le 5\pi$

Solution

(*a*) % Use of plot command

```
>> fplot('x.*cos(x)', [0, 10*pi])
```

(*b*) % Semilog x command

```
>> t = linspace(0, 2*pi, 200);
>> x = exp(–2*t); y = t;
>> semilogx(x, y), grid
```

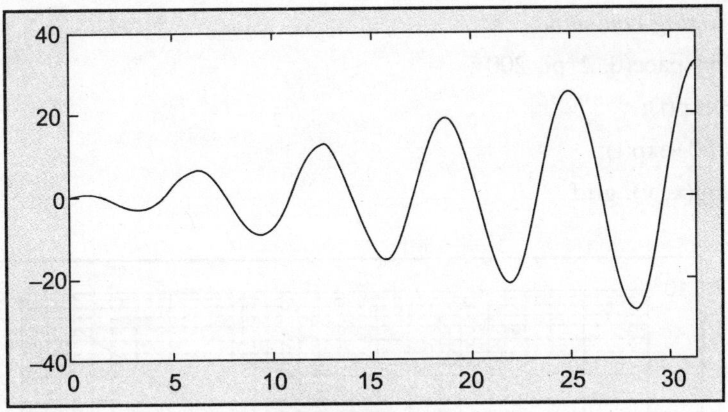

Fig. E2.16 (a)

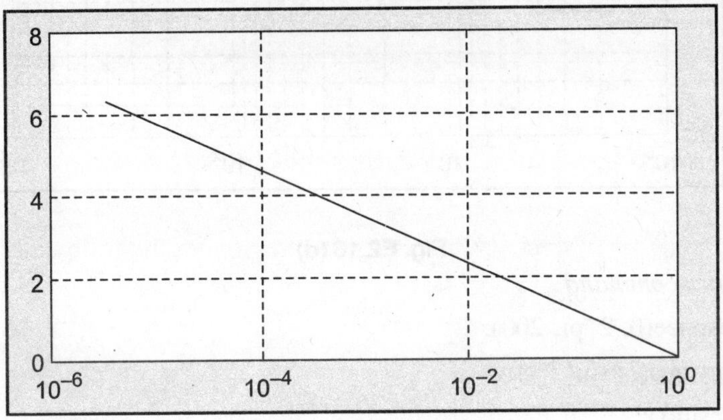

Fig. E2.16 (b)

(*c*) % Semilog y command

t = linspace(0, 2*pi, 200);

```
>> semilogy(t, exp(–2*t)), grid
```

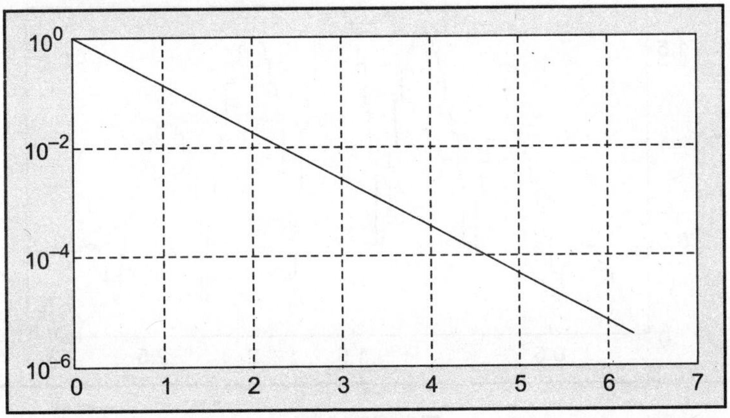

Fig. E2.16 (c)

(*d*) *% Use of loglog command*

```
>> t = linspace(0, 2*pi, 200);
>> x = exp(t);
>> y = 50+exp(t);
>> loglog(x, y), grid
```

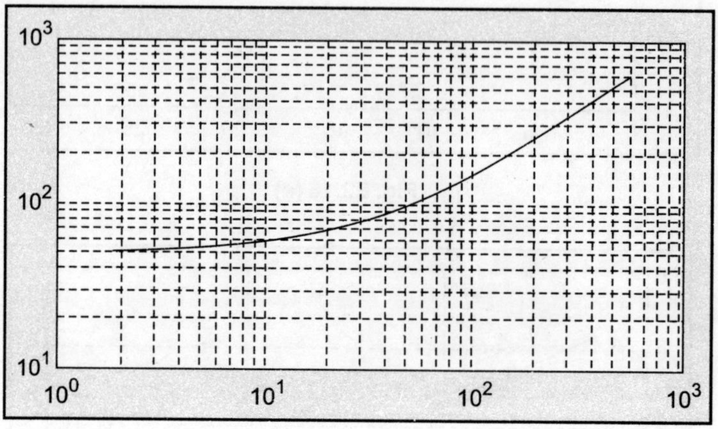

Fig. E2.16 (d)

(*e*) *% Use of stairs command*

```
>> t = linspace(0, 2*pi, 200);
>> r = sqrt(abs(3*sin(7*t)));
>> y = r.*sin(t);
>> stairs(t, y)
>> axis([0 pi 0 inf]);
```

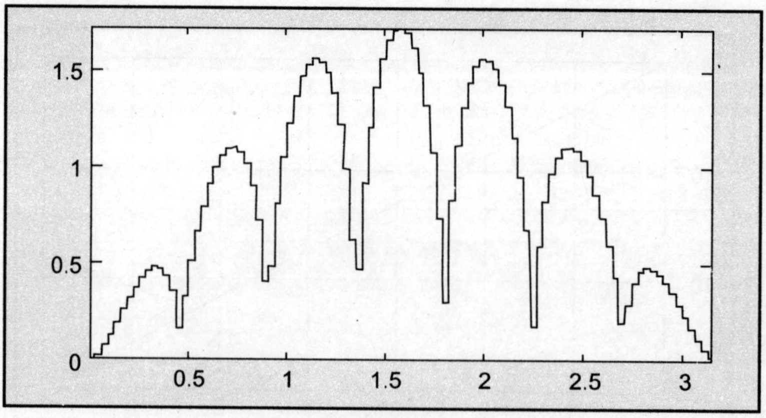

Fig. E2.16 (e)

(*f*) *% Use of bar command*

```
>> t = linspace(0, 2*pi, 200);
>> r = sqrt(abs(3*sin(4*t)));
>> y = r.*sin(t);
>> bar(t, y)
>> axis([0 pi 0 inf ]);
```

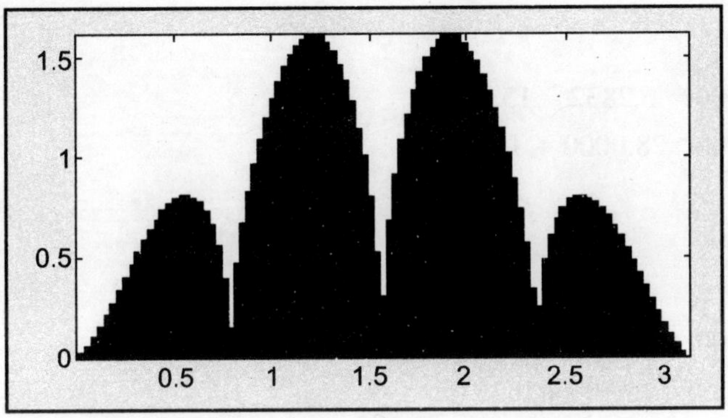

Fig. E2.16 (f)

(*g*) *% use of comet command*

```
>> q = linspace(0, 5*pi, 200);
>> y = q.*sin(q);
>> comet(q, y)
```

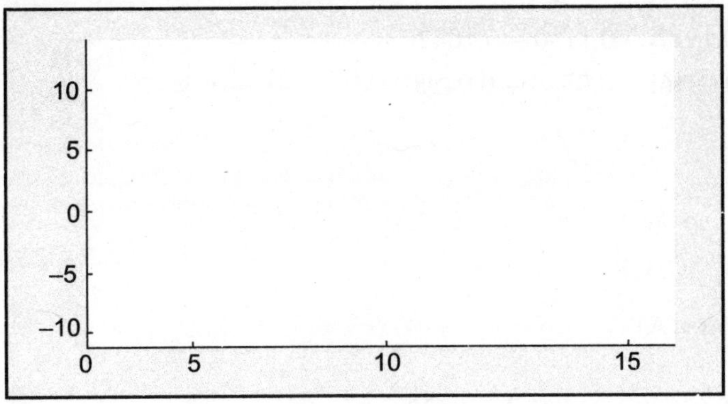

Fig. E2.16 (g)

Example E2.17

Consider the two matrices

$$A = \begin{bmatrix} 3 & 2\pi \\ 5j & 10+\sqrt{2}\,j \end{bmatrix}; \quad B = \begin{bmatrix} 7j & -15j \\ 2\pi & 18 \end{bmatrix}$$

Using MATLAB, determine the following:

(*a*) A + B (*b*) AB (*c*) A^2 (*d*) A^T

(*e*) B^{-1} (*f*) B^TA^T (*g*) $A^2 + B^2 - AB$

Solution

```
>> A = [3 2*pi; 5j 10 + sqrt(2)*j];
>> B = [7j –15j; 2*pi 18];\
```

(*a*) A + B

```
ans =
   3.0000 + 7.0000i   6.2832 – 15.0000i
   6.2832 + 5.0000i  28.0000 + 1.4142i
```

(*b*) >> A * B

```
ans =
   1.0e + 002 *
   0.3948 + 0.2100i   1.1310 – 0.4500i
   0.2783 + 0.0889i   2.5500 + 0.2546i
```

(*c*) >> A^2

```
ans =
    9.0000 + 31.4159i  81.6814 + 8.8858i
   –7.0711 + 65.0000i  98.0000 + 59.7002i
```

(*d*) >> inv(A)

```
ans =
   0.1597 + 0.1917i  –0.1150 – 0.1042i
   0.0829 – 0.0916i   0.0549 + 0.0498i
```

(*e*) >> B^–1

```
ans =
   0 – 0.0817i   0.0681
   0 + 0.0285i   0.0318
```

(*f*) >> inv(B) * inv(A)

```
ans =
    0.0213 – 0.0193i  –0.0048 + 0.0128i
   –0.0028 + 0.0016i   0.0047 – 0.0017i
```

(*g*) >> (A^2 + B^2) – (A * B)

```
ans =
   1.0e + 002 *
   –0.7948 – 0.8383i   0.7358 – 2.1611i
    0.7819 + 1.0010i   1.6700 – 0.6000i
```

Example E2.18

Find the inverse of the following matrices using MATLAB:

$$(a)\begin{bmatrix}3 & 2 & 0\\ 2 & -1 & 7\\ 5 & 4 & 9\end{bmatrix} \qquad (b)\begin{bmatrix}-4 & 2 & 5\\ 7 & --1 & 6\\ 2 & 3 & 7\end{bmatrix} \quad \text{and} \quad (c)\begin{bmatrix}-1 & 2 & -5\\ 4 & 3 & 7\\ 7 & -6 & 1\end{bmatrix}.$$

Solution

```
>> clear % Clears the workspace
>> A = [3 2 0; 2 –1 7; 5 4 9]; % Spaces separate matrix columns – semicolons separate matrix rows
>> B = [–4 2 5; 7 –1 6; 2 3 7]; % Spaces separate matrix columns – semicolons separate matrix rows
>> C = [–1 2 –5; 4 3 7; 7 –6 1]; % Spaces separate matrix columns – semicolons separate matrix rows
>> inv(A); % Finds the inverse of the selected matrix
>> inv(B); % Finds the inverse of the selected matrix
>> inv(C) % Finds the inverse of the selected matrix
  % Inverse of A
  ans =
     0.4805    0.2338   –0.1818
    –0.2208   –0.3506    0.2727
    –0.1688    0.0260    0.0909
  % Inverse of B
  ans =
    –0.1773    0.0071    0.1206
    –0.2624   –0.2695    0.4184
     0.1631    0.1135   –0.0709
  % Inverse of C
  ans =
     0.1667    0.1037    0.1074
     0.1667    0.1259   –0.0481
    –0.1667    0.0296   –0.0407
```

Example E2.19

Determine the eigenvalues and eigenvectors of matrix **A** using MATLAB

$$(a)\ A = \begin{bmatrix}4 & -1 & 5\\ 2 & 1 & 3\\ 6 & -7 & 9\end{bmatrix} \quad \text{and} \quad (b)\ A = \begin{bmatrix}3 & 5 & 7\\ 2 & 4 & 8\\ 5 & 6 & 10\end{bmatrix}$$

Solution

(*a*)
```
A=[4 –1 5; 2 1 3; 6 –7 9]
A =
    4  –1   5
    2   1   3
    6  –7   9
%The eigenvalues of A
format short e
eig(A)
ans =
    1.0000e + 001
    5.8579e – 001
    3.4142e + 000
%The eigenvectors of A
[Q,d] = eig(A)
Q =
    –5.5709e–001  –8.2886e–001  –7.3925e–001
    –3.7139e–001  –3.9659e–002  –6.7174e–001
    –7.4278e–001   5.5805e–001  –4.7739e–002
d =
    1.0000e + 001        0              0
         0         5.8579e – 001        0
         0               0        3.4142e + 000
```

(*b*)
```
A =
    3   5   7
    2   4   8
    5   6  10
%The eigenvalues of A
format short e
eig(A)
ans =
    1.7686e+001
    –3.4295e–001 +1.0066e + 000i
    –3.4295e–001 –1.0066e + 000i
%The eigenvectors of A
[Q, d] = eig(A)
Q =
```

Column 1

5.0537e – 001

4.8932e – 001

7.1075e – 001

Column 2

–2.0715e–001 –5.2772e–001i

7.1769e–001

–3.3783e-001 + 2.2223e–001i

Column 3

–2.0715e–001 + 5.2772e–001i

7.1769e–001

–3.3783e–001 – 2.2223e–001i

d =

Column 1

1.7686e + 001

0

0

Column 2

0

–3.4295e–001 + 1.0066e + 000i

0

Column 3

0

0

–3.4295e–001 –1.0066e + 000i

Example E2.20

Determine the eigenvalues and eigenvectors of **AB** using MATLAB.

$$\mathbf{A} = \begin{bmatrix} 3 & 0 & 2 & 1 \\ 1 & 2 & 5 & 4 \\ 7 & -1 & 2 & 6 \\ 1 & -2 & 3 & 4 \end{bmatrix} \quad \text{and} \quad \mathbf{B} = \begin{bmatrix} 1 & 3 & 5 & 7 \\ 2 & -1 & -2 & 4 \\ 3 & 2 & 1 & 1 \\ 4 & 1 & 0 & 6 \end{bmatrix}$$

Solution

```
% MATLAB Program
    % The matrix "a" = A*B
  >> A = [ 3 0 2 1; 1 2 5 4; 7 –1 2 6; 1 –2 3 4 ];
```

```
>> B = [ 1 3 5 7; 2 –1 –2 4; 3 2 1 1; 4 1 0 6 ];
>> a = A*B
 a =
   13   14   17   29
   36   15    6   44
   35   32   39   83
   22   15   12   26
>> eig (a)
Ans. =
   98.5461
    2.2964
   –1.3095
   –6.5329
```

The eigenvectors are:

```
>> [Q, d] = eig (a)
Q =
   –0.3263  –0.2845   0.3908   0.3413
   –0.3619   0.7387  –0.7816  –0.9215
   –0.8168  –0.6026   0.4769   0.0962
   –0.3089   0.1016  –0.0950   0.1586
d =
        98.5461         0          0          0
              0    2.2964          0          0
              0         0    –1.3095          0
              0         0          0    –6.5329
```

Example E2.21

Solve the following set of equations using MATLAB.

(*a*)
$$x_1 + 2x_2 + 3x_3 + 5x_4 = 21$$
$$-2x_1 + 5x_2 + 7x_3 - 9x_4 = 18$$
$$5x_1 + 7x_2 + 2x_3 - 5x_4 = 25$$
$$-x_1 + 3x_2 - 7x_3 + 7x_4 = 30$$

(*b*)
$$x_1 + 2x_2 + 3x_3 + 4x_4 = 8$$
$$2x_1 - 2x_2 - x_3 - x_4 = -3$$
$$x_1 - 3x_2 + 4x_3 - 4x_4 = 8$$
$$2x_1 + 2x_2 - 3x_3 + 4x_4 = -2$$

Solution

(*a*)

```
>> A = [1 2 3 5; –2 5 7 –9; 5 7 2 –5; –1 –3 –7 7];
>> B = [21; 18; 25; 30];
> S = A\B
S =
   –8.9896
   14.1285
   –5.4438
    3.6128
```

% Therefore x_1 = –8.9896, x_2 = 14.12.85, x_3 = –5.4438, x_4 = 3.6128.

(*b*)

```
>> A = [1 2 3 4; 2 –2 –1 1; 1 –3 4 –4; 2 2 –3 4];
>> B = [8; –3; 8; –2];
>> S = A\B
S =
    2.0000
    2.0000
    2.0000
   –1.0000
```

% Therefore x_1 = 2.0000, x_2 = 2.0000, x_3 = 2.0000, x_4 = –1.0000.

Example E2.22

Use *diff* command for symbolic differentiation of the following functions:

(*a*) $S_1 = e^{x^8}$

(*b*) $S_2 = 3x^3 e^{x^5}$

(*c*) $S_3 = 5x^3 - 7x^2 + 3x + 6$

Solution

(*a*)

```
>> syms x
>> S1 = exp(x^8);
>> diff (S1)
ans =
   8*x^7*exp(x^8)
```

(*b*)

```
>> S2 = 3*x^3*exp(x^5);
>> diff (S2)
ans =
   9*x^2*exp(x^5) + 15*x^7*exp(x^5)
```

(*c*)

```
>> S3 = 5*x^3 – 7*x^2 + 3*x + 6;
>> diff (S3)
ans =
   15*x^2 – 14*x + 3
```

Example E2.23

Use MATLAB's symbolic commands to find the values of the following integrals:

(*a*) $\int_{0.2}^{0.7} |x| dx$

(*b*) $\int_{0}^{\pi} (\cos y + 7y^2) dy$

(*c*) $\sqrt{x}$

(*d*) $7x^5 - 6x^4 + 11x^3 + 4x^2 + 8x + 9$

(*e*) cos a

Solution

(*a*)

```
>> syms x, y, a, b
>> S1 = abs(x)
>> int (S1, 0.2, 0.7)
ans =
   9/40
```

(*b*)

```
>> S2 = cos (y) + 7*y^2
>> int (S2, 0, pi)
ans =
   7/3*pi^3
```

(*c*)

```
>> S3 = sqrt (x)
>> int (S3)
```

```
ans =
    2/3*x^ (3/2)
      >>  int (S3, 'a', 'b')
ans =
    2/3*b^ (3/2) – 2/3*a^ (3/2)
      >> int (S3, 0.4, 0.7)
ans =
    7/150*70^ (1/2) – 4/75*10^ (1/2)
```

(*d*)

```
      >> S4 = 7*x^5 – 6*x^4 + 11*x^3 + 4*x^2 + 8*x – 9
      >> int (S4)
ans =
    7/6*x^6 – 6/5*x^5 + 11/4*x^4 + 4/3*x^3 + 4*x^2 – 9*x
```

(*e*)

```
      >> S5 = cos (a)
      >>  int (S5)
ans =
    sin (a)
```

Example E2.24

Obtain the general solution of the following first order differential equations:

(*a*) $\frac{dy}{dt} = 5t - 6y$

(*b*) $\frac{d^2y}{dt^2} + 3\frac{dy}{dt} + y = 0$

(*c*) $\frac{ds}{dt} = Ax^3$

(*d*) $\frac{ds}{dA} = Ax^3$

Solution

(*a*)

```
      >> solve ('Dy = 5*t – 6*y')
ans =
    5/6*t – 5/36 + exp (–6*t)*C1
```

(*b*)

```
>> dsolve ('D2y + 3*Dy + y = 0')
ans =
C1*exp (1/2*(5^ (1/2) – 3)*t) + C2*exp (–1/2*(5^ (1/2) + 3)*t)
```

(*c*)

```
>> dsolve ('Ds = A*x^3', 'x')
ans =
1/4*A*x^4 + C1
```

(*d*)

```
>> dsolve ('Ds = A*x^3', 'A')
ans =
1/2*A^2*x^3 + C1
```

Example E2.25

Determine the solution of the following differential equations that satisfies the given initial conditions:

(*a*) $\frac{dy}{dx} = -7x^2 \qquad y(1) = 0.7$

(*b*) $\frac{dy}{dx} = 5x\cos^2 y \qquad y(0) = \pi/4$

(*c*) $\frac{dy}{dx} = -y + e^{3x} \qquad y(0) = 2$

(*d*) $\frac{dy}{dt} + 5y = 35 \qquad y(0) = 4$

Solution

(*a*)

```
>> dsolve ('Dy = –7*x^2', 'y (1) = 0.7')
ans =
–7*x^2*t + 7*x^2 + 7/10
```

(*b*)

```
>> dsolve ('Dy = 5*x*cos (y) ^2', 'y (0) = pi/4')
ans =
atan (5*t*x + 1)
```

(*c*)

```
>> dsolve ('Dy = –y+ exp (3*x)', 'y (0) = 2')
ans =
exp (3*x) + exp (–t)*(–exp (3*x) + 2)
```

(*d*)

```
>> dsolve ('Dy + 5*y = 35', 'y (0) = 4')

ans =

   7–3*exp (–5*t)
```

Example E2.26

Given the differential equation

$$\frac{d^2x}{dt^2} + 7\frac{dx}{dt} + 5x = 8\ u\ (t)\ t \geq 0$$

Using MATLAB program, find

(*a*) x(t) when all the initial conditions are zero

(*b*) x(t) when x (0) = 1 and $\dot{x}(0)$ = 2.

Solution

(*a*) x (t) when all the initial conditions are zero

```
>> x = dsolve ('D2x = –7*Dx – 5*x + 8', 'x (0) = 0')

x =

   8/5 + (–8/5–C2)*exp (1/2*(–7 + 29^ (1/2))*t) + C2*exp (–1/2*(7 + 29^ (1/2))*t)
```

(*b*) x (t) when x (0) = 1 and $\dot{x}(0)$ = 2

```
>> x = dsolve ('D2x = –7*Dx – 5*x +8', 'x (0) = 1', 'Dx (0) = 2')

x = 8/5 + (–3/10 – 1/290*29^ (1/2))*exp (1/2*(–7 + 29^ (1/2))*t)
   – 1/290*(–1 + 3*29^ (1/2))*29^ (1/2)      *exp (–1/2*(7 + 29^ (1/2))*t)
```

Example E2.27

Given the differential equation

$$\frac{d^2x}{dt^2} + 12\frac{dx}{dt} + 15x = 35\ t \geq 0$$

Using MATLAB program, find

(*a*) x(t) when all the initial conditions are zero

(*b*) x(t) when x (0) = 0 and $\dot{x}(0)$ = 1.

Solution

(*a*) x (t) when all the initial conditions are zero

```
>> x = dsolve ('D2x = –12*Dx – 15*x + 35', 'x (0) = 0')

x =

   7/3 + (–7/3 – C2)*exp ((–6 + 21^ (1/2))*t) + C2*exp (–(6 + 21^ (1/2))*t)
```

(*b*) x (t) when x (0) = 0 and $\dot{x}(0) = 1$.

```
>> x = dsolve ('D2x = –12*Dx – 15*x + 35', 'x (0) = 0', 'Dx (0) = 1')

x =

7/3+ (–7/6–13/42*21^ (1/2))*exp ((–6 + 21^ (1/2))*t)–1/126*(–39 + 7*21^ (1/2))*21^ (1/2)
*exp (–(6 + 21^ (1/2))*t)
```

Example E2.28

Find the inverse of the following matrix using MATLAB:

$$A = \begin{bmatrix} s & 2 & 0 \\ 2 & s & -3 \\ 3 & 0 & 1 \end{bmatrix}$$

Solution

```
>> A = [s 2 0; 2 s –3; 3 0 1];
>> inv (A)

ans =

[s/(s^2–22),        –2/(s^2–22),      –6/(s^2–22)]
[–11/(s^2–22),      s/(s^2–22),        3 *s/(s^2–22)]
[–3*s/(s^2–22),     6/(s^2–22),       (s^2–4)/(s^2–22)]
```

Example E2.29

Expand the following function F(s) into partial fractions using MATLAB. Determine the inverse Laplace transform of F(s).

$$F(s) = \frac{1}{s^4 + 5s^3 + 7s^2}$$

The MATLAB program for determining the partial-fraction expansion is given below:

Solution

```
>> b = [0 0 0 0 1];
>> a = [1 5 7 0 0];
>> [r, p, k] = residue (b, a)

r =

    0.0510 – 0.0648i
    0.0510 + 0.0648i
   –0.1020
    0.1429
```

p =

−2.5000 + 0.8660i

−2.5000 − 0.8660i

0

0

k = [ ]

% From the above MATLAB output, we have the following expression:

$$F(s) = \frac{r_1}{s-p_1} + \frac{r_2}{s-p_2} + \frac{r_3}{s-p_3} + \frac{r_4}{s-p_4}$$

$$F(s) = \frac{0.0510-0.0648i}{s-(-2.5000+0.8660i)} + \frac{(0.0510+0.0648i)}{s-(-2.5000-0.8660i)} + \frac{-0.1020}{s-0} + \frac{0.1429}{s-0}$$

% Note that the row vector k is zero implies that there is no constant term in this example problem.

% The MATLAB program for determining the inverse Laplace transform of F(s) is given below:

```
>> syms s
>> f = 1/(s^4 + 5*s^3 + 7*s^2);
>> ilaplace (f)
```

ans =

1/7*t–5/49 + 5/49*exp (–)*cos (1/2*3^ (1/2)*t) + 11/147*exp (–5/2*t)*3^ (1/2) *sin(1/2*3^(1/2)*t)

Example E2.30

Expand the following function F(s) into partial fractions using MATLAB. Determine the inverse Laplace transform of F(s).

$$F(s) = \frac{5s^2+3s+6}{s^4+3s^3+7s^2+9s+12}$$

Solution

The MATLAB program for determining the partial-fraction expansion is given below:

```
>> b = [0 0 5 3 6];
>> a = [1 3 7 9 12];
>> [r, p, k] = residue(b, a)
```

r =

−0.5357 − 1.0394i

−0.5357 + 1.0394i

0.5357 − 0.1856i

0.5357 + 0.1856i

```
p =
    -1.5000 + 1.3229i
    -1.5000 - 1.3229i
    -0.0000 + 1.7321i
    -0.0000 - 1.7321i
k = [ ]
```

% From the above MATLAB output, we have the following expression:

$$F(s) = \frac{r_1}{s-p_1} + \frac{r_2}{s-p_2} + \frac{r_3}{s-p_3} + \frac{r_4}{s-p_4}$$

$$F(s) = \frac{-0.5357-1.0394i}{s-(-1.500+1.3229i)} + \frac{(-0.5357+1.0394i)}{s-(-1.5000-1.3229i)} + \frac{0.5357-0.1856i}{s-(-0+1.7321i)} + \frac{0.5357-0.1856i}{s-(-0-1.7321i)}$$

% Note that the row vector k is zero implies that there is no constant term in this example problem.

% The MATLAB program for determining the inverse Laplace transform of F(s) is given below:

```
>> syms s
>> f = (5*s^2 + 3*s + 6)/(s^4 + 3*s^3 + 7*s^2 + 9*s +12);
>> ilaplace(f)
ans =
    11/14*exp(-3/2*t)*7^(1/2)*sin(1/2*7^(1/2)*t)-15/14*exp(3/2*t)*cos(1/2*7^(1/2)*t)
    + 3/14*3^(1/2)
*sin(3^(1/2)*t) + 15/14*cos(3^(1/2)*t)
```

Example E2.31

For the following function F(s):

$$F(s) = \frac{s^4+3s^3+5s^2+7s+25}{s^4+5s^3+20s^2+40s+45}$$

Using MATLAB, find the partial-fraction expansion of F(s). Also, find the inverse Laplace transformation of F(s).

Solution

$$F(s) = \frac{s^4+3s^3+5s^2+7s+25}{s^4+5s^3+20s^2+40s+45}$$

The partial-fraction expansion of F(s) using MATLAB program is given as follows:

```
num = [ 1  3  5  7  25];
den = [1  5  20  40  45];
[r, p, k] = residue(num, den)
```

```
r =
   -1.3849 + 1.2313i
   -1.3849 - 1.2313i
    0.3849 - 0.4702i
    0.3849 + 0.4702i
p =
   -0.8554 + 3.0054i
   -0.8554 - 3.0054i
   -1.6446 + 1.3799i
   -1.6446 - 1.3799i
k =
   1
```

From the MATLAB output, the partial-fraction expansion of F(s) can be written as follows:

$$F(s) = \frac{r_1}{(s-p_1)} + \frac{r_2}{(s-p_2)} + \frac{r_3}{(s-p_3)} + \frac{r_4}{(s-p_4)} + k$$

$$F(s) = \frac{(-1.3849 + j1.2313)}{(s + 0.8554 - j3.005)} + \frac{(-1.3849 - j1.2313)}{(s + 0.8554 + j3.005)}$$

$$+ \frac{(0.3849 - j0.4702)}{(s + 1.6446 - j1.3799)} + \frac{(0.3849 + j0.4702)}{(s + 1.6446 + j1.3779)} + 1$$

Example E2.32

Obtain the partial-fraction expansion of the following function using MATLAB:

$$F(s) = \frac{8(s+1)(s+3)}{(s+2)(s+4)(s+6)^2}$$

Solution

$$F(s) = \frac{8(s+1)(s+3)}{(s+2)(s+4)(s+6)^2} = \frac{(8s+8)(s+3)}{(s^2+6s+8)(s^2+12s+36)}$$

The partial fraction expansion of F(s) using MATLAB program is given as follows:

```
EDU >> num = conv([8 8], [1 3]);
EDU >> den = conv([1 6 8], [1 12 36]);
EDU >> [r, p, k] = residue(num, den)
r =
    3.2500
   15.0000
   -3.0000
   -0.2500
```

p =

–6.0000

–6.0000

–4.0000

–2.0000

k = [ ]

From the above MATLAB result, we have the following expansion:

$$F(s) = \frac{r_1}{(s-p_1)} + \frac{r_2}{(s-p_2)} + \frac{r_3}{(s-p_3)} + \frac{r_4}{(s-p_4)} + k$$

$$F(s) = \frac{3.25}{(s+6)} + \frac{15}{(s-15)} + \frac{-3}{(s+3)} + \frac{-0.25}{(s+0.25)} + 0$$

It should be noted here that the row vector k is zero, because the degree of the numerator is lower than that of the denominator.

$$F(s) = 3.25e^{-6t} + 15e^{15t} - 3e^{-3t} - 0.25e^{-0.25t}$$

Example E2.33

Find the Laplace transform of the following function using MATLAB:

(*a*) $f(t) = 7t^3 \cos(5t + 60°)$

(*b*) $f(t) = -7t\, e^{-5t}$

(*c*) $f(t) = -3 \cos 5t$

(*d*) $f(t) = t \sin 7t$

(*e*) $f(t) = 5\, e^{-2t} \cos 5t$

(*f*) $f(t) = 3 \sin(5t + 45°)$

(*g*) $f(t) = 5\, e^{-3t} \cos(t - 45°)$

Solution

% MATLAB Program

(*a*)
```
>> syms t    % tell MATLAB that "t" is a symbol.
>> f = 7 * t^3*cos (5*t + (pi/3)); % define the function.
>> laplace(f)
ans =
–84/(s^2 + 25)^3*s^2 + 21/(s^2+25)^2 + 336*(1/2*s–5/2*3^(1/2))/(s^2 + 25)^4*s^3–168
*(1/2*s–5/2*3^(1/2))/(s^2 + 25)^3*s
>> pretty(laplace(f)) % the pretty function prints symbolic output
% in a format that resembles typeset mathematics.
```

$$-84\frac{s^2}{(s^2+25)^3} + \frac{21}{(s^2+25)^2} + 336\frac{(1/2-5/23)^{1/2}s^3}{(s^2+25)^4} - 168\frac{(1/2-5/23)^{1/2}s}{(s^2+25)^3}$$

(*b*)
```
>> syms t x
>> f = –7*t*exp(–5*t);
>> laplace(f, x)
ans =
   –7/(x + 5)^2
```

(*c*)
```
>> syms t x
>> f = –3*cos(5*t);
>> laplace(f, x)
ans =
   –3*x/(x^2 + 25)
```

(*d*)
```
>>syms t x
>> f = t*sin(7*t);
>> laplace(f, x)
ans =
   1/(x^2 + 49)*sin(2*atan(7/x))
```

(*e*)
```
>>syms t x
>> f = 5*exp(–2*t)*cos(5*t);
>> laplace(f, x)
ans =
   5*(x + 2)/((x + 2)^2 + 25)
```

(*f*)
```
>>syms t x
>> f = 3*sin(5*t + (pi/4));
>> laplace(f, x)
ans =
   3*(1/2*x*2^(1/2) + 5/2*2^(1/2))/(x^2 + 25)
```

(*g*)
```
>>syms t x
>> f = 5*exp(–3*t)*cos(t–(pi/4));
>> laplace(f, x)
ans =
   5*(1/2*(x + 3)*2^(1/2) + 1/2*2^(1/2))/((x + 3)^2 + 1)
```

Example E2.34

Generate partial-fraction expansion of the following function:

$$F(s) = \frac{10^5(s+7)(s+13)}{s(s+25)(s+55)(s^2+7s+75)(s^2+7s+45)}$$

Solution

Generate the partial fraction expansion of the following function:

```
numg = poly[–7 –13];
numg = poly([–7 –13]);
deng = poly([0 –25 –55 roots([1 7 75])' roots([1 7 45])']);
[numg, deng] = zp2tf(numg', deng', 1e5);
Gtf = (numg, deng);
Gtf = tf(numg, deng);
G = zpk(Gtf);
[r, p, k] = residue(numg, deng)
r =
   1.0e – 017 *
   0.0000
  –0.0014
   0.0254
  –0.1871
   0.1621
  –0.0001
   0.0000
   0.0011
p =
   1.0e + 006 *
   4.6406
   1.4250
   0.3029
   0.0336
   0.0027
   0.0001
   0.0000
        0
k = [ ]
```

Example E2.35

Determine the inverse Laplace transform of the following functions using MATLAB:

(*a*) $F(s) = \dfrac{s}{s(s+2)(s+6)}$ (*b*) $F(s) = \dfrac{1}{s^2(s+5)}$

(*c*) $F(s) = \dfrac{3s+1}{(s^2+2s+9)}$ (*d*) $F(s) = \dfrac{s-25}{s(s^2+3s+20)}$

Solution

(*a*)
```
>> syms s
>> f = s/(s*((s + 2)*(s + 6)));
>> ilaplace(f)
ans =
1/2*exp(–4*t)*sinh(2*t)
```

(*b*)
```
>> syms s
>> f = 1/((s^2)*(s + 5));
>> ilaplace(f)
ans =
1/3*t–2/9*exp(–3/2*t)*sinh(3/2*t)
```

(*c*)
```
>>syms s
>> f = (3*s+1)/s^2 + 2*s + 9);
>> ilaplace(f)
ans =
3*exp(–t)*cos(2*2^(1/2)*t)–1/2*2^(1/2)*exp(–t)*sin(2*2^(1/2)*t)
```

(*d*)
```
>>syms s
>> f = (s – 25)/(s*(s^2 + 3*s + 25));
>> ilaplace(f)
ans =
5/4*exp(–3/2*t)*cos(1/2*71^(1/2)*t) + 23/284*71^(1/2)*exp(–3/2*t)*sin(1/2*71^(1/2)*t)
– 5/4
```

Example E2.36

Find the inverse Laplace transform of the following function using MATLAB:

$$G(s) = \frac{(s^2+9s+7)(s+7)}{(s+2)(s+3)(s^2+12s+150)}$$

Solution

% MATLAB Program

```
>> syms s    % tell MATLAB that "s" is a symbol.
>> G = (s^2 + 9*s + 7)*(s + 7)/[(s + 2)*(s + 3)*(s^2 + 12*s + 150)]; % define the
function.
>> pretty(G) % the pretty function prints symbolic output
% in a format that resembles typeset mathematics.
```

$$G(s) = \frac{(s+9s+7)(s+7)}{(s+2)(s+3)(s+12s+150)}$$

```
>> g = ilaplace(G); % inverse Laplace transform
>> pretty(g)
```

$$- 7/26 \exp(-2t) + \frac{44}{123} \exp(-3t) + \frac{2915}{3198} \exp(-6t) \cos(114^{1/2} t)$$

$$+ \frac{889}{20254} \exp(-6t)\ 114^{1/2} \sin(114^{1/2} t)$$

Example E2.37

Generate the transfer function using MATLAB:

$$G(s) = \frac{3(s+9)(s+21)(s+57)}{s(s+30)(s^2+5s+35)(s^2+28s+42)}$$

using

(*a*) the ratio of factors

(*b*) the ratio of polynomials

Solution

% MATLAB Program:

```
% 'a. The ratio of factors'
    >> Gzpk = zpk([-9 -21 -57], [0 -30 roots([1 5 35])'roots([1 28 42])'], 3)
% zpk is used to create zero-pole-gain models or to convert TF or
% SS models to zero-pole-gain form.
% 'b. The ratio of polynomials'
    >> Gp = tf(Gzpk)  % generate the transfer function
% Computer response:
ans =
```

(*a*) The ratio of factors

Zero-pole-gain:

$$\frac{3\,(s+9)\,(s+21)\,(s+57)}{s\,(s+30)\,(s+26.41)\,(s+1.59)\,(s\verb|^|2+5s+35)}$$

ans =

(*b*) The ratio of polynomials

Transfer function:

$$\frac{3\,s\verb|^|3+261\,s\verb|^|2+5697\,s+32319}{s\verb|^|6+63\,s\verb|^|5+1207\,s\verb|^|4+7700\,s\verb|^|3+37170\,s\verb|^|2+44100\,s}$$

Example E2.38

Generate the transfer function using MATLAB:

$$G(s) = \frac{s^4 + 20s^3 + 27s^2 + 17s + 35}{s^5 + 8s^4 + 9s^3 + 20s^2 + 29s + 32}$$

using

(*a*) the ratio of factors

(*b*) the ratio of polynomials

Solution

% MATLAB Program

```
% a. the ratio of factors
    >> Gtf = tf([1 20 27 17 35], [1 8 9 20 29 32]) % generate the
% transfer function
% Computer response:
```

Transfer function:

$$\frac{s\text{^}4 + 20\,s\text{^}3 + 27\,s\text{^}2 + 17\,s + 35}{s\text{^}4 + 8\,s\text{^}3 + 9\,s\text{^}2 + 20\,s + 29}$$

```
% b. the ratio of polynomials
    >> Gzpk = zpk(Gtf)  % zpk is used to create zero-pole-gain models
% or to convert TF or SS models to zero-pole-gain form.
% Computer response:
```

Zero-pole-gain:

$$\frac{(s+18.59)\,(s+1.623)\,(s\text{^}2-0.214s+1.16)}{(s+7.042)\,(s+1.417)\,(s\text{^}2-0.4593s+2.906)}$$

SUMMARY

In this chapter the MATLAB environment which is an interactive environment for numeric computation, data analysis, and graphics was presented. Arithmetic operations, display formats, elementary built-in functions, arrays, scalars, vectors or matrices, operations with arrays including dot product, array multiplication, array division, inverse and transpose of a matrix, determinants, element by element operations, eigenvalues and eigenvectors, random number generating functions, polynomials, system of linear equation, script files, programming in MATLAB, the commands used for printing information and generating 2-D and 3-D plots, input/output in MATLAB was presented with illustrative examples. MATLAB's functions for symbolic mathematics were introduced. These functions are useful in performing symbolic operations and developing closed-form expressions for solutions to linear algebraic equations, ordinary differential equations and systems of equations. Symbolic mathematics for determining analytical expressions for the derivative and integral of an expression was also presented. Solutions to all the problems at the end of this chapter are presented in Chapter 4.

PROBLEMS

P2.1 Compute the following quantity using MATLAB in the Command Window:

$$\frac{17\left[\sqrt{5}-1\right]}{\left[15^2-13^2\right]}+\frac{5^7\log_{10}(e^3)}{\pi\sqrt{121}}+\ln(e^4)+\sqrt{11}.$$

P2.2 Compute the following quantity using MATLAB in the Command Window:

$$B=\frac{\tan x+\sin 2x}{\cos x}+\log\left|x^5-x^2\right|+\cosh x-2\tanh x$$

for $x = 5\pi/6$.

P2.3 Compute the following quantity using MATLAB in the Command Window:

$$x=a+\frac{ab\,(a+b)}{c\,\sqrt{|ab|}}+c^a+\frac{\sqrt{14\,b}}{e^{3c}}+\ln(2)+\frac{\log_{10}c}{\log_{10}(a+b+c)}+2\sinh a-3\tanh b$$

for a = 1, b = 2 and c = 1.8.

P2.4 Use MATLAB to create:

(*a*) a row and column vectors that has the elements: 11, –3, $e^{7.8}$, ln (59), tan(π/3), 5 $\log_{10}(26)$.

(*b*) a row vector with 20 equally spaced elements in which the first element is 5.

(*c*) a column vector with 15 equally spaced elements in which the first element is –2.

P2.5 Enter the following matrix A in MATLAB and create:

$$A=\begin{bmatrix}1&2&3&4&5&6&7&8\\9&10&11&12&13&14&15&16\\17&18&19&20&21&22&23&24\\25&23&27&28&29&30&31&32\\33&34&35&36&37&38&39&40\end{bmatrix}.$$

(*a*) a 4 × 5 matrix B from the 1st, 3rd, and the 5th rows, and the 1st, 2nd, 4th, and 8th columns of the matrix A.

(*b*) a 16 element-row vector C from the elements of the 5th row, and the 4th and 6th columns of the matrix A.

P2.6 Given the function $y = \left(x^{\sqrt{2}+0.02} + e^{x}\right)^{1.8} \ln x$. Determine the value of y for the following values of x: 2, 3, 8, 10, –1, –3, –5, –6.2. Solve the problem using MATLAB by first creating a vector **x**, and creating a vector **y**, using element-by-element calculations.

P2.7 Define a and b as scalars, a = 0.75, and b = 11.3, and x, y and z as the vectors, x = 2, 5, 1, 9, y = 0.2, 1.1, 1.8, 2 and z = –3, 2, 5, 4. Use these variables to calculate A given below using element-by-element computations for the vectors with MATLAB.

$$A = \frac{x^{1.1} y^{-2} z^{5}}{(a+b)^{b/3}} + a\frac{\left(\frac{z}{x} + \frac{y}{2}\right)}{z^{a}}.$$

P2.8 Enter the following three matrices in MATLAB and show that:

$$A = \begin{bmatrix} 1 & 2 & 3 \\ -8 & 5 & 7 \\ -8 & 4 & 6 \end{bmatrix} \quad B = \begin{bmatrix} 12 & -5 & 4 \\ 7 & 11 & 6 \\ 1 & 8 & 13 \end{bmatrix} \quad C = \begin{bmatrix} 7 & 13 & 4 \\ -2 & 8 & -5 \\ 9 & -6 & 11 \end{bmatrix}$$

(*a*) A + B = B + A

(*b*) A + (B + C) = (A + B) + C

(*c*) 7(A + C) = 7(A) + 7(C)

(*d*) A * (B + C) = A * B + A * C

P2.9 Consider the polynomials following:

$p_1(s) = s^3 + 5s^2 + 3s + 10$

$p_2(s) = s^4 + 7s^3 + 5s^2 + 8s + 15$

$p_3(s) = s^5 + 15s^4 + 10s^3 + 6s^2 + 3s + 9$

Determine $p_1(2)$, $p_2(2)$, and $p_3(3)$.

P2.10 The following polynomials are given:

$p_1(x) = x^5 + 2x^4 - 3x^3 + 7x^2 - 8x + 7$

$p_2(x) = x^4 + 3x^3 - 5x^2 + 9x + 11$

$p_3(x) = x^3 - 2x^2 - 3x + 9$

$p_4(x) = x^2 - 5x + 13$

$p_5(x) = x + 5$

Use MATLAB functions with polynomial coefficient vectors to evaluate the expressions at x = 2.

P2.11 Determine the roots of the following polynomials:

(*a*) $p_1(x) = x^7 + 8x^6 + 5x^5 + 4x^4 + 3x^3 + 2x^2 + x + 1$

(*b*) $p_2(x) = x^6 - 7x^6 + 7x^5 + 15x^4 - 10x^3 - 8x^2 + 7x + 15$

(*c*) $p_3(x) = x^5 - 13x^4 + 10x^3 + 12x^2 + 8x - 15$

(*d*) $p_4(x) = x^4 + 7x^3 + 12x^2 - 25x + 8$

(*e*) $p_5(x) = x^3 + 15x^2 - 23x + 105$

(*f*) $p_6(x) = x^2 - 18x + 23$

(*g*) $p_7(x) = x + 7$

P2.12 An aluminum thin-walled sphere is used as a marker buoy. The sphere has a radius of 65 cm and a wall thickness of 10 mm. The density of aluminum is 2700 kg/m³. The buoy is placed in the ocean where the density of the water is 1050 kg/m³. Determine the height H between the top of the buoy and the surface of the water.

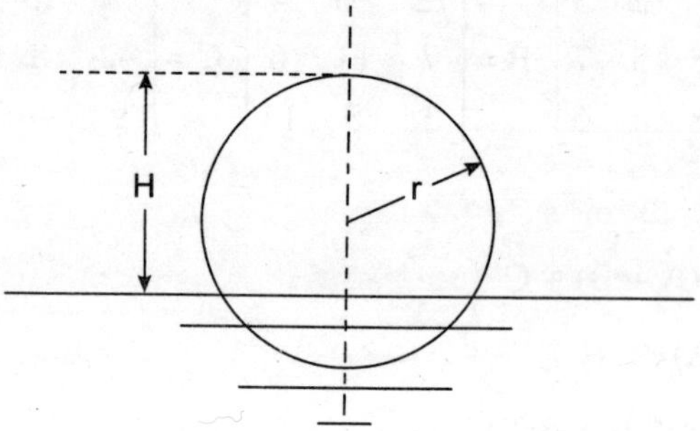

Fig. P2.12

P2.13 Determine the values of x, y, and z for the following set of linear algebraic equations:

$$x_2 - 3x_3 = -7$$

$$2x_1 + 3x_2 - x_3 = 9$$

$$4x_1 + 5x_2 - 2x_3 = 15$$

P2.14 Write a simple script file to find (*a*) dot product (*b*) cross-product of 2 vectors: $a = \hat{j} - \hat{k}$ and $b = 3\hat{i} - 2\hat{j}$.

P2.15 Write a function to find gradient of $f(x, y) = x^2 + y^2 - 2xy + 4$ at (*a*) (1, 1) (*b*) (1, –2) and (*c*) (0, –3). Use the function name from command prompt.

P2.16 Write MATLAB functions $f = x^2 - 3x + 1$ and $g = e^x - 4x + 6$ and find the result f(127)/g(5) from a script file.

P2.17 Plot the function $y = |x| \cos(x)$ for $-200 \le x \le 200$.

P2.18 Plot the following functions on the same plot for $0 \le x \le 2\pi$ using the plot function:

(*a*) $\sin^2 (x)$ (*b*) $\cos^2 x$ (*c*) $\cos (x)$

P2.19 Plot a graph of the function $y = 45 \sin (0.4t)$ for $t \in [0, 3]$.

P2.20 Consider the function $z = 0.56 \cos (xy)$. Draw a surface plot showing variation of z with x and y. Given $x \in [0, 10]$ and $y \in [0,100]$.

P2.21 Figure P2.21 shows two boats: boat A travels south at a speed of 10 mph, and boat B travels east at a speed of 19 mph. The ships are positioned at 8 a.m. are also shown in the figure. Write a MATLAB program to plot the distance between the ships as a function of time for the next 5 hours.

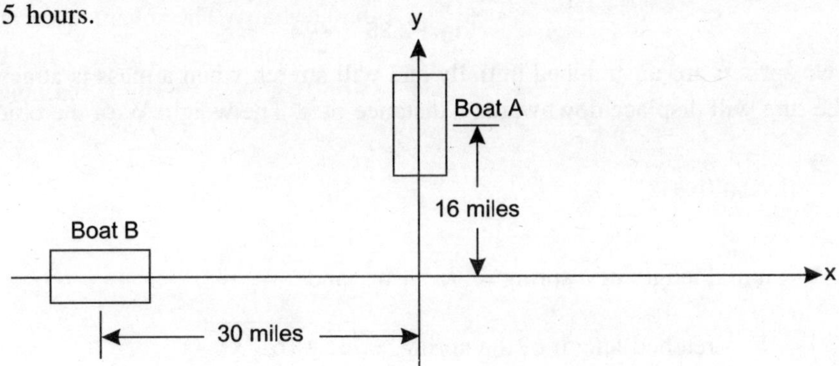

Fig. P2.21

P2.22 Consider the given symbolic expressions defined below:

S1 = '2/(x – 5)'; S2 = 'x ^ 5 + 9 * x – 15'; S3 = '(x ^ 3 + 2 * x +9) * (x * x – 5)';

Perform the following symbolic operations using MATLAB:

(*a*) S1S2/S3 (*b*) S1/S2S3 (*c*) $S1/(S2)^2$

(*d*) S1S3/S2 (*e*) $(S2)^2/(S1S3)$

P2.23 Solve the following equations using symbolic mathematics:

(*a*) $x^2 + 9 = 0$

(*b*) $x^2 + 5x - 8 = 0$

(*c*) $x^3 + 11x^2 - 7x + 8 = 0$

(*d*) $x^4 + 11x^3 + 7x^2 - 19x + 28 = 0$

(*e*) $x^7 - 8x^5 + 7x^4 + 5x^3 - 8x + 9 = 0$

P2.24 Determine the values of x, y, and z for the following set of linear algebraic equations:

$$2x + y - 3z = 11$$
$$4x - 2y + 3z = 8$$
$$-2x + 2y - z = -6$$

P2.25 Figure P2.25 shows a scale with two springs.

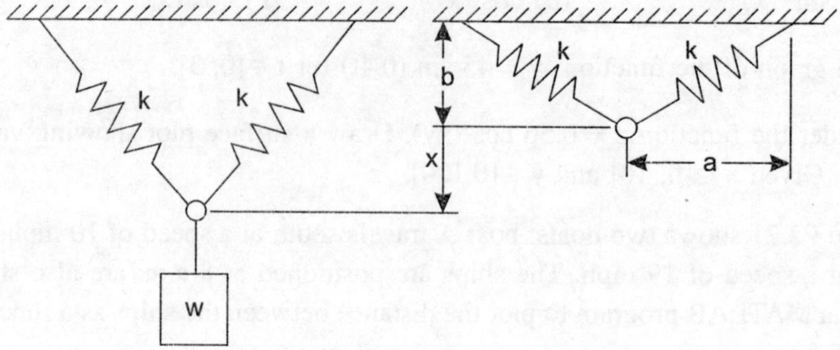

Fig. P2.25

The two springs are unstretched initially and will stretch when a mass is attached to the ring and the ring will displace downwards a distance of x. The weight W of the object is given by

$$W = \frac{2k}{l}(l - l_0)(b + x)$$

where l_0 = initial length of a spring = $\sqrt{a^2 + b^2}$ and

l = the stretched length of the spring = $\sqrt{a^2 + (b + x)^2}$.

If k = spring constant, write a MATLAB program to determine the distance x when W = 350 N. Given: a = 0.16 m, b = 0.045 m, and the spring constant k = 3000 N/m.

P2.26 Determine the solutions of the following first-order ordinary differential equations using MATLAB's symbolic mathematics.

(*a*) $y' = 8x^2 + 5$ with initial condition $y(2) = 0.5$.

(*b*) $y' = 5x \sin^2(y)$ with initial condition $y(0) = \pi/5$.

(*c*) $y' = 7x \cos^2(y)$ with initial condition $y(0) = 2$.

(*d*) $y' = -5x + y$ with initial condition $y(0) = 3$.

(*e*) $y' = 3y + e^{-5x}$ with initial condition $y(0) = 2$.

P2.27 For the following differential equations, use MATLAB to find x (t) when (*a*) all the initial conditions are zero, (*b*) x (t) when x (0) = 1 and $\dot{x}(0) = -1$.

(*a*) $$\frac{d^2x}{dt^2} + 10\frac{dx}{dt} + 5x = 11$$

(*b*) $$\frac{d^2x}{dt^2} - 7\frac{dx}{dt} - 3x = 5$$

(*c*) $$\frac{d^2x}{dt^2} + 3\frac{dx}{dt} + 7x = -15$$

(*d*) $$\frac{d^2x}{dt^2} + \frac{dx}{dt} + 7x = 26$$

P2.28 Figure P2.28 shows a water tank (shaped as an inverted frustum cone with a circular hole at the bottom on the side).

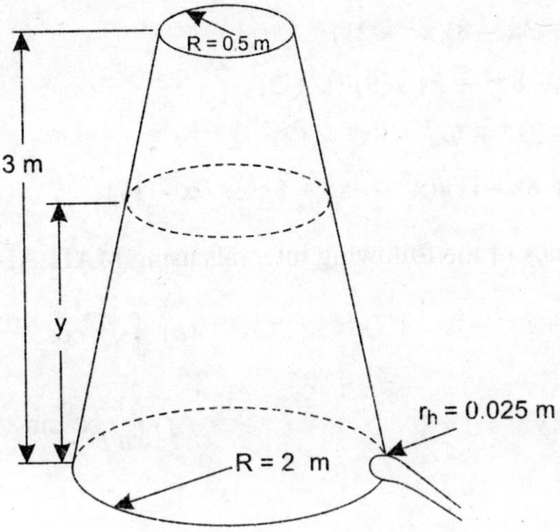

Fig. P2.28 Water-tank

The velocity of water discharged through the hole is given by $v = \sqrt{2gy}$ where h = height of the water and g = acceleration due to gravity (9.81 m/s^2). The rate of discharge of water in the tank as the water drains out through the hole is given by: $\frac{dy}{dt} = -\frac{\sqrt{2gy}r_h^2}{(2-0.5y)^2}$ where y = height of water and r_h = radius of the hole. Write a MATLAB program to solve and plot the differential equation. Assume, that the initial height of the water is 2.5 m.

P2.29 An airplane uses a parachute (See Fig. P2.29) and other means of braking as it slow down on the runway after landing. The acceleration of the airplane is given by $a = -0.005v^2 - 4$ m/s^2.

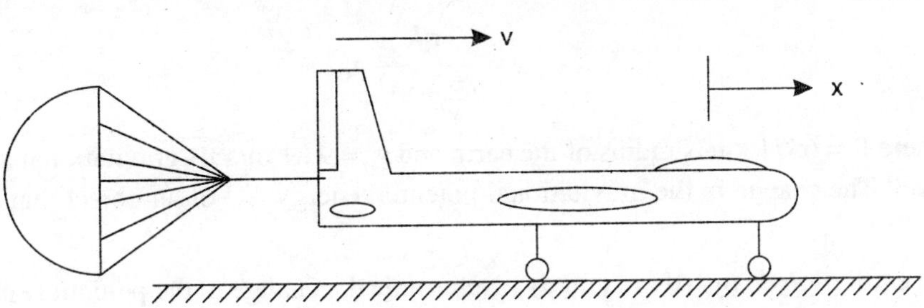

Fig. P2.29

Consider the airplane with a velocity of 500 km/h opens its parachute and starts decelerating at t = 0 seconds, write a MATLAB program to solve the differential equation and plot the velocity from t = 0 seconds until the airplane stops.

P2.30 Obtain the first and second derivatives of the following functions using MATLAB's symbolic mathematics.

(*a*) $F(x) = x^5 - 8x^4 + 5x^3 - 7x^2 + 11x - 9$

(*b*) $F(x) = (x^3 + 3x - 8)(x^2 + 21)$

(*c*) $F(x) = (3x^3 - 8x^2 + 5x + 9)/(x + 2)$

(*d*) $F(x) = (x^5 - 3x^4 + 5x^3 + 8x^2 - 13)^2$

(*e*) $F(x) = (x^2 + 8x - 11)/(x^7 - 7x^6 + 5x^3 + 9x - 17)$

P2.31 Determine the values of the following integrals using MATLAB's symbolic functions:

(*a*) $\int (5x^7 - x^5 + 3x^3 - 8x^2 + 7)dx$ (*b*) $\int \sqrt{x} \cos x$

(*c*) $\int x^{2/3} \sin^2 2x$ (*d*) $\int_{0.2}^{1.8} x^2 \sin x \, dx$

(*e*) $\int_{-1}^{-0.2} |x| \, dx$

P2.32 Use MATLAB to calculate the following integral:

$$\int_0^5 \frac{1}{0.8x^2 + 0.5x + 2} dx.$$

P2.33 Use MATLAB to calculate the following integral:

$$\int_0^{10} \cos^2(0.5x)\sin^4(0.5x)dx.$$

P2.34 The variation of gravitational acceleration g with altitude y is given by:

$$g = \frac{R^2}{(R+y)^2} g_0,$$

where R = 6371 km is radius of the earth and g_0 = 9.81 m/s^2 is gravitational acceleration at sea level. The change in the gravitational potential energy ΔU of an object that is raised up from the earth is given by: $\Delta U = \int_0^y mg\,dy$. Determine the change in the potential energy of a satellite with a mass of 500 kg that is raised from the surface of the earth to a height of 800 km.

P2.35 Find the Laplace transform of the following function using MATLAB:

$$f(t) = 7t^3 \cos(5t + 60°)$$

P2.36 Use MATLAB program to find the transforms of the following functions:

(*a*) $f(t) = -7t\, e^{-5t}$

(*b*) $f(t) = -3 \cos 5t$

(*c*) $f(t) = t \sin 7t$

(*d*) $f(t) = 5\, e^{-2t} \cos 5t$

(*e*) $f(t) = 3 \sin(5t + 45°)$

(*f*) $f(t) = 5\, e^{-3t} \cos(t - 45°)$

P2.37 Consider the two matrices:

$$\mathbf{A} = \begin{bmatrix} 1 & 0 & 2 \\ 2 & 5 & 4 \\ -1 & 8 & 7 \end{bmatrix} \quad \text{and } \mathbf{B} = \begin{bmatrix} 7 & 8 & 2 \\ 3 & 5 & 9 \\ -1 & 3 & 1 \end{bmatrix}$$

Using MATLAB, determine the following:

(*a*) $\mathbf{A} + \mathbf{B}$ (*b*) $\mathbf{AB}$ (*c*) $\mathbf{A}^2$

(*d*) $\mathbf{A}^T$ (*e*) $\mathbf{B}^{-1}$ (*f*) $\mathbf{B}^T\mathbf{A}^T$

(*g*) $\mathbf{A}^2 + \mathbf{B}^2 - \mathbf{AB}$

(*h*) determinant of **A**, determinant of **B** and determinant of **AB**.

P2.38 Use MATLAB to define the following matrices:

$$\mathbf{A} = \begin{bmatrix} 2 & 1 \\ 0 & 5 \\ 7 & 4 \end{bmatrix} \qquad \mathbf{B} = \begin{bmatrix} 5 & 3 \\ -2 & -4 \end{bmatrix}$$

$$\mathbf{C} = \begin{bmatrix} 2 & 3 \\ -5 & -2 \\ 0 & 3 \end{bmatrix} \quad \text{and} \quad \mathbf{D} = [1 \;\; 2]$$

Compute matrices and determinants if they exist.

(*a*) $(\mathbf{AC}^T)^{-1}$ (*b*) $|\mathbf{B}|$

(*c*) $|\mathbf{AC}^T|$ and (*d*) $(\mathbf{C}^T\mathbf{A})^{-1}$

P2.39 Consider the two matrices:

$$\mathbf{A} = \begin{bmatrix} 1 & 0 & 1 \\ 2 & 3 & 4 \\ -1 & 6 & 7 \end{bmatrix} \text{ and } \mathbf{B} = \begin{bmatrix} 7 & 4 & 2 \\ 3 & 5 & 6 \\ -1 & 2 & 1 \end{bmatrix}$$

Using MATLAB, determine the following:

(*a*) $\mathbf{A} + \mathbf{B}$ (*b*) $\mathbf{AB}$ (*c*) $\mathbf{A}^2$

(*d*) $\mathbf{A}^T$ (*e*) $\mathbf{B}^{-1}$ (*f*) $\mathbf{B}^T\mathbf{A}^T$

(*g*) $\mathbf{A}^2 + \mathbf{B}^2 - \mathbf{AB}$ (*h*) det **A**, det **B**, and det of **AB**.

P2.40 Find the inverse of the following Matrices:

(*a*) $\mathbf{A} = \begin{bmatrix} 3 & 2 & 1 \\ -1 & 5 & 4 \\ 5 & 7 & -9 \end{bmatrix}$, (*b*) $\mathbf{B} = \begin{bmatrix} 1 & 6 & 3 \\ -4 & -5 & 7 \\ 8 & 4 & 2 \end{bmatrix}$ and

(*c*) $\mathbf{C} = \begin{bmatrix} -1 & -2 & 5 \\ -4 & 7 & 2 \\ 7 & -8 & -1 \end{bmatrix}$

P2.41 Determine the eigenvalues and eigenvectors of the following matrices using MATLAB:

$$\mathrm{A} = \begin{bmatrix} 1 & -2 \\ 1 & 5 \end{bmatrix}, \ \mathrm{B} = \begin{bmatrix} 1 & 5 \\ -2 & 7 \end{bmatrix}$$

P2.42 If $\mathrm{A} = \begin{bmatrix} 4 & 6 & 2 \\ 5 & 6 & 7 \\ 10 & 5 & 8 \end{bmatrix}$

Use MATLAB to determine the following:

(*a*) the three eigenvalues of **A**

(*b*) the eigenvectors of **A**

(*c*) Show that **AQ** = **Qd** where Q is the matrix containing the eigenvectors as columns and **d** is the matrix containing the corresponding eigenvalues on the main diagonal and zeros elsewhere.

P2.43 Determine eigenvalues and eigenvector of **A** using MATLAB.

$$(a)\ \mathbf{A} = \begin{bmatrix} 0.5 & -0.8 \\ 0.75 & 1.0 \end{bmatrix} \qquad (b)\ \mathbf{A} = \begin{bmatrix} 8 & 3 \\ -3 & 4 \end{bmatrix}$$

P2.44 Determine the eigenvalues and eigenvectors of the following matrices using MATLAB:

$$(a)\ \mathbf{A} = \begin{bmatrix} 1 & -2 \\ 1 & 3 \end{bmatrix} \qquad (b)\ \mathbf{A} = \begin{bmatrix} 1 & 5 \\ -2 & 4 \end{bmatrix}$$

P2.45 Determine the eigenvalues and eigenvectors of A * B using MATLAB.

$$A = \begin{bmatrix} 3 & -1 & 2 & 1 \\ 1 & 2 & 7 & 4 \\ 7 & -1 & 8 & 6 \\ 1 & -2 & 3 & 4 \end{bmatrix} \quad \text{and} \quad B = \begin{bmatrix} 1 & 2 & 5 & 7 \\ 2 & -1 & -2 & 4 \\ 3 & 2 & 5 & 1 \\ 4 & 1 & -3 & 6 \end{bmatrix}$$

P2.46 Determine the eigenvalues and eigenvectors of A and B using MATLAB:

$$\mathbf{A} = \begin{bmatrix} 4 & 5 & -3 \\ -1 & 2 & 3 \\ 2 & 5 & 7 \end{bmatrix} \quad \text{and} \quad \mathbf{B} = \begin{bmatrix} 1 & 2 & 3 \\ 8 & 9 & 6 \\ 5 & 3 & -1 \end{bmatrix}$$

P2.47 Determine the eigenvalues and eigenvectors of A = a * b using MATLAB:

$$\mathbf{a} = \begin{bmatrix} 6 & -3 & 4 & 1 \\ 0 & 4 & 2 & 6 \\ 1 & 3 & 8 & 5 \\ 2 & 2 & 1 & 4 \end{bmatrix} \quad \text{and} \quad \mathbf{b} = \begin{bmatrix} 0 & 1 & 2 & 3 \\ 4 & 5 & 6 & -1 \\ 1 & 5 & 4 & 2 \\ 2 & -3 & 6 & 7 \end{bmatrix}$$

P2.48 Determine the values of x, y, and z for the following set of linear algebraic equations:

$$x_2 - 3x_3 = -7$$

$$2x_1 + 3x_2 - x_3 = 9$$

$$4x_1 + 5x_2 - 2x_3 = 15$$

P2.49 Determine the values of x, y, and z for the following set of linear algebraic equations:

$$2x - y = 10$$

$$-x + 2y - z = 0$$

$$-y + z = -50$$

P2.50 Solve the following set of equations using MATLAB.

(*a*)

$$2x_1 + x_2 + x_3 - x_4 = 12$$
$$x_1 + 5x_2 - 5x_3 + 6x_4 = 35$$
$$-7x_1 + 3x_2 - 7x_3 - 5x_4 = 7$$
$$x_1 - 5x_2 + 2x_3 + 7x_4 = 21$$

(*b*)

$$x_1 - x_2 + 3x_3 + 5x_4 = 7$$
$$2x_1 + x_2 - x_3 + x_4 = 6$$
$$-x_1 - x_2 - 2x_3 + 2x_4 = 5$$
$$x_1 + x_2 - x_3 + 5x_4 = 4$$

P2.51 Solve the following set of equations using MATLAB.

(*a*)

$$2x_1 + x_2 + x_3 - x_4 = 10$$
$$x_1 + 5x_2 - 5x_3 + 6x_4 = 25$$
$$-7x_1 + 3x_2 - 7x_3 - 5x_4 = 5$$
$$x_1 - 5x_2 + 2x_3 + 7x_4 = 11$$

(*b*)

$$x_1 - x_2 + 3x_3 + 5x_4 = 5$$
$$2x_1 + x_2 - x_3 + x_4 = 4$$
$$-x_1 - x_2 + 2x_3 + 2x_4 = 3$$
$$x_1 + x_2 - x_3 + 5x_4 = 1$$

P2.52 Solve the following set of equations using MATLAB.

(*a*)

$$x_1 + 2x_2 + 3x_3 + 5x_4 = 21$$
$$-2x_1 + 5x_2 + 7x_3 - 9x_4 = 17$$
$$5x_1 + 7x_2 + 2x_3 - 5x_4 = 23$$
$$-x_1 - 3x_2 - 7x_3 + 7x_4 = 26$$

(*b*)

$$x_1 + 2x_2 + 3x_3 + 4x_4 = 9$$
$$2x_1 - 2x_2 - x_3 + x_4 = -5$$
$$x_1 - 3x_2 + 4x_3 - 4x_4 = 7$$
$$2x_1 + 2x_2 - 3x_3 + 4x_4 = -6$$

P2.53 Determine the inverse of the following matrix using MATLAB:

$$A = \begin{bmatrix} 3s & 2 & 0 \\ 7s & -s & -5 \\ 3 & 0 & -3s \end{bmatrix}$$

P2.54 Expand the following function F(s) into partial fractions with MATLAB:

$$F(s) = \frac{5s^3 + 7s^2 + 8s + 30}{s^4 + 15s^3 + 62s^2 + 85s + 25}$$

P2.55 Determine the Laplace transform of the following time functions using MATLAB:

(*a*) f (t) = u (t + 9)

(*b*) f (t) = e^{5t}

(*c*) f (t) = (5t + 7)

(*d*) f (t) = 5u (t) + $8e^{7t}$ – $12e^{-8t}$

(*e*) f (t) = e^{-t} + $9t^3$ – $7t^{-2}$ + 8

(*f*) f (t) = $7t^4$ + $5t^2$ – e^{-7t}

(*g*) f (t) = 9ut + $5e^{-3t}$

P2.56 Determine the inverse Laplace transform of the following rotational function using MATLAB:

$$F(s) = \frac{7}{s^2 + 5s + 6} = \frac{7}{(s+2)(s+3)}$$

P2.57 Determine the inverse transform of the following function having complex poles:

$$F(s) = \frac{15}{(s^3 + 5s^2 + 11s + 10)}$$

P2.58 Determine the inverse Laplace transform of the following functions using MATLAB:

(*a*) $F(s) = \dfrac{s}{s(s+2)(s+3)(s+5)}$

(*b*) $F(s) = \dfrac{1}{s^2(s+7)}$

(*c*) $F(s) = \dfrac{5s+9}{(s^3 + 8s + 5)}$

(*d*) $F(s) = \dfrac{s-28}{s(s^2 + 9s + 33)}$

REFERENCES

Chapman, S.J., *MATLAB Programming for Engineers,* 2nd ed., Brooks/Cole, Thomson Learning, Pacific Grove, CA, 2002.

Dukkipati, R.V., *MATLAB for Mechanical Engineers*, New Age Science, UK.

Etter, D.M., *Engineering Problem Solving with MATLAB,* Prentice-Hall, Englewood Cliffs, NJ, 1993.

Gilat, Amos., *MATLAB—An Introduction with Applications*, 2nd ed., Wiley, New York, 2005.

Hanselman, D., and Littlefield, B.R., *Mastering MATLAB 6*, Prentice-Hall, Upper Saddle River, New Jersey, 2001.

Herniter, M.E., *Programming in MATLAB*, Brooks/Cole, Pacific Grove, CA, 2001.

Magrab, E.B., *An Engineers Guide to MATLAB*, Prentice Hall, Upper Saddle River, New Jersey, 2001.

Marchand, P., and Holland, O.T., *Graphics and GUIs with MATLAB*, 3rd ed., CRC Press, Boca Raton, FL, 2003.

Moler, C., *The Student Edition of MATLAB for MS-DOS Personal Computers with 3½" Disks,* MATLAB Curriculum Series, The MathWorks, Inc., 2002.

Palm, W.J. III., *Introduction to MATLAB 7 for Engineers*, McGraw Hill, New York, 2005.

Pratap, Rudra., *Getting Started with MATLAB–A Quick Introduction for Scientists and Engineers,* Oxford University Press, New York, 2002.

Sigman, K., and Davis, T.A., *MATLAB Primer*, 6th ed, Chapman & Hall/CRC Press, Boca Raton, FL, 2002.

The MathWorks, *MATLAB*: *Application Program Interface Reference,* Version 6, The MathWorks, Inc., Natick, 2000.

The MathWorks, Inc., *MATLAB*: *Creating Graphical User Interfaces,* Version 1, The MathWorks, Inc., Natick, 2000.

The MathWorks, Inc., *MATLAB*: *Function Reference,* The MathWorks, Inc., Natick, 2000.

The MathWorks, Inc., *MATLAB: Release Notes for Release 12*, The MathWorks, Inc., Natick, 2000.

The MathWorks, Inc., *MATLAB*: *Symbolic Math Toolbox User's Guide,* Version 2, The MathWorks, Inc., Natick, 1993-1997.

The MathWorks, Inc., MATLAB: *Using MATLAB Graphics,* Version 6, The MathWorks, Inc., Natick, 2000.

CHAPTER 3

MATLAB Tutorial

3.1 INTRODUCTION

The application of MATLAB to the analysis and design of control systems is presented in this chapter with a number of illustrative examples. The MATLAB computational approach to the transient response analysis, steps response, impulse response, ramp response, and response to the simple inputs are presented. Plotting root loci, Bode diagrams, polar plots, Nyquist plot, Nichols plot, and state space method are obtained using MATLAB.

3.2 TRANSIENT RESPONSE ANALYSIS

When the numerator and denominator of a closed-loop transfer function are known, the commands **step (num, den), step (num, den, t)** in MATLAB can be used to generate plots of unit- step responses. Here, t is the user specified time.

3.3 RESPONSE TO INITIAL CONDITION

3.3.1 Case 1: State Space Approach

Consider a system defined in state-space given by

$$\dot{\mathbf{x}} = \mathbf{A}\mathbf{x} \tag{3.1}$$

$$\mathbf{x}\ (0) = \mathbf{x}_0$$

Assuming that there is no external input acting on the system, the response **x (t)** knowing the initial condition x (0) and that **x** is an n-vector, is obtained as follows:

Taking Laplace transform of both sides of Eq. (3.1), we obtain

$$s\,\mathbf{x}\ (s) - \mathbf{x}\ (0) = \mathbf{AX}\ (s) \tag{3.2}$$

Equation (3.2) can be rearranged as

$$s\,\mathbf{x}\ (s) = \mathbf{AX}\ (s) + \mathbf{x}\ (0) \tag{3.3}$$

Taking inverse Laplace transform of Eqn. (3.3), we get

$$\dot{\mathbf{x}} = A\,\mathbf{x} + \mathbf{x}(0)\,d(t) \tag{3.4}$$

Defining $\dot{\mathbf{z}} = \mathbf{x}$, Eq. (3.4) can be written as

$$\ddot{z}\,\mathbf{z} = \mathbf{A}\dot{z} + \mathbf{x}(0)\,d(t) \tag{3.5}$$

Integrating Eq. (3.5), we obtain

$$\dot{\mathbf{z}} = A\,\mathbf{z} + \mathbf{x}(0)\,1(t) = \mathbf{A}\,\mathbf{z} + \mathbf{B}\,u \tag{3.6}$$

where

$\mathbf{B} = \mathbf{x}(0)$

and $u = 1(t)$

Noting that $\dot{\mathbf{z}} = \mathbf{x}$ and $x(t) = \dot{\mathbf{z}}(t)$, we have

$$\mathbf{x} = \dot{\mathbf{z}} = A\,\mathbf{z} + \mathbf{B}\,u \tag{3.7}$$

The response to initial condition is obtained by solving Eqns. (3.6) and (3.7).

The corresponding MATLAB command used to obtain the response curves are given as follows:

```
[x, z, t] = step (A, B, A, B);
x1 = [1 0 0 ...0] * x';
x2 = [1 0 0 ...0] * x';
      ⋮
xn = [0 0 0 ...1] * x';
plot (t, x1, x2,..., t, xn )
```

3.3.2 Case 2: State Space Approach

Consider the system defined in state space is by

$$\dot{\mathbf{x}} = \mathbf{A}\,\mathbf{x} \qquad \mathbf{x}(0) = \mathbf{x_0} \tag{3.8}$$

$$\mathbf{y} = \mathbf{C}\,\mathbf{x} \tag{3.9}$$

where $\mathbf{x}$ is an n vector and $\mathbf{y}$ is an m vector.

By defining $\dot{\mathbf{z}} = \mathbf{x}$ (3.10)

we obtain

$$\dot{\mathbf{z}} = \mathbf{A}\,\mathbf{z} + \mathbf{x}(0)\,1(t) = \mathbf{A}\mathbf{z} + \mathbf{B}\,u \tag{3.11}$$

where

$$\mathbf{B} = \mathbf{x}(0) \text{ and } u = 1(t) \tag{3.12}$$

Since $\mathbf{x} = \mathbf{z}$, Eqn. (3.9) becomes

$$\mathbf{y} = \mathbf{C}\dot{\mathbf{z}} \tag{3.13}$$

From Eqns. (3.11) and (3.13), we obtain

$$\mathbf{y} = \mathbf{C}(\mathbf{A}\mathbf{z} + \mathbf{B}\,u) = \mathbf{C}\mathbf{A}\mathbf{z} + \mathbf{C}\mathbf{B}\,u \tag{3.14}$$

The response of the system is obtained from the Equs. (3.11) and (3.14) to a given initial condition The following MATLAB commands may be used to obtain the response curves:

```
[y, z, t ] = step (A, B, C*A, C*B);
y1 = [1  0  0 ...0] * y';
y2 = [0  1  0 ...0] * y';                                   (3.15)
:
ym = [0  0  0 ...1] * y';
plot (t, y1, t, y2, ........, t, ym)
```

where the output curves are y1, y2, ..., ym verses t.

3.4 SECOND ORDER SYSTEMS

The standard form of a second order system is defined by

$$G(s) = \frac{\omega_n{}^2}{s^2 + 2\xi\omega_n s + \omega_n^2} \tag{3.16}$$

where ξ is the damping ratio of the system and ω_n is the undamped natural frequency of the system.

The dynamic behavior of the second order system is then described in terms of two parameters ξ and ω_n. If $0 < \xi < 1$, the closed loop poles are complex conjugates and lie in the left-half s plane. The system is called underdamped, and the transient response is oscillatory, If $\xi = 0$, the transient response does not die out. If $\xi = 1$, the system is called critically damped. Overdamped system correspond to $\xi = 1$.

Given ω_n and ξ, then the MATLAB command

```
printsys (num, den)
```

or

```
printsys(num, den, s)
```

prints the num/den as a ratio of polynomials in s.

The unit-step response of the transfer-function system using MATLAB is obtained with the use of step-response commands with left-hand arguments.

```
c = step (num, den, t)
```

or

```
[y, x, t ] = step (num, den, t)
```

3.5 ROOT LOCUS PLOTS

Consider the system equation

$$1 + \frac{K(s+z_1)(s+z_2)...(s+z_n)}{(s+p_1)(s+p_2)...(s+p_n)} = 0 \tag{3.17}$$

Equation (3.17) can be written as

$$1 + K\frac{num}{den} = 0 \tag{3.18}$$

where *num* is the numerator of the polynomial and *den* is the denominator polynomial, and K is the gain (K > 0). The vector K contains all the gain values for which the closed loop poles are to be computed.

The root loci is plotted by using the MATLAB command

rlocus (num, den)

The gain vector K is supplied by the user.

The matrix r and gain vector K are obtained by the following MATLAB commands:

```
[r, k] = rlocus (num, den)
[r, k] = rlocus (num, den, k)
[r, k] = rlocus (A, B, C, D)
[r, k] = rlocus (A, B, C, D, K)        (3.19)
[r, k] = rlocus (sys)
```

In Eqns. (3.19), r has length K rows and length [den – 1] columns containing the complex root locations.

- For plotting the root loci, the MATLAB command plot (r, ' ') is used.

The following MATLAB command are used for plotting the root loci with mark '0' or 'x':

```
r = rlocus (num, den)
plot (r, '0')  or  plot (r, 'x')
```

MATLAB provides its own set of gain values used to compute a root locus plot. It also uses the automatic axis scaling features of the plot command.

3.6 BODE DIAGRAMS

Bode diagrams are rectangular plots. Bode diagram are also known as logarithmic plot and consist of two graphs: the first one is a plot of the logarithmic of the magnitude of a sinusoidal transfer function, the second one is a plot of the phase angle. Both these graphs are plotted against the frequency on a logarithmic scale.

The MATLAB command 'bode' obtains the magnitudes and phase angles of the frequency response of continuous-time, linear, time-invariant systems.

The MATLAB bode commands commonly used are:

```
bode(num, den)
bode(num, den, W)
bode(A, B, C, D)        (3.20)
bode(A, B, C, D, W)
bode(sys)
```

where w is the frequency vector.

MATLAB bode commands with left hand arguments commonly used are:

[mag, phase, w] = bode (num, den)

[mag, phase, w] = bode (num, den, w)

[mag, phase, w] = bode (A, B, C, D)

[mag, phase, w] = bode (A, B, C, D, w) (3.21)

[mag, phase, w] = bode (A, B, C, D, iu, w)

[mag, phase, w] = bode (sys)

The MATLAB commands given in Eq. (3.21) returns the frequency response of the system in matrices mag, phase, and w. The plot is not drawn on the screen. The matrices mag, phase provide the magnitudes and phase angles of frequency response of the system, computed at the specified frequency points.

The magnitude may be converted into decibles using the MATLAB statement

magdB = 20 * log 10 (mag) (3.22)

In MATLAB, the following command

logspace (d1, d2) (3.23)

or logspace(d1, d2, n). logspace(d1, d2) (3.24)

are used to specify the frequency range that will generate a vector of 50 points logarithmically equally speed between decades 10^{d1} and 10^{d2}

The MATLAB command

w = logspace (–1, 2) (3.25)

may be used to generate 50 points between 0.1 and 100 rad/sec.

Similarly, the MATLAB command

logspace (d1, d2, n) (3.26)

generates n points logarithmically equally spaced between 10^{d1} and 10^{d2} where by the n points include both the end points.

3.7 NYQUIST PLOTS

Nyquist plots are also used in the frequenc-response representation of linear, time invariant, continuous-time feedback control systems. Nyquist plots are polar plots.

The MATLAB command

nyquist (num, den) (3.27)

Draw the Nyquist plot of the transfer function

$$G(s) = \frac{\text{num}(s)}{\text{den}(s)} \tag{3.28}$$

where num and den contain the polynomial coefficients in descending powers of s. The other MATLAB command uses for drawing Nyquist plots are:

```
nyquist (num, den, w)
nyquist (A, B, C, D)
nyquist (A, B, C, D, w)
nyquist (A, B, C, D, iu, w)          (3.29)
nyquist (sys)
```

where w is the frequency vector.

The MATLAB command involving the user-specified vector w in Eq. (3.29) computes the frequency response at the specified frequency points.

The following MATLAB commands:

```
[re, im, w] = nyquist (num, den)
[re, im, w] = nyquist (num, den, w)
[re, im, w] = nyquist (A, B, C, D)
[re, im, w] = nyquist (A, B, C, D, w)          (3.30)
[re, im, w] = nyquist (A, B, C, D, iu, w)
[re, im, w] = nyquist (sys)
```

are used to obtain the frequency response of the system in the matrices Re, im, and w. The plot is not drawn on the screen. The matrices Re and im contain the real and imaginary parts of the frequency response of the system, computed at the frequency points specified in the vector w.

3.8 NICHOLS CHART

The chart consisting of the M and N loci in the log magnitude verses phase diagram is called the Nichols chart. The G (jw) locus drawn on the Nichols chart gives both the gain characteristics and phase characteristics of the closed-loop transfer function at the same time. The Nichols chart contains curves of constant closed-loop magnitude and phase angle. The Nichols chart is symmetric about the 180° axis. The M loci are centered about the critical point (0 dB, – 180). The Nichols chart is useful in determining the frequency response of the closed-loop from that of the open loop. The Nichols chart is produced by using the MATLAB command nichols(num, den). The command ngrid creates the dotted lines that allow reading closed-loop gain and phase from the Nichols chart. In order to customize the axes of the Nichols chart, the MATLAB command ***axis*** is used.

3.9 GAIN MARGIN, PHASE MARGIN, PHASE CROSSOVER FREQUENCY, AND GAIN CROSSOVER FREQUENCY

The MATLAB command

```
[Gm, pm, wcp, wcg] = margin (sys)          (3.31)
```

can be used to obtain the gain margin, phase margin, phase crossover frequency, and gain crossover frequency.

In Equation (3.31), Gm is the gain margin, pm is the phase margin, wcp is the phase-crossover frequency, and wcg is the gain crossover frequency.

The following MATLAB command is commonly used for obtaining the resonant peak and resonant frequency:

[mag, phase, w] = bode (num, den, w)

or [mag, phase, w] = bode (sys, w)

[Mp, k] = max (mag) (3.32)

resonant peak = 20 * log 10 (Mp)

resonant frequency = w (k)

The following lines are used in MATLAB program to obtain bandwidth:

n = 1

while 20 * log 10 (mag (n)) > – 3

n = n + 1

end (3.33)

bandwidth = w (n)

3.10 TRANSFORMATION OF SYSTEM MODELS

In this section, we consider two cases of transformation of system models.

1. Transformation of system model from transfer function to state space.
2. Transformation of system model from state space to transfer function.

3.10.1 Transformation of System Model from Transfer Function to State Space

The closed-loops transfer function can be written as

$$\frac{Y(s)}{U(s)} = \frac{\text{numerator of polynominal in s}}{\text{denomintor of polynominal in s}} = \frac{\text{num}}{\text{den}} \quad (3.34)$$

The state-space representation is obtained by the MATLAB command

[A, B, C, D] = tf 2ss (num, den) (3.35)

3.10.2 Transformation of System Model from State Space to Transfer Function

The transfer function from state-space equations is obtained by using the MATLAB command:

[num, den] = ss2tf (A, B, C, D, iu) (3.36)

where iu corresponds to the system with more than one input. iu is either 1, 2, or 3, where 1 implies input u_1, 2 implies input u_2, and 3 implies input u_3.

For system with only one input, the MATLAB command

[num, den] = ss2tf (A, B, C, D) (3.37)

or [num, den] = ss2tf (A, B, C, D, 1) (3.38)

may be used

3.11 BODE DIAGRAMS OF SYSTEMS DEFINED IN STATE SPACE

Let the control system defined in State Space be

$$\dot{\mathbf{x}} = \mathbf{Ax} + \mathbf{Bu}$$
$$\mathbf{y} = \mathbf{Cx} + \mathbf{Du} \quad (3.39)$$

where

$\mathbf{A}$ = state matrix ($n \times n$ matrix)
$\mathbf{B}$ = control matrix ($n \times r$ matrix)
$\mathbf{C}$ = output matrix ($m \times n$ matrix)
$\mathbf{D}$ = output matrix ($m \times n$ matrix)
$\mathbf{u}$ = control vector (r-vector)
$\dot{\mathbf{x}}$ **or** $\mathbf{x}$ = state vector (n-vector)
$\mathbf{y}$ = output vector (m-vector)

The MATLAB command **bode[A, B, C, D]** may be used to obtain the Bode diagram of this system. In fact, the command **bode[A, B, C, D]** gives a series of Bode plots, one for each input of the system, with the frequency range automatically determined.

If we use the scalar iu as an index into the inputs of the control system that specifies which input is to be used for the Bode plot, Then the MATLAB command **Bode[A, B, C, D, iu]** produces the Bode plots from the input iu to all the outputs (y_1, y_2, ..., y_m) of the system with the frequency range automatically determined.

If the system has three inputs, then $\mathbf{u} = \begin{bmatrix} u_1 \\ u_2 \\ u_3 \end{bmatrix}$

For a system with only one input u, then the MATLAB command

Bode[A, B, C, D] (3.40)

or **Bode [A, B, C, D, 1]** can be used (3.41)

3.12 NYQUIST PLOTS OF A SYSTEM DEFINED IN STATE SPACE

Consider the system defined in state space given by Equation (3.39). Nyquist plots of the system defined in Eq. (3.39) may be obtained by using the MATLAB command.

nyquist (A, B, C, D) (3.42)

The MATLAB command given by Eq. (3.42) produces a series of Nyquist plots one corresponding to each input and output combination of the system, with the frequency range automatically determined. If we used the scalar iu as an index to the inputs of the control system that specifies which input is to be used for the Nyquist plot, then the MATLAB command nyquist (A, B, C, D, iu, ω) produces Nyquist plots from the input to all the outputs (y_1, y_2, ..., y_m) of the system with the frequency range automatically determined .

The MATLAB command

$$\text{nyquist (A, B, C, D, iu, } \omega) \tag{3.43}$$

considers the user-supplied frequency vector ω. The vector ω specifies the frequency at which the frequency response should be determined.

3.13 TRANSIENT-RESPONSE ANALYSIS IN STATE SPACE

In this section, we present the transient-response analysis of systems in state space using MATLAB. Specifically, we present the step response, impulse, ramp response, and responses to other forms of simple inputs.

3.13.1 Unit Step Response

For a control system defined in a state space form as in Eq. (3.39), the MATLAB command

$$\text{step (A, B, C, D)} \tag{3.44}$$

will generate plots of unit step responses, with the time vector automatically determined provided t is not explicitly provided in the step commands.

The MATLAB command step (sys) may also be used to obtain the unit-step response of a system.

The command

$$\text{step (sys)} \tag{3.45}$$

can be used where the system is defined by

$$\text{sys = tf (num, den)} \tag{3.46}$$

or

$$\text{sys = ss (A, B, C, D)} \tag{3.47}$$

The following MATLAB step commands with left hand arguments are used then no plot is shown on the screen.

$$\begin{aligned} &[\text{y, x, t}] = \text{step [num, den, t]} \\ &[\text{y, x, t}] = \text{step (A, B, C, D, iu)} \\ &[\text{y, x, t}] = \text{step (A, B, C, D, iu, t)} \end{aligned} \tag{3.48}$$

Hence, in order to obtain the response curves, plot commands should be used. The matrices x, and y contain the state response of the system and the output respectively, computed at the time points t. In Eq. (3.48), iu is a scalar index of the inputs of the system, which specifies the input to be used for the response, and t is the user specified time. The step command in Eq. (3.48) can be used to obtain a series of step response plots, one for each input and output combination of

$$\begin{aligned} \dot{\mathbf{x}} &= \mathbf{Ax} + \mathbf{Bu} \\ \mathbf{y} &= \mathbf{Cx} + \mathbf{Du} \end{aligned} \tag{3.49}$$

when the system involves multiple inputs and multiple outputs

3.13.2 Impulse Response

The following MATLAB commands may be used to obtain the unit impulse response of a control system:

impulse (num, den) (3.50)

impulse(A, B, C, D) (3.51)

[y, x, t] = impulse (num, den) (3.52)

[y, x, t] = impulse (num, den, t) (3.53)

[y, x, t] = impulse (A, B, C, D) (3.54)

[y, x, t] = impulse (A, B, C, D, iu) (3.55)

[y, x, t] = impulse (A, B, C, D, iu, t) (3.56)

The command in Eq. (3.50) impulse (num, den) shows the plots of the unit impulse response on the monitor (screen). The command in Eq. (3.51), impulse (A, B, C, D) produces a series of unit impulse-response plots one for each input and output combination of the system defined in Eq. (3.39) with the time vector automatically obtained. The vector t in Eqns. (3.53) and (3.56) is the user supplied time vector, which specifies the times at which the impulse response is to be obtained. The scalar iu in Eqns. (3.55) and (3.56) is an index into the inputs of the system and specifies which input is to be used for the impulse response. The matrices x and y in Eqns. (3.52) to (3.56) contain the state responses of the system and the output respectively, evaluated at the time points t.

3.13.3 Unit Ramp Response

Consider the system described in state space as

$$\dot{\mathbf{x}} = \mathbf{Ax} + \mathbf{Bu}$$
$$\mathbf{y} = \mathbf{Cx} + \mathbf{Du} \qquad (3.57)$$

where u is the unit-ramp function.

When all the initial conditions are zeros, the unit ramp response is the integral of the unit step response. Therefore, the unit ramp response is given by

$$z = \int_0^t y\,dt \qquad (3.58)$$

or

$$\dot{\mathbf{z}} = \mathbf{y} = \mathbf{x}_1 \qquad (3.59)$$

Defining

$$\mathbf{z} = \mathbf{x}_3 \qquad (3.60)$$

Equation (3.59) can be written as

$$\dot{\mathbf{x}}_3 = \mathbf{x}_1 \qquad (3.61)$$

Combining Eqns. (3.57) and (3.61), we can write

$$\dot{\mathbf{x}} = \mathbf{AAx} + \mathbf{BBu}$$
$$\mathbf{z} = \mathbf{CCx} + \mathbf{DDu} \qquad (3.62)$$

The MATLAB command

[z, x, t] = step (AA, BB, CC, DD) (3.63)

can be used to obtain the unit-ramp response curve z (t).

3.13.4 Response to Arbitrary Input

The response to an arbitrary input can be obtained by using the following MATLAB commands:

lsim (num, den, t) (3.64)

lsim (A, B, C, D, u, t) (3.65)

y = lsim (num, den, r, t) (3.66)

y = lsim (A, B, C, D, u, t) (3.67)

The MATLAB commands in Eqns.(3.64) to (3.67) will generate the response to input time function r or u.

3.14 RESPONSE TO INITIAL CONDITION IN STATE SPACE

Consider the system defined in state space by

$$\dot{\mathbf{x}} = \mathbf{Ax} + \mathbf{Bu}, \quad \mathbf{x}\,(0) = \mathbf{x}_0 \tag{3.68}$$

$$y = \mathbf{cx} + \mathrm{Du} \tag{3.69}$$

The MATLAB command

initial (A, B, C, D, [initial condition], t) (3.70)

may be used to provide the response to the initial condition.

EXAMPLES WITH SOLUTIONS

Example E3.1

Reduce the system shown in Fig. E3.1 to a single transfer function, T(s) = C(s)/R(s) using MATLAB. The transfer functions are given as:

$$G_1(s) = \frac{1}{(s+7)}$$

$$G_2(s) = \frac{1}{(s^2+6s+5)}$$

$$G_3(s) = \frac{1}{(s+8)}$$

$$G_4(s) = \frac{1}{s}$$

$$G_5(s) = \frac{7}{(s+3)}$$

$$G_6(s) = \frac{1}{(s^2+7s+5)}$$

$$G_7(s) = \frac{5}{(s+5)}$$

$$G_8(s) = \frac{1}{(s+9)}$$

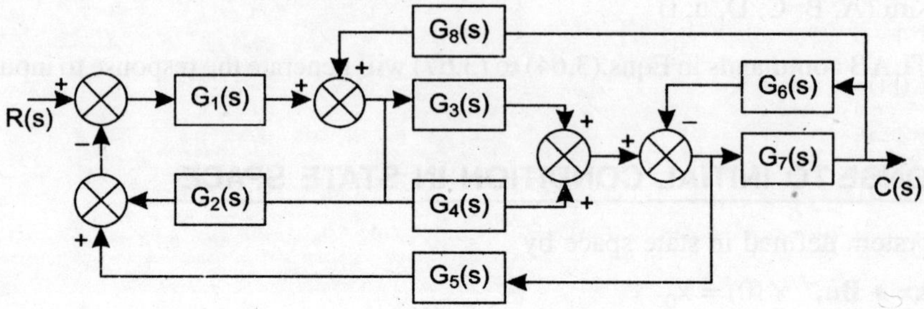

Fig. E3.1

The transfer functions are given as:

G_1 (s) = 1/(s + 7)

G_2 (s) = 1/(s^2 + 3s + 5)

G_3 (s) = 1/(s + 8)

G_4 (s) = 1/s

G_5 (s) = 7/(s + 3)

G_6 (s) = 1/(s^2 + 7s + 5)

G_7 (s) = 5/(s + 5)

G_8 (s) = 1/(s + 9)

Solution

```
% MATLAB Program
G1 = tf ([0 0 1], [0 1 7]);
G2 = tf ([0 0 1], [1 6 5]);
G3 = tf ([0 0 1], [0 1 8]);
G4 = tf ([0 0 1], [0 1 0]);
G5 = tf ([0 0 7], [0 1 3]);
G6 = tf ([0 0 1], [1 7 5]);
G7 = tf ([0 0 5], [0 1 5]);
G8 = tf ([0 0 1], [0 1 9]);
G9 = tf ([0 0 1], [0 0 1]);
```

```
T1 = append (G1, G2, G3, G4, G5, G6, G7, G8, G9);
Q = [ 1 -2 -5 9 ]
2 1 8 0
31 8 0
4 1 8 0
5 3 4 -6
6 7 0 0
7 3 4 -6
8 7 0 0];
Inputs = 9;
Outputs = 7;
Ts = connect (T1, Q, Inputs, Outputs);
T = Tf (Ts) computer response
```

Transfer function

10s^7 + 290s^6 + 3350s^5 + 1.98e004s^4 + 6.369e004s^3 + 1.089e005s^2 + 8.895e004s + 2.7e004s^10 + 45s^9 + 866s^8 + 9305s^7 + 6.116e004s^6 + 2.533e005s^5 + 6.57e005s^4 + 1.027e006s^3 + 8.909e005s^2 + 3.626e005s + 4.2e004

Example E3.2

For each of the second order systems below, find ξ, ωn, Ts, Tp, Tr, % overshoot, and plot the step response using MATLAB.

(*a*) $T(s) = \dfrac{130}{s^2 + 15s + 130}$

(*b*) $T(s) = \dfrac{0.045}{s^2 + 0.025s + 0.045}$

(*c*) $T(s) = \dfrac{10^8}{s^2 + 1.325 \times 10^3 s + 10^8}$

Solution

(*a*)

```
>> clf
>> numa = 130;
>> dena = [1 15 130];
>> Ta = tf(numa, dena)
```

Transfer function

$$\frac{130}{s\text{^}2+15s+130}$$

```
>> omegana = sqrt (dena(3))
omegana =
        11.4018
>> zetaa = dena(2)/(2*omegana)
zetaa =
    0.6578
>> Tsa = 4/(zetaa*omegana)
Tsa =
    0.5333
>> Tpa = pi/(omegana*sqrt(1 – zetaa^2))
Tpa =
    0.3658
>> Tra = (1.76*zetaa^3 – 0.417*zetaa^2 + 1.039*zetaa + 1)/omegana
Tra =
    0.1758
>> percenta = exp(–zetaa*pi/sqrt(1 – zetaa^2))*100
percenta =
    6.4335
>> subplot(221)
>> step(Ta)
>> title('(a)')
>> '(b)'
ans =
(b)
>> numb = 0.045;
>> denb = [1 .025 0.045];
>> Tb = tf(numb, denb)
```

Transfer function

$$\frac{0.045}{s\text{^}2+0.025s+0.045}$$

```
>>  omeganb = sqrt(denb(3))
 omeganb =
    0.2121
>> zetab = denb(2)/(2*omeganb)
 zetab =
    0.0589
>> Tsb = 4/(zetab*omeganb)
 Tsb =
    320
>> Tpb = pi/(omeganb*sqrt(1 – zetab^2))
 Tpb =
    14.8354
>> Trb = (1.76*zetab^3 – 0.417*zetab^2 + 1.039*zetab + 1)/omeganb
 Trb =
    4.9975
>>  percentb = exp(–zetab*pi/sqrt(1 – zetab^2))*100
 percentb =
    83.0737
>> subplot(222)
>> step(Tb)
>> title('(b)')
>> '(c)'
 ans =
 (c)
>> numc = 10E8;
>> denc = [1 1.325*10E3 10E8];
>> Tc = tf(numc, denc)
```

Transfer function

```
        le009
  ------------------
  s^2+13250s+le009
```

```
>> omeganc = sqrt(denc(3))
 omeganc =
    3.1623e+004
>> zetac = denc (2)/(2*omeganc)
 zetac =
    0.2095
```

```
>> Tsc = 4/(zetac*omeganc)
 Tsc =
    6.0377e – 004
>> Tpc = pi/(omeganc*sqrt (1 – zetac^2))
 Tpc =
    1.0160e – 004
>> Trc = (1.76*zetac^3 – 0.417*zetac^2 + 1.039*zetac + 1)/omeganc
 Trc =
    3.8439e – 005
>> percentc = exp (–zetac*pi/sqrt (1 – zetac^2))*100
 percentc =
    51.0123
>> subplot (223)
>> step (Tc)
>> title ('(c)')
```

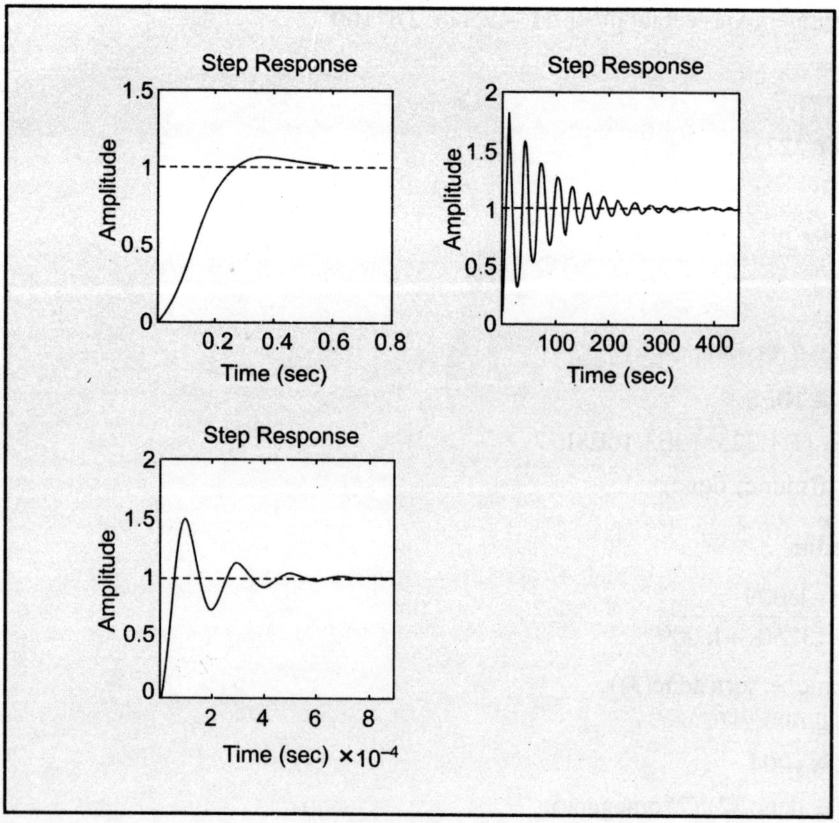

Fig. E3.2

Example E3.3

Determine the pole locations for the system shown below using MATLAB.

$$\frac{C(s)}{R(s)} = \frac{s^3 - 6s^2 + 7s + 15}{s^5 + s^4 - 5s^3 - 9s^2 + 11s - 12}$$

Solution

```
>> % MATLAB Program
>> den = [11 –5 –9 11 –12];
>> A = roots (den)
A =
    –2.1586 + 1.2396i
    –2.1586 – 1.2396i
     2.3339
     0.4917 + 0.7669i
     0.4917 – 0.7669i
```

Example E3.4

Determine the pole locations for the unity feedback system shown below using MATLAB.

$$G(s) = \frac{150}{(s+5)(s+7)(s+9)(s+11)}$$

Solution

```
>> % MATLAB Program
>> numg = 1 50
numg =
    150
>> deng = poly ([–5 –7 –9 –11]);
>> 'G(s)'
ans =
    G(s)
>> G = tf (numg, deng)
```

Transfer function

$$\frac{150}{s\text{^}4 + 32s\text{^}3 + 374s\text{^}2 + 1888s + 3465}$$

```
>> 'Poles of G(s)'

ans =

   Poles of G(s)

>> pole (G)

ans =

   -11.0000
   -9.0000
   -7.0000
   -5.0000

>> 'T(s)'

ans =

   T(s)

>> T = feedback (G, 1)
```

Transfer function

$$\frac{150}{s^4 + 32s^3 + 374s^2 + 1888s + 3415}$$

```
>> pole (T)

ans =

   -10.9673 + 1.9506i
   -10.9673 - 1.9506i
   -5.0327 + 1.9506i
   -5.0327 - 1.9506i
```

Example E3.5

A plant to be controlled is described by a transfer function

$$G(s) = \frac{s+7}{s^2 + 9s + 30}$$

Obtain the root locus plot using MATLAB.

Solution

```
>> % MATLAB Program
>> clf
```

```
>> num = [1 7];
>> den = [1 9 30];
>> rlocus (num, den);
```

Computer response is shown in Fig. E3.5

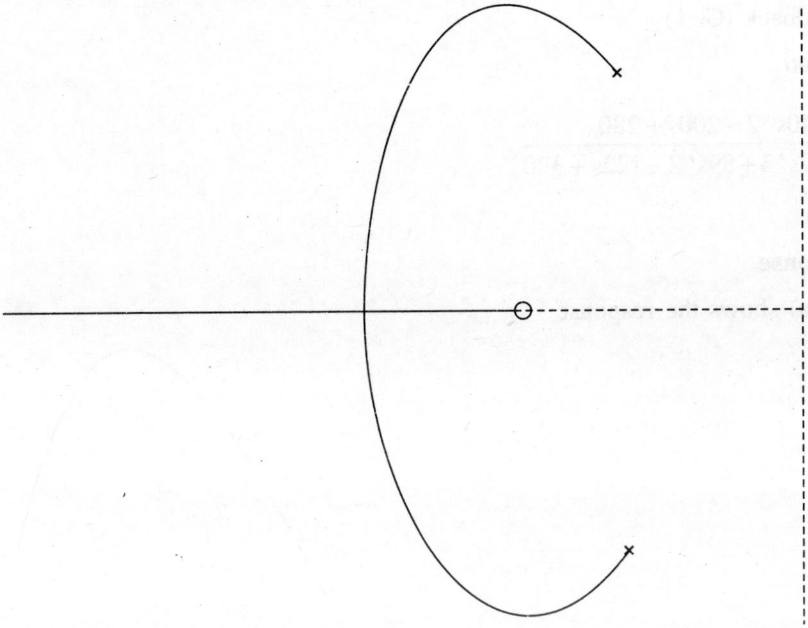

Fig. E3.5

Example E3.6

For the unity feedback system shown in Fig. E3.6, G(s) is given as:

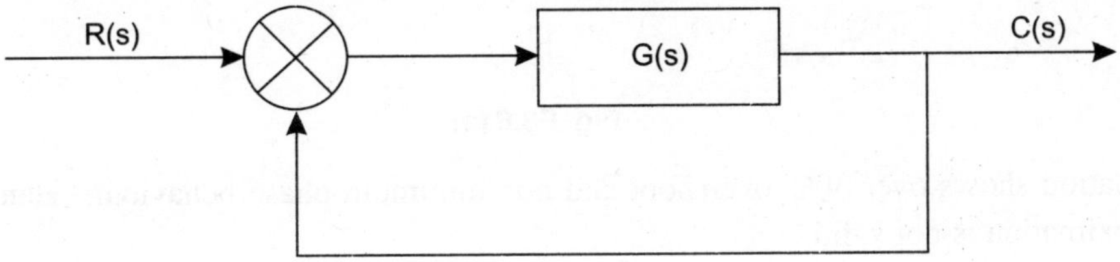

Fig. E3.6

$$G(s) = \frac{30(s^2 - 5s + 3)}{(s+1)(s+2)(s+4)(s+5)}$$

Determine the closed-loop step response using MATLAB.

Solution

```
>> % MATLAB Program
>> numg = 40*[1 –5 7];
>> deng = poly ([–1 –2 –4 –5]);
>> G = tf (numg, deng);
>> T = feedback (G, 1)
```

Transfer function

$$\frac{40s^2 - 200s + 280}{s^4 + 12s^3 + 89s^2 - 122s + 320}$$

```
>> step (T)
```

Computer response

Fig. E3.6 (a) shows the response

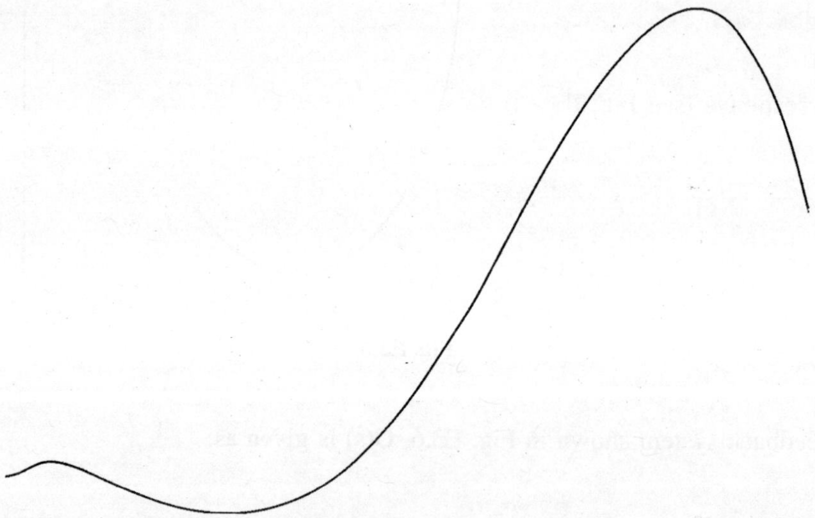

Fig. E3.6 (a)

Simulation shows over 30% overshoot and non minimum-phase behaviour. Hence the second-order approximation is not valid.

Example E3.7

Determine the accuracy of the second-order approximation using MATLAB to simulate the unity feedback system shown in Fig. E3.7 where

$$G(s) = \frac{12(s^2 + 3s + 9)}{(s^2 + 3s + 9)(s + 1)(s + 5)}$$

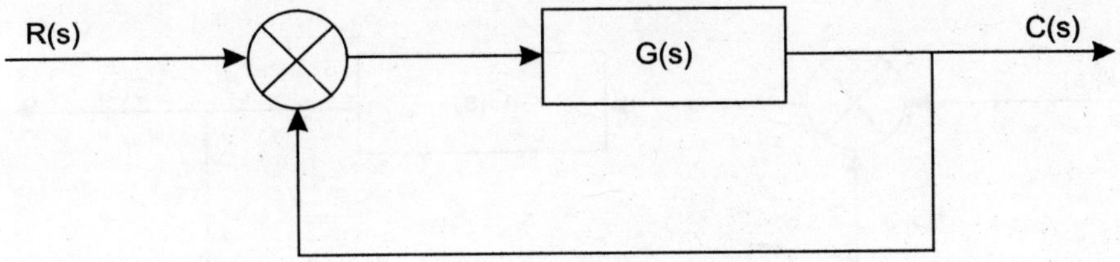

Fig. E3.7

Solution

```
>> % MATLAB Program
>> numg = 12*[1 3 9];
>> deng = conv ([1 3 9], poly ([–1 –5]));
>> G = tf (numg, deng);
>> T = feedback (G, 1);
>> step (T)
```

Computer response [see Fig. E3.7 (a)].

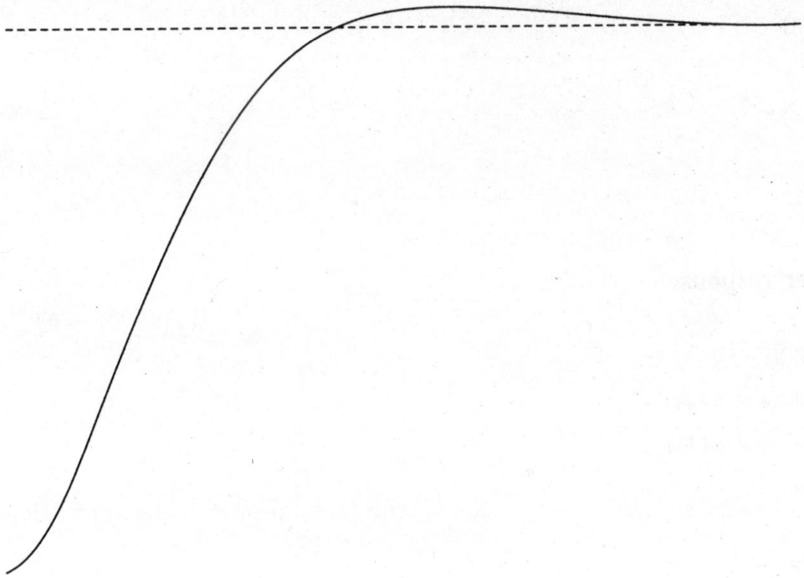

Fig. E3.7 (a)

Example E3.8

For the unity feedback system shown in Fig. E3.8 with

$$G(s) = \frac{K(s+1)}{s(s+1)(s+5)(s+6)}$$

determine the range of K for stability using MATLAB.

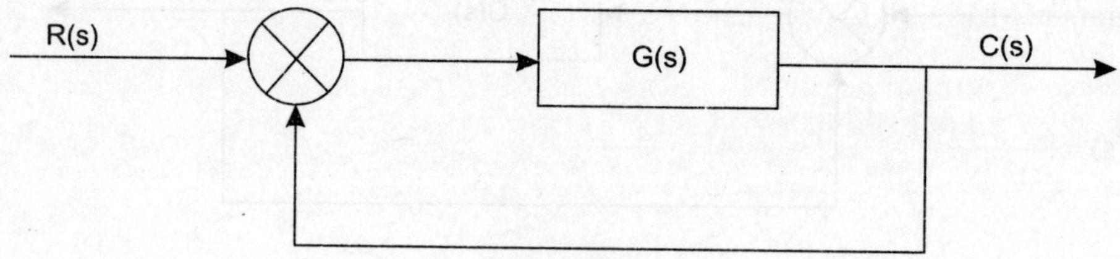

Fig. E3.8

Solution

```
>> % MATLAB Program
>> K = [0:0.2:200];
>> for i = 1: length (K);
>> deng = poly ([0 –1 –5 –6]);
>> dent = deng + [0 0 0 K (i) K (i)];
>> R = roots (dent);
>> A = real(R);
>> B = max (A);
>> if B > 0
>> R
>> K = K (i)
>> break
>> end
>> end
```

Computer response

```
R =
    –10.0000
    –0.5000 + 4.4441i
    –0.5000 – 4.4441i
    –1.0000
A =
    –10.0000
    –0.5000
    –0.5000
    –1.0000
B =
    –0.5000
```

Example E3.9

Write a program in MATLAB to obtain the Nyquist and Nichols plots for the following transfer function for k=30.

$$G(s) = \frac{k(s+1)(s+3+7i)(s+3-7i)}{(s+1)(s+3)(s+5)(s+3+7i)(s+3-7i)}$$

Solution

```
>> %MATLAB Program
>> %Simple Nyquist and Nichols plots
>> clf
>> z = [–1 –3+7*i –3–7*i];
>> p = [–1 –3 –5 –3+7*i –3–7*i];
>> k = 30;
>> [num, den] = zp2tf (z', p', k);
>> subplot (211), nyquist (num, den)
>> subplot (212), Nichols (num, den)
>> ngrid
>> axis ([50 360 –40 30])
```

Computer response: The Nyquist and Nichols plots are shown in Fig. E3.9.

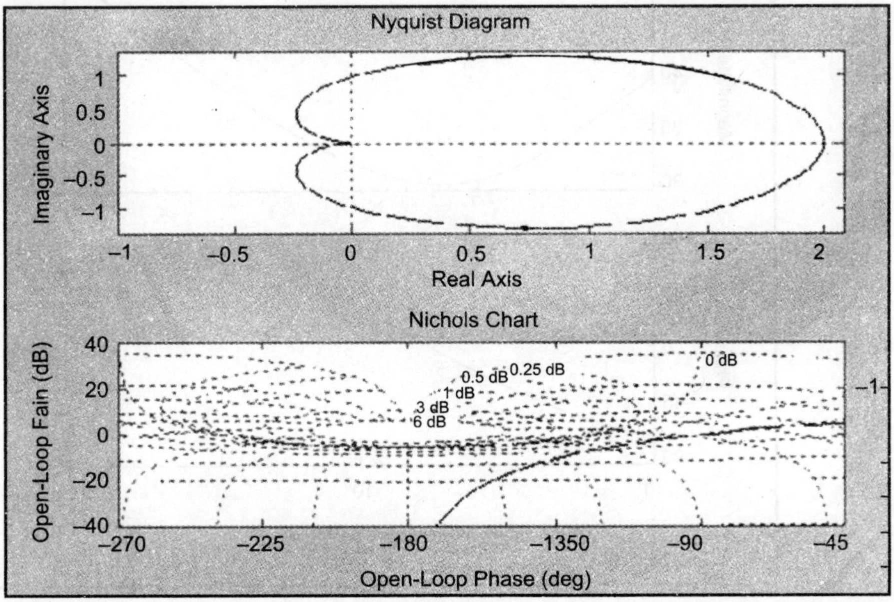

Fig. E3.9

Example E3.10

A PID controller is given by

$$G_c(s) = 29.125\frac{(s+0.57)^2}{s}$$

Draw a Bode diagram of the controller using MATLAB.

Solution

$$G_c(s) = \frac{29.125(s^2+1.14s+0.3249)}{s} = \frac{29.125s^2+33.2025s+9.4627}{s}$$

The following MATALB program produces the Bode diagram:

```
>> % MATLAB Program
>> %Bode diagram
>> num = [29.125 33.2025 9.4627];
>> den = [0 1 0];
>> bode (num, den)
>> title ('Bode diagram of G(s)')
```

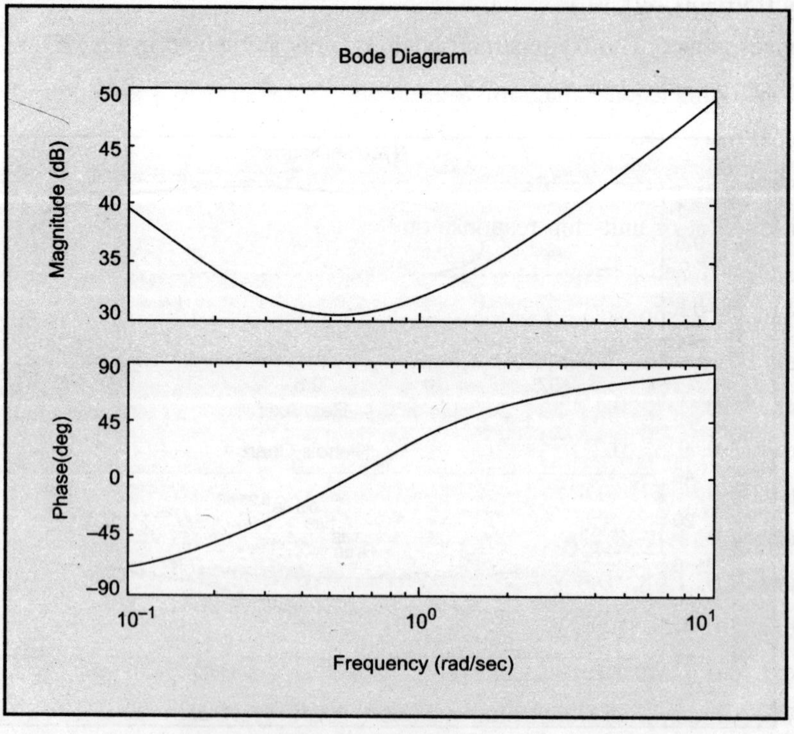

Fig. E3.10 Bode diagram of G(s)

Example E3.11

For the closed-loop system defined by

$$\frac{C(s)}{R(s)} = \frac{1}{s^2 + 2\zeta s + 1}$$

(*a*) plot the unit-step response curves c (t) for ξ = 0, 0.1, 0.2, 0.4, 0.5, 0.6, 0.8, and 1.0. ω_n is normalized to 1.

(*b*) plot a three dimensional plot of (a).

Solution

```
>> %Two-dimensional plot and three-dimensional plot of unit-step
>> %response curves for the standard second-order system with ωn =1
>> %and zeta = 0, 0.1, 0.2, 0.4, 0.5, 0.6, 0.8, and 1.0
>> t = 0:0.2:10;
>> zeta = [0 0.1 0.2 0.4 0.5 0.6 0.8 1.0];
>> for n = 1:8;
>> num = [0 0 1];
>> den = [1 2*zeta (n) 1];
>> [y (1:51, n), x, t] = step (num, den, t);
>> end
>> %Two-dimensional diagram with the command plot (t, y)
>> plot (t, y)
>> grid
>> title ('Plot of unit-step response curves')
>> xlabel ('t Sec')
>> ylabel ('Response')
>> text (4.1, 1.86, '\zeta = 0')
>> text (3.0, 1.7, '0.1')
>> text (3.0, 1.5, '0.2')
>> text (3.0, 1.22, '0.4')
>> text (2.9, 1.1, '0.5')
>> text (4.0, 1.08, '0.6')
>> text (3.0, 0.9, '0.8')
>> text (4.0, 0.9, '1.0')
>> %For three dimensional plot, we use the command mesh (t, eta, y')
>> mesh (t, eta, y')
>> title ('Three-dimensional plot of unit-step response curves')
```

```
>> xlabel ('t Sec')
>> ylabel ('\zeta')
>> zlabel ('Response')
```

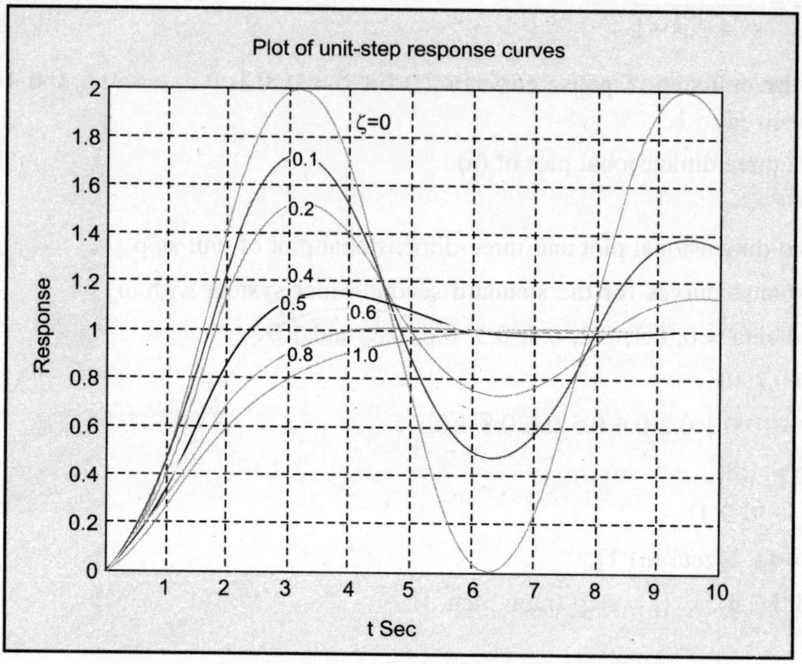

Fig. E3.11 (a) Plot of unit-step response curves

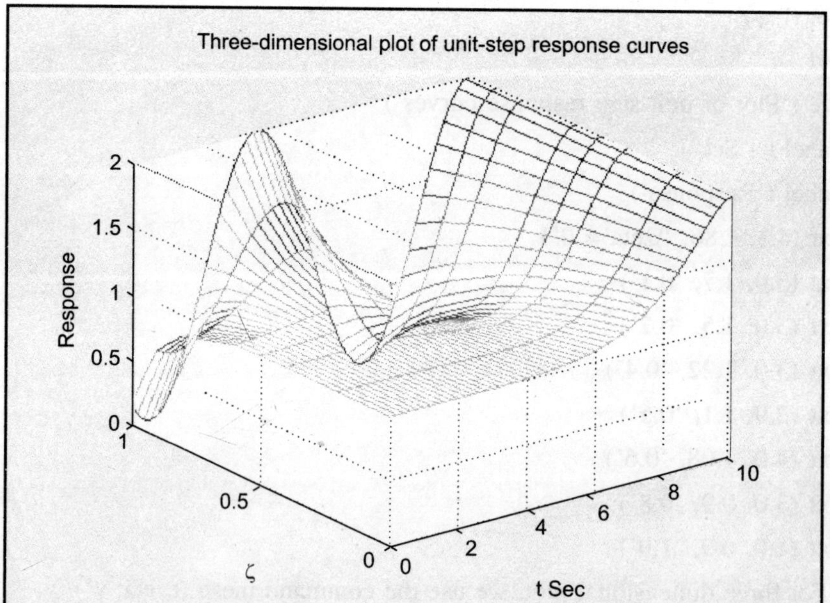

Fig. E3.11 (b) Three-dimensional plot of unit-step response curves

Example E3.12

A closed-loop control system is defined by.

$$\frac{C(s)}{R(s)} = \frac{2\zeta s}{s^2 + 2\zeta s + 1}$$

where ζ is the damping ratio. For ζ = 0.1, 0.2, 0.3, 0.4, 0.5, 0.6, 0.7, 0.8, 0.9, and 1.0 using MATLAB. Plot

(*a*) a two-dimensional diagram of unit-impulse response curves

(*b*) a three-dimensional plot of the response curves.

Solution

A MATLAB program that produces a two-dimensional diagram of unit-impulse response curves and a three-dimensional plot of the response curves is given below:

```
>> %To plot a two-dimensional diagram
>> t = 0:0.2:10;
>> zeta = [0.1 0.2 0.3 0.4 0.5 0.6 0.7 0.8 0.9 1.0];
>> for n = 1:10;
>> num = [0 2*zeta (n) 1];
>> den = [1 2*zeta (n) 1];
>> [y (1:51, n), x, t] = impulse (num, den, t);
>> end
>> plot (t, y)
>> grid
>> title ('Plot of unit-impulse response curves')
>> xlabel ('t Sec')
>> ylabel ('Response')
>> text (2.0, 0.85, '0.1')
>> text (1.5, 0.75, '0.2')
>> text (1.5, 0.6, '0.3')
>> text (1.5, 0.5, '0.4')
>> text (1.5, 0.38, '0.5')
>> text (1.5, 0.25, '0.6')
>> text (1.7, 0.12, '0.7')
>> text (2.0, –0.1, '0.8')
>> text (1.5, 0.0, '0.9')
>> text (.5, 1.5, '1.0')
>> %Three-dimensional plot
>> mesh (t, eta, y')
>> title ('Three-dimensional plot')
```

```
>> xlabel ('t Sec')
>> ylabel ('\zeta')
>> zlabel ('Response')
```

The two-dimensional diagram and three-dimensional diagram produced by this MATLAB program are shown in Figs. E3.12 (a) and (b) respectively.

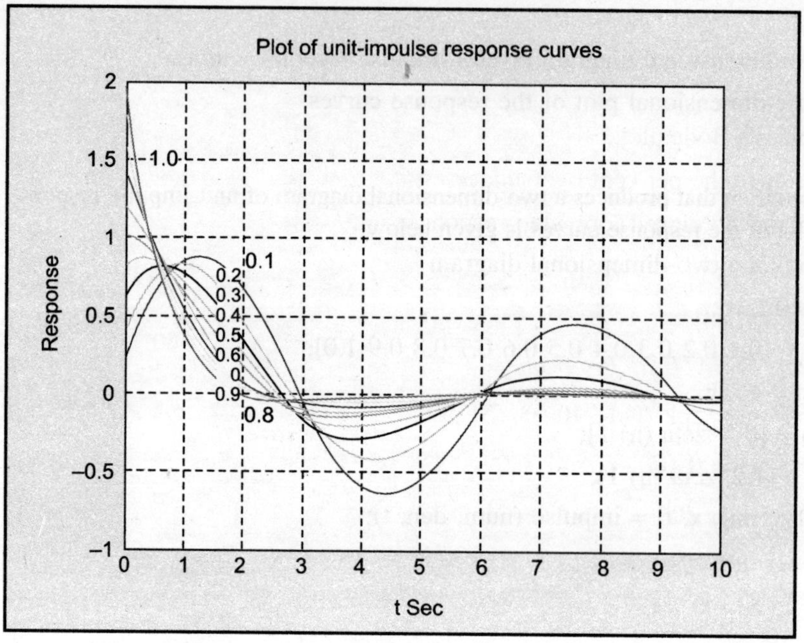

Fig. E3.12 (a) Two-dimensional plot

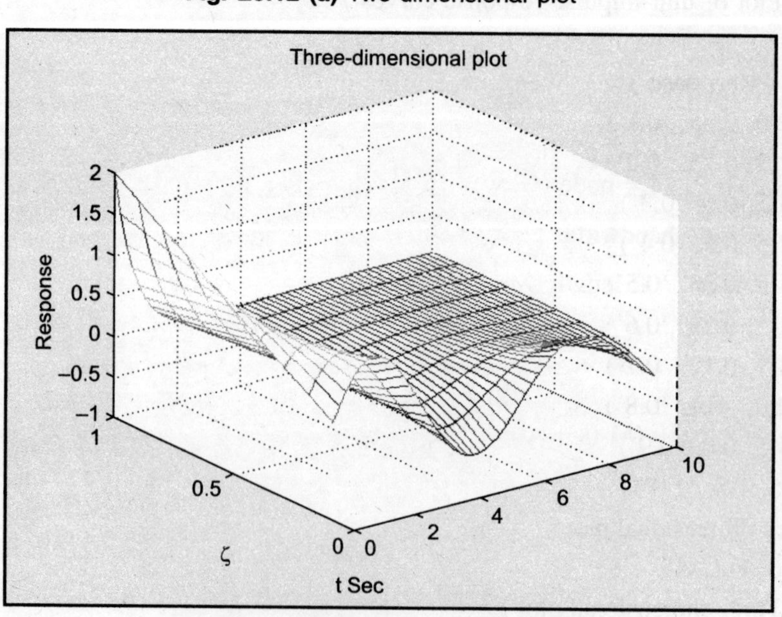

Fig. E3.12 (b) Three-dimensional plot

Example E3.13

For the system shown in Fig. E3.13 write a program in MATLAB that will use an open-loop transfer function G(s):

$$G(s) = \frac{50(s+1)}{s(s+3(s+5)}$$

$$G(s) = \frac{25(s+1)(s+7)}{s(s+2)(s+4)(s+8)}$$

(*a*) Obtain a Bode plot.

(*b*) Estimate the per cent overshoot, settling time, and peak time.

(*c*) Obtain the closed-loop step response.

Solution

(*a*)

```
>> %MATLAB Program
>> G = zpk ([–1], [0 –3 –5], 50)
>> G = tf (G)
>> bode (G)
>> title ('System 1')
>> %title ('System 1')
>> pause
>> %Find phase margin
>> [Gm, Pm, Wcg, Wcp] = margin (G);
>> w = 1:.01:20;
>> [M, P, w] = bode (G, w);
>> %Find bandwidth
>> for k = 1:1: length (M);
>> if 20*log10 (M (k)) + 7 < = 0;
>> 'Mag'
>> 20*log10 (M (k))
>> 'BW'
>> wBW = w (k)
>> break
```

```
>> end
>> end
>> %Find damping ratio, per cent overshoot, settling time, and peak time
>> for z = 0:01:10
>> Pt = atan (2*z/(sqrt (–2*z^2 + sqrt (1 + 4*z^4))))*(180/pi);
>> if (Pm – Pt) < = 0
>> z;
>> Po = exp (–z*pi/sqrt (1 – z^2));
>> Ts = (4/(wBW*z))*sqrt ((1 – 2*z^2) + sqrt (4*z^4 – 4*z^2 + 2));
>> Tp = (pi/(wBW*sqrt (1 – z^2)))*sqrt ((1 – 2*z^2) + sqrt (4*z^4 – 4*z^2 + 2));
>> fprintf ('Bandwidth = %g', wBW)
>> fprintf ('Phase margin = %g', Pm)
>> fprintf (', Damping ratio = %g', z)
>> fprintf (', Per cent overshoot = %g', Po*100)
>> fprintf (', Settling time = %g', Ts)
>> fprintf (', Peak time = %g', Tp)
>> break
>> end
>> end
>> T = feedback (G, 1);
>> step (T)
>> title ('Step response system 1')
>> %title ('Step response system 1')
```

Computer response

Zero/pole/gain

$$\frac{50(s+1)}{s(s+3)(s+3)}$$

Transfer function

$$\frac{50s+50}{s^3+8s^2+15s}$$

The Bode plot is shown in Fig. E3.13 (a).

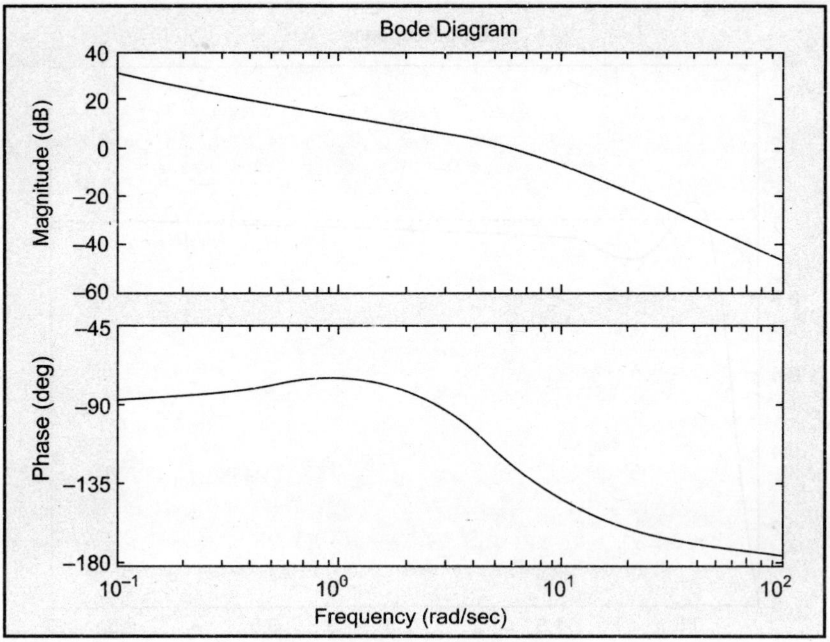

Fig. E3.13 (a)

```
ans =
        Mag
ans =
        -3.0032
ans =
    BW
wBW =
        9.7900
```

Bandwidth = 9.79, Phase margin = 53.892, Damping ratio ≐ 0.59, Per cent overshoot = 10.0693, Settling time = 0.804303, Peak time = 0.461606.

The step response is shown in Fig. 3.13(b).

(*b*) Likewise, for this problem

```
>> G=zpk ([-1 -7], [0 -2 -4 -8], 25)
>> G=tf (G)
```

The following Bode plot and step response are obtained [see Figs. E3.13(c) and (d).

Zero/pole/gain:

$$\frac{25(s+1)(s+7)}{s(s+2)(s+4)(s+8)}$$

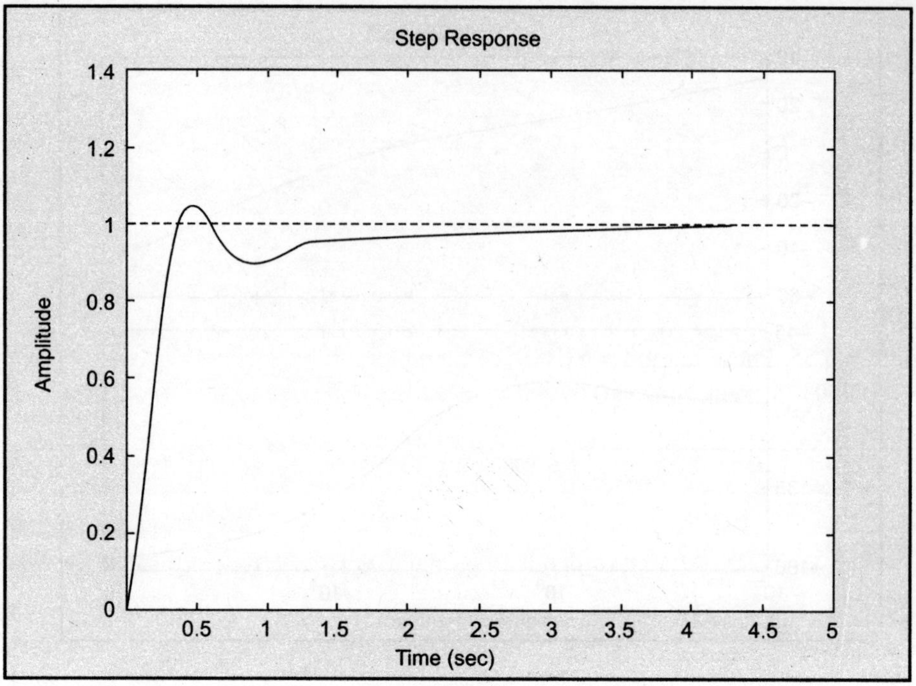

Fig. E3.13 (b)

Transfer function

$$\frac{25s^2 + 200s + 175}{s^4 + 14\,s^3 + 56\,s + 2 + 64\,s}$$

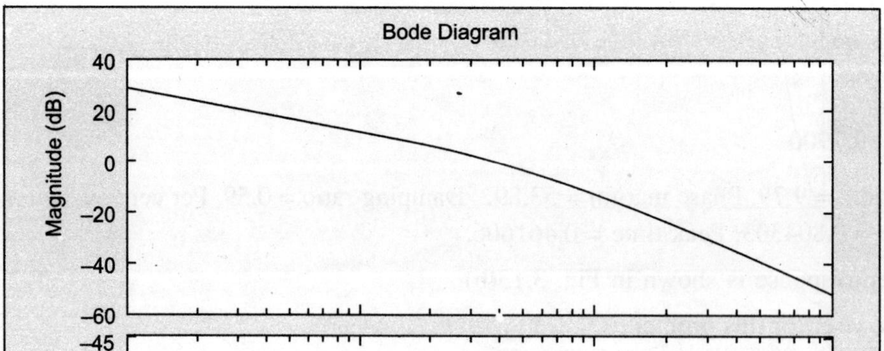

Fig. E3.13(c)

ans =

Mag

ans =

-7.0110

ans =

BW

wBW =

6.5500

Bandwidth = 6.55, Phase margin = 63.1105, Damping ratio = 0.67, Per cent overshoot = 5.86969, Settling time = 0.959175, Peak time = 0.679904.

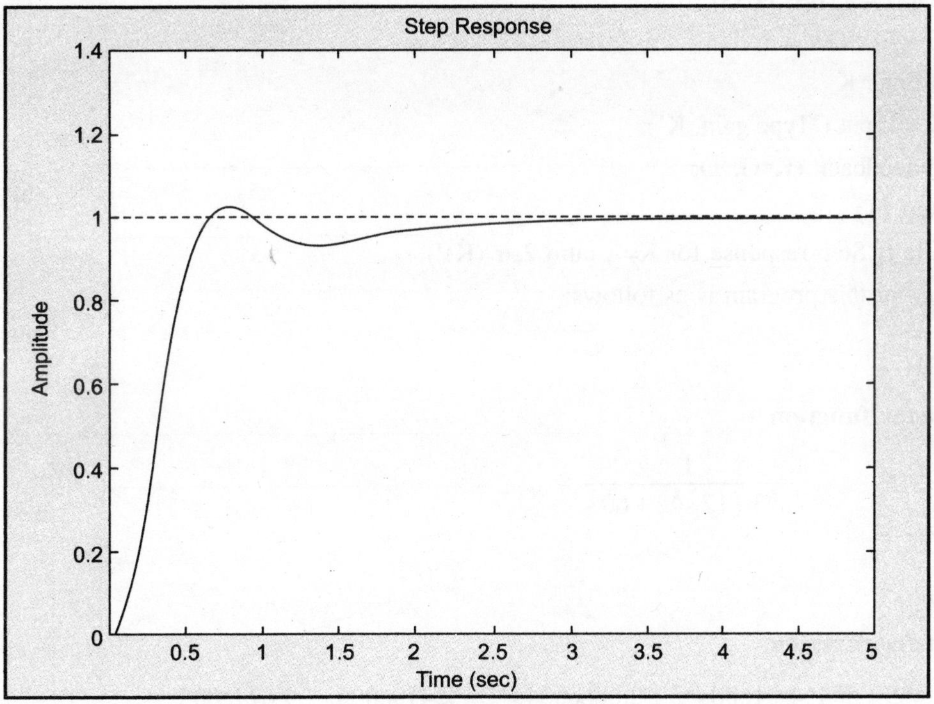

Fig. E3.13 (d)

Example E3.14

For a unit feedback system with the forward-path transfer function

$$G(s) = \frac{K}{s(s+5)(s+12)}$$

and a delay of 0.5 second, estimate the per cent overshoot for K = 40 using a second-order approximation. Model the delay using MATLAB function pade (T, n). Determine the unit step response and check the second-order approximation assumption made.

Solution

```
>> %MATLAB Program
>> %Enter G(s)
>> numg1 = 1;
>> deng1 = poly ([0 –5 –12]);
>> 'G1(s)'
>> G1 = tf (numg1, deng1)
>> [numg2, deng2] = pade (0.5, 5);
>> 'G2(s)'
>> G2 = tf (numg2, deng2)
>> 'G(s) = G1(s) G2(s)'
>> G = G1*G2
>> %Enter K
>> K = input ('Type gain, K');
>> T=feedback (K*G, 1);
>> step (T)
>> title (['Step response for K=', num 2str (K)])
```

Output of this program is as follows:

ans =

G1(s)

Transfer function

$$\frac{1}{s^3+17\,s^2+60\,s}$$

ans =

G2(s)

Transfer function

$$\frac{-s^5+60s^4-1680s^3+2.688e004\,s^2-2.419e005\,s+9.677e005}{s^5+60s^4+1680s^3+2.688e004\,s^2+2.419e005\,s+9.677e005}$$

ans =

G(s) = G1(s) G2(s)

Transfer function

$$\frac{-s^5+60\,s^4-1680s^3+2.688e004s^2-2.419e005s+9.677e005}{s^8+77s^7+2760s^6+5.904e004s^5+7.997e005s^4+6.693e006s^3+3.097e007s^2+5.806e007s}$$

Type Gain, K 40

The following Fig. E3.14 is obtained.

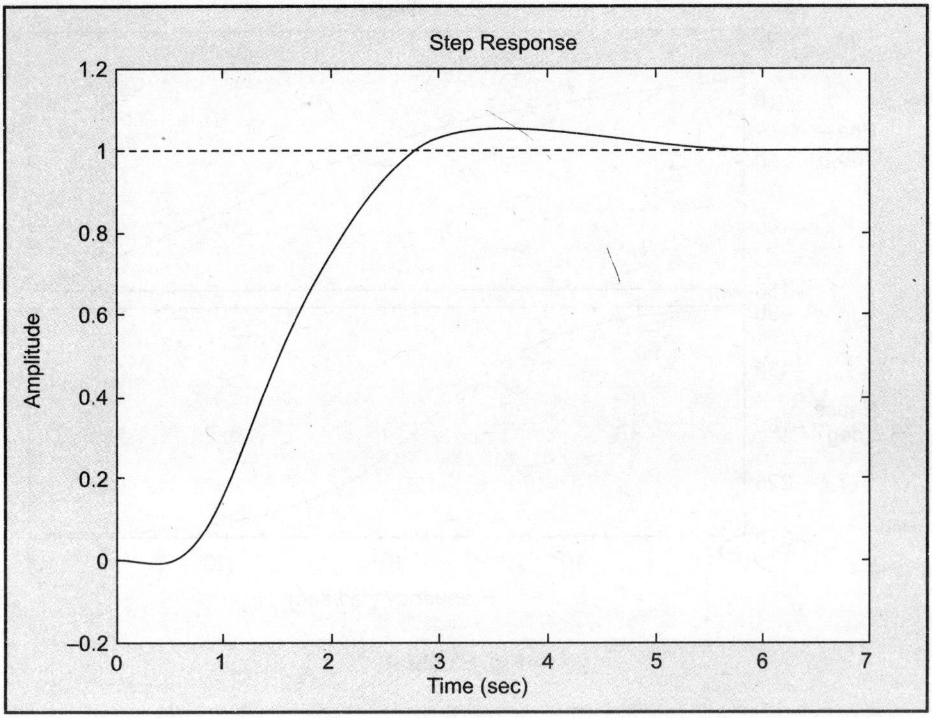

Fig. E3.14

Example E3.15

Write a program in MATLAB to obtain a Bode plot for the transfer function

(*a*) $G(s) = \dfrac{15}{s(s+5)(0.7s+6)}$

(*b*) $G(s) = \dfrac{(7s^3 + 15s^2 + 9s + 80)}{(s^4 + 8s^3 + 15s^2 + 70s + 100)}$

Solution (a)

```
>> %MATLAB Program
>> %Bode plot generation
>> clf
>> num = 15;
>> den = conv ([1 0], conv ([1 5], [0.7 6]));
>> bode (num, den)
```

Computer response: The Bode plot is shown in Fig. E3.15(a)

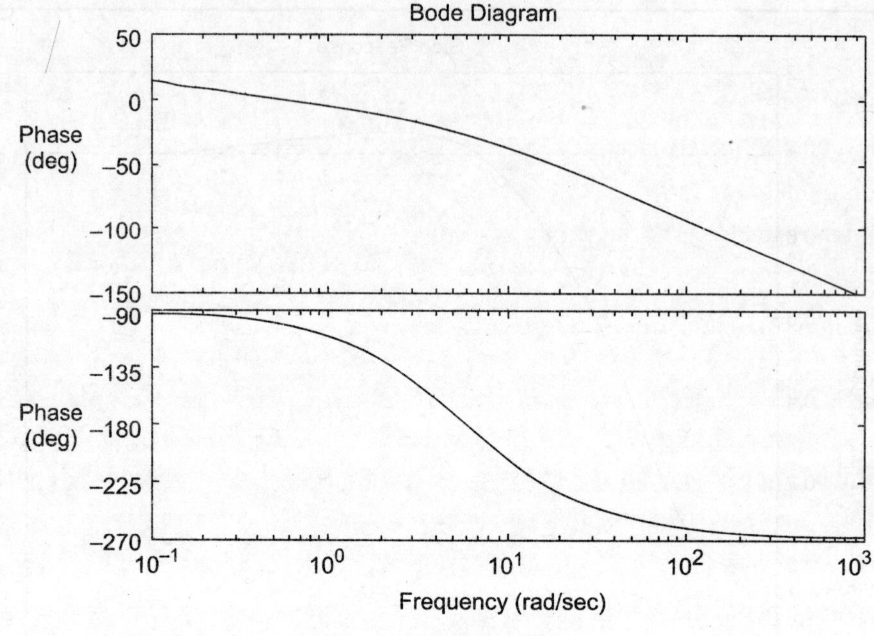

Fig. E3.15(a)

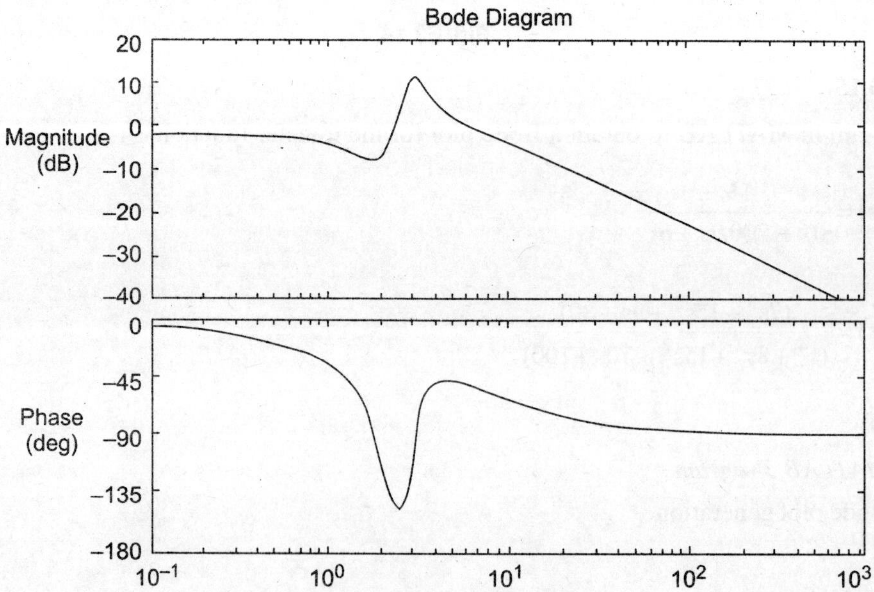

Fig. E3.15 (b)

Solution

```
>> %MATLAB Program
>> %Bode plot
>> clf
>> num = [0 7 15 7 80];
>> den = [1 8 12 70 110];
>> bode (num, den)
```

Computer response: The Bode plot is shown in Fig. E3.15 (b)

Example E3.16

Write a program in MATLAB for a unity-feedback system with

$$G(s) = \frac{K(s+7)}{(s^2+3s+52)(s^2+2s+35)}$$

(*a*) Plot the Nyquist diagram

(*b*) Display the real-axis crossing value and frequency.

Solution

```
>> % MATLAB Program
>> numg = [1 7]
>> deng = conv ([1 3 52], [1 2 35]);
>> G = tf (numg, deng)
>> 'G(s)'
>> Gap = zpk (G)
>> inquest (G)
>> axis ([-3e-3, 4e-3, -5e-3, 5e-3])
>> w = 0:0.1:100;
>> [re, im] = nyquist (G, w);
>> for i = 1:1: length (w)
>> M (i) = abs (re (i) + j*im (i));
>> A (i) = atan2 (im (i), re (i))*(180/pi);
>> if 180 – abs (A (i)) < = 1;
>> re (i);
>> im (i);
>> K=1/abs (re (i));
>> fprintf ('\nw = %g', w (i))
>> fprintf (', Re = %g', re (i))
>> fprintf (', Im = %g', im (i))
```

```
>> fprintf (', M = %g', M (i))
>> fprintf (', K = %g', K)
>> Gm = 20*log10 (1/M (i));
>> fprintf (', Gm = &G', Gm)
>> break
>> end
>> end
```

Computer response

numg=
17

Transfer function

$$\frac{s+7}{s^4+5s^3+93s^2+209s+1820}$$

ans =
G(s)

Zero/pole/gain:

$$\frac{s+7}{(s^2+2s+35)(s^2+3s+52)}$$

The Nyquist plot is shown in Fig. E3.16.

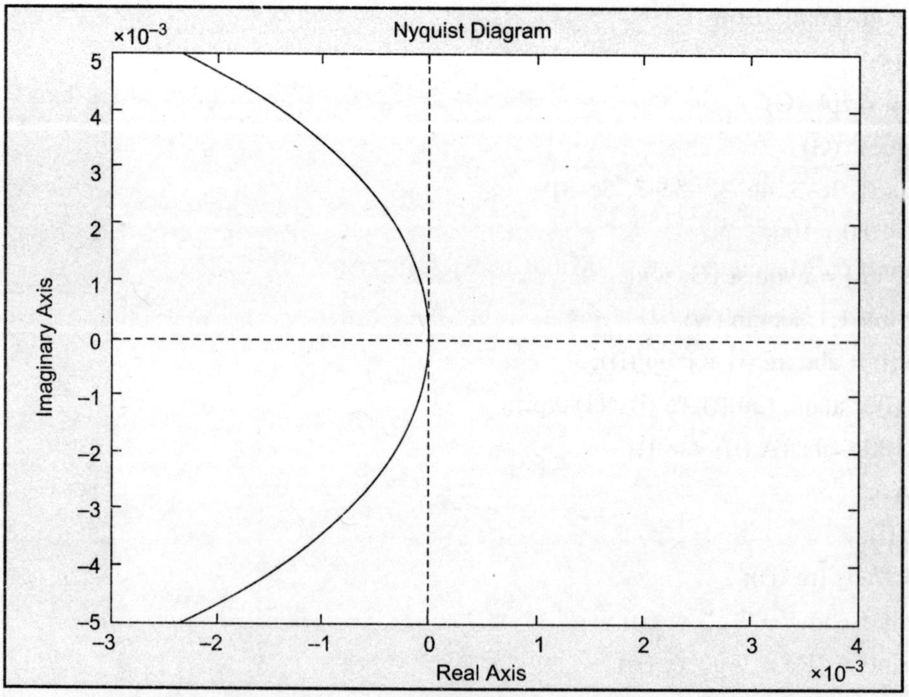

Fig. E3.16

Example E3.17

Write a program in MATLAB for the unity feedback system with

$$G(s) = \frac{K}{[s(s+3)(s+12)]}$$

so that the value of gain K can be input. Display the Bode plots of a system for the input value of K. Determine and display the gain and phase margin for the input value of K.

Solution

```
>> %Enter G(s)
>> numg = 1;
>> deng = poly ([0 –3 –12]);
>> 'G(s)'
>> G = tf (numg, deng)
>> w = 0.01:0.1:100;
>> %Enter K
>> K = input ('Type gain, K');
>> bode (K*G, w)
>> pause
>> [M, P] = bode (K*G, w);
>> %Calculate gain margin
>> for i = 1:1: length (P);
>> if P (i) < = –180;
>> fprintf ('\nGain K = %g', K)
>> fprintf (', Frequency (180 deg) = %g', w (i))
>> fprintf (', Magnitude = %g', M (i))
>> fprintf (', Magnitude(dB) = %g', 20*log10(M(i)))
>> fprintf(', Phase = %g', P(i))
>> Gm = 20*log10(1/M(i));
>> fprintf(', Gain margin(dB) = %g', Gm)
>> break
>> end
>> end
>> %Calculate phase margin
>> for i=1:1:length(M);
```

```
>> if M(i) < = 1;
>> fprintf('\nGain K = %g', K)
>> fprintf(', Frequency(0 dB) = %g', w(i))
>> fprintf(', Magnitude = %g', M(i))
>> fprintf(', Magnitude(dB) = %g', 20*log10(M(i)))
>> fprintf(', Phase = %g', P(i))
>> Pm = 180 + P(i);
>> fprintf(', Phase margin(dB) = %g', Pm)
>> break
>> end
>> end
>> 'Alternate program using MATLAB margin function:'
>> clear
>> clf
>> %Bode plot and find points
>> %Enter G(s)
>> numg = 1;
>> deng = poly([0 -3 -12]);
>> 'G(s)'
>> G = tf(numg,deng)
>> w = 0.01:0.1:100;
>> %Enter K
>> K = input('Type gain,K');
>> bode(K*G,w)
>> [Gm,Pm,Wcp,Wcg] = margin(K*G)
>> 'Gm(dB)'
>> 20*log10(Gm)
```

Computer response

ans =

G(s)

Transfer function

$$\frac{1}{s^3+15\,s^2+36\,s}$$

Type gain, K 40

The Bode plot is shown in Fig. E3.17(a).

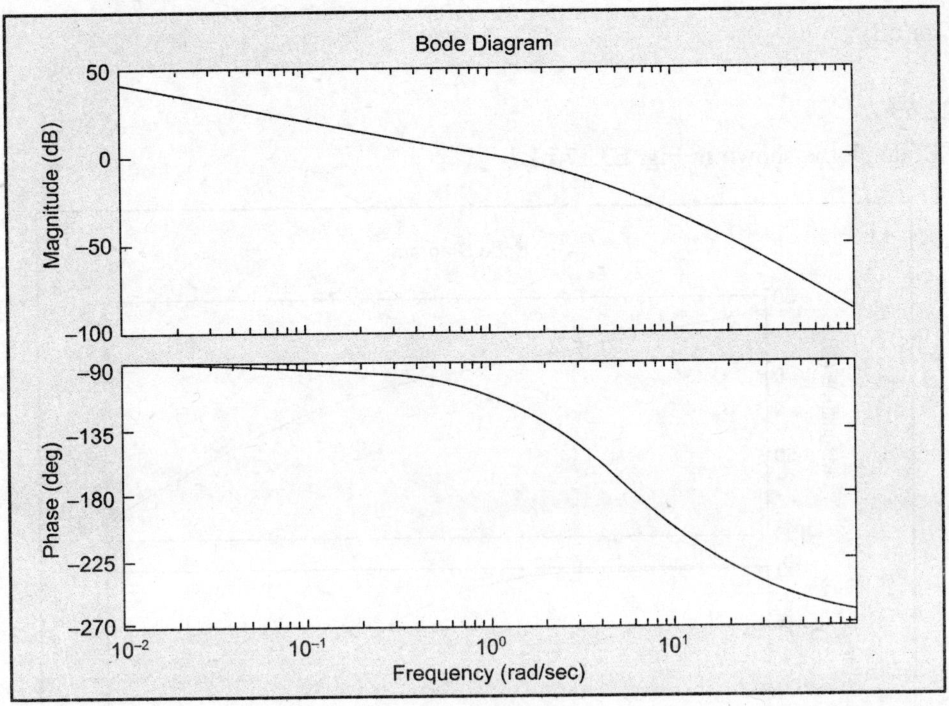

Fig. E3.17(a)

Gain K = 40, Frequency(180 deg) = 6.01, Magnitude = 0.0738277, Magnitude(dB) = –22.6356, Phase = –180.076, Gain margin(dB) = 22.6356.

Gain K = 40, Frequency(0 dB) = 1.11, Magnitude = 0.93481, Magnitude(dB) = –0.585534, Phase = –115.589, Phase margin(dB) = 64.4107

Alternate program using MATLAB margin function:

ans =

G(s)

Transfer function

$$\frac{1}{s^3+15\,s^2+36\,s}$$

Type gain, K 40

Gm =

13.5000

Pm =

65.8119

Wcp =

6

Wcg =

1.0453

```
ans =
    Gm(dB)
ans =
    22.6067
```

The Bode plot is shown in Fig. E3.17(b).

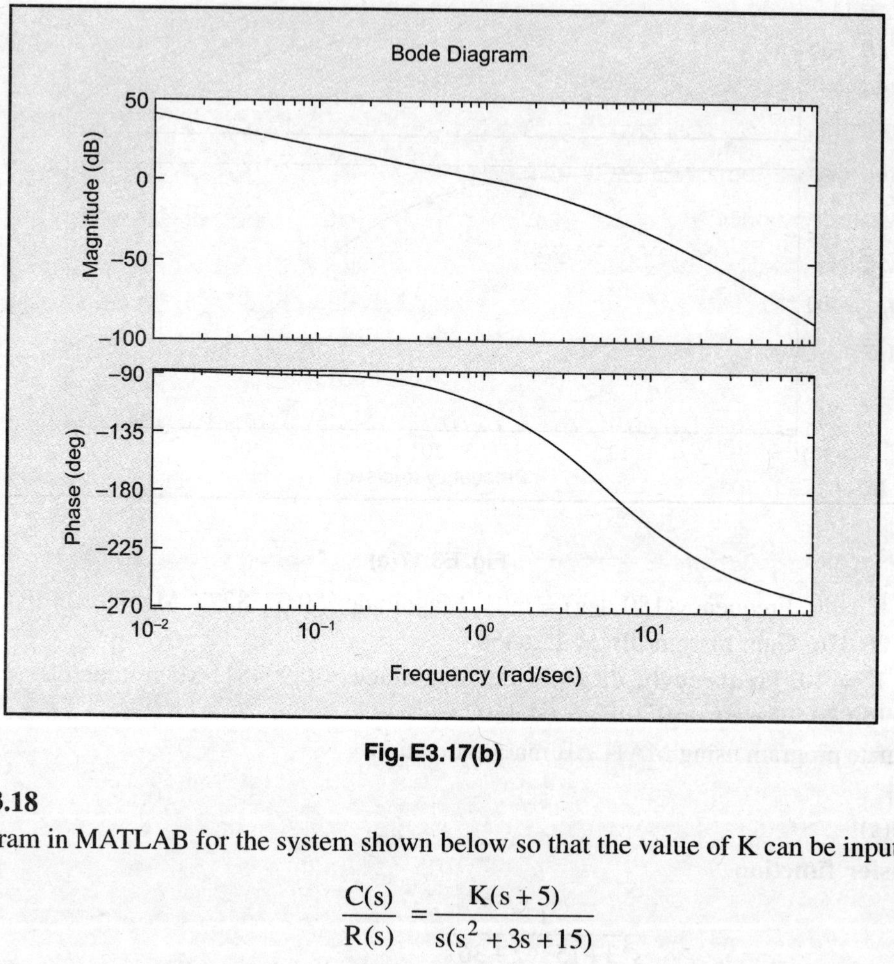

Fig. E3.17(b)

Example E3.18

Write a program in MATLAB for the system shown below so that the value of K can be input (K = 40).

$$\frac{C(s)}{R(s)} = \frac{K(s+5)}{s(s^2+3s+15)}$$

(*a*) Display the closed-loop magnitude and phase frequency response for unity feedback system with an open-loop transfer function, KG(s).

(*b*) Determine and display the peak magnitude, frequency of the peak magnitude, and bandwidth for the closed-loop frequency response for the input value of K.

Solution

```
>> %MATLAB Program
>> %Enter G(s)
>> numg = [1 5];
```

```
>> deng = [1 3 15 0];
>> 'G(s)'
>> G = tf(numg,deng)
>> %Enter K
>> K = input('Type gain,K');
>> 'T(s)'
>> T = feedback(K*G,1)
>> bode(T)
>> title('Closed-loop frequency response')
>> [M,P,w] = bode(T);
>> [Mp i] = max(M);
>> Mp
>> MpdB = 20*log10(Mp)
>> wp = w(i)
>> for i = 1:1:length(M);
>> if M(i) < = 0.707;
>> fprintf('Bandwidth = %g', w(i))
>> break
>> end
>> end
```

Computer response

```
ans =
   G(s)
```

Transfer function

$$\frac{s+5}{s^3+3s^2+15s}$$

```
Type gain, K 40
ans =
   T(s)
```

Transfer function

$$\frac{40s+200}{s^3+3s^2+55s+200}$$

```
Mp =
   11.1162
```

MpdB =

20.9192

wp =

7.5295

Bandwidth = 10.8036

The Bode plot is shown in Fig. E3.18(a).

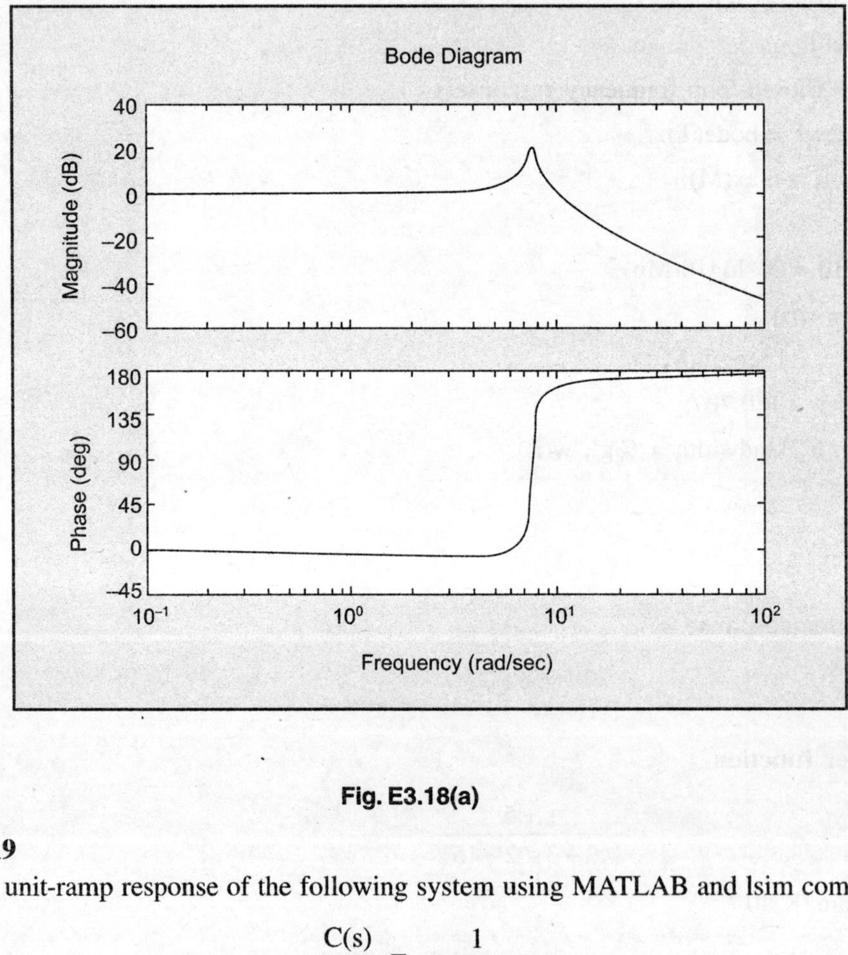

Fig. E3.18(a)

Example E3.19

Determine the unit-ramp response of the following system using MATLAB and lsim command.

$$\frac{C(s)}{R(s)} = \frac{1}{3s^2 + 2s + 1}$$

Solution

```
>> %MATLAB Program
>> %Unit-ramp response
>> num = [0 0 1];
>> den = [3 2 1];
```

```
>> t = 0:0.1:10;
>> r = t;
>> y = lsim(num,den,r,t);
>> plot(t, r, '–', t, y, 'o')
>> grid
>> title('Unit-ramp response')
>> xlabel('t Sec')
>> ylabel('Unit-ramp input and output')
>> text(1.0, 4.0, 'Unit-ramp input')
>> text(5.0, 2.0, 'Output')
```

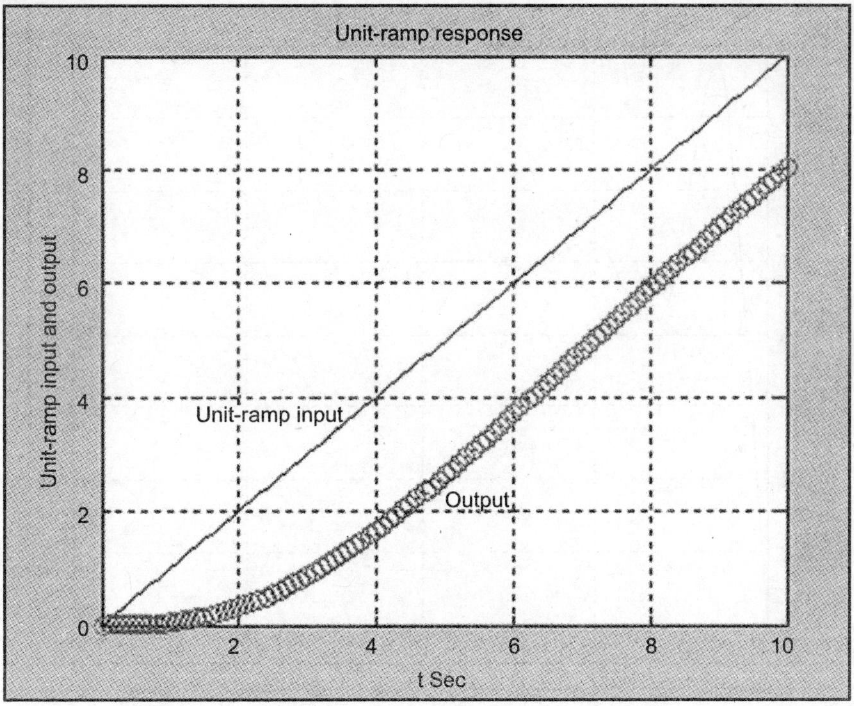

Fig. E3.19 Unit-ramp response

Example E3.20

A higher-order system is defined by

$$\frac{C(s)}{R(s)} = \frac{7s^2 + 16s + 10}{s^4 + 5s^3 + 11s^2 + 16s + 10}$$

(*a*) plot the unit-step response curve of the system using MATLAB

(*b*) obtain the rise time, peak time, maximum overshoot, and settling time using MATLAB.

Solution

```
>> %Unit-step response curve
>> num = [0 0 7 16 10];
>> den = [1 5 11 16 10];
>> t = 0:0.02:20;
>> [y, x, t] = step(num, den,t);
>> plot(t, y)
>> grid
>> title('Unit-step response')
>> xlabel('t Sec')
>> ylabel('Output y(t)')
```

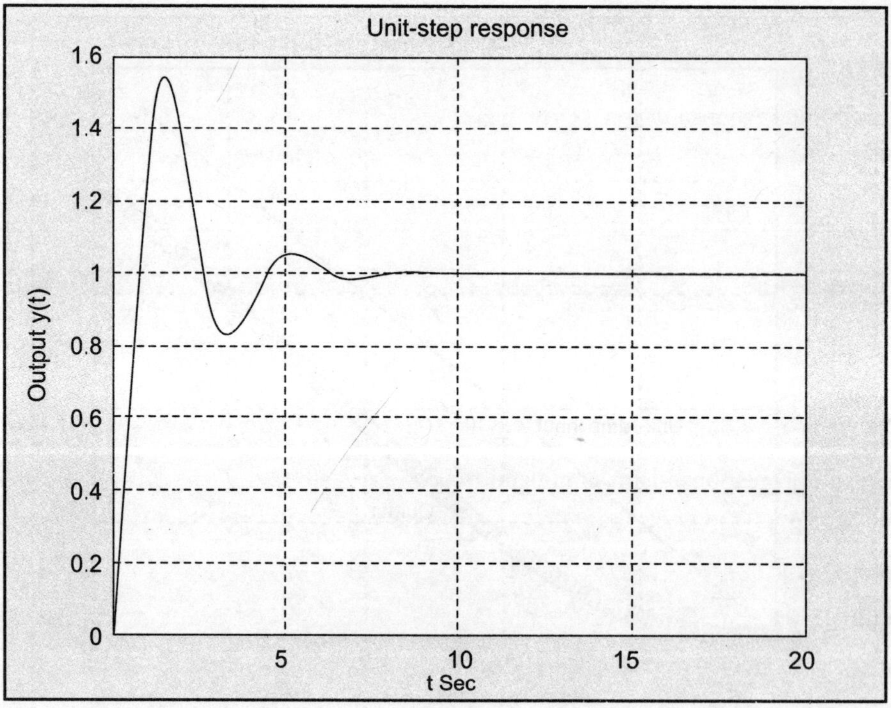

Fig. E3.20 Unit-step response

```
>> %Response to rise from 10% to 90% of its final value
>> r1 = 1; while y(r1) < 0.1, r1 = r1 + 1; end
>> r2 = 1; while y(r2) < 0.9, r2 = r2 +1; end
>> rise_time = (r2 – r1)*0.02
 rise_time =
       0.5400
```

```
>> [ymax, tp] = max(y);
>> peak_time = (tp – 1)*0.02
  peak_time =
          1.5200
>> max_overshoot = ymax – 1
   max_overshoot =
            0.5397
>> s = 1001; while y(s) > 0.98 & y(s) < 1.02; s = s – 1; end
>> settling_time = (s – 1)*0.02
  settling_time =
          6.0200
```

Example E3.21

Obtain the unit-ramp response of the following closed-loop control system whose closed-loop transfer function is given by

$$\frac{C(s)}{R(s)} = \frac{s+12}{s^3+5s^2+8s+12}$$

Determine also the response of the system when the input is given by

$$r = e^{-0.7t}$$

Solution

```
>> %Unit-ramp response-lsim command
>> num = [0 0 1 12];
>> den = [1 5 8 12];
>> t = 0:0.1:10;
>> r = t;
>> y = lsim(num, den, r, t);
>> plot(t, r, '–', t, y, '0')
>> grid
>> title('Unit-ramp response')
>> xlabel('t Sec')
>> ylabel('Output')
>> text(3.0, 6.5, 'Unit-ramp input')
>> text(6.2, 4.5, 'Output')
```

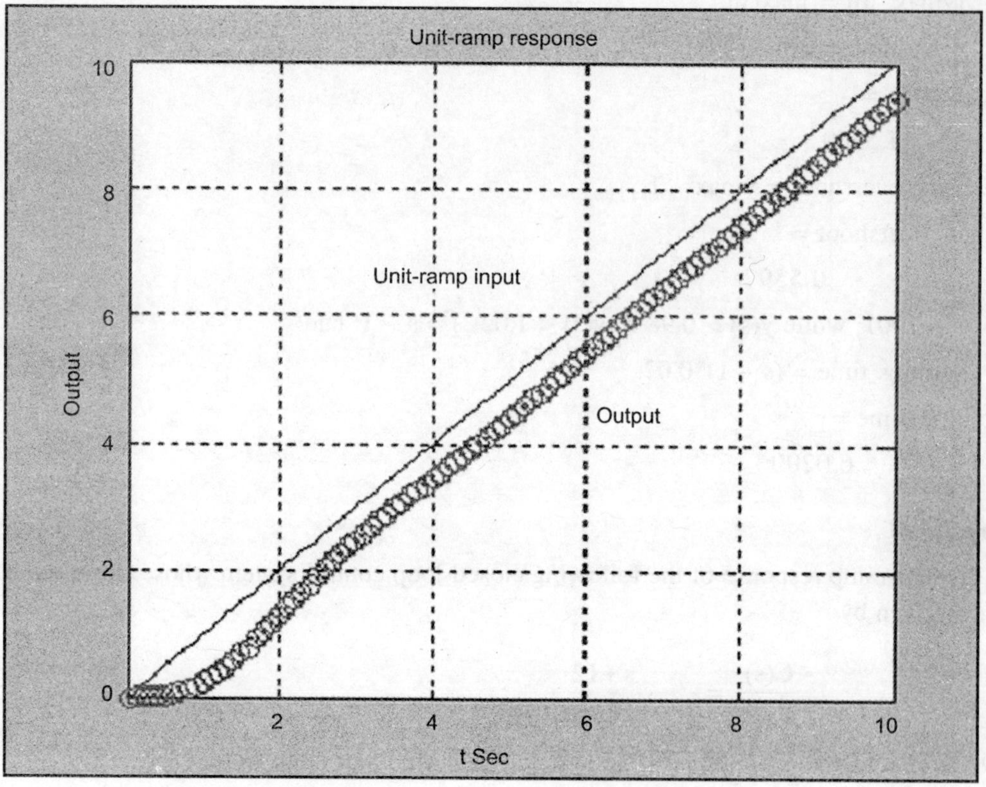

Fig. E3.21(a) Unit-ramp response curve.

```
>> %Input r1 = exp(–0.7t)
>> num = [0 0 1 12];
>> den = [1 5 8 12];
>> t = 0:0.1:12;
>> r1 = exp(–0.7*t);
>> y1 = lsim(num,den,r1,t);
>> plot(t, r1, '–', t, y1, '0')
>> grid
>> title('Response to input r1 = exp(–0.7t)')
>> xlabel('t Sec')
>> ylabel('Input and output')
>> text(0.5, 0.9, 'Input r1 = exp(–0.7t)')
>> text(6.3, 0.1, 'Output')
```

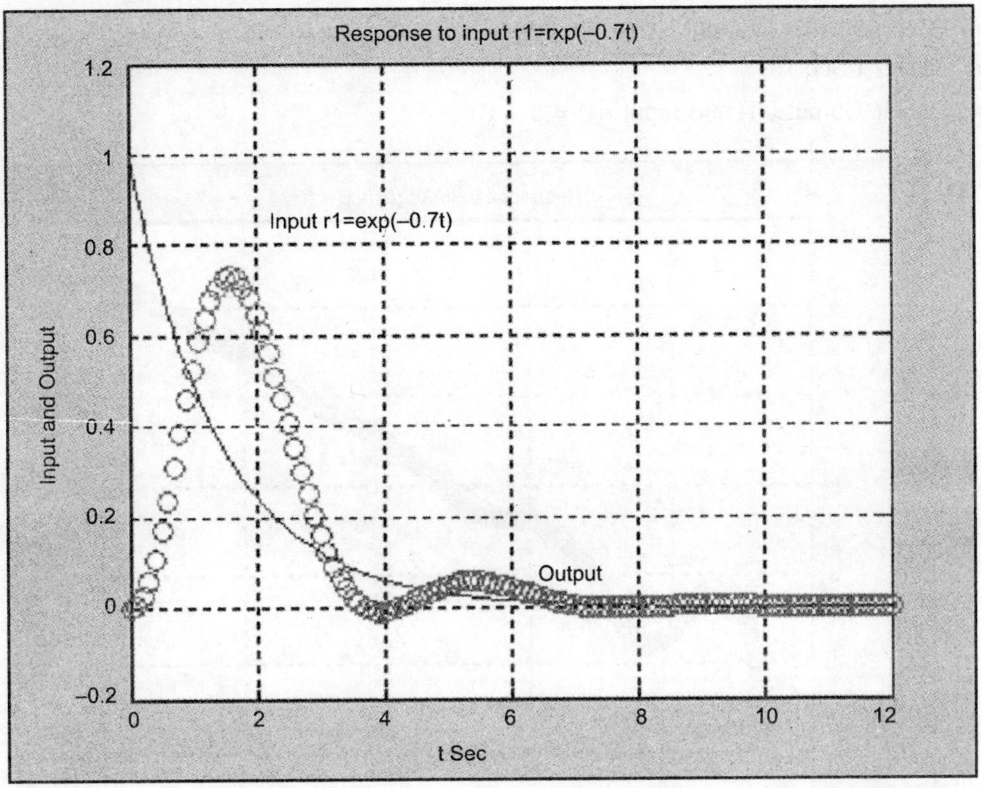

Fig. E3.21(b) Response curve for input r = $e^{-0.7t}$

Example E3.22

Obtain the response of the closed-loop system using MATLAB. The closed-loop system is defined by

$$\frac{C(s)}{R(s)} = \frac{7}{s^2 + s + 7}$$

The input r(t) is a step input of magnitude 3 plus unit-ramp input, r(t) = 3 + t.

Solution

```
>> %MATLAB Program
>> num = [0 0 7];
>> den = [1 1 7];
>> t = 0:0.05:10;
>> r = 3 + t;
>> c = lsim(num, den, r, t);
>> plot(t, r, '–', t, c, '0')
>> grid
```

```
>> title('Response to input r(t) = 3 + t')
>> xlabel('t Sec')
>> ylabel('Output c(t) and input r(t) = 3 + t')
```

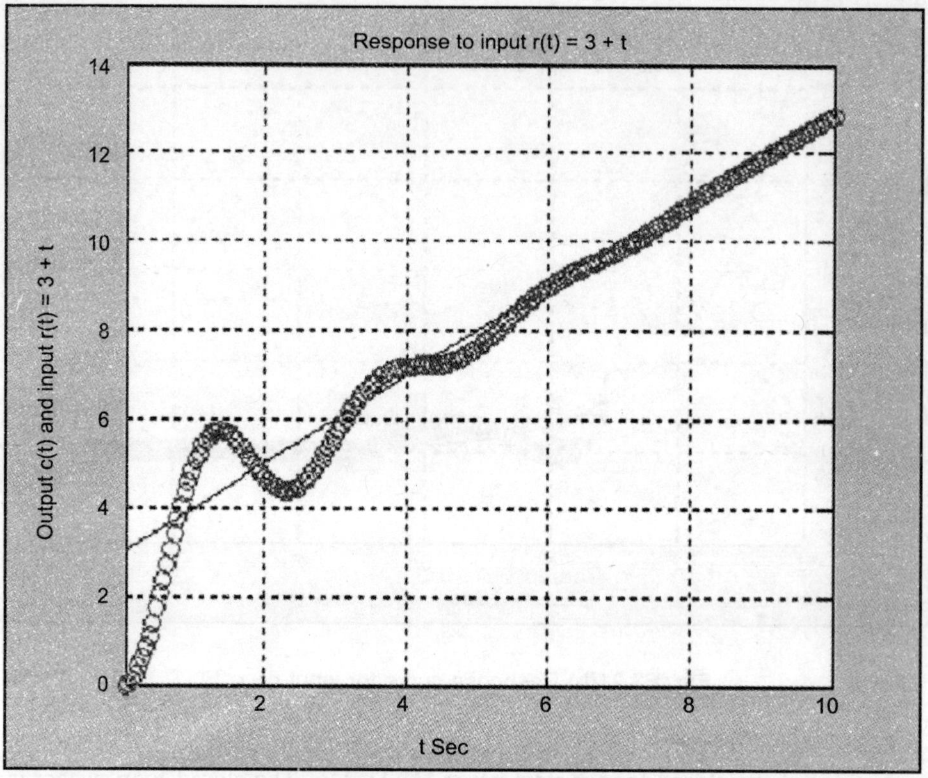

Fig. E3.22 Response to input r(t) = 3 + t

Example E3.23

Plot the root-locus diagram using MATLAB for a system whose open-loop transfer function G(s) H(s) is given by

$$G(s)H(s) = \frac{K(s+3)}{(s^2+3s+4)(s^2+2s+7)}$$

Solution

$$G(s)H(s) = \frac{K(s+3)}{(s^2+3s+4)(s^2+2s+7)} = \frac{K(s+3)}{(s^4+5s^3+17s^2+29s+28)}$$

```
>> % MATLAB Program
>> num = [0 0 0 1 3];
>> den = [1 5 17 29 28];
```

```
>> K1 = 0:0.1:2;
>> K2 = 2:0.02:2.5;
>> K3 = 2.5:0.5:10;
>> K4 = 10:1:50;
>> K5 = 50:5:800;
>> K = [K1 K2 K3 K4 K5];
>> r = rlocus(num, den, K);
>> plot(r, '0')
>> v = [–10 5 –8 8]; axis(v)
>> grid
>> title('Root-locus plot of G(s)H(s)')
>> xlabel('Real axis')
>> ylabel('Imaginary axis')
```

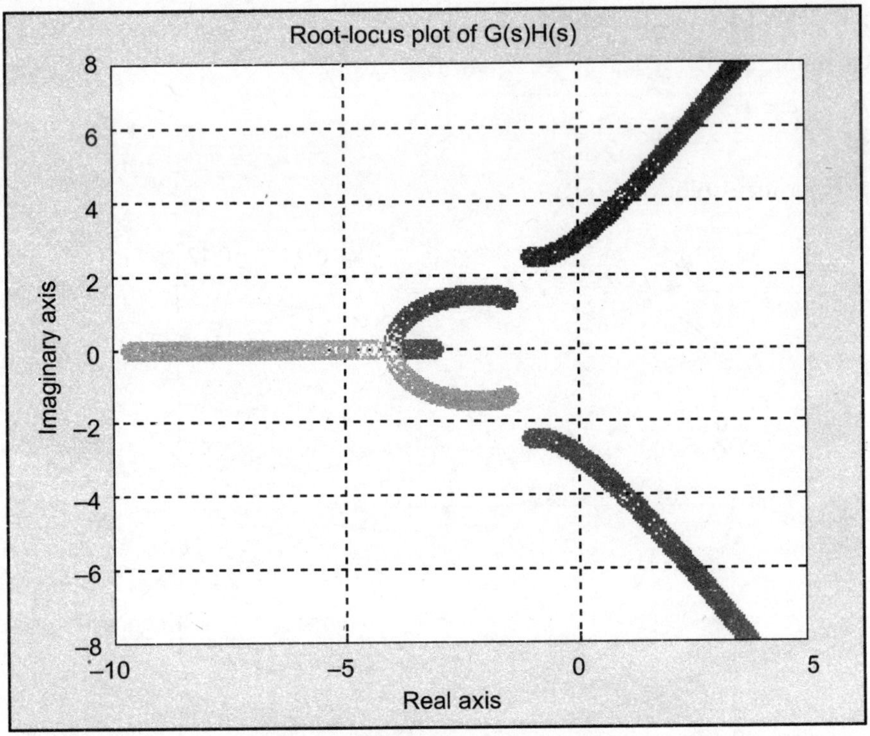

Fig. E3.23 Root-locus diagram

Example E3.24

A unity-feedback control system is defined by the following feed forward transfer function:

$$G(s) = \frac{K}{s(s^2 + 7s + 9)}.$$

(*a*) Determine the location of the closed-loop poles, if the value of gain is equal to 3.

(*b*) Plot the root loci for the system using MATLAB.

Solution

```
>> %MATLAB Program to find the closed-loop poles
>> p = [1 7 9 3];
>> roots(p)
   ans =
     –5.4495
     –1.0000
     –0.5505
>> %MATLAB Program to plot the root-loci
>> num = [0 0 0 1];
>> den = [1 5 9 0];
>> rlocus(num, den);
>> axis('square')
>> grid
>> title('Root-locus plot of G(s)')
```

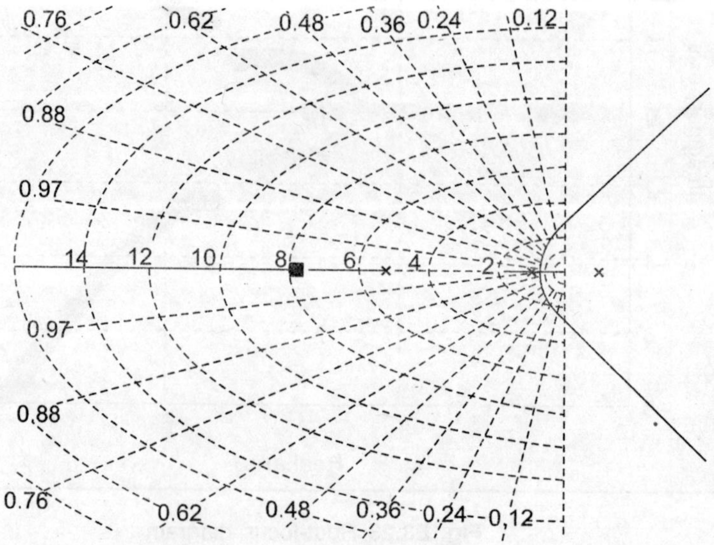

Fig. E3.24 Root-locus plot of G(s)

Example E3.25

The open-loop transfer function of a unity-feedback control system is given by

$$G(s) = \frac{1}{s^3 + 0.4s^2 + 7s + 1}$$

(*a*) Draw a Nyquist plot of G(s) using MATLAB.

(*b*) Determine the stability of the system.

Solution

```
>> % Open-loop poles
>> p = [1 0.4 7 1];
>> roots(p)
  ans =
      -0.1282 + 2.6357i
      -0.1282 - 2.6357i
      -0.1436
>> % Nyquist plot
>> num = [0 0 0 1];
>> den = [1 0.4 7 1];
>> nyquist(num,den)
>> v = [-3 3 -2 2]; axis(v); axis('square')
>> grid
>> title('Nyquist plot of G(s)')
```

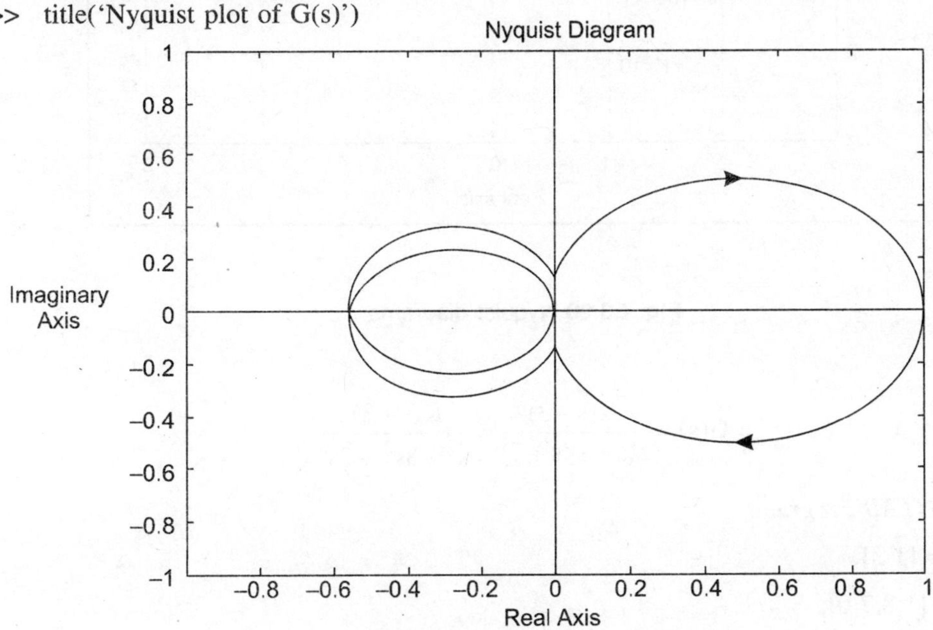

Fig. E3.25 Nyquist plot of G(s)

There are two open-loop poles in the right half s-plane and no encirclement of the critical point, the closed-loop system is unstable.

Example E3.26

The open-loop transfer function of a unity-feedback control system is given by

$$G(s) = \frac{K(s+3)}{s(s+1)(s+7)}.$$

Plot the Nyquist diagram of G(s) for K = 1, 10, and 100 using MATLAB.

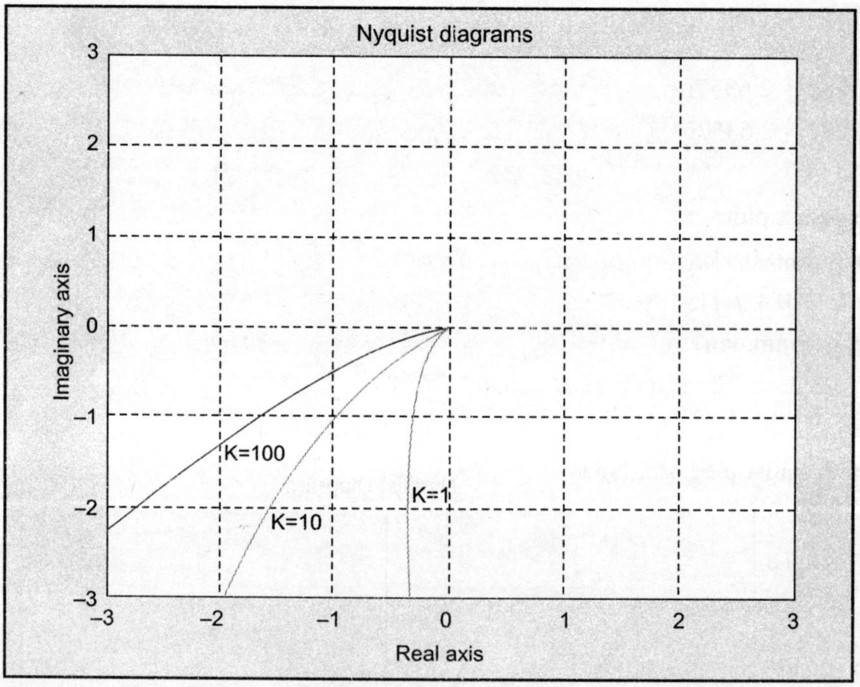

Fig. E3.26 Nyquist diagrams

Solution

$$G(s) = \frac{K(s+3)}{s(s+1)(s+7)} = \frac{K(s+3)}{s^3+8s^2+7s}$$

```
>> % MATLAB Program
>> num = [1 3];
>> den = [1 8 7 0];
```

```
>> w = 0.1:0.1:100;
>> [re1, im1, w] = nyquist(num, den, w);
>> [re2, im2, w] = nyquist(10*num, den, w);
>> [re3, im3, w] = nyquist(100*num, den, w);
>> plot(re1, im1, re2, im2, re3, im3)
>> v = [–3 3 –3 3]; axis(v)
>> grid
>> title('Nyquist diagrams')
>> xlabel('Real axis')
>> ylabel('Imaginary axis')
>> text(–0.2, –2, 'K = 1')
>> text(–1.5, –2.0, 'K=10')
>> text(–2, –1.5, 'K = 100')
```

Example E3.27

The open-loop transfer function of a negative feedback system is given by

$$G(s) = \frac{5}{s(s+1)(s+3)}$$

Plot the Nyquist diagram for

(*a*) G(s) using MATLAB

(*b*) Same open-loop transfer function. Use G(s) of a positive feedback system using MATLAB.

Solution

$$G(s) = \frac{5}{s(s+1)(s+3)} = \frac{5}{s^3 + 4s^2 + 3s}$$

```
>> %Nyquist diagrams of G(s) and –G(s)
>> num1 = [0 0 0 5];
>> den1 = [1 4 3 0];
>> num2 = [0 0 0 –5];
>> den2 = [1 4 3 0];
>> nyquist(num1, den1)
>> hold
   Current plot held
>> nyquist(num2, den2)
>> v = [–5 5 –5 5]; axis(v)
```

```
>> grid
>> text(–3, –1.8, 'G(s)')
>> text(1.9, –2, '–G(s)')
```

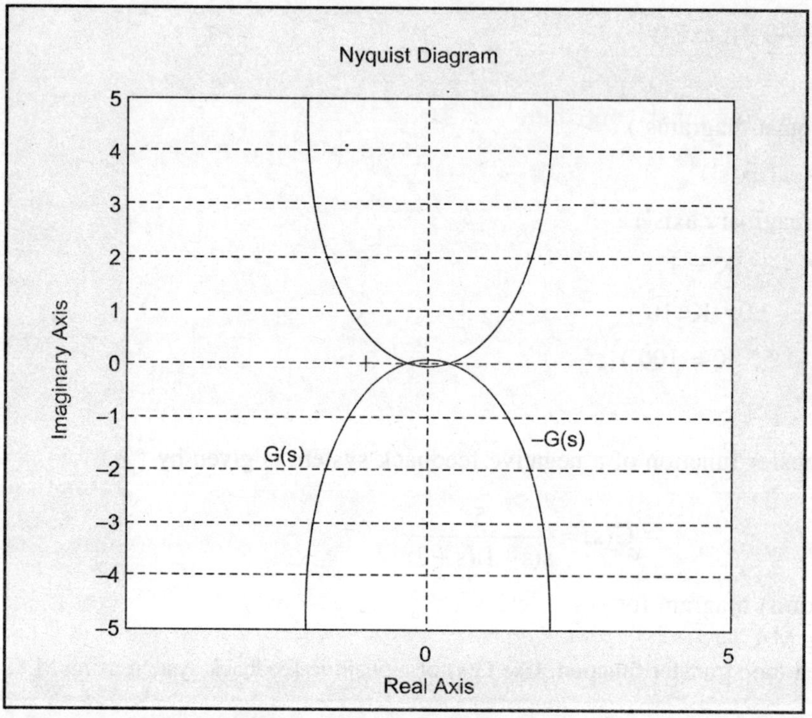

Fig. E3.27 Nyquist diagrams

Example E3.28

For the system shown in Fig. E3.28, design a compensator such that the dominant closed-loop poles are located at $s = -2 \pm j\sqrt{3}$. Plot the unit-step response curve of the designed system using MATLAB.

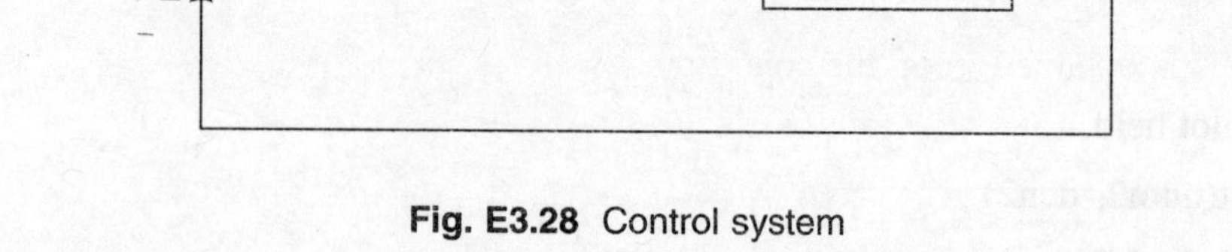

Fig. E3.28 Control system

Solution

From Fig. E3.28(a), for the closed-loop pole is to be located at $s = -2 + j\sqrt{3}$, the sum of the angle contributions of the open-loop poles (at s = 0, and s = –2) is given by –120° – 90° = –210°. For the closed-loop pole at $s = -2 + j\sqrt{3}$ we need to add 30° to the open-loop transfer function. In other words, the angle deficiency of the given open-loop transfer function at the desired closed-loop pole $s = -2 + j\sqrt{3}$ is given by

$$180° - 120° - 90° = -30°$$

The compensator must contribute 30° (lead compensator). The simplest form of a lead compensator is

$$G_c(s) = K\frac{s+a}{s+b}$$

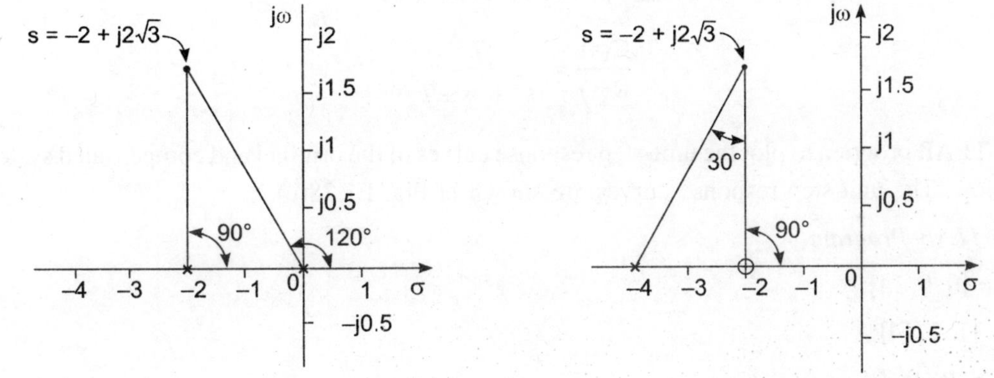

(a) Open-loop poles and a desired closed-loop pole.

(b) Compensator pole-zero configuration to contribute phase lead angle of 30º.

Fig. E3.28(a) and (b)

If we select the zero of the lead compensator at s = –2, then the pole of the compensator must be located at s = –4 in order to have a phase lead angle of 30° (see Fig. E3.28(b)).

Hence

$$G_c(s) = K\frac{s+2}{s+4}$$

The gain K is obtained from the condition

$$\left| K\frac{s+2}{s+4}\,\frac{7}{s(0.5s+1)} \right|_{s=-2+j\sqrt{3}} = 1$$

or
$$K = \left| \frac{s(s+4)}{14} \right|_{s=-2+j\sqrt{3}} = 0.5$$

or
$$G_c(s) = 0.5\frac{s+2}{s+4}$$

The open-loop transfer function of the compensated system is given by

$$G_c(s) \cdot \frac{7}{s(0.5s+1)} = 0.5\frac{s+2}{s+4}\,\frac{14}{s(s+2)} = \frac{7}{s(s+4)}$$

The closed-loop transfer function of the original system is

$$\frac{C(s)}{R(s)} = \frac{14}{s^2+2s+14}$$

The compensated system's closed-loop transfer function is

$$\frac{C(s)}{R(s)} = \frac{7}{s^2+4s+7}$$

A MATLAB program to plot the unit-step response curves of the original and compensated systems is given below. The unit-step response curves are shown in Fig. E3.28(c).

```
% MATLAB Program
num = [0 0 14];
den = [1 2 14];
numc = [0 0 7];
denc = [1 47];
t = 0: 0.01: 5;
c1 = step(num, den, t);
c2 = step(numc, denc, t );
plot(t, c1, '.', t, c2, '–')
xlabel('t Sec')
ylabel('Outputs')
text(1.5, 1.3, 'Original system')
text(1.7, 1.14, 'Compensated system')
grid
title('Unit-Step Responses of Original System and Compensated System')
```

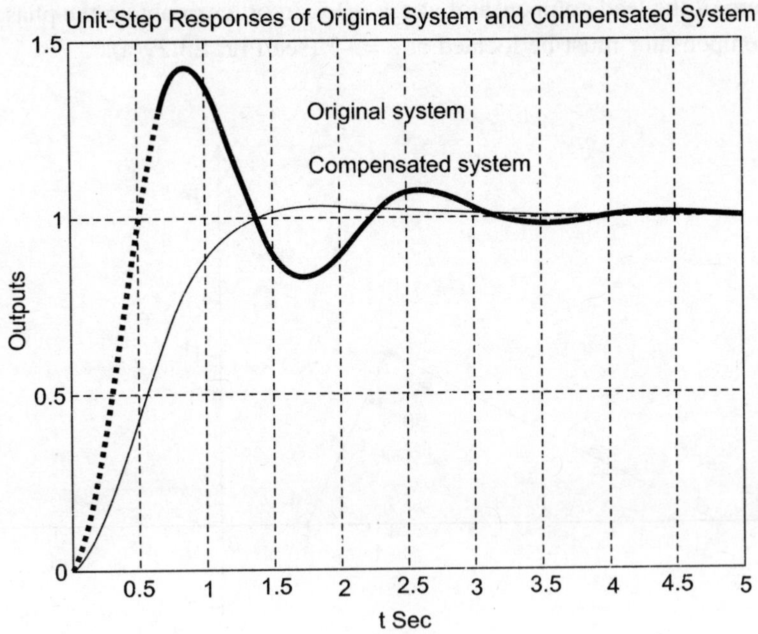

Fig. E3.28(c)

Example E3.29

For the control system shown in Fig. E3.29 design a compensator such that the dominant closed-loop poles are located at s = –1 + j1. Determine also the unit-step and unit-ramp responses of the uncompensated and compensated systems.

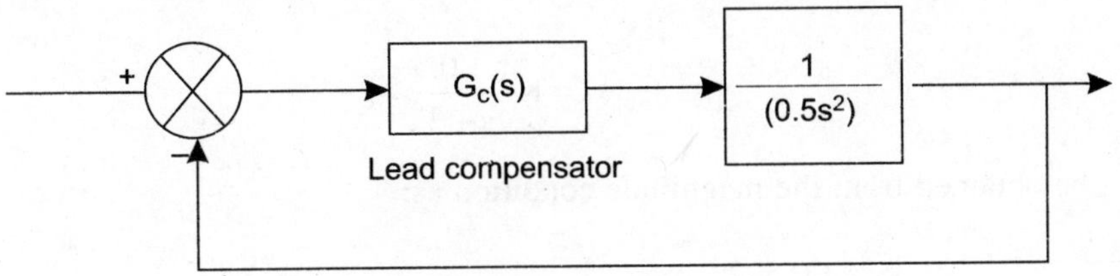

Fig. E3.29

Solution

For a desired closed-loop pole at s = –1 + j1, the angle contribution of the two open-loop poles at the origin is given by –135° – 135° = –270°. Therefore, the angel deficiency is given by

$$180° - 135° - 135° = -90°$$

Hence, the compensator must contribute 90°.

We select a lead compensator of the form

$$G_c(s) = K\frac{s+a}{s+b}$$

and choose the zero of the lead compensator at s = –0.5. In order to obtain the phase lead angle of 90°, the pole of the compensator must be located at s = –3 (see Fig. E3.29(a).

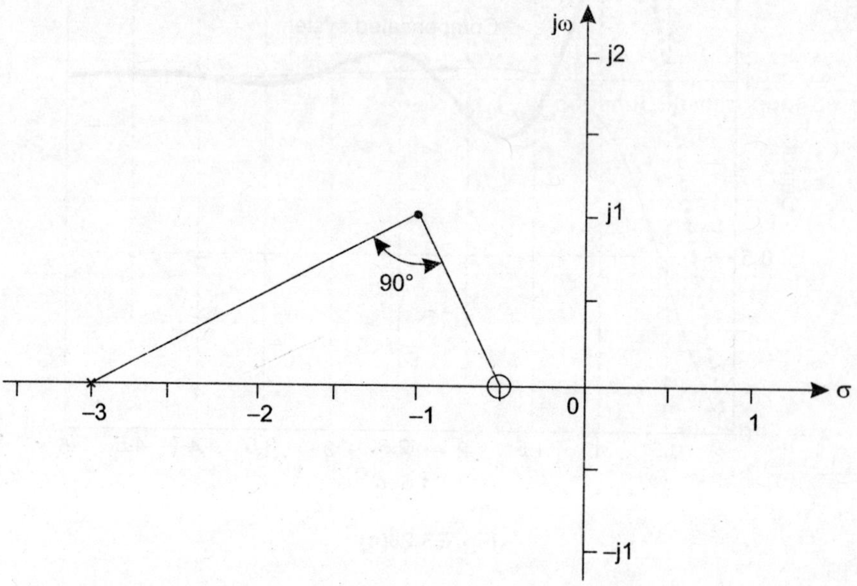

Fig. E3.29(a) Pole-zero location of lead compensator contributing 90º phase lead

Therefore,

$$G_c(s) = K\frac{s+0.5}{s+3}$$

where K must be obtained from the magnitude condition as:

$$\left|K\frac{s+0.5}{s+3}\frac{2}{s^2}\right|_{s=-1+j1} = 1$$

or
$$K = \left|\frac{(s+3)s^2}{2(s+0.5)}\right|_{s=-1+j1} = 2$$

Therefore, the lead compensator becomes

$$G_c(s) = 2\frac{s+0.5}{s+3}$$

The feed forward transfer function is

$$G_c(s)\frac{1}{0.5s^2} = \frac{4s+2}{s^3+3s^2}$$

The root-locus plot of the system is shown in Fig. E3.29(b).

The closed-loop transfer function is given by

$$\frac{C(s)}{R(s)} = \frac{4s+2}{s^3+3s^2+4s+2}$$

The closed-loop poles are located at $s = -1 \pm j1$ and $s = -1$.

Now we determine the unit-step and unit-ramp responses of the uncompensated and compensated systems.

A MATLAB program is written to obtain unit-step response curve. The resulting curves are shown in Fig.E3.29(b).

```
% MATLAB Program
num = [0 0 2];
den = [1 0 2];
nume = [0  0 4 2];
dene = [1 3 4 2];
t = 0:0.02:10;
c1 = step(num, den, t);
c2 = step(numc, denc, t);
plot(t, c1,'.', t, c2, '–')
grid
title('Unit-Step Responses of Uncompensated and Compensated Systems')
xlabel('t Sec')
ylabel('Outputs')
text(2, 0.88, 'Compensated system')
text(3.1, 1.48, 'Uncompensated system')
```

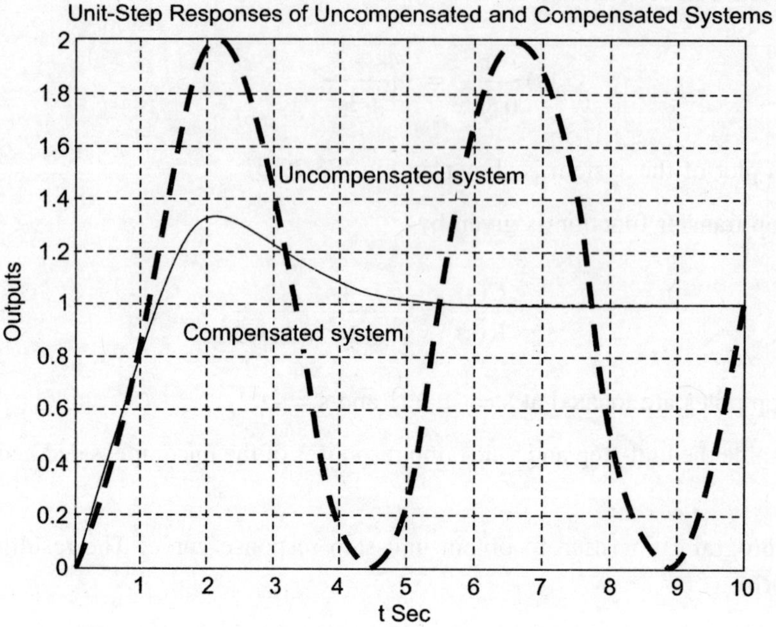

Fig.E3.29(b) Unit step response

A MATLAB program to obtain unit-ramp response curve is given below. The resulting response curves are shown in Fig. E3.29(c).

```
% MATLAB Program
num = [0 0 0 1];
den = [1 0 1 0];
nume = [0 0 0 4 2];
dene = [1 3 4 2 0];
t = 0:0.02:15;
c1 = step(num, den, t);
c2 = step(numc, denc, t);
plot(,t, c1, '.', t, c2, '–')
grid
title('Unit-Ramp Responses of Uncompensated and Compensated Systems')
xlabel('t Sec')
ylabel('Input and Outputs')
legend('.', 'uncompensated system', '–', 'compensated system')
```

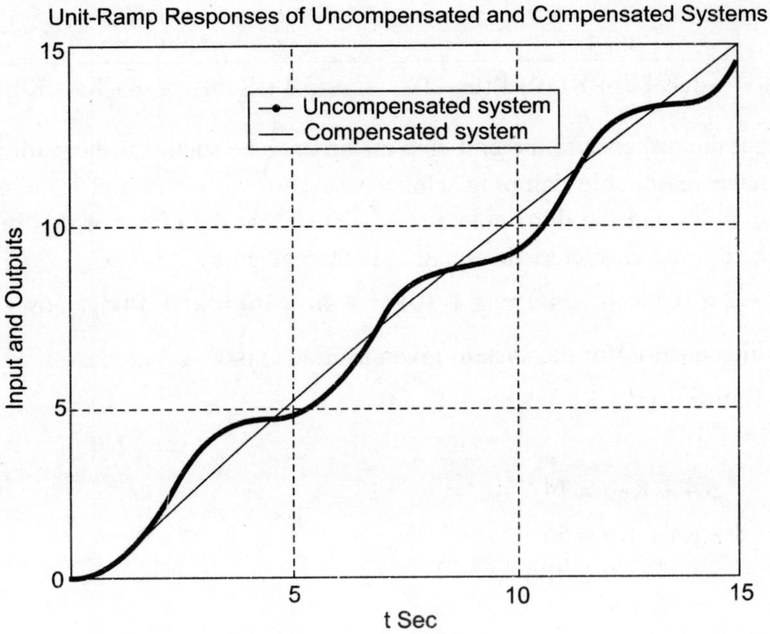

Fig. E3.29 (c) Unit Ramp response

Example E3.30

The PID control of a second-order plant G(s) control system is shown in Fig. E3.30. Consider the reference input R(s) is held constant. Design a control system such that the response to any step disturbance will be damped out in 2 to 3 secs. in terms of the 2% settling time. Select the configuration of the closed-loop poles such that there is a pair of dominant closed-loop poles. Obtain the response to the unit-step disturbance input and to the unit-step reference input.

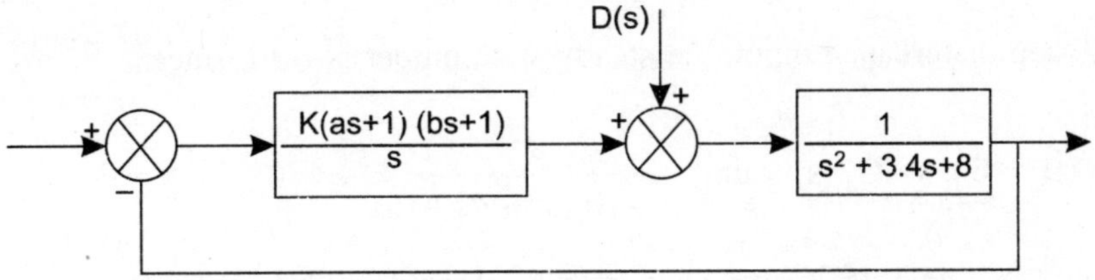

Fig. E3.30

Solution

The transfer function is

$$G_c(s) = \frac{K(as+1)(bs+1)}{s}$$

The closed-loop transfer function is given by

$$\frac{C_d(s)}{D(s)} = \frac{s}{s(s^2+3.4s+8)+K(as+1)(bs+1)} = \frac{s}{s^3+(3.4+Kab)s^2+(8+Ka+Kb)s+K} \quad (1)$$

It is required that the response to the unit-step disturbance be such that the settling time be 2 to 3s and the system have reasonable damping. Hence, we chose $\xi = 0.5$ and $\omega_n = 4$ rad/s for the dominant closed-loop poles and the third pole at $s = -10$ so that the effect of this real pole on the response is small. The desired characteristic equation is then given by

$$(s + 10)(s^2 + 2 \times 0.5 \times 4s + 4^2) = (s + 10)(s^2 + 4s + 16) = s^3 + 14s^2 + 56s + 160$$

The characteristic equation for the system given by Eq.(1) is

$$s^3 + (3.4 + Kab)s^2 + (8 + Ka + Kb)s + K = 0$$

Therefore

$$3.4 + Kab = 14$$

$$8 + Ka + Kb = 56$$

$$K = 160$$

which gives

$$ab = 0.06625,\ a + b = 0.3$$

The PID controller now is given by

$$G_c(s) = \frac{K[abs^2+(a+b)s+1]}{s} = \frac{160(0.06625s^2+0.3s+1)}{s} = \frac{10.6(s^2+4.528s+15.09)}{s}$$

With this PID controller, the response to the disturbance is

$$C_d(s) = \frac{s}{s^3+14s^2+56s+160}D(s) = \frac{s}{(s+10)(s^2+4s+16)}D(s)$$

For a unit-step disturbance input, the steady-state output is zero, since

$$\lim_{t\to\infty} c_d(t) = \lim_{s\to 0} s\ C_d(s) = \lim_{s\to 0} \frac{s^2}{(s+10)(s^2+4s+16)}\frac{1}{s} = 0$$

The response to a unit-step disturbance input is obtained with MATLAB program. The response curve is shown in Fig. E3.30(a). From the response curve we note that the settling time is approximately 2.7 s. The response damps out rather quickly. Hence, the system designed is acceptable.

```
% Response to unit-step disturbance input
numd = [0 0 1 0];
 dend = [1 14 56 160];
   t = 0:0.01:5;
```

```
[c1, x1, t] = step(numd, dend, t);
plot(t, c1)
grid
title('Response to Unit-Step Disturbance Input')
xlabel('t Sec')
ylabel('Output to Disturbance Input')
```

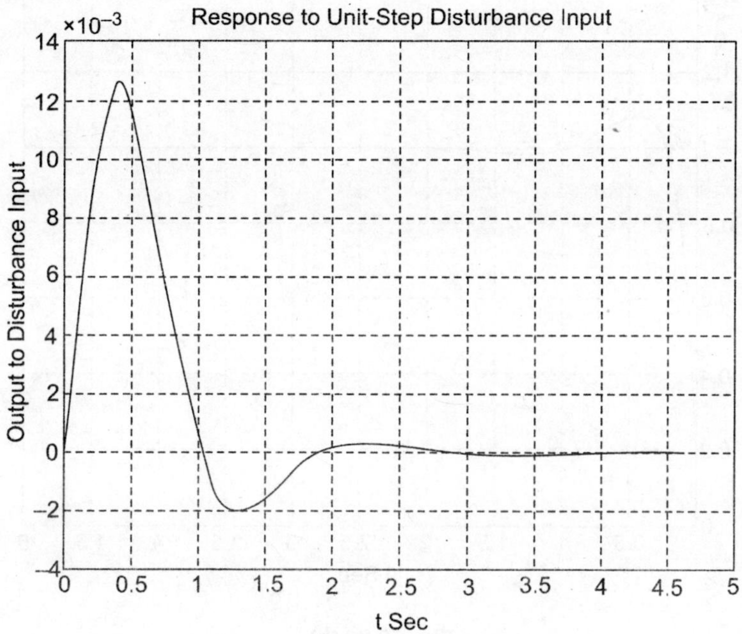

Fig. E3.30 (a)

For the reference input r(t), the closed-loop transfer function is

$$\frac{C_r(s)}{R(s)} = \frac{10.6(s^2 + 4.528s + 15.09)}{s^3 + 14s^2 + 56s + 160} = \frac{10.6s^2 + 48s + 160}{s^3 + 14s^2 + 56s + 160}$$

The response to a unit-step ***reference*** input is obtained by the MATLAB program. The resulting response curve is shown in Fig. E3.30(b). The response curve shows that the maximum overshoot is 7.3% and the settling is 1.7s. Thus, the system has quite acceptable response characteristics.

```
% Response to unit-step reference input
numr = [0 10.6 48 160];
denr = [1 14 56 160];
t = 0:0.01:5;
```

```
[c2, x2, t] = step(numr, denr, t);
plot(t, c2)
grid
title('Response to Unit-Step Reference Input')
xlabel('t Sec')
ylabel('Output to Reference Input')
```

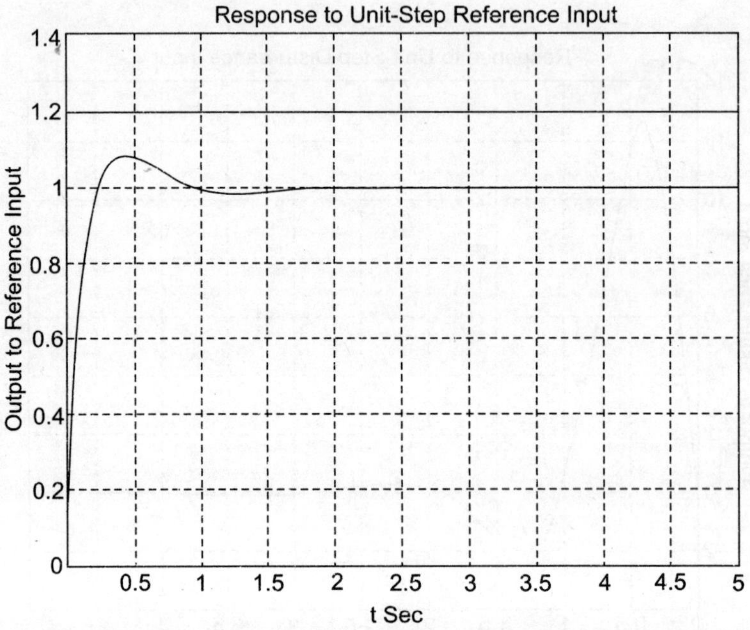

Fig. E3.30 (b)

Example E3.31

For the closed-loop control system shown in Fig. E3.31, obtain the range of gain K for stability and plot a root-locus diagram for the system.

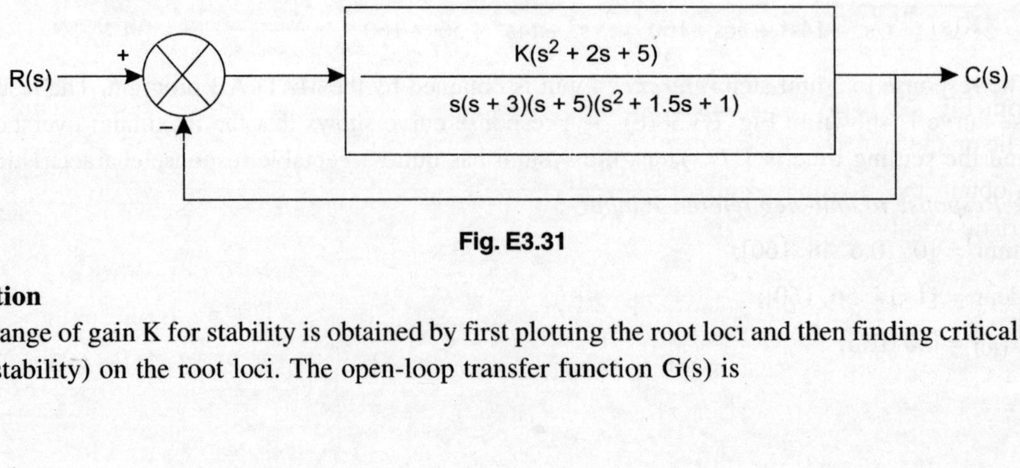

Fig. E3.31

Solution

The range of gain K for stability is obtained by first plotting the root loci and then finding critical points (for stability) on the root loci. The open-loop transfer function G(s) is

$$G(s) = \frac{K(s^2+2s+5)}{s(s+3)(s+5)(s^2+1.5s+1)} = \frac{K(s^2+2s+5)}{s^5+9.5s^4+28s^3+20s^2+15s}$$

A MATLAB program to generate generate a plot of the root loci for the system is given below. The resulting root-locus plot is shown in Fig. E3.31(a).

```
% MATLAB Program
num = [0 0 0 1 2 5];
den = [1 9.5 28 20 15 0];
rlocus(num, den)
v = [-8 2 -5 5]; axis(v); axis('square')
grid
title('Root-Locus Plot')
```

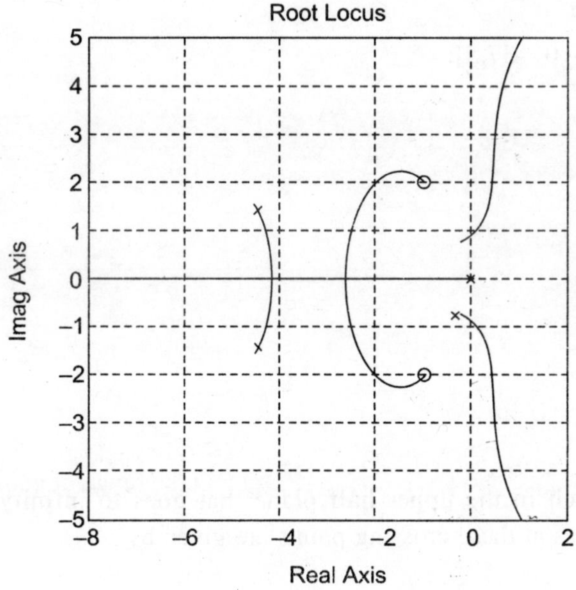

Fig. E3.31 (a)

From Fig. E3.31(a), we notice that the system is conditionally stable. All critical points for stability lie on the jω axis.

To obtain the crossing points of the root loci with the jω axis, we substitute s = jω into the characteristic equation

$$s^5 + 9.5s^4 + 28s^3 + 20s^2 + 15s + K(s^2 + 2s + 5) = 0$$

or $$(j\omega)^5 + 9.5(j\omega)^4 + 28(j\omega)^3 + (20 + K)(j\omega)^2 + (15 + 2K)(j\omega) + 5K = 0$$

or $$[9.5\omega^4 - (20 + K)\,\omega^2 + 5K] + j[\omega^5 - 28\omega^3 + (15 + 2K)\,\omega] = 0$$

Equating the real part and imaginary part equal to zero, respectively, we get

$$9.5\omega^4 - (20 + K)\,\omega^2 + 5K = 0 \quad (1)$$

$$\omega^5 - 28\omega^3 + (15 + 2K)\,\omega = 0 \quad (2)$$

Eqn. (2) can be written as

$$\omega = 0$$

or $$\omega^4 - 28\omega^2 + 15 + 2K = 0 \quad (3)$$

$$K = \frac{-\omega^4 + 28\omega^2 - 15}{2} \quad (4)$$

Substituting Eqn. (4) into Eqn. (1), we obtain

$$9.5\omega^4 - [20 + 1/2(-\omega^4 + 28\omega^2 - 15)]\,\omega^2 - 2.5\omega^4 + 70\omega^2 - 37.5 = 0$$

or $$0.5\omega^6 - 2\omega^4 + 57.5\omega^2 - 37.5 = 0$$

The roots of the above equation can be obtained by MATLAB program given below:

```
% MATLAB program
a = [0.5 0 –20 57.5 0 –37.5];
roots(a)
```

Output is:

```
ans =
  –2.4786 + 2.1157i
  –2.4786 – 2.1157i
   2.4786 + 2.1157i
   2.4786 – 2.1157i
   0.8155
  –0.8155
```

The root-locus branch in the upper half plane that goes to infinity crosses the $j\omega$ axis at $\omega = 0.8155$. The gain values at these crossing points are given by

$$K = \frac{-0.8155^4 + 28 \times 0.8155^2 - 15}{2} = 1.5894 \quad \text{for } \omega = 0.8155$$

For this K value, we obtain the range of gain K for stability as

$$1.5894 > K > 0$$

Example E3.32

For the control system shown in Fig. E3.32:

(*a*) Plot the root loci for the system

(*b*) Find the range of gain K for stability.

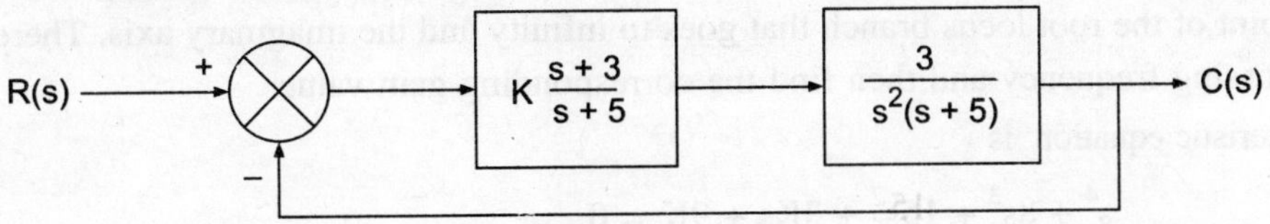

Fig. E3.32

Solution

The open-loop transfer function G(s) is given by

$$G(s) = K\frac{s+3}{s+5}\,\frac{3}{s^2(s+3)} = \frac{3K(s+3)}{s^4+8s^3+15s^2}$$

A MATLAB program to generate the root-locus plot is given below. The resulting plot is shown in Fig. E3.32(a).

```
% MATLAB Program
num = [0 0 0 1 3];
den = [1 8 15 0 0];
rlocus(num, den)
v = [–64 –5 5]; axis(v); axis('square')
grid
title('Root-Locus Plot')
```

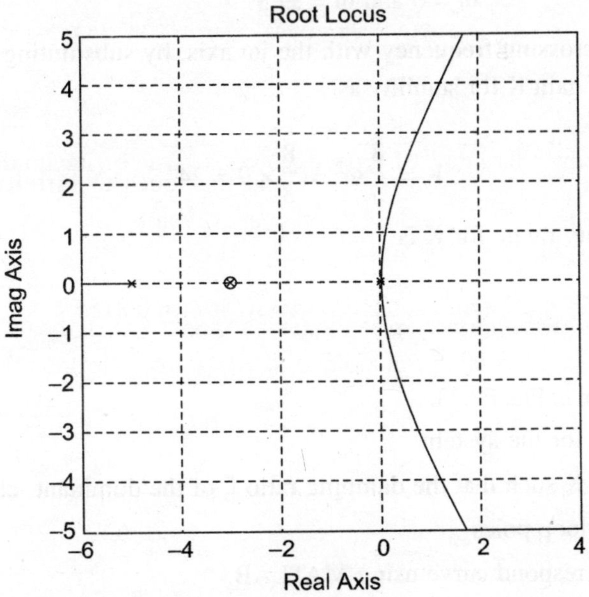

Fig. E3.32(a)

From Fig. E3.32 (a), we notice that the critical value of gain K for stability corresponds to the crossing point of the root locus branch that goes to infinity and the imaginary axis. Therefore, we first find the crossing frequency and then find the corresponding gain value.

The characteristic equation is

$$s^4 + 8s^3 + 15s^2 + 3Ks + 9K = 0$$

Substituting s = jω into the characteristic equation, we get

$$(j\omega)^4 + 8(j\omega)^3 + 15(j\omega)^2 + 3K(j\omega) + 9K = 0$$

or

$$(\omega^4 - 15\omega^2 + 9K) + j\omega(-8\omega^2 + 3K) = 0$$

Equating the real part and imaginary part of the above equation to zero, respectively, we obtain

$$\omega^4 - 15\omega^2 + 9K = 0 \quad (1)$$

$$\omega(-8\omega^2 + 3K) = 0 \quad (2)$$

Eq.(2) can be rewritten as

$$\omega = 0$$

or

$$-8\omega^2 + 3K = 0 \quad (3)$$

Substituting the value of K in Eq.(1), we get

$$\mu\omega^4 - 15\omega^2 + 9\text{x}\frac{8}{3}\omega^2 = 0$$

or

$$\omega^4 + 9\omega^2 = 0$$

which gives

$$\omega = 0 \text{ and } \omega = \pm j\,3$$

Since ω = j3 is the crossing frequency with the jω axis, by substituting ω = 3 into Eq.(E.3) we obtain the critical value of gain K for stability as

$$K = \frac{8}{3}\omega^2 = \frac{8}{3} \times 9 = 24$$

Therefore, the stability range for K is

$24 > K > 0$.

Example E3.33

For the control system shown in Fig. E3.33:

(*a*) Plot the root loci for the system

(*b*) Find the value of K such that the damping ratio ζ of the dominant closed-loop poles is 0.6

(*c*) Obtain all closed-loop poles

(*d*) Plot the unit-step respond curve using MATLAB.

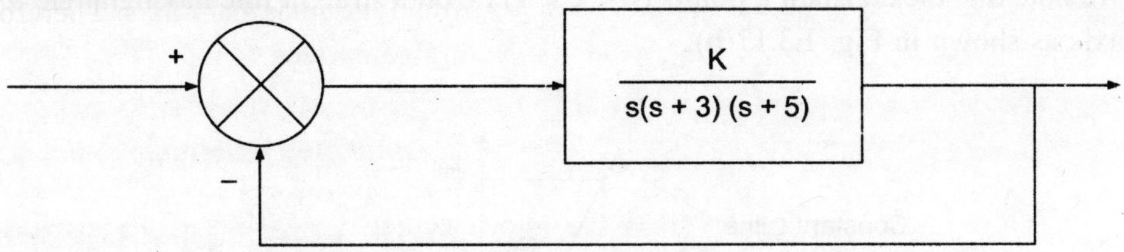

Fig. E3.33

Solution

(*a*) The MATLAB program given below generates a root-locus plot for the given system. The resulting plot is shown in Fig. E3.33(a).

```
% MATLAB Program
num = [0 0 0 1];
den = [1 8 15 0];
rlocus(num, den)
v = [–6 4 –5 5]; axis(v); axis('square')
grid
title('Root-Locus Plot')
```

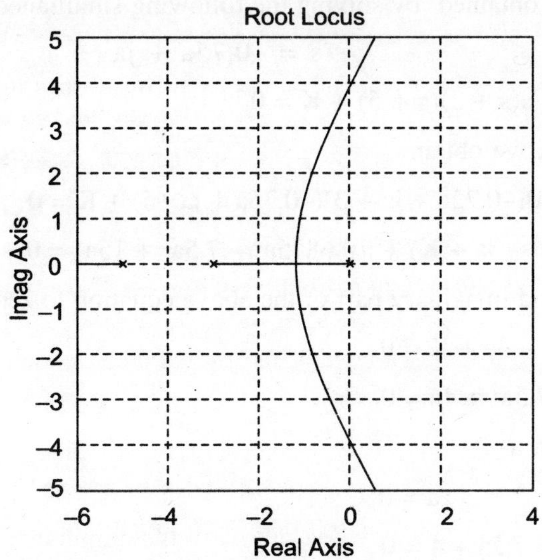

Fig. E3.33(a)

(*b*) We note that the constant ζ points $(0 < \zeta < 1)$ lie on a straight line having angle θ from the $j\omega$ axis as shown in Fig. E3.17(b).

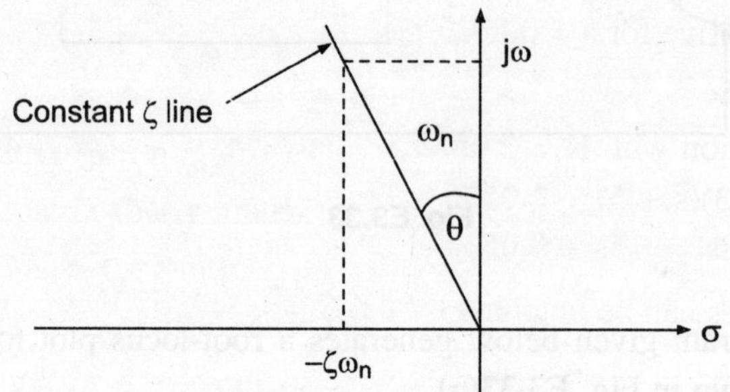

Fig. E3.33(b)

From Fig. E3.33(b), we obtain

$$\sin\theta = \frac{\zeta\omega_n}{\omega_n} = \zeta$$

Also that $\zeta = 0.6$ line can be defined by

$$s = -0.75a + ja$$

where a is a variable $(0 < a < \infty)$. To obtain the value of K such that the damping ratio ζ of the dominant closed-loop poles is 0.6 we determine the intersection of the line $s = -0.75a + ja$ and the root locus. The intersection point can be obtained by solving the following simultaneous equations for a.

$$s = -0.75a + ja \qquad (1)$$

$$s(s + 3)(s + 5) + K = 0 \qquad (2)$$

From Eqns. (1) and (2), we obtain

$$(-0.75a + ja)(-0.75a + ja + 3)(-0.75a + ja + 5) + K = 0$$

or $$(1.8281a^3 - 2.1875a^2 - 3a + K) + j(0.6875a^3 - 7.5a^2 + 15a) = 0$$

Equating the real part and imaginary part of the above equation to zero, respectively, we obtain

$$1.8281a^3 - 2.1875a^2 - 3a + K = 0 \qquad (3)$$

$$0.6875a^3 - 7.5a^2 + 4a = 0 \qquad (4)$$

Eqn.(4) can be rewritten as

$$a = 0$$

or $$0.6875a^2 - 7.5a + 4 = 0$$

or $$a^2 - 10.90991a + 5.8182 = 0$$

or $$(a - 0.5623)(a - 10.3468) = 0$$

Therefore, $a = 0.5323$ or $a = 10.3468$

From Eqn. (3), we obtain

$$K = -1.8281a^3 + 2.1875a^2 + 3a = 2.0535 \quad \text{for } a = 0.5626$$

$$K = -1.8281a^3 + 2.1875a^2 + 3a = -1759.74 \quad \text{for } a = 10.3468$$

Since the K value is positive for a = 0.5623 and negative for a = –10.3468, we select a = 0.5623. The required gain K is 2.0535.

The characteristic equation with K = 2.0535 is then

$$s(s + 3)(s + 5) + 2.0535 = 0$$

or

$$s^3 + 8s^2 + 15s + 2.0535 = 0$$

(*c*) The closed-loop poles can be obtained by the following MATLAB program.

```
% MATLAB Program
p = [1 8 15 2.0535];
roots(p)

ans =
     -5.1817
     -2.6699
     -0.1484
```

Hence, the closed-loop poles are located at

$$s = -5.1817, \quad s = -2.6699, \quad s = -4.1565$$

(*d*) The unit-step response of the system for K = 2.0535 can be obtained from the following MATLAB program. The resulting unit-step response curve is shown in Fig. E3.33(c).

```
% MATLAB Program
num = [0 0 0 2.0535];
den = [1 8 15 2.0535];
step(num, den)
grid
title('Unit-Step Response')
xlabel('t Sec')
ylabel('Output')
```

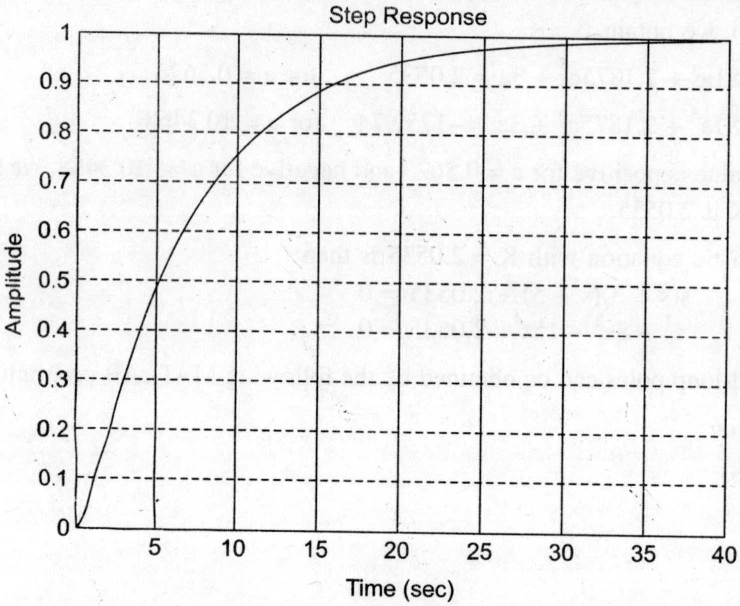

Fig. E3.33 (c)

Example E3.34

For the control system shown in Fig. E3.34, the open-loop transfer function is given by

$$G(s) = \frac{1}{s(s+2)(0.6s+1)}$$

Design a compensator for the system such that the static velocity error constant K_v is 5 s^{-1}, the phase margin is at least 50°, and the gain margin is at least 10 dB.

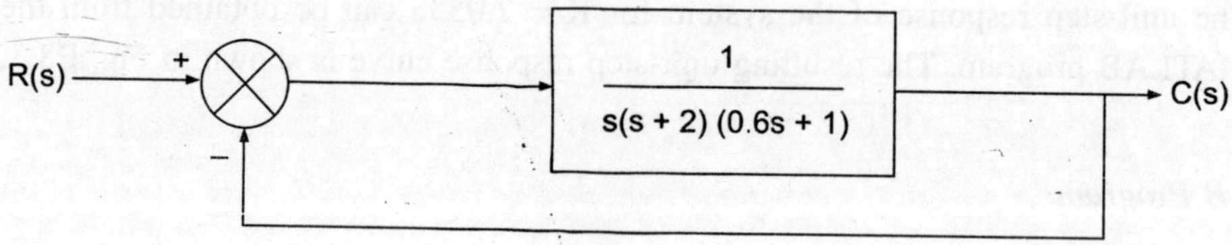

Fig. E3.34

Solution

We can use a lag compensator of the form

$$G_c(s) = K_c\beta\frac{Ts+1}{\beta Ts+1} = K_c\frac{s+\frac{1}{T}}{s+\frac{1}{\beta T}} \qquad \beta > 1$$

Defining $K_c\beta = K$

and $G_1(s) = KG(s) = \dfrac{K}{s(s+2)(0.6s+1)}$

we adjust the gain K to meet the required static velocity error constant.

Hence

$$K_v = \lim_{s\to 0} sG_c(s)G(s) = \lim_{s\to 0} s\frac{Ts+1}{\beta Ts+1}G_1(s) = \lim_{s\to 0} sG_1(s) = \lim_{s\to 0}\frac{sK}{s(s+2)(0.6s+1)} = K/2 = 5$$

or $K = 10$

With K = 10, the compensated system satisfies the steady-state performance requirement.

We can now plot the Bode diagram of

$$G_1(j\omega) = \frac{10}{j\omega(j\omega+2)(0.6j\omega+1)}$$

The magnitude curve and phase-angle curve of $G_1(j\omega)$ are shown in Fig. E3.34(a). From this plot, the phase margin is found to be –20°, which shows that the system is unstable.

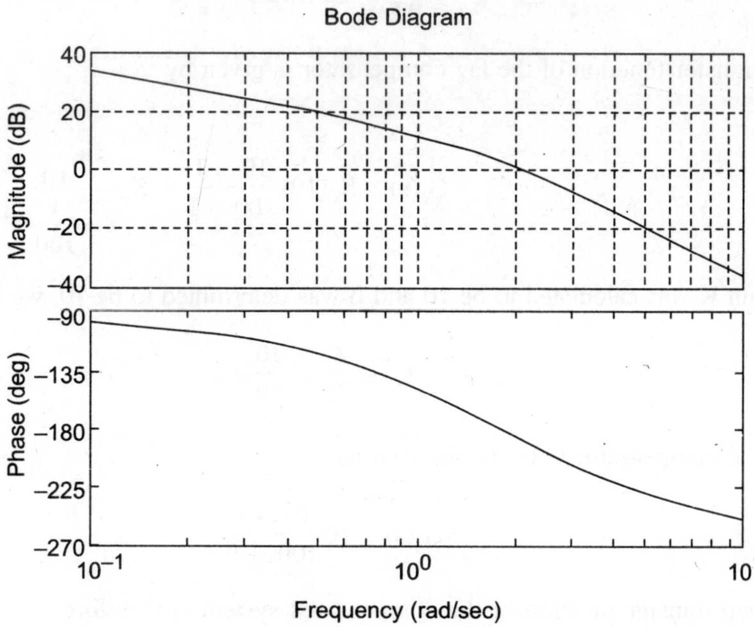

Fig. E3.34(a) Bode diagrams for G_1 = KG (gain-adjusted but uncompensated system), G_c/K (gain-adjusted compensator), and G_cG (compensated system)

The addition of a lag compensator modifies the phase curve of the Bode diagram and therefore we must allow 5° to 12° to the specified phase margin to compensate for the modification of the phase curve. Since the frequency corresponding to a phase margin of 50° is 0.7 rad/s, the new gain crossover frequency (of the compensated system) must be selected near this value. We choose the corner frequency ω = 1/T. Since this corner frequency is not too far below the new gain crossover frequency, the modification in the phase curve may not be small. Also, we add about 12° to the given phase margin as an allowance to account for the lag angle introduced by the lag compensator. The required phase margin is now 52°. The phase angle of the uncompensated open-loop transfer function is –128° at about ω = 0.5 rad/s. Hence, we choose the new gain crossover frequency to be 0.5 rad/s. In order to bring the magnitude curve down to 0 dB, the lag compensator is given the necessary attenuation, which in this case is –20 dB.

Therefore,

$$20\log\frac{1}{\beta} = -20$$

or

$$\beta = 10$$

The other corner frequency ω = 1(βT). This corresponds to the pole of the lag compensator and is obtained as

$$\frac{1}{\beta T} = 0.01 \text{ rad/s}$$

Hence, the transfer function of the lag compensator is given by

$$G_c(s) = K_c(10)\frac{10s+1}{100s+1} = K_c\frac{s+\frac{1}{10}}{s+\frac{1}{100}}$$

Since the gain K was calculated to be 10 and β was determined to be 10, we have

$$K_c = \frac{K}{\beta} = \frac{10}{10} = 1$$

Therefore, the compensator $G_c(s)$ is obtained as

$$G_c(s) = 10\frac{10s+1}{100s+1}$$

The open-loop transfer function of the compensated system is therefore

$$G_c(s)G(s) = \frac{10(10s+1)}{s(100s+1)(s+2)(0.6s+1)}$$

The magnitude and phase-angle curves of $G_c(j\omega)G(j\omega)$ are shown in Fig. E3.34(b).

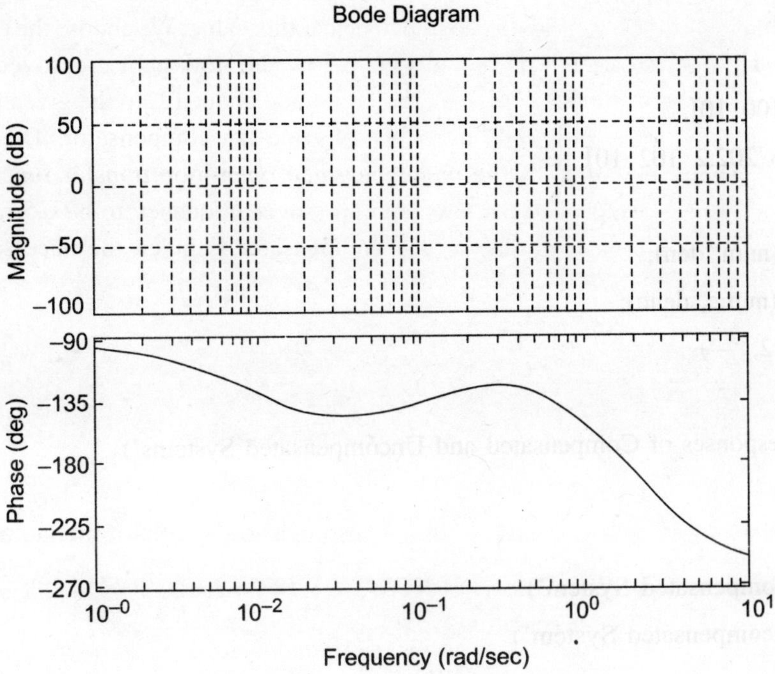

Fig. E3.34(b)

The phase margin of the compensated system is about 50º(the required value). The gain margin is about 11 dB (acceptable). The static velocity error constant is $5s^{-1}$. Thus, the compensated system satisfies the requirements on both the steady state and the relative stability.

We determine now the unit-step response and unit-ramp response of the compensated system and the original uncompensated system. The closed-loop transfer functions of the compensated and uncompensated systems are given by

$$\frac{C(s)}{R(s)} = \frac{100s + 10}{60s^4 + 220.6s^3 + 202.2s^2 + 102s + 10}$$

and

$$\frac{C(s)}{R(s)} = \frac{1}{0.6s^3 + 2.2s^2 + 2s + 1}$$

respectively.

A MATLAB program to obtain the unit-step and unit-ramp responses of the compensated and uncompensated systems is given below. The resulting unit-step response curves and unit-ramp response curves are shown in Fig. E3.34(c) and E3.34 (d) respectively.

```
% MATLAB Program
%       Unit-step response
num = [0 0 0 1];
den = [0.6 2.2 2 1];
numc = [0 0 0 100 10];
denc = [60 220.6 202.2 102 10];
t = 0:0.1:40;
[c1, x1, t] = step(num, den);
[c2, x2, t] = step(numc, denc);
plot(t, c1, '.', t, c2, '–')
grid
title('Unit-Step Responses of Compensated and Uncompensated Systems')
xlabel('t Sec')
ylabel('Outputs')
text(12.2,1.27, 'Compensated System')
text(12.2,0.7, 'Uncompensated System')
```

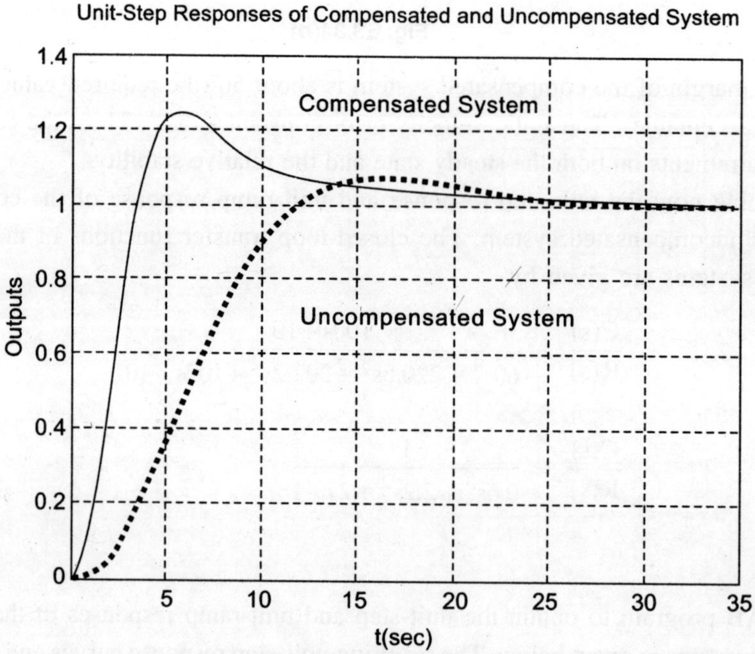

Fig. E3.34 (c)

```
%     Unit-ramp response
num1 = [0  0  0  0 1];
den1 = [0.6  2.2  2  1 0];
num1c = [0  0 0 0  100  10];
den1c = [60 220.6 202.2 102 10 0];
t = 0:0.1:20;
[y1, z1, t] = step(num1, den1, t);
[y2, z2, t] = step(num1c, den1c, t);
plot(t, y1, '.', t, y2, '–', t, t, '—')
grid
title('Unit-Ramp Responses of Compensated and Uncompensated Systems')
xlabel('t Sec')
ylabel('Outputs')
text(8.4, 3, 'Compensated System')
text(8.4, 5, 'Uncompensated System')
```

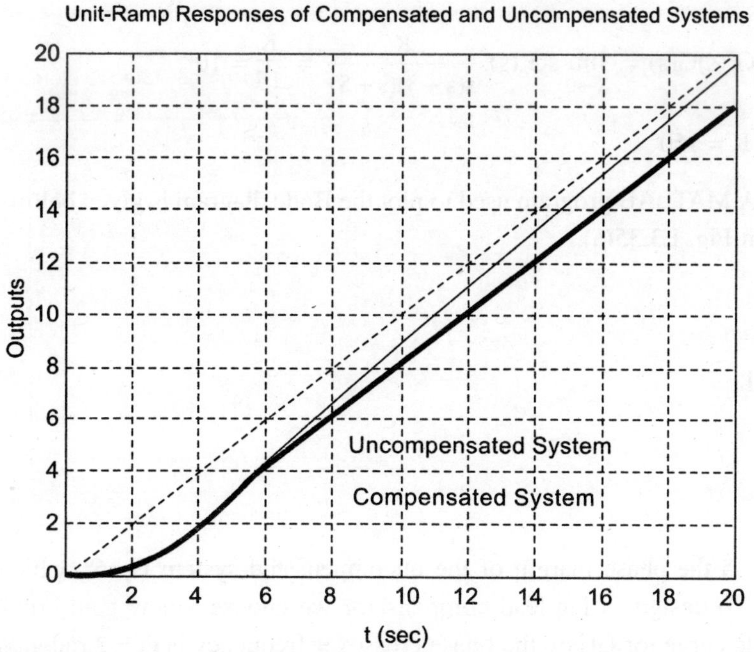

Fig. E3.34 (d)

Example E3.35

The open-loop transfer function of a unit-feedback system is given by

$$G(s) = \frac{K}{s(s+3)(s+5)}$$

Design a compensator $G_c(s)$ such that the static velocity error constant is $10s^{-1}$, the phase margin is 50°, and the gain margin is 10 dB or more.

Solution

We consider a lag-lead compensator of the form

$$G_c(s) = K_c \frac{\left(s+\frac{1}{T_1}\right)\left(s+\frac{1}{T_2}\right)}{\left(s+\frac{\beta}{T_1}\right)\left(s+\frac{\beta}{T_2}\right)}$$

The open-loop transfer function of the compensated system is $G_c(s)G(s)$. For $K_c = 1$, $\lim_{S\to 0} G_c(s) = 1$. For the static velocity error constant, we have

$$K_v = \lim_{S\to 0} sG_c(s)G(s) = \lim_{S\to 0} sG_c(s).\frac{K}{s(s+3)(s+5)} = \frac{K}{15} = 10$$

Therefore, $K = 150$

For $K = 150$, A MATLAB program used to plot the Bode diagram is given below and the diagram obtained is shown in Fig. E3.35(a).

```
% MATLAB Program
num = [0 0 0 150];
den = [1 8 15 0];
bode(num, den, w)
```

From Fig. E3.35 the phase margin of the uncompensated system is –6°, which shows that the system is unstable. To design a lag-lead compensator we choose a new gain crossover frequency. From the phase-angle curve for $G(j\omega)$, the phase crossover frequency is $\omega = 2$ rad/s. We can select the new gain crossover frequency to be 2 rad/s such that the phase-lead angle required at $\omega = 2$ rad/s is about 50°. A single lag-lead compensator can provide this amount of phase-lead angle.

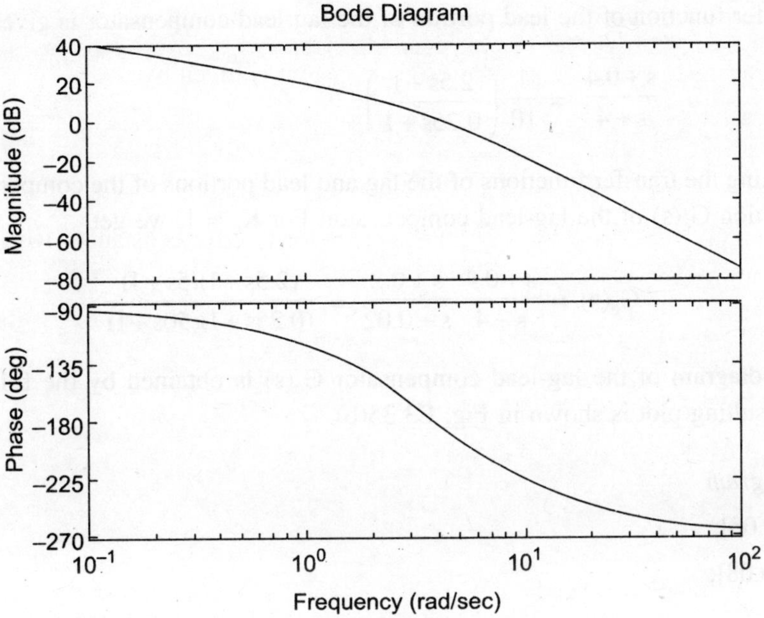

Fig. E3.35(a) Bode diagram of G(s) = 150/[s(s + 3)(s + 5)]

We can find the corner frequencies of the phase-lag portion of the lag-lead compensator. Choosing the corner frequency $\omega = 1/T_2$, corresponding to the zero of the phase-lag portion of the compensator as 1 decade below the new gain crossover frequency, or at $\omega = 0.2$ rad/s. For another corner frequency $\omega = 1/(\beta T_2)$, we need the value of β. The value of β can be obtained from the consideration of the lead portion of the compensator.

The maximum phase-lead angle f_m is given by Eq.(9.10). For a = 1/b, we have given

$$\sin \phi_m = \frac{\beta - 1}{\beta + 1}$$

$\beta = 10$ corresponds to $\phi_m = 54.9°$. We require a 50° phase margin, so we can select $\beta = 10$.

Hence $$\beta = 10$$

Then the corner frequency $\omega = 1/(\beta T_2)$ and $\omega = 0.02$.

The transfer function of the phase-lag portion of the lag-lead compensator is

$$\frac{s + 0.2}{s + 0.02} = 10\left(\frac{5s + 1}{50s + 1}\right)$$

The new gain crossover frequency is $\omega = 2$ rad/s, and $|G(j2)|$ is found to be 6 dB. Therefore, if the lag-lead compensator contributes –6 dB at $\omega = 2$ rad/s, then the new gain crossover frequency is as desired. From this requirement, it is possible to draw a straight line of slope 20 dB/decade passing through the point (–6 dB, 2 rad/s). The intersections of this line and the 0 dB line and –20 dB line gives the corner frequencies. The corner frequencies for the lead portion are $\omega = 0.4$ rad/s and $\omega = 4$ rad/s.

Hence, the transfer function of the lead portion of the lag-lead compensator is given by

$$\frac{s+0.4}{s+4} = \frac{1}{10}\left(\frac{2.5s+1}{0.25s+1}\right)$$

By combining the transfer functions of the lag and lead portions of the compensator, we can find the transfer function $G_c(s)$ of the lag-lead compensator. For $K_c = 1$, we get

$$G_c(s) = \frac{s+0.4}{s+4}\,\frac{s+0.2}{s+0.02} = \frac{(2.5s+1)(5s+1)}{(0.25s+1)(50s+1)}$$

The Bode diagram of the lag-lead compensator $G_c(s)$ is obtained by the following MATLAB program. The resulting plot is shown in Fig. E3.35(b).

```
% MATLAB Program
num = [1 0.6 0.08];
den = [1 4.02 0.08];
bode(num, den)
```

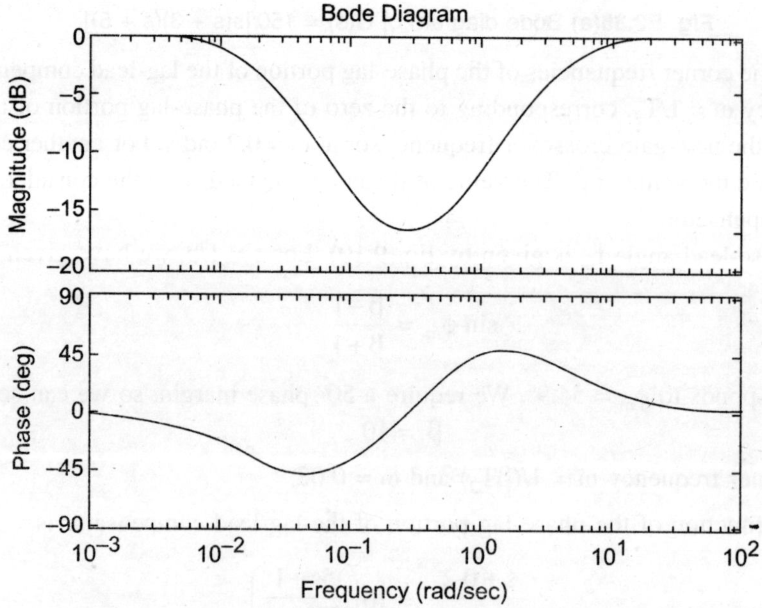

Fig. E3.35 (b) Bode diagram of the designed lag-lead compensator

The open-loop transfer function of the compensated system is

$$G_c(s)G(s) = \frac{(s+0.4)(s+0.2)}{(s+4)(s+0.02)}\,\frac{150}{s(s+3)(s+5)} = \frac{150s^2+90s+12}{s^5+12.02s^4+47.24s^3+60.94s^2+1.2s}$$

The magnitude and phase-angle curves of the designed open-loop transfer function $G_c(s)G(s)$ are shown in the Bode diagram of Fig. E3.35(c). This diagram is obtained using following MATLAB program. Note that the denominator polynomial den was obtained using the conv command, as follows:

```
a = [1 4.02 0.08];
b = [1 8 15 0];

conv(a, b)

ans =

1.0000  12.0200  47.2400  60.9400  1.2000  0
```

```
% MATLAB Program
num = [0 0 0 150 90 12];
den = [1 12.02 47.24 60.94 1.2 0];
bode(num, den)
```

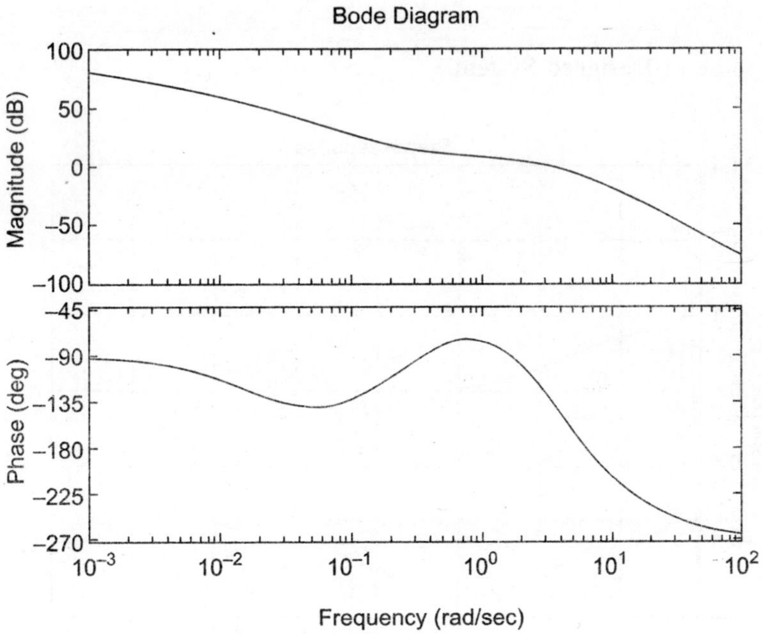

Fig. E3.35(c) Bode diagram of $G_c(s).G(s)$

From Fig. E3.35(c), the requirements on the phase margin, gain margin, and static velocity error constant are all satisfied.

Unit-step response

Now

$$G_c(s)G(s) = \frac{(s+0.4)(s+0.2)}{(s+4)(s+0.02)} \, \frac{150}{s(s+3)(s+5)}$$

and
$$\frac{C(s)}{R(s)} = \frac{G_c(s)G(s)}{1+G_c(s)G(s)} = \frac{150s^2+90s+12}{s^5+12.02s^4+47.24s^3+210.94s^2+91.2s+15.2}$$

The unit-step response is obtained by the following MATLAB program and the unit-step response curve is shown in Fig. E3.35(d).

```
% MATLAB Program
num = [0 0 0 150 90 12];
den = [1 12.02 47.24 210.94 91.2 15.2];
t = 0:0.2:40;
step(num, den, t)
grid
title('unit-Step Response of Designed System')
```

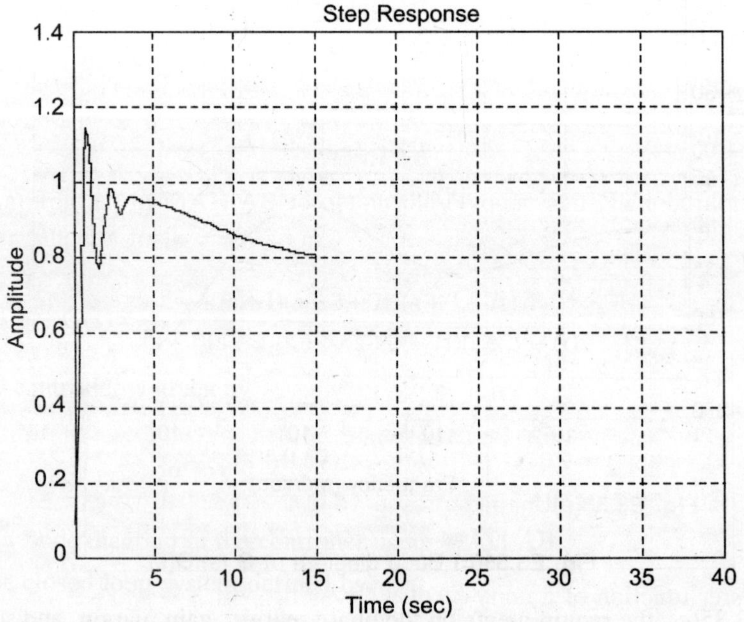

Fig. E3.35(d) Unit-step response of designed system $G_c(s)G(s)$

Unit-ramp response

The unit-ramp response of this system is obtained by the following MATLAB. The unit-ramp response of $G_c(G/(1 + G_cG)$ converted into the unit-step response of $G_cG/[s(1 + G_cG)]$. The unit-ramp response curve obtained is shown in Fig. E3.35(e).

```
% MATLAB Program
num = [0 0 0 0 150 90 12];
den = [1 12.02 47.24 210.94 91.2 15.2 0];
t = 0:0.2:20;
c = step(num, den, t)
plot(t, c, t, t, '.')
grid
title('Unit-Ramp Response of the Designed System')
xlabel('Time (sec)')
ylabel('Amplitude')
```

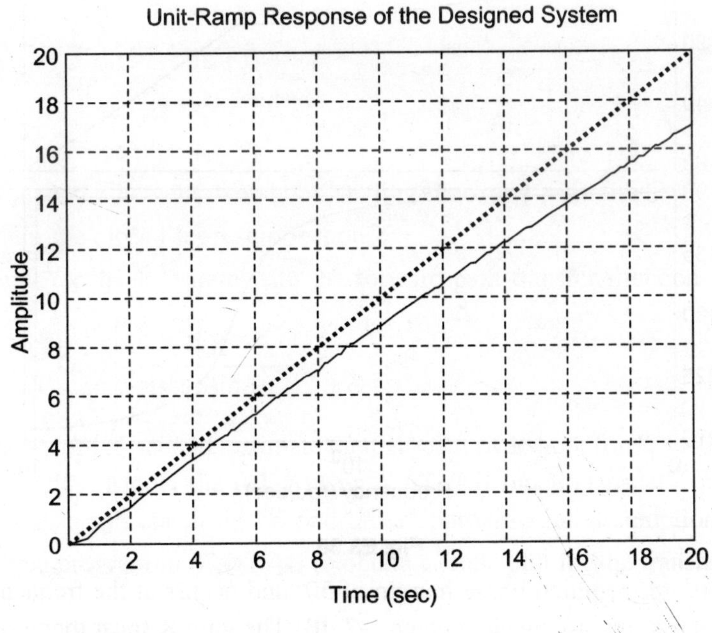

Fig. E3.35(e) Unit-ramp response of the designed system

Example E3.36

The open-loop transfer function of a unity-feedback control system is given by

$$G(s)\ 0 = \frac{K}{s(s^2 + s + 5)}$$

(*a*) determine the value of gain K such that the phase margin is 50°

(*b*) find the gain margin for the gain K obtained in (a).

Solution

$$G(s) = \frac{K}{s(s^2 + s + 5)}$$

The undamped natural frequency is $\sqrt{5}$ rad/s and the damping ratio of $0.1.\sqrt{5}$ from the denominator.

Let the frequency corresponding to the angle of –130° (Phase Margin of 50) be ω_1 and therefore

$$\angle G(j\omega_1) = -130°.$$

The Bode diagram is shown in Fig. E3.36 from MATLAB program.

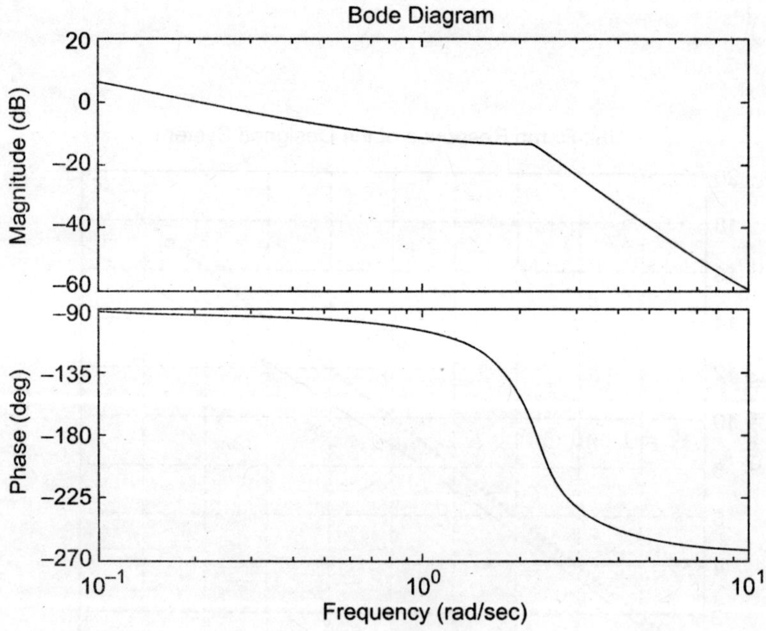

Fig. E3.36

From Fig. E3.36, the required phase margin of 50° and occurs at the frequency ω = 1.06 rad/s. The magnitude of G(jω) at this frequency is then –7 dB. The gain K must then satisfy

$$20 \log K = 7 \text{ dB}$$

or

$$K = 2.23$$

Example E3.37

For the control system shown in Fig. E3.37:

(*a*) Design a lead-compensator $G_c(s)$ such that the phase margin is 45°, gain margin is not less than 8 dB, and the static velocity error constant K_v is 4 s^{-1}

(*b*) plot unit-step and unit-ramp response curves of the compensated system using MATLAB.

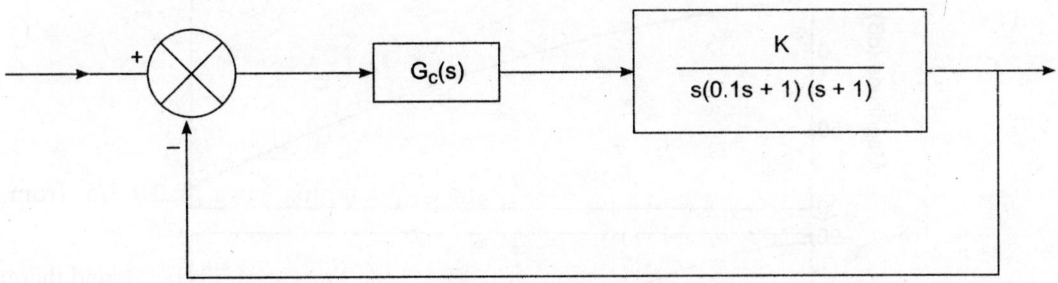

Fig. E3.37

Solution

Consider the lead compensator

$$G_c(s) = K_c a \frac{Ts+1}{\alpha Ts+1} = K_c \frac{s+\frac{1}{T}}{s+\frac{1}{\alpha T}}$$

Since K_v is given as 4 s^{-1}, we have

$$K_v = \lim_{s \to 0} sK_c a \frac{Ts+1}{\alpha Ts+1} \frac{K}{s(0.1s+1)(s+1)} = K_c aK = 4$$

Let K = 1 and define $K_c a = \hat{K}$. Then

$$\hat{K} = 4$$

The Bode diagram of

$$\frac{4}{s(0.1s+1)(s+1)} = \frac{4}{0.1s^3 + 1.1s^2 + s}$$

is obtained by the following MATLAB program. The Bode diagram is shown in Fig. E3.37(a).

```
% MATLAB program .
num = [0 0 0 4];
den = [0.1 1.1 1 0];
bode(num, den)
```

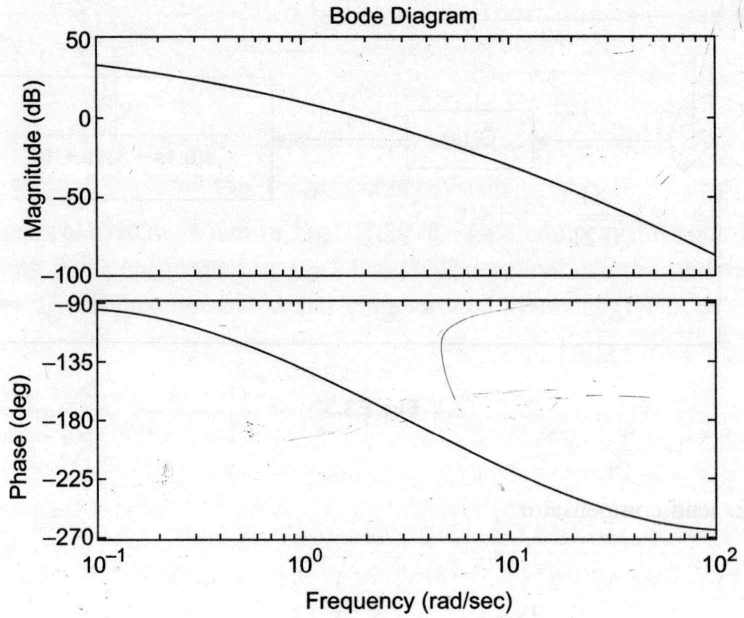

Fig. E3.37 (a)

From Fig. E3.37(a), the phase and gain margins are 17° and 8.7 dB, respectively. For a phase margin of 45°, let us select

$$\phi_m = 45° - 17° + 12° = 40°$$

The maximum phase lead is 40°. Since

$$\sin \phi_m = \frac{1-\alpha}{1+\alpha} \qquad (\phi_m = 40°)$$

α is obtained as 0.2174. Let us choose

$$\alpha = 0.21$$

To determine the corner frequencies $\omega = 1/T$ and $\omega = 1/(\alpha T)$ of the lead compensator we note that the maximum phase-lead angle ϕ_m occurs at the geometric mean of the two corner frequencies, or $\omega = 1/(\sqrt{\alpha}\,T)$. The amount of the modification in the magnitude curve at $\omega = 1/(\sqrt{\alpha}\,T)$ due to the inclusion of the term $(Ts + 1)/(\alpha Ts + 1)$ is then given by

$$\left|\frac{1+j\omega T}{1+j\omega\alpha T}\right|_{\omega=\frac{1}{\sqrt{\alpha}T}} = \frac{1}{\sqrt{\alpha}}$$

Since $$\frac{1}{\sqrt{\alpha}} = \frac{1}{\sqrt{0.21}} = 2.1822 = 6.7778 \text{ dB}$$

The magnitude of $|G(j\omega)|$ is –6.7778 dB which corresponds to ω = 2.81 rad/s. Therefore, we select this as the new gain crossover frequency w_c.

$$\frac{1}{T} = \sqrt{\alpha}\,\omega_c = \sqrt{0.21} \times 2.81 = 1.2877$$

$$\frac{1}{\alpha T} = \frac{\omega_c}{\sqrt{\alpha}} = \frac{2.81}{\sqrt{0.21}} = 6.1319$$

or $$G_c(s) = K_c \frac{s+1.2877}{s+6.1319}$$

and $$K_c = \frac{\hat{K}}{\alpha} = \frac{4}{0.21}$$

Hence $$Gc(s) = \frac{4}{0.21}\,\frac{s+1.2877}{s+6.1319} = 4\frac{0.7768s+1}{0.16308s+1}$$

The open-loop transfer function is

$$G_c(s)G(s) = 4\frac{0.7768s+1}{0.16308s+1}\,\frac{1}{s(0.1s+1)(s+1)} = \frac{3.1064s+4}{0.01631s^4+0.2794s^3+1.2631s^2+s}$$

The closed-loop transfer function is

$$\frac{C(s)}{R(s)} = \frac{3.1064s+4}{0.01631s^4+0.2794s^3+1.2631s^2+4.1064s+4}$$

The following MATLAB program produces the unit-step response curve as shown in Fig. E3.37(b).

```
% MATLAB Program
num = [0 0 0 3.1064 4];
den = [0.01631 0.2794 1.2631 4.1064 4];
step(num, den)
grid
title('Unit-Step Response of Compensated System')
xlabel('t Sec')
ylabel('Output c(t)')
```

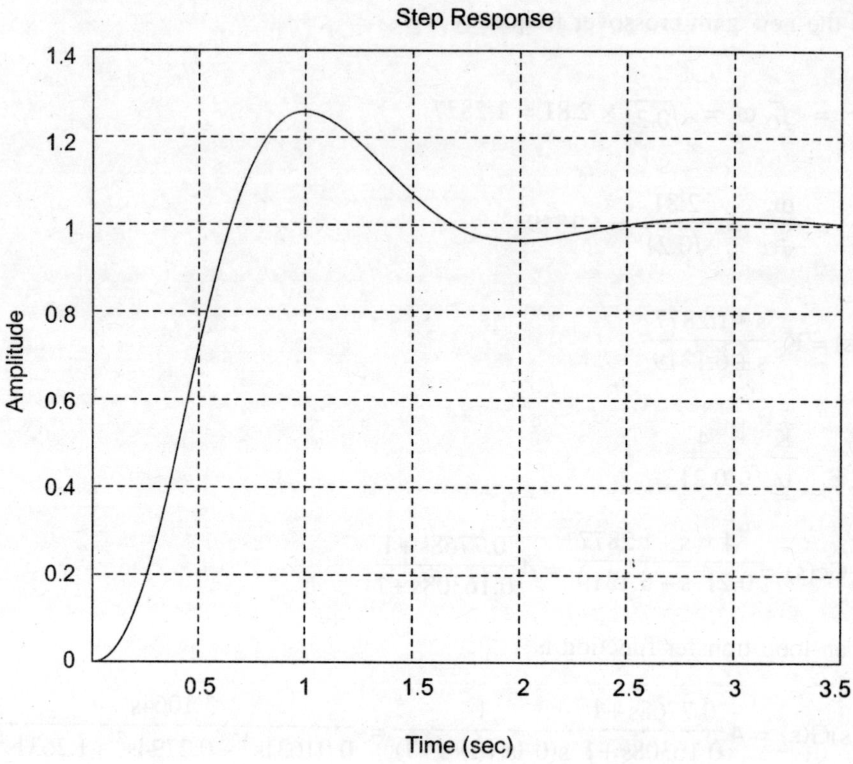

Fig. E3.37(b)

The following MATLAB program produces the unit-ramp response curves as shown in Fig. E3.37(c).

```
% MATLAB Program
num = [0 0 0 0 3.1064 4];
den = [0.01631 0.2794 1.2631 4.1064 4 0];
t = 0:0.01:5;
c = step(num, den, t);
plot(t, c, t, t)
grid
title('Unit-Ramp Response of Compensated System')
xlabel('t Sec')
ylabel('Unit-Ramp Input and System Output c(t)')
```

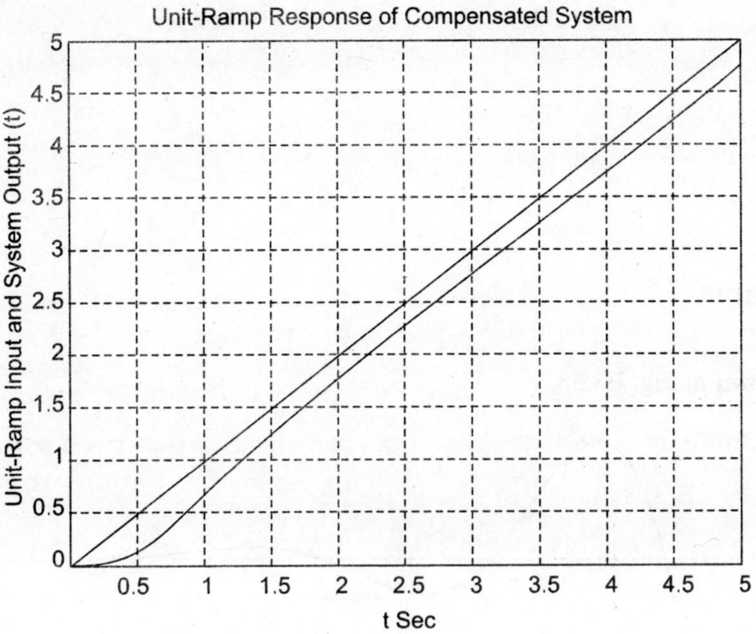

Fig. E3.37(c)

Example 3.38

Obtain the unit-step response and unit-impulse response for the following control system using MATLAB. The initial conditions are all zero.

$$\begin{bmatrix} \dot{x}_1 \\ \dot{x}_2 \\ \dot{x}_3 \\ \dot{x}_4 \end{bmatrix} = \begin{bmatrix} 0 & 1 & 0 & 0 \\ 0 & 0 & 1 & 0 \\ 0 & 0 & 0 & 1 \\ -0.0069 & -0.0789 & -0.5784 & -1.3852 \end{bmatrix} \begin{bmatrix} x_1 \\ x_2 \\ x_3 \\ x_4 \end{bmatrix} + \begin{bmatrix} 0 \\ 0 \\ 0 \\ 2 \end{bmatrix} [u]$$

$$y = \begin{bmatrix} 1 & 0 & 0 & 0 \end{bmatrix} \begin{bmatrix} x_1 \\ x_2 \\ x_3 \\ x_4 \end{bmatrix}$$

Solution

Unit-step response: The following MATLAB program yields the unit-step response of the given system. The resulting unit-step response curve is shown in Fig. E3.38(a).

```
% MATLAB Program
A = [0 1 0 0; 0 0 1 0; 0 0 0 1; –0.0083 –0.06953 –0.6342 –1.4158];
```

```
B = [0; 0; 0; 2];
C = [1 0 0 0];
D = [0];
step(A, B, C, D);
grid
xlabel('t Sec')
ylabel('Output y(t)')
```

The output is shown in Fig. E3.38.

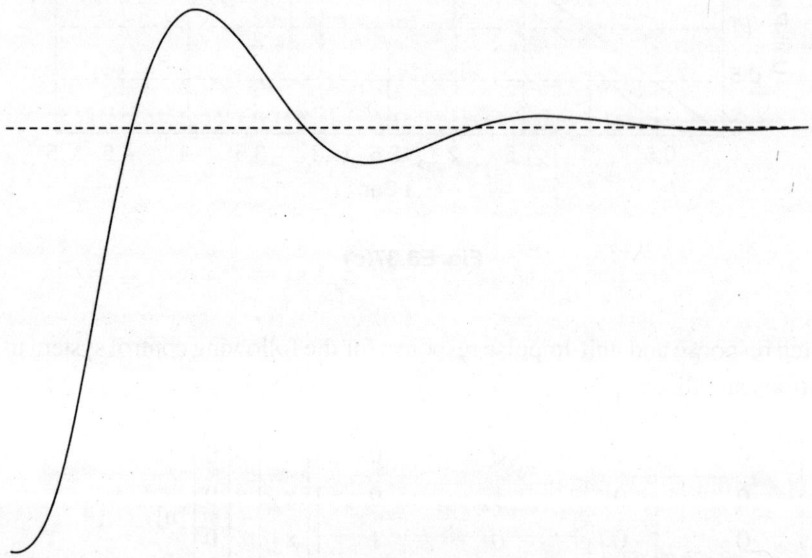

Fig. E3.38

Example 3.39

Obtain the state-space representation of the following system using MATLAB.

$$\frac{C(s)}{R(s)} = \frac{35s + 7}{s^3 + 5s^2 + 36s + 7}$$

Solution

A MATLAB program to obtain a state-space representation of this system is given below:

```
% MATLAB Program
>> num = [0 0 35 7];
```

```
>> den = [1 5 36 7];
>> g = tf(num, den)
```

Transfer function

$$\frac{35s+7}{s^3+5s^2+36s+7}$$

```
>>    [A, B, C, D] = tf2ss(num, den)
A =
    -5   -36   -7
     1     0    0
     0     1    0
B =
     1
     0
     0
C =
     0    35    7
D =
     0
```

From the MATLAB output we obtain the following state space equations:

$$\begin{bmatrix} \dot{x}_1 \\ \dot{x}_2 \\ \dot{x}_3 \end{bmatrix} = \begin{bmatrix} -5 & -36 & -7 \\ 1 & 0 & 0 \\ 0 & 1 & 0 \end{bmatrix} \begin{bmatrix} x_1 \\ x_2 \\ x_3 \end{bmatrix} + \begin{bmatrix} 1 \\ 0 \\ 0 \end{bmatrix} u$$

$$y = [0 \quad 35 \quad 7] \begin{bmatrix} x_1 \\ x_2 \\ x_3 \end{bmatrix} + [0]u$$

Example 3.40

Represent the system shown in Fig. E3.40 using MATLAB in

(*a*) State space in phase-variable form

(*b*) State space in modal form.

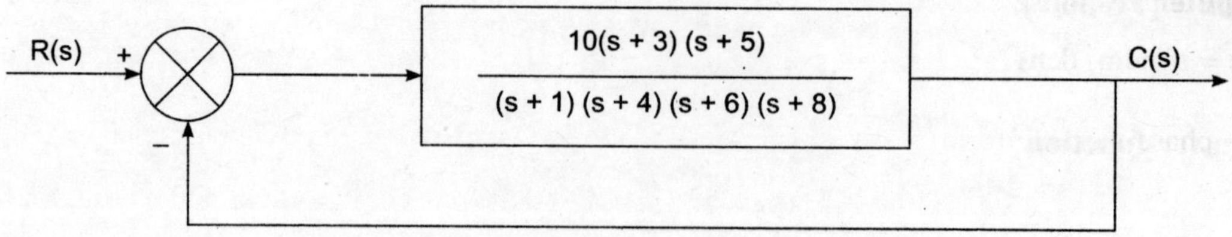

Fig. E3.40

Solution

```
%       MATLAB Program
(a)     phase-variable form'
'G(s)'
G = zpk([-3 -5], [-1 -4 -6 -8], 10)
'T(s)'
T = feedback(G, 1, -1)
[numt, dent] = tfdata(T, 'V');
'Controller canonical form determination'
[AC, BC, CC, DC] = tf2ss(numt, dent)
A1 = flipud(AC);
'Phase-variable form representation'
Apv = fliplr(A1)
Bpv = flipud(BC)
Cpv = fliplr(CC)
(b)     Modal form'
'G(s)'
G = zpk([-3 -5], [-1 -4 -6 -8], 10)
'T(s)'
T = feedback(G, 1, -1)
[numt, dent] = tfdata(T, 'V');
'Controller canonical form'
[AC, BC, CC, DC] = tf2ss(numt, dent)
'Modal form'
[A, B, C, D] = canon(AC, BC, CC, DC, 'modal')
```

Computer response

ans =

(*a*) phase-variable form

ans =

G(s)

Zero/pole/gain

$$\frac{10\,(s+3)\,(s+5)}{(s+1)\,(s+4)\,(s+6)\,(s+8)}$$

ans =

T(s)

Zero/pole/gain

$$\frac{10\,(s+5)\,(s+3)}{(s+1.69)\,(s+4.425)\,(s\text{^}2+12.88s+45.73)}$$

ans =

Controller canonical form determination

```
AC=
   -19.0000  -132.0000  -376.0000  -342.0000
     1.0000          0          0          0
          0     1.0000          0          0
          0          0     1.0000          0

BC=
   1
   0
   0
   0

CC =
   0  10.0000  80.0000  150.0000

DC =
   0
```

ans =

Phase-variable form representation

Apv =

0	1.0000	0	0
0	0	1.0000	0
0	0	0	1.0000
–342.0000	–376.0000	–132.0000	–19.0000

Bpv =

0
0
0
1

Cpv =

150.0000 80.0000 10.0000 0

ans =

(*b*) Modal form

ans =

G(s)

Zero/pole/gain:

$$\frac{10\,(s+3)\,(s+5)}{(s+1)\,(s+4)\,(s+6)\,(s+8)}$$

ans =

T(s)

Zero/pole/gain :

$$\frac{10\,(s+5)\,(s+3)}{(s+1.69)\,(s+4.425)\,(s\verb|^|2+12.88s+45.73)}$$

ans =

Controller canonical form

```
AC =
   -19.0000   -132.0000   -376.0000   -342.0000
     1.0000           0           0           0
          0      1.0000           0           0
          0           0      1.0000           0
BC =
     1
     0
     0
     0

CC =
          0     10.0000     80.0000    150.0000

DC =
     0

ans =

Modal form

A =
    -6.4425      2.0551           0           0
    -2.0551     -6.4425           0           0
          0           0     -4.4249           0
          0           0           0     -1.6902

B =
    -2.7844
    -9.8159
     3.9211
     0.0811
C =
    -0.2709    0.1739    0.0921    7.2936

D =
     0
```

Example 3.41

Determine the state-space representation in phase-variable form for the system shown in Fig. E3.41.

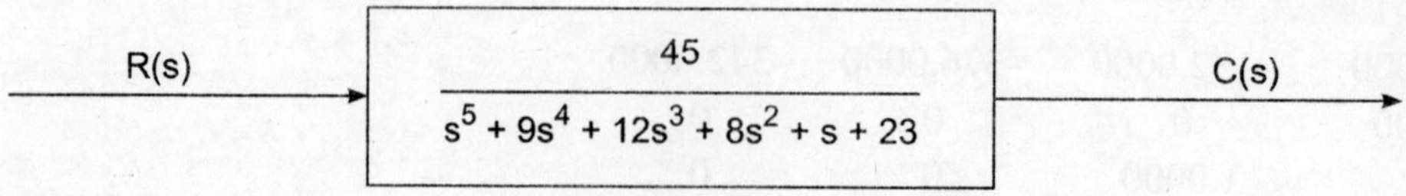

Fig. E3.41

Solution Computer program is as follows:

```
% MATLAB Program
% 'State-space representation'
>>    num = 45

num =
      45

>>    den = [1 9 12 8 1 23];
>>    G = tf(num, den)

Transfer function
                    45
      s^5+9 s^4+12 s^3+8 s^2+s+23

>>    [Ac, Bc, Cc, Dc] = tf2ss(num, den);
>>    Af = flipud(Ac)

Af =
       0    0    0    1    0
       0    0    1    0    0
       0    1    0    0    0
       1    0    0    0    0
      -9  -12   -8   -1  -23

>>    A = fliplr(Af)

A =
        0    1    0    0    0
        0    0    1    0    0
        0    0    0    1    0
        0    0    0    0    1
      -23   -1   -8  -12   -9
>>    B = flipud(Bc)
```

```
B =
      0
      0
      0
      0
      1

>>    C = fliplr(Cc)

C =
      45   0   0   0   0
```

Example 3.42

Using MATLAB, write the state equations and the output equation for the phase-variable representation for the following systems in Fig. E3.42.

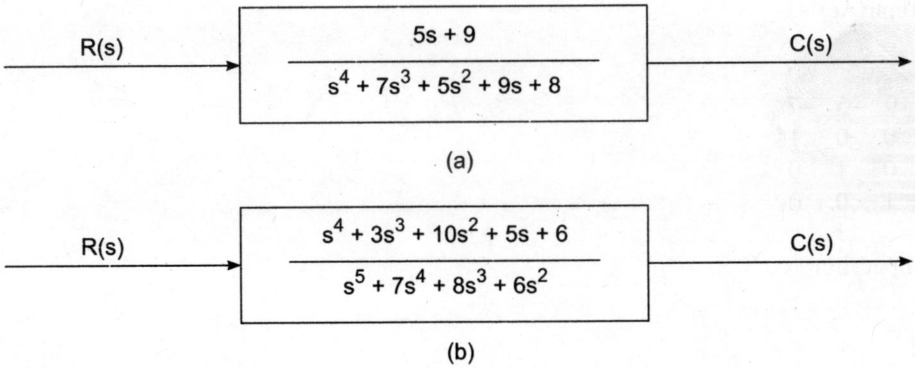

Fig. E3.42

Solution

(*a*)

```
>>    num = [ 5 9]

num =
      5    9

>>    den = [1 7 5 9 8]

den =
```

```
      1    7    5    9    8

>>    G = tf(num, den)
```

Transfer function

$$\frac{5s+9}{s^4+7s^3+5s^2+9s+8}$$

```
>>    [Ac, Bc, Cc, Dc] = tf2ss(num, den);
>>    Af = flipud(Ac)

Af =

      0    0    1    0
      0    1    0    0
      1    0    0    0
     -7   -5   -9   -8

>>  A = fliplr(Ac)

A =
     -8   -9   -5   -7
      0    0    0    1
      0    0    1    0
      0    1    0    0

>>  B = flipud(Bc)

B =
     0
     0
     0
     1

>>  C = fliplr(Cc)

C =
     9   5   0   0
```

Part 2

```
num = [1 3 10 5 6];
den = [1 7 8 6 0 0];
G = tf(num,den)
```

Transfer function

```
s^4 + 3 s^3 + 10 s^2 + 5 s + 6
------------------------------
s^5 + 7 s^4 + 8 s^3 + 6 s^2
```

```
[Ac, Bc, Cc, Dc] = tf2ss(num, den);
Af = flipud(Ac);
A = fliplr(Af)

A =
     0     1     0     0     0
     0     0     1     0     0
     0     0     0     1     0
     0     0     0     0     1
     0     0    -6    -8    -7

B = flipud(Bc)

B =
     0
     0
     0
     0
     1

C = fliplr(Cc)

C =
     6     5    10     3     1
```

Example 3.43

Find the transfer function for the following system using MATLAB:

$$\begin{bmatrix} \dot{x}_1 \\ \dot{x}_2 \\ \dot{x}_3 \end{bmatrix} = \begin{bmatrix} 0 & 1 & 0 \\ -5 & -2 & 0 \\ 0 & 2 & -6 \end{bmatrix} \begin{bmatrix} x_1 \\ x_2 \\ x_3 \end{bmatrix} + \begin{bmatrix} 0 & 0 \\ 3 & -1 \\ 5 & 0 \end{bmatrix} u$$

$$y = \begin{bmatrix} 1 & 0 & 0 \\ 0 & 0 & 1 \end{bmatrix} \begin{bmatrix} x_1 \\ x_2 \\ x_3 \end{bmatrix}$$

Solution

The transfer function matrix is given by

$$G(s) = C[sI - A]^{-1}B$$

where

$$A = \begin{bmatrix} 0 & 1 & 0 \\ -5 & -2 & 0 \\ 0 & 2 & -6 \end{bmatrix} \quad B = \begin{bmatrix} 0 & 0 \\ 3 & -1 \\ 5 & 0 \end{bmatrix} \quad C = \begin{bmatrix} 1 & 0 & 0 \\ 0 & 0 & 1 \end{bmatrix}$$

$$\text{Hence } G(s) = \begin{bmatrix} 1 & 0 & 0 \\ 0 & 0 & 1 \end{bmatrix} \begin{bmatrix} s & -1 & 0 \\ 5 & s+2 & 0 \\ 0 & -2 & s+6 \end{bmatrix} \begin{bmatrix} 0 & 0 \\ 3 & -1 \\ 5 & 0 \end{bmatrix}$$

```
>> % MATLAB Program
>> syms s
>> C = [1 0 0; 0 0 1];
>> M = [s –1 0; 5 s + 2 0; 0 –2 s + 6];
>> B = [0 0; 3 –1; 5 0];
>> C*inv(M)*B

ans =

[3/(s^2 + 2*s + 5),                                  –1/(s^2+2*s+5)]
[6*s/(s^3 + 8*s^2 + 17*s + 30) + 5/(s + 6),          –2*s/(s^3 + 8*s^2 + 17*s + 30)]
```

Example 3.44

A control system is defined by the following state space equations:

$$\begin{bmatrix} \dot{x}_1 \\ \dot{x}_2 \end{bmatrix} = \begin{bmatrix} -4 & -1 \\ 2 & -3 \end{bmatrix} \begin{bmatrix} x_1 \\ x_2 \end{bmatrix} + \begin{bmatrix} 1 \\ 3 \end{bmatrix} u$$

$$y = [1 \quad 2] \begin{bmatrix} x_1 \\ x_2 \end{bmatrix}$$

Find the transfer function G(s) of the system using MATLAB.

Solution

$$A = \begin{bmatrix} -4 & -1 \\ 2 & -3 \end{bmatrix} \quad B = \begin{bmatrix} 1 \\ 3 \end{bmatrix} \quad C = [1 \;\; 2]$$

The transfer function G(s) of the system is

$$G(s) = C(sI - A)^{-1}B = [1 \;\; 2]\begin{bmatrix} s+4 & 1 \\ -2 & s+3 \end{bmatrix}\begin{bmatrix} 1 \\ 3 \end{bmatrix} = [1 \;\; 2]\frac{1}{[(s+4)(s+3)+2]}\begin{bmatrix} s+3 & -1 \\ 2 & s+4 \end{bmatrix}\begin{bmatrix} 2 \\ 5 \end{bmatrix}$$

$$= \frac{1}{[s^2 + 7s + 14]}[1 \;\; 2]\begin{bmatrix} 2s+1 \\ 5s+24 \end{bmatrix} = \frac{[12s + 49]}{[s^2 + 7s + 14]}$$

```
>>    % MATLAB Program
>>    A = [-4 -1; 2 -3];
>>    B = [1; 3];
>>    C = [1 2];
>>    D = 0;
>>    [num,den] = ss2tf(A, B, C, D)

num =
      0    7.0000   28.0000

den =
      1.0000    7.0000   14.0000
```

The result is same as the one derived above.

Example 3.45

Determine the transfer function G(s) = Y(s)/R(s), for the following system representation in state space form.

$$\dot{x} = \begin{bmatrix} 0 & 3 & 7 & 0 \\ 0 & 0 & 1 & 0 \\ 0 & 0 & 0 & 1 \\ -5 & -6 & 9 & 5 \end{bmatrix} x + \begin{bmatrix} 0 \\ 5 \\ 7 \\ 2 \end{bmatrix} r$$

$$y = [1 \;\; 3 \;\; 6 \;\; 5]\, x$$

Solution

```
A = [0 3 5 0; 0 0 1 0; 0 0 0 1; –5 –6 8 5];
B = [0; 5; 7; 2];
C = [1 3 7 5];
D = 0;
state space = ss(A, B, C, D)

a =

          x1     x2     x3     x4
    x1    0      3      5      0
    x2    0      0      1      0
    x3    0      0      0      1
    x4    –5     –6     8      5

b =

          u1
    x1    0
    x2    5
    x3    7
    x4    2

c =

          x1     x2     x3     x4
    y1    1      3      7      5

d =

          u1
    y1    0

Continuous-time model.

[A, B, C, D] = tf2ss(num, den);
          G = tf(num, den)
```

Transfer function

$$\frac{s^4+3s^3+10s^2+5s+6}{s^5+7s^4+8s^3+6s^2}$$

Example 3.46

Determine the transfer function and poles of the system represented in state space as follows using MATLAB.

$$\dot{x} = \begin{bmatrix} 9 & -3 & -1 \\ -3 & 2 & 0 \\ 6 & 8 & -2 \end{bmatrix} + \begin{bmatrix} 1 \\ 2 \\ 3 \end{bmatrix} u(t)$$

$$y = [2 \;\; 9 \;\; -12]x; \; x(0) = \begin{bmatrix} 0 \\ 0 \\ 0 \end{bmatrix}$$

Solution

% MATLAB Program

```
>>    A = [8 –3 4; –7 1 0; 3 4 –7]
A =

      8  –3   4
     –7   1   0
      3   4  –7

>>    B = [1; 3; 8]
B =

      1
      3
      8

>>    C = [1 7 –2]
C =

      1   7  –2

>>    D = 0
D =

      0
```

```
>>    [numg, deng] = ss2tf(A, B, C, D, 1)

numg =
        1.0e+003 *

             0    0.0060    0.0730   -2.8770

deng =
        1.0000   -2.0000   -88.0000   33.0000

>>    G = tf(numg, deng)
```

Transfer function

$$\frac{6s\,^\wedge 2 + 73s - 2877}{s\,^\wedge 3 - 2s\,^\wedge 2 - 88s + 33}$$

```
>> poles = roots(deng)

poles =
        10.2620
        -8.6344
         0.3724
```

Example 3.47

Represent the system shown in Fig. E3.47 using MATLAB in

(*a*) State space in phase-variable form.

(*b*) State space in model form.

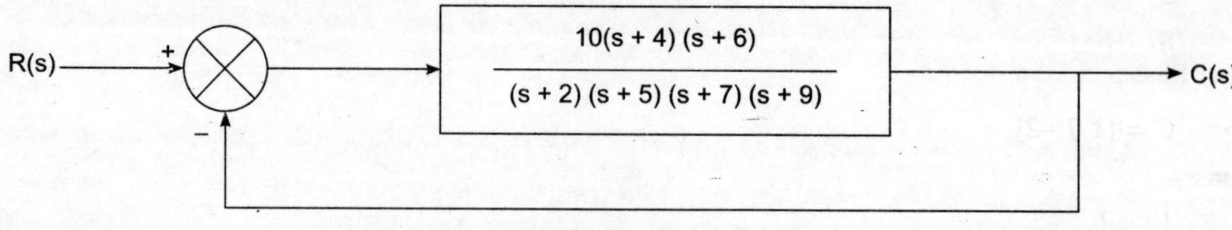

Fig. E3.47

Solution

% MATLAB Program

'(*a*) Phase-variable form'

```
'G(s)'
G = zpk ([-4  -6] , [-2 -5 -7 -9], 10)
'T(s)'
T = feedback (G, 1, -1)
[numt, dent] = tfdata (T, 'V');
'controller  canonical form determination'
[AC, BC, CC, DC]  =  tf2ss (numt, dent)
A1 = flipud (AC);
'Phase-variable form representation'
APV = fliplr (A1)
BPV = flipud (BC)
CPV = fliplr (CC)
'(b)   Modal form'
'G(s)'
G = zpk ([-4  -6] , [-2 -5 -7 -9], 10)
'T(s)'
T =   feedback (G, 1, -1)
[numt, dent] = tfdata (T, 'V');
'controller canonical form'
[AC, BC, CC, DC] = tf2ss (numt, dent)
' Modal form'
[A, B, C, D] = canon (AC, BC, CC, DC, 'modal')
```

Computer response

(*a*) Phase-variable form

ans =

G(s)

Zero/pole/gain:

$$\frac{10\,(s+4)\,(s+6)}{(s+2)\,(s+5)\,(s+7)\,(s+9)}$$

```
ans =
      T(s)

Zero/pole/gain:
               10 (s + 6) (s + 4)
------------------------------------------------
(s + 2.69) (s + 5.425) (s^2 + 14.88s + 59.61)

ans =

Controller canonical form determination

AC =
     -23.0000   -195.0000   -701.0000   -870.0000
      1.0000          0           0           0
           0     1.0000           0           0
           0          0      1.0000           0

BC =
     1
     0
     0
     0

CC =
     0   10.0000   100.0000   240.0000

DC =
     0

ans =

Phase-variable form representation

APV =
     0           1.0000          0          0
     0                0     1.0000          0
     0                0          0     1.0000
  -870.0000   -701.0000   -195.0000   -23.0000
```

BPV =

0
0
0
1

CPV =

240.0000	100.0000	10.0000	0

(*b*) *Modal form*

ans =

G(s)

Zero/pole/gain:

$$\frac{10\,(s+4)\,(s+6)}{(s+2)\,(s+5)\,(s+7)\,(s+9)}$$

ans =

T(s)

Zero/pole/gain:

$$\frac{10\,(s+6)\,(s+4)}{(s+2.69)\,(s+5.425)\,(s\text{^}2+14.88s+59.61)}$$

ans =

Controller canonical form:

AC =

–23.0000	–195.0000	–701.0000	–870.0000
1.0000	0	0	0
0	1.0000	0	0
0	0	1.0000	0

```
BC =
     1
     0
     0
     0

CC =
     0        10.0000        100.0000        240.0000

DC =
     0

ans =
```

Modal form

```
A =
     -7.4425     2.0551        0          0
     -2.0551    -7.4425        0          0
      0          0            -5.4249     0
      0          0             0         -2.6902

B =
     -5.8222
    -13.9839
      7.1614
      0.2860

C =
     -0.1674     0.1378     0.0504     2.0676

D =
     0
```

Example 3.48

Plot the step response using MATLAB for the following system represented in state space, where u(t) is the unit step.

$$\dot{x} = \begin{bmatrix} -5 & 2 & 0 \\ 0 & -9 & 1 \\ 0 & 0 & -3 \end{bmatrix} + \begin{bmatrix} 0 \\ 2 \\ 1 \end{bmatrix} u(t)$$

$$y = [0 \;\; 1 \;\; 1]x \;\; ; x(0) = \begin{bmatrix} 0 \\ 0 \\ 0 \end{bmatrix}$$

Solution

```
>>    A = [–5 3 0; 0 –9 2; 0 0 –3];
>>    B = [0; 2; 1];
>>    C = [0 1 1];
>>    D = 0;
>>    S = ss(A, B, C, D)

a =

          x1   x2   x3
    x1    –5    3    0
    x2     0   –9    2
    x3     0    0   –3

b =

          u1
    x1    0
    x2    2
    x3    1

c =

         x1  x2  x3
    y1   0   1   1

d =

         u1
         y1   0
```

Continuous-time model.
step(S)

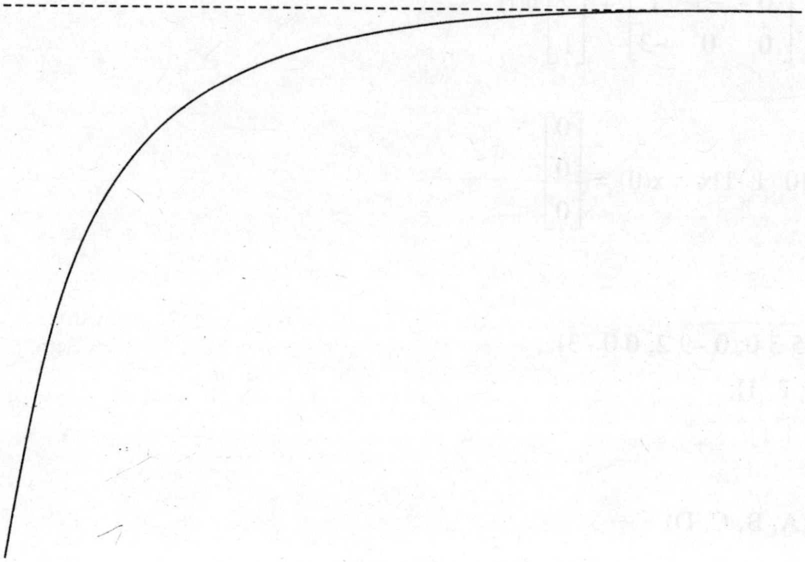

Fig. E3.48

Example 3.49

A control system is defined by

$$\begin{bmatrix} \dot{x}_1 \\ \dot{x}_2 \end{bmatrix} = \begin{bmatrix} 0 & 1 \\ -25 & -9 \end{bmatrix} \begin{bmatrix} x_1 \\ x_2 \end{bmatrix} + \begin{bmatrix} 1 & 1 \\ 0 & 1 \end{bmatrix} \begin{bmatrix} u_1 \\ u_2 \end{bmatrix}$$

$$\begin{bmatrix} y_1 \\ y_2 \end{bmatrix} = \begin{bmatrix} 1 & 0 \\ 0 & 1 \end{bmatrix} \begin{bmatrix} x_1 \\ x_2 \end{bmatrix}$$

Plot the four sets of Bode diagrams for the system [two for input1, and two for input2] using MATLAB.

Solution

There are four sets of Bode diagrams (2 for input1 and 2 for input2)

```
>>    %Bode Diagrams
>>    A = [0 1; –25 –9];
>>    B = [1 1; 0 1];
>>    C = [1 0; 0 1];
>>    D = [0 0; 0 0];
>>    bode(A, B, C, D)
```

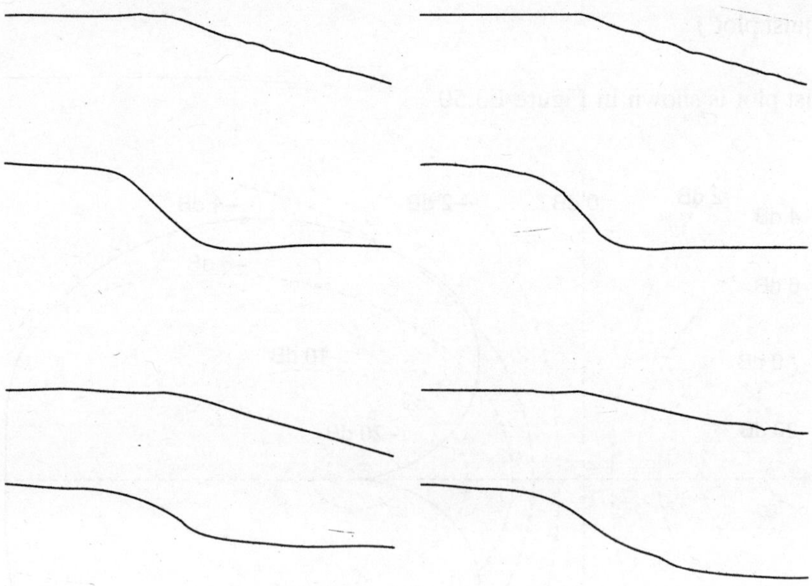

Fig. E3.49 Bode diagrams

Example 3.50

Draw a Nyquist plot for a system defined by

$$\begin{bmatrix} \dot{x}_1 \\ \dot{x}_2 \end{bmatrix} = \begin{bmatrix} 0 & 1 \\ -25 & 5 \end{bmatrix} \begin{bmatrix} x_1 \\ x_2 \end{bmatrix} + \begin{bmatrix} 0 \\ 20 \end{bmatrix} u$$

$$y = \begin{bmatrix} 1 & 0 \end{bmatrix} \begin{bmatrix} x_1 \\ x_2 \end{bmatrix} + [0]u$$

using MATLAB.

Solution

Since the system has a single input u and a single output y, a Nyquist plot can be obtained by using the command nyquist (A, B, C, D) or nyquist (A, B, C, D, 1).

```
>>   %MATLAB Program
>>   A = [0 1; –25 5];
>>   B = [0; 20];
>>   C = [1 0];
>>   D = [0];
>>   nyquist(A, B, C, D)
```

```
>>    grid
>>    title('Nyquist plot')
```

The Nyquist plot is shown in Figure E3.50.

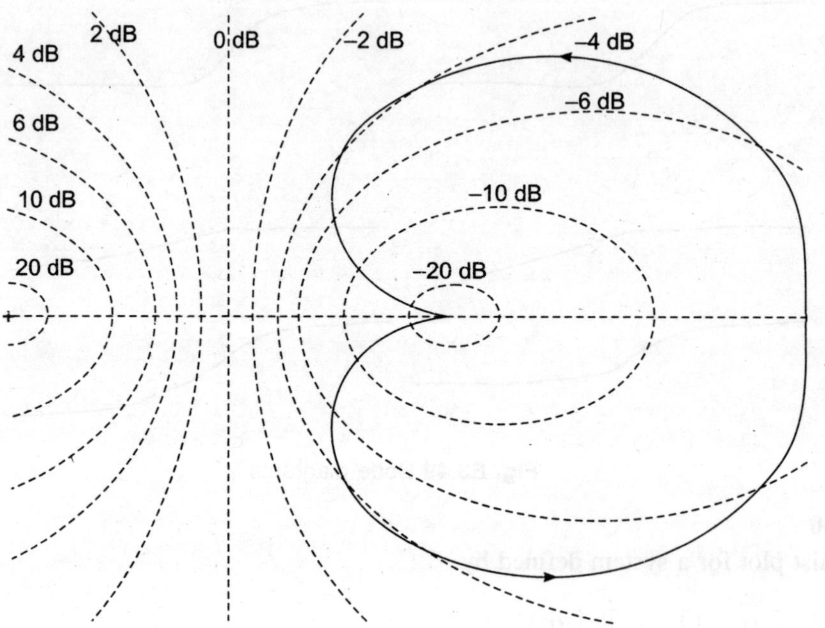

Fig. E3.50 Nyquist plot

Example 3.51

A control system is defined by

$$\begin{bmatrix} \dot{x}_1 \\ \dot{x}_2 \end{bmatrix} = \begin{bmatrix} -1 & -1 \\ 7 & 0 \end{bmatrix} \begin{bmatrix} x_1 \\ x_2 \end{bmatrix} + \begin{bmatrix} 1 & 1 \\ 1 & 0 \end{bmatrix} \begin{bmatrix} u_1 \\ u_2 \end{bmatrix}$$

$$\begin{bmatrix} y_1 \\ y_2 \end{bmatrix} = \begin{bmatrix} 1 & 0 \\ 0 & 1 \end{bmatrix} \begin{bmatrix} x_1 \\ x_2 \end{bmatrix} + \begin{bmatrix} 0 & 0 \\ 0 & 0 \end{bmatrix} \begin{bmatrix} u_1 \\ u_2 \end{bmatrix}$$

The system has two inputs and two outputs. The four sinusoidal output-input relationships are given by

$$\frac{y_1(j\omega)}{u_1(j\omega)}, \frac{y_2(j\omega)}{u_1(j\omega)}, \frac{y_1(j\omega)}{u_2(j\omega)}, \text{and} \frac{y_2(j\omega)}{u_2(j\omega)}$$

Draw the Nyquist plots for the system by considering the input u_1 with input u_2 as zero and vice versa.

Solution

The four individual plots are obtained by using the MATLAB command nyquist (A, B, C, D).

```
>>    %MATLAB Program
>>    A = [-1 -1; 9 0];
>>    B = [1 1; 1 0];
>>    C = [1 0; 0 1];
>>    D = [0 0; 0 0];
>>    nyquist(A, B, C, D)
```

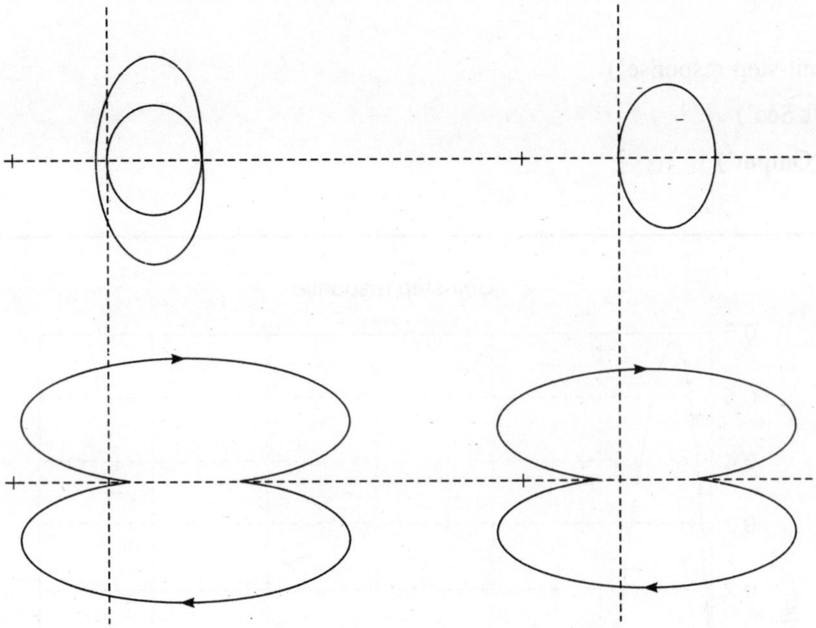

Fig. E3.51 Nyquist plots

Example 3.52

Obtain the unit-step response, unit-ramp response, and unit-impulse response of the following system using MATLAB.

$$\begin{bmatrix} \dot{x}_1 \\ \dot{x}_2 \end{bmatrix} = \begin{bmatrix} -1 & -1.5 \\ 2 & 0 \end{bmatrix} \begin{bmatrix} x_1 \\ x_2 \end{bmatrix} + \begin{bmatrix} 1.5 \\ 0 \end{bmatrix} u$$

$$y = [1 \quad 0] \begin{bmatrix} x_1 \\ x_2 \end{bmatrix}$$

where u is the input and y is the output.

Solution

```
>>    %Unit-step response
>>    A = [-1 -1.5; 2 0];
>>    B = [1.5; 0];
>>    C = [1 0];
>>    D = [0];
>>    [y, x, t] = step(A, B, C, D);
>>    plot(t, y)
>>    grid
>>    title('Unit-step response')
>>    xlabel('t Sec')
>>    ylabel('Output')
```

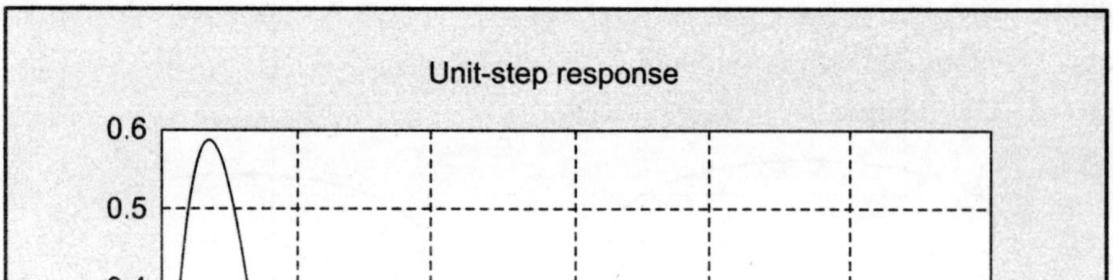

Fig. E3.52 (a) Unit-step response

```
>>    %Unit-ramp response
>>    A = [–1 –1.5; 2 0];
>>    B = [1.5; 0];
>>    C = [1 0];
>>    D = [0];
>>    % New enlarged state and output equations
>>    AA = [A zeros (2, 1); C 0];
>>    BB = [B; 0];
>>    CC = [0 1];
>>    DD = [0];
>>    [z, x, t] = step (AA, BB, CC, DD);
>>    x3 = [0 0 1]*x'; plot (t, x3, t, t, '–')
>>    grid
>>    title ('Unit-ramp response')
>>    xlabel ('t Sec')
>>    ylabel ('Output and unit-ramp input')
>>    text (12, 1.2, 'Output')
```

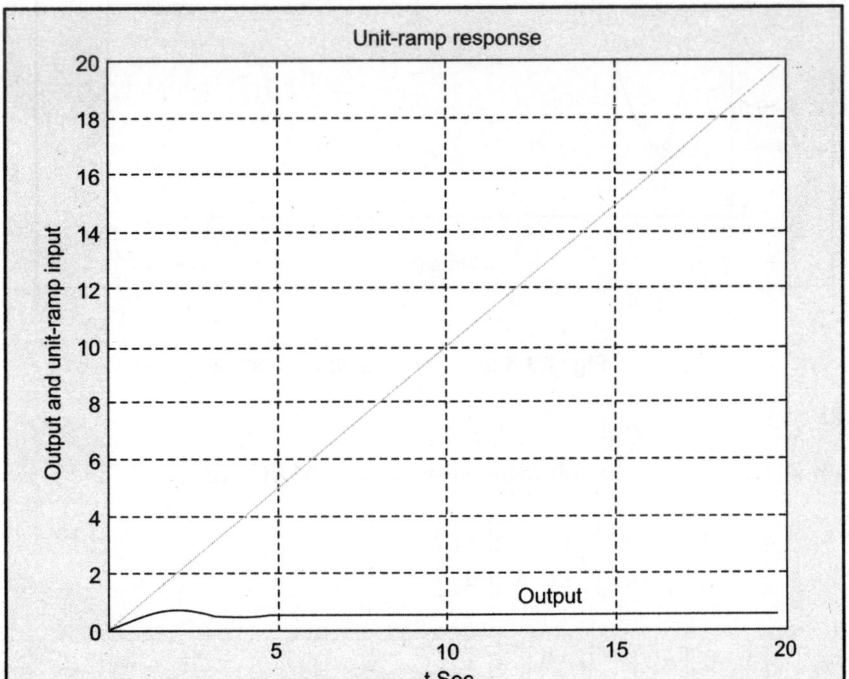

Fig. E3.52 (b) Unit-ramp response

```
>> %Unit-impulse response
>> A = [-1 -1.5; 2 0];
>> B = [1.5; 0];
>> C = [1 0];
>> D = [0];
>> impulse (A, B, C, D)
```

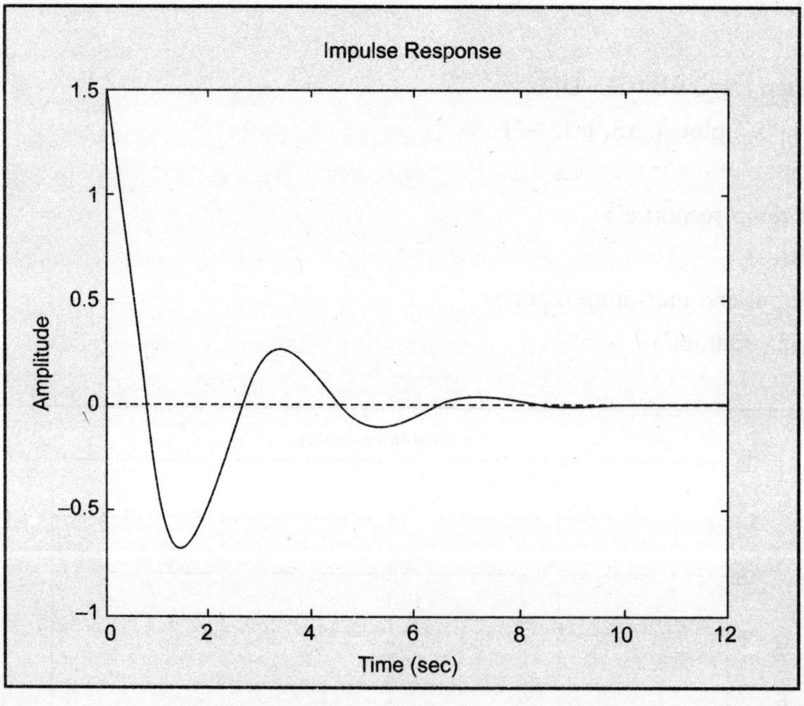

Fig. E3.52(c) Unit-impulse response

Example 3.53

Obtain the unit-step curves for the following system using MATLAB:

$$\begin{bmatrix} \dot{x}_1 \\ \dot{x}_2 \end{bmatrix} = \begin{bmatrix} -1 & -1 \\ 9 & 0 \end{bmatrix} \begin{bmatrix} x_1 \\ x_2 \end{bmatrix} + \begin{bmatrix} 1 & 1 \\ 1 & 0 \end{bmatrix} \begin{bmatrix} u_1 \\ u_2 \end{bmatrix}$$

$$\begin{bmatrix} y_1 \\ y_2 \end{bmatrix} = \begin{bmatrix} 1 & 0 \\ 0 & 1 \end{bmatrix} \begin{bmatrix} x_1 \\ x_2 \end{bmatrix} + \begin{bmatrix} 0 & 0 \\ 0 & 0 \end{bmatrix} \begin{bmatrix} u_1 \\ u_2 \end{bmatrix}$$

Solution

```
>>    % MATLAB Program
>>    A = [–1, –1; 9 0];
>>    B = [1 1; 1 0];
>>    C = [1 0; 0 1];
>>    D = [0 0; 0 0];
>>    step (A, B, C, D)
```

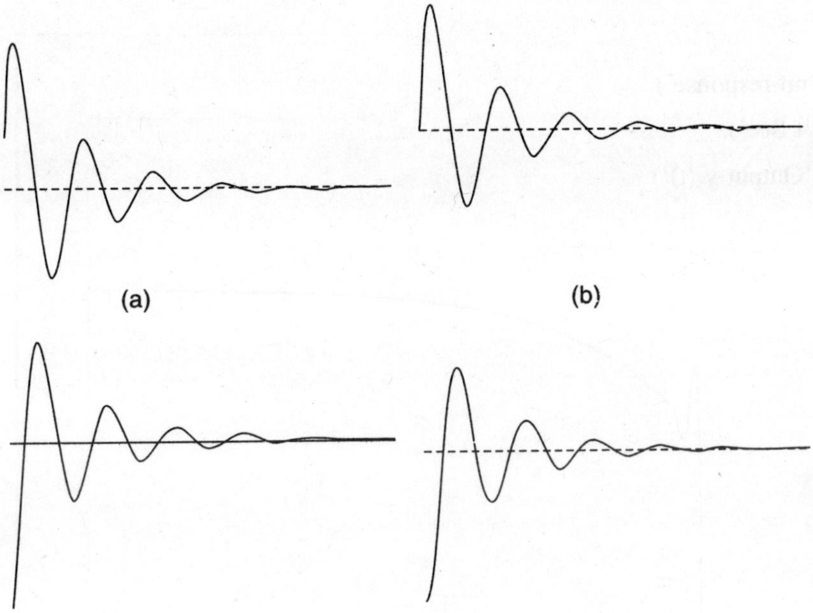

(a) (b)

(c) (d)

Fig. E3.53 Step response

Example 3.54

Obtain the unit-step response and unit-ramp response of the following system using MATLAB:

$$\begin{bmatrix} \dot{x}_1 \\ \dot{x}_2 \\ \dot{x}_3 \end{bmatrix} = \begin{bmatrix} -5 & -30 & -5 \\ 1 & 0 & 0 \\ 0 & 1 & 0 \end{bmatrix} \begin{bmatrix} x_1 \\ x_2 \\ x_3 \end{bmatrix} + \begin{bmatrix} 1 \\ 0 \\ 0 \end{bmatrix} u$$

$$y = \begin{bmatrix} 0 & 20 & 5 \end{bmatrix} \begin{bmatrix} x_1 \\ x_2 \\ x_3 \end{bmatrix} + [0]u$$

Solution

```
>>    %MATLAB Program
>>    A = [–5 –30 –5; 1 0 0; 0 1 0];
>>    B = [1; 0; 0];
>>    C = [0 20 5];
>>    D = [0];
>>    [y, x, t] = step (A, B, C, D);
>>    plot (t, y)
>>    grid
>>    title ('Unit-response')
>>    xlabel ('t Sec')
>>    ylabel ('Output y (t)')
```

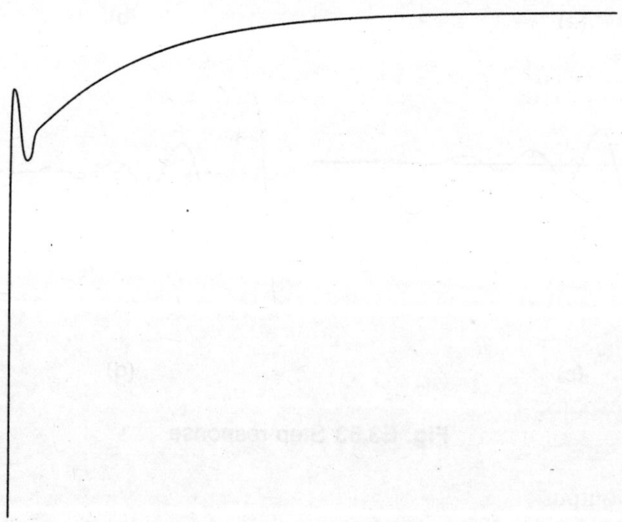

Fig. E3.54 (a) Unit-step response

Unit-ramp response:

$$AA = \begin{bmatrix} -5 & -30 & -5 & 0 \\ 1 & 0 & 0 & 0 \\ 0 & 1 & 0 & 0 \\ 0 & 25 & 5 & 0 \end{bmatrix} = \begin{bmatrix} & A & & \begin{matrix} 0 \\ 0 \\ 0 \end{matrix} \\ 0 & 25 & 5 & 0 \end{bmatrix} = \text{A zeros (2, 1); C 0]}$$

$$BB = \begin{bmatrix} 1 \\ 0 \\ 0 \\ 0 \end{bmatrix} = \begin{bmatrix} B \\ \\ 0 \end{bmatrix}$$

$$CC = \begin{bmatrix} 0 & 25 & 5 & 0 \end{bmatrix} = \begin{bmatrix} C & 0 \end{bmatrix}$$

```
>>    %MATLAB Program
>>    A = [–5 –30 –5; 1 0 0; 0 1 0];
>>    B = [1; 0; 0];
>>    C = [0 25 5];
>>    D = [0];
>>    AA = [A zeros (3, 1); C 0];
>>    BB = [B; 0];
>>    CC = [C 0];
>>    DD = [0];
>>    t = 0:0.01:5;
>>    [z, x, t] = step (AA, BB, CC, DD, 1, t);
>>    P = [0 0 0 1]*x';
>>    plot (t, P, t, t)
>>    grid
>>    title ('Unit-ramp response')
>>    xlabel ('t Sec')
>>    ylabel ('Input and output')
```

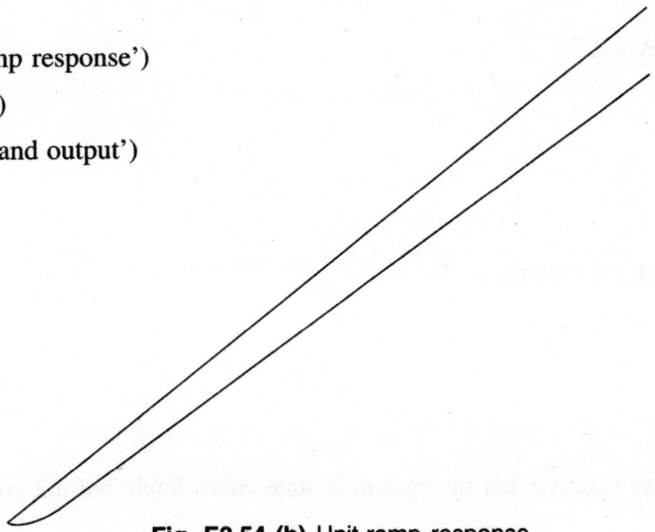

Fig. E3.54 (b) Unit-ramp response

Example 3.55

A control system is given by

$$\begin{bmatrix} \dot{x}_1 \\ \dot{x}_2 \\ \dot{x}_3 \end{bmatrix} = \begin{bmatrix} 3 & 0 & 0 \\ 0 & 1 & 0 \\ 0 & 4 & 5 \end{bmatrix} \begin{bmatrix} x_1 \\ x_2 \\ x_3 \end{bmatrix} + \begin{bmatrix} 0 & 2 \\ 2 & 0 \\ 0 & 1 \end{bmatrix} \begin{bmatrix} u_1 \\ u_2 \end{bmatrix}$$

$$y = \begin{bmatrix} 1 & 2 & 0 \\ 0 & 1 & 0 \end{bmatrix} \begin{bmatrix} x_1 \\ x_2 \\ x_3 \end{bmatrix}$$

Determine the controllability and observability of the system using MATLAB.

Solution

```
>>    %MATLAB Program
>>    A = [3 0 0; 0 1 0; 0 4 5];
>>    B = [0 2; 2 0; 0 1];
>>    C = [1 2 0; 0 1 0];
>>    D = [0 0; 0 0];
>>    rank ([B A*B A^2*B])

ans =

      3

>>    rank ([C' A*C' A^2*C'])

ans =

      3

>>    rank ([C*B C*A*B C*A^2*B])

ans =

      2
```

From the above, we observe that the system is state controllable but not completely observable. It is output controllable.

Example 3.56

Consider the system

$$\begin{bmatrix} \dot{x}_1 \\ \dot{x}_2 \\ \dot{x}_3 \end{bmatrix} = \begin{bmatrix} 3 & 0 & 0 \\ 0 & 1 & 0 \\ 0 & 3 & 2 \end{bmatrix} \begin{bmatrix} x_1 \\ x_2 \\ x_3 \end{bmatrix}$$

The output is given by

$$y = [1 \;\; 1 \;\; 1] \begin{bmatrix} x_1 \\ x_2 \\ x_3 \end{bmatrix}$$

(*a*) Determine the observability of the system using MATLAB.

(*b*) Show that the system is completely observable if the output is given by

$$\begin{bmatrix} y_1 \\ y_2 \end{bmatrix} = \begin{bmatrix} 1 & 1 & 1 \\ 1 & 3 & 2 \end{bmatrix} \begin{bmatrix} x_1 \\ x_2 \\ x_3 \end{bmatrix}$$

using MATLAB.

Solution

```
>>    %MATLAB Program
>>    A = [3 0 0; 0 1 0; 0 3 2];
>>    C = [1 1 1];
>>    rank ([C' A'*C' A'^2*C'])

ans =

      3

>>    A= [3 0 0; 0 1 0; 0 3 2];
>>    C= [1 1 1; 1 3 2];
>>    rank ([C' A'*C' A'^2*C'])

ans =

      3
```

From the above, we observe that the system is observable and controllable.

Example 3.57

Consider the following state equation and output equation:

$$\begin{bmatrix} \dot{x}_1 \\ \dot{x}_2 \\ \dot{x}_3 \end{bmatrix} = \begin{bmatrix} -1 & -3 & -2 \\ 0 & -2 & 1 \\ 1 & 0 & -1 \end{bmatrix} \begin{bmatrix} x_1 \\ x_2 \\ x_3 \end{bmatrix} + \begin{bmatrix} 3 \\ 0 \\ 1 \end{bmatrix} u$$

$$y = \begin{bmatrix} 1 & 1 & 0 \end{bmatrix} \begin{bmatrix} x_1 \\ x_2 \\ x_3 \end{bmatrix}$$

Determine if the system is completely state controllable and completely observable using MATLAB.

Solution

The controllability and observability of the system can be obtained by examining the rank condition of

[B AB A^2B] and [C' A'C' (A') $^{2C'}$]

```
>>    % MATLAB Program
>>    A = [–1 –3 –2; 0 –2 1; 1 0 –1];
>>    B = [3; 0; 1];
>>    C = [1 1 0];
>>    D = [0];
>>    rank ([B A*B A^2*B])

ans =

      3

>>    rank ([C' A'*C' A'^2*C'])

ans =

      3
```

We observe the rank of [B AB A^2B] is 3 and the rank of **[C' A'*C' (A')^2*C']** is 3, the system is completely state controllable and observable.

Example 3.58

Diagonalize the following system using MATLAB:

$$\dot{x} = \begin{bmatrix} -7 & -5 & 5 \\ 15 & 6 & -12 \\ -8 & -3 & 4 \end{bmatrix} x + \begin{bmatrix} -1 \\ 4 \\ 2 \end{bmatrix} r$$

$$y = [1 \quad -3 \quad 5]\, x$$

Solution

```
% MATLAB Program
      A = [-7 -5 5; 15 6 -12; -8 -3 4];
      B = [-1; 4; 2;];
      C = [1; -3; 5;];
  [P, D] = eig (A);
     Ad = inv (P) * A * P
     Bd = inv (P) * B
     Cd = inv (P)* C
```

Computer response

```
>>    Ad = inv (P)*A*P

Ad =

      2.4555 + 6.0296i – 0.0000 – 0.0000i – 0.0000 + 0.0000i
     –0.0000 + 0.0000i  2.4555 – 6.0296i – 0.0000 – 0.0000i
      0.0000 + 0.0000i  0.0000 – 0.0000i – 1.9110 – 0.0000i

>>    Bd = inv (P)*B

Bd =

      1.8397 + 2.1026i
      1.8397 – 2.1026i
      3.3254 + 0.0000i
```

Cd =

−2.4324 + 5.4360i

−2.4324 − 5.4360i

2.6093 + 0.0000i

Example 3.59

Determine the eigenvalues of the following system using MATLAB:

$$\dot{x} = \begin{bmatrix} 0 & 2 & 0 \\ 0 & 2 & -9 \\ -2 & 2 & 5 \end{bmatrix} x + \begin{bmatrix} 0 \\ 0 \\ 2 \end{bmatrix} r$$

$$y = [0\ 0\ 1]\ x$$

Solution

```
>>    A = [0 2 0; 0 2 –7; –2 2 5]; %Define the matrix above
>>    eig (A) %Calculate the eigenvalues of matrix A.

ans =

      2.0000
      2.5000 + 3.4278i
      2.5000 – 3.4278i
```

Example 3.60

For the following forward path of a unity feedback system in state-space representation, determine if the closed-loop system is stable using the Routh-Hurwitz criterion and MATLAB.

$$\dot{x} = \begin{bmatrix} 0 & 2 & 0 \\ 0 & 1 & 9 \\ -2 & -4 & -6 \end{bmatrix} x + \begin{bmatrix} 0 \\ 0 \\ 2 \end{bmatrix} r$$

$$y = [0\ 1\ 1]\ x$$

Solution

```
>>    A = [0 2 0; 0 1 9; –2 –4 –6]; %Define the matrix
>>    B = [0; 0; 2]; %Define the matrix.
```

```
>>    C = [0 1 1]; %Define the matrix
>>    D = 0;
>>    'G';
>>    G = ss (A, B, C, D); %Create a state-space model
>>    'T';
>>    T = Feedback (G, 1);
>>    'Eigenvalues of T are';
>>    ssdata (T); % Create a state-space model
>>    eig (T) % Determine Eigenvalues

ans =

    –0.8872
    –3.0564 + 5.5888i
    –3.0564 – 5.5888i
```

The closed loop system is stable as the numbers are all negative with regards the to axis coordinate system used for Routh-Hurwitz. Negative values are stable, positive values are unstable.

Example 3.61

For the following path of a unity feedback system in state space representation, determine if the closed-loop system is stable using the Routh-Hurwitz criterion and MATLAB.

$$\dot{x} = \begin{bmatrix} 0 & 1 & 0 \\ 0 & 1 & 7 \\ -3 & -4 & -6 \end{bmatrix} x + \begin{bmatrix} 0 \\ 0 \\ 2 \end{bmatrix} u$$

$$y = [0 \quad 1 \quad 1]\, x$$

Solution

```
% MATLAB Program
A = [0 1 0; 0 1 7; –3 –4 –6];
B = [0 0 2];
C = [0 1 1];
D = 0;
'G'
G = ss (A, B, C, D)
```

```
'T'
T = feedback (G, 1)
'Eigenvalues of T are'
ssdata (T);
eig (T)
```

Computer response

```
ans =

      G

a =

            x1      x2      x3
      x1    0       1       0
      x2    0       1       5
      x3    –3      –4      –5

b =

            u1
      x1    0
      x2    0
      x3    1

c =

            x1      x2      x3
      y1    0       1       1

d =

            u1
      y1    0
```

Continuous-time model:

```
ans =

      T
```

```
a =

        x1  x2  x3
   x1    0   1   0
   x2    0   1   7
   x3   -3  -6  -8


b =

        u1
   x1    0
   x2    0
   x3    2


c =

        x1  x2  x3
   y1    0   1   1


d =

        u1
   y1    0
```

Continuous-time model:

```
ans =
```

Eigenvalues of T are

```
ans =

   -0.7112
   -3.1444 + 4.4317i
   -3.1444 - 4.4317i
```

SUMMARY

The classical methods of control systems engineering using MATLAB including the root locus analysis and design, Routh-Hurwitz stability analysis, frequency response methods of analysis, Bode, Nyquist, and Nichols plots, steady-state error analysis, second order systems approximations, phase and gain margin and bandwidth, state space variable method, and controllability and observability are covered in this chapter. With this foundation of basic application of MATLAB, the Chapter provides opportunities to explore advanced topics in control systems engineering.

Extensive worked examples are included with a great number of exercise problems to guide the student to understand and as an aid for learning about the analysis and design of control systems using MATLAB.

PROBLEMS

P3.1 [Reduction of Multiple Subsystems]

Reduce the system shown in Fig. P3.1 to a single transfer function, T(s) = C(s)/R(s) using MATLAB.

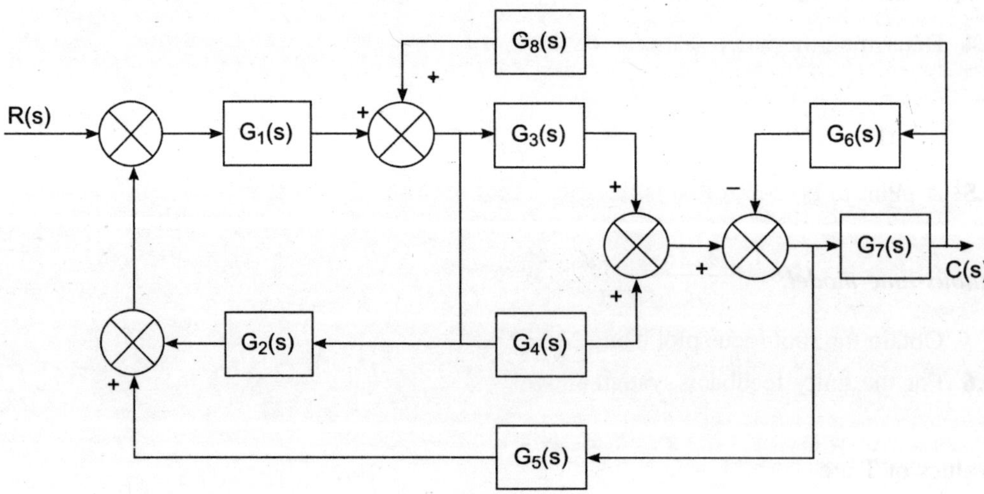

Fig. P3.1

The transfer functions are given as:

$G_1(s) = 1/(s + 3)$

$G_2(s) = 1/(s^2 + 3s + 5)$

$G_3(s) = 1/(s + 7)$

$G_4(s) = 1/s$

$G_5(s) = 7/(s + 5)$

$G_6(s) = 1/(s^2 + 3s + 5)$

$G_7(s) = 5/(s + 6)$

$G_8(s) = 1/(s + 8)$

P3.2 For each of the second-order systems below, find ξ, ωn, Ts, Tp, Tr, % overshoot, and plot the step response using MATLAB.

(*a*) $T(s) = \dfrac{130}{s^2 + 15s + 130}$

(*b*) $T(s) = \dfrac{0.045}{s^2 + 0.025s + 0.045}$

(*c*) $T(s) = \dfrac{10^8}{s^2 + 1.325\times10^3 s + 10^8}$

P3.3 Determine the pole locations for the system shown below using MATLAB.

$$\frac{C(s)}{R(s)} = \frac{s^3 - 5s^2 + 7s + 12}{s^5 + s^4 - 5s^3 - 7s^2 + 9s - 10}.$$

P3.4 Determine the pole locations for the unity feedback system shown below using MATLAB.

$$G(s) = \frac{180}{(s+3)(s+5)(s+7)(s+9)}.$$

P3.5 A plant to be controlled is described by a transfer function

$$G(s) = \frac{s+5}{s^2 + 7s + 25}.$$

Obtain the root locus plot using MATLAB.

P3.6 For the unity feedback system shown in Fig. P3.6, G(s) is given as

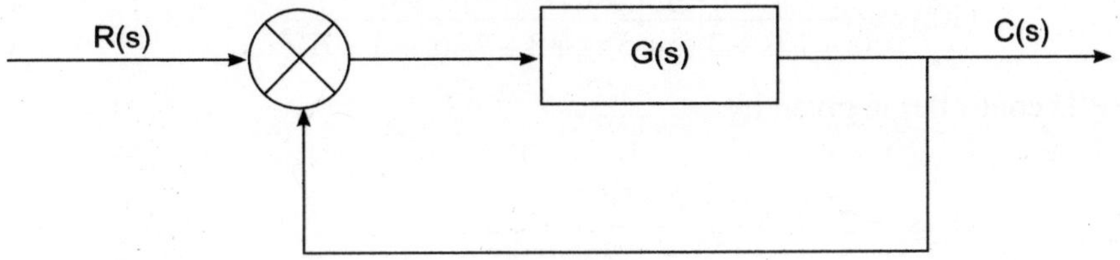

Fig. P3.6

$$G(s) = \frac{30(s^2 - 5s + 3)}{(s+1)(s+2)(s+4)(s+5)}.$$

Determine the closed-loop step response using MATLAB.

P3.7 Determine the accuracy of the second-order approximation using MATLAB to simulate the unity feedback system shown in Fig. P3.7 where

$$G(s) = \frac{15(s^2 + 3s + 7)}{(s^2 + 3s + 7)(s + 1)(s + 3)}.$$

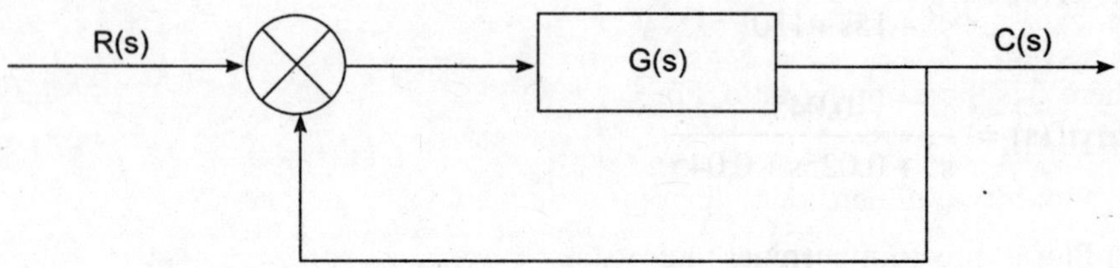

Fig. P3.7

P3.8 For the unity feedback system shown in Fig. P3.8 with

$$G(s) = \frac{K(s + 1)}{s(s + 1)(s + 5)(s + 6)}.$$

Determine the range of K for stability using MATLAB.

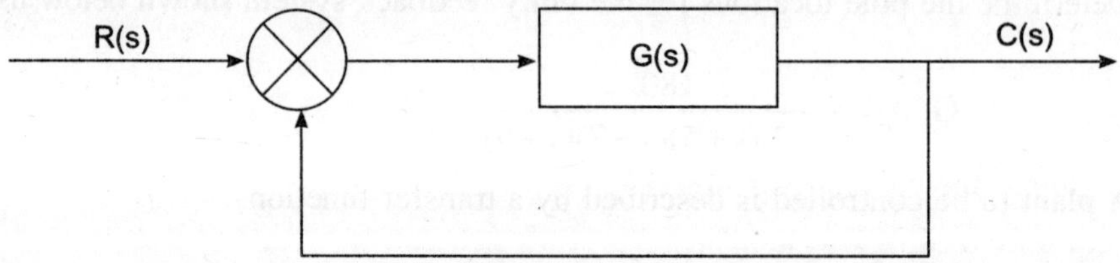

Fig. P3.8

P3.9 Write a program in MATLAB to obtain the Nyquist and Nichols plots for the following transfer function for k = 30.

$$G(s) = \frac{k(s + 1)(s + 3 + 7i)(s + 3 - 7i)}{(s + 1)(s + 3)(s + 5)(s + 3 + 7i)(s + 3 - 7i)}.$$

P3.10 A PID controller is given by

$$G_c(s) = 29.125\frac{(s + 0.57)^2}{s}.$$

Draw a Bode diagram of the controller using MATLAB.

P3.11 For the closed-loop system defined by

$$\frac{C(s)}{R(s)} = \frac{1}{s^2 + 2\zeta s + 1}$$

(*a*) plot the unit-step response curves c(t) for $\xi = 0, 0.1, 0.2, 0.4, 0.5, 0.6, 0.8$, and 1.0 ω_n is normalized to 1.

(*b*) plot a three dimensional plot of (*a*).

P3.12 A closed-loop control system is defined by

$$\frac{C(s)}{R(s)} = \frac{2\zeta s}{s^2 + 2\zeta s + 1}$$

where ζ is the damping ratio. For $\zeta = 0.1, 0.2, 0.3, 0.4, 0.5, 0.6, 0.7, 0.8, 0.9$, and 1.0 using MATLAB:

(*a*) Plot a two-dimensional diagram of unit-impulse response curves.

(*b*) Plot a three-dimensional plot of the response curves.

P3.13 For the system shown in Fig. P3.13 write a program in MATLAB that will use an open-loop transfer function G(s):

$$G(s) = \frac{50(s+1)}{s(s+3(s+5)}$$

$$G(s) = \frac{25(s+1)(s+7)}{s(s+2)(s+4)(s+8)}$$

(*a*) Obtain a Bode plot

(*b*) Estimate the percent overshoot, settling time, and peak time.

(*c*) Obtain the closed-loop step response.

P3.14 For a unit feedback system with the forward-path transfer function

$$G(s) = \frac{K}{s(s+5)(s+12)}$$

and a delay of 0.5 second, estimate the per jcent overshoot for K = 40 using a second-order approximation. Model the delay using MATLAB function pade(T, n). Determine the unit step response and check the second-order approximation assumption made.

P3.15 (*a*) Write a program in MATLAB to obtain a Bode plot for the transfer function

$$G(s) = \frac{15}{s(s+3)(0.7s+5)}.$$

P3.15 (*b*) Write a program in MATLAB to obtain a Bode plot for the transfer function

$$G(s) = \frac{(7s^3 + 15s^2 + 7s + 80)}{(s^4 + 8s^3 + 12s^2 + 70s + 110)}.$$

P3.16 Write a program in MATLAB for a unity-feedback system with

$$G(s)=\frac{K(s+7)}{(s^2+3s+52)(s^2+2s+35)}$$

(*a*) Plot the Nyquist diagram

(*b*) Display the real-axis crossing value and frequency.

P3.17 Write a program in MATLAB for the unity feedback system with

$$G(s)=\frac{K}{[s(s+3)(s+12)]}$$

so that the value of gain K can be input. Display the Bode plots of a system for the input value of K. Determine and display the gain and phase margin for the input value of K.

P3.18 Write a program in MATLAB for the system shown below so that the value of K can be input (K = 40).

$$\frac{C(s)}{R(s)}=\frac{K(s+5)}{s(s^2+3s+15)}.$$

(*a*) Display the closed-loop magnitude and phase frequency response for unity feedback system with an open-loop transfer function, KG(s).

(*b*) Determine and display the peak magnitude, frequency of the peak magnitude, and bandwidth for the closed-loop frequency response for the input value of K.

P3.19 Determine the unit-ramp response of the following system using MATLAB and lsim command.

$$\frac{C(s)}{R(s)}=\frac{1}{3s^2+2s+1}.$$

P3.20 A higher-order system is defined by

$$\frac{C(s)}{R(s)}=\frac{7s^2+16s+10}{s^4+5s^3+11s^2+16s+10}.$$

(*a*) Plot the unit-step response curve of the system using MATLAB.

(*b*) Obtain the rise time, peak time, maximum overshoot, and settling time using MATLAB.

P3.21 Obtain the unit-ramp response of the following closed-loop control system whose closed-loop transfer function is given by

$$\frac{C(s)}{R(s)}=\frac{s+12}{s^3+5s^2+8s+12}.$$

Determine also the response of the system when the input is given by $r=e^{-0.7t}$.

P3.22 Obtain the response of the closed-loop system using MATLAB. The closed-loop system is defined by

$$\frac{C(s)}{R(s)} = \frac{7}{s^2 + s + 7}$$

The input r(t) is a step input of magnitude 3 plus unit-ramp input, r(t) = 3 + t.

P3.23 Plot the root-locus diagram using MATLAB for a system whose open-loop transfer function G(s) H(s) is given by

$$G(s)H(s) = \frac{K(s+3)}{(s^2 + 3s + 4)(s^2 + 2s + 7)}.$$

P3.24 A unity-feedback control system is defined by the following feed forward transfer function

$$G(s) = \frac{K}{s(s^2 + 5s + 9)}.$$

(*a*) Determine the location of the closed-loop poles, if the value of gain is equal to 3.

(*b*) Plot the root loci for the system using MATLAB.

P3.25 The open-loop transfer function of a unity-feedback control system is given by

$$G(s) = \frac{1}{s^3 + 0.3s^2 + 5s + 1}.$$

(*a*) Draw a Nyquist plot of G(s) using MATLAB.

(*b*) Determine the stability of the system.

P3.26 The open-loop transfer function of a unity-feedback control system is given by

$$G(s) = \frac{K(s+3)}{s(s+1)(s+7)}$$

Plot the Nyquist diagram of G(s) for K = 1, 10, and 100 using MATLAB.

P3.27 The open-loop transfer function of a negative feedback system is given by

$$G(s) = \frac{5}{s(s+1)(s+3)}$$

Plot the Nyquist diagram for

(*a*) G(s) using MATLAB

(*b*) same open-loop transfer function use G(s) of a positive feedback system using MATLAB.

P3.28 For the system shown in Fig. P3.28, design a compensator such that the dominant closed-loop poles are located at $s = -2 \pm j\sqrt{3}$. Plot the unit-step response curve of the designed system using MATLAB.

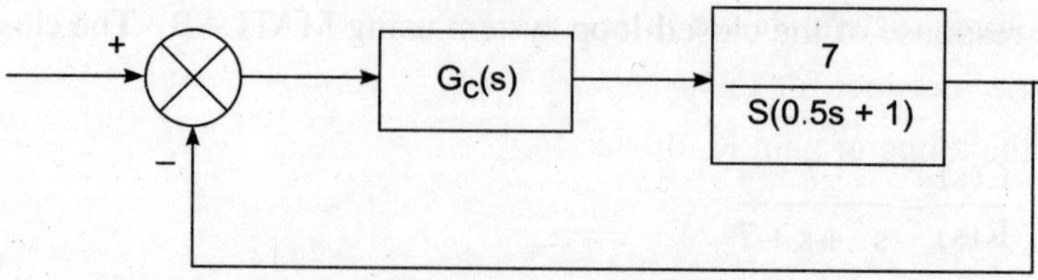

Fig. P3.28 Control system

P3.29 For the control system shown in Fig. P3.29 design a compensator such that the dominant closed-loop poles are located at s = −1 + j1. Determine also the unit-step and unit-ramp responses of the uncompensated and compensated systems.

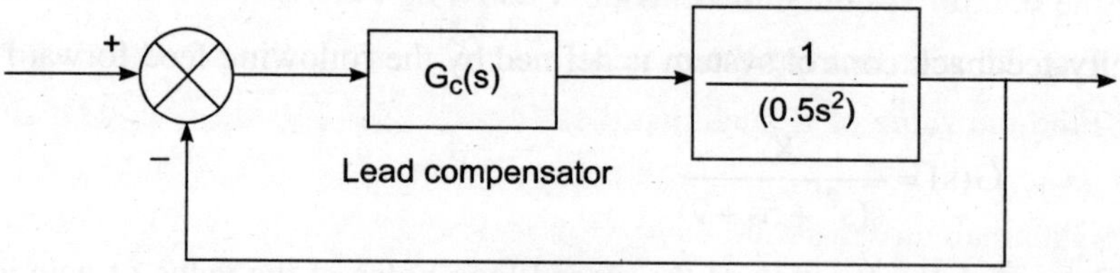

Fig. P3.29

P3.30 The PID control of a second-order plant G(s) control system is shown in Fig. P3.30. Consider the reference input R(s) is held constant. Design a control system such that the response to any step disturbance will be damped out in 2 to 3 secs in terms of the 2% settling time. Select the configuration of the closed-loop poles such that there is a pair of dominant closed-loop poles. Obtain the response to the unit-step disturbance input and to the unit-step reference input.

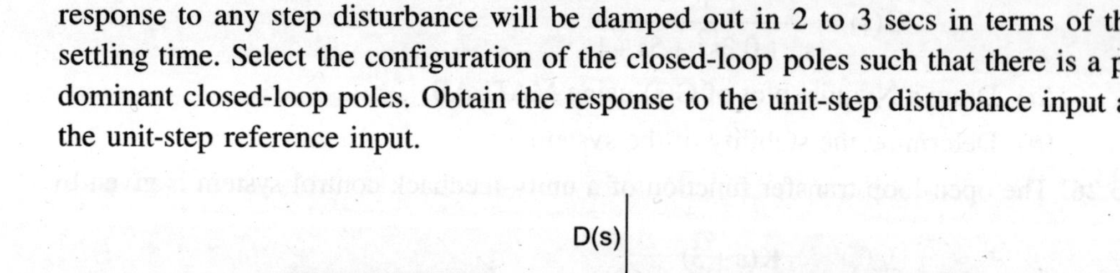

Fig. P3.30

P3.31 For the closed-loop control system shown in Fig. P3.31, obtain the range of gain K for stability and plot a root-locus diagram for the system.

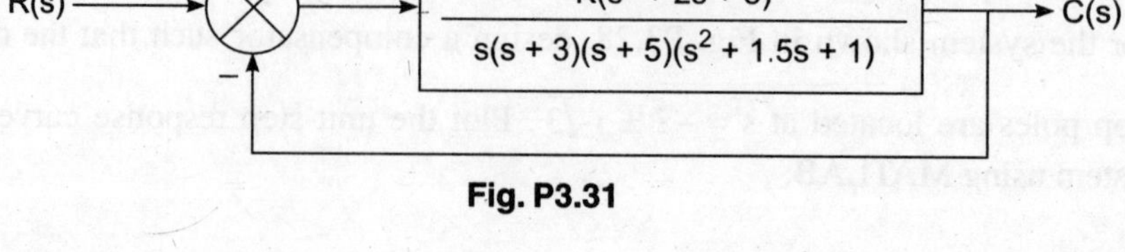

Fig. P3.31

P3.32 For the control system shown in Fig. P3.32:

(*a*) Plot the root loci for the system.

(*b*) Find the range of gain K for stability.

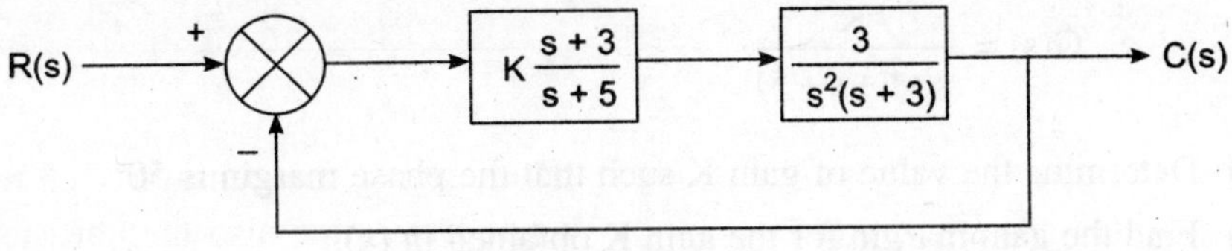

Fig. P3.32

P3.33 For the control system shown in Fig. P3.33:

(*a*) Plot the root loci for the system.

(*b*) Find the value of K such that the damping ratio z of the dominant closed-loop poles is 0.6.

(*c*) Obtain all closed-loop poles.

(*d*) Plot the unit-step respond curve using MATLAB.

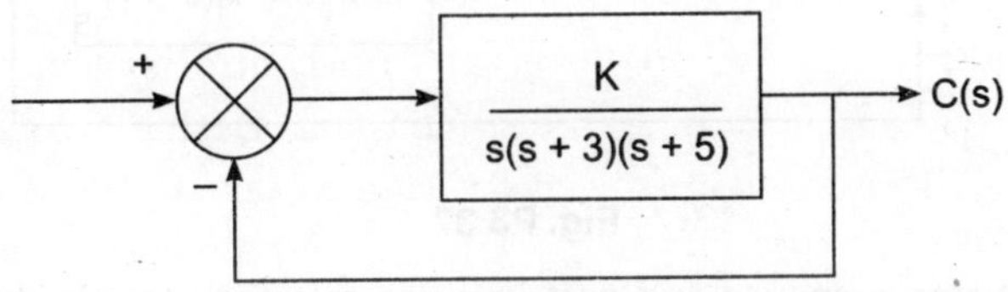

Fig. P3.33

P3.34 For the control system shown in Fig. P3.34, the open-loop transfer function is given by

$$G(s) = \frac{1}{s(s+2)(0.6s+1)}.$$

Design a compensator for the system such that the static velocity error constant K_v is $5s^{-1}$, the phase margin is at least 50°, and the gain margin is at least 10 dB.

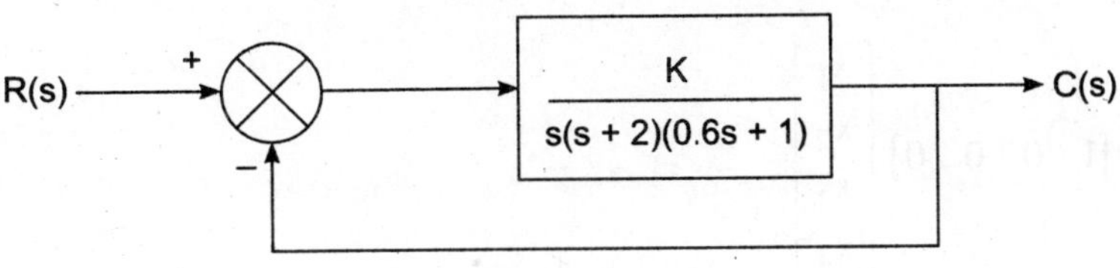

Fig. P3.34

P3.35 The open-loop transfer function of a unit-feedback system is given by

$$G(s) = \frac{K}{s(s+3)(s+5)}.$$

Design a compensator $G_c(s)$ such that the static velocity error constant is $10s^{-1}$, the phase margin is 50°, and the gain margin is 10 dB or more.

P3.36 The open-loop transfer function of a unity-feedback control system is given by

$$G(s) = \frac{K}{s(s^2 + s + 5)}.$$

(*a*) Determine the value of gain K such that the phase margin is 50°.

(*b*) Find the gain margin for the gain K obtained in (a).

P3.37 For the control system shown in Fig. P3.37:

(*a*) Design a lead-compensator $G_c(s)$ such that the phase margin is 45°, gain margin is not less than 8 dB, and the static velocity error constant K_v is 4 s^{-1}.

(*b*) Plot unit-step and unit-ramp response curves of the compensated system using MATLAB.

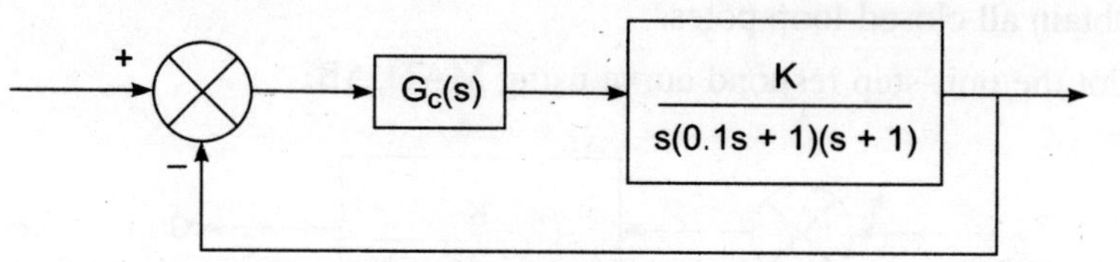

Fig. P3.37

P3.38 Obtain the unit-step response and unit-impulse response for the following control system using MATLAB. The initial conditions are all zero.

$$\begin{bmatrix} \dot{x}_1 \\ \dot{x}_2 \\ \dot{x}_3 \\ \dot{x}_4 \end{bmatrix} = \begin{bmatrix} 0 & 1 & 0 & 0 \\ 0 & 0 & 1 & 0 \\ 0 & 0 & 0 & 1 \\ -0.0069 & -0.0789 & -0.5784 & -1.3852 \end{bmatrix} \begin{bmatrix} x_1 \\ x_2 \\ x_3 \\ x_4 \end{bmatrix} + \begin{bmatrix} 0 \\ 0 \\ 0 \\ 2 \end{bmatrix} [u]$$

$$y = [1 \ \ 0 \ \ 0 \ \ 0] \begin{bmatrix} x_1 \\ x_2 \\ x_3 \\ x_4 \end{bmatrix}$$

P3.39 Obtain the state-space representation of the following system using MATLAB.

$$\frac{C(s)}{R(s)} = \frac{25s + 5}{s^3 + 5s^2 + 26s + 5}.$$

P3.40 Represent the system shown in Fig. P3.40 using MATLAB in

(*a*) State-space in phase-variable form.

(*b*) State-space in modal form.

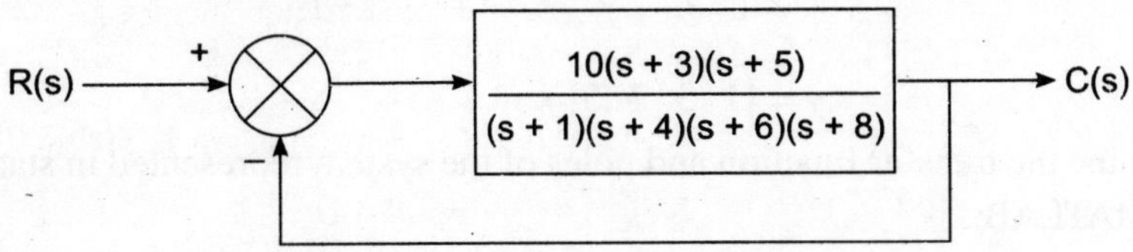

Fig. P3.40

P3.41 Determine the state-space representation in phase-variable form for the system shown in Fig. P3.41.

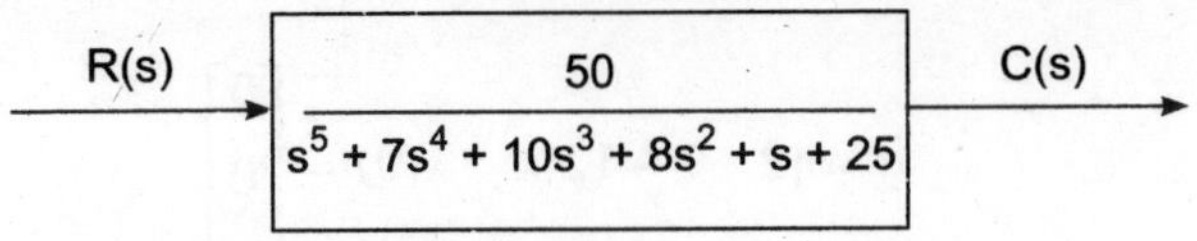

Fig. P3.41

P3.42 Find the transfer function for the following system using MATLAB.

$$\begin{bmatrix} \dot{x}_1 \\ \dot{x}_2 \\ \dot{x}_3 \end{bmatrix} = \begin{bmatrix} 0 & 1 & 0 \\ -5 & -2 & 0 \\ 0 & 2 & -6 \end{bmatrix} \begin{bmatrix} x_1 \\ x_2 \\ x_3 \end{bmatrix} + \begin{bmatrix} 0 & 0 \\ 3 & -1 \\ 5 & 0 \end{bmatrix} u$$

$$y = \begin{bmatrix} 1 & 0 & 0 \\ 0 & 0 & 1 \end{bmatrix} \begin{bmatrix} x_1 \\ x_2 \\ x_3 \end{bmatrix}$$

P3.43 A control system is defined by the following state space equations:

$$\begin{bmatrix} \dot{x}_1 \\ \dot{x}_2 \end{bmatrix} = \begin{bmatrix} -4 & -1 \\ 2 & -3 \end{bmatrix} \begin{bmatrix} x_1 \\ x_2 \end{bmatrix} + \begin{bmatrix} 1 \\ 3 \end{bmatrix} u$$

$$y = [1 \quad 2] \begin{bmatrix} x_1 \\ x_2 \end{bmatrix}$$

Find the transfer function G(s) of the system using MATLAB.

P3.44 Determine the transfer function G(s) = Y(s)/R(s), for the following system representation in state-space form:

$$\dot{x} = \begin{bmatrix} 0 & 3 & 5 & 0 \\ 0 & 0 & 1 & 0 \\ 0 & 0 & 0 & 1 \\ -5 & -6 & 8 & 5 \end{bmatrix} x + \begin{bmatrix} 0 \\ 5 \\ 7 \\ 2 \end{bmatrix} r$$

$$y = [1 \ \ 3 \ \ 7 \ \ 5] \ x$$

P3.45 Determine the transfer function and poles of the system represented in state space as follows using MATLAB:

$$\dot{x} = \begin{bmatrix} 9 & -3 & -1 \\ -3 & 2 & 0 \\ 6 & 8 & -2 \end{bmatrix} + \begin{bmatrix} 1 \\ 2 \\ 3 \end{bmatrix} u(t)$$

$$y = [2 \ \ 9 \ \ -12]x \ \ ; \ x(0) = \begin{bmatrix} 0 \\ 0 \\ 0 \end{bmatrix}$$

P3.46 Represent the system shown in Fig. P3.46 using MATLAB in

(*a*) state-space in phase-variable form

(*b*) state-space in model form.

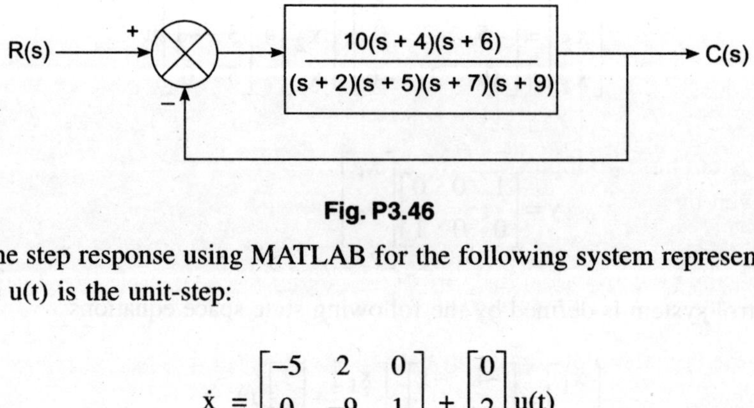

Fig. P3.46

P3.47 Plot the step response using MATLAB for the following system represented in state space, where u(t) is the unit-step:

$$\dot{x} = \begin{bmatrix} -5 & 2 & 0 \\ 0 & -9 & 1 \\ 0 & 0 & -3 \end{bmatrix} + \begin{bmatrix} 0 \\ 2 \\ 1 \end{bmatrix} u(t)$$

$$y = [0 \ \ 1 \ \ 1]x \ \ ; \ x(0) = \begin{bmatrix} 0 \\ 0 \\ 0 \end{bmatrix}$$

P3.48 A control system is defined by

$$\begin{bmatrix} \dot{x}_1 \\ \dot{x}_2 \end{bmatrix} = \begin{bmatrix} 0 & 1 \\ -30 & -7 \end{bmatrix} \begin{bmatrix} x_1 \\ x_2 \end{bmatrix} + \begin{bmatrix} 1 & 1 \\ 0 & 1 \end{bmatrix} \begin{bmatrix} u_1 \\ u_2 \end{bmatrix}$$

$$\begin{bmatrix} y_1 \\ y_2 \end{bmatrix} = \begin{bmatrix} 1 & 0 \\ 0 & 1 \end{bmatrix} \begin{bmatrix} x_1 \\ x_2 \end{bmatrix}.$$

Plot the four sets of Bode diagrams for the system [two for input1, and two for input2] using MATLAB.

P3.49 Draw a Nyquist plot for a system defined by

$$\begin{bmatrix} \dot{x}_1 \\ \dot{x}_2 \end{bmatrix} = \begin{bmatrix} 0 & 1 \\ -30 & 7 \end{bmatrix} \begin{bmatrix} x_1 \\ x_2 \end{bmatrix} + \begin{bmatrix} 0 \\ 30 \end{bmatrix} u$$

$$y = [1 \quad 0] \begin{bmatrix} x_1 \\ x_2 \end{bmatrix} + [0]u$$

using MATLAB.

P3.50 A control system is defined by

$$\begin{bmatrix} \dot{x}_1 \\ \dot{x}_2 \end{bmatrix} = \begin{bmatrix} -1 & -1 \\ 7 & 0 \end{bmatrix} \begin{bmatrix} x_1 \\ \dot{x}_2 \end{bmatrix} + \begin{bmatrix} 1 & 1 \\ 1 & 0 \end{bmatrix} \begin{bmatrix} u_1 \\ u_2 \end{bmatrix}$$

$$\begin{bmatrix} y_1 \\ y_2 \end{bmatrix} = \begin{bmatrix} 1 & 0 \\ 0 & 1 \end{bmatrix} \begin{bmatrix} x_1 \\ x_2 \end{bmatrix} + \begin{bmatrix} 0 & 0 \\ 0 & 0 \end{bmatrix} \begin{bmatrix} u_1 \\ u_2 \end{bmatrix}$$

The system has two inputs and two outputs. The four sinusoidal output-input relationships are given by

$$\frac{y_1(j\omega)}{u_1(j\omega)}, \frac{y_2(j\omega)}{u_1(j\omega)}, \frac{y_1(j\omega)}{u_2(j\omega)}, \text{ and } \frac{y_2(j\omega)}{u_2(j\omega)}$$

Draw the Nyquist plots for the system by considering the input u_1 with input u_2 as zero and vice versa.

P3.51 Obtain the unit-step response, unit-ramp response, and unit-impulse response of the following system using MATLAB:

$$\begin{bmatrix} \dot{x}_1 \\ \dot{x}_2 \end{bmatrix} = \begin{bmatrix} -1 & -1.5 \\ 2 & 0 \end{bmatrix} \begin{bmatrix} x_1 \\ x_2 \end{bmatrix} + \begin{bmatrix} 1.5 \\ 0 \end{bmatrix} u$$

$$y = [1 \quad 0]\begin{bmatrix} x_1 \\ x_2 \end{bmatrix}$$

where u is the input and y is the output.

P3.52 Obtain the unit-step curves for the following system using MATLAB:

$$\begin{bmatrix} \dot{x}_1 \\ \dot{x}_2 \end{bmatrix} = \begin{bmatrix} -1 & -1 \\ 7 & 0 \end{bmatrix}\begin{bmatrix} x_1 \\ x_2 \end{bmatrix} + \begin{bmatrix} 1 & 1 \\ 1 & 0 \end{bmatrix}\begin{bmatrix} u_1 \\ u_2 \end{bmatrix}$$

$$\begin{bmatrix} y_1 \\ y_2 \end{bmatrix} = \begin{bmatrix} 1 & 0 \\ 0 & 1 \end{bmatrix}\begin{bmatrix} x_1 \\ x_2 \end{bmatrix} + \begin{bmatrix} 0 & 0 \\ 0 & 0 \end{bmatrix}\begin{bmatrix} u_1 \\ u_2 \end{bmatrix}$$

P3.53 Obtain the unit-step response and unit-ramp response of the following system using MATLAB:

$$\begin{bmatrix} \dot{x}_1 \\ \dot{x}_2 \\ \dot{x}_3 \end{bmatrix} = \begin{bmatrix} -5 & -25 & -5 \\ 1 & 0 & 0 \\ 0 & 1 & 0 \end{bmatrix}\begin{bmatrix} x_1 \\ x_2 \\ x_3 \end{bmatrix} + \begin{bmatrix} 1 \\ 0 \\ 0 \end{bmatrix} u$$

$$y = [0 \quad 25 \quad 5]\begin{bmatrix} x_1 \\ x_2 \\ x_3 \end{bmatrix} + [0]u$$

P3.54 A control system is given by

$$\begin{bmatrix} \dot{x}_1 \\ \dot{x}_2 \\ \dot{x}_3 \end{bmatrix} = \begin{bmatrix} 3 & 0 & 0 \\ 0 & 1 & 0 \\ 0 & 4 & 5 \end{bmatrix}\begin{bmatrix} x_1 \\ x_2 \\ x_3 \end{bmatrix} + \begin{bmatrix} 0 & 2 \\ 2 & 0 \\ 0 & 1 \end{bmatrix}\begin{bmatrix} u_1 \\ u_2 \end{bmatrix}$$

$$y = \begin{bmatrix} 1 & 2 & 0 \\ 0 & 1 & 0 \end{bmatrix}\begin{bmatrix} x_1 \\ x_2 \\ x_3 \end{bmatrix}$$

Determine the controllability and observability of the system using MATLAB.

P3.55 Consider the system

$$\begin{bmatrix} \dot{x}_1 \\ \dot{x}_2 \\ \dot{x}_3 \end{bmatrix} = \begin{bmatrix} 3 & 0 & 0 \\ 0 & 1 & 0 \\ 0 & 3 & 2 \end{bmatrix}\begin{bmatrix} x_1 \\ x_2 \\ x_3 \end{bmatrix}$$

The output is given by

$$y = [1 \quad 1 \quad 1]\begin{bmatrix} x_1 \\ x_2 \\ x_3 \end{bmatrix}$$

(*a*) determine the observability of the system using MATLAB

(*b*) show that the system is completely observable if the output is given by

$$\begin{bmatrix} y_1 \\ y_2 \end{bmatrix} = \begin{bmatrix} 1 & 1 & 1 \\ 1 & 3 & 2 \end{bmatrix}\begin{bmatrix} x_1 \\ x_2 \\ x_3 \end{bmatrix}$$

using MATLAB.

P3.56 Consider the following state equation and output equation:

$$\begin{bmatrix} \dot{x}_1 \\ \dot{x}_2 \\ \dot{x}_3 \end{bmatrix} = \begin{bmatrix} -1 & -3 & -2 \\ 0 & -2 & 1 \\ 1 & 0 & -1 \end{bmatrix}\begin{bmatrix} x_1 \\ x_2 \\ x_3 \end{bmatrix} + \begin{bmatrix} 3 \\ 0 \\ 1 \end{bmatrix}u$$

$$y = [1 \quad 1 \quad 0]\begin{bmatrix} x_1 \\ x_2 \\ x_3 \end{bmatrix}$$

Determine if the system is completely state controllable and completely observable using MATLAB.

P3.57 Diagonalize the following system using MATLAB:

$$\dot{x} = \begin{bmatrix} -9 & -5 & 5 \\ 15 & 6 & -12 \\ -8 & -3 & 4 \end{bmatrix}x + \begin{bmatrix} -1 \\ 3 \\ 2 \end{bmatrix}r$$

$$y = [1 \quad -3 \quad 5]\,x$$

P3.58 Determine the eigenvalues of the following system using MATLAB:

$$\dot{x} = \begin{bmatrix} 0 & 2 & 0 \\ 0 & 2 & -7 \\ -2 & 2 & 5 \end{bmatrix}x + \begin{bmatrix} 0 \\ 0 \\ 2 \end{bmatrix}r$$

$$y = [0 \quad 0 \quad 1]\,x$$

P3.59 For the following forward path of a unity feedback system in state space representation, determine if the closed-loop system is stable using the Routh-Hurwitz criterion and MATLAB:

$$\dot{x} = \begin{bmatrix} 0 & 2 & 0 \\ 0 & 1 & 7 \\ -2 & -6 & -5 \end{bmatrix} x + \begin{bmatrix} 0 \\ 0 \\ 2 \end{bmatrix} r$$

$$y = [0 \quad 1]\, x$$

P3.60 For the following path of a unity feedback system in state space representation, determine if the closed-loop system is stable using the Routh-Hurwitz criterion and MATLAB:

$$\dot{x} = \begin{bmatrix} 0 & 1 & 0 \\ 0 & 1 & 5 \\ -3 & -4 & -5 \end{bmatrix} x + \begin{bmatrix} 0 \\ 0 \\ 1 \end{bmatrix} u$$

$$y = [0 \quad 1 \quad 1]x$$

CHAPTER 4

Solutions to Problems in MATLAB Basics

The solutions for all the exercise problems at the end of Chapter 2 are presented here in this Chapter.

P2.1 Compute the following quantity using MATLAB in the Command Window:

$$\frac{17\left[\sqrt{5}-1\right]}{\left[15^2-13^2\right]}+\frac{5^7\log_{10}(e^3)}{\pi\sqrt{121}}+\ln(e^4)+\sqrt{11}$$

Solution

```
>> term1 = 17*(sqrt(5) – 1)/(15^2 – 13^2);
>> term2 = 5^7*log10(exp(3))/(pi*sqrt(121));
>> term3 = log(exp(4));
>> term4 = sqrt(11);
>> result = term1 + term2 + term3 + term4
   result =
            2.9532e + 003
```

P2.2 Compute the following quantity using MATLAB in the Command Window:

$$B=\frac{\tan x+\sin 2x}{\cos x}+\log\left|x^5-x^2\right| + \cos h\ x - 2\tan h\ x$$

for x = 5π/6.

Solution

```
>> x = 5*pi/6;
>> term1 =  (tan(x) + sin(2*x))/cos(x);
```

```
>> term2 = log(abs(x^5 – x^2)) + cos h(x) – 2*tan h(x);
>> term = term1 + term2
```

Output:

```
>> term =
        11.3331
```

P2.3 Compute the following quantity using MATLAB in the Command Window:

$$x = a + \frac{ab\,(a+b)}{c\,\sqrt{|ab|}} + c^a + \frac{\sqrt{14\,b}}{e^{3c}} + \ln(2) + \frac{\log_{10} c}{\log_{10}(a+b+c)} + 2 \sin h\ a - 3 \tan h\ b$$

for a = 1, b = 2 and c = 1.8.

Solution

```
>> a = 1; b = 2; c = 1.8;
>> x1 = a + (a*b)*(a + b)/(c*sqrt(abs(a*b)));
>> x2 = c^a + sqrt(14)*b/exp(3*c) + log(2);
>> x3 = log10(c)/log10(a + b + c) + 2*sin h(a) – 3*tan h(b);
>> x = x1 + x2 + x3
```

The output is

```
>> x = 5.7170
```

P2.4 Use MATLAB to create

(*a*) a row and column vectors that has the elements: 11, –3, $e^{7.8}$, ln(59), tan(π/3), 5 $\log_{10}(26)$.

(*b*) a row vector with 20 equally spaced elements in which the first element is 5.

(*c*) a column vector with 15 equally spaced elements in which the first element is –2.

Solution

(*a*)

```
»A = [11 – 3 exp(7.8) log(59) tan(pi/3) 5*log10(26)] % ROW–VECTOR
B = A'                                                % COLUMN–VECTOR

A =
    1.0e + 003 *
        0.0110
       –0.0030
        2.4406
        0.0041
        0.0017
        0.0071
B =
    1.0e + 003 *
        0.0110
       –0.0030
```

2.4406
0.0041
0.0017
0.0071

(*b*) » B = [5:1:24] % Each separated by one

B =

Columns 1 through 12

5 6 7 8 9 10 11 12 13 14 15 16

Columns 13 through 20

17 18 19 20 21 22 23 24

Length of B can be checked as follows:

» c = length(B)

Output is 20

(*c*) » len = 15;

A = [–2:4:(len*4 – 4)]

Output is as follows:

A =

Columns 1 through 12

–2 2 6 10 14 18 22 26 30 34 38 42

Columns 13 through 15

46 50 54

P2.5 Enter the following matrix A in MATLAB and create:

$$A = \begin{bmatrix} 1 & 2 & 3 & 4 & 5 & 6 & 7 & 8 \\ 9 & 10 & 11 & 12 & 13 & 14 & 15 & 16 \\ 17 & 18 & 19 & 20 & 21 & 22 & 23 & 24 \\ 25 & 26 & 27 & 28 & 29 & 30 & 31 & 32 \\ 33 & 34 & 35 & 36 & 37 & 38 & 39 & 40 \end{bmatrix}$$

(*a*) a 4 × 5 matrix B from the 1st, 3rd, and the 5th rows, and the 1st, 2nd, 4th, and 8th columns of the matrix A.

(*b*) a 16 element-row vector C from the elements of the 5th row, and the 4th and 6th columns of the matrix A.

Solution

Here matrix A contains numbers in rows in increasing order of 1.

» A = [1:8; 9:16; 17:24; 25:32; 33:40];

```
A =
     1    2    3    4    5    6    7    8
     9   10   11   12   13   14   15   16
    17   18   19   20   21   22   23   24
    25   26   27   28   29   30   31   32
    33   34   35   36   37   38   39   40
```

(*a*) » x = A(:, 1:2);

```
y = A(:, 4);
z = A(:, 8);
b = [x y z]
b =
     1    2    4    8
     9   10   12   16
    17   18   20   24
    25   26   28   32
    33   34   36   40
» B = reshape(b, 4, 5)
     1   33   26   20   16
B =
     9    2   34   28   24
    17   10    4   36   32
    25   18   12    8   40
```

(*b*)

```
» X = A(5, :);
x = reshape(X, 8, 1)
Y = A(:, 4);
y = Y(1: 4);
Z = A(:, 6);
z = Z(1: 4);
c = [x; y; z];
C = reshape(c, 1, 16)
C =
Columns 1 through 12
    33   34   35   36   37   38   39   40    4   12   20   28
Columns 13 through 16
     6   14   22   30
```

P2.6 Given the function $y = \left(x^{\sqrt{2}+0.02} + e^x\right)^{1.8} \ln x$. Determine the value of y for the following values of x: 2, 3, 8, 10, –1, –3, –5, –6.2. Solve the problem using MATLAB by first creating a vector **x**, and creating a vector **y**, using element-by-element calculations.

Solution

» x = [2; 3; 8; 10; –1; –3; –5; –6.2];

» y = x.^(sqrt(2) + 0.02) + exp(x)).^1.8.*log(x) % Vector (y) is vectorized using the rules in Table 2.18

»for i = 1:length(x)

fprintf('x = %f\ty = %f\n', x(i), y(i));

end

```
x = 2.000000     y = 44.456815
x = 3.000000     y = 358.601333
x = 8.000000     y = 3775247.017492
x = 10.000000    y = 151523614.007320
x = –1.000000    y = 1.775947
x = –3.000000    y = –20.763918
x = –5.000000    y = –113.745299
x = –6.200000    y = –222.404752
```

P2.7 Define a and b as scalars, $a = 0.75$, and $b = 11.3$, and x, y and z as the vectors, $x = 2, 5, 1, 9$, $y = 0.2, 1.1, 1.8, 2$ and $z = –3, 2, 5, 4$. Use these variables to calculate A given below using element-by-element computations for the vectors with MATLAB.

$$A = \frac{x^{1.1} y^{-2} z^5}{(a+b)^{b/3}} + a\frac{\left(\frac{z}{x} + \frac{y}{2}\right)}{z^a}$$

Solution

» a = 0.75;

» b = 11.3;

» x = [2; 5; 1; 9]; y = [0.2; 1.1; 1.8; 2]; z = [–3; 2; 5; 4];

» A = inline('x^1.1*y^–2*z^5/(a + b)^(b/3) + a*(z/x + y/2)/z^a');

» vectorize(A)

This gives output as follows:

ans(a, b, x, y, z) = x.^1.1.*y.^ – 2.*z.^5./(a + b).^(b./3) + a.*(z./x + y./2)./z.^a

Use this function and paste it as again A to get its value

» A = (x.^1.1*y.^ – 2*z.^5)/(a + b)^(b/3) + a.*(z./x + y./2)./z.^a

A =

–0.7783 + 0.3257i

0.4368

1.4052

0.6263

P2.8 Enter the following three matrices in MATLAB and show that:

$$A = \begin{bmatrix} 1 & 2 & 3 \\ -8 & 5 & 7 \\ -8 & 4 & 6 \end{bmatrix},\ B = \begin{bmatrix} 12 & -5 & 4 \\ 7 & 11 & 6 \\ 1 & 8 & 13 \end{bmatrix},\ C = \begin{bmatrix} 7 & 13 & 4 \\ -2 & 8 & -5 \\ 9 & -6 & 11 \end{bmatrix}$$

(*a*) A + B = B + A

(*b*) A + (B + C) = (A + B) + C

(*c*) 7(A + C) = 7(A) + 7(C)

(*d*) A * (B + C) = A * B + A * C

Solution

(*a*) A + B = B + A

```
» A+B
          13   –3    7
ans =
          –1   16   13
          –7   12   19
» B + A
          13   –3    7
ans =
          –1   16   13
          –7   12   19
```

(*b*) A + (B + C) = (A + B) + C

```
» A + (B + C)
          20   10   11
ans =
          –3   24    8
           2    6   30
» (A + B) + C
          20   10   11
ans =
          –3   24    8
           2    6   30
```

(*c*) 7(A + C) = 7A + 7C

```
» 7*(A + C)
        56  105   49
ans =
       –70   91   14
         7  –14  119
» 7*A + 7*C
        56  105   49
ans =
       –70   91   14
         7  –14  119
```

(*d*) A(B + C) = AB + AC

```
» A*(B + C)
        59   52   82
ans =
       –57   45  109
       –72   24   84
» A*B + A*C
        59   52   82
ans =
       –57   45  109
       –72   24   84
```

P2.9 Consider the polynomials

$p_1(s) = s^3 + 5s^2 + 3s + 10$

$p_2(s) = s^4 + 7s^3 + 5s^2 + 8s + 15$

$p_3(s) = s^5 + 15s^4 + 10s^3 + 6s^2 + 3s + 9$

Determine $p_1(2)$, $p_2(2)$, and $p_3(3)$

Solution

```
» p1 = [1 5 3 10]; p2 = [1 7 5 8 15]; p3 = [1 15 10 6 3 9];
» polyval(p1, 2)
Output is ans = 44
» polyval(p2, 2)
Output is ans = 123
» polyval(p3, 2)
Output is ans = 391
```

P2.10 The following polynomials are given:

$p_1(x) = x^5 + 2x^4 - 3x^3 + 7x^2 - 8x + 7$

$p_2(x) = x^4 + 3x^3 - 5x^2 + 9x + 11$

$p_3(x) = x^3 - 2x^2 - 3x + 9$

$p_4(x) = x^2 - 5x + 13$

$p_5(x) = x + 5$

Use MATLAB functions with polynomial coefficient vectors to evaluate the expressions at $x = 2$.

Solution

Define

```
» p1 = [1 2 –3 7 –8 7]; p2 = [1 3 –5 9 11]; p3 = [1 –2 –3 9]; p4 = [1 –5 13]; p5 = [1 5];
» polyval(p1, 2)
Output is ans = 59

» polyval (p2, 2)
Output is ans = 49

» polyval(p3, 2)
Output is ans = 3

» polyval(p4, 2)
Output is ans = 7

» polyval(p5, 2)
Output is ans = 7
```

P2.11 Determine the roots of the following polynomials:

(*a*) $p_1(x) = x^7 + 8x^6 + 5x^5 + 4x^4 + 3x^3 + 2x^2 + x + 1$

(*b*) $p_2(x) = x^6 - 7x^6 + 7x^5 + 15x^4 - 10x^3 - 8x^2 + 7x + 15$

(*c*) $p_3(x) = x^5 - 13x^4 + 10x^3 + 12x^2 + 8x - 15$

(*d*) $p_4(x) = x^4 + 7x^3 + 12x^2 - 25x + 8$

(*e*) $p_5(x) = x^3 + 15x^2 - 23x + 105$

(*f*) $p_6(x) = x^2 - 18x + 23$

(*g*) $p_7(x) = x + 7$

Solution

Define

```
»p1 = [1 8 5 4 3 2 1 1]; p2 = [1 –7 7 15 –10 –8 7 15]; p3 = [1 –13 10 12 8 –15];
»p4 = [1 7 12 –25 8]; p5 = [1 15 –23 105]; p6 = [1 –18 23]; p7 = [1 7];
```

» a = roots(p1)

Output is a =

–7.3898

–0.6570 + 0.3613i

–0.6570 – 0.3613i

0.4268 + 0.5473i

0.4268 – 0.5473i

–0.0749 + 0.7030i

–0.0749 – 0.7030i

» b = roots(p2)

Output is b =

5.1625

2.4906

0.8961 + 0.6912i

0.8961 – 0.6912i

–1.2191

–0.6131 + 0.6094i

–0.6131 – 0.6094i

» c = roots(p3)

Output is c =

12.0867

1.4875

–0.7057 + 0.7061i

–0.7057 – 0.7061i

0.8371

» d = roots(p4)

Output is d =

–4.1331 + 2.2411i

–4.1331 – 2.2411i

0.8305

0.4358

» e = roots(p5)

Output is e =

16.7477

0.8738 + 2.3465i

0.8738 – 2.3465i

```
» f = roots(p6)
Output is f =
        16.6158
        1.3842
» g = roots(p7)
Output is g = –7
```

P2.12 An aluminum thin-walled sphere is used as a marker buoy. The sphere has a radius of 65cm and a wall thickness of 10 mm. The density of aluminum is 2700 kg/m^3. The buoy is placed in the ocean where the density of the water is 1050 kg/m^3. Determine the height H between the top of the buoy and the surface of the water.

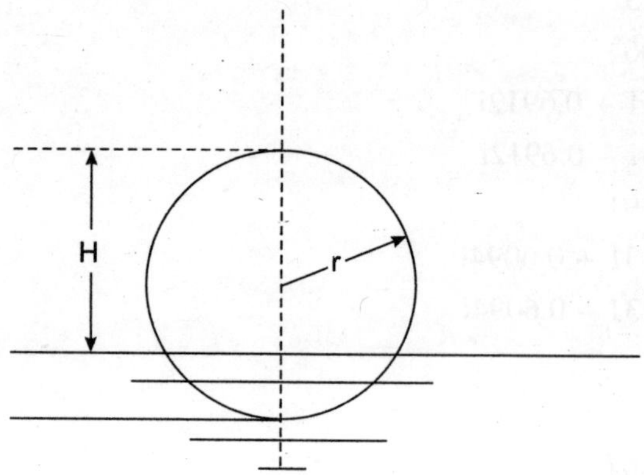

Fig. P2.12

Solution

According to Archimedes principle, the buoyancy force is equal to the weight of the fluid displaced by the body.

Weight of the sphere Ws = ρAlg 4π(ro3 – ri3)/3

Weight of water displaced Ww = ρwπ(2ro – H)2(ro + H)g/3

Setting the two weights equal to each other gives the following:

H3 – 3roH2 + 4ro3 – 4ρA1(ro3 – ri3)/ρw = 0

Last equation is a third degree polynomial in H.

```
ro = 0.65; rin = 0.5;
rhoal = 2700; rhow = 1050;
a0 = 4*ro^3 – 4*rhoal*(ro^3 – rin^3)/rhow;
p = [1 –3*ro 0 a0];
```

```
H = roots(p);
%%%%%%%%%%%%%%%%%%
» H =
        2.0544
       –0.0522 + 0.4601i
       –0.0522 – 0.4601i
```

P2.13 Determine the values of x, y, and z for the following set of linear algebraic equations:

$$x_2 - 3x_3 = -7$$
$$2x_1 + 3x_2 - x_3 = 9$$
$$4x_1 + 5x_2 - 2x_3 = 15$$

Solution

This set of equations can be written as: AX = B and X is obtained through matrix inversion

```
» A = [0 1 –3; 2 3 –1; 4 5 –2];
» B = [–7; 9; 15];
» X = inv(A)*B;
» fprintf('solution is %f\n%f\%f\n', X);
```

Output is as follows:

solution is 1.666667 3.000000 3.333333

P2.14 Write a simple script file to find (*a*) dot product (*b*) crossproduct of 2 vectors: $a = \hat{j} - \hat{k}$ and $b = 3\hat{i} - 2\hat{j}$.

Solution

```
a = [0 1 –1];
b = [3 –2 0];
d = dot(a, b);
c = cross(a, b);
fprintf('dot product of vectors is %f\n', d);
fprintf('cross product is\n'); disp(c);
%%%%%%%%%%%%%%%%%%%%%%%%%%%%%
» vector
dot product of vectors is –2.000000
cross product is
        –2   –3   –3
```

P2.15 Write a function to find gradient of $f(x, y) = x^2 + y^2 - 2xy + 4$ at (*a*) (1, 1) (*b*) (1, –2) and (*c*) (0, –3). Use the function name from command prompt.

Solution

```
function y = grad(X)
y = [2*X(1) – 2*X(2); 2*X(2) – 2*X(1)];  % vector of partial derivatives (gradient)
» grad([1 1])
ans =
     0
     0
» grad([1 –2])
ans =
     6
    –6
» grad([0 –3])
ans =
     6
    –6
```

P2.16 Write MATLAB functions $f = x^2 - 3x + 1$ and $g = e^x - 4x + 6$ and find the result f(127)/g(5) from a script file.

Solution

```
function p = f(x)
p = x^2 – 3*x + 1;
function q = g(x)
q = exp(x) – 4*x + 6;
r = f(127)/g(5);
disp(r);
» result
» 117.1686
```

P2.17 Plot the function $y = |x| \cos(x)$ for $-200 \le x \le 200$.

Solution

First define the range variable and then obtain corresponding values of y.

```
» x = [–200 : 1 : 200];
```

```
» y = abs(x) .* cos(x);
» plot (x, y)
```

Things like title, x-axis and y-axis, grid can be given after this.

```
»title('lxl cos(x) for –200 \leq x \leq 200')
»xlabel('x')
»ylabel('y')
```

Output is shown in Fig. P2.17.

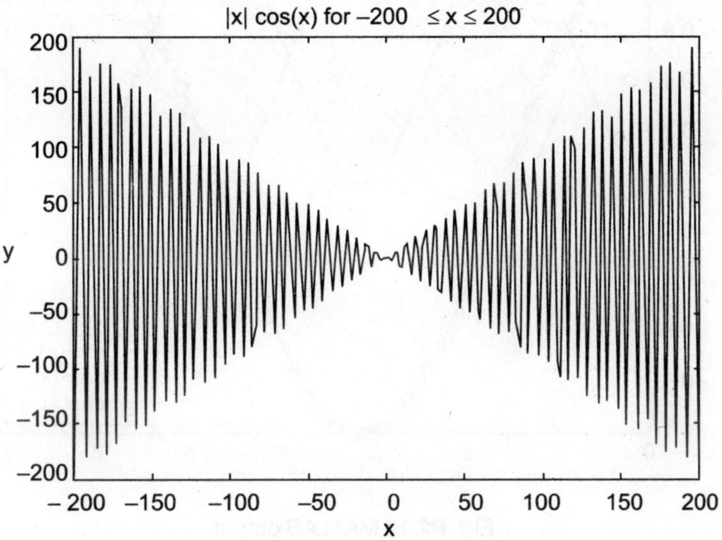

Fig. P2.17

P2.18 Plot the following functions on the same plot for $0 \leq x \leq 2\pi$ using the plot function:

(*a*) $\sin^2 (x)$

(*b*) $\cos^2 x$

(*c*) $\cos (x)$

Solution

```
»x = [0 : .01 : 2*pi];
»ys2 = (sin(x)).^2;
»yc2 = (cos(x)).^2;
```

»yc = cos(x);

»plot (x, ys2, x, yc2, '—', x, yc, '–0');

»legend('sin^2(x)', 'cos^2(x)', 'cos(x)', 4) % 4 refers to quadrant number (right bottom)

»xlabel('x')

The plot obtained is shown in Fig. P2.18.

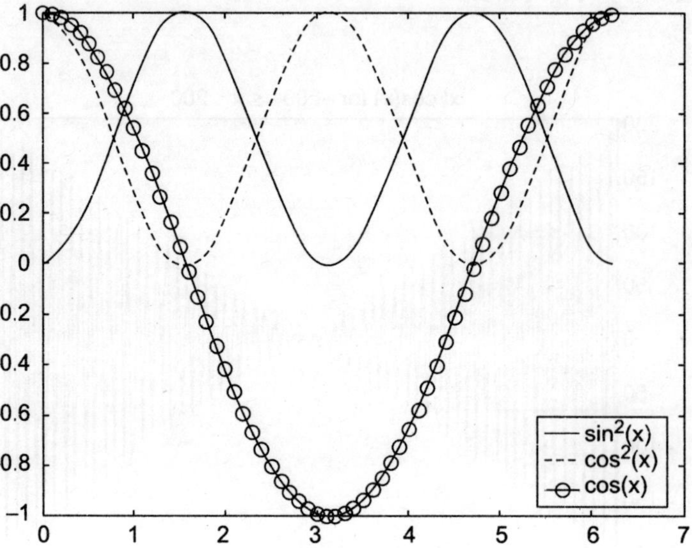

Fig. P2.18 MATLAB output

P2.19 Plot a graph of the function y = 45 sin(0.4t) for t ∈ [0, 3].

Solution

» i = 1;

» for t = 0:0.2:3

y(i) = 45*sin(0.4*t);

i = i+1;

end

» T = [0:0.2:3];

» plot(T, y, '–p');

```
» xlabel('t'); ylabel('y(t)');
» grid on;
```

Output is shown in Fig. P2.19:

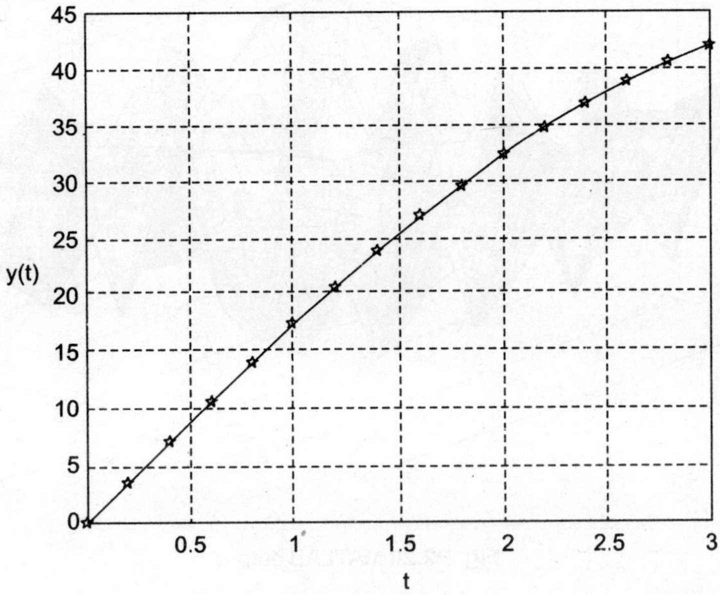

Fig. P2.19 MATLAB output

P2.20 Consider the function z = 0.56 cos(xy). Draw a surface plot showing variation of z with x and y. Given x∈[0, 10] and y∈[0,100]

Solution

```
x = 0:1:10;
y = 0:5:100;
[x, y] = meshgrid(x, y);
z = 0.56.*cos(x.*y);
mesh(x, y, z)
surf(x, y, z)
xlabel('x'); ylabel('y'); zlabel('z')
title('\bfPlot of variation of amplitude in time and frequency domain');
```

Output is shown in Fig. P2.20.

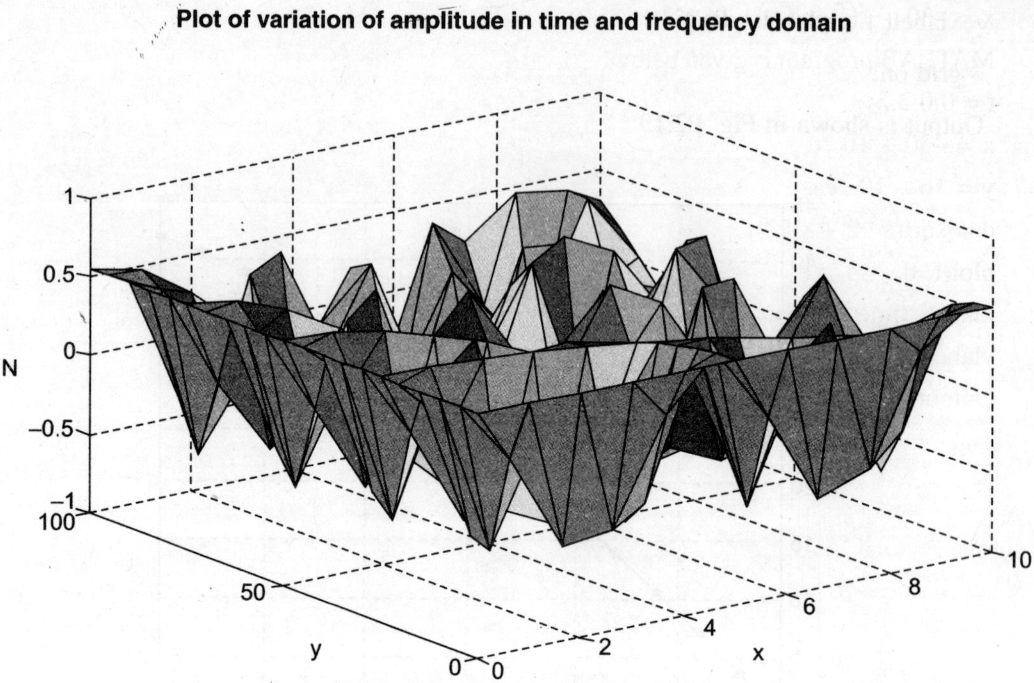

Fig. P2.20 MATLAB output

P2.21 Figure P2.21 shows two boats: boat A travels south at a speed of 10 mph, and boat B travels east at a speed of 19 mph. The ships are positioned at 8 am are also shown in figure. Write a MATLAB program to plot the distance between the ships as a function of time for the next 5 hours.

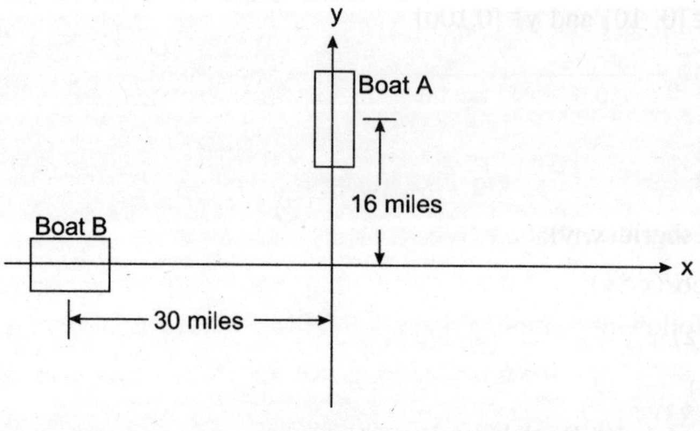

Fig. P2.21

Solution

From basic physics, distance is $d = \sqrt{x^2 + y^2}$, where (x, y) are coordinates of boats which can be written as:

x = –30 + 10t and y = 16 – 19t

MATLAB program is given below:

```
t = 0:0.2:5;
x = –30 + 10.*t;
y = 16 – 19.*t;
d = sqrt(x.^2 + y.^2);
plot(t, d, '–p');
xlabel('time (hrs)');
ylabel('distance between ships(miles)');
```

Output is as shown in Fig. P2.21(a).

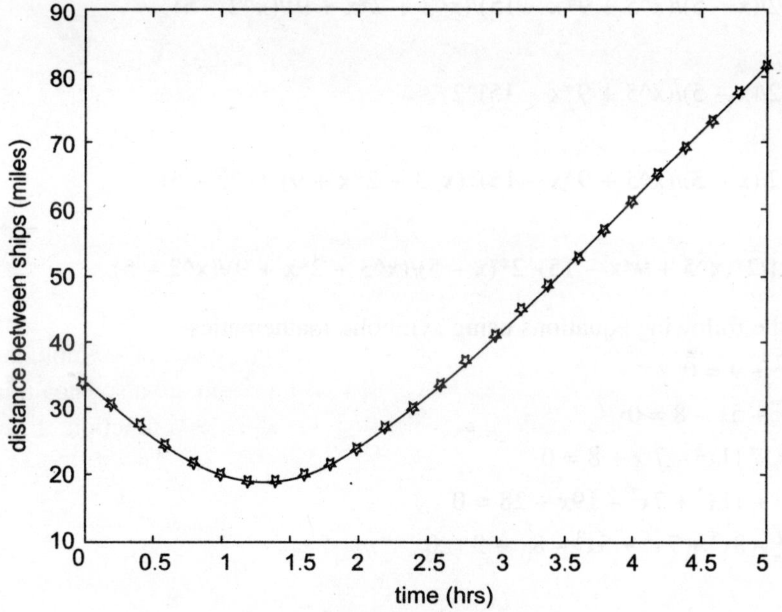

Fig. P2.21(a) MATLAB output

P2.22 Consider the given symbolic expressions defined below:

S1 = '2/(*x* – 5)'; S2 = '*x* ^ 5 + 9 * *x* – 15'; S3 = '(*x* ^ 3 + 2 * *x* +9) * (*x* * *x* – 5)';

Perform the following symbolic operations using MATLAB.

(*a*) S1S2/S3 (*b*) S1/S2S3 (*c*) S1/(S2)^2 (*d*) S1S3/S2

(*e*) (S2)^2/(S1S3)

Solution

```
syms x S1 S2 S3 a b c d e % Shortcut for constructing symbolic objects
»S1 = 2/(x – 5);
»S2 = x ^ 5 + 9 * x – 15;
```

```
»S3 = (x ^ 3 + 2 * x + 9) * (x * x – 5);
»a = S1*S2/S3
»b = S1/(S2*S3)
»c = S1/S2^2
»d = S1*S3/S2
»e = S2^2/(S1*S3)
```

Output is as follows:

```
a =
      2/(x – 5)*(x^5 + 9*x – 15)/(x^3 + 2*x + 9)/(x^2 – 5)
b =
      2/(x – 5)/(x^5 + 9*x – 15)/(x^3 + 2*x + 9)/(x^2 – 5)
c =
      2/(x – 5)/(x^5 + 9*x – 15)^2
d =
      2/(x – 5)/(x^5 + 9*x – 15)*(x^3 + 2*x + 9)*(x^2 – 5)
e =
      1/2*(x^5 + 9*x – 15)^2*(x – 5)/(x^3 + 2*x + 9)/(x^2 – 5)
```

P2.23 Solve the following equations using symbolic mathematics.

(*a*) $x^2 + 9 = 0$

(*b*) $x^2 + 5x - 8 = 0$

(*c*) $x^3 + 11x^2 - 7x + 8 = 0$

(*d*) $x^4 + 11x^3 + 7x^2 - 19x + 28 = 0$

(*e*) $x^7 - 8x^5 + 7x^4 + 5x^3 - 8x + 9 = 0$

Solution

(*a*) `»f = 'x^2+9 = 0'; solve(f, 'x')`

```
ans =
    [ 3*i]
    [ –3*i]
```

(*b*) `»f = 'x^2 + 5*x – 8 = 0'; solve(f, 'x')`

```
ans =
    [ –5/2 + 1/2*57^(1/2)]
    [ –5/2 – 1/2*57^(1/2)]
```

(*c*) » f = 'x^3 + 11*x^2 – 7*x + 8 = 0'; solve(f, 'x')

»ans =

[–1/6*(14284 + 12*144321^(1/2))^(1/3) – 284/3/(14284 + 12*144321^(1/2))^(1/3)–11/3]

[1/12*(14284 + 12*144321^(1/2))^(1/3) + 142/3/(14284 + 12*144321^(1/2))^(1/3) –11/3 + 1/2*i*3^(1/2)*

(–1/6*(14284 + 12*144321^(1/2))^(1/3) + 284/3/(14284 + 12*144321^(1/2))^(1/3))]

[1/12*(14284 +12*144321^(1/2))^(1/3) + 142/3/(14284 + 12*144321^(1/2))^(1/3) – 11/3 – 1/2*i*3^(1/2)*

(–1/6*(14284 + 12*144321^(1/2))^(1/3) + 284/3/(14284 + 12*144321^(1/2))^(1/3))]

This is difficult to read. Thus we can write as eval(ans) to evaluate this solution.

» eval(ans)

ans =

```
–11.6592
 0.3296 – 0.7599i
 0.3296 + 0.7599i
```

(*a*) »f = 'x^4 + 11*x^3 + 7*x^2 – 19*x + 28 = 0'; solve(f, 'x'); eval(ans)

ans =

```
0.7152 + 0.8217i
0.7152 – 0.8217i
–2.3378
–10.0927
```

(*b*) »f = 'x^7 – 8*x^5 + 7*x^4 + 5*x^3 – 8*x + 9'; solve(f, 'x'); eval(ans)

ans =

```
–3.1362
–0.8007 – 0.6944i
–0.8007 + 0.6944i
 0.6139 – 0.6513i
 0.6139 + 0.6513i
 1.7549 – 0.3308i
 1.7549 + 0.3308i
```

P2.24 Determine the values of x, y, and z for the following set of linear algebraic equations:

$$2x + y - 3z = 11$$
$$4x - 2y + 3z = 8$$
$$-2x + 2y - z = -6$$

Solution

```
»syms x y z
»% ANOTHER WAY OF WRITING EQUATIONS AS FUNCTION
»eqn1 = 2*x + y – 3*z – 11;
»eqn2 = 4*x – 2*y + 3*z – 8;
»eqn3 = –2*x + 2*y – z + 6;
» [x, y, z] = solve(eqn1, eqn2, eqn3)
```

Output is as follows:

```
x =
        3
y =
        –1
z =
        –2
```

P2.25 Figure P2.25 shows a scale with two springs.

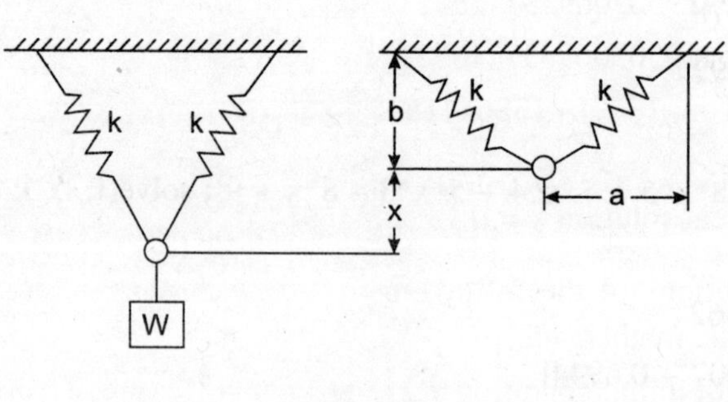

Fig. P2.25

The two springs are unstretched initially and will stretch when a mass is attached to the ring and the ring will displace downwards a distance of x. The weight W of the object is given by

$$W = \frac{2k}{\ell}(\ell - \ell_0)(b + x)$$

where ℓ_0 = initial length of a spring = $\sqrt{a^2+b^2}$ and ℓ = the stretched length of the spring $=\sqrt{a^2+(b+x)^2}$. If k = spring constant, write a MATLAB program to determine the distance x when W = 350 N. Given: a = 0.16 m, b = 0.045 m, and the spring constant k = 3000 N/m.

Solution

Substituting the expressions for ℓ in terms of x into W, we get

$$W - 2k\left(1-\frac{\ell_0}{\sqrt{a^2+(b+x)^2}}\right)(b+x)=0,$$

$$\Rightarrow \quad 350 - 6000\left(1-\frac{0.1662}{\sqrt{0.0256+(0.045+x)^2}}\right)(0.045+x)=0,$$

where $\ell_0=\sqrt{a^2+b^2}=0.1662$

```
syms x
    a = 0.16; b = 0.045; W = 350; k = 3000;
    l0 = sqrt(a^2 + b^2);
    eqn = 350 – 6000*(1 – 0.1662/sqrt(0.0256 + (0.045 + x)^2))*(0.045 + x);
» x = solve(eqn)
x =
[–0.92911489530951193030693377153214e–1 – 0.11894920892604858985051553592798*i]
[–0.92911489530951193030693377153214e–1 + 0.11894920892604858985051553592798*i]
[                                   .13864416954998267806469927987985]
```

There is only one real solution x = 0.13864416954 m

P2.26 Determine the solutions of the following first-order ordinary differential equations using MATLAB's symbolic mathematics.

(*a*) $y' = 8x^2 + 5$ with initial condition $y(2) = 0.5$.

(*b*) $y' = 5x\sin^2(y)$ with initial condition $y(0) = \pi/5$.

(*c*) $y' = 7x\cos^2(y)$ with initial condition $y(0) = 2$.

(*d*) $y' = -5x + y$ with initial condition $y(0) = 3$.

(*e*) $y' = 3y + e^{-5x}$ with initial condition $y(0) = 2$.

Solution

```
» y = dsolve('Dy = 8*x^2 + 5', 'y(2) = 0.5','x')
```

Output is as follows:

y =

8/3*x^3 + 5*x – 185/6

(*a*) » y = dsolve('Dy = 5*x*sin(y)^2', 'y(0) = pi/5', 'x')

Output contains 2 solutions as follows:

y =

[2*atan(5/2*x^2 – 1/(5 – 2*5^(1/2))^(1/2) + 1/2*(25*x^4 – 20*x^2/(5 – 2*5^(1/2))^(1/2) + 4/(5 – 2*5^(1/2)) + 4)^(1/2))]

[2*atan(5/2*x^2 – 1/(5 – 2*5^(1/2))^(1/2) – 1/2*(25*x^4 – 20*x^2/(5–2*5^(1/2))^(1/2) + 4/(5 – 2*5^(1/2)) + 4)^(1/2))]

(*b*) » y = dsolve('Dy = 7*x*cos(y)^2', 'y(0) = 2', 'x')

Output is as follows:

y =

atan(7/2*x^2 + tan(2))

(*c*) » y = dsolve('Dy = –5*x + y', 'y(0) = 3', 'x')

y =

5*x+5–2*exp(x)

(*d*) » y = dsolve('Dy = 3*y + exp(–5*x)', 'y(0) = 2', 'x')

Output is as follows:

y =

–1/8*exp(–5*x) + 17/8*exp(3*x)

P2.27 For the following differential equations, use MATLAB to find x (t) when (*a*) all the initial conditions are zero, (*b*) x (t) when x (0) = 1 and $\dot{x}(0) = -1$.

(*a*) $\frac{d^2x}{dt^2} + 10\frac{dx}{dt} + 5x = 11$

(*b*) $\frac{d^2x}{dt^2} - 7\frac{dx}{dt} - 3x = 5$

(*c*) $\frac{d^2x}{dt^2} + 3\frac{dx}{dt} + 7x = -15$

(*d*) $\frac{d^2x}{dt^2} + \frac{dx}{dt} + 7x = 26$

Solution

(*a*) »x = dsolve('D2x = 11 – 10*Dx – 5*x', 'x(0) = 0', 'Dx(0) = 0')

y = dsolve('D2x = 11 – 10*Dx – 5*x', 'x(0) = 0', 'Dx(0) = –1')

Output is as follows:

x =

11/5 + (–11/10 – 11/20*5^(1/2))*exp((–5 + 2*5^(1/2))*t) – 11/100*(–5 + 2*5^(1/2))*5^(1/2) *exp(–(5 + 2*5^(1/2))*t)

y =

11/5 + (–11/10 – 3/5*5^(1/2))*exp((–5 + 2*5^(1/2))*t) – 1/50*(–30 + 11*5^(1/2))*5^(1/2)*exp(–(5 + 2*5^(1/2))*t)

(*b*) »x = dsolve('D2x = 5 + 7*Dx + 3*x', 'x(0) = 0', 'Dx(0) = 0')

y = dsolve('D2x = 5 + 7*Dx + 3*x', 'x(0) = 0', 'Dx(0) = –1')

Output is as follows:

x =

–5/3 + (5/6 + 35/366*61^(1/2))*exp(–1/2*(–7 + 61^(1/2))*t) + 5/366*(–7 + 61^(1/2))*61^(1/2) *exp(1/2*(7 + 61^(1/2))*t)

y =

–5/3 + (5/6 + 41/366*61^(1/2))*exp(–1/2*(–7 + 61^(1/2))*t) + 1/366*(–41+ 5*61^(1/2))*61^ (1/2) *exp(1/2*(7 + 61^(1/2))*t)

(*c*) »x = dsolve('D2x = –15 – 3*Dx–7*x', 'x(0) = 0', 'Dx(0) = 0')

y = dsolve('D2x = –15 – 3*Dx – 7*x', 'x(0) = 0', 'Dx(0) = –1')

Output is as follows:

x =

–15/7 + 15/7*exp(–3/2*t)*cos(1/2*19^(1/2)*t) + 45/133*19^(1/2)*exp(–3/2*t)*sin (1/2*19^(1/2)*t)

y =

–15/7 + 15/7*exp(–3/2*t)*cos(1/2*19^(1/2)*t) + 31/133*19^(1/2)*exp(–3/2*t)*sin (1/2*19^(1/2)*t)

(*d*) »x = dsolve('D2x = 26 – Dx – 7*x', 'x(0) = 0', 'Dx(0) = 0')

y = dsolve('D2x = 26 – Dx – 7*x', 'x(0) = 0', 'Dx(0) = –1')

Output is as follows:

x =

26/7 – 26/7*exp(–1/2*t)*cos(3/2*3^(1/2)*t) – 26/63*3^(1/2)*exp(–1/2*t)*sin(3/2*3^(1/2)*t)

y =

26/7 – 40/63*3^(1/2)*exp(–1/2*t)*sin(3/2*3^(1/2)*t) – 26/7*exp(–1/2*t)*cos(3/2*3^(1/2)*t)

They give solution of x in terms of default variable time t.

Here, we have to specify the differential equation in a string, using Dy for y′(t) and y for y(t). The last argument 't' is the name of the independent variable. If MATLAB can't find a solution it will return an empty symbol. If MATLAB finds several solutions it returns a vector of solutions. Sometimes MATLAB can't find an explicit solution, but returns the *solution in* **implicit form**.

E.g., dsolve('Dy = 1/(y – exp(y))', 't') returns

t – 1/2*y^2 + exp(y) + C1 = 0

Unfortunately MATLAB cannot handle initial conditions in this case. The solution will contain a constant C1. We can substitute values for the constant using **subs(sol, 'C1', value)**, e.g., to set C1 to 5 and plot this solution for t = –2 to 2 use ezplot(subs(sol, 'C1', 5), [–2 2]).

Sometimes it is better to solve differential equations numerically.

P2.28 Figure P2.28 shows a water tank (shaped as an inverted frustum cone with a circular hole at the bottom on the side).

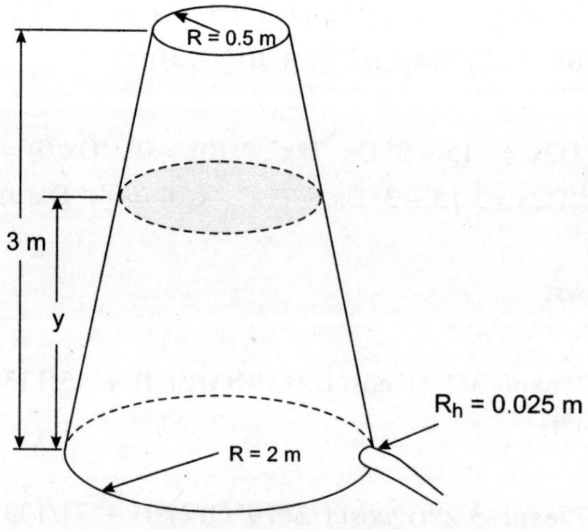

Fig. P2.28 Water-tank

The velocity of water discharged through the hole is given by $v = \sqrt{2gy}$ where h = height of the water and g = acceleration due to gravity (9.81 m/s^2). The rate of discharge of water in the tank as the water drains out through the hole is given by: $\frac{dy}{dt} = -\frac{\sqrt{2gyr_h^2}}{(2-0.5y)^2}$ where y = height of water and r_h = radius of the hole. Write a MATLAB program to solve and plot the differential equation. Assume, that the initial height of the water is 2.5 m.

Solution

```
y0 = 2.5; % Initial level
tspan = [0:1:5000]; % time-span
[t y] = ode45('flow', tspan, y0); % Solving the ODE
for i = 1:length(tspan)
   if y(i)> = 1e–5 T = t(i); end
end
plot(t, y);
xlabel('t(s)'); ylabel('level of water (m)'); grid on;
axis([0 T 0 y0])
```

The function file with the differential equation named flow.m is listed below:

```
function dydt = flow(y, t)
rh = 0.025; g = 9.81;
dydt = –abs(sqrt(2*g*y))*rh^2/(2 – 0.5*y)^2;
```

Output is shown in Fig. P2.28(a) below:

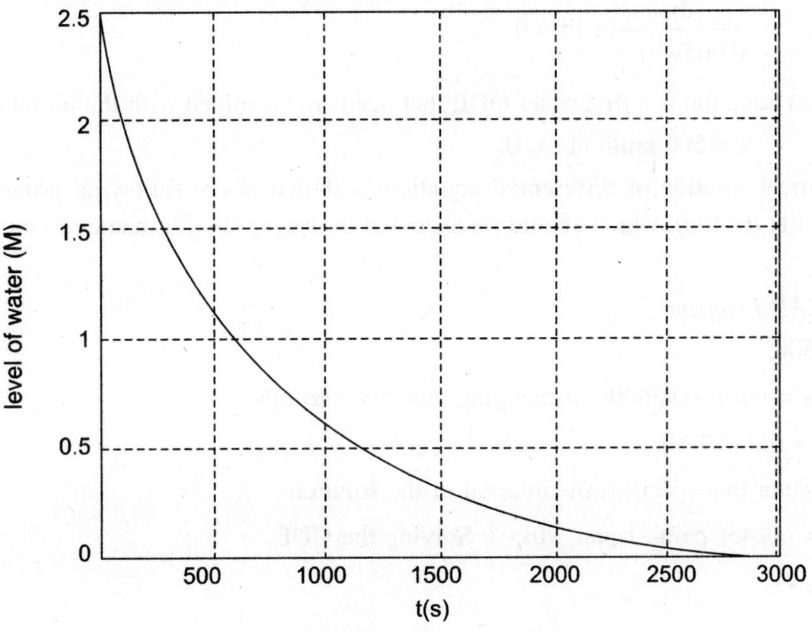

Fig. P2.28 (a) MATLAB output

P2.29 An airplane uses a parachute (See Fig. P2.29) and other means of braking as it slow down on the runway after landing. The acceleration of the airplane is given by $a = -0.005v^2 - 4$ m/s^2

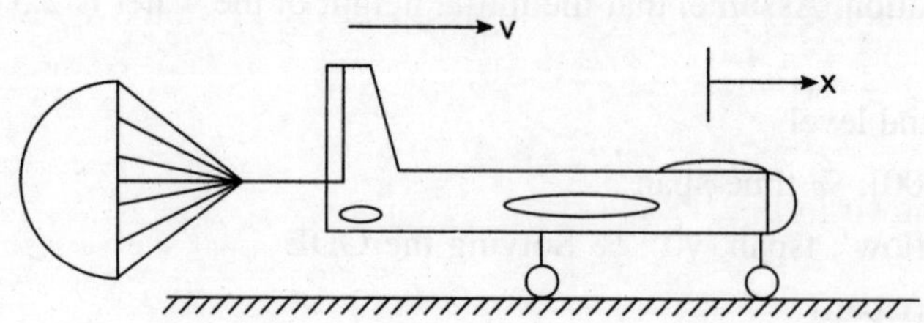

Fig. P2.29

Consider the airplane with a velocity of 500 km/h opens its parachute and starts decelerating at t = 0 seconds, write a MATLAB program to solve the differential equation and plot the velocity from t = 0 seconds until the airplane stops.

Solution

The deceleration of the air-plane is:

$$a = -0.005v2 - 4$$

or
$$\frac{dv}{dt} = -0.005v2 - 4$$

Further it can be written as

$$\frac{dv}{0.005v^2 + 4} + dt = 0$$

The last equation is a first order ODE that needs to be solved with the initial condition:

v = 500 km/h at t = 0.

Numerical solution of differential equation is shown in the following program written in a script file (m-file), which should be executed by typing the file name in command prompt.

MATLAB Program

```
v0 = 500;
v0mps = v0*1000/3600; % changing velocity into m/s
tspan = [0:0.2:100];
% a vector that specifies the interval of the solution
[t v] = ode45('para', tspan, v0); % Solving the ODE
plot(t, v)
```

```
xlabel('t(s)'); ylabel('velocity(m/s)')
axis([0 100 0 v0])
```

The function file with the differential equation named para.m is listed below:

```
function dtdv = para(v, t)
dtdv = -(0.005*v^2 + 4);
```

The output is shown in Fig. P2.29(a).

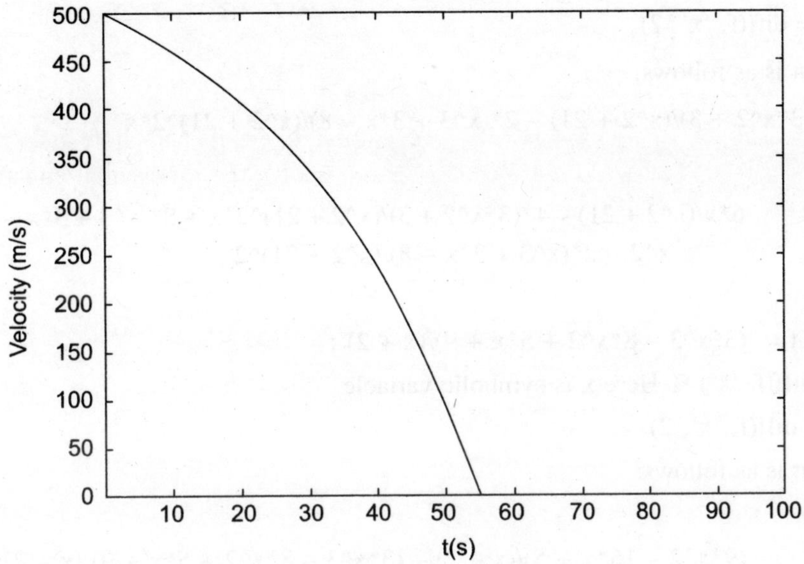

Fig. P2.29 (a) MATLAB output

P2.30 Obtain the first and second derivatives of the following functions using MATLAB's symbolic mathematics:

(*a*) $F(x) = x^5 - 8x^4 + 5x^3 - 7x^2 + 11x - 9$

(*b*) $F(x) = (x^3 + 3x - 8)(x^2 + 21)$

(*c*) $F(x) = (3x^3 - 8x^2 + 5x + 9)/(x + 2)$

(*d*) $F(x) = (x^5 - 3x^4 + 5x^3 + 8x^2 - 13)^2$

(*e*) $F(x) = (x^2 + 8x - 11)/(x^7 - 7x^6 + 5x^3 + 9x - 17)$

Solution

(*a*)
```
» f = 'x^5 - 8*x^4 + 5*x^3 - 7*x^2 + 11*x - 9';
» df = diff(f, 'x') % Here x is symbolic variable
» ddf = diff(f, 'x', 2)
```

Output is as follows:

df =

5*x^4 – 32*x^3 + 15*x^2 – 14*x + 11

ddf =

20*x^3 – 96*x^2 + 30*x – 14

(*b*) » f = '(x^3 + 3*x – 8)/(x^2 + 21)';

df = diff(f, 'x') % Here x is symbolic variable

ddf = diff(f, 'x', 2)

Output is as follows:

df = (3*x^2 + 3)/(x^2 + 21) – 2*(x^3 + 3*x – 8)/(x^2 + 21)^2*x

ddf =

6*x/(x^2 + 21) – 4*(3*x^2 + 3)/(x^2 + 21)^2*x + 8*(x^3 + 3*x – 8)/(x^2 +21)^3*
x^2 – 2*(x^3 + 3*x – 8)/(x^2 + 21)^2

(*c*) » f = '(3*x^3 – 8*x^2 + 5*x + 9)/(x + 2)';

df = diff(f, 'x') % Here x is symbolic variable

ddf = diff(f, 'x', 2)

Output is as follows:

» df =

(9*x^2 – 16*x + 5)/(x + 2) – (3*x^3 – 8*x^2 + 5*x + 9)/(x + 2)^2

» ddf =

(18*x – 16)/(x + 2) – 2*(9*x^2 – 16*x + 5)/(x + 2)^2 + 2*(3*x^3 –
8*x^2 + 5*x+9)/(x+2)^3

(*d*) » f = '(x^5 – 3*x^4 + 5*x^3 + 8*x^2 – 13)^2';

df = diff(f, 'x') % Here x is symbolic variable

ddf = diff(f, 'x', 2)

Output is as follows:

df =

2*(x^5 – 3*x^4 + 5*x^3 + 8*x^2 – 13)*(5*x^4 – 12*x^3 + 15*x^2 + 16*x)

ddf =

2*(5*x^4 – 12*x^3 + 15*x^2 + 16*x)^2 + 2*(x^5 – 3*x^4 + 5*x^3 + 8*x^2
–13)*(20*x^3 – 36*x^2 + 30*x + 16)

(*e*) » f = '(x^2 + 8*x – 11)/(x^7 – 7*x^6 + 5*x^3 + 9*x – 17)';

df = diff(f, 'x')

ddf = diff(f, 'x', 2)

Output is as follows:

df =

(2*x + 8)/(x^7 – 7*x^6 + 5*x^3 + 9*x – 17) – (x^2 + 8*x – 11)/(x^7 – 7*x^6 + 5*x^3 + 9*x – 17)^2*(7*x^6 – 42*x^5 + 15*x^2 + 9)

ddf =

2/(x^7 – 7*x^6 + 5*x^3 + 9*x – 17) – 2*(2*x + 8)/(x^7 – 7*x^6 + 5*x^3 + 9*x – 17)^2 *(7*x^6 – 42*x^5 + 15*x^2 + 9) + 2*(x^2 + 8*x – 11)/(x^7 – 7*x^6 + 5*x^3 + 9*x – 17)^3 *(7*x^6 – 42*x^5 + 15*x^2 + 9)^2 – (x^2 + 8*x – 11)/(x^7 – 7*x^6 + 5*x^3 + 9*x – 17)^2 *(42*x^5 – 210*x^4 + 30*x)

P2.31 Determine the values of the following integrals using MATLAB's symbolic functions:

(*a*) $\int (5x^7 - x^5 + 3x^3 - 8x^2 + 7)dx$

(*b*) $\int \sqrt{x} \cos x$

(*c*) $\int x^{2/3} \sin^2 2x$

(*d*) $\int_{0.2}^{1.8} x^2 \sin x \, dx$

(*e*) $\int_{-1}^{-0.2} |x| \, dx$

Solution

(*a*) int('5*x^7 – x^5 + 3*x^3 – 8*x^2 + 7')

output is as follows

» 5/8*x^8 – 1/6*x^6 + 3/4*x^4 – 8/3*x^3 + 7*x

(*b*) » int('sqrt(x)*cos(x)')

Output is

sin(x)*x^(1/2) – 1/2*2^(1/2)*pi^(1/2)*FresnelS(2^(1/2)/pi^(1/2)*x^(1/2))

(*c*) » int('x^(2/3)*sin(2*x)^2')

Output is

ans =

12/11*x^(11/3)*hypergeom([1, 11/6], [2, 3/2, 17/6], –4*x^2)

(*d*) » int('x^2*sin(x)', 0.2, 1.8)

ans =

−31/25*cos(9/5) + 18/5*sin(9/5) − 49/25*cos(1/5) − 2/5*sin(1/5)

» eval(ans)

ans =

1.7872

(*e*) » int('abs(x)', −1, −0.2)

ans =

12/25

P2.32 Use MATLAB to calculate the following integral: $\int_0^5 \frac{1}{0.8x^2 + 0.5x + 2} dx$

Solution

» int('1/(0.8*x^2 + 0.5*x + 2)', 0, 5)

ans =

.87742237464484169324612512790706

P2.33 Use MATLAB to calculate the following integral: $\int_0^{10} \cos^2(0.5x)\sin^4(0.5x)dx$

Solution

» int('cos(0.5*x)^2*sin(0.5*x)^4', 0, 10)

Output will come like this

ans =

0.60317912454575379882393952215336

P2.34 The variation of gravitational acceleration g with altitude y is given by: $g = \frac{R^2}{(R+y)^2} g_0$, where R = 6371 km is radius of the earth and $g_0 = 9.81$ m/s^2 is gravitational acceleration at sea level. The change in the gravitational potential energy ΔU of an object that is raised up from the earth is given by: $\Delta U = \int_0^y mg dy$. Determine the change in the potential energy of a satellite with a mass of 500 kg that is raised from the surface of the earth to a height of 800 km.

Solution

» ΔU = int('500*(6371e3)^2/(6371e3 + y)^2*9.81', 0, 800e3)

ΔU =

3486236787.0589875888997350439269

P2.35 Find the Laplace transform of the following function using MATLAB:

$f(t) = 7t^3 \cos(5t + 60°)$

Solution

```
» syms t % tell MATLAB that "t" is a symbol.
» f = 7 * t^3*cos(5*t + (pi/3)); % define the function.
» laplace(f)
ans =
      -84/(s^2 + 25)^3*s^2 + 21/(s^2 + 25)^2 + 336*(1/2*s – 5/2*3^(1/2))/(s^2
          + 25)^4*s^3 – 168 *(1/2*s – 5/2*3^(1/2))/(s^2 + 25)^3*s
» pretty(laplace(f)) % the pretty function prints symbolic output % in a format that resembles
typeset mathematics.
```

$$-84\frac{s^2}{(s^2+25)^3}+\frac{21}{(s^2+25)^2}+336\frac{(1/2s-5/23)^{1/2}s^3}{(s^2+25)^4}$$

$$-168\frac{(1/2s-5/23)s}{(s^2+25)^3}$$

P2.36 Use MATLAB program to find the transforms of the following functions:

(*a*) $f(t) = -7t\, e^{-5t}$

(*b*) $f(t) = -3 \cos 5t$

(*c*) $f(t) = t \sin 7t$

(*d*) $f(t) = 5\, e^{-2t} \cos 5t$

(*e*) $f(t) = 3 \sin(5t + 45°)$

(*f*) $f(t) = 5\, e^{-3t} \cos(t - 45°)$

Solution

(*a*)
```
»syms t x
» f = –7*t*exp(–5*t);
» laplace(f, x)
ans =
      –7/(x+5)^2
```

(*b*)
```
»syms t x
»f = –3*cos(5*t);
» laplace(f, x)
ans =
      –3*x/(x^2+25)
```

(*c*) »syms t x

» f = t*sin(7*t);

» laplace(f, x)

ans =

1/(x^2 + 49)*sin(2*atan(7/x))

(*d*) » syms t x

» f = 5*exp(–2*t)*cos(5*t);

» laplace(f, x)

ans =

5*(x + 2)/((x + 2)^2 + 25)

(*e*) »syms t x

» f = 3*sin(5*t + (pi/4));

» laplace(f, x)

ans =

3*(1/2*x*2^(1/2) + 5/2*2^(1/2))/(x^2 + 25)

(*f*) »syms t x

» f = 5*exp(–3*t)*cos(t–(pi/4));

» laplace(f, x)

ans =

5*(1/2*(x + 3)*2^(1/2) + 1/2*2^(1/2))/((x + 3)^2 + 1)

P2.37 Consider the two matrices:

$$\mathbf{A} = \begin{bmatrix} 1 & 0 & 2 \\ 2 & 5 & 4 \\ -1 & 8 & 7 \end{bmatrix} \quad \text{and} \quad \mathbf{B} = \begin{bmatrix} 7 & 8 & 2 \\ 3 & 5 & 9 \\ -1 & 3 & 1 \end{bmatrix}$$

Using MATLAB, determine the following:

(*a*) $\mathbf{A} + \mathbf{B}$

(*b*) $\mathbf{AB}$

(*c*) $\mathbf{A}^2$

(*d*) $\mathbf{A}^T$

(*e*) $\mathbf{B}^{-1}$

(*f*) $\mathbf{B}^T\mathbf{A}^T$

(*g*) $A^2 + B^2 - AB$

(*h*) Determinant of **A**, determinant of **B** and determinant of **AB**.

Solution

```
» A = [1 0 2; 2 5 4; –1 8 7];
» B = [7 8 2; 3 5 9; –1 3 1];
```

(*a*) A + B

```
» A + B
        8     8     4
ans =
        5    10    13
       –2    11     8
```

(*b*) A * B

```
» A * B
        5    14     4
ans =
       25    53    53
       10    53    77
```

(*c*) A2

```
» A^2
       –1    16    16
ans =
        8    57    52
        8    96    79
```

(*d*) AT

```
» A'
        1     2    –1
ans =
        0     5     8
        2     4     7
```

(*e*) B – 1

```
» inv(B)
        0.0991    0.0090   –0.2793
```

```
ans =

      0.0541  -0.0405   0.2568
     -0.0631   0.1306  -0.0495
```

(*f*) BTAT

```
» B'*A'
         5       25       10
ans =
        14       53       53
         4       53       77
```

(*g*) A2 + B2 – AB

```
» A^2 + B^2 – A*B
        65      104      100
w =
        10       80       59
        -1       53       28
```

(*h*) det A, det B and det of AB

```
» det(A)
ans =
      45
» det(B)
ans =
    -222
» det(A*B)
ans =
   -9990
```

P2.38 Use MATLAB to define the following matrices:

$$A = \begin{bmatrix} 2 & 1 \\ 0 & 5 \\ 7 & 4 \end{bmatrix} \qquad B = \begin{bmatrix} 5 & 3 \\ -2 & -4 \end{bmatrix} \qquad C = \begin{bmatrix} 2 & 3 \\ -5 & -2 \\ 0 & 3 \end{bmatrix} \qquad D = [1 \;\; 2]$$

Compute matrices and determinants if they exist.

(*a*) $(AC^T)^{-1}$ (*b*) $|B|$ (*c*) $|AC^T|$ (*d*) $(C^TA)^{-1}$

Solution

```
» A = [2 1; 0 5; 7 4];
» B = [5 3; –2 –4];
» C = [2 3; –5 –2; 0 3];
» D = [1 2];
```

(*a*) (ACT) – 1

```
» inv(A*C')
        8.8765    0.2536   –2.5361

ans =
        1.0e + 014 * 3.5506    0.1014   –1.0145
                    –6.5094   –0.1860    1.8598
```

(*b*) |B|

```
» abs(B)

ans =
        5    3
        4
```

(*c*) |ACT|

```
» abs(A*C')
       7    12    3
ans =
      15    10    15
      26    43    12
```

(*d*) (CTA) – 1

```
» inv(C'*A)
ans =
       0.0078      0.0359
      –0.0421      0.0062
```

P2.39 Consider the two matrices:

$$A = \begin{bmatrix} 1 & 0 & 1 \\ 2 & 3 & 4 \\ -1 & 6 & 7 \end{bmatrix} \text{ and } B = \begin{bmatrix} 7 & 4 & 2 \\ 3 & 5 & 6 \\ -1 & 2 & 1 \end{bmatrix}$$

Using MATLAB, determine the following:

(*a*) $A + B$ (*b*) AB (*c*) A^2 (*d*) A^T

(*e*) B^{-1} (*f*) B^TA^T (*g*) $A^2 + B^2 - AB$

(*h*) det A, det B, and det of AB.

Solution

```
» A = [1 0 1; 2 3 4; –1 6 7];
» B = [7 4 2; 3 5 6; –1 2 1];
```

(*a*) A + B

```
» A+B
        8     4     3
ans =
        5     8    10
       –2     8     8
```

(*b*) A * B

```
» A*B
        6     6     3
ans =
       19    31    26
        4    40    41
```

(*c*) A2

```
» A^2
        0     6     8
ans =
        4    33    42
        4    60    72
```

(*d*) AT

```
» A'
        1     2    –1
```

ans =

```
     0     3     6
     1     4     7
```

(*e*) B – 1

» inv(B)

```
    0.1111    0.0000   –0.2222
ans =
    0.1429   –0.1429    0.5714
   –0.1746    0.2857   –0.3651
```

(*f*) BTAT

» B'*A'

```
     6    19     4
ans =
     6    31    40
     3    26    41
```

(*g*)A2 + B2 – AB

» A^2 + B^2 – A*B

```
    53    52    45
w =
    15    51    58
    –2    28    42
```

(*h*) det A, det B and det of AB

» det(A)

ans =

12

» det(B)

ans =

–63

» det(A*B)

ans =

–756

P2.40 Find the inverse of the following matrices:

(a) $\mathbf{A} = \begin{bmatrix} 3 & 2 & 1 \\ -1 & 5 & 4 \\ 5 & 7 & -9 \end{bmatrix}$

(b) $\mathbf{B} = \begin{bmatrix} 1 & 6 & 3 \\ -4 & -5 & 7 \\ 8 & 4 & 2 \end{bmatrix}$

(c) $\mathbf{C} = \begin{bmatrix} -1 & -2 & 5 \\ -4 & 7 & 2 \\ 7 & -8 & -1 \end{bmatrix}$

Solution

(a)
```
» A = [3 2 1; –1 5 4; 5 7 –9];
» w = inv(A)

         0.3188     –0.1092     –0.0131
w =
        –0.0480      0.1397      0.0568
         0.1397      0.0480     –0.0742
```

(b)
```
          1      6      3
B =
         –4     –5      7
          8      4      2

» B = [1 5 3; –4 –5 7; 8 4 2];
» w = inv(B)
        –0.1073      0.0056      0.1412
w =
         0.1808     –0.0621     –0.0537
         0.0678      0.1017      0.0424
```

(c)
```
         –1     –2      5
```

```
C =
    -4    7    2
     7   -8   -1

» C = [-1 -2 5; -4 7 2; 7 -8 -1];
» w = inv(C)
   -0.0789   0.3684   0.3421

w =
   -0.0877   0.2982   0.1579
    0.1491   0.1930   0.1316
```

P2.41 Determine the eigenvalues and eigenvectors of the following matrices using MATLAB:

$$A = \begin{bmatrix} 1 & -2 \\ 1 & 5 \end{bmatrix}, \quad B = \begin{bmatrix} 1 & 5 \\ -2 & 7 \end{bmatrix}$$

Solution

```
» A = [1 -2; 1 5];
» [V, D] = eig(A)

V =
   -0.9597    0.5054
    0.2811   -0.8629

D =
    1.5858    0
    0         4.4142

» B = [1 5; -2 7];
» [V, D] = eig(B)

V =
   0.2673 + 0.8018i    0.2673 - 0.8018i
        0 + 0.5345i         0 - 0.5345i

D =
   4.0000 + 1.0000i    0
   0                   4.0000 - 1.0000i
```

P2.42 If $A = \begin{bmatrix} 4 & 6 & 2 \\ 5 & 6 & 7 \\ 10 & 5 & 8 \end{bmatrix}$

Use MATLAB to determine the following:

(*a*) The three eigenvalues of **A**

(*b*) The eigenvectors of **A**

(*c*) Show that **AQ** = **Qd** where Q is the matrix containing the eigenvectors as columns and **d** is the matrix containing the corresponding eigenvalues on the main diagonal and zeros elsewhere.

Solution

```
» A = [4 6 2; 5 6 7; 10 5 8];
» [V, D] = eig(A)

V =

    0.3723        –0.0271 + 0.5859i      –0.0271 – 0.5859i
    0.5972        –0.4405 – 0.2391i      –0.4405 + 0.2391i
    0.7104         0.4831 – 0.4140i       0.4831 + 0.4140i

D =

   17.4432              0                     0
         0         0.2784 + 3.0348i           0
         0              0                0.2784 – 3.0348i

» x = A*V
    6.4934        –1.7855 + 0.0808i      –1.7855 – 0.0808i
x =
   10.4178         0.6030 – 1.4035i       0.6030 + 1.4035i
   12.3923         1.3910 + 1.3509i       1.3910 – 1.3509i

» y = V*D
    6.4934        –1.7855 + 0.0808i      –1.7855 – 0.0808i
y =
   10.4178         0.6030 – 1.4035i       0.6030 + 1.4035i
   12.3923         1.3910 + 1.3509i       1.3910 – 1.3509i
```

P2.43 Determine eigenvalues and eigenvector of **A** using MATLAB.

(*a*) $\mathbf{A} = \begin{bmatrix} 0.5 & -0.8 \\ 0.75 & 1.0 \end{bmatrix}$ (*b*) $\mathbf{A} = \begin{bmatrix} 8 & 3 \\ -3 & 4 \end{bmatrix}$

Solution

(*a*) » A = [0.5 –0.8; 0.75 –1.0];

» [V, D] = eig(A)

```
V =
      -0.1796 + 0.6956i      -0.1796 - 0.6956i
            0 + 0.6956i            0 - 0.6956i

D =
      -0.2500 + 0.1936i                 0
                      0      -0.2500 - 0.1936i
```

(*b*)

» A = [8 3; –3 4];

» [V, D] = eig(A)

```
V =
      0.5270 - 0.4714i      0.5270 + 0.4714i
           0 + 0.7071i           0 - 0.7071i

D =
      6.0000 + 2.2361i                 0
                     0      6.0000 - 2.2361i
```

P2.44 Determine the eigenvalues and eigenvectors of the following matrices using MATLAB.

(*a*) $A = \begin{bmatrix} 1 & -2 \\ 1 & 3 \end{bmatrix}$ (*b*) $A = \begin{bmatrix} 1 & 5 \\ -2 & 4 \end{bmatrix}$

Solution

(*a*) » A=[1 –2; 1 3];

» [V, D] = eig(A)

```
V =
      -0.5774 - 0.5774i      -0.5774 + 0.5774i
            0 + 0.5774i            0 - 0.5774i
```

```
D =

    2.0000 + 1.0000i         0
         0              2.0000 - 1.0000i
```

(*b*)

```
» A = [1 5; -2 4];
» [V, D] = eig(A)

V =

    0.7440 + 0.4009i    0.7440 - 0.4009i
         0 + 0.5345i         0 - 0.5345i

D =

    2.5000 + 2.7839i         0
         0              2.5000 - 2.7839i
```

(*c*)

```
» A = [4 -1 5; 2 1 3; 6 -7 9];
» [V, D] = eig(A)

V =

    0.5571   -0.8289    0.7392
    0.3714   -0.0397    0.6717
    0.7428    0.5580    0.0477

D =

    10.0000        0          0
         0     0.5858         0
         0         0     3.4142
```

(*d*)

```
» A = [3 5 7; 2 4 8; 5 6 10];
» [V, D] = eig(A)
```

```
V =

    -0.5054    -0.0923 - 0.5594i   -0.0923 + 0.5594i
    -0.4893     0.7018 + 0.1500i    0.7018 - 0.1500i
    -0.7108    -0.3768 + 0.1467i   -0.3768 - 0.1467i

D =

    17.6859          0                  0
          0   -0.3430 + 1.0066i         0
          0          0            -0.3430 - 1.0066i
```

(*e*)

```
» A = [3 0 2 1; 1 2 5 4; 7 -1 2 6; 1 -2 3 4];
» [V, D] = eig(A)

V =

    -0.1953    0.3325   -0.0211 + 0.4078i   -0.0211 - 0.4078i
    -0.4090    0.7695   -0.4810 + 0.6075i   -0.4810 - 0.6075i
     0.7741    0.5261   -0.1631 + 0.2657i   -0.1631 - 0.2657i
    -0.4420    0.1433   -0.1475 - 0.3375i   -0.1475 + 0.3375i
D =
    -2.6635         0           0                   0
          0    6.5954           0                   0
          0         0    3.5341 + 1.1341i           0
          0         0           0            3.5341 - 1.1341i
```

(*f*)

```
» A = [1 3 5 7; 2 -1 -2 4; 3 2 1 1; 4 1 0 6];
» [V, D] = eig(A)

V =

     0.6752    0.8466   -0.2233 - 0.3064i   -0.2233 + 0.3064i
     0.2650   -0.3291    0.5062 + 0.5125i    0.5062 - 0.5125i
     0.3207   -0.2962   -0.3335 - 0.4542i   -0.3335 + 0.4542i
     0.6092   -0.2952    0.0599 + 0.1273i    0.0599 - 0.1273i
```

```
D =

    10.8684          0                  0                  0
          0    -4.3563                  0                  0
          0          0    0.2440 + 0.3308i                 0
          0          0                  0    0.2440 - 0.3308i
```

P2.45 Determine the eigenvalues and eigenvectors of A * B using MATLAB.

$$A = \begin{bmatrix} 3 & -1 & 2 & 1 \\ 1 & 2 & 7 & 4 \\ 7 & -1 & 8 & 6 \\ 1 & -2 & 3 & 4 \end{bmatrix} \qquad B = \begin{bmatrix} 1 & 2 & 5 & 7 \\ 2 & -1 & -2 & 4 \\ 3 & 2 & 5 & 1 \\ 4 & 1 & -3 & 6 \end{bmatrix}$$

Solution

```
» A = [3 -1 2 1; 1 2 7 4; 7 -1 8 6; 1 -2 3 4];
» B = [1 2 5 7; 2 -1 -2 4; 3 2 5 1; 4 1 -3 6];
» C = A*B;
» [V, D] = eig(C)

V =

   -0.2817    0.3810 - 0.2370i    0.3810 + 0.2370i   -0.3945
   -0.4157   -0.3597 - 0.3784i   -0.3597 + 0.3784i    0.9114
   -0.8327    0.5153 + 0.1438i    0.5153 - 0.1438i   -0.0528
   -0.2333   -0.4274 + 0.2391i   -0.4274 - 0.2391i   -0.1049

D =

   1.0e + 002 * 1.2034          0                  0                  0
          0    0.0026 + 0.0615i                    0                  0
          0                  0    0.0026 - 0.0615i                    0
          0                  0                  0              -0.0686
```

P2.46 Determine the eigenvalues and eigenvectors of A and B using MATLAB.

(*a*) $A = \begin{bmatrix} 4 & 5 & -3 \\ -1 & 2 & 3 \\ 2 & 5 & 7 \end{bmatrix}$ and $B = \begin{bmatrix} 1 & 2 & 3 \\ 8 & 9 & 6 \\ 5 & 3 & -1 \end{bmatrix}$

Solution

```
» A = [4 5 -3; -1 2 3; 2 5 7];
```

```
» [V, D] = eig(A)

V =

   0.0413 + 0.8753i   0.0413 – 0.8753i   –0.1344
  –0.2890 – 0.2916i  –0.2890 + 0.2916i    0.4083
   0.2450 + 0.0591i   0.2450 – 0.0591i    0.9029

D =

   2.0184 + 2.3967i        0                  0
        0             2.0184 – 2.3967i        0
        0                  0             8.9633
» B = [1 2 3; 8 9 6; 5 3 –1];
» [V, D] = eig(B)

V =

  –0.2299   –0.5452   –0.4718
  –0.9305    0.7528   –0.1126
  –0.2852   –0.3688    0.8745

D =

  12.8161        0          0
        0   0.2675          0
        0        0    –4.0836
```

P2.47 Determine the eigenvalues and eigenvectors of A = a * b using MATLAB.

$$\mathbf{a} = \begin{bmatrix} 6 & -3 & 4 & 1 \\ 0 & 4 & 2 & 6 \\ 1 & 3 & 8 & 5 \\ 2 & 2 & 1 & 4 \end{bmatrix} \text{ and } \mathbf{b} = \begin{bmatrix} 0 & 1 & 2 & 3 \\ 4 & 5 & 6 & -1 \\ 1 & 5 & 4 & 2 \\ 2 & -3 & 6 & 7 \end{bmatrix}$$

Solution

```
» a = [6 –3 4 1; 0 4 2 6; 1 3 8 5; 2 2 1 4];
» b = [0 1 2 3; 4 5 6 –1; 1 5 4 2; 2 –3 6 7];
» A = a * b;
» [V, D] = eig(A)
```

```
V =

    -0.1925   0.7337  -0.7417  -0.7156
    -0.5384  -0.5918  -0.1826  -0.1102
    -0.7413   0.1627   0.5595   0.5710
    -0.3515  -0.2915  -0.3217  -0.3870

D =

143.7552        0          0          0          0
                0   -23.2047          0          0
                0          0    -0.4838          0
                0          0          0     1.9333
```

P2.48 Determine the values of x, y, and z for the following set of linear algebraic equations:

$$x_2 - 3x_3 = -7$$
$$2x_1 + 3x_2 - x_3 = 9$$
$$4x_1 + 5x_2 - 2x_3 = 15$$

Solution

Method #1

```
» A = [0 1 –3; 2 3 –1; 4 5 –2];
» B = [–7 9 15]';
» w = A\B
```

Method #2

```
» A = [0 1 –3; 2 3 –1; 4 5 –2];
» B = [–7 9 15]';
» w = inv(A)*B

w =

    1.6667
    3.0000
    3.3333
```

P2.49 Determine the values of x, y, and z for the following set of linear algebraic equations:

$$2x - y = 10$$
$$-x + 2y - z = 0$$
$$-y + z = -50$$

Solution

Method #1

```
» A = [2 –1 0; –1 2 –1; 0 –1 1];
```

```
» B = [10 0 –50]';
» w = A\B
```

Method #2

```
» A = [2 –1  0; –1 2 –1; 0  –1 1];
» B = [10 0 –50]';
» w = inv(A)*B

w =

        –40.0000
        –90.0000
       –140.0000
```

P2.50 Solve the following set of equations using MATLAB.

(*a*)
$$2x_1 + x_2 + x_3 - x_4 = 12$$
$$x_1 + 5x_2 - 5x_3 + 6x_4 = 35$$
$$-7x_1 + 3x_2 - 7x_3 - 5x_4 = 7$$
$$x_1 - 5x_2 + 2x_3 + 7x_4 = 21$$

(*b*)
$$x_1 - x_2 + 3x_3 + 5x_4 = 7$$
$$2x_1 + x_2 - x_3 + x_4 = 6$$
$$-x_1 - x_2 - 2x_3 + 2x_4 = 5$$
$$x_1 + x_2 - x_3 + 5x_4 = 4$$

Solution

(*a*) **Method #1**

```
» A = [2 1 1 –1; 1 5 –5 6; –7 3 –7 –5; 1 –5 2 7];
» B = [12 35 7 21]';
» w = A\B
```

Method #2

```
» A = [2 1 1 –1; 1 5 –5 6; –7 3 –7 –5; 1 –5 2 7];
» B = [12 35 7 21]';
» w = inv(A)*B

w =

         35.2780
        –28.2511
        –40.8520
        –10.5471
```

(*b*)

Method #1

```
» A = [2 --1 3 5; 2 1 –1 1; –1 –1 –2 2; 1 1 –1 5];
» B = [7 6 5 4]';
» w = A\B
```

Method #2

```
» A = [2 –1 3 5; 2 1 –1 1; –1 –1 –2 2; 1 1 –1 5];
» B = [7 6 5 4]';
» w = inv(A)*B

w =

        3.6500
       –3.7500
       –2.0375
        0.4125
```

P2.51 Solve the following set of equations using MATLAB:

(*a*)

$$2x_1 + x_2 + x_3 - x_4 = 10$$
$$x_1 + 5x_2 - 5x_3 + 6x_4 = 25$$
$$-7x_1 + 3x_2 - 7x_3 - 5x_4 = 5$$
$$x_1 - 5x_2 + 2x_3 + 7x_4 = 11$$

(*b*)

$$x_1 - x_2 + 3x_3 + 5x_4 = 5$$
$$2x_1 + x_2 - x_3 + x_4 = 4$$
$$-x_1 - x_2 + 2x_3 + 2x_4 = 3$$
$$x_1 + x_2 - x_3 + 5x_4 = 1$$

Solution

(*a*) **Method #1**

```
» A = [2 1 1 –1; 1 5 –5 6; –7 3 –7 –5; 1 –5 2 7];
» B = [10 25 5 11]';
» w = A\B
```

Method #2

```
» A = [2 1 1 –1; 1 5 –5 6; –7 3 –7 –5; 1 –5 2 7];
» B = [10 25 5 11]';
» w = inv(A)*B
```

```
w =

   25.3587
  -19.6143
  -28.9058
   -7.8027
```

(*b*)

Method #1

```
» A = [2 -1 3 5; 2 1 -1 1; -1 -1 2 2; 1 1 -1 5];
» B = [5 4 3 1]';
» w = A\B
```

Method #2

```
» A = [2 -1 3 5; 2 1 -1 1; -1 -1 2 2; 1 1 -1 5];
» B = [5 4 3 1]';
» w = inv(A)*B

w =

   -2.5000
   24.0000
   13.6250
   -1.3750
```

P2.52 Solve the following set of equations using MATLAB:

(*a*)
$$x_1 + 2x_2 + 3x_3 + 5x_4 = 21$$
$$-2x_1 + 5x_2 + 7x_3 - 9x_4 = 17$$
$$5x_1 + 7x_2 + 2x_3 - 5x_4 = 23$$
$$-x_1 - 3x_2 - 7x_3 + 7x_4 = 26$$

(*b*)
$$x_1 + 2x_2 + 3x_3 + 4x_4 = 9$$
$$2x_1 - 2x_2 - x_3 + x_4 = -5$$
$$x_1 - 3x_2 + 4x_3 - 4x_4 = 7$$
$$2x_1 + 2x_2 - 3x_3 + 4x_4 = -6$$

Solution

(*a*) **Method #1**

```
» A = [1 2 3 5; -2 5 7 -9; 5 7 2 -5; -1 -3 -7 7];
» B = [21 17 23 26]';
» w = A\B
```

Method #2

(*a*) » A = [1 2 3 5; –2 5 7 –9; 5 7 2 –5; –1 –3 –7 7];

» B = [21 17 23 26]';

» w = inv(A)*B

w =

–8.0756
12.8353
–4.6128
3.4487

(*b*)

Method #1

» A = [1 2 3 4; 2 –2 –1 1; 1 –3 4 –4; 2 2 –3 4];

» B = [9 –5 7 –6]';

» w = A\B

Method #2

» A = [1 2 3 4; 2 –2 –1 1; 1 –3 4 –4; 2 2 –3 4];

» B = [9 –5 7 –6]';

» w = inv(A)*B

w =

–0.1355
1.0710
2.4774
–0.1097

P2.53 Determine the inverse of the following matrix using MATLAB:

$$A = \begin{bmatrix} 3s & 2 & 0 \\ 7s & -s & -5 \\ 3 & 0 & -3s \end{bmatrix}$$

Solution

» syms s

» A = [3*s 2 0; 7*s –1*s –5; 3 0 –3*s];

» w = inv(A)

Ans =

[s^2/(3*s^3 + 14*s^2 – 10), 2*s/(3*s^3 + 14*s^2 – 10), –10/3/(3*s^3 + 14*s^2 – 10)]
[(7*s^2 – 5)/(3*s^3 + 14*s^2 – 10), –3*s^2/(3*s^3 + 14*s^2 – 10), 5*s/(3*s^3 + 14*s^2–10)]
[s/(3*s^3 + 14*s^2 – 10), 2/(3*s^3 + 14*s^2–10), –1/3*s*(3*s + 14)/(3*s^3 + 14*s^2 – 10)]

>> pretty(w)

Manual "pretty"

$[s^2/(3s^3+14s^2-10),\quad 2s/(3s^3+14s^2-10),\quad -10/3/(3s^3+14s^2-10)]$

$[(7s^2-5)/(3s^3+14s^2-10),\quad -3s^2/(3s^3+14s^2-10),\quad 5s/(3s^3+14s^2-10)]$

$[s/(3s^3+14s^2-10),\quad 2/(3s^3+14s^2-10),\quad -1/3s(3s+14)/(3s^3+14s^2-10)]$

P2.54 Expand the following function F(s) into partial fractions with MATLAB:

$$F(s) = \frac{5s^3 + 7s^2 + 8s + 30}{s^4 + 15s^3 + 62s^2 + 85s + 25}$$

Solution

```
>> b = [0 5 7 8 30];
>> a = [1 15 62 85 25];
>> [r, p, k] = residue (b, a)

r =

     8.9278
    –4.6370
     0.0578
     0.6514

p =

    –9.2690
    –3.2633
    –2.0680
    –0.3997

k =

  []
```

Ans =>

$$F(s) = \frac{8.9278}{s+9.2690} + \frac{-4.6370}{s+3.2633} + \frac{0.0578}{s+2.0680} + \frac{0.6214}{s+0.3997}$$

P2.55 Determine the Laplace transform of the following time functions using MATLAB:

(*a*) f (t) = u (t + 9)

(*b*) f (t) = e^{5t}

(*c*) f (t) = (5t + 7)

(*d*) f (t) = 5u (t) + $8e^{7t} - 12e^{-8t}$

(*e*) f (t) = $e^{-t} + 9t^3 - 7t^{-2} + 8$

(*f*) f (t) = $7t^4 + 5t^2 - e^{-7t}$

(*g*) f (t) = 9ut + $5e^{-3t}$

Solution

(*a*) f(t0 = u(t + 9)

```
>>  sym s t u
>>  f = u*t+0*u;
>>  laplace(f, u)

ans =
        1/u*(1+9*u)

>>  pretty(laplace(f))
```

$$\frac{u(1+9s)}{s^2}$$

(*b*) f(t) = e^{5t}

```
>>  sym s t x
>>  f = exp(5*t);
>>  laplace(f, x)

ans =
        1/(x – 5)
```

```
>> pretty(laplace(f))
```

$$\frac{1}{s-5}$$

(*c*) f(t) = (5t + 7)

```
>> sym s t x
>> f = 5*t + 7;
>> laplace(f, x)

ans =
    (5 + 7*x)/x^2

>> pretty(laplace(f))
```

$$\frac{5+7s}{s^2}$$

(*d*) f(t) = 5u(t) + $8e^{7t}$ – $12e^{-St}$

```
>> sym s t x
>> f = 5*ut + 8*exp(7*t) – 12*exp(–8*t);
>> laplace(f, x)

ans =
          5/u + 8/(u – 7) – 12/(u + 8)

>> pretty(laplace(f))
```

$$\frac{5u}{s2}+\frac{8}{s-7}-\frac{12}{s+8}$$

(*e*) f(t) = $e^{-t} + 9t^3 - 7t^{-2} + 8$

```
>> sym s t x
>> f = exp(–t) + 9*t^3 – 7*t^(–2) + 8;
>> laplace(f, x)

ans =
          1/(1 + x) + 54/x^4–7*laplace(1/t^2, t, x) + 8/x
```

```
>> pretty(laplace(f))
```

$$\frac{1}{1+s}+\frac{54}{s^4}-7\ \text{laplace}\ (\frac{1}{t^2},\ t,\ s)+8/x$$

P2.56 Determine the inverse Laplace transform of the following rotational function using MATLAB:

$$F(s)=\frac{7}{s^2+5s+6}=\frac{7}{(s+2)(s+3)}.$$

Solution

```
>> syms s
>> num = 7;
>> den = s^2 + 5*s + 6;
>> F = num/den

F = 7/(s^2 + 5*s + 6)

>> invlaplaceF = ilaplace(F)
      invlaplaceF = –7*exp(–3*t) + 7*exp(–2*t)

>> pretty(invlaplaceF)
            –7 exp(–3 t) + 7 exp(–2 t)
```

P2.57 Determine the inverse transform of the following function having complex poles:

$$F(s)=\frac{15}{(s^3+5s^2+11s+10)}$$

Solution

```
>> syms s
>> num =15;
>> den = s^3 + 5*s^2 + 11*s + 10;
>> F = num/den

F = 15/(s^3 + 5*s^2 + 11*s + 10)

>> invlaplaceF = ilaplace(F)
```

```
invlaplaceF = 5*exp(-2*t) + 5/11*exp(-3/2*t) * (-11*cos(1/2*11^(1/2)*t)
              + 11^(1/2)*sin(1/2*11^(1/2)*t))

>> pretty(invlaplaceF)
```

$5e^{-2t} + 5/11\ e^{-3/2\ t}\ (-11\ \cos(1/2*11^{1/2}t) + 11^{1/2}\sin(1/2*11^{1/2}t))$

P2.58 Determine the inverse Laplace transform of the following functions using MATLAB:

(*a*) $F(s) = \dfrac{s}{s(s+2)(s+3)(s+5)}$

(*b*) $F(s) = \dfrac{1}{s^2(s+7)}$

(*c*) $F(s) = \dfrac{5s+9}{(s^3+8s+5)}$

(*d*) $F(s) = \dfrac{s-28}{s(s^2+9s+33)}$

Solution

(*a*)

```
>> syms s
>> num = s;
>> den = s^4 + 10*s^3 + 31*s^2 + 30*s;
>> F = num/den

F = s/(s^4 + 10*s^3 + 31*s^2 + 30*s)

>> invlaplaceF = ilaplace(F)
   invlaplaceF = 1/6*exp(-5*t) + 1/3*exp(-2*t)-1/2*exp(-3*t)

>> pretty(invlaplaceF)
```

$1/6\ e^{-5\,t} + 1/3\ e^{-2\,t} - 1/2\ e^{-3\,t}$

(*b*)

```
>> syms s
>> num = 1;
>> den = s^3 + 7*s^2;
>> F = num/den
```

```
F = 1/(s^3 + 7*s^2)

>> invlaplaceF = ilaplace(F)
   invlaplaceF = 1/49*exp(-7*t) - 1/49 + 1/7*t
>> pretty(invlaplaceF)
   1/49 e^(-7 t) - 1/49 + 1/7 t
```

(*c*)
```
>> syms s
>> num = 5*s + 9;
>> den = s^3 + 8*s + 5;
>> F = num/den

F = 5*s + 9/(s^3 + 8*s + 5)

>> invlaplaceF = ilaplace(F)
   invlaplaceF = 1/2723*sum((-1045*_alpha + 1104 + 207*_alpha^2)*exp(_alpha*t),_alpha
               = RootOf(_Z^3+8*_Z+5))
```

(*d*)
```
>> syms s
>> num = s - 28;
>> den = s^3 + 9*s^2 + 33*s;
>> F = num/den

F = s - 28/(s^3 + 9*s^2 + 33*s)

>> invlaplaceF = ilaplace(F)

   invlaplaceF = -28/33 + 2/561*exp(-9/2*t)*(238*cos(1/2*51^(1/2)*t)
                 +53*51^(1/2)*sin(1/2*51^(1/2)*t))

>> pretty(invlaplaceF)
```

$$\frac{28}{33} + 2/561\,\exp(-\,^{9/2\,t})\ (238\ \cos(1/2*51^{1/2}\ t) + 53*51^{1/2}*\sin(1/2*51^{1/2}\ t))$$

CHAPTER 5

MATLAB Tutorial Solutions

P3.1 [Reduction of Multiple Subsystems]

Reduce the system shown in Fig. P3.1 to a single transfer function, T(s) = C(s)/R(s) using MATLAB.

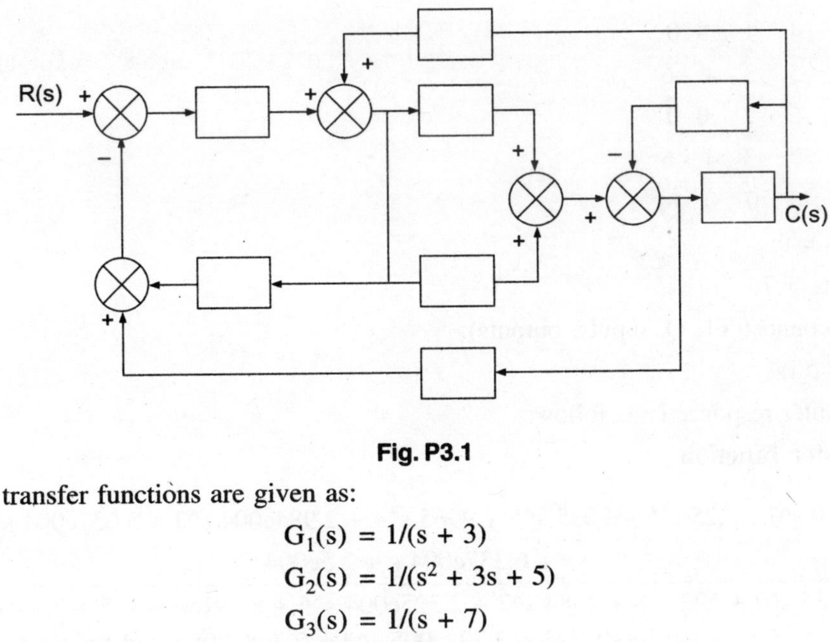

Fig. P3.1

The transfer functions are given as:

$$G_1(s) = 1/(s + 3)$$
$$G_2(s) = 1/(s^2 + 3s + 5)$$
$$G_3(s) = 1/(s + 7)$$
$$G_4(s) = 1/s$$
$$G_5(s) = 7/(s + 5)$$
$$G_6(s) = 1/(s^2 + 3s + 5)$$
$$G_7(s) = 5/(s + 6)$$
$$G_8(s) = 1/(s + 8)$$

Solution

```
% MATLAB Program
        G1 = tf([0 1], [1 3]);
        G2 = tf([0 0 1], [1 3 5]);
        G3 = tf([0 1], [1 7]);
        G4 = tf([0 1], [1 0]);
        G5 = tf([0 7], [1 5]);
        G6 = tf([0 0 1], [1 3 5]);
        G7 = tf([0 5], [1 6]);
        G8 = tf([0 1], [1 8]);
        G9 = tf([1], [1]);
% Transducer at the input
T1 = append(G1, G2, G3, G4, G5, G6, G7, G8, G9);
Q = [1 -2 -5 9
     2  1  8 0
     3  1  8 0
     4  1  8 0
     5  3  4 -6
     6  7  0 0
     7  3  4 -6
     8  7  0 0];
inputs = 9;
outputs = 7;
Ts = connect(T1, Q, inputs, outputs);
T = Tf(Ts)
```

Computer response is as follows:

Transfer function

```
 10 s^7 + 225 s^6 + 2035 s^5 + 9965 s^4 + 2.984e004 s^3 + 5.637e004 s^2
                       + 6.337e004 s + 3.5e004
----------------------------------------------------------------------------
s^10 + 35 s^9 + 522 s^8 + 4384 s^7 + 2.325e004 s^6 + 8.291e004 s^5 + 2.045e005 s^4
          +3.455e005 s^3 + 3.794e005 s^2 + 2.348e005 s + 4.568e004
```

P3.2 For each of the second-order systems below, find ξ, ωn, Ts, Tp, Tr, % overshoot, and plot the step-response using MATLAB.

(*a*) $T(s) = \dfrac{130}{s^2 + 15s + 130}$

(*b*) $T(s) = \dfrac{0.045}{s^2 + 0.025s + 0.045}$

(*c*) $T(s) = \dfrac{10^8}{s^2 + 1.325\times10^3 s + 10^8}$

Solution

(*a*)
```
>> clf
>> numa = 130;
>> dena = [1 15 130];
>> Ta = tf(numa, dena)
```

Transfer function: $\dfrac{130}{s\text{^}2 + 15s + 130}$

```
>> omegana = sqrt(dena(3))
   omegana =
              5.4018
>> zetaa = dena(2)/(2*omegana)
   zetaa =
              0.6578
>> Tsa = 4/(zetaa*omegana)
   Tsa =
              0.5333
>> Tpa = pi/ (omegana*sqrt(1-zetaa^2))
   Tpa =
              0.3658
>> Tra = (1.76*zetaa^3 – .417*zetaa^2 + 1.039*zetaa + 1)/omegana
   Tra =
              0.1758
>> percenta = exp(–zetaa*pi/sqrt(1–zetaa^2))*100
   percenta =
              6.4335
>> subplot(221)
>> step(Ta)
>> title('(a)')
>> '(b)'
   ans =
```

(*b*)
```
>> numb =0.045;
>> denb = [1 .025 0.045];
```

```
>> Tb = tf(numb, denb)
   Transfer function

          0.045
   -------------------
   s^2 + 0.025s + 0.045

>> omeganb = sqrt(denb(3))
   omeganb =
             0.2121
>> zetab = denb(2)/(2*omeganb)
   zetab =
             0.0589
>> Tsb = 4/(zetab*omeganb)
   Tsb =
             320
>> Tpb = pi/(omeganb*sqrt(1–zetab^2))
   Tpb =
             14.8354
>> Trb = (1.76*zetab^3 – 0.417*zetab^2 + 1.039*zetab + 1)/omeganb
   Trb =
             4.9975
>> percentb = exp(–zetab*pi/ sqrt(1 – zetab^2))*100
   percentb =
             83.0737
>> subplot(222)
>> step(Tb)
>> title('(b)')
>> '(c)'
ans =
```

(*c*)

```
>> numc = 10E8;
>> denc = [1 1.325*10E3 10E8];
>> Tc = tf(numc, denc)
```

Transfer function:

```
          1e009
   ----------------------
   s ^ 2 + 13250 s + 1e009

>> omeganc = sqrt(denc(3))
   omeganc =
             3.1623e + 004
```

```
>> zetac = denc(2)/(2*omeganc)
   zetac =
             0.2095
>> Tsc = 4/(zetac*omeganc)
   Tsc =
             6.0377e – 004
>> Tpc = pi/(omeganc*sqrt(1 – zetac^2))
   Tpc =
             1.0160e – 004
>> Trc = (1.76*zetac^3 – 0.417*zetac^2 + 1.039*zetac + 1)/omeganc
   Trc =
             3.8439e – 005
>> percentc = exp(–zetac*pi/sqrt(1 – zetac^2))*100
   percentc =
             51.0123
>> subplot(223)
>> step(Tc)
>> title('(c)')
```

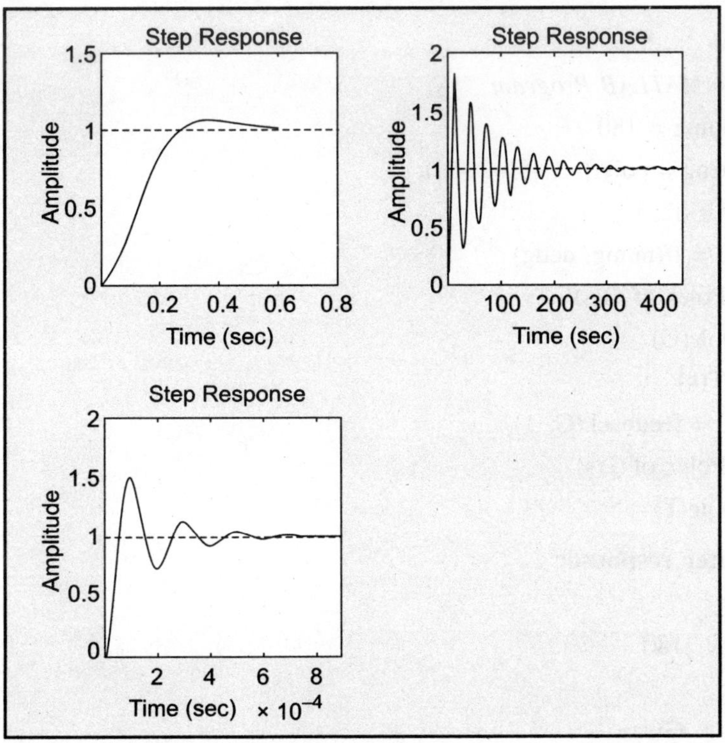

Fig. P3.2

P3.3 Determine the pole locations for the system shown below using MATLAB.

$$\frac{C(s)}{R(s)} = \frac{s^3 - 5s^2 + 7s + 12}{s^5 + s^4 - 5s^3 - 7s^2 + 9s - 10}$$

Solution

```
>> %MATLAB Program
>> den = [1 1 –5 –7 9 –10];
>> A = roots(den)
```

Computer response:

```
A =
      –2.1066 + 1.0515i
      –2.1066 – 1.0515i
       2.2343
       0.4894 + 0.7535i
       0.4894 – 0.7535i
```

P3.4 Determine the pole locations for the unity feedback system shown below using MATLAB.

$$G(s) = \frac{180}{(s+3)(s+5)(s+7)(s+9)}$$

Solution

```
>> % MATLAB Program
>> numg = 180
>> deng = poly([–3 –5 –7 –9]);
>> 'G(s)'
>> G = tf(numg, deng)
>> 'Poles of G(s)'
>> pole(G)
>> 'T(s)'
>> T = feedback(G, 1)
>> 'Poles of T(s)'
>> pole(T)
```

Computer response:

```
numg =
        180
ans =
        G(s)
```

Transfer function

$$\frac{180}{s^4 + 24s^3 + 206s^2 + 744s + 945}$$

ans =

Poles of G(s)

ans =

-9.0000

-7.0000

-5.0000

-3.0000

ans =

T(s)

Transfer function

$$\frac{180}{s^4 + 24s^3 + 206s^2 + 744s + 1125}$$

ans =

Poles of T(s)

ans =

-9.0617 + 2.0914i

-9.0617 – 2.0914i

-2.9383 + 2.0914i

-2.9383 – 2.0914i

P3.5 A plant to be controlled is described by a transfer function

$$G(s) = \frac{s+5}{s^2 + 7s + 25}$$

Obtain the root locus plot using MATLAB.

Solution

```
>> %MATLAB Program
>> clf
>> num = [1 5];
>> den = [1 7 25];
>> rlocus(num, den);
```

Computer response is shown in Fig. P3.5.

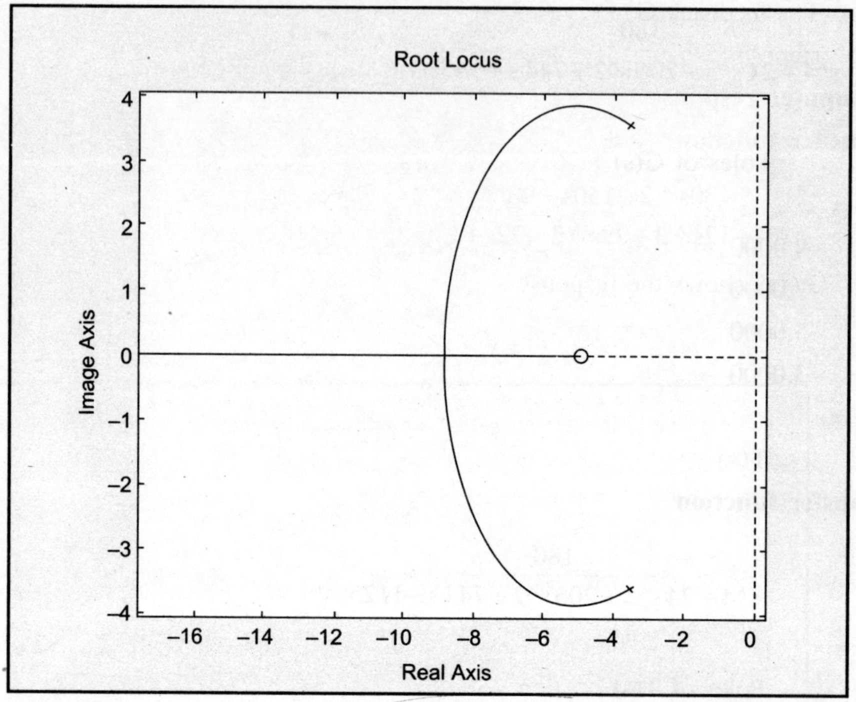

Fig. P3.5

P3.6 For the unity feedback system shown in Fig. P3.6, G(s) is given as:

$$G(s) = \frac{30(s^2 - 5s + 3)}{(s+1)(s+2)(s+4)(s+5)}$$

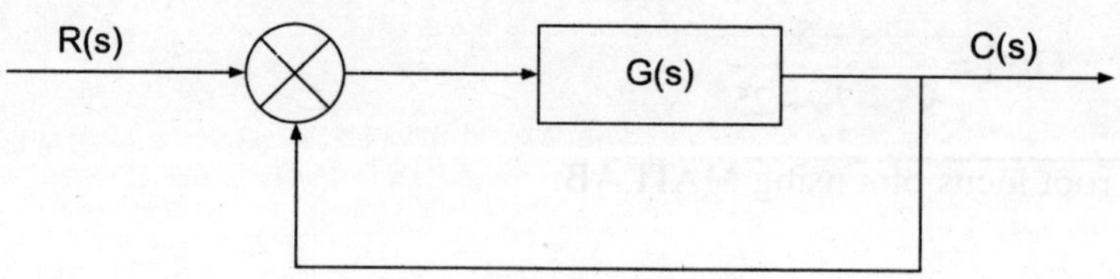

Fig. P3.6

Determine the closed-loop step response using MATLAB.

Solution

```
>> %MATLAB Program
>> numg = 30*[1 –5 3];
>> deng = poly([–1 –2 –4 –5]);
```

```
>> G = tf(numg, deng);
>> T = feedback(G, 1)
>> step(T)
```

Computer response

Transfer function

$$\frac{30s\,^\wedge 2-150s+90}{s\,^\wedge 4+12s\,^\wedge 3+79s\,^\wedge 2-72s+130}$$

Fig. P3.6(a) shows the response

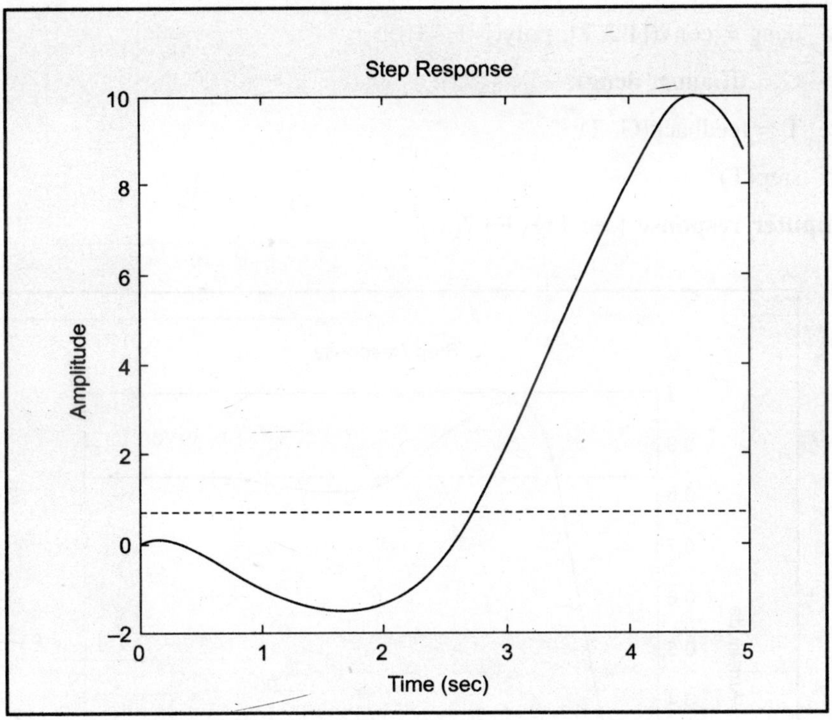

Fig. P3.6(a)

Simulation shows over 30% overshoot and non minimum-phase behaviour. Hence the second-order approximation is not valid.

P3.7 Determine the accuracy of the second-order approximation using MATLAB to simulate the unity feedback system shown in Fig. P3.7 where

$$G(s) = \frac{15(s^2+3s+7)}{(s^2+3s+7)(s+1)(s+3)}.$$

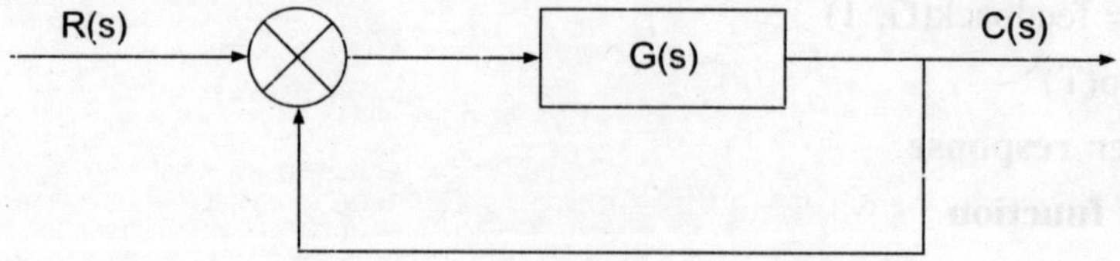

Fig. P3.7

Solution

```
>> %MATLAB Program
>> numg = 15*[1 3 7];
>> deng = conv([1 3 7], poly([-1 -3]));
>> G = tf(numg, deng);
>> T = feedback(G, 1);
>> step(T)
```

Computer response [see Fig. P3.7(a)].

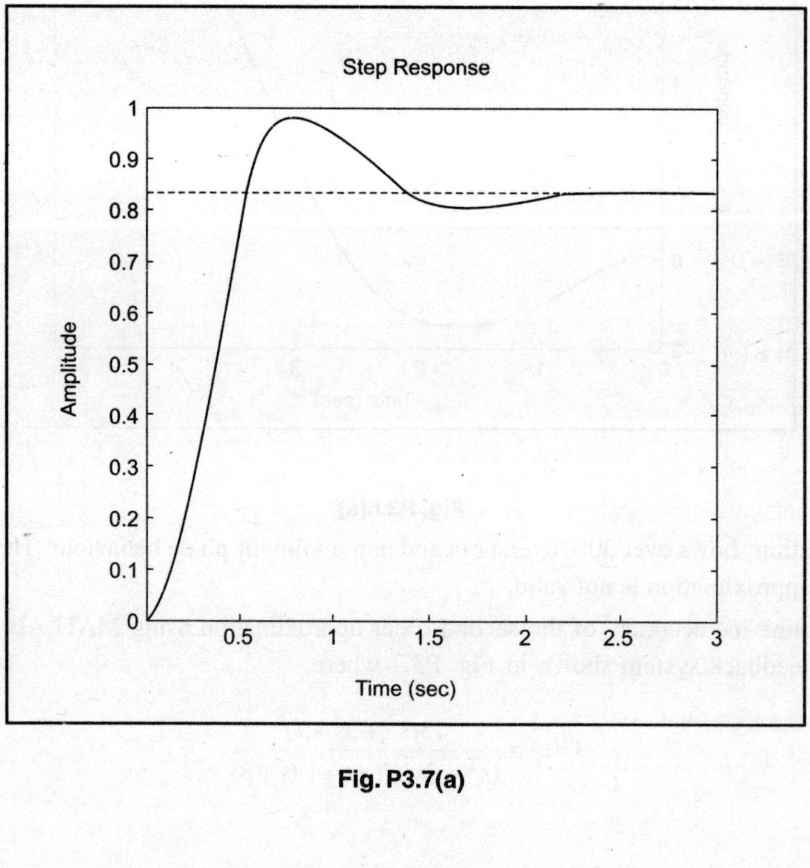

Fig. P3.7(a)

P3.8 For the unity feedback system shown in Fig. P3.8 with

$$G(s) = \frac{K(s+1)}{s(s+1)(s+5)(s+6)}.$$

Determine the range of K for stability using MATLAB.

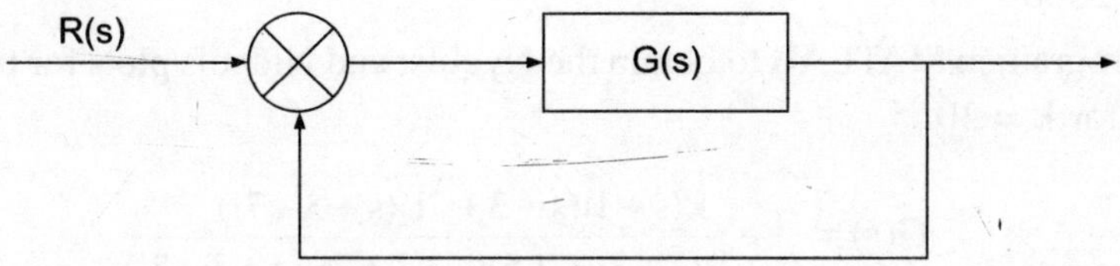

Fig. P3.8

Solution

```
>> %MATLAB Program
>> K = [0:0.2:200];
>> for i = 1:length(K);
>> deng = poly([0 –1 –5 –6]);
>> dent = deng + [0 0 0 K(i) K(i)];
>> R = roots(dent);
>> A = real(R);
>> B = max(A);
>> if B > 0
>> R
>> K = K(i)
>> break
>> end
>> end
```

Computer response:

```
R =
     –10.0000
     –0.5000 + 4.4441i
     –0.5000 – 4.4441i
     –1.0000
```

A =

−10.0000

−0.5000

−0.5000

−1.0000

B =

−0.5000

P3.9 Write a program in MATLAB to obtain the Nyquist and Nichols plots for the following transfer function for k = 30.

$$G(s) = \frac{k(s+1)(s+3+7i)(s+3-7i)}{(s+1)(s+3)(s+5)(s+3+7i)(s+3-7i)}$$

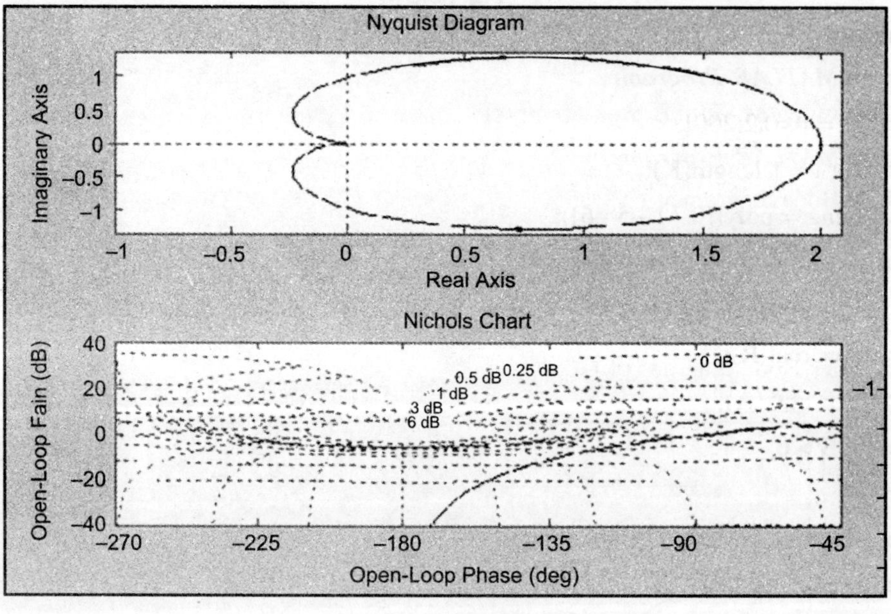

Fig. P3.9

Solution

```
>> %MATLAB Program
>> %Simple Nyquist and Nichols plots
>> clf
>> z = [–1 –3 + 7*i –3 – 7*i];
>> p = [–1 –3 –5 –3 + 7*i  –3–7*i];
>> k = 30;
```

```
>> [num, den] = zp2tf(z', p', k);
>> subplot(211), nyquist(num, den)
>> subplot(212), Nichols(num, den)
>> ngrid
>> axis([50 360 –40 30])
```

Computer response: The Nyquist and Nichols plots are shown in Fig. P3.9.

P3.10 A PID controller is given by

$$G_c(s) = 29.125\frac{(s+0.57)^2}{s}$$

Draw a Bode diagram of the controller using MATLAB.

Solution

$$G_c(s) = \frac{29.125(s^2+1.14s+0.3249)}{s} = \frac{29.125s^2+33.2025s+9.4627}{s}$$

The following MATLAB program produces the Bode diagram

```
>> %MATLAB Program
>> %Bode diagram
>> num = [29.125 33.2025 9.4627];
>> den = [0 1 0];
>> bode(num, den)
>> title('Bode diagram of G(s)')
```

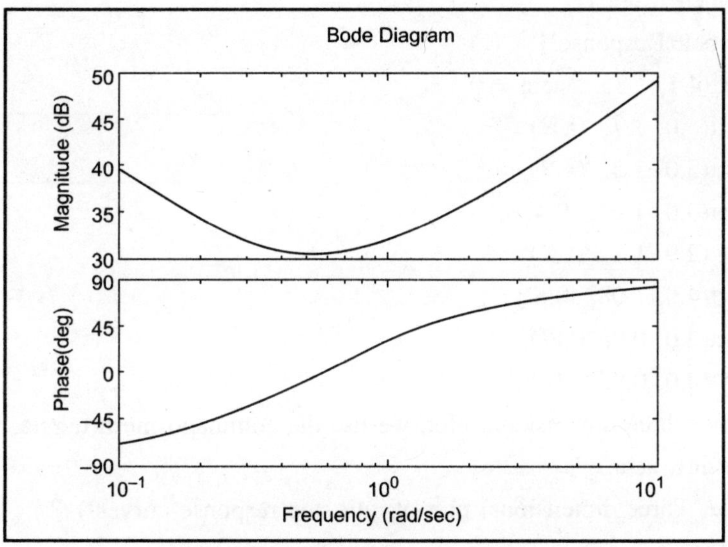

Fig. P3.10 Bode diagram of G(s)

P3.11 For the closed-loop system defined by

$$\frac{C(s)}{R(s)} = \frac{1}{s^2 + 2\zeta s + 1}.$$

(*a*) Plot the unit-step response curves c(t) for $\xi = 0, 0.1, 0.2, 0.4, 0.5, 0.6, 0.8$, and 1.0. ω_n is normalized to 1.

(*b*) Plot a three dimensional plot of (a).

Solution

```
>> %Two-dimensional plot and three-dimensional plot of unit-step
>> %response curves for the standard second-order system with ωn = 1
>> %and zeta = 0, 0.1, 0.2, 0.4, 0.5, 0.6, 0.8, and 1.0
>> t = 0:0.2:10;
>> zeta = [0 0.1 0.2 0.4 0.5 0.6 0.8 1.0];
>> for n = 1:8;
>> num = [0 0 1];
>> den = [1 2*zeta(n) 1];
>> [y(1:51, n), x, t] = step(num, den, t);
>> end
>> %Two-dimensional diagram with the command plot(t, y)
>> plot(t, y)
>> grid
>> title('Plot of unit-step response curves')
>> xlabel('t Sec')
>> ylabel('Response')
>> text(4.1, 1.86, '\zeta = 0')
>> text(3.0, 1.7, '0.1')
>> text(3.0, 1.5, '0.2')
>> text(3.0, 1.22, '0.4')
>> text(2.9, 1.1, '0.5')
>> text(4.0, 1.08, '0.6')
>> text(3.0, 0.9, '0.8')
>> text(4.0, 0.9, '1.0')
>> %For three dimensional plot, we use the command mesh(t, zeta, y')
>> mesh(t, zeta, y')
>> title('Three-dimensional plot of unit-step response curves')
>> xlabel('t Sec')
```

```
>> ylabel('\zeta')
>> zlabel('Response')
```

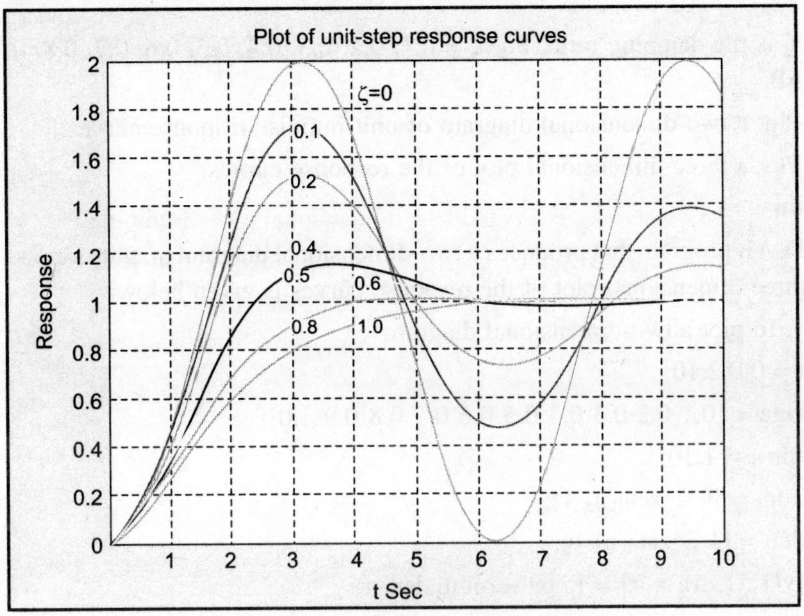

Fig. P3.11(a) Plot of unit-step response curves

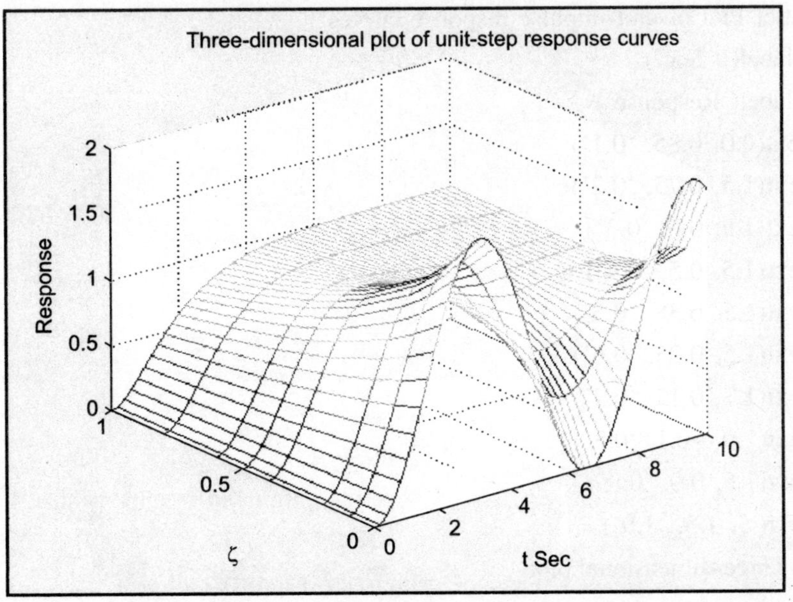

Fig. P3.11(b) Three-dimensional plot of unit-step response curves

3.12 A closed-loop control system is defined by

$$\frac{C(s)}{R(s)} = \frac{2\zeta s}{s^2 + 2\zeta s + 1}$$

where ζ is the damping ratio. For ζ = 0.1, 0.2, 0.3, 0.4, 0.5, 0.6, 0.7, 0.8, 0.9, and 1.0 using MATLAB:

(*a*) Plot a two-dimensional diagram of unit-impulse response curves.

(*b*) Plot a three-dimensional plot of the response curves.

Solution

A MATLAB program that produces a two-dimensional diagram of unit-impulse response curves and a three-dimensional plot of the response curves is given below:

```
>> %To plot a two-dimensional diagram
>> t = 0:0.2:10;
>> zeta = [0.1 0.2 0.3 0.4 0.5 0.6 0.7 0.8 0.9 1.0];
>> for n = 1:10;
>> num = [0 2*zeta(n) 1];
>> den = [1 2*zeta(n) 1];
>> [y(1:51, n), x, t] = impulse(num,den, t);
>> end
>> plot(t, y)
>> grid
>> title('Plot of unit-impulse response curves')
>> xlabel('t Sec')
>> ylabel('Response')
>> text(2.0, 0.85, '0.1')
>> text(1.5, 0.75, '0.2')
>> text(1.5, 0.6, '0.3')
>> text(1.5, 0.5, '0.4')
>> text(1.5, 0.38, '0.5')
>> text(1.5, 0.25, '0.6')
>> text(1.7, 0.12, '0.7')
>> text(2.0, –0.1, '0.8')
>> text(1.5, 0.0, '0.9')
>> text(.5, 1.5, '1.0')
>> %Three-dimensional plot
>> mesh(t, zeta, y')
>> title('Three-dimensional plot')
```

```
>> xlabel('t Sec')
>> ylabel('\zeta')
>> zlabel('Response')
```

The two-dimensional diagram and three-dimensional diagram produced by this MATLAB program are shown in Figures. P3.12(a) and (b) respectively.

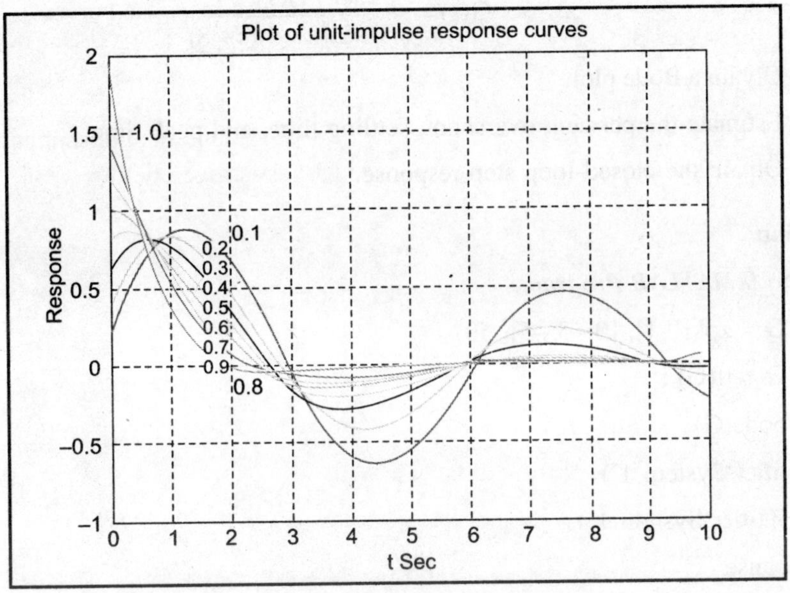

Fig. P3.12(a) Two-dimensional plot

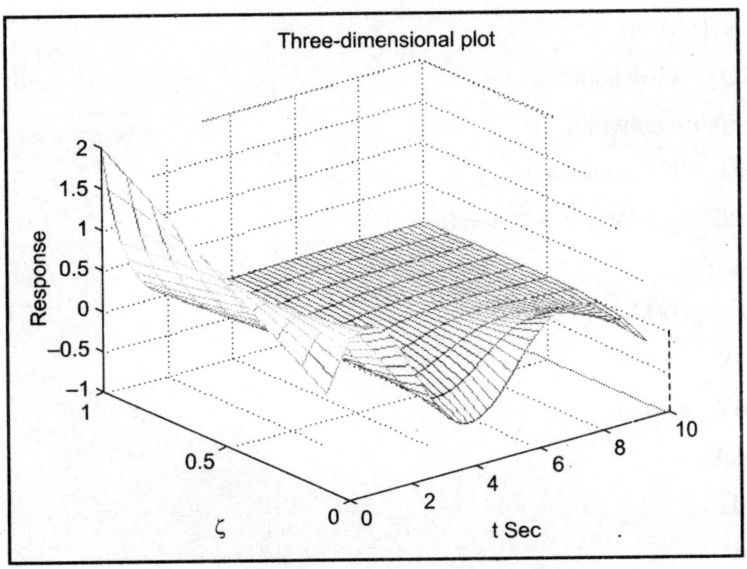

Fig. P3.12(b) Three-dimensional plot

P3.13 For the system shown in Fig. P3.13 write a program in MATLAB that will use an open-loop transfer function G(s):

$$G(s) = \frac{50(s+1)}{s(s+3(s+5)}$$

$$G(s) = \frac{25(s+1)(s+7)}{s(s+2)(s+4)(s+8)}$$

(*a*) Obtain a Bode plot.

(*b*) Estimate the per cent overshoot, settling time, and peak time.

(*c*) Obtain the closed-loop step response.

Solution

(*a*)
```
>> %MATLAB Program
>> G = zpk([–1], [0 –3 –5], 50)
>> G = tf(G)
>> bode(G)
>> title('System 1')
>> %title('System 1')
>> pause
>> %Find phase margin
>> [Gm, Pm, Wcg, Wcp] = margin(G);
>> w = 1:.01:20;
>> [M, P, w] = bode(G, w);
>> %Find bandwidth
>> for k = 1:1:length(M);
>> if 20*log10(M(k)) + 7 < = 0;
>> 'Mag'
>> 20*log10(M(k))
>> 'BW'
>> wBW = w(k)
>> break
>> end
>> end
```

```
>> %Find damping ratio, per cent overshoot, settling time, and peak time
>> for z = 0:01:10
>> Pt = atan(2*z/(sqrt(–2*z^2 + sqrt(1 + 4*z^4))))*(180/pi);
>> if(Pm – Pt)< = 0
>> z;
>> Po = exp(–z*pi/sqrt(1 – z^2));
>> Ts = (4/(wBW*z))*sqrt((1 – 2*z^2) + sqrt(4*z^4 – 4*z^2 + 2));
>> Tp = (pi/(wBW*sqrt(1 – z^2)))*sqrt((1 – 2*z^2) + sqrt(4*z^4 – 4*z^2 + 2));
>> fprintf('Bandwidth = %g', wBW)
>> fprintf('Phase margin = %g', Pm)
>> fprintf(', Damping ratio = %g', z)
>> fprintf(', Per cent overshoot = %g', Po*100)
>> fprintf(', Settling time = %g', Ts)
>> fprintf(', Peak time = %g', Tp)
>> break
>> end
>> end
>> T = feedback(G, 1);
>> step(T)
>> title('Step response system 1')
>> %title('Step response system 1')
```

Computer response

Zero/pole/gain:

$$\frac{50(s+1)}{s(s+3)(s+5)}$$

Transfer function

$$\frac{50s+50}{s\verb|^|3+8s\verb|^|2+15s}$$

The Bode plot is shown in Fig. P3.13(a).

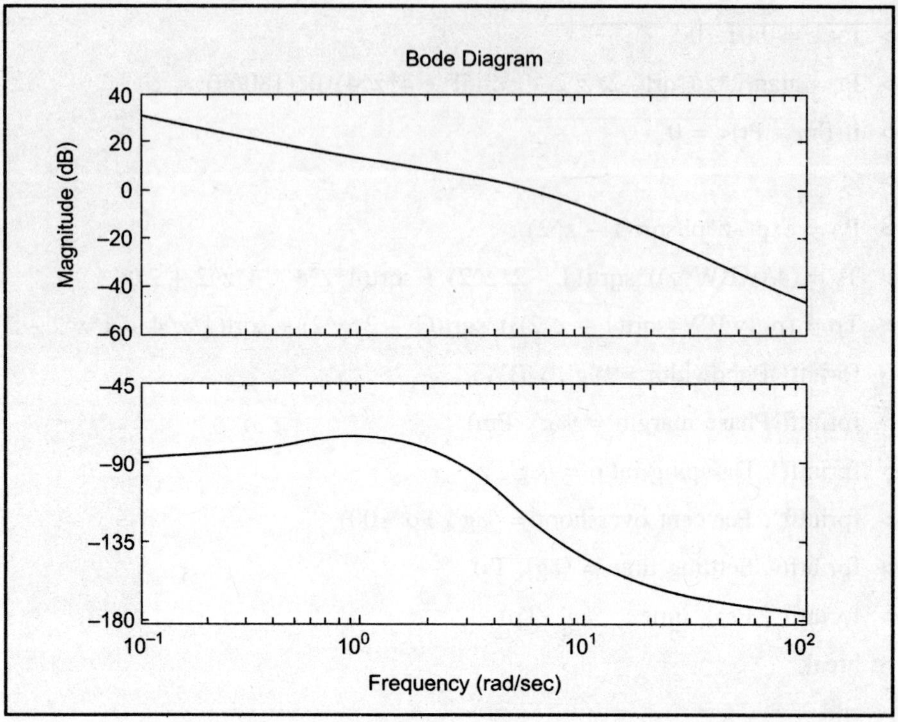

Fig. P3.13(a)

```
ans =

      Mag

ans =

      -7.0032

ans =

      BW

wBW =

      9.7900
```

Bandwidth = 9.79, Phase margin = 57.892, Damping ratio = 0.59, Per cent overshoot = 10.0693, Settling time = 0.804303, Peak time = 0.461606

The step response is shown in Fig. 3.13(b).

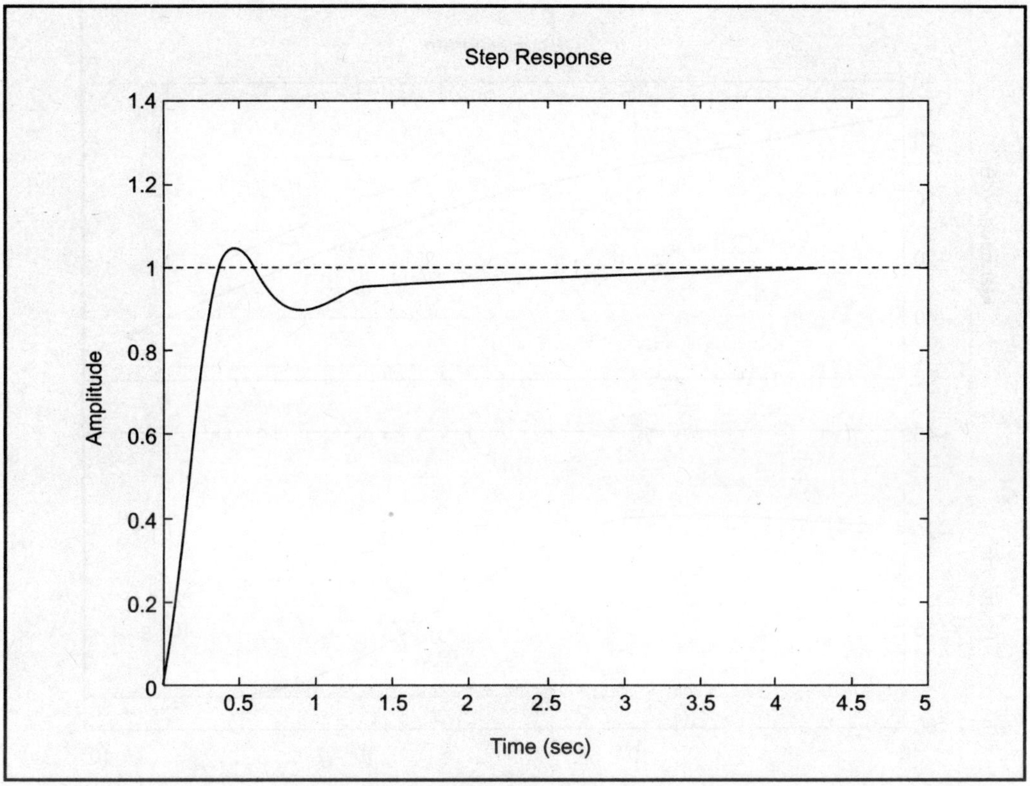

Fig. P3.13(b)

(*b*) Likewise, for this problem

```
>> G = zpk([–1 –7],[0 –2 –4 –8], 25)
>> G = tf(G)
```

The following Bode plot and step response are obtained [see Figures. P3.13(c) and (d).

Zero/pole/gain:

$$\frac{25(s+1)(s+7)}{s(s+2)(s+4)(s+8)}$$

Transfer function

$$\frac{25s^\wedge 2+200s+175}{s^\wedge 4+14s^\wedge 3+56s^\wedge 2+64s}$$

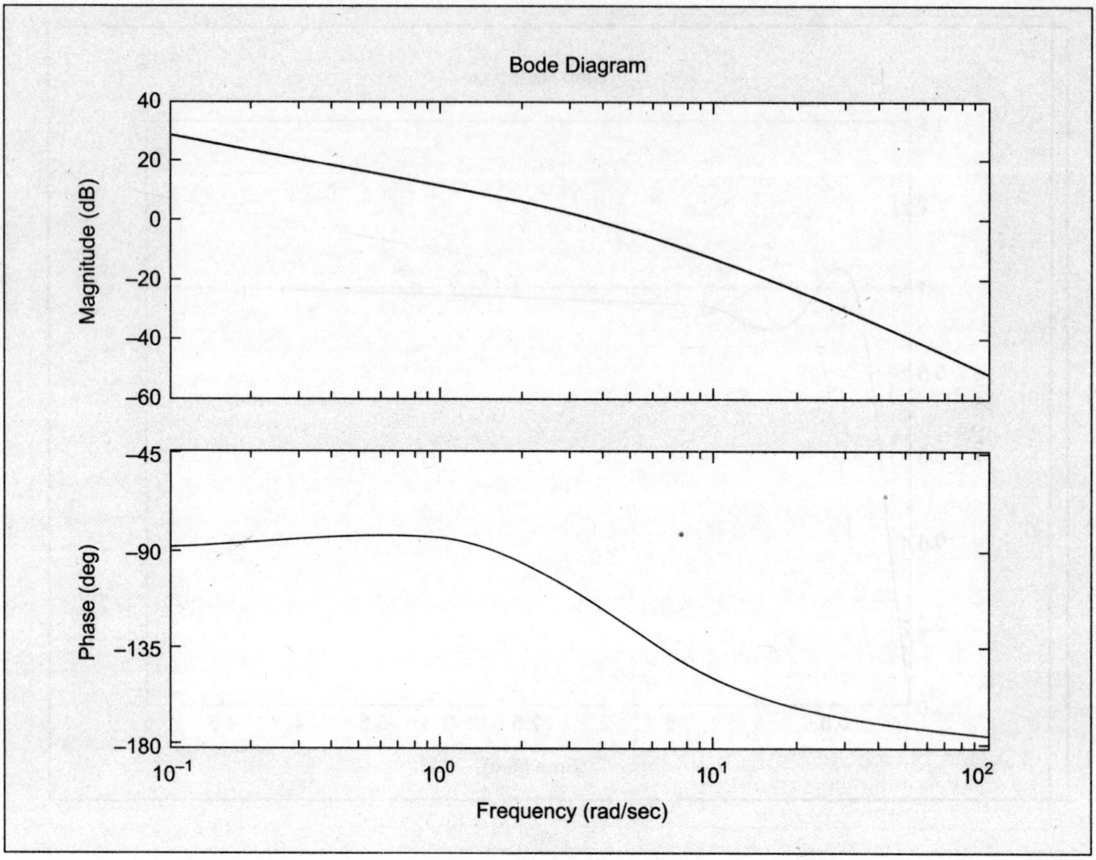

Fig. P3.13(c)

ans =

Mag

ans =

–7.0110

ans =

BW

wBW =

6.5500

Bandwidth = 6.55Phase margin = 63.1105, Damping ratio = 0.67, Percent overshoot = 5.86969, Settling time = 0.959175, Peak time = 0.679904

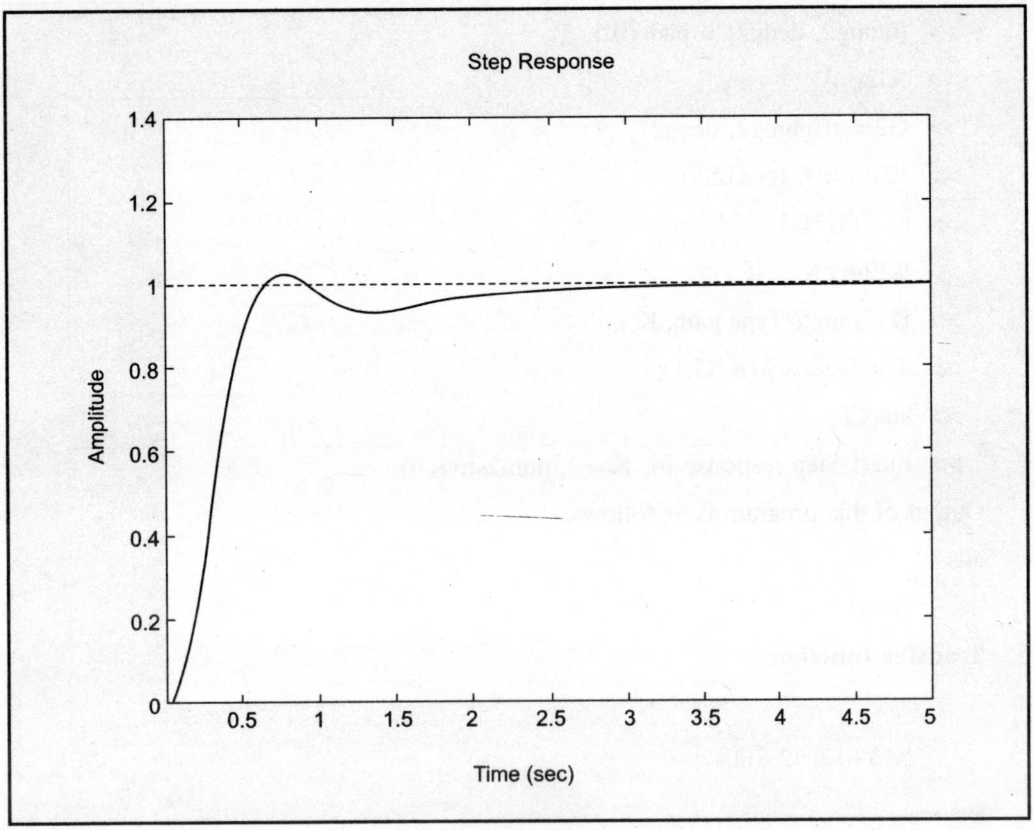

Fig. P3.13(d)

P3.14 For a unit feedback system with the forward-path transfer function

$$G(s) = \frac{K}{s(s+5)(s+12)}$$

and a delay of 0.5 second, estimate the percent overshoot for K = 40 using a second-order approximation. Model the delay using MATLAB function pade(T, n). Determine the unit step response and check the second-order approximation assumption made.

Solution

```
>> %MATLAB Program
>> %Enter G(s)
>> numg1 = 1;
>> deng1 = poly([0 –5 –12]);
>> 'G1(s)'
```

```
>> G1 = tf(numg1, deng1)
>> [numg2, deng2] = pade(0.5, 5);
>> 'G2(s)'
>> G2 = tf(numg2, deng2)
>> 'G(s) = G1(s)G2(s)'
>> G = G1*G2
>> %Enter K
>> K = input('Type gain, K');
>> T = feedback(K*G,1);
>> step(T)
>> title(['Step response for K = ', num2str(K)])
```

Output of this program is as follows:

```
ans =

     G1(s)

Transfer function

            1
     ---------------
     s^3+17s^2+60s

ans =

     G2(s)

Transfer function

 -s^5 + 60 s^4 - 1680 s^3 + 2.688e004 s^2 - 2.419e005 s + 9.677e005
 -------------------------------------------------------------------
  s^5 + 60 s^4 + 1680 s^3 + 2.688e004 s^2 + 2.419e005 s + 9.677e005

ans =

     G(s) = G1(s)G2(s)

Transfer function

    -s^5 + 60 s^4 - 1680 s^3 + 2.688e004 s^2 - 2.419e005 s + 9.677e005
 ------------------------------------------------------------------------
 s^8 + 77 s^7 + 2760 s^6 + 5.904e004 s^5 + 7.997e005 s^4 + 6.693e006 s^3
                          + 3.097e007 s^2 + 5.806e007 s

Type Gain, K 40
```

The following Fig. P3.14 is obtained.

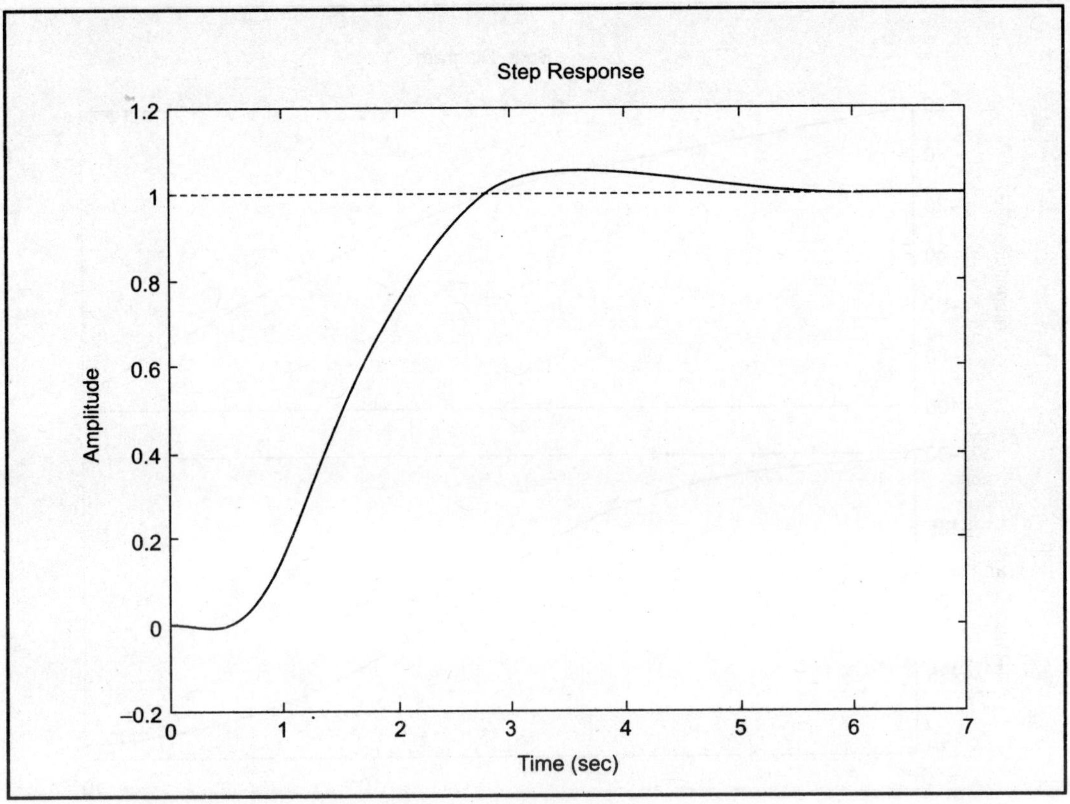

Fig. P3.14

P3.15(a) Write a program in MATLAB to obtain a Bode plot for the transfer function

$$G(s) = \frac{15}{s(s+3)(0.7s+5)}$$

Solution

```
>> %MATLAB Program
>> %Bode plot generation
>> clf
>> num = 15;
>> den = conv([1 0], conv([1 3], [0.7 5]));
>> bode(num, den)
```

Computer response: The Bode plot is shown in Fig. P3.15.

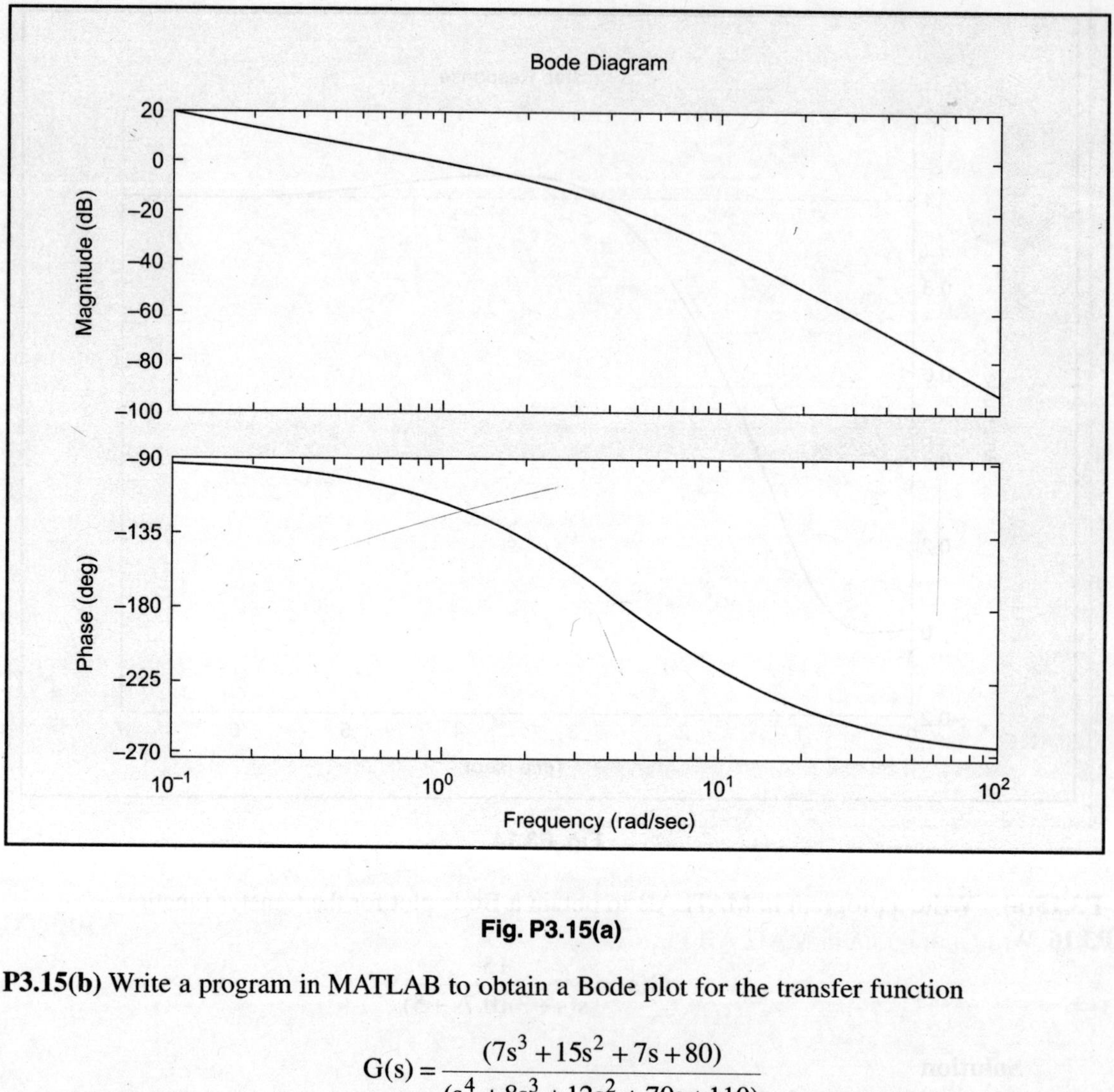

Fig. P3.15(a)

P3.15(b) Write a program in MATLAB to obtain a Bode plot for the transfer function

$$G(s) = \frac{(7s^3 + 15s^2 + 7s + 80)}{(s^4 + 8s^3 + 12s^2 + 70s + 110)}$$

Solution

```
>> %MATLAB Program
>> %Bode plot
>> clf
>> num = [0 7 15 7 80];
>> den = [1 8 12 70 110];
>> bode(num, den)
```

Computer response: The Bode plot is shown in Fig. P3.15(b).

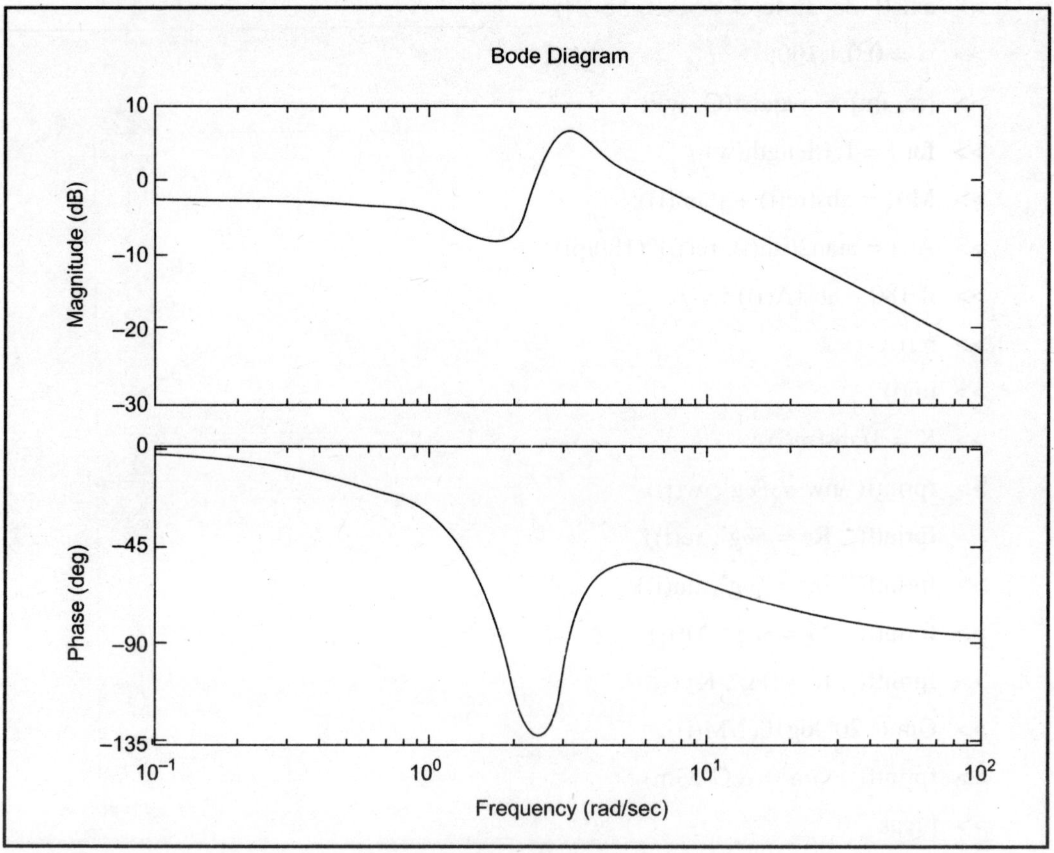

Fig. P3.15(b)

P3.16 Write a program in MATLAB for a unity-feedback system with

$$G(s) = \frac{K(s+7)}{(s^2+3s+52)(s^2+2s+35)}.$$

(*a*) Plot the Nyquist diagram.

(*b*) Display the real-axis crossing value and frequency.

Solution

```
>> %MATLAB Program
>> numg = [1 7]
>> deng = conv([1 3 52], [1 2 35]);
>> G = tf(numg, deng)
>> 'G(s)'
>> Gzpk = zpk(G)
>> nyquist(G)
```

```
>> axis([–3e–3, 4e–3, –5e–3, 5e–3])
>> w = 0:0.1:100;
>> [re, im] = nyquist(G, w);
>> for i = 1:1:length(w)
>> M(i) = abs(re(i) + j*im(i));
>> A(i) = atan2(im(i), re(i))*(180/pi);
>> if 180 – abs(A(i))< = 1;
>> re(i);
>> im(i);
>> K = 1/abs(re(i));
>> fprintf('\nw = %g', w(i))
>> fprintf(', Re = %g', re(i))
>> fprintf(', Im = %g', im(i))
>> fprintf(', M = %g', M(i))
>> fprintf(', K = %g', K)
>> Gm = 20*log10(1/M(i));
>> fprintf(', Gm = &G',Gm)
>> break
>> end
>> end
```

Computer response

numg =

1 7

Transfer function

$$\frac{s+7}{s^4+5s^3+93s^2+209s+1820}$$

ans =

G(s)

Zero/pole/gain:

$$\frac{s+7}{(s^2+2s+35)(s^2+3s+52)}$$

The Nyquist plot is shown in Fig. P3.16.

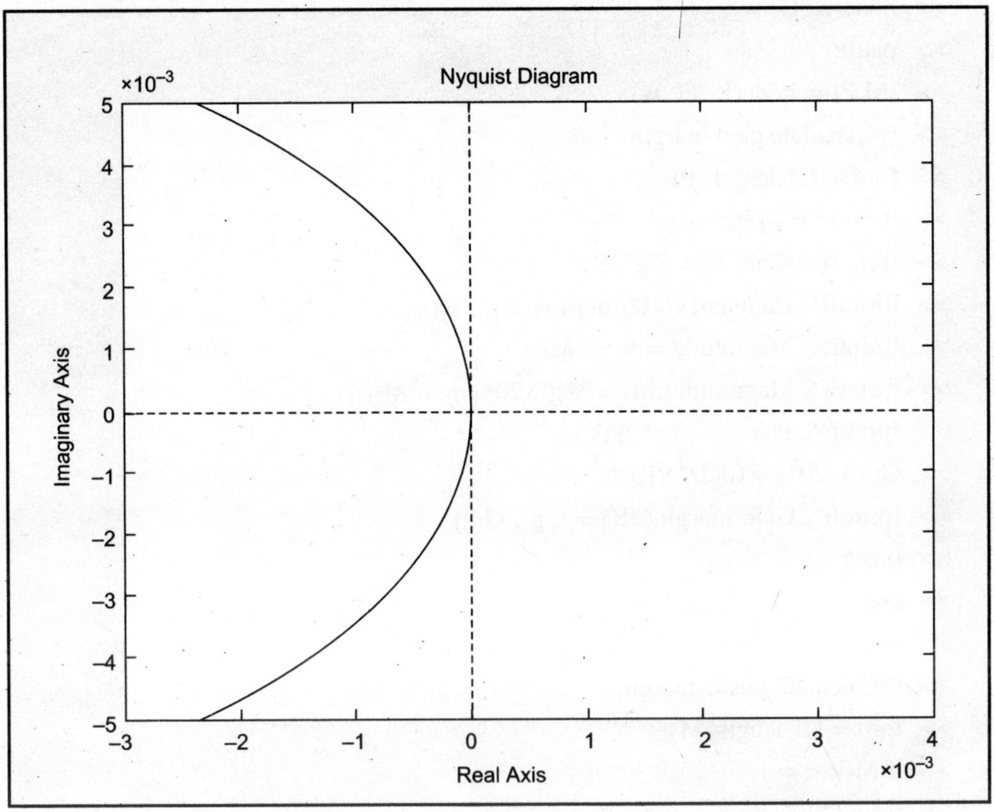

Fig. P3.16

P3.17 Write a program in MATLAB for the unity feedback system with

$$G(s) = \frac{K}{[s(s+3)(s+12)]}$$

so that the value of gain K can be input. Display the Bode plots of a system for the input value of K. Determine and display the gain and phase margin for the input value of K.

Solution

```
>> %Enter G(s)
>> numg = 1;
>> deng = poly([0 –3 –12]);
>> 'G(s)'
>> G = tf(numg, deng)
>> w = 0.01:0.1:100;
>> %Enter K
>> K = input('Type gain, K');
```

```
>> bode(K*G, w)
>> pause
>> [M,P] = bode(K*G, w);
>> %Calculate gain margin
>> for i = 1:1:length(P);
>> if P(i)< = --180;
>> fprintf('\nGain K = %g', K)
>> fprintf(', Frequency(180 deg) = %g', w(i))
>> fprintf(', Magnitude = %g', M(i))
>> fprintf(', Magnitude(dB) = %g', 20*log10(M(i)))
>> fprintf(', Phase = %g', P(i))
>> Gm = 20*log10(1/M(i));
>> fprintf(', Gain margin(dB) = %g', Gm)
>> break
>> end
>> end
>> %Calculate phase margin
>> for i = 1:1:length(M);
>> if M(i) < = 1;
>> fprintf('\nGain K = %g', K)
>> fprintf(', Frequency(0 dB) = %g', w(i))
>> fprintf(', Magnitude = %g', M(i))
>> fprintf(', Magnitude(dB) = %g', 20*log10(M(i)))
>> fprintf(', Phase = %g', P(i))
>> Pm = 180 + P(i);
>> fprintf(', Phase margin(dB) = %g', Pm)
>> break
>> end
>> end
>> 'Alternate program using MATLAB margin function:'
>> clear
>> clf
>> %Bode plot and find points
>> %Enter G(s)
>> numg = 1;
>> deng = poly([0 –3 –12]);
>> 'G(s)'
```

```
>> G = tf(numg, deng)
>> w = 0.01:0.1:100;
>> %Enter K
>> K = input('Type gain, K');
>> bode(K*G,w)
>> [Gm, Pm, Wcp, Wcg] = margin(K*G)
>> 'Gm(dB)'
>> 20*log10(Gm)
```

Computer response

ans =

G(s)

Transfer function

$$\frac{1}{s^3+15s^2+36s}$$

Type gain, K 40

The Bode plot is shown in Fig. P3.17(a).

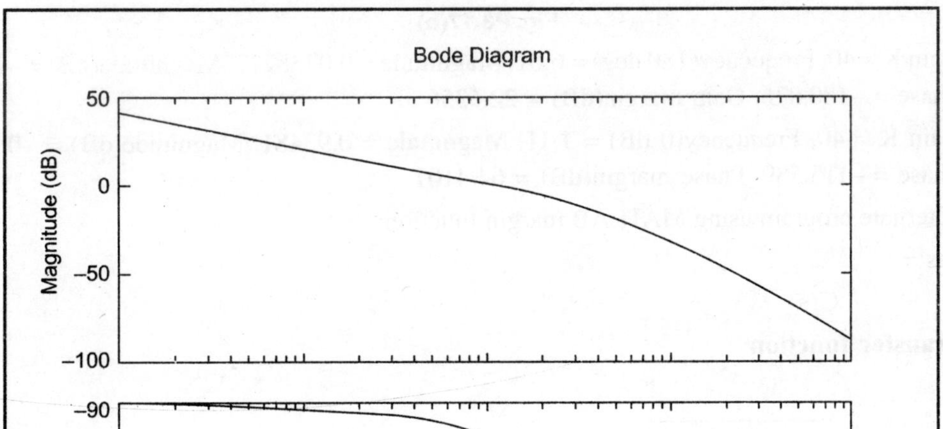

Fig. P3.17(a)

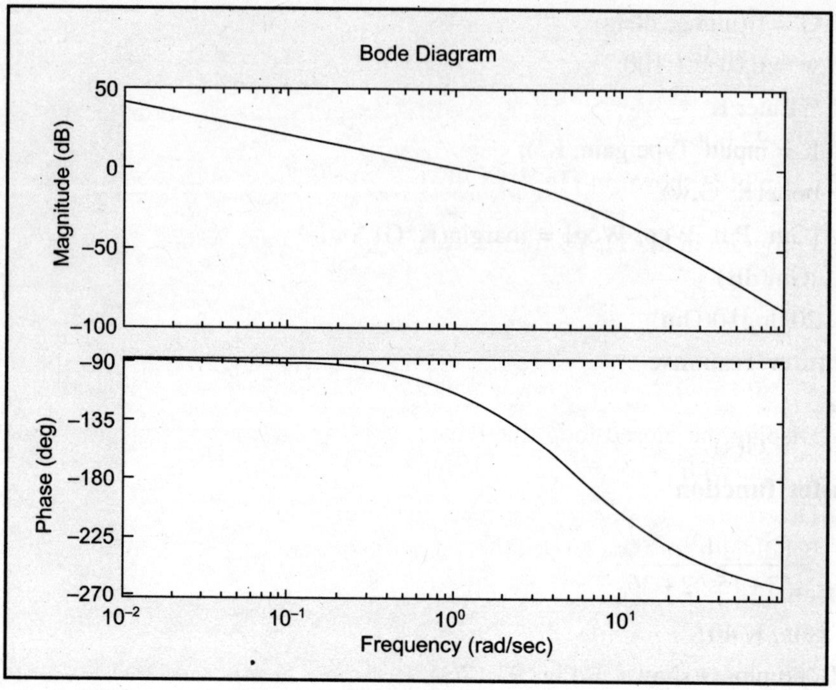

Fig. P3.17(b)

Gain K = 40, Frequency(180 deg) = 6.01, Magnitude = 0.0738277, Magnitude(dB) = –22.6356, Phase = –180.076, Gain margin(dB) = 22.6356

Gain K = 40, Frequency(0 dB) = 1.11, Magnitude = 0.93481, Magnitude(dB) = –0.585534, Phase = –115.589, Phase margin(dB) = 64.4107

Alternate program using MATLAB margin function:

ans =

G(s)

Transfer function

$$\frac{1}{s^3 + 15s^2 + 36s}$$

Type gain, K 40

Gm =

13.5000

Pm =

65.8119

Wcp =

6

Wcg =

1.0453

```
ans =
        Gm(dB)
ans =
        22.6067
```

The Bode plot is shown in Fig. P3.17(b).

P3.18 Write a program in MATLAB for the system shown below so that the value of K can be input (K = 40).

$$\frac{C(s)}{R(s)} = \frac{K(s+5)}{s(s^2+3s+15)}.$$

(*a*) Display the closed-loop magnitude and phase frequency response for unity feedback system with an open-loop transfer function, KG(s).

(*b*) Determine and display the peak magnitude, frequency of the peak magnitude, and bandwidth for the closed-loop frequency response for the input value of K.

Solution

```
>> %MATLAB Program
>> %Enter G(s)
>> numg = [1 5];
>> deng = [1 3 15 0];
>> 'G(s)'
>> G = tf(numg, deng)
>> %Enter K
>> K = input('Type gain, K');
>> 'T(s)'
>> T = feedback(K*G, 1)
>> bode(T)
>> title('Closed-loop frequency response')
>> [M,P,w] = bode(T);
>> [Mp i] = max(M);
>> Mp
>> MpdB = 20*log10(Mp)
>> wp = w(i)
>> for i = 1:1:length(M);
>> if M(i)< = 0.707;
>> fprintf('Bandwidth = %g', w(i))
>> break
>> end
>> end
```

Computer response

ans =

G(s)

Transfer function

$$\frac{s+5}{s^3+3s^2+15s}$$

Type gain, K 40

ans =

T(s)

Transfer function

$$\frac{40s+200}{s^3+3s^2+55s+200}$$

Mp =

11.1162

MpdB =

20.9192

wp =

7.5295

Bandwidth = 10.8036

The Bode plot is shown in Fig. P3.18(a).

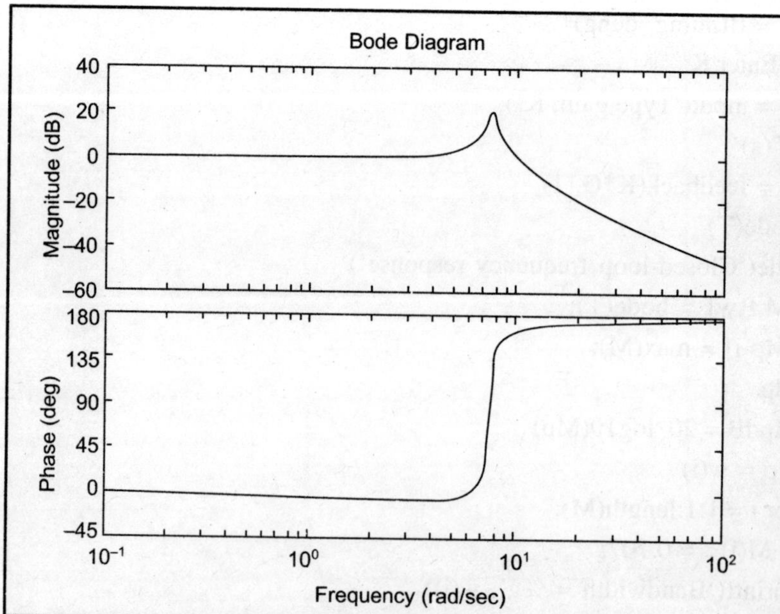

Fig. P3.18(a)

P3.19 Determine the unit-ramp response of the following system using MATLAB and lsim command:

$$\frac{C(s)}{R(s)} = \frac{1}{3s^2 + 2s + 1}.$$

Solution

```
>> %MATLAB Program
>> %Unit-ramp response
>> num = [0 0 1];
>> den = [3 2 1];
>> t = 0:0.1:10;
>> r = t;
>> y = lsim(num, den, r, t);
>> plot(t, r, '–', t, y, '0')
>> grid
>> title('Unit-ramp response')
>> xlabel('t Sec')
>> ylabel('Unit-ramp input and output')
>> text(1.0, 4.0, 'Unit-ramp input')
>> text(5.0, 2.0, 'Output')
```

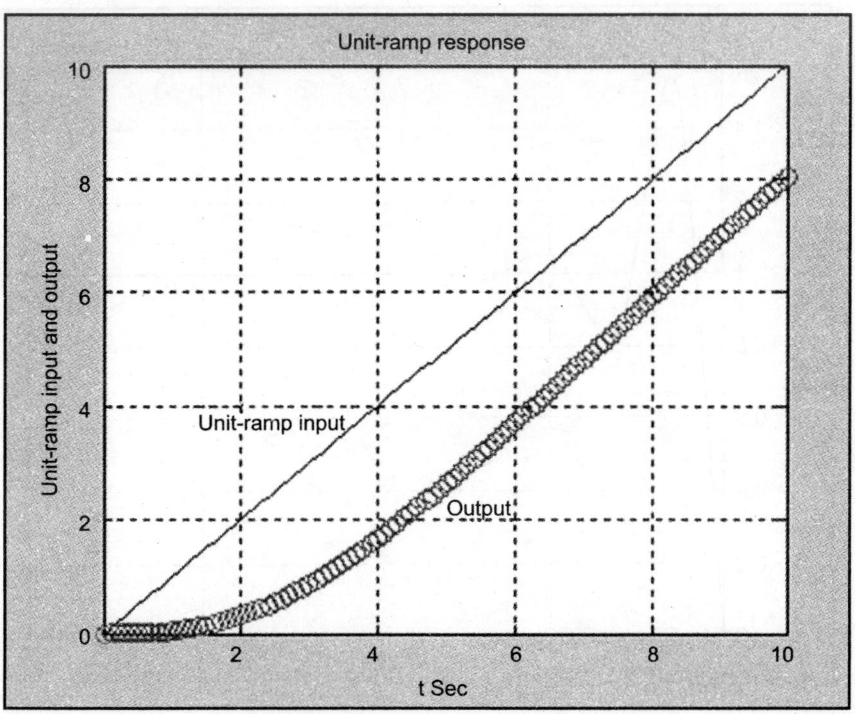

Fig. P3.19 Unit-ramp response

P3.20 A higher-order system is defined by

$$\frac{C(s)}{R(s)} = \frac{7s^2 + 16s + 10}{s^4 + 5s^3 + 11s^2 + 16s + 10}.$$

(*a*) Plot the unit-step response curve of the system using MATLAB.

(*b*) Obtain the rise time, peak time, maximum overshoot, and settling time using MATLAB.

Solution

```
>> %Unit-step response curve
>> num = [0 0 7 16 10];
>> den = [1 5 11 16 10];
>> t = 0:0.02:20;
>> [y, x, t] = step(num, den, t);
>> plot(t, y)
>> grid
>> title('Unit-step response')
>> xlabel('t Sec')
>> ylabel('Output y(t)')
```

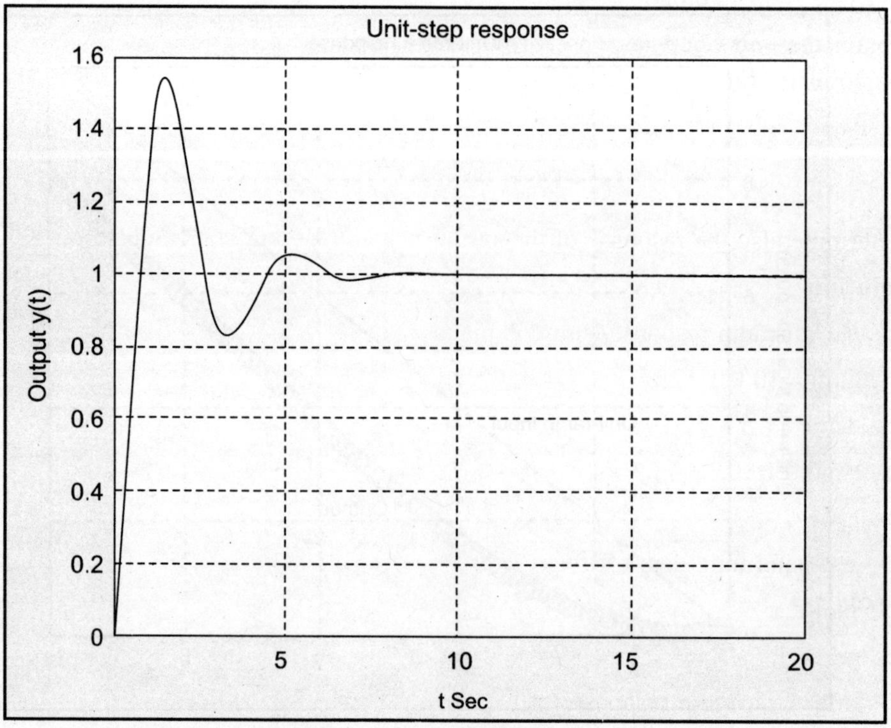

Fig. P3.20 Unit-step response

```
>> %Response to rise from 10% to 90% of its final value
>> rl = 1; while y(rl) < 0.1, rl = rl + 1; end
>> r2 = 1; while y(r2) < 0.9, r2 = r2 + 1; end
>> rise_time = (r2 – rl)*0.02
   rise_time =
              0.5400
>> [ymax, tp] = max(y);
>> peak_time = (tp – 1)*0.02
   peak_time =
              1.5200
>> max_overshoot = ymax – 1
   max_overshoot =
              0.5397
>> s = 1001; while y(s) > 0.98 & y(s) < 1.02; s = s–1; end
>> settling_time = (s – 1)*0.02
   settling_time =
              6.0200
```

P3.21 Obtain the unit-ramp response of the following closed-loop control system whose closed-loop transfer function is given by:

$$\frac{C(s)}{R(s)} = \frac{s+12}{s^3+5s^2+8s+12}.$$

Determine also the response of the system when the input is given by $r = e^{-0.7t}$.

Solution

```
>> %Unit-ramp response-lsim command
>> num = [0 0 1 12];
>> den = [1 5 8 12];
>> t = 0:0.1:10;
>> r = t;
>> y = lsim(num, den, r, t);
>> plot(t, r, '–', t, y, '0')
>> grid
>> title('Unit-ramp response')
>> xlabel('t Sec')
```

```
>> ylabel('Output')
>> text(3.0, 6.5, 'Unit-ramp input')
>> text(6.2, 4.5, 'Output')
```

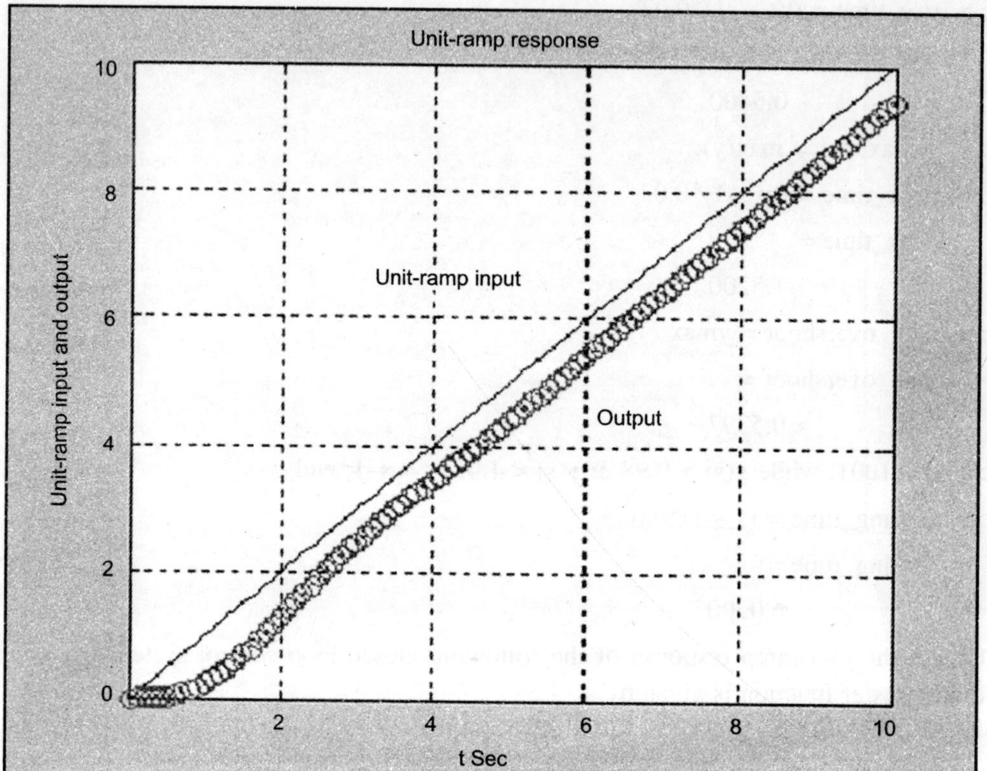

Fig. P3.21(a) Unit-ramp response curve

```
>> %Input r1 = exp(–0.7t)
>> num = [0 0 1 12];
>> den = [1 5 8 12];
>> t = 0:0.1:12;
>> r1 = exp(–0.7*t);
>> y1 = lsim(num,den,r1,t);
>> plot(t, r1, '–', t, y1, '0')
>> grid
>> title('Response to input r1 = exp(–0.7t)')
>> xlabel('t Sec')
>> ylabel('Input and output')
>> text(0.5, 0.9, 'Input r1 = exp(–0.7t)')
>> text(6.3, 0.1, 'Output')
```

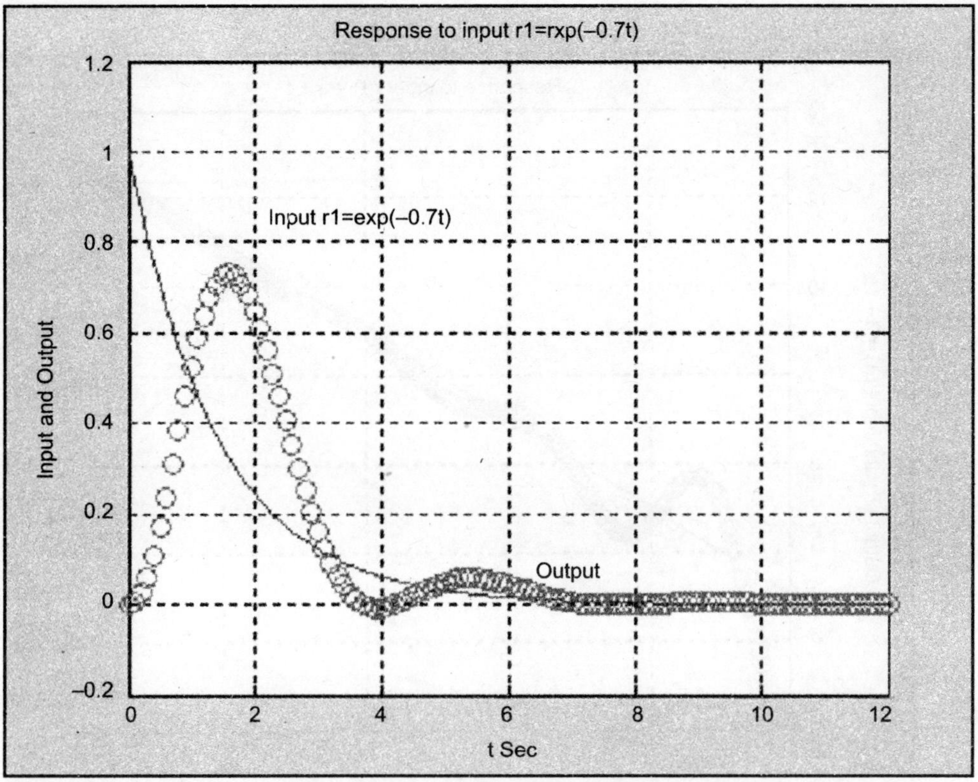

Fig. P3.21(b) Response curve for input r = $e^{-0.7t}$

P3.22 Obtain the response of the closed-loop system using MATLAB. The closed-loop system is defined by

$$\frac{C(s)}{R(s)} = \frac{7}{s^2 + s + 7}.$$

The input r(t) is a step input of magnitude 3 plus unit-ramp input, r(t) = 3 + t.

Solution

```
>> %MATLAB Program
>> num = [0 0 7];
>> den = [1 1 7];
>> t = 0:0.05:10;
>> r = 3 + t;
>> c = lsim(num, den, r, t);
>> plot(t, r, '–', t, c, '0')
>> grid
>> title('Response to input r(t) = 3 + t')
>> xlabel('t Sec')
>> ylabel('Output c(t) and input r(t) = 3 + t')
```

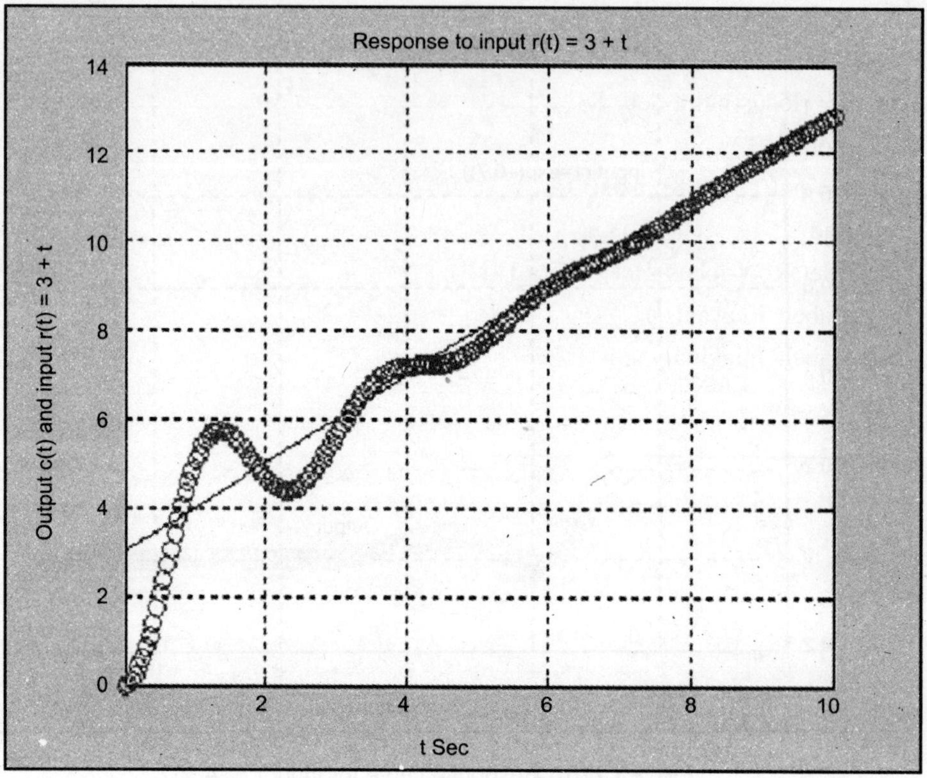

Fig. P3.22 Response to input r(t) = 3 + t

P3.23 Plot the root-locus diagram using MATLAB for a system whose open-loop transfer function G(s) H(s) is given by

$$G(s)H(s) = \frac{K(s+3)}{(s^2+3s+4)(s^2+2s+7)}$$

Solution

$$G(s)H(s) = \frac{K(s+3)}{(s^2+3s+4)(s^2+2s+7)} = \frac{K(s+3)}{(s^4+5s^3+17s^2+29s+28)}$$

```
>> %MATLAB Program
>> num = [0 0 0 1 3];
>> den = [1 5 17 29 28];
>> K1 = 0:0.1:2;
>> K2 = 2:0.02:2.5;
>> K3 = 2.5:0.5:10;
```

```
>> K4 = 10:1:50;
>> K5 = 50:5:800;
>> K = [K1 K2 K3 K4 K5];
>> r = rlocus(num, den, K);
>> plot(r, '0')
>> v = [–10 5 –8 8]; axis(v)
>> grid
>> title('Root-locus plot of G(s)H(s)')
>> xlabel('Real axis')
>> ylabel('Imaginary axis')
```

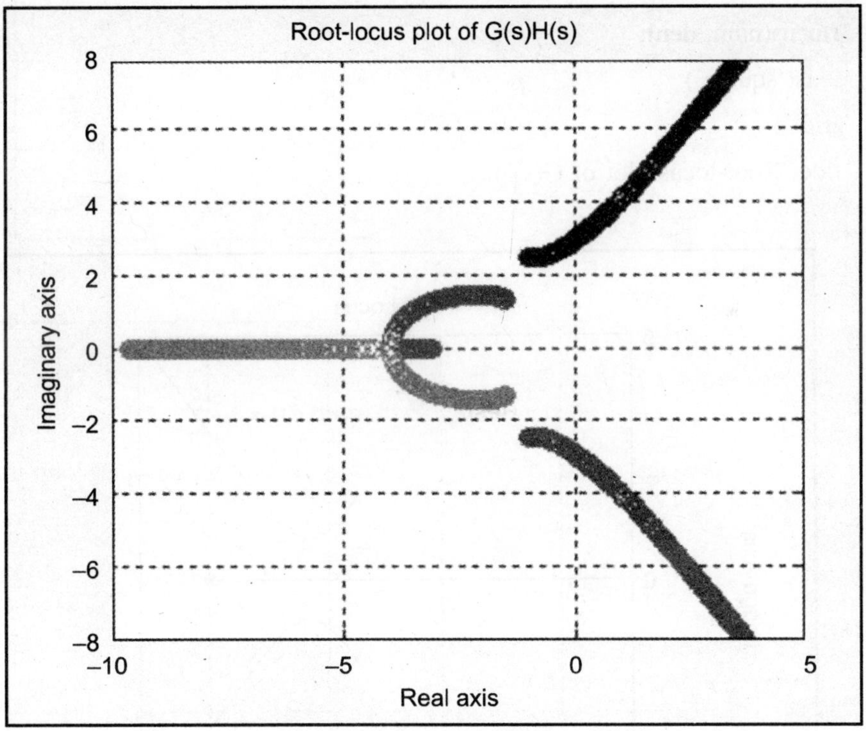

Fig. P3.23 Root-locus diagram

P3.24 A unity-feedback control system is defined by the following feed forward transfer function:

$$G(s) = \frac{K}{s(s^2 + 5s + 9)}.$$

(*a*) Determine the location of the closed-loop poles, if the value of gain is equal to 3.

(*b*) Plot the root loci for the system using MATLAB.

Solution

```
>> %MATLAB Program to find the closed-loop poles
>> p = [1 5 9 3];
>> roots(p)
ans =
        –2.2874 + 1.3500i
        –2.2874 – 1.3500i
        –0.4253
>> %MATLAB Program to plot the root-loci
>> num = [0 0 0 1];
>> den = [1 5 9 0];
>> rlocus(num, den);
>> axis('square')
>> grid
>> title('Root-locus plot of G(s)')
```

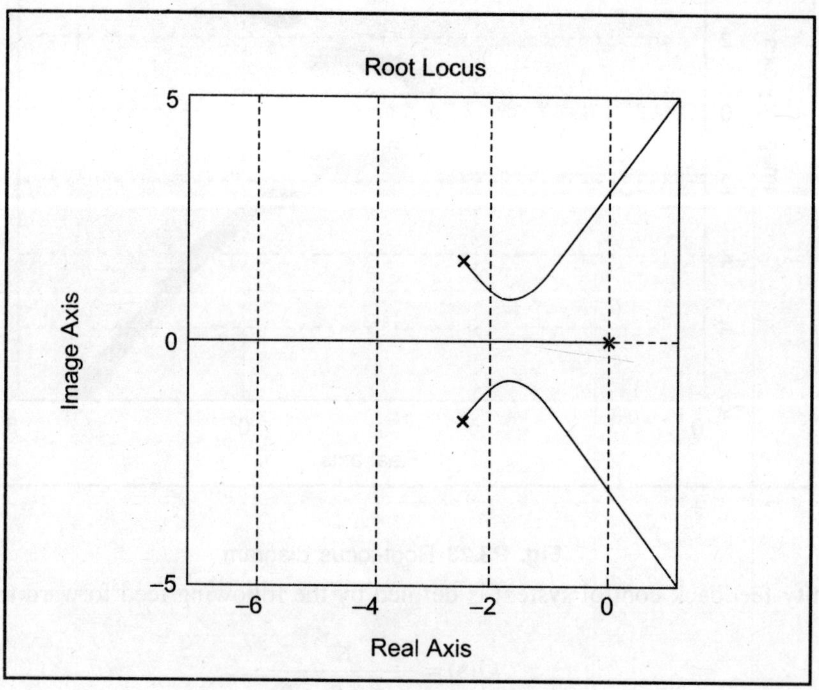

Fig. P3.24 Root-locus plot of G(s)

P3.25 The open-loop transfer function of a unity-feedback control system is given by

$$G(s) = \frac{1}{s^3 + 0.3s^2 + 5s + 1}.$$

(*a*) Draw a Nyquist plot of G(s) using MATLAB.

(*b*) Determine the stability of the system.

Solution

```
>> % Open-loop poles
>> p = [1 0.3 5 1];
>> roots(p)
ans =
        -0.0496 + 2.2311i
        -0.0496 - 2.2311i
        -0.2008
>> % Nyquist plot
>> num = [0 0 0 1];
>> den = [1 0.3 5 1];
>> nyquist(num,den)
>> v = [-3 3 -2 2]; axis(v); axis('square')
>> grid
>> title('Nyquist plot of G(s)')
```

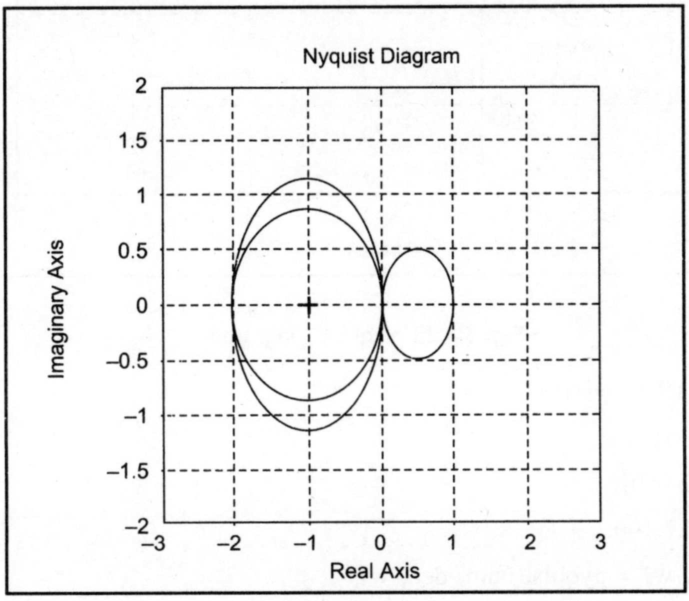

Fig. P3.25 Nyquist plot of G(s)

There are two open-loop poles in the right half s plane and no encirclement of the critical point, the closed-loop system is unstable.

P3.26 The open-loop transfer function of a unity-feedback control system is given by

$$G(s) = \frac{K(s+3)}{s(s+1)(s+7)}$$

Plot the Nyquist diagram of G(s) for K = 1, 10, and 100 using MATLAB.

Solution

$$G(s) = \frac{K(s+3)}{s(s+1)(s+7)} = \frac{K(s+3)}{s^3+8s^2+7s}$$

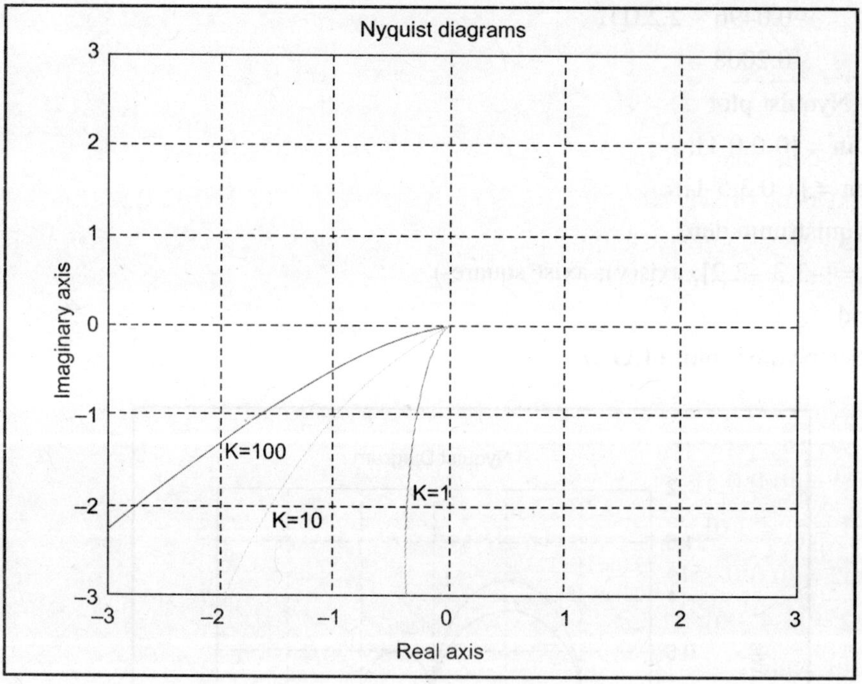

Fig. P3.26 Nyquist Diagrams

```
>> % MATLAB Program
>> num = [1 3];
>> den = [1 8 7 0];
>> w = 0.1:0.1:100;
>> [re1, im1, w] = nyquist(num, den, w);
>> [re2, im2, w] = nyquist(10*num, den, w);
```

```
>> [re3, im3, w] = nyquist(100*num, den, w);
>> plot(re1, im1, re2, im2, re3, im3)
>> v = [–3 3 –3 3]; axis(v)
>> grid
>> title('Nyquist diagrams')
>> xlabel('Real axis')
>> ylabel('Imaginary axis')
>> text(–0.2, –2, 'K = 1')
>> text(–1.5, –2.0, 'K = 10')
>> text(–2, –1.5, 'K = 100')
```

P3.27 The open-loop transfer function of a negative feedback system is given by

$$G(s) = \frac{5}{s(s+1)(s+3)}$$

Plot the Nyquist diagram for

(*a*) G(s) using MATLAB

(*b*) Same open-loop transfer function use G(s) of a positive feedback system using MATLAB.

Solution

$$G(s) = \frac{5}{s(s+1)(s+3)} = \frac{5}{s^3 + 4s^2 + 3s}$$

```
>> %Nyquist diagrams of G(s) and –G(s)
>> num1 = [0 0 0 5];
>> den1 = [1 4 3 0];
>> num2 = [0 0 0 –5];
>> den2 = [1 4 3 0];
>> nyquist(num1, den1)
>> hold
Current plot held
>> nyquist(num2, den2)
>> v = [–5 5 –5 5]; axis(v)
>> grid
>> text(–3, --1.8, 'G(s)')
>> text(1.9, –2, '–G(s)')
```

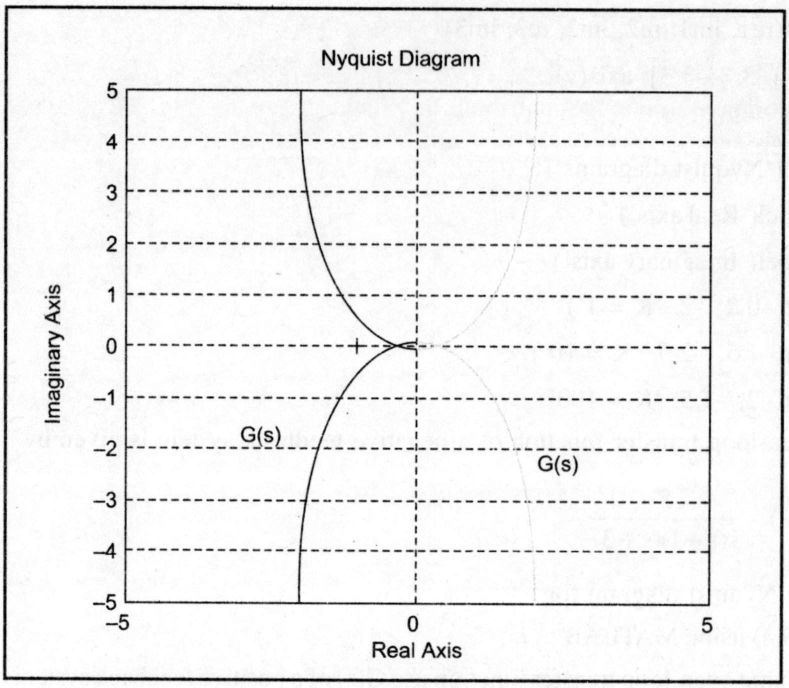

Fig. P3.27 Nyquist diagrams

P3.28 For the system shown in Fig. P3.28, design a compensator such that the dominant closed-loop poles are located at $s = -2 \pm j\sqrt{3}$. Plot the unit-step response curve of the designed system using MATLAB.

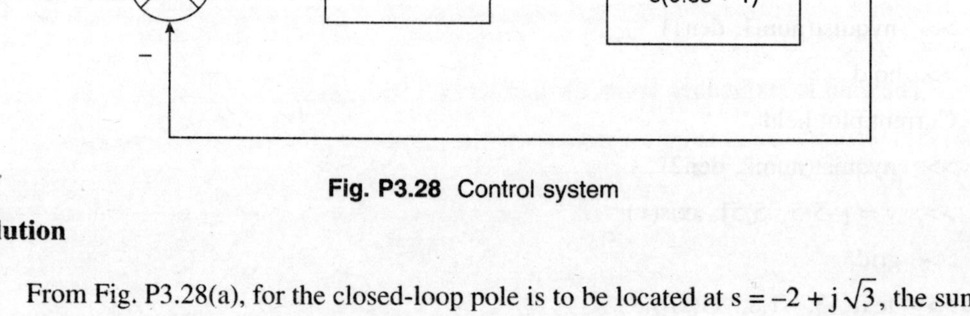

Fig. P3.28 Control system

Solution

From Fig. P3.28(a), for the closed-loop pole is to be located at $s = -2 + j\sqrt{3}$, the sum of the angle contributions of the open-loop poles (at s = 0, and s = −2) is given by −120° − 90° = −210°. For the closed-loop pole at $s = -2 + j\sqrt{3}$ we need to add 30° to the open-loop transfer function. In other words, the angle deficiency of the given open-loop transfer function at the desired closed-loop pole $s = -2 + j\sqrt{3}$ is given by

$$180^\circ - 120^\circ - 90^\circ = -30^\circ$$

The compensator must contribute 30° (lead compensator). The simplest form of a lead compensator is

$$G_c(s) = K\frac{s+a}{s+b}$$

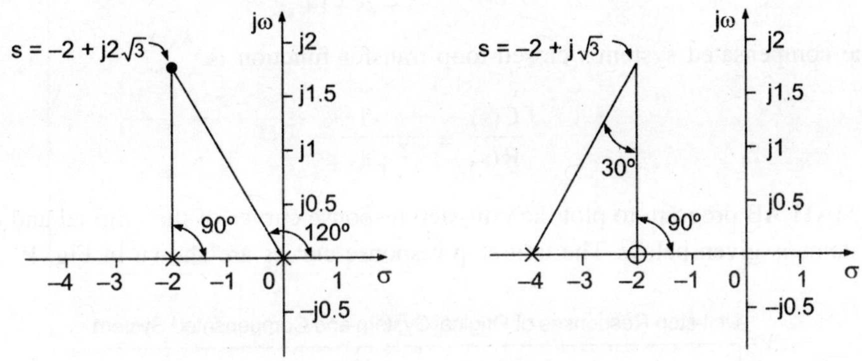

(a) Open-loop poles and a desired closed-loop pole.

(b) Compensator pole-zero configuration to contribute phase lead angle of 30°.

Fig. P3.28(a) and **(b)**

If we select the zero of the lead compensator at $s = -2$, then the pole of the compensator must be located at $s = -4$ in order to have a phase lead angle of 30° (see Fig. P3.28(b)). Hence

$$G_c(s) = K\frac{s+2}{s+4}$$

The gain K is obtained from the condition

$$\left| K\frac{s+2}{s+4}\,\frac{7}{s(0.5s+1)} \right|_{s=-2=j\sqrt{3}} = 1$$

or

$$K = \left| \frac{s(s+4)}{14} \right|_{s=-2=j\sqrt{3}} = 0.5$$

or
$$G_c(s) = 0.5\frac{s+2}{s+4}$$

The open-loop transfer function of the compensated system is given by

$$G_c(s)\,.\,\frac{7}{s(0.5s+1)} = 0.5\frac{s+2}{s+4}\,\frac{14}{s(s+2)} = \frac{7}{s(s+4)}$$

The closed-loop transfer function of the original system is

$$\frac{C(s)}{R(s)} = \frac{14}{s^2+2s+14}$$

The compensated system's closed-loop transfer function is

$$\frac{C(s)}{R(s)} = \frac{7}{s^2+4s+7}$$

A MATLAB program to plot the unit-step response curves of the original and compensated systems is given below. The unit-step response curves are shown in Fig. P3.28(c).

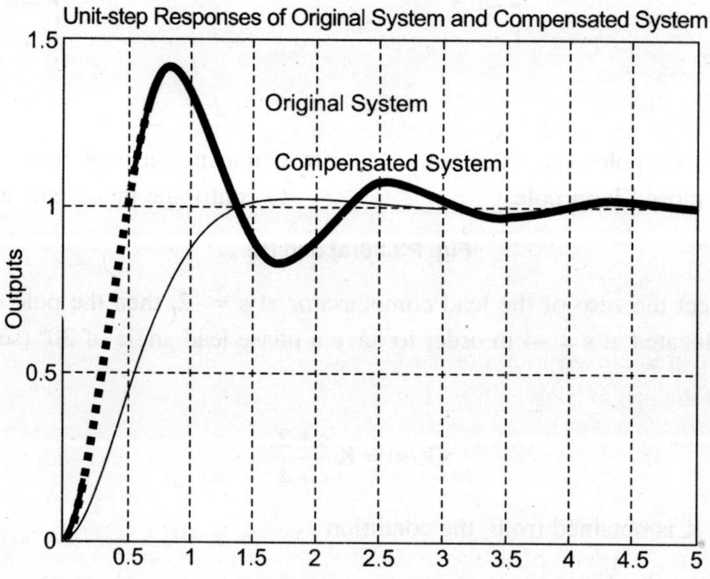

Fig. P3.28(c)

% MATLAB Program

num = [0 0 14];

den = [1 2 14];

numc = [0 0 7];

```
denc = [1 4 7];
t = 0: 0.01: 5;
c1 = step(num, den,t);
c2 = step(numc, denc, t);
plot(t, c1, '.', t, c2, '–')
xlabel('t Sec')
ylabel('Outputs')
text(1.5, 1.3, 'Original system')
text(1.7, 1.14, 'Compensated system')
grid
title('Unit-Step Responses of Original System and Compensated System')
```

P3.29 For the control system shown in Fig. P3.29 design a compensator such that the dominant closed-loop poles are located at s = –1 + j1. Determine also the unit-step and unit ramp responses of the uncompensated and compensated systems.

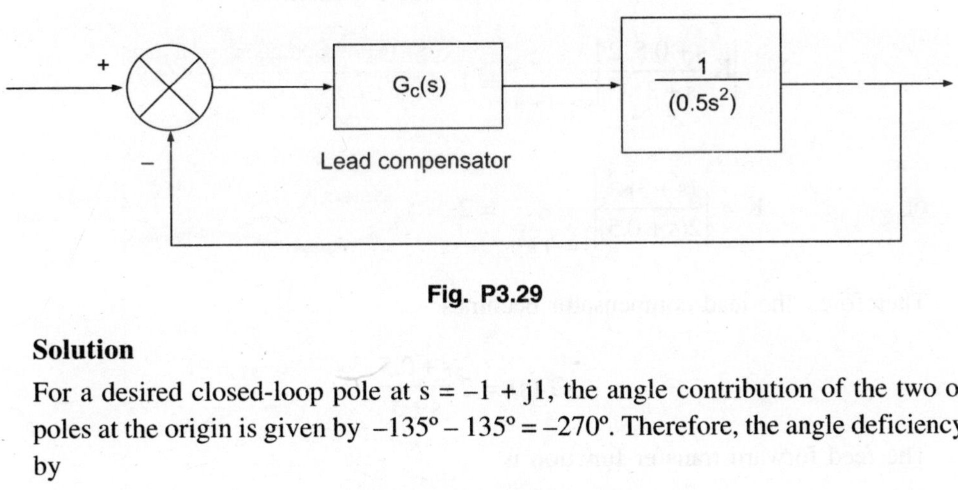

Fig. P3.29

Solution

For a desired closed-loop pole at s = –1 + j1, the angle contribution of the two open-loop poles at the origin is given by –135° – 135° = –270°. Therefore, the angle deficiency is given by

$$180° - 135° - 135° = -90°$$

Hence, the compensator must contribute 90°.

We select a lead compensator of the form

$$G_c(s) = K\frac{s+a}{s+b}$$

and choose the zero of the lead compensator at s = –0.5. In order to obtain the phase lead angle of 90°, the pole of the compensator must be located at s = –3 (see Fig. P3.29(a).

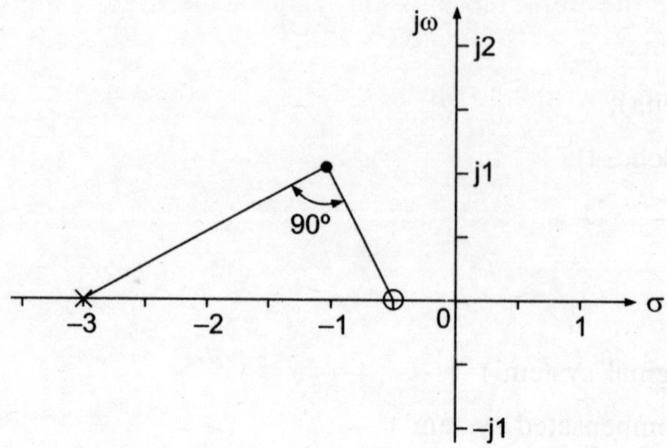

Fig. P3.29(a) Pole-zero location of lead compensator contributing 90º phase lead

Therefore

$$G_c(s) = K\frac{s+0.5}{s+3}$$

where K must be obtained from the magnitude condition as

$$\left|K\frac{s+0.5}{s+3}\frac{2}{s^2}\right|_{s=-1+j1} = 1$$

or
$$K = \left|\frac{(s+3)s^2}{2(s+0.5)}\right|_{s=-1+j1} = 2$$

Therefore, the lead compensator becomes

$$G_c(s) = 2\frac{s+0.5}{s+3}$$

The feed forward transfer function is

$$G_c(s)\frac{1}{0.5s^2} = \frac{4s+2}{s^3+3s^2}$$

The root-locus plot of the system is shown in Fig. P3.29(b).

The closed-loop transfer function is given by

$$\frac{C(s)}{R(s)} = \frac{4s+2}{s^3+3s^2+4s+2}$$

The closed-loop poles are located at s = –1 ± j1 and s = –1.

Now we determine the unit-step and unit-ramp responses of the uncompensated and compensated systems.

A MATLAB program is written to obtain unit-step response curve. The resulting curves are shown in Fig. P3.29(b).

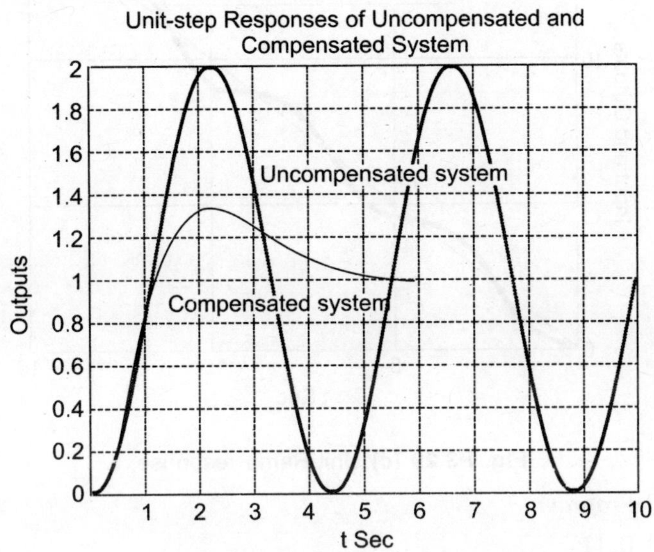

Fig. P3.29(b) Unit-step response

```
% MATLAB Program
num = [0 0 2];
den = [1 0 2];
nume = [0 0 4 2];
dene = [1 3 4 2];
t = 0:0.02:10;
c1 = step(num, den, t);
c2 = step(numc, denc, t);
plot(t, c1,‘.’, t, c2, ‘–’)
grid
title(‘Unit-Step Responses of Uncompensated and Compensated Systems’)
xlabel(‘t Sec’)
ylabel(‘Outputs’)
text(2, 0.88, ‘Compensated system’)
text(3.1, 1.48, ‘Uncompensated system’)
```

A MATLAB program to obtain unit-ramp response curve is given below. The resulting response curves are shown in Fig. P3.29(c).

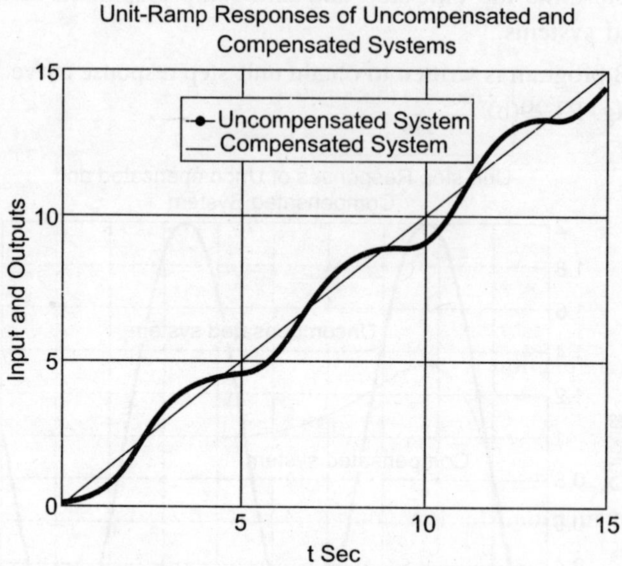

Fig. P3.29 (c) Unit-Ramp response

```
% MATLAB Program
num = [0 0 0 1];
den = [1 0 1 0];
nume = [0 0 0 4 2];
dene = [1 3 4 2 0];
t = 0:0.02:15;
c1 = step(num, den, t);
c2 = step(numc, denc, t);
plot(, t, c1, '.', t, c2, '–')
grid
title('Unit-Ramp Responses of Uncompensated and Compensated Systems')
xlabel('t Sec')
ylabel('Input and Outputs')
legend('.', 'uncompensated system', '–', 'compensated system')
```

P3.30 The PID control of a second-order plant G(s) control system is shown in Fig. P3.30. Consider the reference input R(s) is held constant. Design a control system such that the response to any step disturbance will be damped out in 2 to 3 secs in terms of the 2% settling time. Select the configuration of the closed-loop poles such that there is a pair of dominant closed-loop poles. Obtain the response to the unit-step disturbance input and to the unit-step reference input.

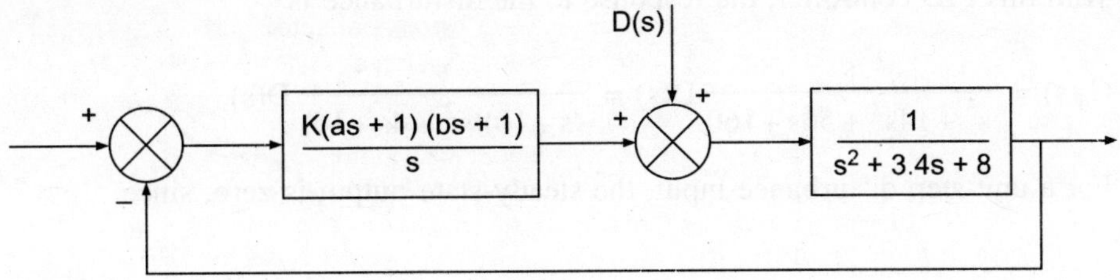

Fig. P3.30

Solution

The transfer function is

$$G_c(s) = \frac{K(as+1)(bs+1)}{s}$$

The closed-loop transfer function is given by

$$\frac{C_d(s)}{D(s)} = \frac{s}{s(s^2+3.4s+8)+K(as+1)(bs+1)} = \frac{s}{s^3(3.4+Kab)s^2+(8+Ka+Kb)s+K} \quad ...(1)$$

It is required that the response to the unit-step disturbance be such that the settling time be 2 to 3s and the system have reasonable damping. Hence, we chose $\xi = 0.5$ and $\omega_n = 4$ rad/s for the dominant closed-loop poles and the third pole at $s = -10$ so that the effect of this real pole on the response is small. The desired characteristic equation is then given by

$$(s + 10)(s^2 + 2 \times 0.5 \times 4s + 4^2) = (s + 10)(s^2 + 4s + 16) = s^3 + 14s^2 + 56s + 160$$

The characteristic equation for the system given by Eq. (1) is

$$s^3 + (3.4 + Kab)s^2 + (8 + Ka + Kb)s + K = 0$$

Therefore

$$3.4 + Kab = 14$$
$$8 + Ka + Kb = 56$$
$$K = 160$$

which gives

$$ab = 0.06625, \; a + b = 0.3$$

The PID controller now is given by

$$G_c(s) = \frac{K[abs^2+(a+b)s+1]}{s} = \frac{160(0.06625s^2+0.3s+1)}{s} = \frac{10.6(s^2+4.528s+15.09)}{s}$$

With this PID controller, the response to the disturbance is

$$C_d(s) = \frac{s}{s^3 + 14s^2 + 56s + 160} D(s) = \frac{s}{(s+10)(s^2 + 4s + 16)} D(s)$$

For a unit-step disturbance input, the steady-state output is zero, since

$$\lim_{t\to\infty} c_d(t) = \lim_{s\to 0} sC_d(s) = \lim_{s\to 0} \frac{s^2}{(s+10)(s^2+4s+16)} \frac{1}{s} = 0$$

The response to a unit-step disturbance input is obtained with MATLAB program. The response curve is shown in Fig. P3.30(a). From the response curve we note that the settling time is approximately 2.7 s. The response damps out rather quickly. Hence, the system designed is acceptable.

```
% Response to unit-step disturbance input
numd = [0 0 1 0];
dend = [1 14 56 160];
t = 0:0.01:5;
[c1, x1, t] = step(numd, dend, t);
plot(t, c1)
grid
title('Response to Unit-Step Disturbance Input')
xlabel('t Sec')
ylabel('Output to Disturbance Input')
```

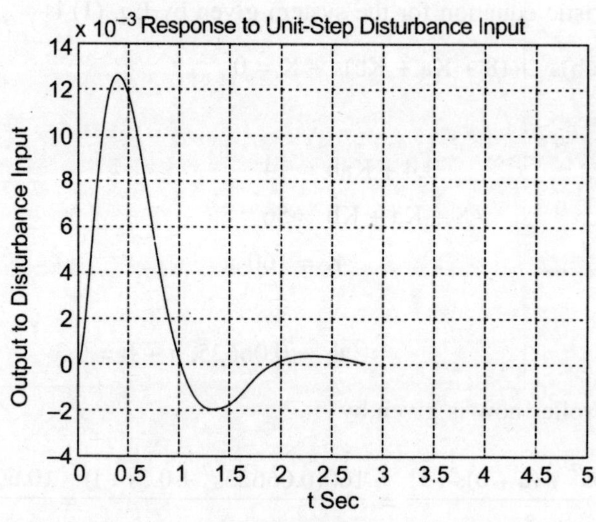

Fig. P3.30 (a)

For the reference input r(t), the closed-loop transfer function is

$$\frac{C_r(s)}{R(s)} = \frac{10.6(s^2 + 4.528s + 15.09)}{s^3 + 14s^2 + 56s + 160} = \frac{10.6s^2 + 48s + 160}{s^3 + 14s^2 + 56s + 160}$$

The response to a unit-step ***reference*** input is obtained by the MATLAB program. The resulting response curve is shown in Fig. P3.30(b). The response curve shows that the maximum overshoot is 7.3% and the settling time is 1.7s. Thus, the system has quite acceptable response characteristics.

```
% Response to unit-step reference input
numr = [0 10.6 48 160];
denr = [1 14 56 160];
t = 0:0.01:5;
[c2, x2, t] = step(numr, denr, t);
plot(t, c2)
grid
title('Response to Unit-Step Reference Input')
xlabel('t Sec')
ylabel('Output to Reference Input')
```

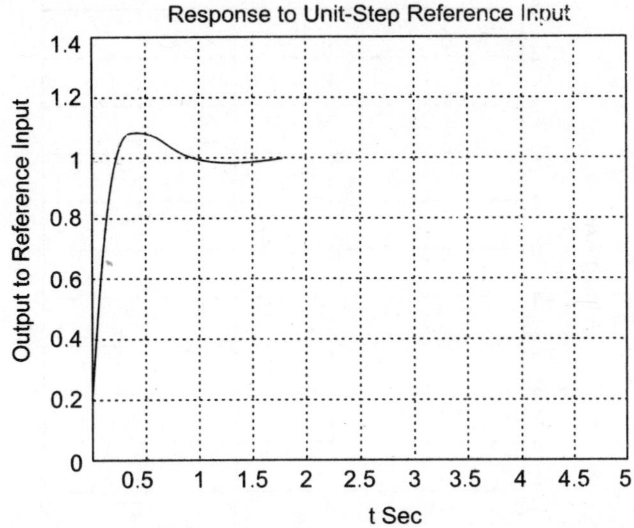

Fig. P3.30 (b)

P3.31 For the closed-loop control system shown in Fig. P3.31, obtain the range of gain K for stability and plot a root-locus diagram for the system.

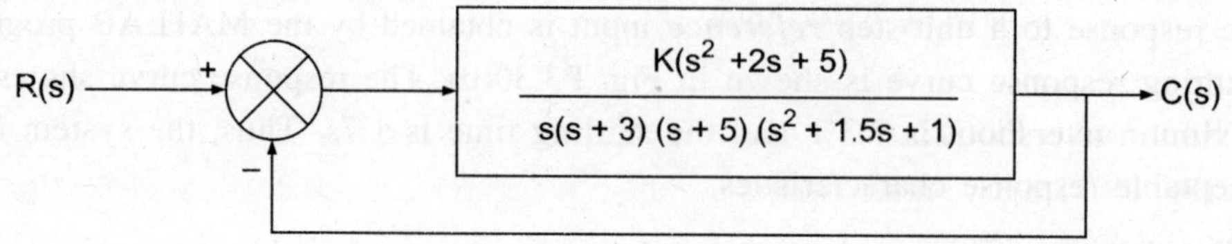

Fig. P3.31

Solution

The range of gain K for stability is obtained by first plotting the root loci and then finding critical points (for stability) on the root loci. The open-loop transfer function G(s) is

$$G(s) = \frac{K(s^2+2s+5)}{s(s+3)(s+5)(s^2+1.5s+1)} = \frac{K(s^2+2s+5)}{s5+9.5s^4+28s^3+20s^2+15s}$$

A MATLAB program to generate generate a plot of the root loci for the system is given below. The resulting root-locus plot is shown in Fig. P3.31(a).

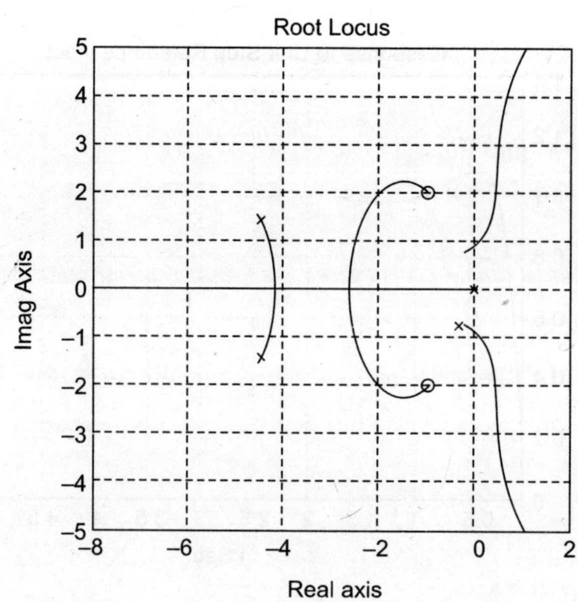

Fig. P3.31 (a)

% MATLAB Program

```
num = [0 0 0 1 2 5];
den = [1 9.5 28 20 15 0];
rlocus(num, den)
v = [–8 2 –5 5]; axis(v); axis('square')
grid
title('Root-Locus Plot')
```

From Fig. P3.31(a), we notice that the system is conditionally stable. All critical points for stability lie on the jω axis.

To obtain the crossing points of the root loci with the jw axis, we substitute s = jω into the characteristic equation

$$s^5 + 9.5s^4 + 28s^3 + 20s^2 + 15s + K(s^2 + 2s + 5) = 0$$

or $$(j\omega)^5 + 9.5(j\omega)^4 + 28(j\omega)^3 + (20 + K)(j\omega)^2 + (15 + 2K)(j\omega) + 5K = 0$$

or $$[9.5\omega^4 - (20 + K)\,\omega^2 + 5K] + j[\omega^5 - 28\omega^3 + (15 + 2K)\,\omega] = 0$$

Equating the real part and imaginary part equal to zero, respectively, we get

$$9.5\omega^4 - (20 + K)\,\omega^2 + 5K = 0 \quad \text{...(1)}$$

$$\omega^5 - 28\omega^3 + (15 + 2K)\,\omega = 0 \quad \text{...(2)}$$

Eqn. (2) can be written as

$$\omega = 0$$

or $$\omega^4 - 28\omega^2 + 15 + 2K = 0 \quad \text{...(3)}$$

$$K = \frac{-\omega^4 + 28\omega^2 - 15}{2} \quad \text{...(4)}$$

Substituting Eqn. (4) into Eqn. (1), we obtain

$$9.5\omega^4 - [20 + \tfrac{1}{2}(-\omega^4 + 28\omega^2 - 15)]\,\omega^2 - 2.5\omega^4 + 70\omega^2 - 37.5 = 0$$

or $$0.5\omega^6 - 2\omega^4 + 57.5\omega^2 - 37.5 = 0$$

The roots of the above equation can be obtained by MATLAB program given below.

% MATLAB Program

```
a = [0.5 0 –2 0 57.50 –37.5];
roots(a)
```

Output is:

```
ans =

    –2.4786 + 2.1157i
    –2.4786 – 2.1157i
     2.4786 + 2.1157i
     2.4786 – 2.1157i
```

0.8155

–0.8155

The root-locus branch in the upper half plane that goes to infinity crosses the jω axis at ω = 0.8155. The gain values at these crossing points are given by

$$K = \frac{-0.8155^4 + 28\times 0.8155^2 - 15}{2} = 1.5894 \quad \text{for } \omega = 0.8155$$

For this K value, we obtain the range of gain K for stability as

$$1.5894 > K > 0$$

P3.32 For the control system shown in Fig. P3.32:

(*a*) Plot the root loci for the system.

(*b*) Find the range of gain K for stability.

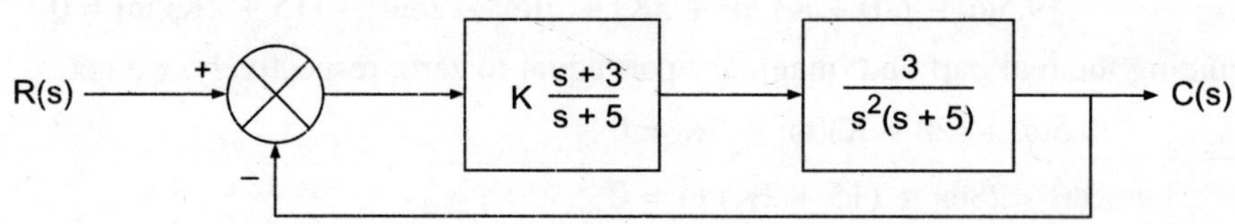

Fig. P3.32

Solution

The open-loop transfer function G(s) is given by

$$G(s) = K\frac{s+3}{s+5}\,\frac{3}{s^2(s+3)} = \frac{3K(s+3)}{s^4 + 8s^3 + 15s^2}$$

A MATLAB program to generate the root-locus plot is given below. The resulting plot is shown in Fig. P3.32(a).

```
% MATLAB Program
num = [0 0 0 1 3];
den = [1 8 15 0 0];
rlocus(num, den)
v = [–6 4 –5 5]; axis(v); axis('square')
grid
title('Root-Locus Plot')
```

From Fig. P3.32 (a), we notice that the critical value of gain K for stability corresponds to the crossing point of the root locus branch that goes to infinity and the imaginary axis. Therefore, we first find the crossing frequency and then find the corresponding gain value.

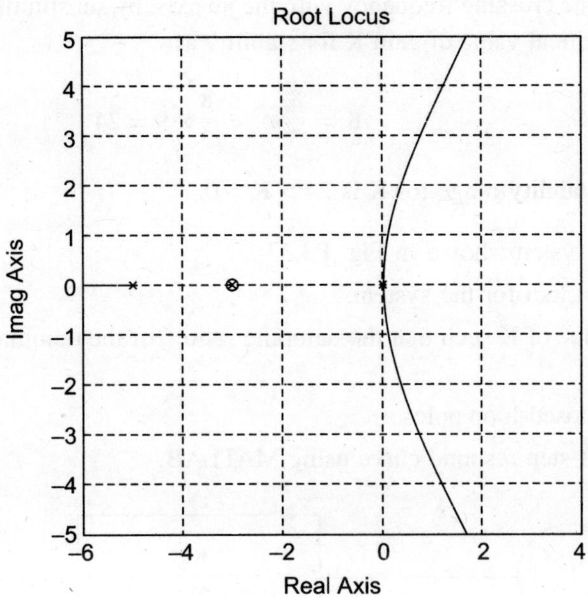

Fig. P3.32(a)

The characteristic equation is

$$s^4 + 8s^3 + 15s^2 + 3Ks + 9K = 0$$

Substituting s = jω into the characteristic equation, we get

$$(j\omega)^4 + 8(j\omega)^3 + 15(j\omega)^2 + 3K(j\omega) + 9K = 0$$

or

$$(\omega^4 - 15\omega^2 + 9K) + j\omega(-8\omega^2 + 3K) = 0$$

Equating the real part and imaginary part of the above equation to zero, respectively, we obtain

$$\omega^4 - 15\omega^2 + 9K = 0 \quad ...(1)$$

$$\omega(-8\omega^2 + 3K) = 0 \quad ...(2)$$

Eq. (2) can be rewritten as

$$\omega = 0$$

or

$$-8\omega^2 + 3K = 0 \quad ...(3)$$

Substituting the value of K in Eq.(1), we get

$$\omega^4 - 15\omega^2 + 9 \times \frac{8}{3}\omega^2 = 0$$

or

$$\omega^4 + 9\omega^2 = 0$$

which gives

$$\omega = 0 \text{ and } \omega = \pm j\,3$$

Since $\omega = j3$ is the crossing frequency with the $j\omega$ axis, by substituting $\omega = 3$ into Eqn. (E.3) we obtain the critical value of gain K for stability as

$$K = \frac{8}{3}\omega^2 = \frac{8}{3} \times 9 = 24$$

Therefore, the stability range for K is $24 > K > 0$.

P3.33 For the control system shown in Fig. P3.33:

(*a*) Plot the root loci for the system.

(*b*) Find the value of K such that the damping ratio ζ of the dominant closed-loop poles is 0.6.

(*c*) Obtain all closed-loop poles.

(*d*) Plot the unit-step respond curve using MATLAB.

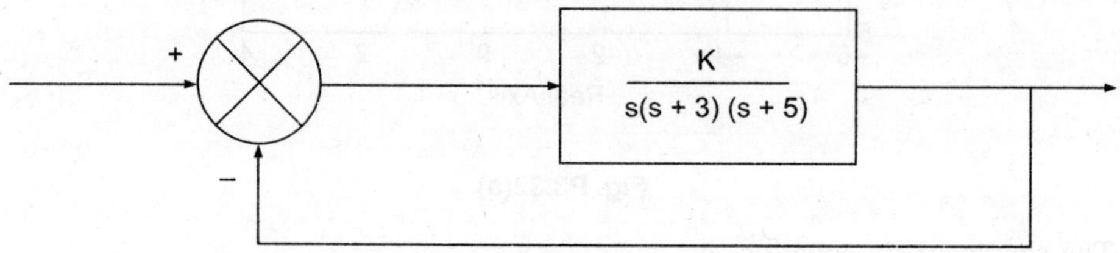

Fig. P3.33

Solution

(*a*) The MATLAB program given below generates a root-locus plot for the given system. The resulting plot is shown in Fig. P3.33(a).

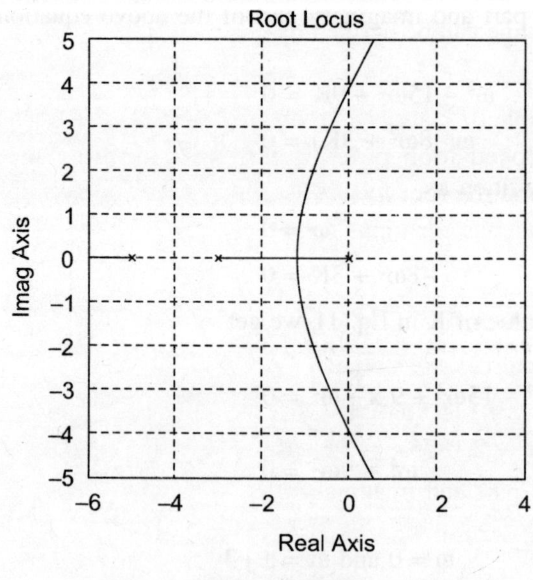

Fig. P3.33(a)

```
% MATLAB Program
num = [0 0 0 1];
den = [1 8 15 0];
rlocus(num,den)
v = [–6 4 –5 5]; axis(v); axis('square')
grid
title('Root-Locus Plot')
```

(*b*) We note that the constant ζ points ($0 < \zeta < 1$) lie on a straight line having angle θ from the $j\omega$ axis as shown in Fig. P3.17(b).

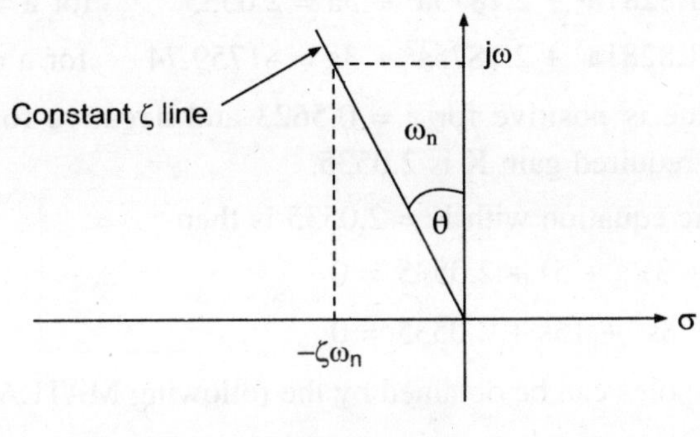

Fig. P3.33(b)

From Fig. P3.33(b), we obtain

$$\sin\theta = \frac{\zeta\omega_n}{\omega_n} = \zeta$$

Also that $\zeta = 0.6$ line can be defined by

$$s = -0.75a + ja$$

where a is a variable ($0 < a < \infty$). To obtain the value of K such that the damping ratio z of the dominant closed-loop poles is 0.6 we determine the intersection of the line $s = -0.75a + ja$ and the root locus. The intersection point can be obtained by solving the following simultaneous equations for a.

$$s = -0.75a + ja \qquad \text{...(1)}$$

$$s(s + 3)(s + 5) + K = 0 \qquad \text{...(2)}$$

From Eqns. (1) and (2), we obtain

$$(-0.75a + ja)(-0.75a + ja + 3)(-0.75a + ja + 5) + K = 0$$

or $$(1.8281a^3 - 2.1875a^2 - 3a + K) + j(0.6875a^3 - 7.5a^2 + 15a) = 0$$

Equating the real part and imaginary part of the above equation to zero, respectively, we obtain

$$1.8281a^3 - 2.1875a^2 - 3a + K = 0 \qquad \text{...(3)}$$

$$0.6875a^3 - 7.5a^2 + 4a = 0 \qquad ...(4)$$

Eqn. (4) can be rewritten as

$$a = 0$$

or $$0.6875a^2 - 7.5a + 4 = 0$$

or $$a^2 - 10.90991a + 5.8182 = 0$$

or $$(a - 0.5623)(a - 10.3468) = 0$$

Therefore a = 0.5323 or a = 10.3468

From Eqn. (3) we obtain

$$K = -1.8281a^3 + 2.1875a^2 + 3a = 2.0535 \qquad \text{for } a = 0.5626$$

$$K = -1.8281a^3 + 2.1875a^2 + 3a = -1759.74 \qquad \text{for } a = 10.3468$$

Since the K value is positive for a = 0.5623 and negative for a = –10.3468, we select a = 0.5623. The required gain K is 2.0535.

The characteristic equation with K = 2.0535 is then

$$s(s + 3)(s + 5) + 2.0535 = 0$$

or $$s^3 + 8s^2 + 15s + 2.0535 = 0$$

(*c*) The closed-loop poles can be obtained by the following MATLAB program:

```
% MATLAB Program
p = [1 8 15 2.0535];
roots(p)
ans =

     -5.1817
     -2.6699
     -0.1484
```

Hence, the closed-loop poles are located at

s = –5.1817, s = –2.6699, s = –4.1565

(*d*) The unit-step response of the system for K = 2.0535 can be obtained from the following MATLAB program. The resulting unit-step response curve is shown in Fig. P3.33(c).

```
% MATLAB Program
num = [0 0 0 2.0535];
den = [1 8 15 2.0535];
step(num, den)
grid
title('Unit-Step Response')
xlabel('t Sec')
ylabel('Output')
```

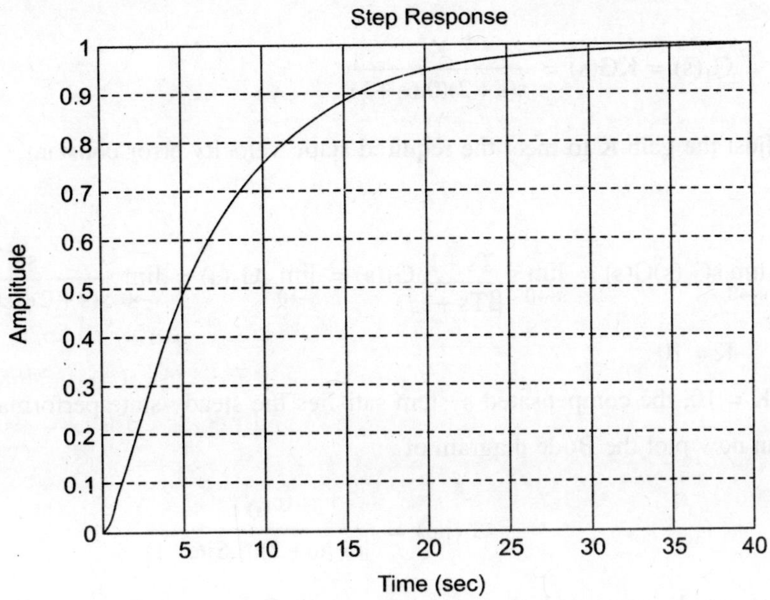

Fig. P3.33 (c)

P3.34 For the control system shown in Fig. P3.34, the open-loop transfer function is given by

$$G(s) = \frac{1}{s(s+2)(0.6s+1)}$$

Design a compensator for the system such that the static velocity error constant K_v is $5s^{-1}$, the phase margin is at least 50°, and the gain margin is at least 10 dB.

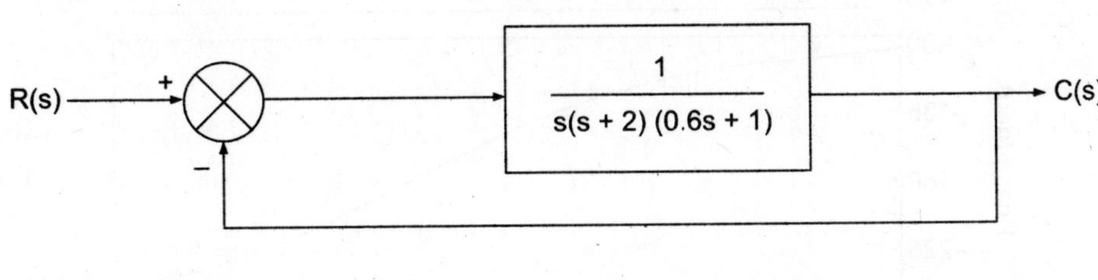

Fig. P3.34

Solution

We can use a lag compensator of the form

$$G_c(s) = K_c\beta\frac{Ts+1}{\beta Ts+1} = K_c\frac{s+\frac{1}{T}}{s+\frac{1}{\beta T}} \quad \beta > 1$$

Defining $\quad K_c\beta = K$

and $\quad G_1(s) = KG(s) = \dfrac{K}{s(s+2)(0.6s+1)}$

we adjust the gain K to meet the required static velocity error constant.

Hence

$$K_v = \lim_{s\to 0} sG_c(s)G(s) = \lim_{s\to 0} s\frac{Ts+1}{\beta Ts+1}G_1(s) = \lim_{s\to 0} sG_1(s) = \lim_{s\to 0}\frac{sK}{s(s+2)(0.6s+1)} = K/2 = 5$$

or $\quad K = 10$

With K = 10, the compensated system satisfies the steady-state performance requirement. We can now plot the Bode diagram of

$$G_1(j\omega) = \frac{10}{j\omega(j\omega+2)(0.6j\omega+1)}$$

The magnitude curve and phase-angle curve of $G_1(j\omega)$ are shown in Fig. P3.34(a). From this plot, the phase margin is found to be –20°, which shows that the system is unstable.

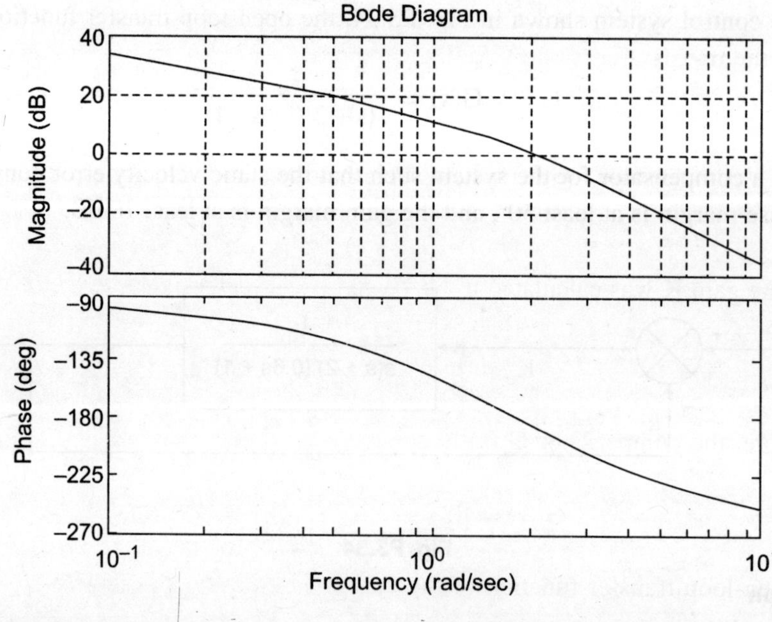

Fig. P3.34(a) Bode diagrams for G_1 = KG (gain-adjusted but uncompensated system), G_c/K (gain-adjusted compensator), and G_cG (compensated system)

The addition of a lag compensator modifies the phase curve of the Bode diagram and therefore we must allow 5° to 12° to the specified phase margin to compensate for the modification of the phase curve. Since the frequency corresponding to a phase margin of 50° is 0.7 rad/s, the new gain crossover frequency (of the compensated system) must be selected near this value. We choose the corner frequency $\omega = 1/T$. Since this corner frequency is not too far below the new gain crossover frequency, the modification in the phase curve may not be small. Also, we add about 12° to the given phase margin as an allowance to account for the lag angle introduced by the lag compensator. The required phase margin is now 52°. The phase angle of the uncompensated open-loop transfer function is –128° at about $\omega = 0.5$ rad/s. Hence, we choose the new gain crossover frequency to be 0.5 rad/s. In order to bring the magnitude curve down to 0 dB, the lag compensator is given the necessary attenuation, which in this case is –20 dB.

Therefore

$$20\log\frac{1}{\beta} = -20\,.$$

or
$$\beta = 10$$

The other corner frequency $\omega = 1(\beta T)$. This corresponds to the pole of the lag compensator and is obtained as

$$\frac{1}{\beta T} = 0.01 \text{ rad/s}$$

Hence, the transfer function of the lag compensator is given by

$$G_c(s) = K_c(10)\frac{10s+1}{100s+1} = K_c\frac{s+\dfrac{1}{10}}{s+\dfrac{1}{100}}$$

Since the gain K was calculated to be 10 and β was determined to be 10, we have

$$K_c = \frac{K}{\beta} = \frac{10}{10} = 1$$

Therefore, the compensator $G_c(s)$ is obtained as

$$G_c(s) = 10\frac{10s+1}{100s+1}$$

The open-loop transfer function of the compensated system is therefore

$$G_c(s)G(s) = \frac{10(10s+1)}{s(100s+1)(s+2)(0.6s+1)}$$

The magnitude and phase-angle curves of $G_c(j\omega)G(j\omega)$ are shown in Fig. P3.34(b).

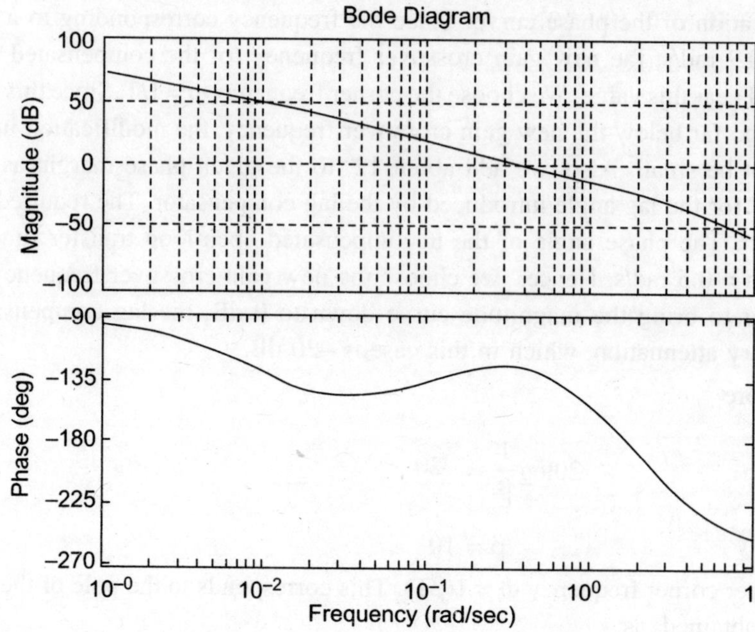

Fig. P3.34(b)

The phase margin of the compensated system is about 50º(the required value). The gain margin is about 11 dB (acceptable). The static velocity error constant is $5s^{-1}$. Thus, the compensated system satisfies the requirements on both the steady state and the relative stability.

We determine now the unit-step response and unit-ramp response of the compensated system and the original uncompensated system. The closed-loop transfer functions of the compensated and uncompensated systems are given by

$$\frac{C(s)}{R(s)} = \frac{100s + 10}{60s^4 + 220.6s^3 + 202.2s^2 + 102s + 10}$$

and

$$\frac{C(s)}{R(s)} = \frac{1}{0.6s^3 + 2.2s^2 + 2s + 1}$$

respectively.

A MATLAB program to obtain the unit-step and unit-ramp responses of the compensated and uncompensated systems is given below. The resulting unit-step response curves and unit-ramp response curves are shown in Fig. P3.34(c) and P3.34 (d) respectively.

```
%MATLAB Program
%Unit-step response
num = [0 0 0 1];
den = [0.6 2.2 2 1];
```

```
numc = [0 0 0 100 10];
denc = [60 220.6 202.2 102 10];
t = 0:0.1:40;
[c1, x1, t] = step(num, den);
[c2, x2, t] = step(numc, denc);
plot(t, c1, '.', t, c2, '–')
grid
title('Unit-Step Responses of Compensated and Uncompensated Systems')
xlabel('t Sec')
ylabel('Outputs')
text(12.2, 1.27, 'Compensated System')
text(12.2, 0.7, 'Uncompensated System')
```

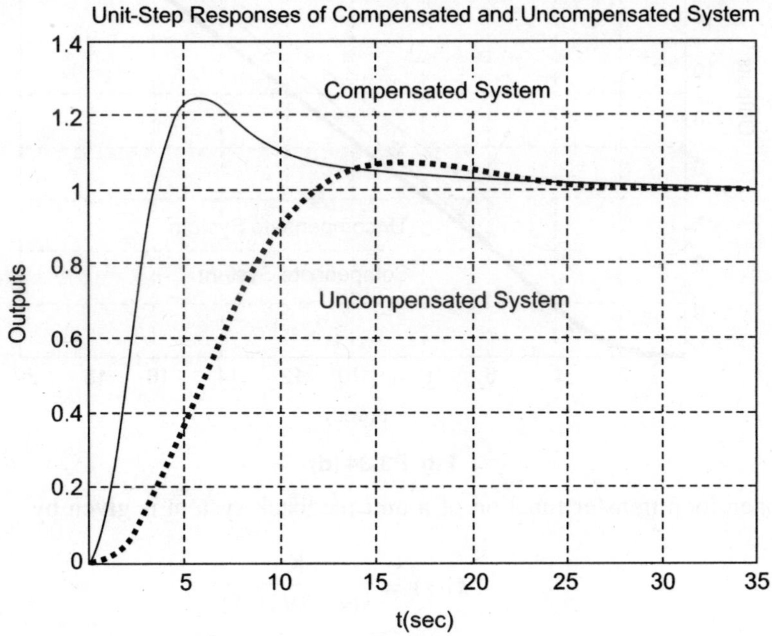

Fig. P3.34(c)

```
%Unit-ramp response
num1 =[0 0 0 0 1];
den1= [0.6 2.2 2 1 0];
num1c = [0 0 0 0 100 10];
den1c = [60 220.6 202.2 102 10 0];
t = 0:0.1:20;
[y1, z1, t] = step(num1, den1, t);
[y2, z2, t] = step(num1c, den1c, t);
```

```
plot(t, y1, '.', t, y2, '-', t, t, '—')
grid
title('Unit-Ramp Responses of Compensated and Uncompensated Systems')
xlabel('t Sec')
ylabel('Outputs')
text(8.4, 3, 'Compensated System')
text(8.4, 5, 'Uncompensated System')
```

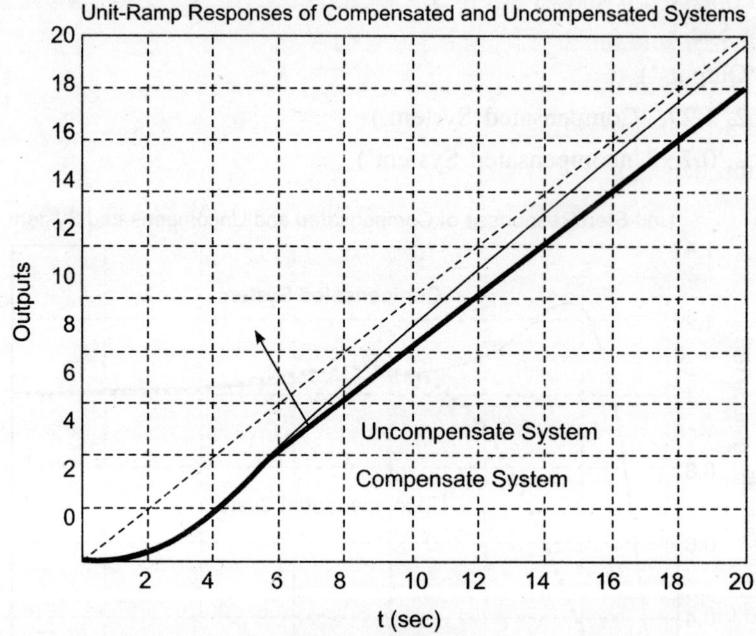

Fig. P3.34 (d)

P3.35 The open-loop transfer function of a unit feedback system is given by

$$G(s) = \frac{K}{s(s+3)(s+5)}.$$

Design a compensator $G_c(s)$ such that the static velocity error constant is $10s^{-1}$, the phase margin is 50°, and the gain margin is 10 dB or more.

Solution

We consider a lag-lead compensator of the form

$$G_c(s) = K_c \frac{\left(s+\frac{1}{T_1}\right)\left(s+\frac{1}{T_2}\right)}{\left(s+\frac{\beta}{T_1}\right)\left(s+\frac{\beta}{T_2}\right)}$$

The open-loop transfer function of the compensated system is $G_c(s)G(s)$. For $K_c = 1$, $\lim_{s \to 0} G_c(s) = 1$. For the static velocity error constant, we have

$$K_u = \lim_{s \to 0} sG_c(s)G(s) = \lim_{s \to 0} sG_c(s).\frac{K}{s(s+3)(s+5)} = \frac{K}{15} = 10$$

Therefore $\quad K = 150$

For K = 150, A MATLAB program used to plot the Bode diagram is given below and the diagram obtained is shown in Fig. P3.35(a).

```
% MATLAB Program
num = [0 0 0 150];
den = [1 8     15     0];
bode(num, den, w)
```

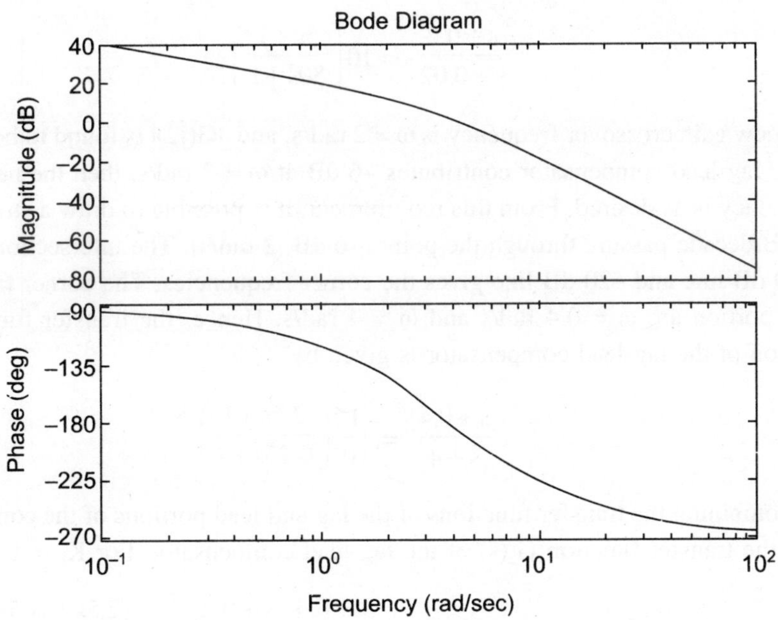

Fig. P3.35(a) Bode diagram of G(s) = 150/[s(s + 3)(s + 5)]

From Fig. P3.35 the phase margin of the uncompensated system is –6°, which shows that the system is unstable. To design a lag-lead compensator we choose a new gain crossover frequency. From the phase-angle curve for G(jω), the phase crossover frequency is ω = 2 rad/s. We can select the new gain crossover frequency to be 2 rad/s such that the phase-lead angle required at ω = 2 rad/s is about 50°. A single lag-lead compensator can provide this amount of phase-lead angle.

We can find the corner frequencies of the phase-lag portion of the lag-lead compensator. Choosing the corner frequency $\omega = 1/T_2$, corresponding to the zero of the phase-lag portion of the compensator as 1 decade below the new gain crossover frequency, or at $\omega = 0.2$ rad/s. For another corner frequency $\omega = 1/(\beta T_2)$, we need the value of β. The value of β can be obtained from the consideration of the lead portion of the compensator. The maximum phase-lead angle ϕ_m is given by Eqn. (9.10). For $\alpha = 1/\beta$, we have gives

$$\sin \phi_m = \frac{\beta - 1}{\beta + 1}$$

$\beta = 10$ corresponds to $\phi_m = 54.9°$. We require a 50° phase margin, so we can select $\beta = 10$. Hence

$$\beta = 10$$

Then the corner frequency $\omega = 1/(\beta T_2)$ and $\omega = 0.02$.

The transfer function of the phase-lag portion of the lag-lead compensator is

$$\frac{s+0.2}{s+0.02} = 10\left(\frac{5s+1}{50s+1}\right)$$

The new gain crossover frequency is $\omega = 2$ rad/s, and $|G(j2)|$ is found to be 6 dB. Therefore, if the lag-lead compensator contributes –6 dB at $\omega = 2$ rad/s, then the new gain crossover frequency is as desired. From this requirement, it is possible to draw a straight line of slope 20 dB/decade passing through the point (–6 dB, 2 rad/s). The intersections of this line and the 0 dB line and –20 dB line gives the corner frequencies. The corner frequencies for the lead portion are $\omega = 0.4$ rad/s and $\omega = 4$ rad/s. Hence, the transfer function of the lead portion of the lag-lead compensator is given by

$$\frac{s+0.4}{s+4} = \frac{1}{10}\left(\frac{2.5s+1}{0.25s+1}\right)$$

By combining the transfer functions of the lag and lead portions of the compensator, we can find the transfer function $G_c(s)$ of the lag-lead compensator. For $K_c = 1$, we get

$$G_c(s) = \frac{s+0.4}{s+4}\,\frac{s+0.2}{s+0.02} = \frac{(2.5s+1)(5s+1)}{(0.25s+1)(50s+1)}$$

The Bode diagram of the lag-lead compensator $G_c(s)$ is obtained by the following MATLAB program. The resulting plot is shown in Fig. P3.35(b).

```
% MATLAB Program
num = [1  0.6  0.08];
den = [1 4.02  0.08];
bode(num, den)
```

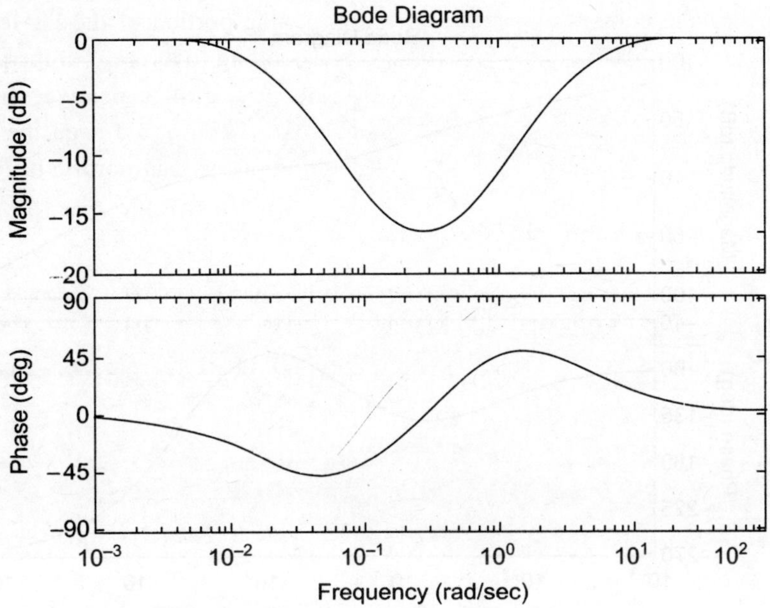

Fig. P3.35 (b) Bode diagram of the designed lag-lead compensator

The open-loop transfer function of the compensated system is

$$G_c(s)G(s) = \frac{(s+0.4)(s+0.2)}{(s+4)(s+0.02)} \frac{150}{s(s+3)(s+5)} = \frac{150s^2+90s+12}{s^5+12.02s^4+47.24s^3+60.94s^2+1.2s}$$

The magnitude and phase-angle curves of the designed open-loop transfer function $G_c(s)G(s)$ are shown in the Bode diagram of Fig. P3.35(c). This diagram is obtained using following MATLAB program. Note that the denominator polynomial den was obtained using the conv command, as follows:

```
a = [1  4.02  0.08];
b = [1  8  15  0];
conv(a, b)
ans =
        1.0000   12.0200   47.2400   60.9400   1.2000   0
```

```
% MATLAB Program
num = [0 0 0  150  90  12];
den = [1 12.02 47.24  60.94 1.2 0];
bode(num, den)
```

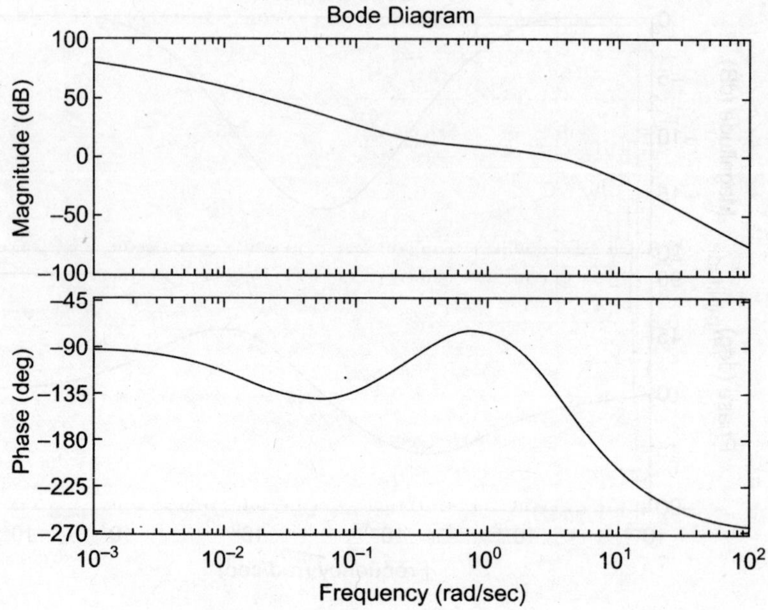

Fig. P3.35(c) Bode Diagram of $G_c(s).G(s)$

From Fig. P3.35(c), the requirements on the phase margin, gain margin, and static velocity error constant are all satisfied.

Unit-step response

Now

$$G_c(s)G(s) = \frac{(s+0.4)(s+0.2)}{(s+4)(s+0.02)} \frac{150}{s(s+3)(s+5)}$$

and
$$\frac{C(s)}{R(s)} = \frac{G_c(s)G(s)}{1+G_c(s)G(s)} = \frac{150s^2+90s+12}{s^5+12.02s^4+47.24s^3+210.94s^2+91.2s+15.2}$$

The unit-step response is obtained by the following MATLAB program and the unit-step response curve is shown in Fig. P3.35(d).

```
% MATLAB Program
num = [0 0 0 150 90 12];
den = [1 12.02 47.24 210.94 91.2 15.2];
t = 0:0.2:40;
step(num, den, t)
grid
title('unit-Step Response of Designed System')
```

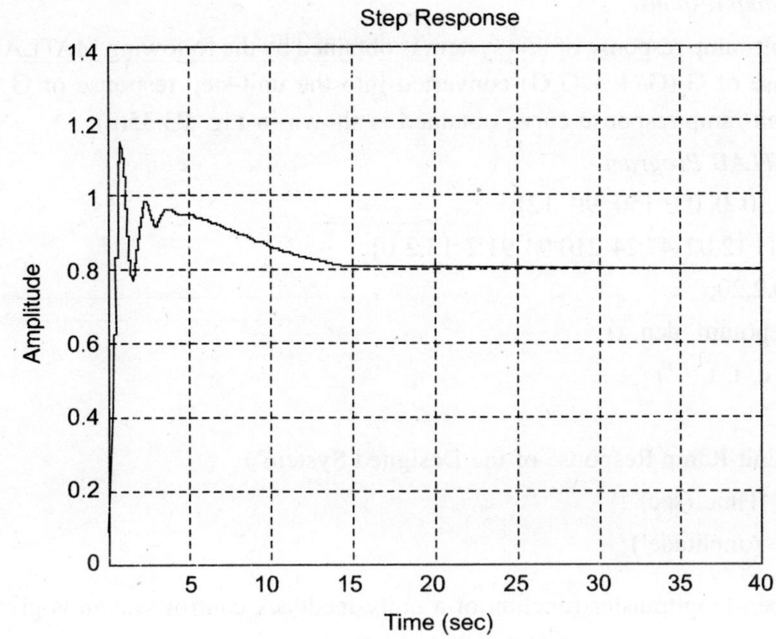

Fig. P3.35(d) Unit-step Response of designed system $G_c(s)G(s)$

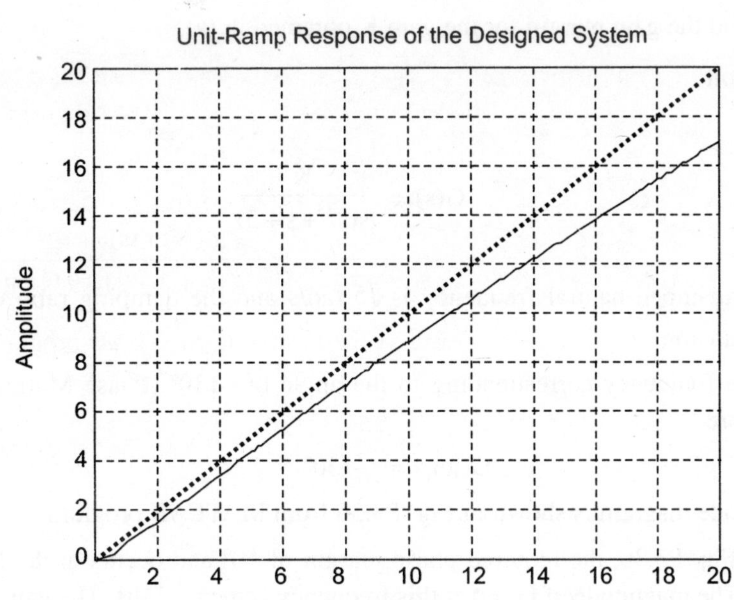

Fig. P3.35(e) Unit-ramp response of the designed system

Unit-ramp response:

The unit-ramp response of this system is obtained by the following MATLAB The unit-ramp response of $G_c(G/(1 + G_cG)$ converted into the unit-step response of $G_cG/[s(1 + G_cG)]$. The unit-ramp response curve obtained is shown in Fig. P3.35(e).

```
% MATLAB Program
num = [0 0 0 0 150 90 12];
den = [1 12.02 47.24 210.94 91.2 15.2 0];
t = 0:0.2:20;
c = step(num, den, t)
plot(t, c, t, t, '.')
grid
title('Unit-Ramp Response of the Designed System')
xlabel('Time (sec)')
ylabel('Amplitude')
```

P3.36 The open-loop transfer function of a unity-feedback control system is given by

$$G(s) = \frac{K}{s(s^2 + s + 5)}$$

(*a*) Determine the value of gain K such that the phase margin is 50º

(*b*) Find the gain margin for the gain K obtained in (a).

Solution

$$G(s) = \frac{K}{s(s^2 + s + 5)}$$

The undamped natural frequency is $\sqrt{5}$ rad/s and the damping ratio of $0.1.\sqrt{5}$ from the denominator.

Let the frequency corresponding to the angle of –130º (Phase Margin of 50) be ω_1 and therefore

$$\angle G(j\omega_1) = -130^\circ$$

The Bode diagram is shown in Fig. P3.36 from MATLAB program.

From Fig. P3.36, the required phase margin of 50º and occurs at the frequency $\omega = 1.06$ rad/s. The magnitude of $G(j\omega)$ at this frequency is then –7 dB. The gain K must then satisfy

$$20\log K = 7 \text{ dB}$$

or

$$K = 2.23$$

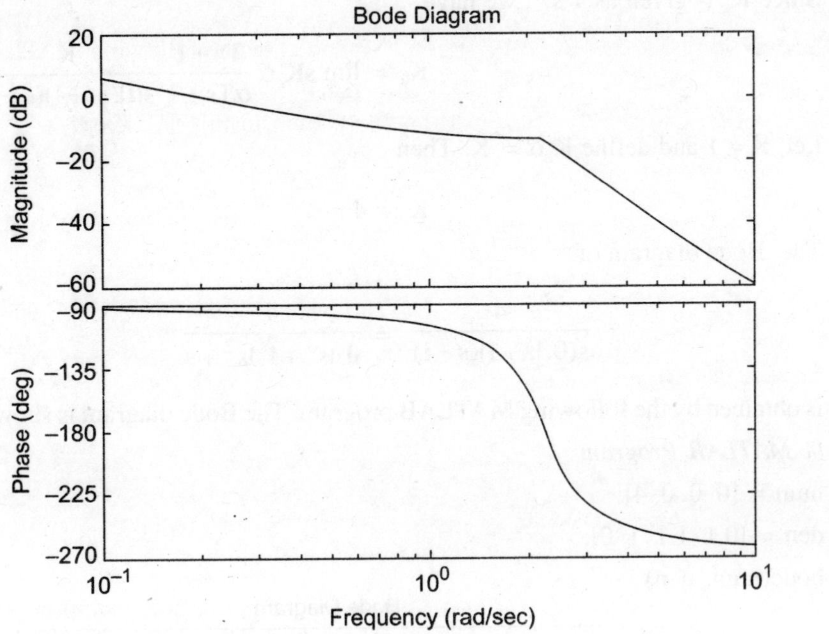

Fig. P3.36

P3.37 For the control system shown in Fig. P3.37:

(*a*) Design a lead-compensator $G_c(s)$ such that the phase margin is 45°, gain margin is not less than 8 dB, and the static velocity error constant K_v is 4 s^{-1}.

(*b*) Plot unit-step and unit-ramp response curves of the compensated system using MATLAB.

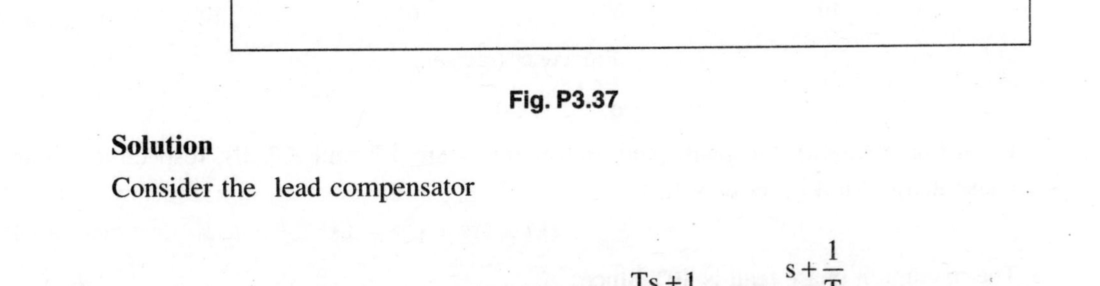

Fig. P3.37

Solution

Consider the lead compensator

$$G_c(s) = K_c\alpha\frac{Ts+1}{\alpha Ts+1} = K_c\frac{s+\frac{1}{T}}{s+\frac{1}{\alpha T}}$$

Since K_v is given as 4 s^{-1}, we have

$$K_v = \lim_{s\to 0} sK_c\alpha \frac{Ts+1}{\alpha Ts+1} \frac{K}{s(0.1s+1)(s+1)} = K_c\alpha K = 4$$

Let $K = 1$ and define $K_c\alpha = \hat{K}$. Then

$$\hat{K} = 4$$

The Bode diagram of

$$\frac{4}{s(0.1s+1)(s+1)} = \frac{4}{0.1s^3 + 1.1s^2 + s}$$

is obtained by the following MATLAB program. The Bode diagram is shown in Fig. P3.37(a).

```
% MATLAB Program
num = [0 0 0 4];
den = [0.1 1.1 1 0];
bode(num, den)
```

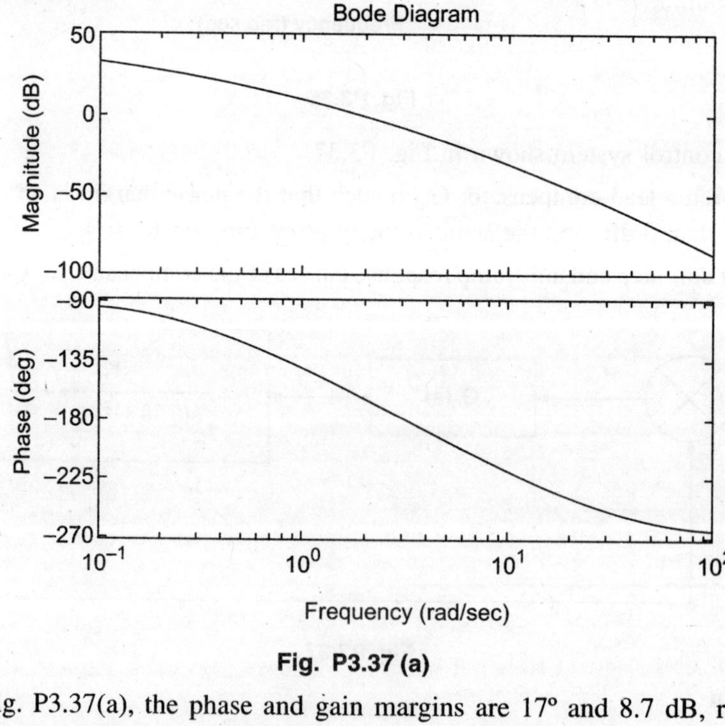

Fig. P3.37 (a)

From Fig. P3.37(a), the phase and gain margins are 17° and 8.7 dB, respectively. For a phase margin of 45°, let us select

$$\phi_m = 45° - 17° + 12° = 40°$$

The maximum phase lead is 40°. Since

$$\sin \phi_m = \frac{1-\alpha}{1+\alpha} \qquad (\phi_m = 40°)$$

α is obtained as 0.2174. Let us choose

$$\alpha = 0.21$$

To determine the corner frequencies $\omega = 1/T$ and $\omega = 1/(\alpha T)$ of the lead compensator we note that the maximum phase-lead angle ϕ_m occurs at the geometric mean of the two corner frequencies, or $\omega = 1/(\sqrt{\alpha}\,T)$. The amount of the modification in the magnitude curve at $\omega = 1/(\sqrt{\alpha}\,T)$ due to the inclusion of the term $(Ts + 1)/(\alpha Ts + 1)$ is then given by

$$\left|\frac{1+j\omega T}{1+j\omega\alpha T}\right|_{\omega=\frac{1}{\sqrt{\alpha}T}} = \frac{1}{\sqrt{\alpha}}$$

Since

$$\frac{1}{\sqrt{\alpha}} = \frac{1}{\sqrt{0.21}} = 2.1822 = 6.7778 \text{ dB}$$

The magnitude of $|G(j\omega)|$ is -6.7778 dB which corresponds to $\omega = 2.81$ rad/s. Therefore, we select this as the new gain crossover frequency ω_c.

$$\frac{1}{T} = \sqrt{\alpha}\,\omega_c = \sqrt{0.21} \times 2.81 = 1.2877$$

$$\frac{1}{\alpha T} = \frac{\omega_c}{\sqrt{\alpha}} = \frac{2.81}{\sqrt{0.21}} = 6.1319$$

or

$$G_c(s) = K_c\frac{s+1.2877}{s+6.1319}$$

and

$$K_c = \frac{\hat{K}}{\alpha} = \frac{4}{0.21}$$

Hence

$$G_c(s) = \frac{4}{0.21}\,\frac{s+1.2877}{s+6.1319} = 4\frac{0.7768s+1}{0.16308s+1}$$

The open-loop transfer function is

$$G_c(s)G(s) = 4\frac{0.7768s+1}{0.16308s+1}\,\frac{1}{s(0.1s+1)(s+1)}$$

$$= \frac{3.1064s+4}{0.01631s^4+0.2794s^3+1.2631s^2+s}$$

The closed-loop transfer function is

$$\frac{C(s)}{R(s)} = \frac{3.1064s + 4}{0.01631s^4 + 0.2794s^3 + 1.2631s^2 + 4.1064s + 4}$$

The following MATLAB program produces the unit-step response curve as shown in Fig. P3.37(b).

```
% MATLAB Program
num = [0 0 0 3.1064 4];
den = [0.01631 0.2794 1.2631 4.1064 4];
step(num, den)
grid
title('Unit-Step Response of Compensated System')
xlabel('t Sec')
ylabel('Output c(t)')
```

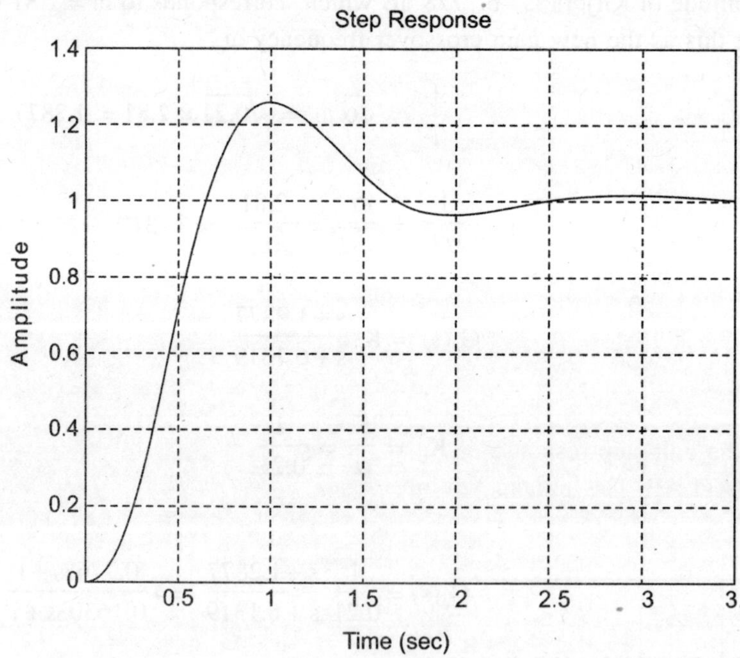

Fig. P3.37(b)

The following MATLAB program produces the unit-ramp response curves as shown in Fig. P3.37(c).

```
% MATLAB Program
num = [0 0 0 0 3.1064 4];
den = [0.01631 0.2794 1.2631 4.1064 4 0];
```

```
t = 0:0.01:5;
c = step(num, den, t);
plot(t, c, t, t)
grid
title('Unit-Ramp Response of Compensated System')
xlabel('t Sec')
ylabel('Unit-Ramp Input and System Output c(t)')
```

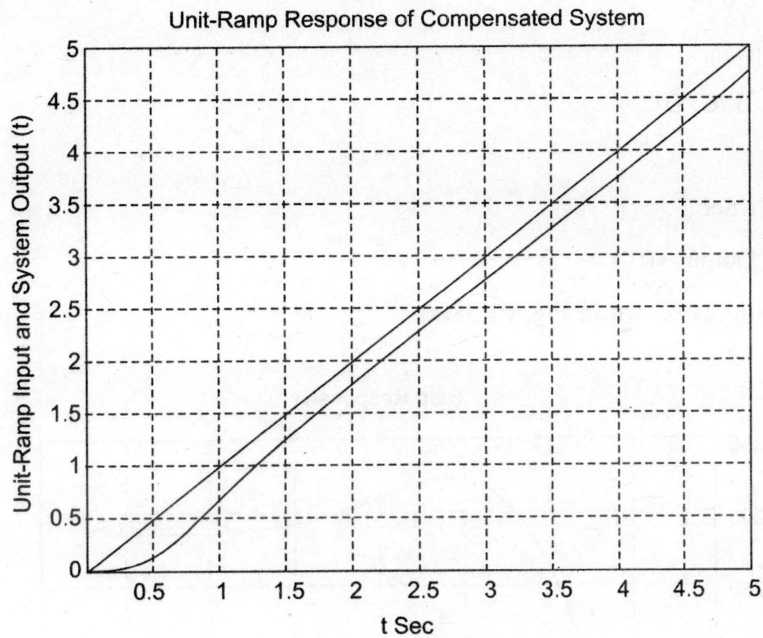

Fig. P3.37(c)

3.38 Obtain the unit-step response and unit-impulse response for the following control system using MATLAB. The initial conditions are all zero.

$$\begin{bmatrix} \dot{x}_1 \\ \dot{x}_2 \\ \dot{x}_3 \\ \dot{x}_4 \end{bmatrix} = \begin{bmatrix} 0 & 1 & 0 & 0 \\ 0 & 0 & 1 & 0 \\ 0 & 0 & 0 & 1 \\ -0.0069 & -0.0789 & -0.5784 & -1.3852 \end{bmatrix} \begin{bmatrix} x_1 \\ x_2 \\ x_3 \\ x_4 \end{bmatrix} + \begin{bmatrix} 0 \\ 0 \\ 0 \\ 2 \end{bmatrix} [u]$$

$$y = [1 \quad 0 \quad 0 \quad 0] \begin{bmatrix} x_1 \\ x_2 \\ x_3 \\ x_4 \end{bmatrix}$$

Solution

Unit-step response: The following MATLAB program yields the unit-step response of the given system. The resulting unit-step response curve is shown in Fig. P3.38(a).

```
% MATLAB Program
A = [0 1 0 0;0 0 1 0; 0 0 0 1; –0.0069 –0.0789 –0.5784 –1.3852];
B = [0; 0; 0; 2];
C = [1 0 0 0];
D = [0];
step(A, B, C, D);
grid
xlabel('t Sec')
ylabel('Output y(t)')
```

The output is shown in Fig. P3.38(a).

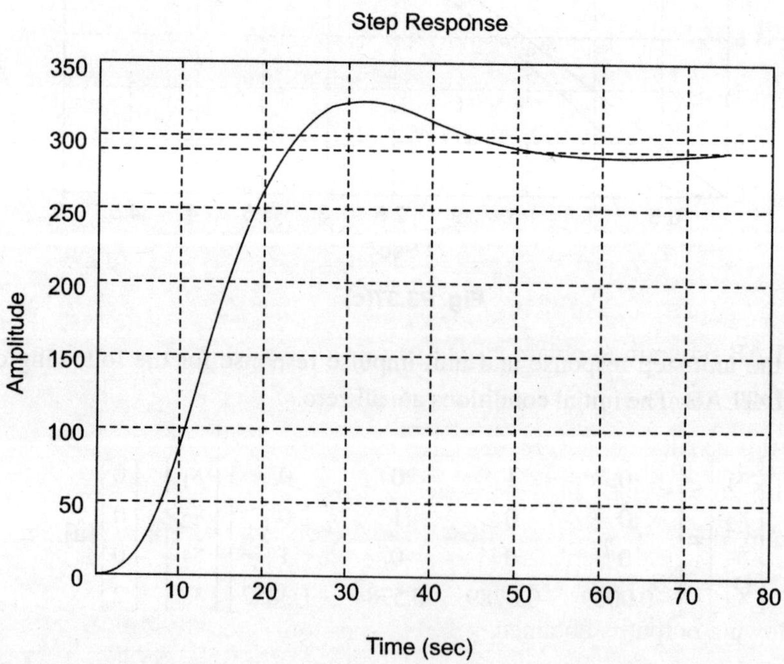

Fig. P3.38 (a)

Similarly with impulse(A, B, C, D) statement, we obtain the response as shown in Fig. P3.38(b).

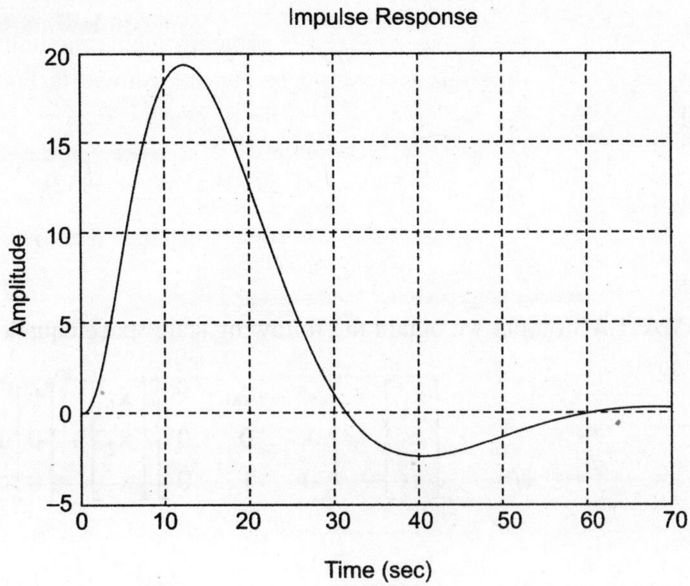

Fig. P3.38(b)

P3.39 Obtain the state-space representation of the following system using MATLAB:

$$\frac{C(s)}{R(s)} = \frac{25s+5}{s^3+5s^2+26s+5}$$

Solution

$$\frac{C(s)}{R(s)} = \frac{25s+5}{s^3+5s^2+26s+5}$$

A MATLAB program to obtain a state-space representation of this system is given below.

```
% MATLAB Program
num = [0 0 25 5];
den = [1 5 26 5];
g = tf(num, den)
[A, B, C, D] = tf2ss(num, den)
```

The following output is obtained.

```
A =
    -5  -26  -5
     1    0   0
     0    1   0
```

B =

1
0
0

C =

0 25 5

D =

0

From the MATLAB output we obtain the following state space equations:

$$\begin{bmatrix} \dot{x}_1 \\ \dot{x}_2 \\ \dot{x}_3 \end{bmatrix} = \begin{bmatrix} -5 & -26 & -5 \\ 1 & 0 & 0 \\ 0 & 1 & 0 \end{bmatrix} \begin{bmatrix} x_1 \\ x_2 \\ x_3 \end{bmatrix} + \begin{bmatrix} 1 \\ 0 \\ 0 \end{bmatrix} u$$

$$y = [0 \quad 25 \quad 5] \begin{bmatrix} x_1 \\ x_2 \\ x_3 \end{bmatrix} + [0]u$$

P3.40 Represent the system shown in Fig. P3.40 using MATLAB in

(*a*) state-space in phase-variable form.

(*b*) state-space in modal form.

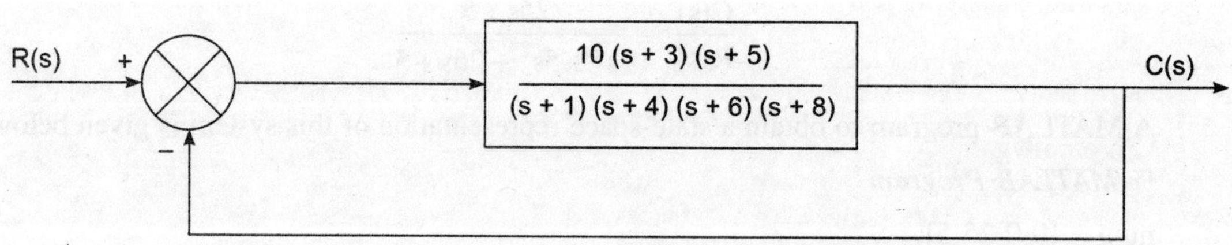

Fig. P3.40

Solution

% MATLAB Program

'(*a*) Phase-variable form'

'G(s)'

G = zpk([–3 –5], [–1 –4 –6 –8], 10)

'T(s)'

```
T = feedback(G, 1, –1)
[numt, dent] = tfdata(T, 'V');
'Controller canonical form determination'
[AC, BC, CC, DC] = tf2ss(numt, dent)
A1 = flipud(AC);
'Phase-variable form representation'
Apv = fliplr(A1)
Bpv = flipud(BC)
Cpv = fliplr(CC)
'(b) Modal form'
'G(s)'
G = zpk([–3 –5], [–1 –4 –6 –8], 10)
'T(s)'
T = feedback(G, 1, –1)
[numt, dent] = tfdata(T, 'V');
'Controller canonical form'
[AC, BC, CC, DC] = tf2ss(numt, dent)
'Modal form'
[A, B, C, D] = canon(AC, BC, CC, DC, 'modal')
```

Computer response:

ans =

(*a*) Phase-variable form

ans =

G(s)

Zero/pole/gain:

$$\frac{10(s+3)(s+5)}{(s+1)(s+4)(s+6)(s+8)}$$

ans =

T(s)

Zero/pole/gain:

$$\frac{10(s+5)(s+3)}{(s+1.69)(s+4.425)(s\text{^}2+12.88s+45.73)}$$

ans =

Controller canonical form determination

```
AC =
     -19.0000   -132.0000   -376.0000   -342.0000
       1.0000           0           0           0
            0      1.0000           0           0
            0           0      1.0000           0
BC =
     1
     0
     0
     0
CC =
     0  10.0000  80.0000  150.0000
DC =
     0
ans =
Phase-variable form representation
Apv =
          0      1.0000           0           0
          0           0      1.0000           0
          0           0           0      1.0000
  -342.0000   -376.0000   -132.0000    -19.0000
Bpv =
     0
     0
     0
     1
Cpv =
     150.0000  80.0000  10.0000    0
ans =
(b) Modal form
ans =
     G(s)
Zero/pole/gain:
```

$$\frac{10(s+3)(s+5)}{(s+1)(s+4)(s+6)(s+8)}$$

```
ans =

        T(s)

Zero/pole/gain:

               10(s+5)(s+3)
    --------------------------------------
    (s+1.69)(s+4.425)(s^2+12.88s+45.73)

ans =
Controller canonical form
AC =
          -19.0000    -132.0000    -376.0000    -342.0000
            1.0000            0            0            0
                 0       1.0000            0            0
                 0            0       1.0000            0
BC =
        1
        0
        0
        0
CC =
        0    10.0000    80.0000    150.0000
DC =
        0
ans =
Modal form
A =
     -6.4425      2.0551            0            0
     -2.0551     -6.4425            0            0
           0           0      -4.4249            0
           0           0            0      -1.6902
B =
       -2.7844
       -9.8159
        3.9211
        0.0811
C =
       -0.2709    0.1739    0.0921    7.2936
D =
        0
```

P3.41 Determine the state-space representation in phase-variable form for the system shown in Fig. P3.41.

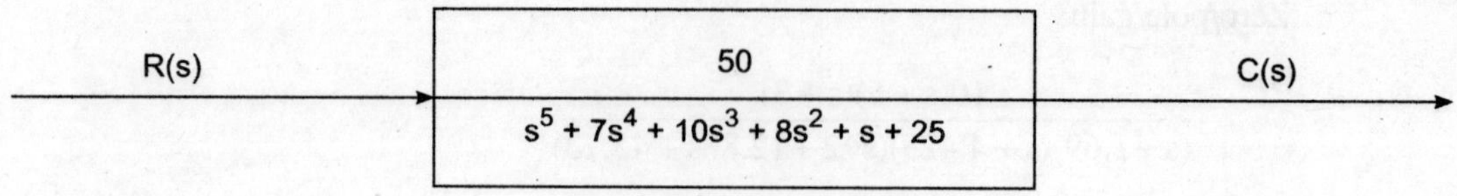

Fig. P3.41

Solution

Computer program is as follows:

```
%MATLAB Program
'State-space representation'
num = 50
den = [1 7    10    8    1    25];
G = tf(num, den)
[AC, BC, CC, DC] = tf2ss(num, den);
Af = flipud(AC)
A = fliplr(Af)
B = flipud(BC)
C = fliplr(CC)
```

Computer response:

```
num =

    50
```

Transfer function:

```
              50
--------------------------------
s^5+7s^4+10s^3+8s^2+s+25

Af =

     0    0    0    1    0
     0    0    1    0    0
     0    1    0    0    0
     1    0    0    0    0
    -7  -10   -8   -1  -25

A =

     0    1    0    0    0
     0    0    1    0    0
```

```
       0    0    0    1    0
       0    0    0    0    1
     -25   -1   -8  -10   -7
B =
           0
           0
           0
           0
           1
C =
      50    0    0    0    0
```

P3.42 Using MATLAB, write the state equations and the output equation for the phase-variable representation for the following systems in Fig. P3.42.

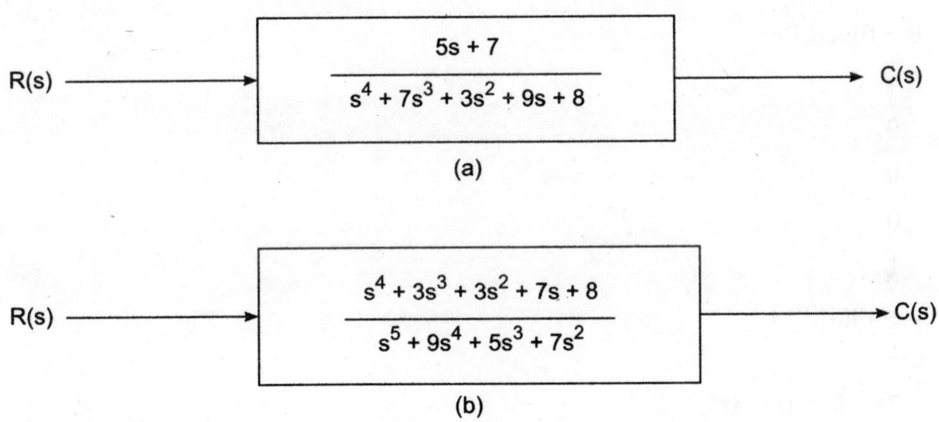

Fig. P3.42

Solution

(*a*) num = [5 7]

```
num =
        5    7
den = [1 7 3 9 8]
den =
     1    7    3    9    8
G = tf(num, den)
```

Transfer function:

$$\frac{5s+7}{s\hat{}4+7s\hat{}3+3s\hat{}2+9s+8}$$

```
[Ac, Bc, Cc, Dc] = tf2ss(num, den);
Af = flipud(Ac)
Af =
     0    0    1    0
     0    1    0    0
     1    0    0    0
    -7   -3   -9   -8
A = fliplr(Ac)
A =
    -8   -9   -3   -7
     0    0    0    1
     0    0    1    0
     0    1    0    0
B = flipud(Bc)
B =
   0
   0
   0
   1
C = fliplr(Cc)
C =
   7    5    0    0
Part 2
num = [1 3 10 5 6];
den = [1 7 8 6 0 0];
G = tf(num, den)
```

Transfer function:

```
s^4+3s^3+10s^2+5s+6
-------------------
s^5+7s^4+8s^3+6s^2
```

```
[Ac, Bc, Cc, Dc] = tf2ss(num, den);
Af = flipud(Ac);
A = fliplr(Af)
```

```
A =
   0   1   0   0   0
   0   0   1   0   0
   0   0   0   1   0
   0   0   0   0   1
   0   0  -6  -8  -7
B = flipud(Bc)
B =
   0
   0
   0
   0
   1
C = fliplr(Cc)
C =
   6   5  10   3   1
```

P3.43 Find the transfer function for the following system using MATLAB:

$$\begin{bmatrix} \dot{x}_1 \\ \dot{x}_2 \\ \dot{x}_3 \end{bmatrix} = \begin{bmatrix} 0 & 1 & 0 \\ -5 & -2 & 0 \\ 0 & 2 & -6 \end{bmatrix} \begin{bmatrix} x_1 \\ x_2 \\ x_3 \end{bmatrix} + \begin{bmatrix} 0 & 0 \\ 3 & -1 \\ 5 & 0 \end{bmatrix} u$$

$$y = \begin{bmatrix} 1 & 0 & 0 \\ 0 & 0 & 1 \end{bmatrix} \begin{bmatrix} x_1 \\ x_2 \\ x_3 \end{bmatrix}$$

Solution

The transfer function matrix is given by

$$G(s) = C[sI - A]^{-1}B$$

where

$$A = \begin{bmatrix} 0 & 1 & 0 \\ -5 & -2 & 0 \\ 0 & 2 & -6 \end{bmatrix} \quad B = \begin{bmatrix} 0 & 0 \\ 3 & -1 \\ 5 & 0 \end{bmatrix} \quad C = \begin{bmatrix} 1 & 0 & 0 \\ 0 & 0 & 1 \end{bmatrix}$$

Hence

$$G(s)=\begin{bmatrix}1 & 0 & 0\\ 0 & 0 & 1\end{bmatrix}\begin{bmatrix}s & -1 & 0\\ 5 & s+2 & 0\\ 0 & -2 & s+6\end{bmatrix}\begin{bmatrix}0 & 0\\ 3 & -1\\ 5 & 0\end{bmatrix}$$

```
>> % MATLAB Program
>> syms s
>> C = [1 0 0; 0 0 1];
>> M = [s –1 0; 5 s + 2 0; 0 –2 s + 6];
>> B = [0 0; 3 –1; 5 0];
>> C*inv(M)*B
ans =
[                    3/(s^2 + 2*s + 5),              –1/(s^2 + 2*s + 5)]
[ 6*s/(s^3 + 8*s^2 + 17*s + 30) + 5/(s + 6),    –2*s/(s^3 + 8*s^2 + 17*s + 30)]
```

P3.44 A control system is defined by the following state-space equations:

$$\begin{bmatrix}\dot{x}_1\\ \dot{x}_2\end{bmatrix}=\begin{bmatrix}-4 & -1\\ 2 & -3\end{bmatrix}\begin{bmatrix}x_1\\ x_2\end{bmatrix}+\begin{bmatrix}1\\ 3\end{bmatrix}u$$

$$y=\begin{bmatrix}1 & 2\end{bmatrix}\begin{bmatrix}x_1\\ x_2\end{bmatrix}$$

Find the transfer function G(s) of the system using MATLAB.

Solution

$$A=\begin{bmatrix}-4 & -1\\ 2 & -3\end{bmatrix}\quad B=\begin{bmatrix}1\\ 3\end{bmatrix}\quad C=\begin{bmatrix}1 & 2\end{bmatrix}$$

The transfer function G(s) of the system is

$$G(s)=C(sI-A)^{-1}B$$

$$=\begin{bmatrix}1 & 2\end{bmatrix}\begin{bmatrix}s+4 & 1\\ -2 & s+3\end{bmatrix}\begin{bmatrix}1\\ 3\end{bmatrix}=\begin{bmatrix}1 & 2\end{bmatrix}\frac{1}{[(s+4)(s+3)+2]}\begin{bmatrix}s+3 & -1\\ 2 & s+4\end{bmatrix}\begin{bmatrix}2\\ 5\end{bmatrix}$$

$$=\frac{1}{[s^2+7s+14]}\begin{bmatrix}1 & 2\end{bmatrix}\begin{bmatrix}2s+1\\ 5s+24\end{bmatrix}=\frac{[12s+49]}{[s^2+7s+14]}$$

```
>> %MATLAB Program
>> A = [-4 -1; 2 -3];
>> B = [1;3];
>> C = [1 2];
>> D = 0;
>> [num, den] = ss2tf(A, B, C, D)
num =
        0        7.0000   28.0000
den =
        1.0000   7.0000   14.0000
```

The result is same as the one derived above.

P3.45 Determine the transfer function G(s) = Y(s)/R(s), for the following system representation in state-space form:

$$\dot{x} = \begin{bmatrix} 0 & 3 & 5 & 0 \\ 0 & 0 & 1 & 0 \\ 0 & 0 & 0 & 1 \\ -5 & -6 & 8 & 5 \end{bmatrix} x + \begin{bmatrix} 0 \\ 5 \\ 7 \\ 2 \end{bmatrix} r$$

$$y = [1 \ \ 3 \ \ 7 \ \ 5]\, x$$

Solution

```
A = [0 3 5 0; 0 0 1 0; 0 0 0 1; -5 -6 8 5];
B = [0; 5; 7; 2];
C = [1 3 7 5];
D = 0;
state-space = ss(A, B, C, D)
a =
        x1    x2    x3    x4
   x1   0     3     5     0
   x2   0     0     1     0
   x3   0     0     0     1
   x4  -5    -6     8     5
```

```
b =
          u1
   x1     0
   x2     5
   x3     7
   x4     2
c =
          x1     x2     x3     x4
   y1     1      3      7      5
d =
          u1
   y1     0
```

Continuous-time model.

[A, B, C, D] = tf2ss(num, den);

G = tf(num, den)

Transfer function:

$$\frac{s\hat{}4+3s\hat{}3+10s\hat{}2+5s+6}{s\hat{}5+7s\hat{}4+8s\hat{}3+6s\hat{}2}$$

P3.46 Determine the transfer function and poles of the system represented in state-space as follows using MATLAB:

$$\dot{x} = \begin{bmatrix} 9 & -3 & -1 \\ -3 & 2 & 0 \\ 6 & 8 & -2 \end{bmatrix} + \begin{bmatrix} 1 \\ 2 \\ 3 \end{bmatrix} u(t)$$

$$y = [2 \quad 9 \quad -12]x \quad ; x(0) = \begin{bmatrix} 0 \\ 0 \\ 0 \end{bmatrix}$$

Solution

% MATLAB Program

```
>> A = [8 –3 4; –7 1 0; 3 4 –7]
A =
   8   –3    4
  –7    1    0
   3    4   –7
```

```
>> B = [1; 3; 8]
B =
  1
  3
  8
>> C = [1 7 -2]
C =
  1   7   -2
>> D = 0
D =
  0
>> [numg, deng] = ss2tf(A, B, C, D, 1)
numg =
      1.0e + 003 *
      0          0.0060       0.0730     -2.8770
deng =
      1.0000     -2.0000     -88.0000    33.0000
>> G = tf(numg, deng)
```

Transfer function:

$$\frac{6s^2 + 73s - 2877}{s^3 - 2s^2 - 88s + 33}$$

```
>> poles = roots(deng)
poles =
  10.2620
  -8.6344
   0.3724
```

P3.47 Represent the system shown in Fig. P3.47 using MATLAB in

(*a*) state space in phase-variable form

(*b*) state space in model form.

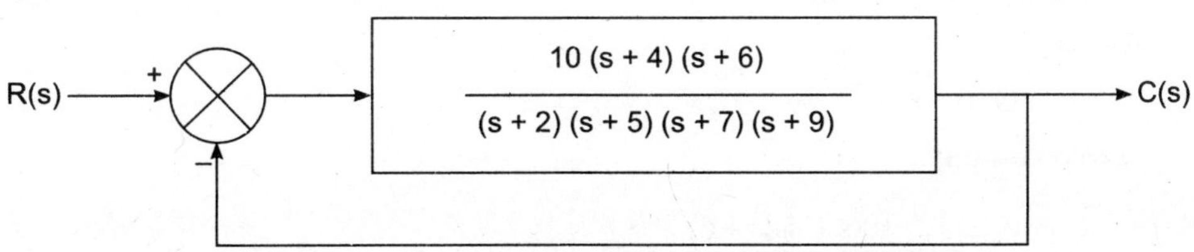

Fig. P3.47

Solution

```
% MATLAB Program
'(a) Phase-variable form'
'G(s)'
G = zpk ([-4  -6], [-2 -5 -7 -9], 10)
'T(s)'
T = feedback (G, 1, -1)
[numt, dent] = tfdata (T, 'V');
'controller canonical form determination'
[AC, BC, CC, DC] = tf2ss (numt, dent)
A1 = flipud (AC);
'Phase-variable form representation'
APV = fliplr (A1)
BPV = flipud (BC)
CPV = fliplr (CC)

'(b) Modal form'
'G(s)'
G = zpk ([-4  -6], [-2 -5 -7 -9], 10)
'T(s)'
T = feedback (G, 1, -1)
[numt, dent] = tfdata (T, 'V');
'controller canonical form'
[AC, BC, CC, DC] = tf2ss (numt, dent)
'Modal form'
[A, B, C, D] = canon (AC, BC, CC, DC, 'modal')
```

Computer response:

(*a*) Phase-variable form

Ans. =

G(s)

Zero/pole/gain:

$$\frac{10(s+4)(s+6)}{(s+2)(s+5)(s+7)(s+9)}$$

Ans. =

T(s)

Zero/pole/gain:

$$\frac{10(s+6)(s+4)}{(s+2.69)(s+5.425)(s^2+14.88s+59.61)}$$

Ans =

Controller canonical form determination

AC =

–23.0000	–195.0000	–701.0000	–870.0000
1.0000	0	0	0
0	1.0000	0	0
0	0	1.0000	0

BC =

1
0
0
0

CC =

0 10.0000 100.0000 240.0000

DC =

0

Ans. =

Phase-variable form representation

APV =

–23.

0	1.0000	0	0
0	0	1.0000	0
0	0	0	1.0000
–870.0000	–701.0000	–195.0000	–23.0000

BPV =

0
0
0
1

CPV =

240.0000 100.0000 10.0000 0

(*b*) Modal form

Ans. =

G(s)

Zero/pole/gain:

$$\frac{10(s+4)(s+6)}{(s+2)(s+5)(s+7)(s+9)}$$

Ans. =

T(s)

Zero/pole/gain:

$$\frac{10(s+6)(s+4)}{(s+2.69)(s+5.425)(s\text{^}2+14.88s+59.61)}$$

Ans. =

Controller canonical form

AC =

–23.0000	–195.0000	–701.0000	–870.0000
1.0000	0	0	0
0	1.0000	0	0
0	0	1.0000	0

BC =

1
0
0
0

CC =

0	10.0000	100.0000	240.0000

DC =

0

Ans. =

Modal form

A =

–7.4425	2.0551	0	0
–2.0551	–7.4425	0	0
0	0	–5.4249	0
0	0	0	–2.6902

```
B =
        -5.8222
       -13.9839
         7.1614
         0.2860
C =
        -0.1674        0.1378         0.0504        2.0676
D =
         0
```

P3.48 Plot the step response using MATLAB for the following system represented in state-space, where u(t) is the unit step.

$$\dot{x} = \begin{bmatrix} -5 & 2 & 0 \\ 0 & -9 & 1 \\ 0 & 0 & -3 \end{bmatrix} + \begin{bmatrix} 0 \\ 2 \\ 1 \end{bmatrix} u(t)$$

$$y = [0 \;\; 1 \;\; 1]x \;\; ; \; x(0) = \begin{bmatrix} 0 \\ 0 \\ 0 \end{bmatrix}$$

Solution

```
>> A = [-5 2 0; 0 -9 1; 0 0 -3];
>> B = [0; 2; 1];
>> C = [0 1 1];
>> D = 0;
>> S = ss(A, B, C, D)
a =
          x1      x2      x3
   x1     -5       2       0
   x2      0      -9       1
   x3      0       0      -3
b =
          u1
   x1      0
   x2      2
   x3      1
```

```
c =
            x1      x2      x3
   y1       0       1       1
d =
            u1
   y1       0
```

Continuous-time model.

```
>> step(S)
```

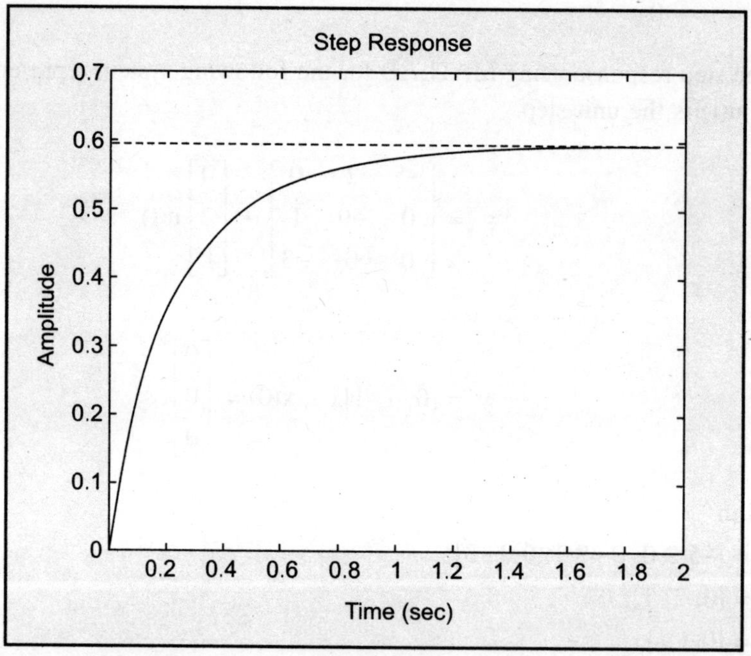

Fig. P3.48

P3.49 A control system is defined by

$$\begin{bmatrix} \dot{x}_1 \\ \dot{x}_2 \end{bmatrix} = \begin{bmatrix} 0 & 1 \\ -30 & -7 \end{bmatrix} \begin{bmatrix} x_1 \\ x_2 \end{bmatrix} + \begin{bmatrix} 1 & 1 \\ 0 & 1 \end{bmatrix} \begin{bmatrix} u_1 \\ u_2 \end{bmatrix}$$

$$\begin{bmatrix} y_1 \\ y_2 \end{bmatrix} = \begin{bmatrix} 1 & 0 \\ 0 & 1 \end{bmatrix} \begin{bmatrix} x_1 \\ x_2 \end{bmatrix}$$

Plot the four sets of Bode diagrams for the system [two for input1, and two for input2] using MATLAB.

Solution

There are 4 sets of Bode diagrams (2 for input1 and 2 for input2)

```
>> %Bode Diagrams
```

```
>> A = [0 1; –30 –7];
>> B = [1 1; 0 1];
>> C = [1 0; 0 1];
>> D = [0 0; 0 0];
>> bode(A, B, C, D)
```

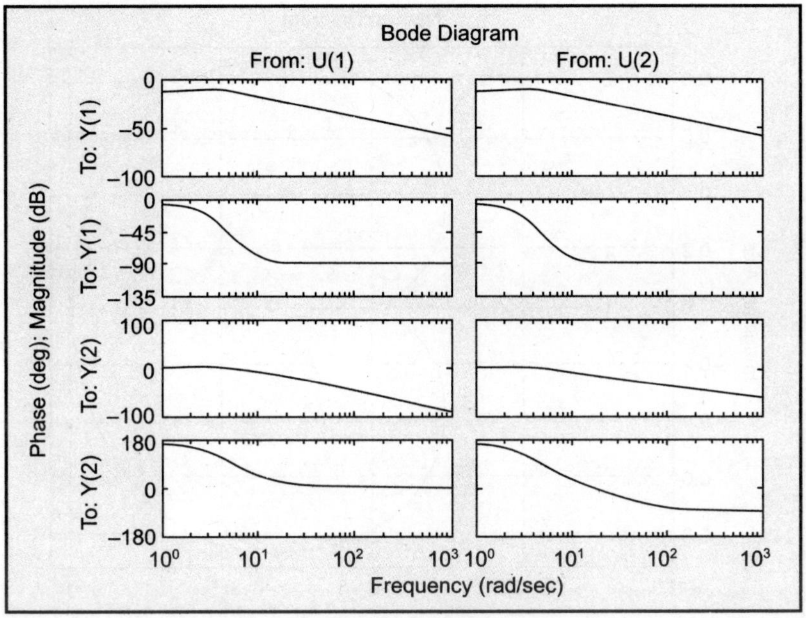

Fig. P3.49 Bode diagrams

P3.50 Draw a Nyquist plot for a system defined by

$$\begin{bmatrix} \dot{x}_1 \\ \dot{x}_2 \end{bmatrix} = \begin{bmatrix} 0 & 1 \\ -30 & 7 \end{bmatrix} \begin{bmatrix} x_1 \\ x_2 \end{bmatrix} + \begin{bmatrix} 0 \\ 30 \end{bmatrix} u$$

$$y = \begin{bmatrix} 1 & 0 \end{bmatrix} \begin{bmatrix} x_1 \\ x_2 \end{bmatrix} + [0]u$$

using MATLAB.

Solution

Since the system has a single input u and a single output y, a Nyquist plot can be obtained by using the command nyquist (A, B, C, D) or nyquist (A, B, C, D, 1).

```
>> %MATLAB Program
>> A = [0 1; –30 7];
>> B = [0; 30];
>> C = [1 0];
>> D = [0];
```

```
>> nyquist(A, B, C, D)
>> grid
>> title('Nyquist plot')
```

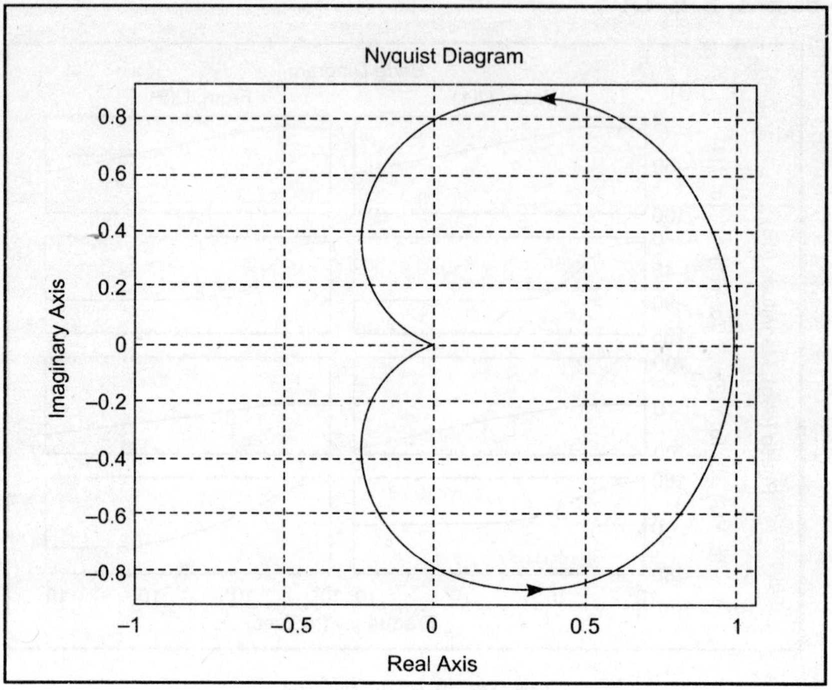

Fig. P3.50 Nyquist plot

P3.51 A control system is defined by

$$\begin{bmatrix} \dot{x}_1 \\ \dot{x}_2 \end{bmatrix} = \begin{bmatrix} -1 & -1 \\ 7 & 0 \end{bmatrix} \begin{bmatrix} x_1 \\ x_2 \end{bmatrix} + \begin{bmatrix} 1 & 1 \\ 1 & 0 \end{bmatrix} \begin{bmatrix} u_1 \\ u_2 \end{bmatrix}$$

$$\begin{bmatrix} y_1 \\ y_2 \end{bmatrix} = \begin{bmatrix} 1 & 0 \\ 0 & 1 \end{bmatrix} \begin{bmatrix} x_1 \\ x_2 \end{bmatrix} + \begin{bmatrix} 0 & 0 \\ 0 & 0 \end{bmatrix} \begin{bmatrix} u_1 \\ u_2 \end{bmatrix}$$

The system has two inputs and two outputs. The four sinusoidal output-input relationships are given by

$$\frac{y_1(j\omega)}{u_1(j\omega)}, \frac{y_2(j\omega)}{u_1(j\omega)}, \frac{y_1(j\omega)}{u_2(j\omega)}, \text{ and } \frac{y_2(j\omega)}{u_2(j\omega)}$$

Draw the Nyquist plots for the system by considering the input u_1 with input u_2 as zero and vice versa.

Solution

The four individual plots are obtained by using the MATLAB command nyquist (A, B, C, D).

```
>> %MATLAB Program
>> A = [–1 –1; 7 0];
>> B = [1 1; 1 0];
>> C = [1 0; 0 1];
>> D = [0 0; 0 0];
>> nyquist(A, B, C, D)
```

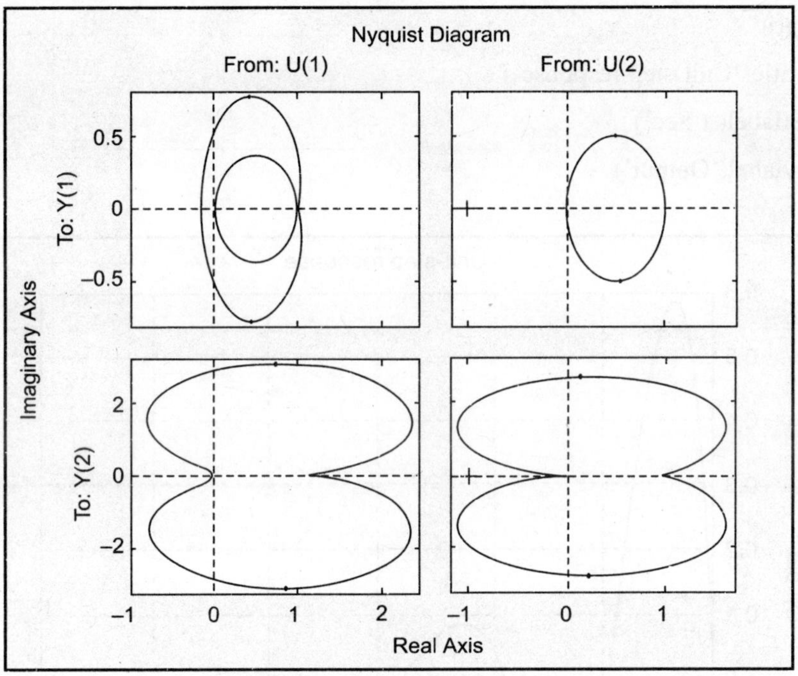

Fig. P3.51 Nyquist plots

P3.52 Obtain the unit-step response, unit-ramp response, and unit-impulse response of the following system using MATLAB:

$$\begin{bmatrix} \dot{x}_1 \\ \dot{x}_2 \end{bmatrix} = \begin{bmatrix} -1 & -1.5 \\ 2 & 0 \end{bmatrix} \begin{bmatrix} x_1 \\ x_2 \end{bmatrix} + \begin{bmatrix} 1.5 \\ 0 \end{bmatrix} u$$

$$y = [1 \quad 0] \begin{bmatrix} x_1 \\ x_2 \end{bmatrix}$$

where u is the input and y is the output.

Solution

```
>> %Unit-step response
>> A = [–1 –1.5; 2 0];
>> B = [1.5; 0];
>> C = [1 0];
>> D = [0];
>> [y, x, t] = step(A, B, C, D);
>> plot(t, y)
>> grid
>> title('Unit-step response')
>> xlabel('t Sec')
>> ylabel('Output')
```

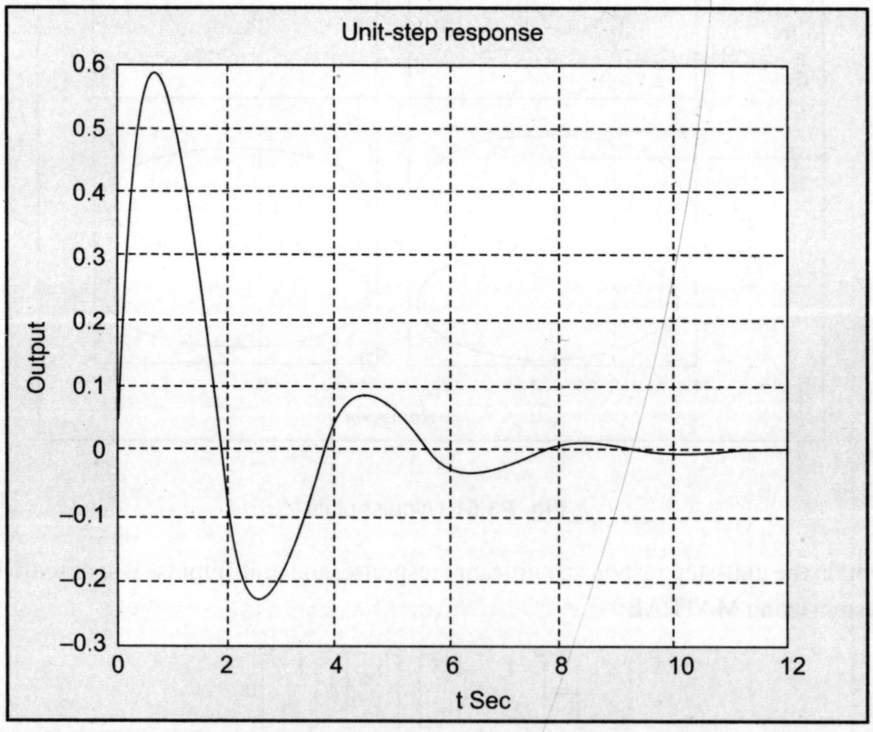

Fig. P3.52(a) Unit-step response

```
>> %Unit-ramp response
>> A = [–1 –1.5; 2 0];
```

```
>> B = [1.5; 0];
>> C = [1 0];
>> D = [0];
>> %New enlarged state and output equations
>> AA = [A zeros(2, 1); C 0];
>> BB = [B; 0];
>> CC = [0 0 1];
>> DD = [0];
>> [z, x, t] = step(AA, BB, CC, DD);
>> x3 = [0 0 1]*x'; plot(t, x3, t, t, '–')
>> grid
>> title('Unit-ramp response')
>> xlabel('t Sec')
>> ylabel('Output and unit-ramp input')
>> text(12, 1.2, 'Output')
```

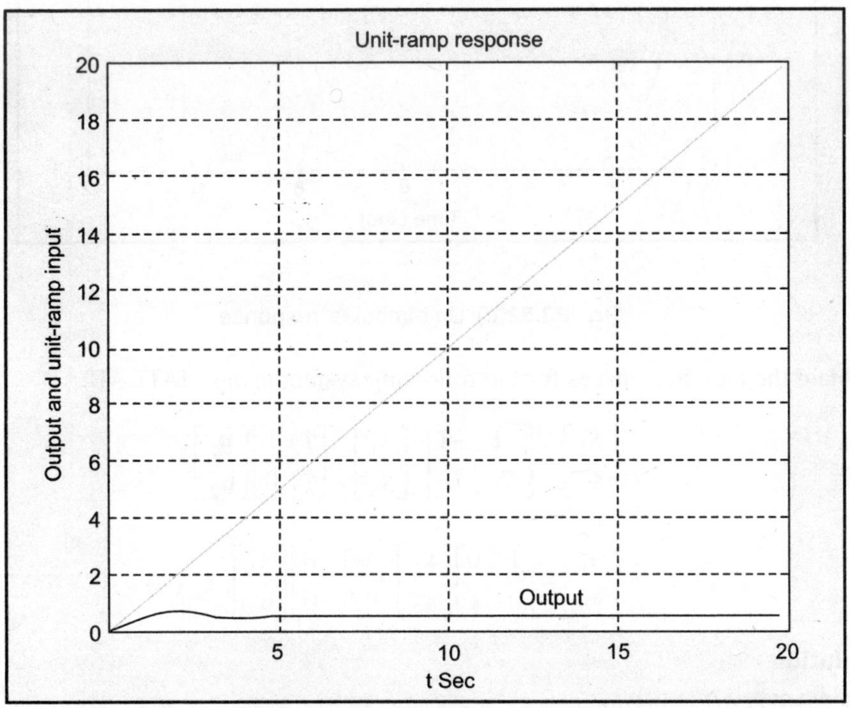

Fig. P3.52(b) Unit-ramp response

```
>> %Unit-impulse response
>> A = [-1 -1.5; 2 0];
>> B = [1.5; 0];
>> C = [1 0];
>> D = [0];
>> impulse(A, B, C, D)
```

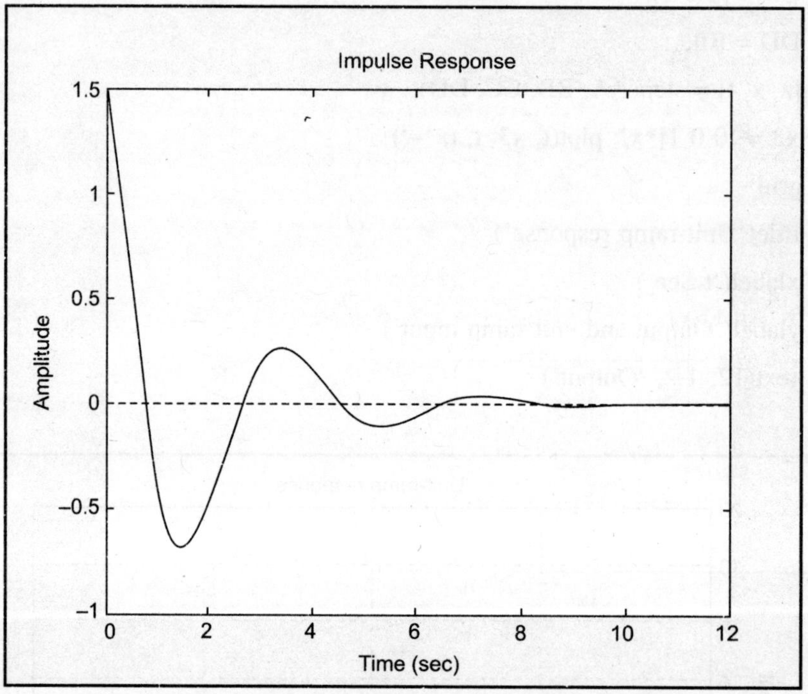

Fig. P3.52(c) Unit-impulse response

P3.53 Obtain the unit-step curves for the following system using MATLAB:

$$\begin{bmatrix} \dot{x}_1 \\ \dot{x}_2 \end{bmatrix} = \begin{bmatrix} -1 & -1 \\ 7 & 0 \end{bmatrix} \begin{bmatrix} x_1 \\ x_2 \end{bmatrix} + \begin{bmatrix} 1 & 1 \\ 1 & 0 \end{bmatrix} \begin{bmatrix} u_1 \\ u_2 \end{bmatrix}$$

$$\begin{bmatrix} y_1 \\ y_2 \end{bmatrix} = \begin{bmatrix} 1 & 0 \\ 0 & 1 \end{bmatrix} \begin{bmatrix} x_1 \\ x_2 \end{bmatrix} + \begin{bmatrix} 0 & 0 \\ 0 & 0 \end{bmatrix} \begin{bmatrix} u_1 \\ u_2 \end{bmatrix}$$

Solution

```
>> %MATLAB Program
>> A = [-1, -1; 7 0];
```

```
>> B = [1 1; 1 0];
>> C = [1 0; 0 1];
>> D = [0 0; 0 0];
>> step(A, B, C, D)
```

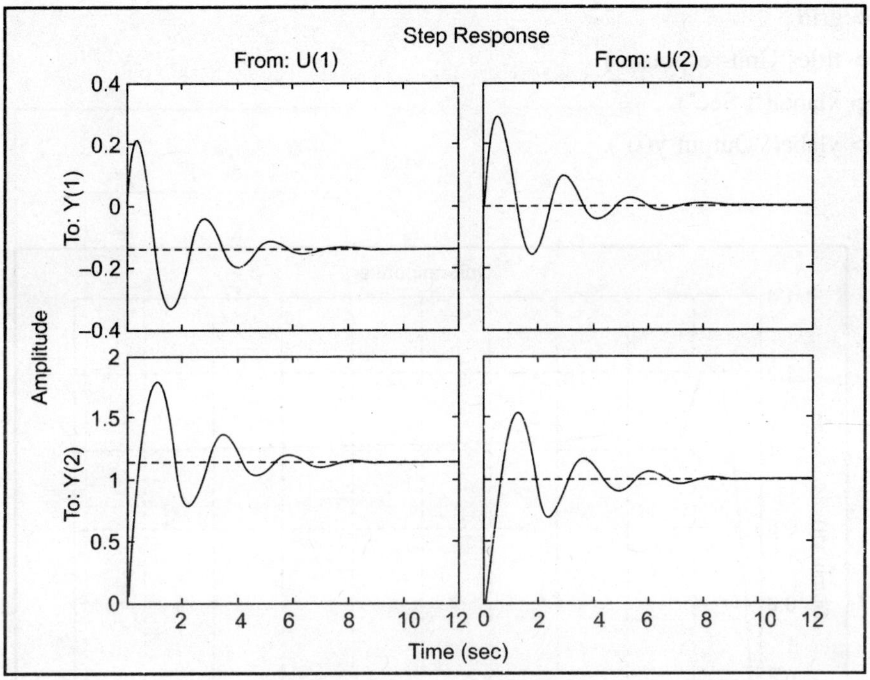

Fig. P3.53 Step response

P3.54 Obtain the unit-step response and unit-ramp response of the following system using MATLAB.

$$\begin{bmatrix} \dot{x}_1 \\ \dot{x}_2 \\ \dot{x}_3 \end{bmatrix} = \begin{bmatrix} -5 & -25 & -5 \\ 1 & 0 & 0 \\ 0 & 1 & 0 \end{bmatrix} \begin{bmatrix} x_1 \\ x_2 \\ x_3 \end{bmatrix} + \begin{bmatrix} 1 \\ 0 \\ 0 \end{bmatrix} u$$

$$y = \begin{bmatrix} 0 & 25 & 5 \end{bmatrix} \begin{bmatrix} x_1 \\ x_2 \\ x_3 \end{bmatrix} + [0]u$$

Solution

```
>> %MATLAB Program
>> A = [-5 -25 -5; 1 0 0; 0 1 0];
```

```
>> B = [1; 0; 0];
>> C = [0 25 5];
>> D = [0];
>> [y, x, t] = step(A, B, C, D);
>> plot(t, y)
>> grid
>> title('Unit-response')
>> xlabel('t Sec')
>> ylabel('Output y(t)')
```

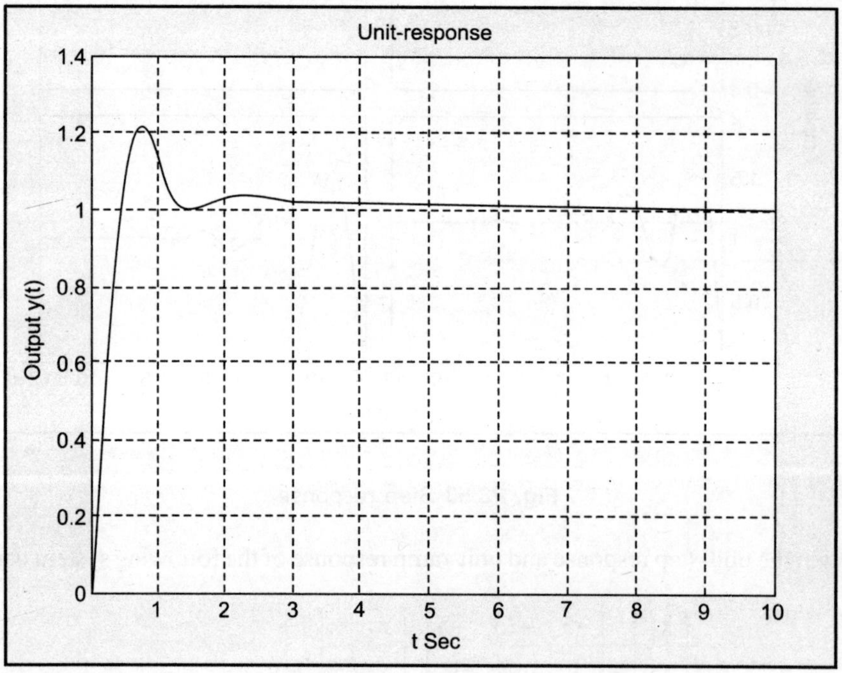

Fig. P3.54(a) Unit-step response

Unit-ramp response:

$$AA = \begin{bmatrix} -5 & -25 & -5 & 0 \\ 1 & 0 & 0 & 0 \\ 0 & 1 & 0 & 0 \\ 0 & 25 & 5 & 0 \end{bmatrix} = \begin{bmatrix} & A & & 0 \\ & & & 0 \\ & & & 0 \\ 0 & 25 & 5 & 0 \end{bmatrix} = \text{A zeros(2, 1); C 0]}$$

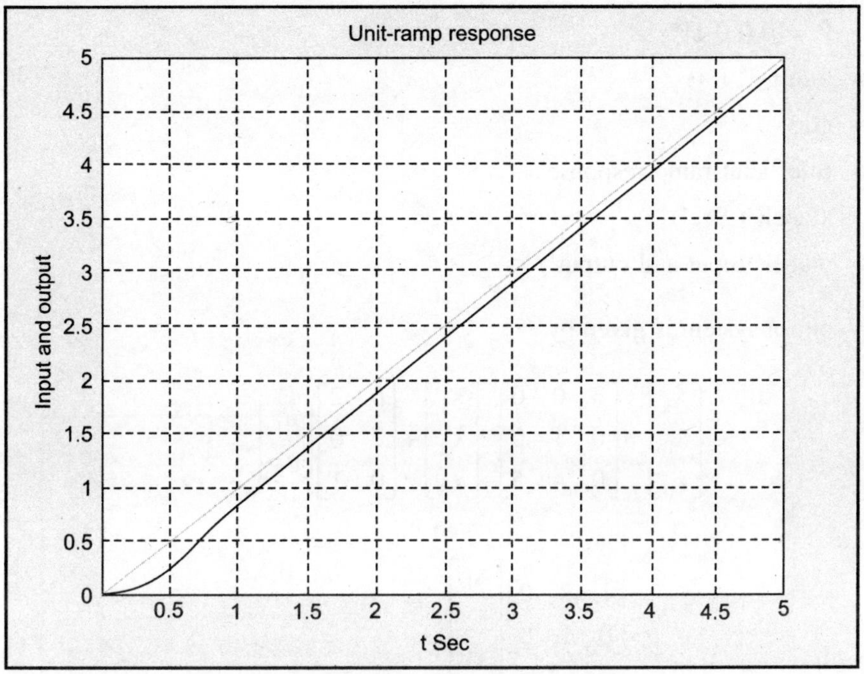

Fig. P3.54(b) Unit-ramp response

$$BB = \begin{bmatrix} 1 \\ 0 \\ 0 \\ 0 \end{bmatrix} = \begin{bmatrix} B \\ \\ 0 \end{bmatrix}$$

$$CC = [0 \quad 25 \quad 5 \quad 0] = [C \quad 0]$$

```
>> %MATLAB Program
>> A = [–5 –25 –5; 1 0 0; 0 1 0];
>> B = [1; 0; 0];
>> C = [0 25 5];
>> D = [0];
>> AA = [A zeros(3, 1); C 0];
>> BB = [B; 0];
>> CC = [C 0];
>> DD = [0];
>> t = 0:0.01:5;
```

```
>> [z, x, t] = step(AA, BB, CC, DD, 1, t);
>> P = [0 0 0 1]*x';
>> plot(t, P, t, t)
>> grid
>> title('Unit-ramp response')
>> xlabel('t Sec')
>> ylabel('Input and output')
```

P3.55 A control system is given by

$$\begin{bmatrix} \dot{x}_1 \\ \dot{x}_2 \\ \dot{x}_3 \end{bmatrix} = \begin{bmatrix} 3 & 0 & 0 \\ 0 & 1 & 0 \\ 0 & 4 & 5 \end{bmatrix} \begin{bmatrix} x_1 \\ x_2 \\ x_3 \end{bmatrix} + \begin{bmatrix} 0 & 2 \\ 2 & 0 \\ 0 & 1 \end{bmatrix} \begin{bmatrix} u_1 \\ u_2 \end{bmatrix}$$

$$y = \begin{bmatrix} 1 & 2 & 0 \\ 0 & 1 & 0 \end{bmatrix} \begin{bmatrix} x_1 \\ x_2 \\ x_3 \end{bmatrix}.$$

Determine the controllability and observability of the system using MATLAB.

Solution

```
>> %MATLAB Program
>> A = [3 0 0; 0 1 0; 0 4 5];
>> B = [0 2; 2 0; 0 1];
>> C = [1 2 0; 0 1 0];
>> D = [0 0; 0 0];
>> rank([B A*B A^2*B])
ans =
        3
>>      rank([C' A*C' A^2*C'])
ans =
        3
>>      rank([C*B C*A*B C*A^2*B])
ans =
        2
```

From the above, we observe that the system is state controllable but not completely observable. It is output controllable.

P3.56 Consider the system

$$\begin{bmatrix} \dot{x}_1 \\ \dot{x}_2 \\ \dot{x}_3 \end{bmatrix} = \begin{bmatrix} 3 & 0 & 0 \\ 0 & 1 & 0 \\ 0 & 3 & 2 \end{bmatrix} \begin{bmatrix} x_1 \\ x_2 \\ x_3 \end{bmatrix}$$

The output is given by

$$y = [1 \quad 1 \quad 1] \begin{bmatrix} x_1 \\ x_2 \\ x_3 \end{bmatrix}$$

(*a*) Determine the observability of the system using MATLAB.

(*b*) Show that the system is completely observable if the output is given by

$$\begin{bmatrix} y_1 \\ y_2 \end{bmatrix} = \begin{bmatrix} 1 & 1 & 1 \\ 1 & 3 & 2 \end{bmatrix} \begin{bmatrix} x_1 \\ x_2 \\ x_3 \end{bmatrix}$$

using MATLAB.

Solution

```
>> %MATLAB Program
>> A = [3 0 0; 0 1 0; 0 3 2];
>> C = [1 1 1];
>> rank([C' A'*C' A'^2*C'])
ans =
     3
>> A = [3 0 0; 0 1 0; 0 3 2];
>> C = [1 1 1; 1 3 2];
>> rank([C' A'*C' A'^2*C'])
ans =
     3
```

P3.57 Consider the following state equation and output equation

$$\begin{bmatrix} \dot{x}_1 \\ \dot{x}_2 \\ \dot{x}_3 \end{bmatrix} = \begin{bmatrix} -1 & -3 & -2 \\ 0 & -2 & 1 \\ 1 & 0 & -1 \end{bmatrix} \begin{bmatrix} x_1 \\ x_2 \\ x_3 \end{bmatrix} + \begin{bmatrix} 3 \\ 0 \\ 1 \end{bmatrix} u$$

$$y = [1 \;\; 1 \;\; 0] \begin{bmatrix} x_1 \\ x_2 \\ x_3 \end{bmatrix}$$

Determine if the system is completely state controllable and completely observable using MATLAB.

Solution

The controllability and observability of the system can be obtained by examining the rank condition of

[B AB A^2B] and [C' A'C' $(A')^2$C']

Solution

```
>> %MATLAB Program
>> A = [–1 –3 –2; 0 –2 1–1 0 –1];
>> B = [3; 0; 1];
>> C = [1 1 0];
>> D = [0];
>> rank([B A*B A^2*B])
ans =
        3
>> rank([C' A'*C' A'^2*C'])
ans =
        3
```

We observe the rank of [B AB A^2B] is 3 and the rank of **[C' A'*C' $(A')^2$*C']** is 3, the **system is completely state controllable and observable.**

P3.58 Diagonalize the following system using MATLAB

$$\dot{x} = \begin{bmatrix} -9 & -5 & 5 \\ 15 & 6 & -12 \\ -8 & -3 & 4 \end{bmatrix} x + \begin{bmatrix} -1 \\ 3 \\ 2 \end{bmatrix} r$$

$$y = [1 \;\; -3 \;\; 5]\, x$$

Solution

```
% MATLAB Program
A = [–9 –5 5; 15 6 –12; –8 –3 4];
B = [–1; 3; 2;];
C = [1; –3; 5;];
```

```
[P, D] = eig (A) ;
Ad = inv (p) * A * P
Bd = inv (p) * B
Cd = C * P
```

Computer response:

```
Ad =

   1.7851   + 4.3577i   0.0000   + 0.0000i   0.0000   - 0.0000i
   0.0000   - 0.0000i   1.7851   - 4.3577i   0.0000   + 0.0000i
  -0.0000   + 0.0000i  -0.0000   - 0.0000i  -2.5703   - 0.0000i

Bd =

  -1.9826   - 3.8569i
  -1.9826   + 3.8569i
   2.7345   - 0.0000i

Cd =

   4.3824   + 0.5969i   4.3824   - 0.5969i   4.6708
```

P3.59 Determine the eigenvalues of the following system using MATLAB:

$$\dot{x} = \begin{bmatrix} 0 & 2 & 0 \\ 0 & 2 & -7 \\ -2 & 2 & 5 \end{bmatrix} x + \begin{bmatrix} 0 \\ 0 \\ 2 \end{bmatrix} r$$

$$y = [0 \;\; 0 \;\; 1]\, x$$

Solution

```
>> A = [0 2 0; 0 2 -7; -2 2 5]; %Define the matrix above
>> eig (A) %Calculate the eigenvalues of matrix A.
ans =

   2.0000
   2.5000 + 2.7839i
   2.5000 - 2.7839i
```

P3.60 For the following forward path of a unity feedback system in state space representation, determine if the closed-loop system is stable using the Routh-Hurwitz criterion and MATLAB.

$$\dot{x} = \begin{bmatrix} 0 & 2 & 0 \\ 0 & 1 & 7 \\ -2 & -6 & -5 \end{bmatrix} x + \begin{bmatrix} 0 \\ 0 \\ 2 \end{bmatrix} r$$

$$y = [0 \quad 1]\, x$$

Solution

```
>> A = [0 2 0; 0 1 7; –2 –6 –5]; %Define the matrix above
>> B = [0; 0; 2]; %Define the matrix above. Semicolon needed because it is a vertical
       matrix.
>> C = [0 1 1]; %Define the matrix above
>> D = 0;
>> 'G';
>> G = ss(A, B, C, D); %Create a state-space model as required
>> 'T';
>> T = Feedback (G, 1);
>> 'Eigenvalues of T are';
>> ssdata(T); %Calculate a state-space model of all the matrices
>> eig(T) % Determine Eigenvalues
ans =

      –0.6127
      –2.6936 + 6.2003i
      –2.6936 – 6.2003i
```

The closed-loop system is stable as the numbers are all negative with regards the to axis coordinate system used for Routh-Hurwitz. Negative values are stable, positive values are unstable.

P3.61 For the following path of a unity feedback system in state-space representation, determine if the closed-loop system is stable using the Routh-Hurwitz criterion and MATLAB:

$$\dot{x} = \begin{bmatrix} 0 & 1 & 0 \\ 0 & 1 & 5 \\ -3 & -4 & -5 \end{bmatrix} x + \begin{bmatrix} 0 \\ 0 \\ 1 \end{bmatrix} u$$

$$y = [0\ 1\ 1]x$$

Solution

%MATLAB Program

```
A = [0 1 0; 0 1 5; –3 –4 –5];
B = [0 0 1];
C = [0 1 1];
D = 0;
'G'
G = ss(A, B, C, D)
'T'
```

```
T = feedback(G, 1)
'Eigenvalues of T are'
ssdata(T);
eig(T)
```

Computer response:

```
ans =
        G
a =
                x1      x2      x3
        x1      0       1       0
        x2      0       1       5
        x3      –3      –4      –5
b =
                u1
        x1      0
        x2      0
        x3      1
c =
                x1      x2      x3
        y1      0       1       1
d =
                u1
        y1      0
```

Continuous-time model:

```
ans =
        T
a =
                x1      x2      x3
        x1      0       1       0
        x2      0       1       5
        x3      –3      –5      –6
b =
                u1
        x1      0
        x2      0
        x3      1
```

c =

	x1	x2	x3
y1	0	1	1

d =

	u1
y1	0

Continuous-time model:

ans =

Eigenvalues of T are

ans =

–1.0000

–2.0000 + 3.3166i

–2.0000 – 3.3166i

Bibliography

There are several outstanding text and reference books on feedback control systems and MATLAB that merit consultation for those readers who wish to pursue these topics further. The following list is but a representative sample of the many excellent references on analysis and design of feedback control systems and MATLAB.

CONTROL SYSTEMS

Anand, D.K., *Introduction to Control Systems,* 2nd ed., Pergamon Press, New York, 1984.

Atkinson, P., *Feedback Control Theory for Engineers,* 2nd ed., Heinemann, 1977.

Bateson, R.N., *Introduction to Control System Technology*, Prentice Hall, Upper Saddle River, NJ, 2002.

Bayliss, L.E., *Living Control Systems*, English Universities Press Limited, London, UK, 1966.

Beards, C.F., *Vibrations and Control System,* Ellis Horwood, 1988.

Benaroya, H., *Mechanical Vibration-Analysis, Uncertainties and Control*, Prentice Hall, Upper Saddle River, NJ, 1998.

Bode, H.W., *Network Analysis and Feedback Design*, Van Nostrand Reinhold, New York, 1945.

Bolton, W., *Control Engineering*, 2nd ed., Addison Wesley Longman Ltd., Reading, MA, 1998.

Brogan, W.L., *Modern Control Theory*, Prentice Hall, Upper Saddle River, NJ, 1985.

Buckley, R.V., *Control Engineering,* Macmillan, New York, 1976.

Burghes, D., and **Graham, A.**, *Introduction to Control Theory including Optimal Control,* Ellis Horwood, 1980.

Cannon, R.H., *Dynamics of Physical Systems*, McGraw Hill, New York, 1967.

Chesmond, C.J., *Basic Control System Technology,* Edward Arnold, 1990.

Clark, R.N., *Introduction to Automatic Control Systems*, Wiley, New York, 1962.

D'Azzo, J.J., and Houpis, C.H., *Linear Control System Analysis and Design: Conventional and Modern*, 4th ed., McGraw Hill, New York, 1995.

Dorf, R.C., and Bishop, R.H., *Modern Control Systems*, 9th ed., Prentice Hall, Upper Saddle River, NJ, 2001.

Dorsey, John., *Continuous and Discrete Control Systems*, McGraw Hill, New York, 2002.

Douglas, J., *Process Dynamics and Control, Volumes I and II*, Prentice Hall, Englewood Cliffs, NJ, 1972.

Doyle, J.C., Francis, B.A., and Tannenbaum, A., *Feedback Control Theory,* Macmillan, New York, 1992.

Dransfield, P., and Habner, D.F., *Introducing Root Locus*, Cambridge University Press, Cambridge, 1973.

Dukkipati, R.V., *Control Systems,* Narosa Publishing House, New Delhi, India, 2005.

Dukkipati, R.V., *Engineering System Dynamics,* Narosa Publishing House, New Delhi, India, 2004.

Dukkipati, R.V., *Vibration Analysis,* Narosa Publishing House, New Delhi, India, 2004.

Evans, W.R., *Control System Dynamics*, McGraw Hill, New York, 1954.

Eveleigh, V.W., *Control System Design,* McGraw Hill, New York, 1972.

Franklin, G.F., David Powell, J., and Abbas Emami-Naeini., *Feedback Control of Dynamic Systems*, 3rd ed., Addison Wesley, Reading, MA, 1994.

Friedland, B., *Control System Design*, McGraw Hill, New York, 1986.

Godwin, Graham E., Graebe, Stefan F., and Salgado, Maria E., *Control System Design*, Prentice Hall, Upper Saddle River, NJ, 2001.

Grimble, Michael J., *Industrial Control Systems Design*, Wiley, New York, 2001.

Gupta, S., *Elements of Control Systems*, Prentice Hall, Upper Saddle River, NJ, 2002.

Guy, J.J., *Solution of Problems in Automatic Control*, Pitman, 1966.

Healey, M., *Principles of Automatic Control*, Hodder and Stoughton, 1975.

Jacobs, O.L.R., *Introduction to Control Theory*, Oxford University Press, 1974.

Johnson, C., and Malki, H., *Control Systems Technology*, Prentice Hall, Upper Saddle River, NJ, 2002.

Kailath, T., *Linear Systems*, Prentice Hall, Upper Saddle River, NJ, 1980.

Kuo, B.C., *Automatic Control Systems*, 6th ed., Prentice Hall, Englewood Cliffs, NJ, 1991.

Leff, P.E.E., *Introduction to Feedback Control Systems*, McGraw Hill, New York, 1979.

Levin, W.S., *Control System Fundamentals*, CRC Press, Boca Raton, FL, 2000.

Levin, W.S., *The Control Handbook*, CRC Press, Boca Raton, FL, 1996.

Lewis, P., and Yang, C., *Basic Control Systems Engineering*, Prentice Hall, Upper Saddle River, NJ, 1997.

Marshall, S.A., *Introduction to Control Theory*, Macmillan, 1978.

Mayr, O., *The Origins of Feedback Control*, MIT Press, Cambridge, MA, 1970.

Mees, A.J., *Dynamics of Feedback Systems,* Wiley, New York, 1981.

Nise, Norman, S., *Control Systems Engineering*, 3rd ed., Wiley, New York, 2000.

Ogata, K., *Modern Control Engineering*, 3rd ed., Prentice Hall, Englewood Cliffs, NJ, 1997.

Ogata, K., *State Space Analysis of Control Systems*, Prentice Hall, Upper Saddle River, NJ, 1967.

Ogata, K., *System Dynamics*, 3rd ed., Prentice Hall, Upper Saddle River, NJ, 1998.

Palm III, W.J., *Control Systems Engineering*, Wiley, New York, 1986.

Paraskevopoulos, P.N., *Modern Control Engineering*, Marcel Dekker, Inc., New York, 2003.

Phillips, C.L., and Harbour, R.D., *Feedback Control Systems,* 4th ed., Prentice Hall, Upper Saddle River, NJ, 2000.

Power, H.M., and Simpson, R.J., *Introduction to Dynamics and Control*, McGraw Hill, New York, 1978.

Raven, F.H., *Automatic Control Engineering*, 4th ed., McGraw Hill, New York, 1987.

Richards, R.J., *An Introduction to Dynamics and Control*, Longman, 1979.

Richards, R.J., *Solving Problems in Control*, Longman Scientific & Technical, Wiley, New York, 1993.

Rohrs, C.E., Melsa, J.L., and Schultz, D.G., *Linear Control Systems*, McGraw Hill, New York, 1993.

Rowell, G., and Wormley, D., *System Dynamics*, Prentice Hall, Upper Saddle River, NJ, 1999.

Schwarzenbach, J., and Jill, K.F., *System Modeling and Control*, 2nd ed., Arnold, 1984.

Shearer, J.L., Kulakowski, B.T., and Gardner, J.F., *Dynamic Modeling and Control of Engineering Systems*, 2nd ed., Prentice Hall, Upper Saddle River, NJ, 1997.

Shinners, S. M., *Modern Control System Theory and Design*, 2nd ed., Wiley Interscience, New York, 1998.

Sinha, N.K., *Control Systems,* Holt Rinehart and Winston, New York, 1986.

Smith, O.J.M., *Feedback Control Systems*, McGraw Hill, New York, 1958.

Stefano, D.III., Stubberud, A.R., and Williams, I.J., *Schaum's Outline Series Theory and Problems of Feedback and Control Systems,* McGraw Hill, New York, 1967.

Thompson, S., *Control Systems: Engineering and Design*, Longman, 1989.

Truxal, J.G., *Control System Synthesis*, McGraw Hill, New York, 1955.

Umez-Eronini, E., *System Dynamics and Control*, Brooks/Cole Publishing Company, Pacific Grove, CA, 1999.

Vu, H.V., *Control Systems*, McGraw Hill Primis Custom Publishing, New York, 2002.

Vukic, Z., Kuljaca, L., Donlagic, D., and Tesnjak, S., *Nonlinear Control Systems*, Marcel Dekker, Inc., New York, 2003.

Welbourn, D.B., *Essentials of Control Theory,* Edward Arnold, 1963.

Weyrick, R.C., *Fundamentals of Automatic Control,* McGraw Hill, New York, 1975.

MATLAB

Chapman, S.J., *MATLAB Programming for Engineers,* 2nd ed., Brooks/Cole, Thomson Learning, Pacific Grove, CA, 2002.

Dabney, J.B., and Harman, T.L., *Mastering SIMULINK 4,* Prentice Hall, Upper Saddle River, NJ, 2001.

Djaferis, T.E., *Automatic Control— The Power of Feedback using MATLAB*, Brooks/Cole, Thomson Learning, Pacific Grove, CA, 2000.

Dukkipati, R.V., *MATLAB for Mechanical Engineers*, New Age Science, UK, 2009.

Etter, D.M., *Engineering Problem Solving with MATLAB,* Prentice-Hall, Englewood Cliffs, NJ, 1993.

Gardner, J.F., *Simulation of Machines using MATLAB and SIMULINK*, Brooks/Cole, Thomson Learning, Pacific Grove, CA, 2001.

Harper, B. D., *Solving Dynamics Problems in MATLAB*, 5th ed., Wiley, New York, 2002.

Harper, B. D., *Solving Statics Problems in MATLAB*, 5th ed., Wiley, New York, 2002.

Herniter, M.E., *Programming in MATLAB*, Brooks/Cole, Pacific Grove, CA, 2001.

Karris, S.T., *Signals and Systems with MATLAB Applications,* Orchard Publications, Fremont, CA, 2001.

Leonard, N.E., and Levine, W.S., *Using MATLAB to Analyze and Design Control Systems*, Addison-Wesley, Redwood City, CA, 1995.

Lyshevski, S.E., *Engineering and Scientific Computations Using MATLAB*, Wiley, New York, 2003.

Moler, C., *The Student Edition of MATLAB for MS-DOS Personal Computers with* $3\frac{1}{2}$" *Disks,* MATLAB Curriculum Series, The MathWorks, Inc., 2002.

Ogata, K., *Designing Linear Control Systems with MATLAB*, Prentice Hall, Upper Saddle River, NJ, 1994.

Ogata, K., *Solving Control Engineering Problems with MATLAB*, Prentice Hall, Upper Saddle River, NJ, 1994.

Pratap, Rudra., *Getting Started with MATLAB—A Quick Introduction for Scientists and Engineers,* Oxford University Press, New York, 2002.

Saadat, Hadi., *Computational Aids in Control Systems using MATLAB*, McGraw Hill, New York, 1993.

Sigman,K., and Davis, T.A., *MATLAB Primer*, 6th ed., Chapman & Hall/CRC Press, Boca Raton, FL, 2002.

The MathWorks, Inc., *SIMULINK, Version 3*, The MathWorks, Inc., Natick, MA, 1999.

The MathWorks, Inc., *MATLAB: Application Program Interface Reference Version 6*, The MathWorks, Inc., Natick, 2000.

The MathWorks, Inc., *MATLAB: Control System Toolbox User's Guide, Version 4*, The MathWorks, Inc., Natick, 1992–1998.

The MathWorks, Inc., *MATLAB: Creating Graphical User Interfaces, Version 1*, The MathWorks, Inc., Natick, 2000.

The MathWorks, Inc., *MATLAB: Function Reference,* The MathWorks, Inc., Natick, 2000.

The MathWorks, Inc., *MATLAB: Release Notes for Release 12*, The MathWorks, Inc., Natick, 2000.

The MathWorks, Inc., *MATLAB: Symbolic Math Toolbox User's Guide, Version 2*, The MathWorks, Inc., Natick, 1993–1997.

The MathWorks, Inc., *MATLAB: Using MATLAB Graphics, Version 6*, The MathWorks, Inc., Natick, 2000.

The MathWorks, Inc., *MATLAB: Using MATLAB, Version 6*, The MathWorks, Inc., Natick, 2000.